Cow Killing And Beef Export

The Master Plan
To Turn India Into A Desert
By 2050

By
Dr. Sahadeva dasa

B.com., FCA., AICWA., PhD
Chartered Accountant

Soul Science University Press

www.cowism.com

Readers interested in the subject matter of this
book are invited to correspond with the publisher at:
SoulScienceUniversity@gmail.com +91 98490 95990
or visit DrDasa.com

First Edition: July 2013

Soul Science University Press expresses its gratitude to the Bhaktivedanta Book Trust International (BBT), for the use of quotes by His Divine Grace A.C.Bhaktivedanta Swami Prabhupada.

ISBN 97893-82947-03- 5

Published by:
Dr. Sahadeva dasa for Soul Science University Press

Printed by:
Rainbow Print Pack, Hyderabad

To order a copy write to chandra@rgbooks.co.in
or buy online: Amazon.com, Rgbooks.co.in

Dedicated to....

His Divine Grace A.C.Bhaktivedanta Swami Prabhupada

yas tvam krsne gate duram saha-gandiva-dhanvana
socyo'sy asocyan rahasi praharan vadham arhasi

You rogue, do you dare beat an innocent cow because Lord Krsna and Arjuna, the carrier of the Gandiva bow, are out of sight? Since you are beating the innocent in a secluded place, you are considered a culprit and therefore deserve to be killed.

In a civilization where God is conspicuously banished, and there is no devotee warrior like Arjuna, the associates of the age of Kali take advantage of this lawless kingdom and arrange to kill innocent animals like the cow in secluded slaughterhouses. Such murderers of animals stand to be condemned to death by the order of a pious king like Maharaja Pariksit. For a pious king, the culprit who kills an animal in a secluded place is punishable by the death penalty, exactly like a murderer who kills an innocent child in a secluded place.

~ Srimad Bhagavatam 9.2.3

By The Same Author

Oil-Final Countdown To A Global Crisis And Its Solutions

End of Modern Civilization And Alternative Future

To Kill Cow Means To End Human Civilization

Cow And Humanity - Made For Each Other

Cows Are Cool - Love 'Em!

Capitalism Communism And Cowism - A New Economics For The 21st Century

Noble Cow - Munching Grass, Looking Curious And Just Hanging Around

Let's Be Friends - A Curious, Calm Cow

Wondrous Glories of Vraja

We Feel Just Like You Do

Tsunami of Diseases Headed Our Way - Know Your Food Before Time Runs Out

(More information on availability : DrDasa.com)

Contents

Preface

Gaia is the the primal Greek goddess personifying the Earth. Gaia is a primordial deity in the ancient Greek pantheon and considered a Mother Goddess.

Etymologically Gaia is a compound word of two elements. Ge, meaning "Earth" and 'aia' is a derivative of an Indo-European stem meaning "Grandmother".

This epical name was revived in 1979 by James Lovelock, in 'Gaia: A New Look at Life on Earth' which proposed a Gaia hypothesis. The hypothesis proposes that living organisms and inorganic material are part of a dynamic system that shapes the Earth's biosphere, and maintains the Earth as a fit environment for life. In some Gaia theory approaches, the Earth itself is viewed as an organism with self-regulatory functions. Further books by Lovelock and others popularized the Gaia Hypothesis, which was widely embraced and passed into common usage as part of the heightened awareness of environmental concerns of the 1990s.

Gaia has been widely held throughout history and has been the basis of a belief which still coexists with the great religions. Today the very word 'Gaia' has come to mean ecology and sustainability.

There is a thriving green community which runs the portal Gaia.com.

Interestingly, in India the cow is known as 'Gai' and Vedic literatures have similar words, 'Gau' or 'Gava'.

The word Gaia has been derived from these words. If we go to Nirukta, the earliest book of etymology from India, and look up its meaning, the two primary meanings of the word 'gau', from which 'gava' is derived, are given in the following order:

1. The planet earth
2. The animal, cow.

By using interchangeable words for cow and Earth, Vedas, the oldest repository of knowledge, emphatically state that cow is a symbolic representation of the planet Earth itself. In almost all Indian languages, cow is knows as gai or go-mata.

Therefore cow has a serious significance for saving a planet in crisis. Of all the man-made crises, probably the worst is the destruction of top soil and desertification of fertile lands.

The history of preceding civilizations and cultures indicate the imbalances that have developed when minerals have been permanently transferred from the soil. There are only a few localities in the world where great civilizations have continued to exist through long periods and these have very distinct characteristics.

It required only a few centuries, and in some profligated systems a few decades to produce so serious a mineral depletion of the soil that progressive plant and animal deterioration resulted. In such instances, regular and adequate replenishment was not taking place.

In nature's program, minerals are loaned temporarily to the plants and animals and their return to the soil is essential. In the case of a forest system, this replenishment is made by its plant and animal life automatically. But in case of agriculture, we have to make a conscious effort to do it. A few intelligent civilizations have done it but the balance of the cultures have largely failed at this point.

One such civilization was Indian (or Vedic) Civilization. According to the available historical records, they have successfully farmed and protected the topsoil for at least 50 centuries. And the entire credit for this goes to humble cow.

But this all has changed in last few decades. Indian government, especially in the post-independence era, has made great efforts to promote cow slaughter and beef export. Their efforts finally paid off when this year India topped the list of beef exporting countries.

But this 'accomplishment' has come with a big price tag. The whole agriculture sector is dying out in a country where 70% of the people directly depend on small farm holdings. This is evidenced by rising food prices of food and a spate of farmers' suicides.

Sahadeva dasa

Dr. Sahadeva dasa
1st June 2013
Secunderabad, India

Section-I

Cow Killing And Beef Export

The Highest National Priority And Truly A National Goal

Of The Present Indian Government

1.

Beef Exports Up 44% In 4 Years

India Is Top Seller In The World

According to a Times of India report dated April 1, 2013, India, homeland of the sacred cow has become the world's leading beef exporter in 2013. Last year itself, USDA's Foreign Agricultural Service forecasts showed that India would ship roughly 1.5 million metric tons of beef, passing reigning export champion Australia. It's a remarkable rise from just three years ago, when this famously bovine-friendly country exported less than half that amount.

The Central government's Pink Revolution to promote meat production and export has led to a 44% increase in meat consumption and export in four years, but it has failed to regulate the industry.

It certainly seems surprising at first, that a nation widely known for revering the cow would be a beef exporter at all.

According to data compiled by the animal husbandry departments of all states, meat from registered slaughterhouses increased from 5.57 lakh tonnes in 2008 to 8.05 lakh tonnes in 2011. Export earnings from bovine (beef and cattle) meat touched Rs 18,000 crore in 2012-2013.

Indian beef exports for 2012 were forecast at 1.525 million MT, 25% higher than the previous year and an almost three fold increase in the past 10 years.

Though beef meeting international standards reaches markets in the Europe, the Gulf and South-East Asia, the way animals are transported and slaughtered is extremely cruel and far from international standards. "There is rampant abuse of animals in transport and slaughter of meat whether for domestic consumption or export," says Arpan Sharma, CEO of Federation of Indian Animal Protection Organisations.

India's Central government has taken up modernization of abattoirs and storage facilities on a war footing. The food processing ministry announced subsidies of over 4000 crores to modernize abattoirs.

There are 38 integrated abattoirs in the country which slaughter for export. This is apart from thousands of other abattoirs which are operating unofficially. Agricultural and Processed Food Exports Development Authority (APEDA) is responsible for overseeing their operations.

Himalayan Academy explains it:

The cow represents the giving nature of life to every Hindu. Honoring this gentle animal, who gives more than she takes, we honor all creatures. Hindus regard all living creatures as sacred—mammals, fishes, birds and more. We acknowledge this reverence for life in our special affection for the cow. At festivals we decorate and honor her. To the Hindu, the cow symbolizes all other creatures. The cow is a symbol of the Earth, the nourisher, the ever-giving, undemanding provider. The cow represents life and the sustenance of life. The cow is so generous, taking nothing but water, grass and grain. She gives and gives and gives of her milk, as does the liberated soul gives of his spiritual knowledge. The cow is so vital to life, the virtual sustainer of life, for many humans. The cow is a symbol of grace and abundance. Veneration of the cow instills in Hindus the virtues of gentleness, receptivity and connectedness with nature.

None of the meat exporters pay attention to the condition of animals. Crammed in lorries, the animals are transported without food and water. Police officers let vehicles through without fining them for overloading as per the Prevention of Cruelty to Animals Act.

The international practice of stunning an animal before slaughter is not followed in India. In Kerala, cows are killed by hammer blows.

India overtakes Australia, Brazil, and the United States in beef export, in that order. Each of those nations will export around 1.2-1.4m metric tons of beef this year. India's beef is mostly sold in the Middle East, North Africa, and Southeast Asia with some portion going to European nations.

International community is shocked that a nation in which cow slaughter is officially prohibited and is an utter anathema to the majority of the population, will overtake these three icons (Australia, Brazil and US) of cattle ranching and beef eating.

This is just an indication of the efforts and planning the central government is putting in to accomplish this 'feat'.

"From government side there is an article that in Iran they want meat, so all these skinny cows should be killed and meat should be exported so that you can get oil economically. One should not think of this religious sentiment. People should be practical. They should not object. Government is going to open many slaughterhouses and kill these loitering, mischief cows.

So government policy is that religion is the opiate of the masses. It is a sentiment. It has no value. That is government conclusion.... To their point of view, it is useless. So under the circumstances, we have to make vigorous propaganda, public opinion. You see? Therefore I suggest that various meetings should be arranged in big, big halls and public meeting so that public may understand, at least, that this movement is very important."
~ Srila Prabhupada (Room Conversation, March 20, 1974, Bombay)

2.

Transforming A Nation

With The Lowest Meat Consumption In The World

According to a report by Rachel Tepper in Huffington Post, Indian meat consumption is lowest in the world, at only seven pounds per person a year.

Tiny European nation Luxembourg tips the scales at 136.5 kg of meat per person a year, or roughly 300 pounds, and occupies the first place in meat consumption. Burger-loving U.S. comes second.

The information, gathered by the U.N. Food And Agriculture Organization (FAO) and analyzed by The Economist, indicates that consumption of meat has been on the rise worldwide over the last 50 years. 177 countries were included in the study.

Tastes have changed, too:

Cow (beef and veal) was top of the menu in the early 1960s, accounting for 40% of meat consumption, but by 2007 its share had fallen to 23%. Pig is now the animal of choice, with around 99m tonnes consumed.

Although Western countries still eat the most meat per person, The Economist notes that it's middle-income countries like China that drive worldwide demand for it.

In addition to being linked to health problems, meat consumption has environmental experts crying foul. In 2008, Time reported that FAO data indicates that 18 percent of the Earth's greenhouse gas emissions were linked to worldwide livestock farming. In contrast, emissions from cars, trains, planes and boats worldwide combined accounted for only 13 percent.

As the world wakes up to the dangers of meat eating and a wave of vegetarianism sweeps through the world, Indian government realizes it's time to promote meat consumption and export. They are going out of their way to get the vegetarian population hooked on to taste of meat.

Policy makers have no regard for India's native food culture, which is one of the richest in the world. They are rolling-out red carpet welcome to western fast food chains.

Of the 7 billion people on the planet, nearly 1.2 billion of them are Indians and if this segment of humanity starts eating meat on American scale, its environmental, economic and moral implications will be catastrophic.

The Race To Make A Meal Of India's Fast-Food Market

When Domino's Pizza Inc. came to India in 1996 – in the first wave of international fast-food brands to enter the country – the company had to start with some basic education of its market.

They had to teach, 'This is a pizza and it's made from ingredients you are familiar with, but the shape is different.' Indians embraced it, enthusiastically enough that Domino's now has 513 outlets across 112 cities in India, with a restaurant and delivery business. But a couple of years ago, Domino's concluded it needed to start a second round of vigorous education: Convincing a new group of Indians that they belong in restaurants.

Domino's, working through its master franchisee Jubilant FoodWorks Ltd., put its product developers to work designing a

The whole process of westernizing, India or materializing India began about two hundred years ago. The Westerners introduced their so-called civilization, with its coffee, tea and meat eating. They built factories and developed large cities that had never been developed before. The entire Indian economy had been based on the villages, but under British rule and then recently more and more, everything moved towards the city. What happened is that the Vedic culture broke down. When it was present, the necessities of life were plentiful; there was no difficulty. But by and by it broke down.
~ Srila Prabhupada (A Cheating Civilization)

pizza they could sell for under a dollar. The big savings came in cheese, when the company replaced mozzarella with what it calls "liquid cheese sauce." In 2008, Domino's India launched its first Pizzamania, priced at 35 rupees (about 65 cents).

It opened doors for a lot of Indians who had never tried Domino's or ordered us at home," Mr. Rajpal, CEO says. "We see a lot of new people who had never tried pizza coming to us – and over time graduating to other products. ... It's democratic consumption now."

This strategy is also being aggressively pursued by the other big players in the $12.5-billion Indian fast-food industry. While organized retail has only 5 per cent of the fast-food market, it is growing with explosive speed, about 36 per cent last year, dominated by a handful of international brands.

McDonald's Corp. is the clear leader, according to a market analysis by Euromonitor released in October, with 2 per cent of the quick-service market. Pizza Hut Inc. and KFC Corp. – which, like McDonald's and Domino's, entered India in 1996 – each have close to 250 outlets. Subway, which arrived in 2002, is playing a fast game of catch-up with 320 stores in 60 cities and plans to top 400 sites next year; Baskin-Robbins has locked up the dessert market, with 425 stores in 95 cities, including many far from the country's major urban hubs.

All of these firms have relied on the international cachet of their brands to get people in the store.

And all are now using a "sub-dollar pricing" strategy to try to convince a new segment of consumers that regular visits to a fast-food outlet are feasible for them.

KFC has been the market leader here, with a "Streetwise" range offering a hot chicken meal starting from 25 rupees. Domino's Pizzamania is now priced at 44 rupees. McDonald's offers a full hot lunch for under a dollar. Pizza Hut has 60-cent "iPan" pizzas for delivery.

Subway, which struggled initially because of the higher cost of its ingredients, this year experimented with a "toastie," a 60-cent open-face sandwich, that marketing manager Sanjiv Pandey says appeals both to Indians' love of hot food and the low-budget market. "It is a phenomenal entry level price point and it's worked fantastically well for us."

All of this ultralow pricing is paired with aggressive print and television marketing, showing people who clearly cover a wide socioeconomic range eating in the outlets.

Domino's pioneered delivery, startling customers with its "30 minutes or it's free" promise (a massive logistics achievement in cities such as New Delhi and Mumbai that regularly experience total traffic gridlock). McDonald's has since taken the lead in delivery, with a 24-hour call centre and online ordering. It has also been the first to experiment with drive-throughs and gas-station outlets.

So people are becoming meat-eaters nowadays. There is no secrecy. Formerly, at least in India, the meat-eaters used to eat meat very secretly. We had seen in our childhood. If somebody will meat-eat, it was not allowed within the house. They, formerly, rich men, they used to keep Muslim servants as the caretaker of the horse or the carriage driver. So in the horse stable they would secretly cook some meat, and the so-called Babu, Zamindar, will eat. It was not allowed. And those who are not rich men -- poor men, sudra class -- they would go to Kali-ghata, and get one goat, sacrifice there, and cook there and eat, then come back. Meat-eating was not at all allowed. The higher caste, especially the brahmanas, they would never touch. Still in some provinces, in Maharastra provinces, in Madras... Of course, they are now taking.

So meat-eaters means mleccha. So now that is increasing, meat-eaters. So when wholesale population will be meat-eaters, mleccha, they'll not understand anything about spiritual matter -- "Why it is forbidden?" Because the meat-eaters, they cannot understand anything about spiritual matter. It is very difficult for them. ~Srila Prabhupada (Lecture, Srimad-Bhagavatam 1.8.34 -- Mayapur, October 14,1974)

The Scramble To Enter India Intensifies

Several U.S. chains have announced plans to enter the country, hoping to tap the growing fast-food market.

Restaurants like Denny's Corp , known for serving pancakes and sausages all day and Pollo Tropical of Carrols Restaurant , known for Caribbean-flavored chicken, Applebee's and Johnny Rockets, known for its hamburgers, are also looking to cash into the Indian quick-service restaurant market.

All brands will face challenges as they compete with incumbent McDonald's and Yum Brands, not the least of which would be adapting a meat-centric menu to a largely vegetarian palate.

Others wanting a foothold include Wendy's, Arby's International, CKE Restaurants with Carl's Jr and Focus Brands with Schlotzsky's Deli, all known for sandwiches and burgers.

Also India may finally get to savour Ikea meat balls. The Swedish giant has all the necessary permissions to set up their furniture showroom and restaurants in India.

BannaStrow's Crepes and Coffee, Moe's Southwest Grill, Starbucks Corp, Dunkin Donuts and Carvel Ice Cream are also in line.

These franchise owners are queuing up at the Ministry of Commerce and Industry and the Ministry of Corporate Affairs. It is not difficult to get a license issued, as long as you are willing to grease a few palms.

When I think about how "fast food" came to be, I think it definitely destroys the art of traditional cooking. Fast food changes the nutritional value and flavor of food. It has to be mass produced to feed so many people (although a lot of food gets thrown away by restaurants). It has to be made in a way so it can be shipped all over the country and then prepared in 5 minutes to eat. A lot of McDonald's food products aren't even real food. They put fillers in the meats with flavor enhancers. Subway has fake chicken and their bread is so cheap it goes bad within hours after being made (it becomes hard as a rock by the end of the day, I use to work at a few subways).

The basic food culture in many countries is actually healthy. The fast food chains sell all but healthy food. Also they puts family owned eateries out of business. ~ Amber Toebosis

Waistlines Surge With A Surging Market

But the increasing consumption of processed food that is high in fat and sugar is causing worries that India is importing the Western disease of obesity, creating a ticking public health bomb that the country can ill-afford.

While undernutrition is rampant – more than 50 percent of children are stunted due to malnutrition, according to a 2008 study in The Lancet medical journal – the over-fed middle class is growing in numbers and in trouser sizes.

A November 2010 study by the National Diabetes, Obesity and Cholesterol Foundation of India found that one in three children in private schools in New Delhi were obese, compared with one in 10 in government schools. Schoolchildren are attracted to the way junk food is advertised. Fast food giants are specifically targeting them.

3.

Massive Nationwide Drive

To Establish New Slaughterhouses And Modernize/Expand Existing Ones

Present Indian government came to power 10 years ago. After assuming office, their first move was to modernize existing slaughterhouses and grant licenses for establishing new slaughterhouses. A lucrative subsidy ranging from 50-90% was offered to lure entrepreneurs in this area. Contacts were established with slaughterhouse machinery suppliers in Europe and China. The whole government machinery was mobilized to usher in a new era of increased meat consumption and export. It was a significant policy shift in last several centuries. Even the British in their 200 years of rule could not accomplish what the present government has accomplished in just 10 years. It helps to have an Italian brain at the top and an agriculture minister who is practically a butcher himself, owning several piggeries and poultries.

This team was able to fulfill the dream of India's founders like Pandit Nehru who can finally rest in peace now. It was their cherished desire to see Indians eat, drink and have sex like Westerners. These founders must be reveling in their graves, having fulfilled their long pending dreams. After independence, it took Indian leaders 65 long years to accomplish this feat.

There's Method In Madness - Targeting The Rural Population

As we saw in the previous chapter, urban population is being 'taken care of' by multinational fast food chains but transforming rural population has presented a considerable challenge.

In India, rural diet mostly consists of locally grown farm products and meat consumption, when compared to cities, is very low. But this is all set to change. Majority of Indian population still lives in villages and smaller towns and the government has decided to target them as potential consumers. And this is no small number - we are talking of 700 million people here, that is 10% of humanity. It's hard to calculate the environmental, health and economic cost of a move of this sort.

A Central Government circular is produced below to give the readers an idea of their modus operandi.

Circular No. 217 /ICD - 44/2009
24 December 2009
The Chairman / Managing Director
All Scheduled Commercial Banks /
All Scheduled (Primary) Urban Cooperative Banks
All RRBs/ADFCs/SCBs/SCARDBs
All other institutions eligible for NABARD refinance

Dear Sir

Centrally Sponsored Scheme - Establishment/Modernisation of Rural Slaughter Houses

As you are aware, meat industry in India has great potential but received very limited attention for its growth and development due to socio-religious factors. Slaughter houses have been under the control of municipal authorities/local bodies but no systematic efforts have been made so far to make meat production a commercial activity. Barring a few export-oriented abattoirs, it has been in the hands of those who have no knowledge of slaughter house hygiene, sanitation and meat quality.

Thus when there is a demoniac rule, everything concerning the Vedic principles is turned upside down, all the religious ceremonies of yajna are stopped, the resources meant to be spent for yajna are taken away by the demoniac government, everything becomes chaotic, and consequently the entire world becomes hell itself.

~ Srila Prabhupada (Srimad Bhagavatam 7.8.44)

2. In this background, it has been decided by Government of India to launch a subsidy based credit linked scheme for establishment/ modernisation of Rural Slaughter Houses on pilot basis during the remaining period of XI Five Year Plan with effect from 2009-10 in three States, viz., Andhra Pradesh, Meghalaya and Uttar Pradesh. The credit linked back-ended subsidy shall be provided on the total financial outlay for the sub-sectors as indicated at para 6.1 of the guidelines.

3. The assistance under the scheme shall be available to any company, partnership firm, NGO and individual entrepreneurs. Capital subsidy @ 50% of the total financial outaly of the project with the upper ceiling as indicated in para 6.1 and 6.2 of the guidelines shall be available for all categories of the promoters.

4. The Department of Animal Husbandry, Dairying and Fisheries, Ministry of Agriculture, Government of India, is the focal department for the scheme. NABARD will be administering the subsidy and monitoring the progress of the scheme besides providing refinance support to the eligible financing banks for the term loan extended under the scheme. Extent and interest rate of refinance will be as per instructions issued by NABARD from time to time.

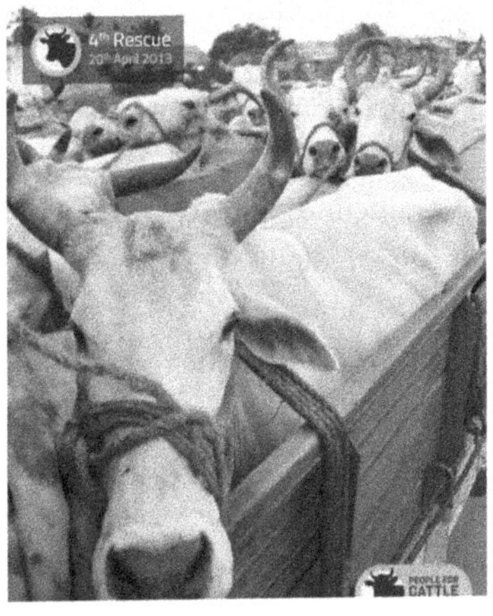

5. The implementation of the scheme shall be monitored by the Central Monitoring Committee (CMC) on a half yearly basis and the State Level Sanctioning and Monitoring Committee (SLSMC) will review the progress on quarterly basis. The participating banks will conduct periodic inspections of the units and give a feedback to the SLSMC on a consolidated basis.

6. The SLSMCs in each State are expected to meet quickly after their constitution and decide whether proposal concerning each beneficiary is to be placed before the Committee for approval or proposals of a district/cluster are to be firmed up and bunched together for consideration of the Committee or the Committee would ratify the action taken by the financial institution on individual projects.

7. We request you to circulate the operational guidelines among your controlling offices and branches in the concerned states with instructions to implement the scheme expeditiously and advise your Controlling offices to submit the proposals to the Regional Offices of NABARD in the respective states. NABARD will release subsidy subject to availability of funds from GoI. You may also take steps for giving wide publicity to the scheme. The State Animal Husbandry Department may also be approached for popularising the scheme and mobilising applications from prospective promoters. A copy of the operational guidelines of the scheme is enclosed. English and Hindi versions of the operational guidelines would be placed in the website of NABARD

Please acknowledge receipt.

Yours faithfully

(S C Kaushik)

Chief General Manager

Guidelines For Establishment /Modernisation Of Rural Slaughter Houses

1. Background

Meat sector is one of the poorly organised sectors in our country. Though the consumption of meat is on the increase, the quality aspects have remained unchanged. Slaughterhouses have been under the control of municipal authorities and no effort had been made to make meat production an economic activity. Lack of finance, poor private participation, and environmental problems are some of the other constraints felt.

It is not just the cow slaughter business that is disturbing. The cruelty of animal transport in India is mind boggling. It would never be permitted by the beef-eaters in the US or EU where strict laws regarding movement of animals by road or train are enforced. I have seen French police stop trucks going into Spain and make the attendants feed and water the cattle before proceeding (that was in the 1960s; the rules are much stricter today). Today I see trucks sneak through the back roads of my town with cows with broken legs dangling off the back of the vehicle as they head for Pondicherry and Chennai.

~ Dinesh Wadhwa, Goa

1.2 With enactment of Food Safety and Standards Act 2006, all the food items produced in the country will have to meet a certain level of quality standards in terms of hygiene prescribed. Meat is probably one item, which has not been paid adequate attention in this regard. At present slaughter houses in rural areas are under the control of local bodies like Panchayats and Municipalities. The slaughterhouses maintained by them get least priority and no standards are being

ma saurabheyatra suco
vyetu te vrsalad bhayam
ma rodir amba bhadram te
khalanam mayi sastari

O son of Surabhi, you need lament no longer now. There is no need to fear this low-class sudra. And, O mother cow, as long as I am living as the ruler and subduer of all envious men, there is no cause for you to cry. Everything will be good for you.

Protection of bulls and cows and all other animals can be possible only when there is a state ruled by an executive head like Maharaja Pariksit. Maharaja Pariksit addresses the cow as mother, for he is a cultured, twice-born, ksatriya king. Surabhi is the name of the cows which exist in the spiritual planets and are especially reared by Lord Sri Krsna Himself. As men are made after the form and features of the Supreme Lord, so also the cows are made after the form and features of the surabhi cows in the spiritual kingdom. In the material world the human society gives all protection to the human being, but there is no law to protect the descendants of Surabhi, who can give all protection to men by supplying the miracle food, milk. But Maharaja Pariksit and the Pandavas were fully conscious of the importance of the cow and bull, and they were prepared to punish the cow-killer with all chastisement, including death. There has sometimes been agitation for the protection of the cow, but for want of pious executive heads and suitable laws, the cow and the bull are not given protection. The human society should recognize the importance of the cow and the bull and thus give all protection to these important animals, following in the footsteps of Maharaja Pariksit. For protecting the cows and brahminical culture, the Lord, who is very kind to the cow and the saintly persons, will be pleased with us and will bestow upon us real peace.

~ Srimad Bhagavatam 1.17.9

insisted on. Production of meat in them cannot be recognized as meat from organized sector.

Schemes to improve slaughterhouses formulated in the past have not been very effective, since most of them concentrated on large urban-based slaughterhouses. Even at present, Ministry of Food Processing has prepared a scheme to support large modern slaughterhouses for supply of meat to cities. These will be units of large outlay and help produce wholesome meat for the consumers in these cities.

1.3 To make this sector dynamic, targeting large slaughterhouses will not suffice. Addition of value at the local level will be more ideal, as it will limit transport of animals, contain environmental pollution to local levels, and help animal owners to earn better income by providing them direct access to market. It is important to introduce private participation and make the activity a business. The past shows that slaughterhouses at industrial scale have been successful only in the private sector where they are run as meat producing centres.

1.4 Service slaughterhouses have not been self-sustaining, as the service charges collected do not meet even the running expenses leading to maintenance of units. Small slaughterhouses have not been tried on commercial lines, except in few cases and even in them no systemic investments have been made. A pilot scheme to encourage establishment of rural slaughterhouses and help entrepreneurs to undertake the activity as a bankable venture is envisaged.

2. Objectives of the Scheme

i. To establish a new system of slaughter of livestock along with network of cold chain and distribution on commercial basis.

ii. To develop models of slaughterhouses which can be run by private entrepreneurs in rural and semi urban areas with population of less than 50,000.

iii. To encourage value addition to the products in rural areas so that livestock owners get better income and wastage of byproducts of slaughterhouses is avoided.

iv. To ensure hygiene in meat production from the slaughterhouse to consumer table by establishing cold chain and distribution system.

v. Minimize clandestine slaughter and provide pollution free environment.

3. Definition

For the purpose of the scheme, rural slaughter houses are those which are located in places with a population of less than 50,000.

4. Implementing period and Area of Operation

The pilot phase will be implemented during the remaining XI plan period in three states viz. Andhra Pradesh, Meghalaya and Uttar Pradesh on a first come first serve basis.

5. Eligibility

5.1. Any company, partnership firm, NGO and individual entrepreneur would be eligible for the assistance if they set up/ modernize the slaughter houses / poultry dressing units as per guidelines laid down. They should have the necessary approval of the local body to take up the work.

5.2. Each entrepreneur would be eligible to avail benefit under the scheme for two units per State with a ceiling of four units under the scheme.

All possible care will be taken to avoid duplication of projects under the scheme with similar projects implemented by Ministry of Food Processing Industries in the same areas.

A signboard displaying "Assisted by Department of Animal Husbandry Dairying and Fisheries, Ministry of Agriculture, Government of India" will be exhibited at the unit.

After reproducing this government circular, now we present several media reports on modernization and expansion of slaughterhouse activities in India.

Hi-Tech Killing In The Ancient City Of Patna

Times News Network | Dec 11, 2012,

If things go according to plans, Patna may soon have a hi-tech slaughter house. An expression of interest on the website of Bihar Urban Infrastructure Development Corporation Limited (BUIDCO) has been posted about setting up a modern slaughter house on a five-acre plot at Rama Chakberia on Patna-Gaya Road. The estimated cost of the slaughter house would be Rs 26.34 crore.

The proposed structure would have the capacity of slaughtering 200 cattle besides 350 sheep and goat on eight-hour shift basis. Ministry of Food Processing Industry, Government of India (MoFPI), has approved Rs 11 crore grant for the project. The bidders can avail the grant subject to the condition that it meets the MoFPI guidelines.

According to the proposal, the selected agency would have to set up backward linkage and livestock reception yard, a lairage, slaughter lines for sheep, goat and cows, effluent treatment plant (ETP), dry rendering plant, forward linkage with meat, transport facility under cold chain system and meat packaging plant. To keep the plant and adjoining areas healthy, the agency would have to install a rendering-cum-carcass utilization plant for disposal of cadavers and meat waste.

However, BUIDCO managing director Anupam Kumar Suman says, "The project has to be implemented in 24 months. It is a semi-mechanized project but the agency would be free to install a fully mechanized plant."

Earlier, Patna Municipal Corporation (PMC) had constructed a boundary wall around the allotted land but due to the local residents' protest they had failed to proceed with the project. The slaughter house will be made under public private partnership (PPP) mode.

PMC maintains one goat abattoir near Ashok Cinema. "Maintaining a goat abattoir is far easier than providing hygiene to the cow abattoir. The existing cow abattoir runs in an unhealthy and unhygienic condition and there is no option than to shift it," says PMC commissioner Pankaj Kumar Pal.

pravrttim ca nivrttim ca
jana na vidur asurah
na saucam napi cacaro
na satyam tesu vidyate

"Those who are demonic do not know what is to be done and what is not to be done. Neither cleanliness nor proper behavior nor truth is found in them" (Bhagavad-gita 16.7).

Because demons do not know what to do and what not to do, they become involved in unclean dealings. As clearly indicated in the Bhagavad-gita, these are classic symptoms of a demonic personality. As long as such demons falsely occupy responsible government posts, the people in general will not be peaceful, prosperous, or happy.
~ Srila Prabhupada (Back To Godhead, 12-7, 1977)

Proposed Ultra Modern Slaughter House For Shimla, The Queen Of Hills

http://www.shimlamc.gov.in/page/Slaughter-House.aspx

The present slaughterhouse is existing since British days and happens to be one of the oldest slaughterhouse in the country. It is in a dilapidated condition. The existing site is not connected to a proper road where trucks/ load wagons can ply. Moreover this site is thickly inhabited and when the meat is transported on head load by coolies, there is resentment amongst the locals.

It is difficult to clean blood and excreta from old floors and walls. Moreover hides are removed manually. Effluent from the existing slaughterhouse is going untreated into the sewerage system and the adjoining nalah.

Considering these demerits, Ministry of Agriculture approved modernization of this slaughterhouse on 50:50 basis.

Project submitted amounted to Rs.19.43 crores. Later the Ministry of Food Processing Industries consented to provide 33% of the project cost or 4.00 Crores whichever was less. Since the tenders amounting to Rs. 13.65 Crores had been finalized hence the balance amount was to be provided by the H.P. Govt. or from any other sources.

Long, Cruel Road To The Slaughterhouse

Bindiya Chari, Times News Network, May 2, 2013,

A committee constituted by the high court of Bombay at Goa has discovered that animals brought to Goa from neighbouring states for slaughtering, often face cruelty during transportation. Animals get injured as vehicles carrying them from Karnataka and Maharashtra are packed beyond their intended capacity.

And if animals are unable stand due to injuries before the slaughter, meat traders put chilli powder in their eyes, says the report.

Meat traders brought animals to Goa without transportation certificate though it is mandatory under the Animal transportation Rules 1978. Animals are slaughtered at the state-run slaughter house, Goa meat complex (GMC) at Usgao in Ponda.

In The Holy City Of Varanasi, Slaughter Houses Get Funds For Modernisation

Rajeev Dikshit, Times News Network, Mar 22, 2013,

Opening of a modern slaughter house to replace old and now closed Kamalgadaha slaughter house will not be done before the end of the current financial year. But the funds to modernize the existing low capacity slaughter houses at Orderly Bazaar and Beniabag have been released.

Municipal commissioner RP Singh said that due to directives of the ministry of environment, Varanasi Municipal Corporation (VMC) has allowed low capacity slaughter houses at Orderly Bazaar and Beniabag to operate till a modern slaughterhouse opens.

Municipal veterinary officer Mohammad Aslam Ansari said that only small animals are butchered at Beniabag while Orderly Bazaar also slaughters big animals. He said that the divisional commissioner had recently sanctioned a budget of Rs 91 lakh to establish bio-digesters at both these slaughter houses. A fund of Rs 5 lakh had also been released for the renovation of Beniabag slaughter house. A proposal of Rs 1.5 crore had been submitted for the modernization of Orderly Bazaar slaughter house.

Pune Gets A Brand New Slaughterhouse, To Be Leased Out

Abhijit Atre, Times News Network, May 17, 2005

The UP state government has done some deal with slaughter house owners and is issuing new licences due to which the population of livestock in the state has come down drastically. Cows are being illegally slaughtered.

Though slaughtering of cow is banned and the animal is worshipped by Hindus, the menace of cow slaughtering has increased in the present regime. As a result of this, the population of cattle and livestock has come down drastically in Uttar Pradesh. (PTI)

~ Hriday Narain Dixit, BJP spokesperson and MLC, May 2, 2011

The recently modernised slaughter house at Kondhwa will be handed over to a private agency on a built operate and transfer (BOT) basis. According to the administration, the Pune Municipal Corporation (PMC) has spent around Rs. 4 crore on modernisation of the slaughter house which stands on a PMC owned land, cost of which is Rs. 3 crore.

The expenses on modernisation were met from the grants issued by the state and the central government. The PMC operates the slaughter house between 4 am to 9 am. After the five hour use the slaughter house is kept unused.

The private agency has shown willingness to operate the slaughter house on a commercial basis by paying an annual rent of Rs 66 lakh to the PMC, provided the agency is allowed to run the slaughter house from 4 am till 10 pm.

Gurgaon And Faridabad: Soon, Wait For High-Tech Slaughterhouse May End

HT Correspondent, Hindustan Times Gurgaon, February 16, 2013

Government is moving fast in the direction of setting up two high-tech slaughterhouses at Gurgaon and Faridabad at the cost of Rs. 60 crore and Rs. 56 crore respectively. The municipal corporations of Gurgaon and Faridabad have submitted a proposal in 2011.

Now for the first time in a kingdom well protected by the arms of the kings of the Kuru dynasty, I see you grieving with tears in your eyes. Up till now no one on earth has ever shed tears because of royal negligence.

The protection of the lives of both the human beings and the animals is the first and foremost duty of a government. A government must not discriminate in such principles. It is simply horrible for a pure-hearted soul to see organized animal-killing by the state in this age of Kali. Maharaja Pariksit was lamenting for the tears in the eyes of the bull, and he was astonished to see such an unprecedented thing in his good kingdom. Men and animals were equally protected as far as life was concerned. That is the way in God's kingdom.

~ Srila Prabhuapda (Srimad Bhagavatam 1.17.8)

Naresh Kadian, a member of a committee set up by the government on slaughterhouses, said illegal slaughtering has been taking place in Gurgaon. According to him, these slaughterhouses were flouting rules framed for prevention of cruelty to animals. The member asked civic agencies to implement the norms effectively.

5 New Mechanized Slaughterhouses Proposed For Bhubaneswar

Times News Network, Apr 18, 2013

Bhubaneswar Municipal Corporation (BMC) has engaged a Kerala-based consultancy to prepare a detailed project report (DPR) of five proposed mechanized slaughterhouses in the city. But the projects are moving at snail's pace, causing resentment among meat vendors.

The proposed modern slaughterhouses at Pandara, Gadakana, Dumduma, Ghatikia and Vani Vihar were supposed to be commissioned in 2012. Though the city has two slaughterhouses at Meherpalli in Laxmisagar area and Gandamunda, they are lying defunct.

The state government has already allotted land for each slaughterhouse. Around Rs.15 crore would be spent for the construction of five slaughterhouses. The state government and Union ministry of food processing industries would equally share the amount. Sources said the Centre was initially insisting for one big slaughterhouse for the entire city. However, the BMC sought several abattoirs to cater to the need of people at different locations.

Therefore I say that today the leaders are all fourth-class men. And that is why the whole world is in a chaotic condition. We require learned spiritual teachers -- first-class men-to lead. If people will take Bhagavad-gita's advice, then everything will be all right. What is the use of fourth-class men leading a confused and chaotic society?

If I speak so frankly, people will be very angry. But basically, their leaders are all fourth class. First-class men are great devotees of the Lord, who can guide the administrators and the citizens through their words and practical example.

~ Srila Prabhupada (JSD 6.5: Slaughterhouse Civilization)

Ludhiana - Slaughterhouse In For A Major Upgrade

Nidhi Singhi, Times News Network, Apr 25, 2010

Following strict directions from Punjab and Haryana High Court, the municipal corporation has shortlisted three companies to upgrade the slaughter house situated at Hambran Road.

Authorities have asked the firms to submit their financial bids so that work could begin soon.

Talking to Times Of India, municipal commissioner A K Sinha said four companies had approached them for the job and after going through their presentations, three were shortlisted. "The bids will be submitted soon, following which tenders will be allotted to the company on BOT basis," he added. He said the work would take at least three months to complete.

Aurangabad Slaughterhouse May Go Hi-Tech

Niraj Chinchkhede, Times News Network, Dec 8, 2012

A German company which specialises in modern slaughter and meat processing systems has evinced interest in developing the city's slaughter house at Padegaon.

The representatives of the company, BANSS Germany, who visited the Aurangabad Municipal Corporation (AMC), gave a

Then he [Maharaja Pariksit] asked the bull: Oh, who are you? Are you a bull as white as a white lotus, or are you a demigod? You have lost three of your legs and are moving on only one. Are you some demigod causing us grief in the form of a bull?

At least up to the time of Maharaja Pariksit, no one could imagine the wretched conditions of the cow and the bull. Maharaja Pariksit, therefore, was astonished to see such a horrible scene. He inquired whether the bull was not a demigod assuming such a wretched condition to indicate the future of the cow and the bull.

~ Srila Prabhuapda (Srimad Bhagavatam 1.17.7)

presentation on how the slaughter house could be developed into a state-of-the-art centre with machines doing most of the work. They also presented how waste generated at the slaughter house could be managed and converted into fertilizers.

That depends on the person. Sometimes...Those who are pious persons, they know that these rats, they are also hungry and they should be given some food. That is the vision of the pious person. And that is stated in the Srimad-Bhagavatam, that in your house you should see not only to the welfare of your children. Even there is a lizard, there is a rat, even there is a snake, you should see how they are also comfortably situated. That is spiritual communism. In Vrndavana still, a snake found in the house is never killed, snake. Still a rat is never killed. If you kill a rat in Vrndavana, then so many people will come: "Oh, you are committing such sinful acts. You are killing a rat." That depends on the mentality of the person. You can take care of this animal, I mean to say, against the disturbance created by this animal, but you cannot kill them. That is not. But when it is unavoidable, we have to do like that. But as far as possible we should avoid. We have heard from our father that his elder brother in the village had a cloth shop, and there were rats. So at night he would keep a big bowl of rice in the middle of the shop, and the rats will eat whole night. They would not commit any harm to the cloth. They respect it. They are also hungry, they are also living entities. They have also right to live, to eat. Isavasyam idam sarvam [Iso mantra 1]. Everything. They are God's creatures. The food is not only meant for you, that you shall simply eat rice and not allow to the rats and cats. No. That is not Vedic injunction. You will find in the Srimad-Bhagavatam. You can take precaution. After all, they are animals. But you cannot kill.

Of course, that is Western philosophy, that because the animals are increasing, they should be killed. We Indians also, we have taken that view—because we cannot give protection to the cows, they must be sent to the slaughterhouse. That is the modern view. But that is not injunction of the Vedas. The Vedas says that everyone has right to live, every living entity. That is going on not only in consideration of the animals—even in human beings. Just like the Americans, they were all Europeans, and they entered this American land, killed so many Red Indians. So these kind of things are going on, but that does not mean that is the law. You killed so many Red Indians for your benefit, but you have to suffer for that.

~ Srila Prabhupada (Lecture, Surat, India, 1970)

The proposed project would cost Rs 33.68 crore, with the central government offering a 50 per cent subsidy. The corporation will have to make arrangements for remaining funding. Highly placed sources in the civic body said it would adopt a public private partnership (PPP) model or a build, operate and transfer (BOT) option to give shape to the project.

The slaughter house at Padegaon will be spread over 36 acres area.

BANSS Germany supplies modern slaughter and meat processing systems as well as storage and cooling room transport systems for cows, pigs and sheep.

Emu Slaughterhouse To Come Up On Hubli Outskirts

Vincent D'Souza, Times News Network, Sep 3, 2011

An emu slaughter house -- where the birds will be slaughtered and their meat processed is taking shape on the outskirts of the city. Indo-Aussie Emu Farm, which is installing the project at Sulla village at a cost of Rs 2 crore has plans to export the meat.

The installation works of the slaughter house and two cold storage units having a storage capacity of two tonnes each will be completed by December end. The slaughtering machine has been imported from Germany. The farm which has helped around 60 farmers take up emu farming in several parts of the state by providing chicks will buy back the grown up birds from them.

Farm proprietor Vinny John said he has got advance orders mainly from Iraq, Iran, Mecca and Goa. The meat which will be exported to Muslim countries will be of purely Halal standard, he added.

According to Vinny John, who is currently doing a research on emu breeding in University of Western Australia, the Australian origin bird was first brought to India by an American NRI about 10 years ago who set up a farm in Andhra Pradesh. Then it spread

> *Starvation, world hunger, cruelty, waste, wars -- we must make a statement against these things. Vegetarianism is my statement. And I think it's a strong one.*
>
> *- Isaac Bashevis Singer, Nobel laureate and Holocaust survivor*

to Maharasthra, Tamil Nadu, Karnataka and northern states. The promoters of emu rearing have been regularly organizing food festivals in metros where emu dishes are served for people to develop a taste for the red meat.

Nagpur To Get A 'Scientific' Slaughterhouse

Times News Network, Jul 27, 2011

The Nagpur Municipal Corporation (NMC) will be constructing an ultra-modern slaughter house on the city outskirts. NMC has dropped its earlier plan to upgrade its old abattoir in Bhandewadi.

Sukrut Nirman Charitable Trust, a social organization working for protection and welfare of animals, has filed a plea claiming that majority of slaughterhouses are running illegally as they haven't sought permission of Maharashtra Pollution Control Board (MPCB) and Animal Welfare Board of India before opening as per rules of Prevention of Cruelty to Animals Act, 1960.

For Slaughterhouse, Chandigarh MC To Cough Up Rs 15cr

Deepak Yadav, Times News Network, Feb 19, 2012

There is fresh hope for city residents to get hygienic meat on their plate. After previous attempt to run a temporary slaughter house failed, MC has finally decided to cough up Rs 15 crore for automatic poultry processing plant in the financial budget for 2012-2013 and approached national meat and poultry processing board of ministry of food processing to provide consultancy on this project.

A senior official of the MC said, "We are in touch with the national meat and poultry processing board to provide consultancy

> *We simply request, "Don't kill. Don't maintain slaughterhouses." That is very sinful. It brings down very severe karmic reactions upon society. Stop these slaughterhouses. We don't say, "Stop eating meat." You can eat meat, but don't take it from the slaughterhouse, by killing. Simply wait, and you'll get the carcasses.*
>
> *After all, how long will the cows live? Their maximum age is twenty years, and there are many cows who live only eighteen, sixteen, or ten years. So wait that much time; then regularly get dead cows and eat. What is the difficulty?*
> *~Srila Prabhupada (JSD 6.5: Slaughterhouse Civilization)*

to us to establish plant and following this board has recently sent their consultancy proposal along with their terms and conditions to us. We will soon visit some of the private giants to establish the plant with latest and environment friendly technology."

Pig Slaughterhouse in Allahabad, The City Of Kumbha Mela

Times News Network, May 26, 2009

The Allahabad Municipal Corporation (AMC) has failed to open a pig slaughterhouse outside the municipal limits of the city though plans for it were finalized long ago.

Even the money sanctioned by the Central government for the construction of the slaughter house is lying unutilised for the last three years. The Central government has sanctioned Rs 26.16 lakh for the purpose. The AMC had to arrange the remaining 50 per cent of the amount from its resources. However, the severe financial crisis grappling the corporation has put brakes on the project.

The land for the construction of the slaughterhouse has been identified at Naini and boundary wall has been constructed. The remaining work had to be stopped due to lack of funds. The AMC officers are hopeful that if amount of Rs 15 lakh is arranged, then the project could see the light of the day.

Pimpri Chinchwad Municipal Corporation Plans Abattoir In Industrial Area

Siddharth Gaikwad, Times News Network Aug 18, 2012

After hunting for a suitable spot for an abattoir for the past many years, the Pimpri Chinchwad Municipal Corporation (PCMC) has proposed to construct a modern abattoir in an industrial area. The civic body's previous proposals for abattoir at various sites had faced opposition in the past for their inconvenient location.

> *This killing of animals is for the non-civilized society. They cannot... They do not know how to grow food. They were killing animals. When man is advanced in his knowledge and education, why they should kill? Especially here, we see so many nice foodstuffs. Fruits, grains, milk. And from milk, you can get hundreds of nice preparations, all nutritious.*
> *-Prabhupada (Room Conversation, July 5, 1975, Chicago)*

At present, Pimpri-Chinchwad has only one small slaughter house located below the Indira Gandhi Railway Over Bridge (ROB). Traders sell meat from rows of shops that the PCMC has constructed under the bridge.

The municipal corporation has now proposed to construct the slaughter house on a hectare of land in survey number 202 at Pimpri Waghire.

The proposed slaughter house will have all modern facilities, including proper disposal of the waste.

Kolkata Municipal Corporation In A Hurry To Build Abattoir

Times News Network, Jan 7, 2011

A year has passed since the Centre sent a Rs15 crore grant to build a modern slaughter house in Tangra, but KMC has not even invited a tender. The money is bound to be returned if nothing is done by end of this fiscal.

Now, in the eleventh hour, MMiC health, Atin Ghosh is on a frantic effort to at least begin the project. Mayor Sovan Chatterjee on Thursday laid the foundation stone of the slaughterhouse, next to the old one, and assured that it would be one of the most modern abattoirs in the country. A KMC source said the new slaughter house will cost Rs 29 crore and be ready by 2012.

Ghosh promised that the meat processed in the slaughter house will be disinfected and pass hygiene tests at a lab to be built in the

Therefore, according to Vedic scripture, those animal-eaters, they should kill them personally so that they can see how much suffering is there, so he will stop. But now the things are being done in the slaughterhouse. They do not see. They purchase very nicely packed. They do not know. And they are becoming implicated. Therefore, according to Vedic injunction, if you want to eat meat, you kill yourself in your front,
~ Srila Prabhupada, (Morning Walk -- June 29, 1974, Melbourne)

facility. The meat will be transported in refrigerated vans. It will also accommodate more animals.

The existing abattoir can hold 700 big animals a day, but the new one can hold 2,000 and process 80-90 animals per hour.

Delhi Goverment Constructs Hi-tech Abattoir, Lands In Trouble

Dhananjay Mahapatra, Times News Network, Mar 5, 2009

The ultra-modern abattoir built at Ghazipur at a cost of Rs 123 crore does not even conform to a 1939 British Raj scheme for a slaughter house at Najafgarh, alleged the apex pollution control board in the Supreme Court on Wednesday.

This startling allegation made by Central Pollution Control Board counsel Vijay Panjwani before a Bench comprising Justices S B Sinha, V S Sirpurkar and Cyriac Joseph startled the

The personality of religious principles, Dharma, was wandering about in the form of a bull. And he met the personality of earth in the form of a cow who appeared to grieve like a mother who had lost her child. She had tears in her eyes, and the beauty of her body was lost.

The bull is the emblem of the moral principle, and the cow is the representative of the earth. When the bull and the cow are in a joyful mood, it is to be understood that the people of the world are also in a joyful mood. The reason is that the bull helps production of grains in the agricultural field, and the cow delivers milk, the miracle of aggregate food values. The human society, therefore, maintains these two important animals very carefully so that they can wander everywhere in cheerfulness. But at the present moment in this age of Kali both the bull and the cow are now being slaughtered and eaten up as foodstuff by a class of men who do not know the brahminical culture. The bull and the cow can be protected for the good of all human society simply by the spreading of brahminical culture as the topmost perfection of all cultural affairs. By advancement of such culture, the morale of society is properly maintained, and so peace and prosperity are also attained without extraneous effort. When brahminical culture deteriorates, the cow and bull are mistreated, and the resultant actions are prominent by the following symptoms.

~ Srila Prabhuapda (Srimad Bhagavatam 1.16.19)

court. Absence of an approach road to the abattoir results in the transporting vehicles whipping up dust clouds, which would defeat the purpose -- supply of hygienic meat to Delhiites.

While stressing that there was no environment management plan prepared by MCD and the Delhi government for the abattoir, CPCB detailed the February 6, 1939 plan prepared by then Delhi Municipal Committee for setting up an abattoir at Najafgarh spread over 277.3 acres with every possible amenity, many of which were not provided for at the Ghazipur slaughter house.

The Ghazipur slaughter house got mired in controversy from 2004 onwards when MCD abruptly decided to increase the animal handling capacity of the abattoir from 2,500 per day to 5,000 without the upward revision of the earlier estimated project cost of Rs 65 crore.

While only 2,500 animals are slaughtered at Idgah, nearly 10,000 would be slaughtered at Ghazipur.

State's First Modern Slaughterhouse On The Cards For Indore

Bagish Jha, Times News Network Mar 18, 2012

Indore Municipal Corporation (IMC) is all set to develop the first of its kind state-of-the-art slaughterhouse in Madhya Pradesh with a zero waste disposal facility. Though the civic body is yet to identify the place for the slaughterhouse, it is likely to come up on eight acres of land on the outskirts of the city at an estimated cost of Rs 50 crore.

A proposal for a similar slaughterhouse for Bhopal is also in the pipeline.

tatas canu-dinam dharmah
satyam saucam ksama daya
kalena balina rajan
nanksyaty ayur balam smrtih

Sukadeva Gosvami said: Then, O King, religion, truthfulness, cleanliness, tolerance, mercy, duration of life, physical strength and memory will all diminish day by day because of the powerful influence of the age of Kali.

~Srila Prabhupada (SB 12.2.1)

The slaughterhouse will be developed on public-private partnership (PPP) basis under which 15% of the cost will be borne by the Union government and the remaining 85% will be shared by the company, which will be picked through tender. The IMC has to allot land for the slaughterhouse.

"The state-of-art slaughterhouse will be operated on a zero waste disposal basis," said the zoo in-charge Dr Uttam Yadav, who is supervising the project, adding that the waste from the slaughterhouse would be disposed scientifically. Other features of the slaughter house include a collection centre, main slaughtering and chilling chambers, storage room, packaging and processing centres. "It will also have provision for a market to sell and purchase animals," said Yadav adding most of the metros have such modern slaughterhouses and soon Indore will join the league.

Interestingly, there are three authorized slaughterhouses in the city at Sadar Bazaar, Khajaran and Junni Adda. But sources said that there 35 unauthorized slaughterhouses operating in the city.

The consumption of meat in Indore is about 500 kg everyday. The proposed slaughterhouse will have the capacity to produce more than the existing demand. The company, which will develop the slaughterhouse, will also export meat from here.

Dutch Know-how For Hyderabad Slaughterhouse, Completion Delayed

Times News Network, Aug 24, 2012

Mayor Mohammed Majid Hussain along with GHMC officials visited Ramanaspura slaughter house on Thursday and took up the issue of delay in completion of modernisation works with the contractor. He asked the contractor to complete work and conduct a trial run in October.

There are four classes: lazy intelligent, busy intelligent, lazy foolish, and active foolish. The active foolish is a fourth-class man. So at the present moment they're very active, but they're all foolish. Therefore the world is in danger. Active foolishness. Foolish, if he stops, he does not work, it is better. But as soon as he becomes active he becomes more dangerous.

-Srila Prabhupada (Lecture, , Los Angeles, December 8, 1973)

Upgradation and modernisation of Ramanaspura slaughter house was handed over to Ramky Enviro Engineers Ltd in 2009. The works were slated to be completed within two years but was delayed. The mayor also informed that technical experts from Netherlands will arrive in Hyderabad in September to install equipment at the slaughterhouse.

Thiruvananthapuram Slaughterhouse To Get A Lease Of Life

Aswin J Kumar, Times News Network, Dec 3, 2012

The corporation-run slaughter house in Kunnukuzhy is likely to get a fresh lease of life following the civic body submitting a fresh proposal to install a rendering plant.

The slaughter house has been facing closure following a pollution control board notice.

The corporation, in its bid to save the unit, had earlier planned to set up a rendering plant to process the waste. The government, however, denied administrative sanction, citing technical hurdles in allotting the necessary funds.

While rejecting the plan, the government had also directed the corporation to submit a fresh proposal.

It was in this backdrop that the corporation submitted the fresh proposal.

Practically there is no mercifulness now, daya. Formerly a man was very charitable, but here, at the present moment, where is the question of charity? He cannot maintain oneself. So these things are reducing. Therefore Vyasadeva thought it wise to give the Vedic knowledge in writings so that we can read, we can hear, and we can utilize, we can take benefit out of it.

-Srila Prabhupada (Sunday Feast Lecture — Los Angeles, January 19, 1969)

The corporation had earlier drawn a detailed project proposal to convert the rendering plant into a major marketing venture. According to that project, the rendering plant was to be set up at a cost of Rs 2 crore, and was to function on a build, operate and transfer basis.

The byproducts from the rendering plant like tallow, (a hard, fatty substance made from rendered animal fat), grease and MBM (meat and bone meals) were to be marketed by a private agency, which would also operate the plant.

Deonar Slaughterhouse, Mumbai

This abattoir is located in Deonar, in the eastern suburb of Mumbai. The abattoir is the largest in Asia. At present it kills 4000 animals daily and employs a workforce of 1200 butchers. 50% of its production is exported to Gulf countries and it uses 1.7 million liters of water everyday. Animals are brought from Gujarat, Rajasthan, MP, Maharashtra and UP.

Run by Municipal Corporation of Greater Mumbai, its operating losses run into crores which are borne by the taxpayers.

Plans have been finalized for a Rs.125 crore makeover of the slaughterhouse to process 14000 animals everyday. Members of public and some lawmakers are opposing the plans.

"I do not want my tax money to fund the death of any more animals," says Yogesh Shah, a Jain who runs the Mumbai-based Himsa Virodhak Sangh, or anti-violence association.

State Run Slaughterhouses

By this, he refers to a law dating back about 130 years, when the British made slaughterhouses a government responsibility, and municipal corporations began running the abattoirs across India. Over the last 60 years, slaughterhouses have increased more than 100-fold, from 345 to about 36,000, and the cattle population has declined by 1.18% a year.

"Now, they want to expand the Deonar slaughterhouse and increase its killing capacity from 4,000 to 14,000 animals," says Shah. He explains that law requires the state to provide meat only for the local population. A Bombay Municipal Corporation resolution of 1983 prohibits the state from exporting "any meat, beef or pork whatsoever from this country".

But, Deonar slaughterhouse records reveal that it has exported the meat of bullocks, goats and sheep. Records show that meat of 387,953 cows and buffaloes and 10,878,424 sheep and goats was illegally exported to West Asian countries between 1990 and 2006. Allegations of financial mismanagement have also dogged the slaughterhouse and records of the same period reveal that the abattoir has made losses to the tune of Rs. 89 crore.

Others such as the municipal corporator Manoj Kotak, question the presence of the state in the meat business. "Just regulate the slaughterhouses and provide them to private, licensed operators. Why should a municipality run them? And if it is doing this for the non-vegetarian citizens, then it should run a vegetable house for the vegetarians, too. Why does it not start that enterprise as well?"

He declares that his party will oppose any move to expand the abattoir. "We will not let it happen. There is no need to kill cattle in India to export them to other countries. Certainly, no need for the state to do it."

4.

Pink Revolution

A Historic Policy Shift, Unprecedented In India's History

India is known all over the world as a peace loving country. It is a historical fact that India never attacked any other country, believing always in the philosophy of peaceful coexistence.

It is also probably the only country that provides for animal care in its constitution. Animals are mentioned as something more than just food. Each citizen is enjoined to care for and preserve nature and its creatures.

Article 48, The Directive Principles of State Policy states, "The state shall, in particular, take steps for ... prohibiting the slaughter of cows and calves and other milch and draught cattle."

India has been a country of farmers and shepherds, lovingly looking after their animals. India was never a country of butchers and murderers. Bloodbath is foreign to Indian culture.

Compassion and non-violence formed the core belief of all the religions that originated in this great land.

Traditional Indian or Vedic way of life teaches respect for all life forms. In their view, all living beings are born of mother nature and

> *And the rascal, blind leaders are leading everyone to hell. They are simply misleaders. People do not like to accept any authority. Still, they have accepted these rascals as leaders and are being misled. In this way both the rascal leaders and their unfortunate followers remain bound up by the stringent laws of material nature.*
> *~Srila Prabhupada (Beyond the Limits of the Body)*

have an equal right to life. Indeed, in Vedic conception, animals are treated like innocent children and are meant to be given all protection.

Srimad Bhagavatam, the foremost of all Vedic texts states, "One should treat animals such as deer, camels, asses, monkeys, mice, snakes, birds and flies exactly like one's own son. How little difference there actually is between children and these innocent animals." (SB 7.14.9)

National Policy Takes A U-turn

10 years ago it marked a significant moment in Indian history when Indian government decided to accord highest priority to meat consumption and export, making it 'truly a national initiative'.

Website of Ministry of Food Processing Industries states:

> There is an urgent need to frame a right strategy for the development of meat and poultry production in the country. This will certainly bring prosperity to millions of our rural citizens and create employment in rural India. Having achieved the Green Revolution, the White Revolution and the Blue Revolution, it is time to ask the question "can the Pink Revolution be far behind?" Certainly this will require large investment in infrastructure, mainly in cold storages, and modern meat processing plants. Without a strong and dependable cold chain, a vital sector like meat industry, which is based mostly on perishable products, cannot survive and grow.
>
> (http://mofpi.nic.in/ContentPage.aspx?CategoryId=173)

These so-called civilized people -- what is the difference between these rascals and vultures? The vultures also enjoy killing and then eating the dead body. "Make it dead and then enjoy" -- people have become vultures. And their civilization is a vulture civilization. Animal-eaters -- they're like jackals, vultures, dogs. Flesh is not proper food for human beings. Here in the Vedic culture is civilized food, human food: milk, fruit, vegetables, nuts, grains. Let them learn it. Uncivilized rogues, vultures, raksasas [demons] -- and they're leaders. ~ Srila Prabhupada (Journey of Self Discover 6.5: Slaughterhouse Civilization)

Also, below we reproduce excerpts from the report of the working group on food processing industries for 12th five year plan by Government of India.

Ministry of Food Processing Industries
Excerpts From Report of the Working Group on Food Processing Industries For 12th Five Year Plan, Government of India

11th Plan (2007-2012)

The total plan outlay of the Ministry rose from 650 crore during the 10th Plan to 4,031 crore during the 11th Plan.

The financial projections for the 12th Plan have to be looked at from the perspective of making growth of food processing sector truly a national goal and reflect both the potential of the sector and demand from the stakeholders.

Likely Impact

The proposed financial outlay of around 15,300 crore would have an aggregate component of around 10,300 crore towards providing part capital assistance to food processing projects. Based on design of the Schemes and experience so far, this may be able to attract a total investment

The foolish leaders of a godless civilization try to devise various plans to bring about peace and prosperity in the godless world under a patent trademark of materialism, and because such attempts are illusory only, the people elect incompetent, blind leaders, one after another, who are incapable of offering solutions. If we want at all to end this anomaly of a godless civilization, we must follow the principles of revealed scriptures like the Srimad-Bhagavatam and follow the instruction of a person like Sri Sukadeva Gosvami who has no attraction for material gain.
~ Srila Prabhupada (Srimad Bhagavatam 2.2.6)

of around 35,000 crore in food processing sector. Considering an Incremental Capital Output ratio of around 4 for Indian Economy, though it may be less for food processing sector, an additional investment of 35,000 crore may lead to an additional output of 8,750 crore.

The Mid-Term Appraisal Report of the 11th Five Year Plan has also recommended accelerating agricultural growth through high value segment (horticulture, livestock and fisheries). To achieve this, it has suggested, inter-alia, the following:

nijagrahaujasa virah
kalim digvijaye kvacit
nrpa-linga-dharam sudram
ghnantam go-mithunam pada

Once, when Maharaja Pariksit was on his way to conquer the world, he saw the master of Kali-yuga, who was lower than a sudra, disguised as a king and hurting the legs of a cow and bull. The King at once caught hold of him to deal sufficient punishment.

The king cannot tolerate insults to the most important animal, the cow...Human civilization means to advance the cause of brahminical culture, and to maintain it, cow protection is essential. There is a miracle in milk, for it contains all the necessary vitamins to sustain human physiological conditions for higher achievements. Brahminical culture can advance only when man is educated to develop the quality of goodness, and for this there is a prime necessity of food prepared with milk, fruits and grains. Maharaja Pariksit was astonished to see that a black sudra, dressed like a ruler, was mistreating a cow, the most important animal in human society.

The age of Kali means mismanagement and quarrel. And the root cause of all mismanagement and quarrel is that worthless men with the modes of lower-class men, who have no higher ambition in life, come to the helm of the state management. Such men at the post of a king are sure to first hurt the cow and the brahminical culture, thereby pushing all society towards hell. Maharaja Pariksit, trained as he was, got the scent of this root cause of all quarrel in the world. Thus he wanted to stop it in the very beginning.

~ Srila Prabhuapda (Srimad Bhagavatam 1.16.4)

i. To encourage "clustering" of farmers in groups through NGOs, be it in the form of "cooperatives", farmer clubs, or contract farming, etc.

ii. To encourage organized logistics players, processors and modern retailers (both domestic and foreign) by freeing them from restrictions, and supporting them to link directly with clusters of farmers.

This is a matter of great satisfaction for the Ministry of Food Processing Industries that the above suggestions have already been the guiding principles of its 11th Five Year Plan.

The Scheme for Modernization of Abattoirs was the third important component of the Infrastructure Development Scheme of the Ministry. This Scheme aimed at creating infrastructure for hygienic and more humane slaughtering of animals leading to availability of hygienic meat to the domestic consumers as well as exports. This Scheme also has requisite flexibility for spirit of Public-Private Partnership and has generated good response from the States.

The 11th Plan approach of the Ministry also gave special stress on creation of institutional structures to guide the growth of the sector in the desired direction. The establishment of National Meat and Poultry Processing Board and Indian Grape Processing Board

Saunaka Rsi inquired: Why did Maharaja Pariksit simply punish him, since he was the lowest of the sudras, having dressed as a king and having struck a cow on the leg?

Saunaka and the rsis were astonished to hear that the pious Maharaja Pariksit simply punished the culprit and did not kill him. This suggests that a pious king like Maharaja Pariksit should have at once killed an offender who wanted to cheat the public by dressing like a king and at the same time daring to insult the purest of the animals, a cow. The rsis in those days, however, could not even imagine that in the advanced days of the age of Kali the lowest of the sudras will be elected as administrators and will open organized slaughterhouses for killing cows.

~ Srila Prabhuapda (Srimad Bhagavatam 1.16.5)

may be considered as significant milestones during this period. The Indian Institute of Crop Processing Technology was also upgraded to a National Centre of Excellence in the country. Above all, a National Institute of Food Technology Entrepreneurship & Management (NIFTEM) has been established by the Ministry as a Centre of Excellence to cater to all aspects of technology, entrepreneurship, research, skill development and management for the sector at the apex level.

Various studies suggest that the industry is grappling with the shortage of refrigeration mechanics, electricians and fitters and food safety professionals etc. There are a few institutions only that provide qualified manpower for food processing sector. Hence, one of the major emphasis of 12th Plan would be on mapping the skill gaps and identify priority areas for human resource development for increasing the productivity of workers/units in the sector.

iii. Scheme for Cold Chain, Value Addition and Preservation Infrastructure

Capital grant of 50% / 75% of the project cost (plant and machinery and technical civil work only) in general areas/difficult areas subject to a maximum of 10 crore.

Cold chain network in India is practically non-existent with stand alone cold storage facilities passing of as cold chain network. Most of the cold stores are single chambered, single product facilities which mainly stock potato and potato seed for about 6 months a year and lie idle during the rest of the year. The entrepreneurs, setting up cold chain projects, have to grapple with the procurement issues as well which lead to low capacity utilization.

People in general are misled by blind leaders. The leaders of human society -- the politicians, philosophers and scientists -- are blind because they are not God conscious. According to Bhagavad-gita, because they are bereft of all factual knowledge due to their atheistic way of life, they are actually sinful rascals and are the lowest among men.

When such atheists become leaders of society, the entire atmosphere is surcharged with nescience.

~ Srila Prabhupada (Nectar of Instruction: verse 7)

The Ministry of Food Processing Industries has been fully aware of the need for comprehensive cold chain solutions for food processors. The Scheme for Integrated Cold Chain, Value Addition and Preservation Infrastructure was therefore launched during 11th Plan to provide integrated cold chain and preservation facilities without any break, from the farm gate to the consumer.

The Scheme is designed to link farms to value addition facilities through an efficient supply chain and includes sectors such as dairy, meat, poultry and fishery too in addition to fruits and vegetables

Out of 164 proposals, 39 cold chain projects have been approved initially which met all eligibility parameters within stipulated timeline. The approved proposals envisage a total investment of about 850 Crore which would be creating an additional aggregate cold chain capacity of about 2.5 lakh MT in the Country. Most of these projects are under implementation and a significant part of them may be completed by end of this year.

Considering very encouraging response from industry, the Ministry has decided to cover more cold chain projects under the Scheme during 11th Plan and has already received in principle approval from the Planning Commission in this regard.

It is being proposed to support 120 more integrated cold chain projects during 12th Plan, out of which 20 projects would be of irradiation facilities.

iv. Scheme for Modernization of Abattoirs

Capital grant of 50% / 75% of the project cost (Plant machinery and technical, civil work only) in general areas/difficult areas subject to a maximum of 15 crore.

Value addition in meat sector has been almost non-existent except in the case of cattle meat processing which is primarily meant

It is a grossest type of sin to eat meat supplied by organized slaughterhouses which are ghastly places for breeding all kinds of material afflictions to society, country and the people in general. The material world is itself a place always full of anxieties, and by encouraging animal slaughter the whole atmosphere becomes polluted more and more by war, pestilence, famine and many other unwanted calamities.
~ Srila Prabhupada (Srimad Bhagavatam 1.7.37)

for the export market. *Livestock markets and abattoirs are mostly in unorganised sector. For the meat sector to be more vibrant, profitable, export oriented and provider of safe meat, it is necessary that a perceptible shift from unorganized to organized sector takes place.*

Mid-Term Appraisal of 11th Five Year Plan

The rise in per capita income in the Country has witnessed an increased demand for meat products in recent years. It is to be noted that meat consumption remains a "luxury" for majority of non-vegetarian population in India. However, as the purchasing

> *O chaste one, the king's good name, duration of life and good rebirth vanish when all kinds of living beings are terrified by miscreants in his kingdom. It is certainly the prime duty of the king to subdue first the sufferings of those who suffer. Therefore I must kill this most wretched man because he is violent against other living beings.*
>
> *When there is some disturbance caused by wild animals in a village or town, the police or others take action to kill them. Similarly, it is the duty of the government to kill at once all bad social elements such as thieves, dacoits and murderers. The same punishment is also due to animal-killers because the animals of the state are also the praja. Praja means one who has taken birth in the state, and this includes both men and animals. Any living being who takes birth in a state has the primary right to live under the protection of the king. The jungle animals are also subject to the king, and they also have a right to live. So what to speak of domestic animals like the cows and bulls.*
>
> *By the law of the Supreme Lord, all living beings, in whatever shape they may be, are the sons of the Lord, and no one has any right to kill another animal, unless it is so ordered by the codes of natural law. The tiger can kill a lower animal for his subsistence, but a man cannot kill an animal for his subsistence. That is the law of God, who has created the law that a living being subsists by eating another living being. Thus the vegetarians are also living by eating other living beings. Therefore, the law is that one should live only by eating specific living beings, as ordained by the law of God. The Isopanisad directs that one should live by the direction of the Lord and not at one's sweet will. A man can subsist on varieties of grains, fruits and milk ordained by God, and there is no need of animal food, save and except in particular cases.*
>
> *~ Srila Prabhupada (Srimad Bhagavatam 1.17.10-11)*

power of the people rise, there has been a perceptible shift towards meat and poultry consumption, which is also being reflected in food inflation figures. The poultry industry has though risen to this challenge and a number of organized players have entered this segment to take optimum advantage of this increasing demand. But the domestic supply chain of the poultry sector also leaves much to be desired.

Unfortunately, the meat sector remains unorganized except cattle meat processing for export market. This has led to not only continuous upward pressure on meat prices, but also increasing concerns regarding hygiene standards of meat products. Quality and hygiene levels in the meat market continue to be major issues due to unscientific breeding, primitive and crude slaughtering and de-feathering techniques, lack of basic infrastructure facilities including facilities for handling carcass/flaying, cross-contamination in slaughter and improper handling during carriage and transportation. These issues lead to high wastages of meat, contamination and deterioration in quality during the whole process. *It was thus felt that both qualitative as well as quantitative capacities of abattoirs need to be upgraded and they are required to be appropriately linked with commercial processing of meat, both for domestic consumption and export markets besides discouraging unauthorized slaughtering.*

Creation of the infrastructure of Meat Testing Laboratories also needs to be looked at.

In view of the above, during 11th Plan, the Ministry had launched a comprehensive Scheme for Modernization of Abattoirs across the Country. The Scheme is mainly aimed at promoting scientific and hygienic slaughtering of animals, by-product utilization and value addition, provision of chilling facility to prevent microbial activity in slaughtered animals and better forward linkage facilities for finished meat and meat products.

> *If man does not allow the animals peaceful coexistence, how can he expect peaceful existence in human society? The blind leaders must therefore understand the laws of the Supreme Being and then try to rule.*
> *~ Srila Prabhupada (Srimad Bhagavatam 1.13.47)*

The Scheme is to be implemented with the involvement of local bodies (Panchayats and Municipal Corporations) and also has the flexibility for facilitating involvement of private investors through competitive bidding. Professional agencies are also being involved by the Ministry for project appraisals, implementation and monitoring of projects.

A. Status Of Implementation

As in the case of Mega Food Parks and Integrated Cold Chain projects, the Ministry initially decided to take up 10 abattoir projects in the first phase. The approved 10 projects are under various stages of implementation in Dimapur (Nagaland), Kolkata (West Bengal), Ranchi (Jharkhand), Shimla (Himachal Pradesh), Hyderabad (Andhra Pradesh), Patna (Bihar), Ahmednagar (Maharashtra), Jammu (Jammu & Kashmir), Srinagar (Jammu & Kashmir) and Shillong (Meghalaya). Two of these projects viz. Dimapur and Ahmednagar have been completed and commissioned. The third project at Hyderabad is likely to be completed by December, 2011.

etam drstim avastabhya
nastatmano 'lpa-buddhayah
prabhavanty ugra-karmanah
ksayaya jagato 'hitah

Following such conclusions, the demoniac, who are lost to themselves and who have no intelligence, engage in unbeneficial, horrible works meant to destroy the world.

The demoniac are engaged in activities that will lead the world to destruction. The Lord states here that they are less intelligent. The materialists, who have no concept of God, think that they are advancing. But according to Bhagavad-gita, they are unintelligent and devoid of all sense. They try to enjoy this material world to the utmost limit and therefore always engage in inventing something for sense gratification. Such materialistic inventions are considered to be advancement of human civilization, but the result is that people grow more and more violent and more and more cruel, cruel to animals and cruel to other human beings. They have no idea how to behave toward one another. Animal killing is very prominent amongst demoniac people.

~ Srila Prabhuapda (Bhagavad-gita 16.9)

Other projects have also received requisite approvals, including environmental clearance, and are under construction.

Major challenges of the Scheme remain identification and acquisition of land and complex regulatory issues related to such projects. Considering the challenges of the sector, though, the progress of the Scheme may be considered satisfactory.

B. Recommendations For 12th Plan

In view of the satisfactory progress and further interest shown by various State Governments, the Sub-group report has recommended continuation and further upscaling of this Scheme.

It is proposed to establish 90 new abattoirs and modernize 150 existing abattoirs during 12th Plan. It is also being recommended that while these projects may remain owned by municipal bodies, the responsibility of Operation and Management (O&M) of these facilities may be ideally done by private sector, appointed through a transparent bidding process.

Finally, this Scheme is recommended to become part of the proposed NMFP (National Mission on Food Processing) to be implemented by State Governments since most of the proposals are from the Municipal Bodies who are closely connected to the State Governments.

However, as the system of approval of abattoir projects at the State level, as a component of NMFP (National Mission on Food Processing), may take some time to come into operation, it is

The cow is not my mother? Who can live without milk? And who has not taken cow's milk? Immediately, in the morning, you require milk. And the animal, she's supplying milk, she's not mother? What is the sense? Mother-killing civilization. And they want to be happy. And periodically there is great war and wholesale massacre, reaction.

-Srila Prabhupada (Garden Conversation, June 14, 1976, Detroit)

proposed that the Scheme for Modernisation of Abattoir may continue to be operated as Central Sector Scheme by the Ministry till 31 March 2014. *It is envisaged that under Central Sector Scheme, during first two years of the 12th Plan, 40 abattoir projects would be take up which would include 20 projects for setting up new abattoirs and 20 others for modenisation of existing abattoirs.* In addition, the Ministry would continue to be directly responsible for remaining grant to be given to projects sanctioned during the 11th Plan.

During 11th Plan, the Ministry has already provided assistance to around 2,000 units under this Scheme with around similar number of units likely to be assisted with proposed enhancement in budget allocation.

Scheme For Supporting Cold Chain Facilities For Non-Horticultural Produces And Reefer Vehicles

At present, NHM/NHB programmes provide funding support for standalone modern cold storage facilities horticultural produces. However, such support is not available for nonhorticultural projects dealing with dairy, fish, poultry, meat etc.

It is proposed to support such projects now under NMFP (National Mission on Food Processing) with the same funding pattern as available under the Central Sector Scheme supporting integrated cold chains, i.e., capital grant of 50% and 75% of the project cost for general areas and difficult areas respectively. This initiative would also support projects for acquisition of reefer vehicles for efficient transportation of food processing products.

Pariksit Maharaja was an ideal king and householder because he was a devotee of the Personality of Godhead. And the Emperor was a typical example of this. Personally he had no attachment for all the worldly opulences in his possession. But since he was king for the all-around welfare of his citizens, he was always busy in the welfare work of the public, not only for this life, but also for the next. He would not allow slaughterhouses or killing of cows. He was not a foolish and partial administrator who would arrange for the protection of one living being and allow another to be killed. Because he was a devotee of the Lord, he knew perfectly well how to conduct his administration for everyone's happiness -- men, animals, plants and all living creatures.
~ Srila Prabhupada (Srimad Bhagavatam 1.4.12)

C. Scheme For Modernization Of Meat Shops

This Scheme has been designed to address increasing concern about public health arising out of contamination and poor quality of meat being made available from meat shops in urban areas. It is believed that small investments by these meat shops in basic infrastructure (e.g. tiles, SS wash basin, exhaust and ventilation systems) and equipment (cutting table with SS base, deep freezer, sealing machine etc.) would go a long way in promoting hygienic meat consumption and thus give further fillip to this sector.

Each meat shop is proposed to be provided with maximum grant of 3 lakh, depending on eligible items, through this Scheme which may be implemented as part of NMFP through local urban bodies. *It is proposed to modernize 10,000 meat shops during the 12th Plan in the Country.*

D. Scheme For Human Resource Development (HRD)

All the activities being conducted by the Ministry under this Scheme would be now made partly available to the State Governments through NMFP. In case of Skill Development for the food processing sector, which is a gigantic task, the same would be implemented through NIFTEM (National Institute of Food Technology Entrepreneurship and Management) which

> *"These blind leaders, they do not know." They are especially mentioned, andha yathandhair upaniyamanah. The leaders, they lead others. So, yad yad acarati srestha tat tad evetaro janah [Bg. 3.21]. Leaders are responsible because yad yad acarati srestha: "Those who are leaders, whatever they do, they perform, common men follow that." Therefore they must be very perfect. Common men follow the leaders. If the leaders are themselves imperfect, then what will be the position of the common men?*
>
> *So here it is said that because the leaders, they do not know what is the aim of life, what is the goal of life, therefore common men, people in general, they are being misguided. They are being misguided. Suppose a blind man leads some other blind men. What will be the result? Both of them will meet danger.*
>
> *~ Srila Prabhupada (Srimad-Bhagavatam 7.5.31 -- Mauritius, October 4, 1975)*

would work as the apex body to plan strategic roll out, implement and monitor this development of around 3 million skilled people for the food processing sector during next 7–8 years. This would be achieved by networking with the existing Government/non-Governmental/private organizations as well as establishing some new structures wherever required.

The Ministry would handle/coordinate all the work pertaining to skill development till such time NIFTEM becomes fully operational and capable enough to handle the skill development as envisaged in the foregoing. The Ministry would continue to give the overall policy framework and monitor progress achieved by NIFTEM in this direction.

I. Creation Of Infrastructure Facilities For Running Degree/ Diploma/Certificate Courses In Food Processing Technology

This is to encourage introduction of specialized courses in food processing technology in recognized Colleges/Educational Institutions. Apart from Degree/Diploma courses, certain short duration Certificate courses may also be considered under the Scheme. These courses may be of duration of 3–6 months and initiated preferably through Industrial Training Institutes/Polytechnics. The level of assistance available for creation of requisite infrastructure is proposed to be enhanced from existing 75 lakh to 1 crore for each proposal.

II. Entrepreneurship Development Programme (EDP)

This is to promote entrepreneurship in food processing sector. Eligible institutions may be provided assistance of 2 lakh per EDP during 12th Plan. The Curriculums for such programmes may be standardized with the assistance of NIFTEM to keep them abreast of developments in the food processing industry and till such time the existing curriculum would be continued.

III. Food Processing Training Centre (FPTC)

These Centres are basically meant for development of rural entrepreneurship and transfer of technology for processing of food products by utilising locally grown raw material and providing hands-on experience at such production–cum-training centres. Thus, these Centres would be helpful in promoting entrepreneurship/skill development as well as transfer of technology

The entire outlay for HRD activities during the 12th Plan would now be implemented under NMFP though the Ministry would be directly releasing remaining assistance for projects sanctioned during 11th Plan, for which 6 crore each for next two years has been provided.

E. Scheme For Promotional Activities

Out of the total proposed budget for various promotional Schemes of the Ministry, 50% of funds would be made available to State Governments through Mission during 12th Plan. Some of

Has this civilization produced anything but quarreling individually and nationally? Has this civilization enhanced the cause of equality and fraternity by sending thousands of men into a hellish factory and the warfields at the whims of a particular man? It is said here that the cows used to moisten the pasturing land with milk because their milk bags were fatty and the animals were joyful. Do they not require, therefore, proper protection for a joyful life by being fed with a sufficient quantity of grass in the field? Why should men kill cows for their selfish purposes? Why should men not be satisfied with grains, fruits and milk, which, combined together, can produce hundreds and thousands of palatable dishes. Why are there slaughterhouses all over the world to kill innocent animals? Maharaja Pariksit, grandson of Maharaja Yudhisthira, while touring his vast kingdom, saw a black man attempting to kill a cow. The King at once arrested the butcher and chastised him sufficiently. Should not a king or an executive head protect the lives of the poor animals who are unable to defend themselves? Is this humanity? Are not the animals of a country citizens also? Then why are they allowed to be butchered in organized slaughterhouses? Are these the signs of equality and fraternity and nonviolence? Therefore, in contrast with the modern, advanced, civilized form of government, an autocracy like Maharaja Yudhisthira's is by far superior to so-called democracy in which animals are killed and a man less than an animal is allowed to cast votes for another less than animal man.
~Srila Prabhupada (Room Conversations -- July 26, 1975, Laguna Beach)

the promotional activities to be funded under Mission would be as follows:

i. Organizing seminar/Workshops

For organizing seminars/workshops, State agencies and industry associations would be eligible for grant up to 50% of the cost, subject to a maximum of 7 lakh per event.

ii. Conducting studies/survey

For conducting studies/surveys or preparation of feasibility reports etc., agencies would be eligible for grant up to 50% of the cost, subject to a maximum of 10 lakh for each proposal.

iii. Support to exhibitions/fairs

In case of financial assistance to any institution/organization for organizing a fair/exhibition or sponsoring/co-sponsoring of a fair/exhibition, quantum of assistance may be decided on merits of the proposal by State Mission, subject to a maximum assistance of 7 lakh.

iv. Advertising And Publicity

Killing is illegal, according to the law of God. But the government does not want to follow God's law. They would rather follow their own cruel whims.

On the one side, the government prohibits the flesh-eaters from eating animals who have died a natural death. On the other side, they allow the flesh-eaters to put millions of animals to most unnatural, painful death in slaughterhouses.

These rascals are in power. But legally -- according to God's law -- they should permit flesh-eaters to eat only animals who have died a natural death.

In India, for example, after some animal has died, people come and take the carcass away -- free. They get it without any cost to themselves. They get the skin for making shoes and so forth. They get the flesh for eating. Let them cook and eat it if they want. The farmer does not charge anything. Why slaughterhouses? Take this."

So some day, when the government is made up of godly men, there will be no more slaughterhouses. And you'll be able to advertise, "Here is a cow carcass -- available free." Those who are butchers and tanners can take the flesh and skins free.

~ Srila Prabhupada (Morning walk, New Orleans)

The proposed activities under the Mission would need to be given adequate publicity to ensure their optimal utilisation. This would be more critical during initial years. Thus, there would be provision for funds for dissemination of information and creation of necessary awareness about various Schemes to be covered under the Mission.

National Meat And Poultry Processing Board (NMPPB)

National Meat and Poultry Processing Board (NMPPB) is another much needed institution for a sector, which is mostly unorganized and has remained neglected, due to both historical and cultural reasons. *The Ministry is though fully seized of the huge potential of this sector in coming years and has therefore mandated NMPPB to guide the sector through its future growth path.* The Board would have focus on evolving and adherence to modern standards of hygiene and quality in this sector, through initiatives for standardization, testing etc. The activities that are proposed for NMPPB during the 12th Plan include:

i. Studies/Surveys/Research

ii. Outreach Activities

iii. Training programs for butchers, municipal officials and entrepreneurs

iv. Establishment expenses of NMPPB

v. Promotional activities like participating in exhibitions, seminars etc in India and abroad

vi. Filling patterns

When we kill the animals to eat them, they end up killing us because their flesh, which contains cholesterol and saturated fat, was never intended for human beings.

~Williams C. Roberts, M.D., editor of The American Journal of Cardiology

vii. Establishing food testing Laboratories

Indian Grape Processing Board (IGBP)

The growth potential of wine sector necessitated creation of Indian Grape Processing Board (IGPB). This Board, located at Pune amidst grape growing area, would be aiming at making Indian wine a preferred product in both domestic and foreign markets. For this purpose, IGPB is creating a detailed Action Plan with special stress on increasing efficiency and quality upgradation.

Academic Programs

The National Meat And Poultry Processing Board (NMPPB) began offering formal degree courses at bachelors, masters and doctoral levels in food process engineering from 2009-10 academic year. In B.Tech program 40 students are admitted every year, 10 students in the M. Tech program and 5 in the Ph.D programs.

In a significant related decision, based on recommendations of the concerned Sub-group report, it is proposed to bifurcate the NMPPB and create separate Boards for meat and poultry. The necessary steps would be taken soon and suitable provisions would be made in the 12th Plan for expanding their activities. *Thus, the existing NMPPB would be converted into a Board looking after meat processing only. This is being proposed as it has been felt that both meat and poultry sectors are sufficiently large, with their own special needs and separate sets of stakeholders, to warrant dedicated Boards.*

It is further proposed to set up a National Meat Processing Training Centre and 20 Meat Quality Labs in the Country to ensure all round development of this sector.

People everywhere are suffering on account of being led by blind leaders who are devoid of all knowledge of the soul. Such foolish men lead other foolish men and all concerned suffer. Andha yathandhair upaniyamana, when one blind man leads another, the result is that both of them fall into the ditch. Therefore there is a requirement for a section of society to become first-class men, free of the influence of the modes of material nature, who can understand the mission of this human form of life and who can teach it to others.
~ Srila Prabhupada (A Transcendental Diary, Vol.4)

Promoting Innovations

The need for innovation has never been felt more as India strives to find a delicate balance between growth aspirations of its poor and increasing concerns about environmental degradation.

The decision to declare 2010–2020 as a "Decade of Innovation" and setting up of National Innovation Council (NIC) may be regarded as significant steps in this direction. In keeping with this national goal, the Ministry has decided to make innovation in food processing, part of its central theme of planning for the 12th Plan.

As mentioned in the previous sections of this Report, dealing with strengthening of institutions and promotion of R&D, the establishment of NIFTEM (National Institute of Food Technology Entrepreneurship and Management) is part of this belief to encourage product and process innovations in food processing sector. Further, the existing Schemes as well as proposed measures for promoting R&D efforts are also expected to promote innovation. It is though felt that encouraging innovations may require much more efforts and thus it is now proposed to introduce some direct measures for this purpose.

Summary Of Financial Projections For 12th Five Year Plan (2012-17)

There is a total financial projection of 15,304 crore for the 12th Five Year Plan. More than 75% of this is accounted for by Infrastructure Development Scheme and National Mission on Food Processing. Further, out of around 11,750 crore under these two initiatives, an amount of 10,300 crore has been proposed towards part capital support to projects like Mega Food Parks, Integrated

mrgostra-khara-markakhu-
sarisrp khaga-maksikah
atmanah putravat pasyet
tair esam antaram kiyat

One should treat animals such as deer, camels, asses, monkeys, mice, snakes, birds and flies exactly like one's own son. How little difference there actually is between children and these innocent animals.
(Srimad Bhagavatam 7.14.9)

Cold Chains, modernization of abattoirs and setting up of other food processing units.

The total financial outlay of around 15,300 crore would have an aggregate component of around 10,300 crore towards providing capital assistance to projects such as food parks, cold chains, abattoirs, on-farm infrastructure and other food processing units.

As has been mentioned earlier, the Ministry would be targeting skill development of 3 million persons under its proposed skill development programme. This programme would thus prepare rural youth for working with food processing industry and ensure that the sector, with above projected investment and growth, does not face any manpower issues.

5.

Subsidies And Tax Rebates

On Meat Processing And Export

Taxes on processed food in India are among the highest in the world. No other country imposes excise duty on processed food.

No country distinguishes between branded and unbranded food sectors for taxation. There is excise duty of 16% in the form of CENVAT levied on food products and then there is sales tax, octroi, mandi samiti, entry tax and customs duty on material, levied by the Central/State/Local bodies. The net effect ranges from 21% to 30% on various food items. India is the only country to have levied excise duty on machinery and equipment for processed foods. Indian consumers are very price-sensitive and cost reductions are imperative to raise demand and consumption of food products. Since the net effect of various taxes falls directly on the price, the off-take of processed food items remains low. Consider the Food and Vegetable sector, where against the installed capacity of 21 lakh tonnes (of the units registered under FPO), present production is only 9.4 lakh tonnes or about 45%.

But all these tax strictures apply only to the non-meat products. When it comes to meat products, it's a different ball game altogether. In fact, meat is the most subsidized commodity and meat sector is the most pampered sector in the entire Indian economy.

Everything related to meat - raising animals, their slaughter, transportation, retail outlets, pre-cooling facilities, cold storage, brand publicity, quality control, packaging development, brand publicity, export and even shipping is subsidized by the government.

Ignoring millions of children who die of malnutrition every year, the central government is spending thousands of crores to subsidize an industry which only serves vested interests - mostly underworld mafia and big agribusinesses. Meat is being made increasingly available to few meat eaters in the country while the prices of vegetables, grains and milk are doubling every year.

Some excerpts from the website of the Ministry of Food Processing Industries:

> There are no restrictions on exports of poultry and poultry products. The government provides some transportation subsidies (Rs 3-15 per kg) for its exports. There are a number of issues that need to be addressed to fructify and ensure the growth for the current markets, industry sources expressed.

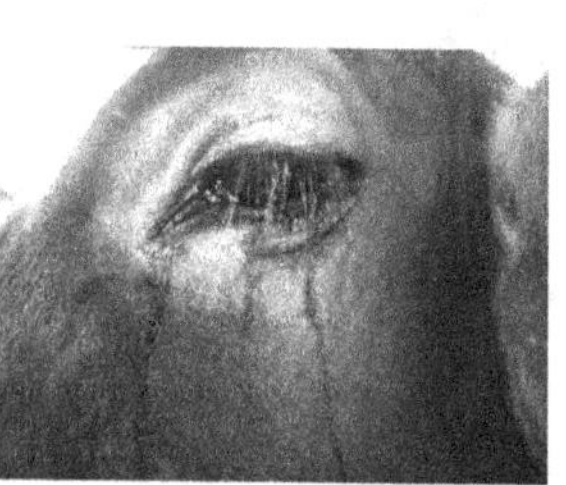

> For the development of meat export from India the industry has demanded some immediate measures like financial assistance for upgradation of export oriented abattoirs/processing plants, inclusion of cattle meat under APEDA's Transport Assistance Scheme for new markets in Africa/CIS where freight cost from India for reefer containers is much higher than from competing countries, restoration of DEPB rates for frozen cattle meat, exemption from Service Tax on transportation of meat products processed for exports.
>
> (http://mofpi.nic.in/ContentPage.aspx?CategoryId=173)

Below is an article which sheds further light on the subject. It was published in Times of India on August 10, 2012.

'Withdraw Subsidies To Meat Exporters'

Times News Network, Aug 10, 2012

The Central government has been urged to abolish subsidies to meat trade and exports which is not only taking toll on productive

> *Cow protection is our life. Krsna has ordered, 'krsi-go-raksya.' Cow protection at any cost. It is Krsna's order. We have to execute it. Any government allowing slaughterhouses should be removed, but we are not so powerful.*
> *~ Srila Prabhupada TKG's Diary: July 13*

cattle but is also creating shortage of milk. "There is an immediate need to arrest the present practice of indiscriminate slaughter of young and productive animals. Otherwise, the problem will intensify and the country will have to face acute shortage of milk," said Kanakrai Savadia, managing trustee of Sukrut Nirman Charitable Trust, an organization working to save cows in Vidarbha.

In a memorandum submitted to Anand Sharma, the union minister of commerce and industry, Savadia has said the prevailing high prices of bovine, milk and meat are strong indication of

The next symptom of the age of Kali is the distressed condition of the cow. Milking the cow means drawing the principles of religion in a liquid form. The great rsis and munis would live only on milk. Srila Sukadeva Gosvami would go to a householder while he was milking a cow, and he would simply take a little quantity of it for subsistence. Even fifty years ago, no one would deprive a sadhu of a quart or two of milk, and every householder would give milk like water. For a Sanatanist (a follower of Vedic principles) it is the duty of every householder to have cows and bulls as household paraphernalia, not only for drinking milk, but also for deriving religious principles. The Sanatanist worships cows on religious principles and respects brahmanas. The cow's milk is required for the sacrificial fire, and by performing sacrifices the householder can be happy. The cow's calf not only is beautiful to look at, but also gives satisfaction to the cow, and so she delivers as much milk as possible. But in the Kali-yuga, the calves are separated from the cows as early as possible for purposes which may not be mentioned in these pages of Srimad-Bhagavatam. The cow stands with tears in her eyes, the sudra milkman draws milk from the cow artificially, and when there is no milk the cow is sent to be slaughtered. These greatly sinful acts are responsible for all the troubles in present society. People do not know what they are doing in the name of economic development. The influence of Kali will keep them in the darkness of ignorance. Despite all endeavors for peace and prosperity, they must try to see the cows and the bulls happy in all respects. Foolish people do not know how one earns happiness by making the cows and bulls happy, but it is a fact by the law of nature. Let us take it from the authority of Srimad-Bhagavatam and adopt the principles for the total happiness of humanity.

~ Srila Prabhuapda (Srimad Bhagavatam 1.17.3)

shortage of supply. Even existing slaughterhouses are not able to meet requirements. Hence, they are procuring buffaloes by illegal means.

The most unfortunate fallout of this has been the deleterious effect on small farmers. They are lured to sell their animals, but soon discover that it is impossible to buy fresh stock again. The slaughterhouses involved in export are killing productive cattle clandestinely to fulfil their export commitments.

Savadia said in India farmers mainly rear cattle for agriculture purpose as well as milk production. When the animal grows old and is not fit for either milk production or agricultural purpose, it is sold at throwaway prices to the traders involved in meat export. Thus the traders get animals at an extremely low cost. To fulfil the demand these animals are even stolen and slaughtered.

In abattoirs even milk-giving animals are slaughtered illegally to meet the export demand of traders. He pointed out that slaughterhouses maintained and run by local bodies are meant for domestic requirement of meat and not export. Yet, these establishments are involved in illegal export of meat.

Savadia said despite violations subsidies are offered by the Central and state governments for construction and upgradation of slaughterhouses and the prevailing meat trade in the country.

At the present, especially on this planet earth, the influence of Lord Brahma has decreased considerably, and the representatives of Hiranyakasipu—the Raksasas and demons—have taken charge. Therefore there is no protection of brahminical culture and cows, which are the basic prerequisites for all kinds of good fortune. This age is very dangerous because society is being managed by demons and Raksasas.

~ Srila Prabhupada (Srimad Bhagavatam 7.3.13)

He said the Agriculture Agricultural and Processed Food Products Export Development Authority (APEDA) is providing 25% to 60% subsidy on transport of meat, pre-cooling facilities, cold storage, brand publicity, quality control, packaging development, brand publicity etc.

In addition, there is exemption from sales tax and income tax. The modern export-oriented slaughterhouses are mostly run by private players who earn huge profits at the cost of our water bodies and environment, causing pollution and diseases.

Savadia urged Sharma to withdraw all the subsidies offered to meat trade. "The subsidy of thousands of crores of rupees from taxpayers' money is not justifiable from any angle," he added.

Centre Slammed Over Subsidy for Beef Exports

October 28, 2012, Outlook

Gujarat chief minister Narendra Modi today reiterated the charge that the Centre was promoting beef exports by providing subsidies even while levying duty on cotton exports.

Speaking at the 4th Annual General Meeting of the Jain International Trade Organisation here, Modi said "The UPA government allows subsidy to open slaughterhouses, whereas cotton farmers are levied duty for exporting cotton".

He alleged that to facilitate mutton exports, tax is waived off for five years. "The union government does not want another green revolution and white revolution, but wants to promote pink revolution," Modi alleged, adding that he had to approach the Supreme Court to get a law enacted to ban cow slaughter in his state.

He said that it is possible to bring change within the system if motives are noble, intentions are clear and policies are coherent.

> *Vegetarians have the best diet. They have the lowest rates of coronary disease of any group in the country... they have a fraction of our heart attack rate and they have only 40 percent of our cancer rate. On the average, they outlive other people by about six years now."*
>
> *~William Castelli, M.D.,*
>
> *Director, Framingham Heart Study, the longest-running epidemiological study in medical history.*

6.

Rail Minister Signs Order

To Resume Cow Carriage Trains

Cancelling an earlier order of the previous government, in September 2004, railway minister Laloo Prasad Yadav permitted the transport of cattle on trains all over the country. The previous government had banned the transport of cattle in 2001.

Railway Ministry officials said the transport of cows, buffaloes and goats would be subject to strict rules like certificates from district authorities and local vets.

Attacking Railway Minister Lalu Prasad for lifting the ban on ferrying of cattle by trains, the BJP alleged he was behaving as a "trader of cows for slaughter" and asked Prime to intervene to stop it.

BJP Vice President and spokesman Mukhtar Abbas Naqvi told reporters that the previous NDA government had put a ban on

> *An uncivilized man can do anything for the satisfaction of his senses. He can kill children, he can kill cows, he can kill old men; he has no mercy for anyone. According to the Vedic civilization, cows, women, children, old men and saintly persons should be excused if they are at fault. But asuras, uncivilized men, do not care about that. At the present moment, the killing of cows and the killing of children is going on unrestrictedly, and therefore this civilization is not at all human, and those who are conducting this condemned civilization are uncivilized demons.*
>
> *~ Srila Prabhupada (Srimad Bhagavatam 10.3.22)*

ferrying of cattle by train in 2002 considering that these are being transported to Bangladesh for slaughter.

"It is a matter of concern that Prasad is trying to give legal sanctity to trafficking of cows for slaughter," he alleged, asserting that his party will oppose it.

Sources said after a series of representations from various bodies, including confidential reports from the RPF and an internal audit report, former Railway Minister Nitish Kumar had imposed a virtual ban on movement of cows via trains. Provisions in the existing laws were made stringent so that it was practically impossible to ferry cows by trains.

Member of Parliament and former union minister, Ms Menaka Gandhi's outburst was widely reported in the press. Following is a press report on the issue.

Railway Minister Took 'Bribe' From Cattle Mafia, Says Maneka

Tribune News Service, New Delhi, September 17

Senior leader and former Central Minister Maneka Gandhi today accused Railway Minister Laloo Prasad Yadav of taking

Unfortunately, our modern materialistic civilization is filled with so-called leaders who are devoid of spiritual knowledge and who refuse to take guidance from genuine spiritual authorities. Such leaders are blind in the truest sense, and therefore both they and their blind followers waste their time in a hopeless, meaningless struggle to be happy by gratifying the senses of the temporary material body. In defiance of God's laws for spiritual life in harmony with the laws of nature, such leaders encourage all sorts of sinful activities, such as gambling, intoxication, meat eating, and illicit sex. As a result they make civilization hellish, and in their next lives both they and their followers are thrown into hellish planets. Such leaders should certainly be known as demons.
~ Srila Prabhuapda (Back To Godhead, 12-07, 1977)

'bribe' for lifting the ban on transport of cattle in railway bogies. "One of the first order that Mr Yadav passed after assuming the charge of the Railway Minister was allowing the transport of cattle in railway bogies. It, in practical terms, means extending support to the cattle mafia that takes these animals to Bangladesh for slaughtering," she said.

The illegal cattle trade is more lucrative and bigger than drug trade, she said.

Giving details of the illegal trade, she said, "The mafia has an organisation called Howrah Cattle Dealer Association in Howrah. It runs the illegal trade by bringing lakhs of cows, buffaloes, bullocks and bulls from northern states like Punjab, Haryana to West Bengal where these animals are slaughtered or smuggled to Bangladesh."

"Bangladesh has thin cattle population of its own, but its exports of beef runs into lakhs of tonnes," she asserted to buttress her claim of smuggling of cattle to Bangladesh.

Suta Gosvami said: After reaching that place, Maharaja Pariksit observed that a lower-caste sudra, dressed like a king, was beating a cow and a bull with a club, as if they had no owner.

The principal sign of the age of Kali is that lower-caste sudras, i.e., men without brahminical culture and spiritual initiation, will be dressed like administrators or kings, and the principal business of such non-ksatriya rulers will be to kill the innocent animals, especially the cows and the bulls, who shall be unprotected by their masters, the bona fide vaisyas, the mercantile community. In the Bhagavad-gita (18.44), it is said that the vaisyas are meant to deal in agriculture, cow protection and trade. In the age of Kali, the degraded vaisyas, the mercantile men, are engaged in supplying cows to slaughterhouses. The ksatriyas are meant to protect the citizens of the state, whereas the vaisyas are meant to protect the cows and bulls and utilize them to produce grains and milk. The cow is meant to deliver milk, and the bull is meant to produce grains. But in the age of Kali, the sudra class of men are in the posts of administrators, and the cows and bulls, or the mothers and the fathers, unprotected by the vaisyas, are subjected to the slaughterhouses organized by the sudra administrators.

~ Srila Prabhuapda (Srimad Bhagavatam 1.17.1)

Rubbishing the claim that the Railways would earn revenue through this, she said this was not correct as a boggy carried over 300 cattle illegally instead of 10 permitted by the law. It resulted in damage to these bogies. Repair of bogies leads to massive loss of revenue to the Railways, she asserted.

Showing a photograph of the cattle being carried in a railway boggy on September 7 at the Mubarakpur railway station in Patiala district, she said 70 per cent of cattle perished during transportation and then their skin and meat were sold.

Sher Khan, the trader who was carrying the cattle to the Howrah railway station, was absconding, she said. He was part of the bigger mafia, she added.

Because every third head of cattle in Bangladesh is smuggled in from India. Many come from as far away as Haryana and Punjab. An estimated 20,000 to 25,000 animals enter Bangladesh almost everyday through West Bengal alone. While the trade is illegal on the Indian side, it becomes legal the moment the livestock enters Bangladesh.

Some estimates put the annual turnover from leather, meat and meat exports from smuggled Indian cattle in Bangladesh at over Rs 25 billion.

prsadhras tu manoh putro
go-palo guruna krtah
palayam asa ga yatto
ratryam virasana-vratah

Among these sons, Prsadhra, following the order of his spiritual master, was engaged as a protector of cows. He would stand all night with a sword to give the cows protection.

One who becomes virasana takes the vow to stand all night with a sword to give protection to the cows. Because Prsadhra was engaged in this way, it is to be understood that he had no dynasty. We can further understand from this vow accepted by Prsadhra how essential it is to protect the cows. Some son of a ksatriya would take this vow to protect the cows from ferocious animals, even at night. What then is to be said of sending cows to slaughterhouses? This is the most sinful activity in human society.

~ Srila Prabhupada (Srimad Bhagavatam 9.2.4)

She said that as per the Cattle Prevention Act, it was illegal to transport cattle across State borders for purposes of slaughter and allowed only in case of draught and milch cattle.

The Indian Railways, she said, has been transporting cattle from North Indian States only in the direction of West Bengal proved that these were then taken to Bangladesh for slaughter. "The fact that they are going to Bangladesh is undisputed," she said.

Since the Railway Ministry could not have done it on its own, so a clearance was taken from the Animal Welfare Board. The board, which is without a full-time chairman since June this year, issued a letter on July two saying the matter has been "reconsidered" and in view of "practical constrains", the rule was being relaxed.

The Transport of Animal Rules says: "As far as possible, cattle may be moved during the nights only. They should be off-loaded during the day and be fed, given water and rested and if in milk, milking should be carried out." Any violation was to be treated as criminal offence.

Only 12 cows were to be put in a bogey with prior permission of the Animal Welfare Board and a medical certificate from designated veterinary doctor was needed before that. The route plan was also to be submitted to the board. The Ministry of Home Affairs, in April, 2003, had directed the BSF (Border Security Force) to keep a vigil on smuggling of cows to Bangladesh.

That the order had been reversed was known on September 7 when activists of former Union Minister Maneka Gandhi's People for Animals stopped a train at the Chagger Railway station near Dera Basi in Punjab and foundthat hundreds of cows were loaded in the train in the most pitiable conditions en route to eastern India (http://www.tribuneindia.com/2004/20040918/nation.htm#1)

In another interview about the whole episode, Ms Gandhi told The Pioneer: "This is a national shame. Actions of the the Congress-led UPA and the Prime Minister, who is responsible for policy making, have from the beginning been anti-national whether it is arresting the people for hoisting the national flag or reversing the laws in existence since 1978 to allow open smuggling of cows to Bangladesh. Bangladesh is eating and exporting beef from Indian cows.

"In 2001, the Railways, after a careful study, came to a conclusion that they had somehow been abetting the crime of sending the cows to West Bengal on false certifications. It thus imposed a ban.

"The new order of the UPA Government effectively means that it was reopening the smuggling route of sending the cows to Bangladesh for slaughter."

Toppling the Congress Party coalition that had ruled India for 48 of the 49 preceding years in 1998, the Hindu nationalist Bharatiya Janata Dal coalition beefed up the Cattle Transport Act by banning cattle transport by train in March 2001, under the 1960 Prevention of Cruelty to Animals Act. The action had long been urged by then-animal welfare minister Maneka Gandhi and then-Animal Welfare Board of India chair Guman Mal Lodha as an essential step toward ending cattle slaughter, which increased 20-fold between 1977 and 1997.

And cruelty to animals means not to be cruel to the cats and dogs. And for the cows, "Oh, there is no question of cruelty. It has no soul. Kill him." This is your civilization, Dog civilization.

One side they're advertising "Stop cruelty to animals," another side they're opening unrestricted slaughterhouse. Just see. Just like a gang of thieves gives a signboard, "Goodman and Company." So there are so many members of the society against cruelty to animals. But they are all meat-eaters.

-Srila Prabhupada (Talk with Bob Cohen - February 27-29, 1972, Mayapura)

7.

White Lies

And Blatant Cover-ups

Even in the face of the facts mentioned so far, the government maintains its stand that it is not doing anything to promote meat consumption and export. Like they say..."You can't fool all the people all the time...but you can fool enough to run a large country." Following news reports might illustrate this point better.

Narendra Modi-Sharad Pawar Squabble Over Meat Export 'Subsidy' Continues

Published: Thursday, Apr 19, 2012, Place: Anand (Gujarat) | Agency: PTI

Gujarat Chief Minister Narendra Modi on Wednesday once again raised the issue of "subsidy" on meat exports, but Union Agriculture Minister Sharad Pawar countered it saying no such concession is being given by the Central government.

Modi and Pawar were present at the unveiling of National Dairy Plan under the Mission Milk. The mission, touted as second white revolution, aims to augment the production of milk to meet its raising demand.

"I am concerned about the UPA government encouraging 'pink revolution'. By pink revolution I mean encouraging export of mutton and also subsiding it," Modi said from the dais in Anand.

Subsidising meat has also affected milk production of the country as animals get killed for their meat without any proper

Make the lie big, make it simple, keep saying it, and eventually they will believe it. ~ Unknown

curbs, he said. There is a "big racket" involving smuggling of cows to Bangladesh, he alleged and said the issue needs serious thinking.

Pawar, reacting to Modi's statement, said after the programme, "Government of India's meat export policy has not changed since the last 15 to 20 years. There has been no new amendments by the UPA government and there is no concession provided for its exports."

"I am surprised the issue was raised today by Modi who spoke of 'pink revolution'. The issue (of subsidy) has never come up before the government in the last seven years."

"I would have given answer to the issue raised by Modi on the dais itself. But I did not do it because I wanted to maintain dignity of the function which was organised by the Government of India where he (Modi) was invited as a guest. Guests can raise their concerns from the dais," Pawar said.

Earlier this month at a public meeting in Rajkot, Modi had said the UPA government was taxing cotton export while giving subsidy on meat exports.

Union Commerce Minister Anand Sharma had termed Modi's remark as "unwarranted" and bereft of facts.

'Modi's Statement On Beef Exports Inflammatory'

PTI New Delhi, August 19, 2012

Commerce and industry minister Anand Sharma has hit out at Gujarat chief minister Narendra Modi accusing him of giving

> *The great masses of the people ... will more easily fall victims to a big lie than to a small one.*
>
> *~Adolf Hitler*

a "political slant" by making "inflammatory" statement on beef exports.

"My attention has been drawn to your public statement regarding the meat export policy alleging that the central government is promoting slaughter of cows and export of beef, which is inaccurate, inflammatory and misleading," Sharma said in his letter to Modi.

"It is unfortunate that in spite of the factual position, you have chosen to give a political slant to Government's stand on meat export policy. Public discourse on policy matters must never be allowed to be trapped in partisan political agenda," Sharma added.

In his Janamashtami message through his blog, Modi appealed to the people to reject 'pink revolution'.

He said the UPA Government led by Congress is "promoting slaughtering of cows"

Sharma said, "You are well aware that slaughter of cows is prohibited in India in harmony with principles enshrined in our Constitution".

He said meat is largely a by-product of livestock, utilising spent animals at the end of their productive life.

"Cattle and buffaloes which account for over 60% of meat production, are primarily reared for milk and towards the end of their productive life, are utilised for meat production.

As there are many parties, Communist party, Congress party, this party, that party, so there must be one Krishna's party. Why not? Then people will be happy, if Krishna's party comes to the governmental post. Immediately there will be peace. In India, there are so many slaughterhouses. There are... It is said that ten thousand cows are being killed everyday, in the land were one cow was being attempted to be killed, immediately Maharaja Pariksit took his sword, "Who are you?" In that land, now ten thousand cows are being killed every day. So you expect peace? You expect prosperity? This is not possible. Therefore if some day Krishna's representative takes the governmental power, then he will immediately stop all these slaughterhouses, all these brothels, all these liquor houses. Then there will be peace and prosperity.

~ Srila Prabhupada (Srimad Bhagavatam 1.10.2 -- Mayapura, June 17, 1973)

“A ban on meat production or export would lead to an abnormal rise of unproductive animals which is inconsistent with sound animal husbandry practices,” Sharma said.

8.

Factory Farms

Coming To India In A Big Way

The majority of the world's farm animals currently live in miserable conditions, raised using 'production line' methods. High output is achieved by subjecting the animals to intense and prolonged suffering.

They live short, barren lives, spent in cages, crates, overcrowded sheds and narrow stalls.

Exporting Factory Farms : The Global Expansion of Industrialized Meat Production

From The Food Empowerment Project

It is frightening that our species now eats more than five times more meat than we did back then in 1950. These days, over 50 billion land animals are killed for food worldwide every year - and that number is expected to double by 2030. Rising incomes in large, rapidly-developing countries are driving a major shift in global dietary patterns as those societies strive to emulate the West's eating habits.

The factory farming techniques that make the mass-production of meat, dairy and eggs possible cause incalculable harm and cruelty to animals, the environment and people—so why would these countries choose to follow this path?

The main reason is that some multinational agribusiness companies see serious profit in expanding their operations to largely untapped emerging markets. These corporations have already saturated the Western world with their products, so in order to maintain their economic superiority, companies must break into countries where consumer demand for meat and animal products is rising, environmental and animal welfare regulations are lax, and labor is enticingly cheap. Namely, established agribusiness giants are actively advancing into Asia and nations in the Global South—threatening to supplant traditional agrarian practices and wreak the very same kind of havoc they have done in the U.S.

A brief look at the past provides a chilling glimpse into the planet's potential food future. Consider the historical precedent of Tyson Foods, the world's largest meat producer, which in the late 1940s essentially invented the system of vertical integration that now serves as the model for industrialized animal agriculture. The core principle behind vertical integration is to have a single corporate entity own and control every aspect of the meat production process—from feed mills and hatcheries to slaughterhouses—so that farmers solely raise animals on contract for the company at reduced prices. This domineering system now sets the standard for the nation's chicken industry, and can increasingly be found in cow and pig production.

Six decades after its introduction, the economic efficiency of virtual integration now allows just four major companies to process over half the chickens, 80% of the cows, and 60% of the pigs consumed in the U.S. And now, this business model is enabling these same few massive corporations to expand into the consumer territories of developing societies.

We can begin to understand what this means for animals, the environment and people in other parts of the world by examining Big Ag's recent commercial activities in some of these countries.

The factory farm attitude is exemplified by the ISE corporation, whose lawyer asserted that it is legally acceptable to dispose of live birds as if they were manure. When the judge asked, 'Isn't there a big distinction between manure and live animals?' ISE's lawyer responded, 'No, your honour.'

India

In 2008, Tyson also bought a majority share in Mumbai-based Godrej Foods Ltd. and expects to reap about $50 million a year in poultry sales throughout India. But the company may find that Indian society is less conducive to their vertical integration schemes than Brazil, because approximately 65% of Indians are employed in the agricultural sector, and vegetarianism is quite common. In a country where about 780 million people make a living producing food, Tyson's top-down domination strategy faces real challenges. However, meat consumption (especially chicken) is rising in India as incomes grow, and drive-through fast food franchises are spreading at an exponential rate, so company heads figure that increasing demand for meat and more convenient means of distribution will work in their favor over the long term.

Officially Stated Government Policy On Vertical integration of poultry industry : The annual per capita consumption in India is only 33 eggs and 630 grams of poultry meat. This is much lower as compared to the world average of 124 eggs and 5.9 kg meat. The National Committee on Human Nutrition in India has recommended per capita of 180 eggs (about one egg every two days) and 10.8 kg meat .To meet this target , it is estimated that by year 2010, the requirements will be 180 billion eggs and 9.1 billion kg poultry meat while the estimated production may only be around 46.2 billion eggs and 3.04 billion kg poultry meat .

The scheme has been introduced recently in few places by private sector hatcheries or feed millers. They provide chicks and feed to the producers and purchase the live broilers at a cost depending upon the body weight. Some incentives for high feed efficiency and good livability are provided. However, in most cases, the purchased birds are sold to the wholesale dealers who often dictate the price and full benefits of the scheme are not available to the farmers. The scheme needs to be supported by providing infrastructure for meat processing, packaging, preservation and marketing with value addition of products and maintaining a cold chain till the product reaches the consumer. The private sector companies including foreign investors have a great opportunity to invest in these schemes, in collaboration with the Indian entrepreneurs.

In India, both intensive and traditional systems of poultry farming are followed, but intensive system is rapidly increasing due to increasing land and other input costs. It is estimated that in India, about 60% of poultry meat and 56% of eggs are currently being produced in the intensive system. It is further estimated that there are about 60000 farms under Intensive system (some of them having more that 100000 birds) while there are about 100000 small farms scattered in rural areas practicing more extensive production systems, having flock sizes ranging from 25 to 250 birds. In case of layers the cage system is rapidly replacing the deep litter system. However in broiler farming, the deep litter system is more prevalent.

It is estimated that in year 2000, Indian Poultry Industry contribution to the GDP was about Rs 80 billion which reached to Rs. 300 billion by the Year 2005.

Lessons From China

Fast food is a $28 billion industry in China today, where there are already more than 900 McDonald's and 2,000 KFC restaurants. This is no surprise, given that China has one of the world's fastest-growing economies, with a burgeoning middle class that sees "meat" as a social status symbol signifying wealth and privilege (much like the upwardly-mobile consumers in many other developing countries). To feed this demand for animal foods, China has courted

We want to stop these killing houses. These are very, very sinful. Therefore in Europe, so many wars. Every ten years, fifteen years, there is a big war and wholesale slaughter of the whole human kind. And these rascals, they do not see it. The reaction must be there. You are killing innocent cows and animals. Nature will take revenge. Wait for that. As soon as the time is ripe, the nature will gather all these rascals, and club, slaughter them. Finished. They will fight amongst themselves, Protestant and Catholic, Russian and America, and France and Germany. This is going on. Why? This is the nature's law. Tit for tat. You have killed. Now you become killed. Amongst yourselves. They are being sent to the slaughterhouse. And here, you'll create slaughterhouse, "Dum! dum!" and killed, be killed.

~ Srila Prabhupada (Room Conversation -- June 11, 1974, Paris)

agribusiness investment from the likes of Tyson, Smithfield Foods and Novus International, and is well on its way to becoming one of the world's top meat-consuming countries. Yet, even as Chinese society increasingly emulates the Western-style diet, a legacy of ecological damage resulting from their currently unsustainable agricultural practices looms behind them, casting a dark shadow over a future that may prove even bleaker. That is, *even though factory farming is not yet the main "meat" production method in China, almost a million acres of Chinese grassland are already reduced to desert annually as a result of overgrazing and intensive farming,* and China surpassed the U.S. as the world's top emitter of greenhouse gasses in 2008. If factory farming becomes widespread in China, these problems—and many others—will become more devastating, not only to this country of 1.3 billion people, but to the rest of the world as well.

For decades, animals, people and the planet have suffered the severe consequences of factory farming as it is conducted in the Western world— and the export of this corporatized method of mass-production can only exacerbate the ethical, ecological and social problems it causes. The implications of Concentrated Animal Feeding Operations expanding across the globe are especially disturbing because most of the countries targeted by agribusinesses have even fewer animal welfare, environmental, health, and labor regulations than the U.S. or Europe, so the abuses inherent to factory farming would only worsen. Even as individuals we can make a positive difference by supporting activists in developing nations who proactively promote a diet free from animal products and work to prevent these industries from gaining a foothold in their countries.

Industrial Mega Dairy Proposal For Andhra Pradesh, Plan Opposed

P S Jayaram, 18 August 2011

The Animal Welfare Board of India (AWBI) has raised objections to the establishment of the ambitious 'Kisan' Special Economic Zone (SEZ) in Nellore district of Andhra Pradesh after environmentalists and animal lovers raised serious concerns over the proposal to set up mega dairies in collaboration with a foreign company as part of the SEZ.

According to AWBI Chairman Dr R M Kharb, the establishment of mega dairies in the coastal district involved several environmental and animal welfare risks and possible violation of rules. The AWBI is a statutory body of Government of India, working under the aegis of Ministry of Environment and Forests.

Dr Kharb, in a letter to the promoters of Kisan SEZ, raised several environmental concerns over the proposed project by a consortium of IFFCO, Fonterra, a New Zealand-based dairy company and Global Dairy Health, an Indian firm. The letter was in response to a petition by the Federation of Indian Animal Protection Organizations (FIAPO), an umbrella body of Indian animal welfare groups across the country, seeking the intervention of AWBI to stop the project.

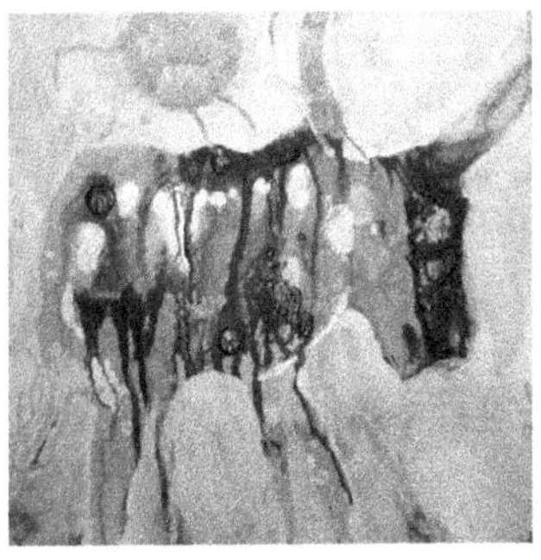

Dr Kharb said: "The proposed project is a corporate farm where animals will come under tremendous stress. The animals will be kept at high stocking densities which might result in them contracting diseases which could lead to an increased likelihood of emergence of novel zoonotic diseases."

The genetically-manipulated high-yielding cows that are proposed to be introduced in the farm have shortened life span, reduced fertility, greater propensity for diseases, physiological and development problems, environmentalists argue. "Cow slaughter and transportation for slaughter results in additional problems. The management of the amount of animal waste is also a key challenge and often results in degradation of local environment," the AWBI Chairman said. According to the convener of FIAPO, Arpan Sharma, the consortium had proposed to import 9,000 high yielding pregnant cows from New Zealand over a three year period. There were also plans to import frozen embryos and semen for subsequent breeding.

"As consumers in developed countries are demanding an end to inhumane confinement systems as is proposed in the SEZ, foreign animal production companies are looking to developing countries like India as a dumping ground for such industrial farm animal production," Sharma alleged.

"The Indian standards lag behind those of some of the developed nations with progressive animal welfare standards not being implemented by foreign companies in Indian markets. This is unfair to Indian consumers, as most of us would prefer products with high animal welfare standards," he said.

In such mega dairies, the cows are typically kept almost exclusively indoors with little or no access to natural surroundings. Cows farmed intensively like this are bred to produce unnaturally large amounts of milk which can make them more susceptible to several health problems.

Sharma pointed out that Lincolnshire in UK had recently refused permission to a cattle farm similar to the one being proposed in AP. "It is clear that the west itself is moving away from such production systems and India should not permit the establishment of such models that have demonstrated negative impacts on the environment," he contended.

A New Jungle

Meat once occupied a very different dietary place in most of the world. Beef, pork, and chicken were considered luxuries, and were eaten on special occasions or to enhance the flavor of other

The mlecchas, however, make plans to install slaughterhouses for killing bulls and cows along with other animals, thinking that they will prosper by increasing the number of factories and live on animal food without caring for performance of sacrifices and production of grains. But they must know that even for the animals they must produce grass and vegetables, otherwise the animals cannot live. And to produce grass for the animals, they require sufficient rains. Therefore they have to depend ultimately on the mercy of the demigods like the sun-god, Indra and Candra, and such demigods must be satisfied by performances of sacrifice (yajna).

~ Srila Prabhupada (Srimad Bhagavatam1.16.20)

foods. But as agriculture became more mechanized, so did animal production. In the United States, livestock raised in the West was herded or transported east to slaughterhouses and packing mills.

Upton Sinclair's The Jungle, written almost a century ago when the United States lacked many food-safety and labor regulations, described the appalling conditions of slaughterhouses in Chicago in the early 20th century and was a shocking expose of meat production and the conditions inflicted on both animals and humans by the industry. Workers were treated much like animals themselves, forced to labor long hours for very little pay under dangerous conditions, and with no job security.

If The Jungle were written today, however, it might not be set in the American Midwest. Today, developing nations like India are becoming the centers of large-scale livestock production and processing to feed the world's growing appetite for cheap meat and other animal products. But the problems Sinclair pointed to a century ago, including hazardous working conditions, unsanitary processing methods, and environmental contamination, still exist. Many have become even worse. And as environmental regulations in the European Union and the United States become stronger, large agribusinesses are moving their animal production operations to nations with less stringent enforcement of environmental laws.

They are sending animals to the slaughterhouse, and now they'll create their own slaughterhouse. [Imitating gunfire:] Tung! Tung! Kill! Kill! You see? Just take Belfast, for example. The Roman Catholics are killing the Protestants, and the Protestants are killing the Catholics. This is nature's law. It's not necessary that you be sent to the ordinary slaughterhouse. You'll make a slaughterhouse at home. You'll kill your own child-abortion. This is nature's law. Who are these children being killed? They are these meat-eaters. They enjoyed themselves when so many animals were killed, and now they're being killed by their mothers. People do not know how nature is working. If you kill, you must be killed. If you kill the cow, who is your mother, then in some future lifetime your mother will kill you. Yes. The mother becomes the child, and the child becomes the mother.
~ Srila Prabhupada (JSD 6.5: Slaughterhouse Civilization)

These intensive and environmentally destructive production methods are spreading all over the globe, to Mexico, India, the former Soviet Union, and most rapidly throughout Asia. Wherever they crop up, they create a web of related food safety, animal welfare, and environmental problems.

9.

Government's Push For Livestock Business

Killing The Soul Of The Nation

According to an ANI (Asian News International) news release dated November 18th 2009, an increasing number of farmers are being motivated to undertake crop diversification and livestock farming in Punjab and other states. As part of its endeavour to ensure the growth of the livestock farming sector, the government is holding various livestock shows.

Departments of Animal Husbandry have been instructed to provide details of various government schemes to farmers. The presence of farmers at such livestock shows reflects a rapidly popularizing livestock business.

Farmers from Amritsar, Gurdaspur, Tarn Taran and Kapurthala districts recently converged in Tarn Taran to participate in the three-day "Livestock and Competition Fair".

Mahga Singh of Sarya village, who arrived here with his award winner "Goat", said: "Now, my sons have started doing this business as their family income has increased. People from all over the Punjab come to them to buy livestock." The department has registered every farmer of the area and is encouraging them to breed "Beetal Goat". They are provided with free medical aid and medicines.

There are countless such schemes to encourage farmers to give up traditional farming and take up animal rearing for meat export.

Rs. 300 Crore Scheme To Rear Male Buffaloes

Jun 29, 2009, PTI

The Centre is considering launching a Rs 300 crore scheme to rear male buffalo calves to boost meat export.

The Department of Animal Husbandry and Dairying under the Agriculture Ministry will soon approach the Cabinet for approval of the scheme, which will be funded by National Bank for Agriculture and Rural Development (NABARD).

"The proposed scheme 'Salvaging and rearing of male buffalo calves', with an estimated outlay of Rs 300 crore for the 11th Five Year Plan period, is aimed at generating employment in rural areas and earning foreign exchange for the country," a senior government official told PTI.

Under the scheme, male buffalo calves will be rescued particularly from the big cities and reared in villages, the official said, adding that this would not only lead to retaining of genetic material but also boosting buffalo meat export.

Farmers will be given incentives for rearing male buffalo calves and provided back-end linkage with export-oriented slaughter houses to buy these animals, the official said.

"There is vast potential for development of meat, by products and leather industry," the official observed.

The implementation of scheme will also lead to an additional output of buffalo meat and hides. Forex earnings will also come through export of the same.

Meat Industry - Evolving Into A Fad

Meat eaters like sexual offenders if not checked, want more and more excitement, more and more fancies to feed their fetish.

More and more Indians are trying out meats which are not supermarket staples. Illegal restaurants have sprung up selling game meat and rare birds. Our increasing interest in pushing boundaries in everything we do means that there is now a market for anything that crawls, runs, flies or swims.

One such segment being popularized is Emu meat. Farmers are selling their lands and cows to invest in emu farms, often with disastrous consequences.

India was not a meat eating or meat producing civilization. Meat eating was rare and for special occasions and confined only to a small section of our people. Today it is an industry, a fad. And that kills the soul of the nation.

India Should Ban Emu Farming

Maneka Gandhi, 07 October 2012

In 1996, an Andhra Pradesh businessman smuggled in emus through the customs, saying they were chickens from Australia. Emus look nothing like chicken but one bribe looks like another so everyone kept quiet. He multiplied these emus and started giving them to people who had poultry farms. Soon, this illegal bird spread throughout India and the animal husbandry department, who were informed again and again of the dangers of keeping this bird, jumped into its promotion enthusiastically. This Government, under Sharad Pawar (who else?) has permitted emu farming. Nabard gives loans for it.

It has spread like a disease from Andhra Pradesh to Tamil Nadu, Maharashtra, Goa, Uttarakhand and even Gujarat. It has taken 15 years and hundreds of bankruptcies to realize that emu farming is a fake – a Ponzi scheme started by clever crooks to defraud farmers. A Ponzi scheme is an investment fraud that involves the payment of so called returns to existing investors from funds contributed by new investors. Ponzi scheme organizers solicit new investors by promising to invest funds in opportunities claimed to generate high returns with little or no risk.

Let me explain to you the Great Emu Game through example:

A man called M. S. Guru started Susi Emu Farms in 2006 in Erode. He cheated 12,000 investors. It was done in two ways:

The company sold emu chicks to a farmer. The farmer was told that that once the birds were reared and adult, the company would buy them back. Many farmers turned their agricultural lands into emu rearing sheds.

Susi also asked people to invest in their emu business, paying to own emus which would be reared by Susi on a contract basis, guaranteeing Rs.1,000 per month as a return to the farmer. Many victims were lured by what appeared to be the success of Susi Farms.

Guru was conferred the Arch of Excellence (Business) Award (2008) and Gem of India Award-2011 by All India Achievers Conference.

This is what his victims have to say: "They said it was a very simple business. They promised to supply chicks and the fodder. The shed was built on my premises claiming it was free, though I had to pay a huge amount in the form of interest free security deposit," recalls P. Subrahmani from Omallaur who invested Rs. 15 lakh with Susi Farms. He got 25 others to invest. "As per the agreement, they had to pay me Rs.7,000 per month on a unit of six birds as maintenance charge. I had ten units. They made one payment and then stopped. They kept the security deposit and had no explanation for not making the payment." Those that invested in Susi directly had to give an initial investment of Rs. 2 lakh and were allocated 20 chicks. They were promised a total return of Rs. 6.5 lakh in five years.

Perunthurai, a town in Erode district is the hub of emu farming with 28 companies who have done the same thing as Susi. According to police estimates, there are over 250 promoters of contract farming of this bird across the state and they all attracted investors promising higher returns. Dozens of emu farms started operations with advertisement campaigns to lure farmers to rear the bird on contract mode in Coimbatore, Krishnagiri, Pollachi, Mettupalayam, Tirupur, Perundurai, Dharapuram and Salem . The district administration and police have now issued press statements warning people off Emu farming or investments. The Susi birds are now being fed by the government but they will all die soon as feeding them is very expensive.

Mam sa khadatiti mamsah. The Sanskrit word is mamsa. Mam means "me," and sa means "he." I am killing this animal; I am eating him. And in my next lifetime he'll kill me and eat me. When the animal is sacrificed, this mantra is recited into the ear of the animal -- "You are giving your life, so in your next life you will get the opportunity of becoming a human being. And I who am now killing you will become an animal, and you will kill me." So after understanding this mantra, who will be ready to kill an animal?
~ Srila Prabhupada (JSD 6.5: Slaughterhouse Civilization)

Tamil Nadu is not alone. For the last three months teams of People For Animals have been going round Uttarakhand checking emu farms. Farmers in Nainital had started breeding emus some years ago. Now, the emus have been abandoned and the farmer ruined. The farmers have stopped feeding them and lakhs of these birds are dying of starvation. Nothing can be done as there is no space to keep them.

The companies insist that the emu is a bird which is easy to keep and is very popular for its meat, oil, leather and eggs. None of these claims are true. The fact is that emu meat is a failure. It is tough and difficult to cook. In fact even Australians do not eat emu meat. Susi farms started a restaurant with emu meat as the main fare. No takers. The emus require lakhs to feed. They grow to 6 feet.

Ganesa: Some people say that in our philosophy, if we do not wish to slaughter the animals, what about the trees? We are killing the plants. They are also living entities.

Prabhupada: If you compare the animals and the trees as the same, then why not kill yourself, your brother? Why do you distinguish? Why don't you slaughter your own son? Why do you distinguish?

Ganesa: He's a relative.

Prabhupada: You discriminate. If you are slaughtering animals and you are comparing that killing of the vegetables and the killing of the animals is the same, then killing your son and killing an animal is also the same. Why do you discriminate? Just kill your own son and eat.

Paramahamsa: He's a human being, though.

Prabhupada: Ah, therefore there is discrimination. Discrimination is the better part of valor. Whom should we kill? It is all right. Jivo jivasya jivanam. But there is important. If you eat vegetables there is no crisis, you can go on. It is a fact that an animal is eating another animal. It may be vegetables or animals, but they are disturbing. Therefore it is said, "As it is allotted." You should eat such and such. Not that indiscriminately you can eat everything. If you think killing of an animal and killing a vegetable is the same, then killing of your son and killing of animals or vegetable is the same. Why do you discriminate? What is your answer?

Ganesa: So if we discriminate between the animals and the plants, well what about the discrimination between the human beings and the

(continued on next page...)

They have to be feed several times a day, 4 kg. of food each. They eat seeds, fruit, insects, young leaves, lizards, other small animals and animal droppings. They do not eat dry grasses or older leaves, even if that's all that is available to them. Emus also need charcoal to help them digest their food.

Each requires 10 litres of water daily. The female lays eggs only during October to March and the maximum number are 10-20 eggs, one every 3-5 days. Emus lay eggs with difficulty. Only a few lay eggs at one time and an incubator is needed to hatch them. But incubators are uneconomical unless there is a reasonable quantity of eggs to sustain the cost of production. They get diseases like encephalitis.

As far as selling them for food, the price of emu meat is Rs. 450 a kg – an impossible price. The egg sells for Rs. 2,200. The eggs are dark green and very difficult to eat at one go and impossible to keep. In 2010 Punjab Agro Tech promoted the emu at its business

(...continued from previous page)

animals? Is it not all right to kill animals and not human beings?

Prabhupada: No. You discriminate actually. You do not kill human beings, but you kill animals. Similarly you discriminate: instead of killing animals, kill vegetables. Importance. Just like this grass. There is enough supply of grass, but you cannot have enough supply of cows. Therefore discrimination is that it is better to live on grass than on animals. Now, still they are eating seventy-five percent other than animals. They are not eating only animals. Why not twenty-five percent more? In the market they are not eating animal. When the animal-eaters I see, they have got a little flesh, surrounded by salad and these peas and so many other things. Why don't you eat only meat?

Srutakirti: Because we require a balanced diet.

Prabhupada: No, you cannot supply. If everyone eats meat only, then one day all animals will be finished.

Paramahamsa: But we want to have a balanced diet with meat, and vegetables and fruit.

Prabhupada: That balance of diet can be done by grains and vegetables. Why should we kill animals? We know that, the balance can be done. You learn from us that balanced food can be done. ~Srila Prabhupada (Morning Walk -- May 7, 1975, Perth) fair, saying that omelettes of its eggs were selling at Rs. 5,000 per omelette in 5 star hotels – a claim found to be utterly false. In fact, 5 stars hotels do not even have emu on their menus.

Now the emu companies are claiming that they will sell feather and nails, cooking oil and beauty products!

If the emu was being grown for meat and oil, any emu business has to have a slaughterhouse to kill the birds hygienically and another unit to process oil. No companies have these. They simply have birds which they contract out, take the money and run.

There is no meat market developed yet for export or for local sale and no symptoms of it so far. In any case there are no foreign offers for the meat. So far the oil processing and other industrial ventures remain only in newspaper and radio advertisements.

An entrepreneur in Anand, Gujarat who expected to reap huge profits from killing the bird, is now selling them away as pets. The farmers of Hoshiarpur are now bankrupt as are the emu farmers of Maharashtra – a scam that broke in 2010 and was ignored.

Uttarakhand, Maharashtra and Tamil Nadu have crashed. But that doesn't prevent more states and more ignorant state administrations from pushing emu meat. Goa, Orissa and Madhya Pradesh are pushing this. Bihar's ignorant animal husbandry and fisheries resources department minister is asking the World Bank to give Bihar money to start emu farming! His department says that they will sell it as a medicine saying that its oil has anti-inflammatory and anti-oxidative effects – a claim that even Australia does not make! Previously he had tried to make rat eating popular.

How many farmers will have to commit suicide before India bans emu farming?

They are now killing animal, but animal lives on this grass and grains. When there will be no grass, no grains, where they will get animal? They'll kill their own son and eat. That time is coming. Nature's law is that you grow your own food. But they are not interested in growing food. They are interested in manufacturing bolts and nuts.

-Srila Prabhupada (Morning Walk — June 22, 1974, Germany)

10.

Promoting Export Of Meat Will Kill Livestock-Driven Farming

Anuradha Dutt, The Pioneer, 24 May 2012

Gujarat Chief Minister Narendra Modi recently expressed concern at the Centre's 'pink revolution' — encouraging exports of meat — describing it as an anti-farmer policy. This is because livestock is diverted from farming to slaughter houses. The blame must first fall on the British, who began the practice. In fact, they changed the traditional farming system for pecuniary reasons. Under the Permanent Settlement Act, 1793, first implemented in Bengal and then in other parts, landowners were assigned fixed revenue targets by the colonial administrators and many were forced to shift to plantation farming such as cotton and indigo in place of food grains. This led to famines in the 19th century.

Cultivators were under greater pressure to meet the zamindars' demands. If the revenue target was not met, the land was auctioned off, ruining both owners and peasants. It altered India's agrarian economy, which was self-sustaining, primarily grew food grains, vegetables and fruits, reared livestock and engaged in organic farming by using animal dung, urine and manure as fertilisers, and plant and cattle derivatives as pesticides. Emphasis shifted to cash crops, and during the Green Revolution, synthetic fertilisers and pesticides. This increased the debt burden on the farmers.

Livestock-driven farming was ruined by the promotion of the meat, bones and leather industries by the British, with butchering of cattle, goat, sheep, pigs, fowls and other creatures acquiring institutional status, and mechanized slaughter houses being set up.

Later, tractors and machines further made cattle redundant among better-off farmers. The age-old ethos of compassion was completely repudiated, with free India's leaders continuing with the meat policy. Many people, overcoming food taboos and religious tenets against wanton killing, took to commerce of meat.

The constitutional directive for a countrywide ban on cow slaughter was never implemented though some States did impose a ban. A Supreme Court order in 1958, dismissing a plea by some Patna butchers that cow slaughter was a religious duty under Islam, had allowed slaughter of impotent bulls but prohibited killing of cows and calves on economic grounds. It said, "Cattle in India has three-fold uses, firstly providing milk for consumption, secondly for draught purposes; and, finally, as provider of manure for agriculture. Dung is cheaper than chemical fertilisers and extremely useful. In short, the cow and bullock are the back bone of India."

However, livestock continued to be diverted to slaughter houses to feed the thriving meat export, leather and derivatives industries. Modern India developed a culture of non-vegetarian food, sharply at variance with its pre-Raj past. Under Muslim rulers, most Hindus, barring the heterodox, shunned flesh and eggs. And cow slaughter was forbidden by many sultans out of respect for Hindu sentiments.

Emperor Akbar was said to be so very impressed by Jain tenets that he forbade killing of animals and fish, and eating of flesh for six months in a year. Foreign travellers testified to the general avoidance of flesh. JT Wheeler quoted John Fires (1678-81) on Hindu food habits in his British History under Mughal Rule, "Hindus eat fruits, vegetables, roots and rice. But they do not eat meat, fish and eggs."

In his Indian History, Part II, Wheeler quoted the late 13th century Venetian Marco Polo's Testimony, "In the entire country spreading from Cape Camorin to the Koromandal coast in the east which was earlier known as Maula Pradesh and which is the area inhabited by the Tamil speaking people; and from there the entire area up to the Bay of Bengal, which is inhabited by the Telugu speaking Telangs; no one except the Parihars (pariahs) ate beef or meat. All these people worship cows and bullocks. They do not slaughter any animal. Hence, if any traveller wishes to eat flesh of goats, he has to carry with him as servant a Syrian for doing the job of a butcher."

Much before, the Chinese Buddhist monks Fa Hien in the fifth century and Hsuang-tsang in the seventh century recorded the absence of violence against animals and consumption of flesh, or, as Fa Hien noted, even liquor.

The British made meat-eating and drinking socially acceptable. They requisitioned the services of some pliant natives. A book by Pandurang Kane, a Bombay advocate, postulated that beef was consumed in the Vedic age. Raja Rajendralal Mitra of Bengal in 1872 brought out an essay, Beef in Ancient India. He was awarded a doctorate by his masters for his effort. He later expanded this into a book, Indo-Aryan, published in 1877.

Bengal, as the seat of the Raj, provided the most fertile ground for such ideas to take root. Left-hand tantrik tradition condoned the consumption of flesh and liquor. 'Beef-eating clubs' sprouted, with English-educated natives readily breaking food taboos. If not beef, they ate other flesh and eggs and freely drank alcohol. The ethos spread throughout India as a mark of modernity.

Mohammed Ali Jinnah, Pakistan's founding father, and the Nehrus, all anglicised, relished both beef and pork. Krishna Hutheesing, Pandit Nehru's youngest sister, recalled in We Nehrus, published in 1967, "Our lunch was always of the British style and that is why we always used to have lunch in a hotel because only the British lunch included beef and pork. If beef and pork were to

> *India is perhaps the only nation state wherein large numbers of people subjugate their desires for the benefit of other species. That this great culture of kindness is being eroded by one of greed is very sad. I hope compassionate vegetarians of every creed are able to join hands and stop this descent into malevolence and moral turpitude. ~ Leroy Schwarz*

be brought into the home, our mother and Muslim servants would have felt bad."

The genesis of the pink revolution lies in such devaluation of animal life, with unfortunate consequences for farmers.

11.

Rant To Legalize

Cattle Smuggling On Bangladesh Border

Deeptiman Tiwary, Times News Network, Dec 1, 2012

In a controversial suggestion, outgoing BSF chief U K Bansal has said that the menace of cattle smuggling on the India-Bangladesh border defies policing and might be best controlled by making the trade legal.

Cattle running mafias abound on the border, making smuggling bovines for meat a highly lucrative but violence-prone illegal business. Bansal seemed to endorse the view that the sheer scale of operations and the economic interests involved make policing a limited option.

Asked if the illegal cattle trade should be legalized given the economic realities in Bangladesh, Bansal said, "We all have to think about it seriously. It is not a problem that can be solved by policing." Bansal was speaking at BSF's annual press conference.

Several Bangladeshis lose their lives smuggling cattle for a remuneration as low as Rs 500. While trying to stop them, BSF men put their lives at risk while reports of corruption have also surfaced.

The massive demand for meat feeding a Rs 2,000 crore industry in Bangladesh has made it difficult for forces to stop the smuggling. The proposal to make cattle trade legal, despite its apparent pragmatism, is sure to attract fire from groups advocating cow protection.

Legalizing the trade is a hot potato that the government is unlikely to consider, but it could throw open a discussion on a taboo subject that might yield results later.

The issue has been contentious, leading to a stand-off between India and Bangladesh at various bilateral meets where charges have been traded. Bangladesh has rarely accepted any illegality, including the large inflow of illegal immigrants into India.

The government has made efforts to bring down casualties of Bangladeshi nationals by introducing non-lethal weapons. But the move has hurt BSF as emboldened smugglers have started attacking force personnel.

In the past three years, while casualties of Bangladeshis on the border came down by over 60%, attacks on personnel of Border Security Force went up by over 100%.

According to government figures, in 2010, as many 32 suspected intruders were shot dead by BSF on the Indo-Bangladesh border while 64 men from the force were injured due to attacks from

gam ca dharma-dugham dinam
bhrsam sudra-padahatam
vivatsam asru-vadanam
ksamam yavasam icchatim

Although the cow is beneficial because one can draw religious principles from her, she was now rendered poor and calfless. Her legs were being beaten by a sudra. There were tears in her eyes, and she was distressed and weak. She was hankering after some grass in the field.

In the age of Kali, the poor helpless animals, especially the cows, which are meant to receive all sorts of protection from the administrative heads, are killed without restriction. Thus the administrative heads under whose noses such things happen are representatives of God in name only. Such powerful administrators are rulers of the poor citizens by dress or office, but factually they are worthless, lower-class men without the cultural assets of the twice-born. No one can expect justice or equality of treatment from once-born (spiritually uncultured) lower-class men. Therefore in the age of Kali everyone is unhappy due to the maladministration of the state.

~ Srila Prabhupada (Srimad Bhagavatam 1.17.5)

smugglers. Due to continued high fatalities of its nationals, Bangladesh had been pushing for softer approach towards border guarding from India.

Thus, in 2010, India had proposed and implemented use of non-lethal weapons such as rubber bullets and pump action guns by the BSF against suspected smugglers.

Bangladeshi fatalities came down to merely 11. However, injuries to BSF men jumped to 150. In 2012, the force has recorded six deaths of Bangladeshis and 100 injuries to its men on the border.

"The problem is that the sheer economics of the trade makes it unstoppable. Close to seven lakh cattle are smuggled every year, and this is only the data collected through arrest of smugglers. The industry is worth thousands of crores of rupees in Bangladesh," said a BSF officer who has served on the Indo-Bangla border.

One of the reasons India has never been able to come to an agreement with Bangladesh on resolving the problem is the latter does not consider it smuggling, calling it cattle trade. Bangladesh has even unofficially offered to help make arrangements so that cattle can be bought at the border without risking the lives of people on either side.

You have become mad and you are engaged in doing all forbidden things which you should not do. You are doing that. And why you are doing that? Nunam pramattah kurute vikarma [SB 5.5.4]. Why? Yad indriya-pritaya aprnoti. Simply for sense gratification. Simply for sense gratification. I have seen one hotel man in Calcutta. He cut the throat of a chicken, and the chicken, half-cut, it was flapping and jumping. The child of the hotel man, he was crying, and the hotel man was laughing. He was taking pleasure, "Oh, how this chicken, half-cut throat, and how he is jumping... Why you are crying? Why you are crying?" And in Western countries I think students are sometimes taken to slaughterhouse to see. Is it a fact? Yes. You see. They take pleasure. Doing something sinful, they take pleasure. For pleasure's sake they do that.

~ Srila Prabhupada (Srimad-Bhagavatam 3.25.16 — Bombay, November 16, 1974)

12.

India-Pak Livestock Export Deal

By A.M. Parekh

India recently signed a deal with Pakistan to transfer 1 million livestock every year to Pakistan. The following is a letter from A.M. Parekh (Trustee of the Viniyog Parivar Trust) to the Prime Minister of India.

Dr. Manmohan Singh
Hon'ble Prime Minister of India,
Prime Minister's Office,
152, South Block,
New Delhi-110 011.

Respected Dr. Manmohan ji,

Re: Export of livestock to Pakistan

We understand from newspaper reports that the Government of India has permitted export of livestock from India to Pakistan. It is reported that the Pakistan administration has approved setting up of four quarantine centres immediately and another 30 to 40 over the next few months to accommodate upto ten thousand animals per quarantine centre, where the animals exported from India will be kept for 15 days before being certified as disease free and fit for slaughter for meat. The preliminary estimates of exports put the figure as 10 lakh animals per annum. Pakistan will permit duty free import of these live animals into its country.

It is also reported that this step is being taken as a measure to improve relations with Pakistan and also to increase the trade with Pakistan.

Meat is one of the 11 items which are reviewed by the Pakistan Price Control Committee and it is reported that these items are priced at 15 to 50% higher in Islamabad than in New Delhi. It is to ease the price situation in Pakistan that live animals from India will be exported.

To say the least, this is a very ill-conceived proposal. Livelihoods of a very vast number of people in rural India is dependent on rearing of animals i.e. cattle, sheep and goat. The 17th livestock census report indicates about 10% decline in population of cattle and a very negligible rise in population of sheep and goat. Even otherwise there is large scale clandestine export of livestock across the border both to Pakistan and to Bangladesh as also to the Middle East from various ports of Gujarat.

Opening up or legalizing export of livestock will be a severe blow to the Animal Husbandry in our country. It will also increase price of meat within the country. Lured by higher prices in the neighbouring country, the traders in livestock will be tempted to export more and more animals and over a period of time India will face the same situation on price front of meat that Pakistan is facing today.

We wonder whether our country has run out of ideas to improve relations with Pakistan and is considering sacrifice of dumb and innocent animals to achieve this object! Our Constitution has imposed a Fundamental Duty to show compassion towards all living beings and these duties are cast equally on the government as on the citizens. Acting against this Fundamental Duty, the

Just like we are taking milk from the cow. We are indebted. "No, we are killing them." They are committing simply sinful life and they want to be happy and peaceful. Just see. We are indebted. I am obliged to you for your service. So instead of feeling obligation, if I cut your throat, how gentleman I am, just see, imagine.

~ Srila Prabhupada (Bhagavad-gita 1.37-39 -- London, July 27, 1973)

Government has decided to export animals knowing fully well that they will be slaughtered.

Our country has adopted meat export as a Policy measure identifying it as a thrust area. This is already playing havoc with our livestock situation and a few entrepreneurs are making huge profits at the cost of our national wealth i.e. our animals. The export earnings of some three thousand crores of rupees is peanuts when compared to the foreign exchange reserve of more than 130 billion USD.

Throughout the country the public sentiment is against the export of meat which is being continued to cater to the vested interests of a few private sector entrepreneurs and their patrons in bureaucracy and politicians. It is painful to note that instead of honoring the public sentiments of banning meat export from the country the Government is taking steps now to export livestock also.

We are not elaborating on how livestock is the backbone of our rural economy as you are well aware of it.

We request you to kindly reconsider the whole issue and reverse the decision to permit export of livestock to Pakistan/Bangladesh and also to consider banning of meat export from the country.

Thanking you,

Yours faithfully, For Viniyog Parivar Trust

(A.M. Parekh) Trustee

Prabhupada: Now Kirtanananda was prosecuted because he is not killing cows.

Brahmananda: By having them grow old, they were saying that "This is cruelty. You should kill them."

Prabhupada: This is their civilization, that "You are not killing? You are cruel." Just see. Christ said, "Thou shall not kill." That is cruel. How can you pull on this civilization? But this is their religion. So what kind of persons they are?

- Srila Prabhupada (Room Conversation - February 28, 1977, Mayapur)

13.

Recognition And Awards

To Meat Exporters

In India, the meat exporter are the cynosure of all eyes. They not only receive subsidies and tax rebates, but also many awards and recognitions. Most of these exporters enjoy the coveted status of 'Star Export House'. They always seem to receive preferential treatment in selection for awards and grants.

Commonly conferred awards to them are : National Productivity Award, Rajiv Gandhi National Quality Award, National Safety Award, Industry Excellence Award, National Award For Export Excellence, APEDA Award, GMP (Good Manufacturing Practices) Award etc. Then there is a whole list of awards instituted by the Council For Leather Exports for leather exporters.

All India Meat & Livestock Exporters Association-AIMLEA claims on its home page : AIMLEA members have world class, state of the art, integrated establishments, incorporating mechanised abattoirs, operated in accordance with the Codex Alimentarius Standards, OIE Terrestrial Animal Health Code, besides having ISO 9001:2000 for Quality Systems, HACCP for Food Safety, ISO 14001 for Environment

Management and ISO 18001 for Occupational Health and Safety Management System accreditations.

India is definitely excelling in this particular area. Some of the award winning Indian meat export houses are:

- Allanasons
- Al-Noor Exports
- Al Drahim Exports Holding Private Limited
- Mirha Exports Pvt. Ltd
- Swetha Exports
- Al Safi Frozen Foods
- Abdul Majeed Qureshi & Co.
- Al Kabeer Exports Pvt. Ltd.
- Al Nafees Proteins Pvt. Ltd.
- Al Quresh Exports

Anyone who takes milk... Everyone takes milk. The cow is the mother. Mother gives milk. And mother, when she cannot supply milk, mother should be cut up. Is that a very good philosophy? Is it human philosophy? What is the answer?

You are eating everything. Except the moving cars, you are eating all the moving animals. The car also moves, but you cannot eat. Otherwise you are killing everything. You have become so civilized rascal that your business is to kill other animals and eat. You are so civilized. You are still in the crude form of human being, just like in the jungles, the aborigines, the Africans, they do not know how to develop civilization -- crude methods, eating the animals. That also, they are not so uncivilized that they keep slaughterhouses. You are so uncivilized that you are keeping slaughterhouses, regularly. These Africans and other jungle people they eat meat, but they directly kill. They have no such civilization as to maintain a slaughterhouse. The tigers eat meat, but they do not keep a slaughterhouse. And you are civilized. You are keeping slaughterhouse. Why should you keep? The government shouldn't allow you to keep slaughterhouses. If anyone wants to eat meat, let them eat like tigers and others. Individually, kill one animal -- a lower animal, not cows. This should be the government law. You kill it in your home, before your children and family, and eat. This is not good civilization.
~ Srila Prabhupada (Morning Walk -- May 10, 1975, Perth)

- Al Tamash Exports Pvt. Ltd.
- DD Marine Exports Pvt. Ltd.
- Hind Agro Industries Ltd.
- VKS Farms Pvt. Ltd.

14.

Locking Horns Over Culture And Business

Are Cattle Commodifiable Without Loss Of Traditional Farm-Life?

Sangeetha Sriram, June 2002

India has a livestock population of 500 million (20% of the world's total), more than half of which is cattle, forming the backbone of Indian agriculture. Mechanisation of agricultural operations has pushed cattle to redundancy in large parts of the country. Short hybrid grain varieties and harvester machines have reduced the availability of cattle fodder. Alongside, meat export almost doubled between 1990 and 95, while livestock population only increased by half that rate. Further, indigenous breeds of cattle have been taken over by foreign breeds introduced during the white revolution, which are treated as milch and meat machines.

From all these changes, India's cattle population is increasingly viewed as a mere economic resource for optimal returns, a transformation that is greatly impacting traditional farm-life. Recognizing this, the government instituted the National Commission on Cattle in August 2001, to suggest ways and means for the preservation and protection of the nation's cattle wealth.

But from the outset, the government's other actions have undermined the commission's work. Within the 10th five-year plan, the government has been constituting sub-committees to design policies on various sectors. Under this scheme, the sub-group on Animal Husbandry -XI - Meat Sector, constituted by the Department of Agriculture, came into being. Even as the cattle commission was drawing up policies for cattle protection, the policy recommendations of the 'meat-sector' were released;

these are clearly at odds with the commission's role and objectives. The document, in which these policy recommendations are stipulated, is peppered with phrases like "in the interest of the farmer" and "cow protection with economic spirit". The actual recommendations, however, show no such interest or spirit. Among the recommendations:

- Removal of all bans on meat export and all restrictions on processed meat import and slaughter machinery.
- Removal of all restrictions on slaughter of buffaloes.
- Reduction in the minimum age for slaughter of bullocks.
- Removal of the ban on beef exports.

The policies clearly provide a thrust towards the creation of a significant meat market supplied by industrial abbattoirs and corporate food marketeres. The main questions that arise from this are:

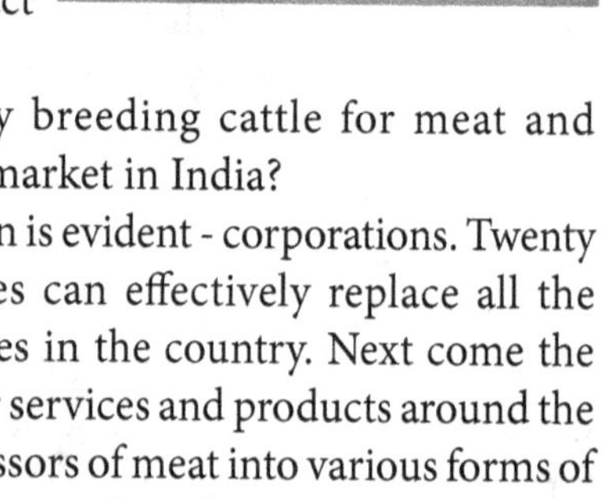

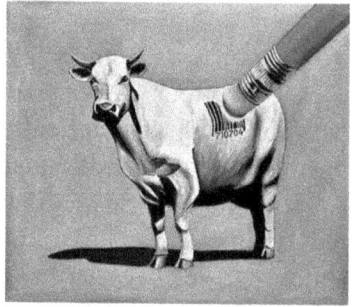

- What are the pros and cons of industrialising slaughter houses and raising more cattle for meat?
- How will these policies impact the typical Indian farmer?
- Who stands to benefit by breeding cattle for meat and expanding the meat-consumer market in India?

The answer to that last question is evident - corporations. Twenty five cattle-slaughtering factories can effectively replace all the existing 140,000 slaughter houses in the country. Next come the corporations that have built their services and products around the meat-consuming market - processors of meat into various forms of fast food, processed meat transporters, deep freezer manufacturers, cattle feed 'enhancers', drug manufacturers who sell 'meat growth

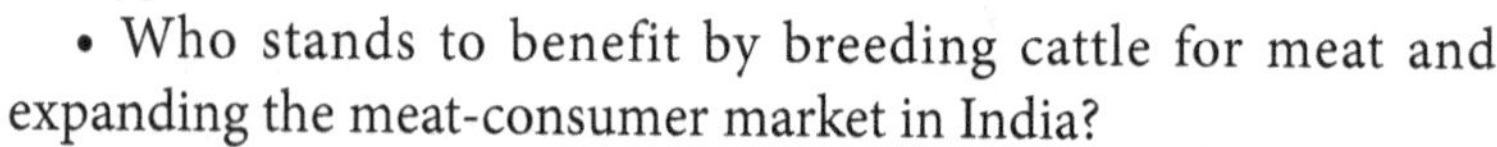

On the street, in your front, if somebody's being killed, nobody will take care; he'll go on. There is no mercifulness. Even the mother has no mercifulness, killing the child. This is Kali-yuga.

~ Srila Prabhupada (Srimad-Bhagavatam 7.6.3 -Toronto, June 19, 1976)

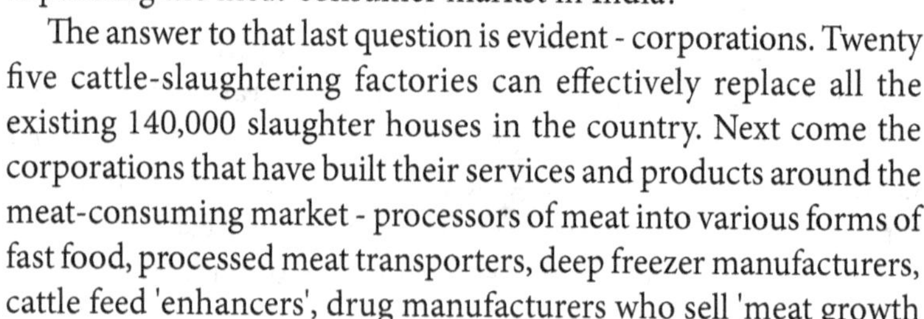

hormones' and antibiotics for cattle and even agri'business' banks that will give loans only for cattle 'producing'. Not to forget the fast-growing biotech industry.

Dimming Prospects In The West

An interesting phenomenon in the globalisation scene is that as the West is waking up and rejecting many harmful technologies like the use of certain chemical pesticides and waste incinerators, the private companies that have invested in them are frantically looking for markets in the less regulated, developing countries. India, with its more than one billion people, is naturally an attractive market.

Inefficient And Uneconomical Choices

The sub-group's document explains the need for India to become a livestock economy thus: "Increase in productivity of land and productivity of definite number of livestock is a necessity to meet the growing needs of human population. Thus the need for increased efficiency in livestock production and utilization is far greater today than in the past". But nothing could be farther from the truth! Vandana Shiva says in her book, Stolen Harvest "Europe's intensive livestock economy requires seven times the area of Europe in other countries for the production of cattle feed. In a complementary economy, the cattle eat the straw and agricultural waste that humans cannot. But, in a competitive model such as the livestock industry, grain is diverted from human consumption to the intensive feed for livestock. It takes eight kilograms of grain to produce one kilogram of meat."

This inefficiency - eating meat that must first be fed grain that could instead be itself eaten directly - is well known. The Meat-subgroup's proposal will move India away from her primarily complementary economy to a competitive livestock economy. By growing the cattle here for unrestricted export, India will be subsidising the meat-based industries dominated by foreign firms. By permitting them to use the natural resources in India to produce meat for export or even inefficient consumption models within India, we are creating the sort of imbalance that will divert resources away from adequate food production for our own people.

In other economic terms, too, the new policies inlcude significant dangers. A story from Stolen Harvest is instructive. "Al-Kabeer, one of the biggest abattoirs in Andhra Pradesh, slaughters 182,400 cattle every year, animals whose dung could have provided for the fuel needs of 90,000 average Indian families of five. Kerosene imports quadrupled in 1993 from 1988. If livestock were not slaughtered in AP, farmyard manure would cultivate 38,400 hectares producing 530,000 tons of food grain. The state of AP must now spend Rs.9.1 billion to import nitrogen, phosphorous and potash previously provided by livestock over the duration of their lives. The projected earnings of Rs.200 million by Al-Kabeer is actually leading to a drain of billions of rupees in foreign exchange. Finally, in a lawsuit against Al-Kabeer, the courts ordered a 50% reduction of its capacity, in order to save the cattle wealth and the rural economy of AP."

An especially anti-democratic move is the recommendation that "animal husbandry Departments under State Govt. should be entrusted with licensing of slaughterhouses as at present, local bodies who are the owners, are also license providers". This proposal essentially asks for the decision-making power to be taken farther away from the people and centralised, so the hassle of manipulating 50 (or so) local bodies in every state could be reduced to that of manipulating just one state department.

"More we try to know the about the reasons responsible for the unreasonable increase in the number of slaughterhouses in 'independent' India, the more painful astonishing facts await us. It is like opening a can of worms... It is a conspiracy, political conspiracy to eternalize India's slavery to West's policy of materialism and mammon worship. Sadly, the politicians are successful as the general people are turning more ignorant and immune, gathering themselves in the selfish cocoon of just their own individual happiness. They do not realize that nobody can be an independent individual, however tiny we are a part of BIG network and this is sensitive to the slightest imbalance that we bring in the natural set-up. Smallest of the action has its reaction; and we are paying the price for that."

The cow has been a symbol of prosperity in India since ancient times and is deeply respected. Indian agriculture is almost philosophically built on integrating cattle into the human lifestyle. Besides helping the farmer, the livestock are the source of many important products (which is different from the factory mindset of man as the 'producer' with the cow just being a machine) - ghee for medicine, dung for fertilizer, milk for food, urine for pesticide and many others.

The Indian farmer has already been pushed to a state of despair by the government's agricultural policies. With the promotion of short stemmed hybrid varieties of paddy and wheat (which have deprived the cattle of their natural feed), agrochemicals, artificial insemination of exotic breeds, hormone injections for more milk production, the government of India has systematically converted the 'localised, environment-friendly, energy- and water-efficient, knowledge-driven agri'culture' into a centralised energy- and water-inefficient, technology- and private-profit-driven agri'business'.

(More information on this issue and an online petition to stop the move towards industrialisation of slaughter is available at www.chennaiorganicfood.com/cow.htm)

So this is our program. Let the cows live. We take sufficient milk. We are getting milk, one thousand pounds. One thousand pounds daily in our, one center, New Vrindaban, Virginia. So we are making various preparations from the milk, and they are very happy, and the cows are also happy. So this is one of our programs, to stop killing this important animal. And the flesh-eaters may wait a little until the cow dies. Then he gets the opportunity. Why there should be slaughterhouse maintained? As you are one of the leading citizens of Paris, we appeal to you to take up this consideration seriously. Why we should maintain slaughterhouse? If we want to eat the flesh, let us wait till the death. And there will be death. There is no doubt about it. So why they should maintain slaughterhouse? And this is most cruelty. A animal which is giving milk, so important foodstuff, and that is being killed, it does not suit any moral sense of any human being.

~ Srila Prabhupada (Room Conversation with Monsieur Mesman, Chief of Law House of Paris — June 11, 1974, Paris)

15.

The New Livestock Policy

A Policy Of Ecocide Of Indigenous Cattle Breeds And A Policy Of Genocide For India's Small Farmers

by Dr.Vandana Shiva

The Livestock Policy Perspective 1995-2020 developed by the Government of India and the Swiss Development Cooperation is a policy for the destruction of India's farm animal biodiversity and a threat to the survival of small farmers who depend on a diversity based decentralised livestock economy.

India's livestock legacy has four unique dimensions :-

- 1. Cows and bulls are treated as sacred and hence are protected.
- 2. The conservation of farm animals is essential for the sustainability of agriculture and the survival of small farmers.

• 3. The conservation and utilisation of farm animals is based on diversity - both diversity of breeds as well as diversity of function of farm animals

• 4. The sustenance of cattle comes from diverse sources of fodder and feed - agricultural by products such as straw and oil cake, fodder trees planted on farms and common property resources such a village pastures and forests.

Thus, the indigenous approach to livestock is based on diversity, decentralisation, sustainability and equity. Our cattle are not just milk machines or meat machines. They are sentient beings who serve human communities through their multidimensional role in agriculture.

On the other hand, externally driven projects, programmes and policies emerging from industrial societies treat cattle as one-dimensional machines which are maintained with capital intensive and environmentally intensive inputs and which provide a single output - either milk or meat. Polices based on this approach are characterized by monocultures, concentration and centralisation, non-sustainability and inequality.

The new livestock policy has been framed in this paradigm of machines and monocultures. It is a serious attack on principles of

Ample food grains can be produced through agricultural enterprises, and profuse supplies of milk, yogurt and ghee can be arranged through cow protection. Abundant honey can be obtained if the forests are protected. Unfortunately, in modern civilization, men are busy killing the cows that are the source of yogurt, milk and ghee, they are cutting down all the trees that supply honey, and they are opening factories to manufacture nuts, bolts, automobiles and wine instead of engaging in agriculture. How can the people be happy? They must suffer from all the misery of materialism. Their bodies become wrinkled and gradually deteriorate until they become almost like dwarves, and a bad odor emanates from their bodies because of unclean perspiration resulting from eating all kinds of nasty things. This is not human civilization. If people actually want happiness in this life and want to prepare for the best in the next life, they must adopt a Vedic civilization.

~ Srila Prabhuapda (Srimad Bhagavatam 5.16.25)

diversity, decentralisation, sustainability and equity in the livestock sector.

The Cattle Economy: The Provider For The Poor

The policy document recognizes that the livestock economy is the economy of the poorest households in India.

As stated in Section 2.3: About 630 million people reside in rural areas (74% of total population) of which 40% have incomes which place them below the poverty line. Some 70 million households (73% of total rural households) keep and own livestock of one kind or another and derive on average 20% of their income from this source. Small and marginal fanners and landless tabourers constitute almost two-thirds of these livestock keeping households. The importance of the livestock sector can therefore not be measured purely in terms of its contribution to GDP but it plays a very crucial role in generating income and employment for the weaker sections of the economy. Rapid growth of the livestock sector can be a deciding factor in the efforts at improving nutrition and relieving poverty. Women provide nearly 90% of all labour for livestock management.

However, all the analysis in the policy is totally insensitive to the systems which allow cattle to serve the needs of the poorest. As a result the recommendations are a direct assault on this survival base of the poor.

An Assault on the Culture of Conservation.

The livestock policy paper is disrespectful to the Indian culture of reverence for farm animals. These cultural beliefs are viewed as block to promoting meat production. At a time when meat consumption is going down in western countries themselves, India's livestock policy is trying to convert a predominantly vegetarian

> *Cruelty to dumb animals is one of the distinguishing vices of low and base minds. Wherever it is found, it is a certain mark of ignorance and meanness; a mark which all the external advantages of wealth, splendour, and nobility, cannot obliterate. It is consistent neither with learning nor true civility.*
>
> *~William Jones*

society into a beef eating culture. In the U.S. beef consumption per capita has declined from 88.9 pounds in 1976 to 63.9 pounds in 1990. Cultural attitudes have been the most significant reason for maintaining vegetarian diets for the large majority in India. The livestock policy would like to undermine these conservation policies to promote a meat culture.

As stated in Section 2.10 on Meat Production: The beef production in India is purely an adjunct to milk and draught power production. The animals slaughtered are the old and the infirm and the sterile and are in all cases malnourished. There is no organized marketing and no grading system and beef prices are at a level which makes feeding uneconomic. There is no instance of feedlots or even individual animals being raised for meat. Religious sentiments (particularly in the Northern and Western parts of India) against cattle slaughter seem to spill over also on buffaloes and prevent the utilization of a large number of surplus male calves.

The policy then recommends government interventions to stimulate meat production even though this will totally undermine the basis of sustainable agriculture. (Section 3.10)

Undermining Sustainability Of Agriculture.

The economics of meat exports is totally flawed in a diversity based culture of animal husbandry and farming. Two thirds and more of the power requirements of Indian villages are met by the 80 million work animals. Indian cattle excrete 700 million tons of recoverable manure. Half of which is used as fuel, saving 27 millions

Now, we must take to agricultural work -- produce food and give protection to the cows. And if we produce a surplus, we can trade. It is a simple thing that we must do. Our people should live peacefully in farming villages, produce grain and fruit and vegetables, protect the cows, and work hard. And if there is a surplus, we can start restaurants. Krsna conscious people will never be losers by following the instructions of Krsna. They will live comfortably, without any material want, and tyaktva deham punar janma naiti [Bhagavad-gita 4.9]: After leaving this body they will go directly to God. This is our way of life.
~ Srila Prabhupada (JSD 6.5: Slaughterhouse Civilization)

of kerosene, 35 million tons of coal or 68 million tons of wood. The remaining half is used as fertiliser.

As Maneka Gandhi has shown in the case of one export slaughter house, the value of nitrogen, phosphate and potassium provided annually by living cattle is fifty times more than the animal earnings from meat exports, which at current rates of slaughter will wipe out Indian farm animals in 10-15 years. If animals are allowed to live, we will get 19,18,562 tonnes of farmyard manure with the help of their dung and urine.

The livestock policy has nothing to say on the role of animals in the maintenance of sustainability in agriculture. In fact, the livestock policy if implemented would convert cow dung from a source of fertility into a major source of pollution since intensive factory farming of cattle for beef leads to concentration of organic waste from livestock in one place. Since such intensive production is not integrated and cannot be integrated with agriculture as in the case of small farms with decentralised livestock economies, the animal waste turns into a pollutant. Nitrogen from cattle waste is converted into Ammonia and Nitrates which leach into and pollute the surface and ground water.

A feedlot of 10,000 cattle produces. as much waste as a city of 110,000 people. This is the reason the Netherlands has been able to export its toxic cow dung to India and is unable to reintegrate this animal waste into its own agricultural systems. Cow dung is a fertilizer only in small scale integrated farming systems. In large scale, concentrated and specialised factory farming systems, this wealth is converted into a hazardous waste. Further, since intensive factory farming of cattle goes hand in hand with intensive feeding and feed production which in turn requires heavy use of fertilizers and pesticides, the cattle waste from factory farms is very heavily contaminated with chemicals.

Animal Energy.

While in decentralised small scale animal husbandry, cow dung is the most significant gift of the cow to sustainable agriculture, there is total neglect of the contribution of cattle to renewal of soil fertility in the livestock policy. While reference is made to draught power, it is only with the objective of wiping out this source of sustainable energy production, without recognising that if animals were replaced by tractors in India we would have to spend more than a thousand million US dollars annually on fossil fuels, worsening our debt crisis and our balance of payment. In total indifference to the huge economic costs to both farmers and the country generated by substituting animal energy by fossil fuel run mechanical energy, the livestock policy blindly proposes such a shift.

As Section 2.4 on Drought Power: The number of work animals continued to increase through 1977 but has since fallen by about 10 million to a level of 70 million in 1987 of which 9% are buffaloes. To ensure replacement every sixth year one needs about 0.67 breedable cows per bullock. The bullocks have been largely replaced by mechanical means in transport and irrigation and are now almost exclusively u@ for land preparation. How much of the gross cropped area (180 m ha) that is cultivated by animal power is uncertain (an estimate of 60 m ha is given in a recent WB report) but it is clear that the bullocks may only be utilized for a short period of the year (at most 100 days). Since bullocks generally are not put out to grazing except possibly during the slack season, feeding them and the necessary replacement stock imposes a major strain. Crossbreds are generally not appreciated as bullocks. Although there are opportunities to introduce improved bullock genes in F2 and subsequent crosses these are seldom utilized. In larger herds one may use some cows for crossbreeding while others are used for bullock (and marginal milk) production. In smaller herds one can however not separately pursue both the power and the dairy objective. The policy of upgrading bullocks and introducing improved implements has met with limited success (some implements like the seeder has been introduced). Where the field sizes, topography etc. allow the farmer has the choice between keeping his own bullocks (and the stock needed for their replacement), disposing of the bullocks and either hire power for cultivation (animal or tractor) with the consequent risk that the timeliness of operations will suffer, or acquiring a tractor and offer its service for transport and cultivation. We have only limited material that illustrates the relative attractiveness of these options for different farm sizes with due consideration to the importance of timeliness of land preparation (see however Sharma and Binswanger). The trend is obviously away from animal power.

As stated in Section 5.2 on Interventions: with respect of animal power further adds, if our aim, as suggested, is to accelerate the trend towards mechanization as well as to promote upgrading of bullock power and improvement of implements we will need to consider interventions for this purpose.

In order to accelerate mechanization one may consider providing credit for tractor (incl.equipment) procurement and to make sure (through training programs and subsidy) that the weaker sections get a fair chance to exploit this opportunity. At a time when as a result of the climate change crisis we should be moving away from fossil fuel use to sustainable sources of energy, the livestock policy recommends the reverse.

It also neglects the fact that even in the affluent state of Punjab, farmers are shifting back from tractors to bullocks because the

tractors have become too expensive to operate due to rise in fuel prices.

The Flawed One-Dimensional, Linear And Monoculture Logic

The livestock policy is based on a flawed logic of one dimensionality and linearity. One dimensional thinking is based on perceiving cattle as linear and mechanical input-output systems with a single function, single output usually limited to milk or meat. Linearity is displayed in treating these inputs and outputs as linear flows. *On this one dimensional and linear logic, it says that India's 70 million work animals have to be fed and managed over a "365 day feeding year" while they give a "100 day working year". On the basis of this flawed logic it is then stated that these "inefficient" work animals can become progressively redundant to the farming sector and cattle population can be reduced to one third of what it is.*

This concept of efficiency applied to cattle is totally misplaced. Firstly, for most rural families, animals are part of their extended families and are not mere work machines. If this misplaced logic of efficiency had to be applied to humans, we too should be totally annihilated and replaced by robots because humans are "inefficient" as they have to be looked after in childhood and old age and during ill health, while they "work" only in adult life and during healthy periods. Treating humans and animals as if they were mere machines with an externally defined single function is ethically outrageous and economically flawed.

Secondly, in any case, in India, farm animals are not single output, single function machines. They have many functions only one of which is to provide work energy. Even when work animals are not pulling ploughs or bullock carts they are giving manure, the most significant contribution that cattle make to agriculture. Thirdly, a comparative energy audit of inputs and useful outputs from U.S. cattle and Indian cattle shows that Indian cattle are far more efficient than their counterparts in industrial economies in using energy. They use 29 per cent of organic matter provided to them, and 22 per cent of the energy and 3 per cent of the protein in contrast to 9, 7 and 5 per cent respectively in the intensive cattle industry in the U.S.

Indian cattle provide food in the excess of the edible food consumed, in contrast to the U.S. where 6 times as much edible food is fed to the cattle as is obtained from them.

It is this wasteful and inefficient system of livestock management that the new livestock policy introduced in India in the name of improving "efficiency" of cattle.

Undermining Farm Animal Biodiversity.

The Biodiversity Convention obliges all member states to protect biodiversity. This includes farm animal biodiversity- India's indigenous livestock policy has been based on a wide diversity of cattle breeds. They are high milk yielders like the Gir, Sindhi, Sahiwal and Deoni. They are dual purpose breeds such as the Haryana, Ongole, Gaolao, Krishna Valley, 'Ibarparkar, Kankrej. Finally there are specialised draught animals such as Nagori, Bachour, Kenkatha, Malvi, Kherigarh, Hallikar, Amritmohal, Kangayam, Khillari etc.

The livestock policy document totally fails to address the issue of conservation of animal biodiversity even though it has been drafted after the Biodiversity Convention was signed. In fact, by recommending the wiping out of draught power, the policy is indirectly writing a death certificate for indigenous breeds which have been evolved as dual purpose breeds for both dairy and drought power or a specialised draught animals. By a one dimensional focus on dairy and meat alone, and a deliberate destruction of the animal energy economy, the policy promotes the replacement of diverse indigenous breeds by uniform breeds from

Moreover, demons must always do the opposite of the demigods. That is their nature. We have actually seen this in relation to our Krsna consciousness movement. We are advocating cow protection and encouraging people to drink more milk and eat palatable preparations made of milk, but the demons, just to protest such proposals, are claiming that they are advanced in scientific knowledge, as described here by the words svadhyaya-sruta-sampannah. They say that according to their scientific way, they have discovered that milk is dangerous and that the beef obtained by killing cows is very nutritious.

~Srimad Bhagavatam 8.7.3

Europe. One-dimensional thinking thus leads to a monoculture of farm animals bred and maintained through external imported inputs for an export oriented economy.

Aggravating The Fodder Crisis.

The primary reason for decline of cattle is the shortage of fodder. The fodder crisis has three roots - one lies in agriculture policy based on Green Revolution technologies which undermined the sources of fodder from agricultural crops. High Yielding Varieties were bred for grain and led to decline in fodder.

The second source of the fodder crisis lies in aid programmes such as "social forestry" and "farm forestry" projects which promoted the planting of monocultures of non-fodder species such as Eucalyptus, thus aggravating the shortage of fodder.

Some rascals put forward the theory that an animal has no soul or is something like dead stone. In this way they rationalize that there is no sin in animal killing. Actually animals are not dead stone, but the killers of animals are stone-hearted. Consequently no reason or philosophy appeals to them. They continue keeping slaughterhouses and killing animals. *-Srila Prabhupada (Srimad-Bhagavatam 4.26.9)*

Finally, the enclosure of the commons has also led to scarcity of grazing lands and pastures. In addition there has been a scarcity of cattle feed both because traditional sources of cattle feed such as oil cakes have declined as a result of the Green Revolution which displaced oil seeds and because new sources such as soya bean cake are largely exported. The Agricultural Minister recently announced that he wanted a special port set up for the export of soya bean cake.

Industrial countries such as Netherlands use seven times more land than their own in Third World countries for fodder and feed to provide inputs to their intensive factory farming. The livestock policy does recognise the crisis of fodder and feed in India but fails to provide solutions. In fact, by promoting intensive factory farming, it is indirectly proposing a system that will intensify the pressure on land, divert land from food for people to food to animals and further erode the scarce environmental resources of the country.

As Section 2.7 states: The feed and fodder resources are of course shared by all livestock. Lactating cows and bullocks receive preferential treatment while sheep and goats, dry and unproductive animals and backyard poultry to a large extent have to fend for themselves. Agricultural residues are currently estimated to provide 40%, grazing 31%, green fodder (cut and cultivated) 26%, and grain and concentrates (mainly for commercial poultry and high producing cows) 3% of total consumption. Over the last decade the straw grain ratio has deteriorated because of the large scale adoption of high yielding varieties which also produce poorer quality straw.

So without being devotee a man will become cruel, cruel, cruel, cruel, cruel, in this way go to hell. And devotee cannot tolerate. We have studied in the life of Lord Jesus Christ. When he saw that in the Jewish synagogue the birds were being killed, he became shocked. He therefore left. Jesus... He inaugurated the Christian religion. Perhaps you know. He was shocked by this animal-killing. And therefore his first commandment is "Thou shall not kill." But the foolish Christians, instead of following his instruction, they are opening daily slaughterhouses.

~ Srila Prabhupada (Srimad-Bhagavatam 7.9.52 — Vrndavana, April 7, 1976)

As Section 2.8 states: The amount of common property grazing land has deteriorated sharply from 78m ha in 1950-51 to 55 m ha in 1988-89 (admittedly very crude estimates) together with the quality of grazing in the remaining areas. This has been at least partly compensated by encroachment into reserved forest areas (67m ha) a large proportion of which (probably more than 50%) now exhibit serious degradation (other factors than grazing may have contributed to this state of affairs).

Cultivated green fodder is estimated at 7 million ha and is gaining in importance (particularly in the NW). The nutritional constraints in dairy production are very real and the conditions under which stall-feeding, concentrate feeding and cultivated fodder become viable options are not very clear.

There is no recommendation in the policy that would improve the natural resource and environmental base for ameliorating the fodder scarcity. Steps in this direction would include:

a) Shift to agricultural crops and crop varieties that produce food for both animals and humans. For example, our seed conservation programme, 'Navadanya' has shown that high fodder yielding varieties are the most popular ones among the farmers.

b) Shift to fodder trees in agroforestry and social forestry programmes.

c) Recover and rejuvenate the commons

d) Stop export of cattle feed.

The policy perspective has no recommendations with respect to (a, b and d) above. With respect to c, it recommends the opposite of what the environment movements have been saying.

As Section 3.4 states:

We are doubtful about the chances of success in relation to the village common (panchayat) lands and would not recommend any major effort to establish management for and to regenerate this resource.

The Government Livestock Policy developed in collaboration with the Swiss Development Corporation is thus the opposite of what an ecologically sound animal husbandry policy should be given the information we now have about the ecological and social externalities of intensive factory farming of animals. Instead of promoting the conservation of indigenous breeds of cattle, the policy prescribes the wiping out of local breeds. Instead of reducing dependence on fossil fuels, the policy recommends replacing ploughs and bullock carts with tractors. Instead of promoting reduction of meat eating it promotes increase of meat production. Instead of recovering the commons it suggests we should let the commons disappear.

This is a prescription for wiping out biodiversity and worsening the climate change crisis. Both the Indian government and the Swiss government are thus acting against their commitments made at the Earth Summit in Rio, in Agenda 21 as well as in the Biodiversity Convention and the Climate Change Convention.

The official policy needs to be totally revised to reflect people's concern, government obligations and full scientific and ecological knowledge that is available about the environmental and economic costs of large scale, centralised and intensive factory farming.

The People's Ecological Agenda.

For the livestock policy to be ecologically sound and socially just the following elements must be urgently addressed.

1. Protection of native breeds and conservation of animal biodiversity.
2. Strengthening the role of farm animals in sustainable agriculture.
3. Stopping the slaughter of cattle for exports.
4. Stopping the export of oil cake and cattle feed.
5. Taking urgent steps to improve the fodder situation through planting appropriate crop species and trees and by rejuvenating the commons.
6. Preventing the import of environmentally unsound methods of intensive factory farming of animals which degrade and pollute the environment and cause health hazards to consumers.

16.

Cow Raids

The Most Lucrative Profession In India

A visitor to India is taken aback by the sight of cows walking unattended or lounging in the busy streets. The traffic skirts round them taking extreme care not to disturb their walk or nap. Cows of all ages roam wherever they like. Some cows are so old that they can hardly stand. But nobody would dare to push them or use a stick to move them from the busiest of intersections.

But these street roaming cows, India's trademark, may soon be history. All over India, butchers have started raiding towns and villages to kidnap cows, both stray as well as privately owned. Government's export policy has made cattle rustling one of the most lucrative businesses today. In each raid, they stand to make lakhs of rupees as each head can fetch upto 10,000 rupees. A dead cow in India now commands better price than a living one.

We only mention a few cases here for the sake of reference. Hundreds of such cases are reported every month from different parts of India.

The Activities Of Butchers In Braja

By Antony Brennan

A recent 'Care for Cows in Vrindavan' newsletter from Kurma Rupa das highlights an issue that warrants the attention of all of us: the increased incidence of cows being kidnapped in Vrindavan and sold for profit.

In the March newsletter (careforcows.org) Kurma Rupa tells about those who make their living by abducting cows for slaughter. He refers to them as butchers.

As if this isn't bad enough there are also accomplices that "pose as sympathisers and offer support but only with intent to win our confidence so they can learn of our plans and thus weaken our defences," Kurma says.

Reportedly the kidnappers can receive up to 10,000 rupees for a single cow. According to villagers the kidnappers are becoming more brazen and better organised. Authorities have done little to prevent the abductions and locals are risking their lives trying to prevent the deadly night raids. "Sorry to say, but it seems that the values of the elite of modern India have changed. It is no longer the cow who is sacred, but it is profit that is sacred. Cow protection is being replaced by profit protection," Kurma Rupa says.

Security had not previously required great effort or resources as cow protection programs once received genuine support from all quarters. Now things are changing and the security of cows requires maximum effort.

In the Match newsletter Kurma Rupa paints a disturbing picture and outlines a shocking chain of events.

"On the cold, damp and foggy night of January 2, 2009 a truck with five or six men stopped in front or our gate. They were armed

These saintly kings gave protection to all the prajas, or living beings, to live and to fulfill their terms of embodiment. Maharaja Pariksit was actually an ideal saintly king because while touring his kingdom he happened to see that a poor cow was about to be killed by the personified Kali, whom he at once took to task as a murderer. This means that even the animals were given protection by the saintly administrators, not from any sentimental point of view, but because those who have taken their birth in the material world have the right to live.

~ Srila Prabhupada (Srimad Bhagavatam 1.12.19)

and hostile and arrived with intent to steal our cows. One of them demanded that our guard surrender the keys to the gate but he secured himself upstairs.

The intruders jumped the gate and performed a thorough search of our facility. Since our cows are not tied up they moved about restlessly in the fog, filling the night with the frantic ringing of their bells.

The thieves next broke the lock on our front gate but then mysteriously left without taking anything. We reported the incident to the local police and they advised us to hire two gunmen. Several of us volunteered to stand guard as well. We were supplied two men armed with shotguns for the next month.

Kurma Rupa says the hired men turned out to have little interest in protecting the cows. Their weapons were poorly maintained and ineffective. Eventually the gunmen were fired.

"In any case the break-in and frustration with the hired guards had a unifying affect on the volunteer go-sevaks at Care for Cows." Kurma Rupa says. Volunteers began taking shifts to protect the cows each night. "Neighbours gave us their phone numbers and invited us to call them in the middle of the night in the case of an emergency and wealthy businessman from Delhi donated flood lights and pledged to arrange siren to distract and scare off any intruders."

At the end of January Care for Cows was reasonably secure. "We received several reports that cows were being stolen in other places around the town," Kurma Rupa says. "We got permission from the local police to patrol the streets by motorcycle as a service to the rest of the community. Every night two or three of our volunteers patrol areas that street cows frequent and at times we are accompanied by police or concerned residents with gun permits. Our objective is to locate the butchers, notify the police and then help chase them out of town."

In February Kurma Rupa learned that two trucks and fifteen men armed with the guns had come to abduct cows. Six armed

> *Our inhumane treatment of livestock is becoming widespread and more and more barbaric... These creatures feel; they know pain. They suffer pain just as we humans feel pain.*
>
> *- Senator Robert Byrd*

men jumped out of the trucks and loudly announced that if anyone came out of their Houses they would meet with death. Five other men forced several street cows on their truck by prodding them with swords. Several men rode in the back of the truck poised to shoot or throw rocks at anyone who attempted to pursue them out of town. "It is interesting to note that this incident took place hardly two hundred meters away from the local police station," Kurma Rupa says.

Volunteers at Care for Cows and other local villagers and well wishers have participated in several confrontations with those who come to steal the cows to be slaughtered for profit. On these occasions the group have been successful in chasing off the dangerous and armed abductors, but not without risk.

"It is most unfortunate that cow protection today in Krishna's holy land means that one has to risk his life to keep them from being abducted for slaughter," Kurma Rupa says.

Devotees and well wishers who wish to help should contact Uttar Pradesh government ministers and demand action be taken against those who kidnap and kill cows. Letters can be faxed to the Chief Minister at the following fax number: +91 522 2237620.

Kidnapping of cows is a criminal offence In Vrindavan. Residents of Vrindavan say the villagers and cows need support and protection whilst the police need resources to stop and catch those who prey on the cows.

If you wish you can send your letter by email to dontkillcows@gmail.com. All the letters sent to this email address will be collected and presented to the Chief Minister with a petition asking his government to take action.

A king or ruler is meant to treat all the living beings in his kingdom as his own self or children. The subjects also lovingly treated the king as their father.

In this age, however, so-called kings and presidents do not treat all other living entities as their own self. Most of them are meat-eaters, and even though they may not be meat-eaters and may pose themselves to be very religious and pious, they still allow cow slaughter within their state.

~ Srila Prabhupada (Srimad Bhagavatam 6.7.24)

How Vrindavan Is Losing Its Cows To Slaughter

By Antony Brennan

Subhangi Devi Dasi lives in Vrindavan, India. Recently she was awoken early in the morning to witness a site none of us would even dream could be happening. Krishna's cows are being violently kidnapped in the night. It is believed the cows are killed and sold for their flesh and leather products.

"I was sleeping," Subhangi Devi Dasi says. "At 2.00 am I hear cows crying, people screaming and yelling. I run out to my balcony and see a truck backing away and cows franticly running in all directions down the lanes, all crying. I have never seen that in Vrindavan."

Subhangi was witnessing the kidnapping of the local cows. "Then I see some local men throwing stones at the trucks and swearing in Hindi, some other men came with machetes and one with a rifle," Subhangi says. These men were coming to protect the cows "The truck backed out of the road and drove off."

Arjuna, one of the men trying to protect the cows says the kidnappers came with several trucks. "They caught and stole 48 cows just here in this area," he says. "The men were ruthless, throwing the cows in the back of their trucks, beating then and in some cases killing them if they were resisting," Arjuna says. "Blood was everywhere."

Villagers say the kidnappers are armed and attack anyone who tries to stop them. "A month or so back." Arjuna says. "The police put up barricades to try to stop the kidnappers. That night they rammed the barricades with their trucks."

"It is so out of control," says Arjuna. "Vrindavan is the land of cows and these demons have become aware that there are so many cows and goshallas just ripe for the picking." The locals are helpless. They can do little without risking their own lives.

It is reported that 15 days ago, when the police tried to stop them, the kidnappers rammed a police jeep. A policeman fired a shot and he got a rock in the head for his effort. It is reported that the police had to pull back as there were only four of them, whilst there were eight heavily armed kidnappers. "They criminals seem to be aware of how much resistance they will encounter and come prepared to meet it," Arjuna says.

"Sometimes they hit the cows in the head with rocks and sometimes shoot them or hack them with machetes if they resist," says Arjuna. "They used to come in one truck now they travel with four trucks at a time."

Subhangi Devi Dasi says she has heard the cows can fetch up to 10,000 rupees. It is no wonder kidnappers are armed and are prepared to injure even the police. Villagers who try to prevent the kidnappings are said to be placing themselves and their families in a very dangerous situation.

My comments: I'm writing with a heavy heart. After reading this article, I was motionless for sometime and still in shock. I don't know how such incidents keep happening. Vrindavan residents should be aggressive and do something concrete (large-scale strike/ road-blocking, notifying media houses) to bring the attention of the nation. If this is not immediately stopped, those murderers will increase their activities.

Ahmedabad Crime Round Up: 25 Cows Stolen In One Night

Monday, Oct 1, 2012, Agency: DNA

In his application with Aslali police on Sunday, Ishwar Rabari said that a 20-strong gang stole his 25 cows late on Saturday night.

Rabari, who hails from Bevdi village of Daskroi taluka, alleged that the gang came in seven vehicles, including mini-trucks and jeeps and broke into the cow shelter adjoining his house.

They tranquilised the cows and hauled them away in the trucks. The incident happened at about 2.30am on Sunday.

Rabari woke up hearing the noise and came out of his house, only to spot the goons run away with the cattle. He gathered other villagers and chased them but the gang was well equipped to handle any such situation.

They pelted stones at the villagers and managed to escape into the darkness in the ensuing melee.

Police sub-inspector with Aslali, DL Dodia has launched investigations in the case.

Gurgaon - 7 Cops Beaten Up By Villagers

Sanjay Yadav, Times News Network, Apr 3, 2012,

Seven policemen were beaten up mercilessly by villagers after they failed to stop cow smugglers early on Monday morning at the Kaliyawas village police barrier. After driving away the policemen, the villagers also blocked the Gurgaon-Badli road near Makdola village.

After getting assurance from ACP (Sadar) Krishna Murari that action will be taken against the cops, the villagers ended the road blockade. Sources said that all the seven cops were suspended on the charge of dereliction of duty and transferred to Police Lines, Gurgaon. Police officials did not confirm the cops' suspension and transfer yet.

According to the police, the incident took place at the Kaliyawas village police barrier around 3AM on Monday. The barrier was installed for the prevention and detection of crime by the Gurgaon crime branch near Kaliyawas village of Farrukhnagar. At this barrier seven cops were deployed. They were EASI Chander Singh, Raghunath, constable Naresh, Dinesh, Sudesh, Roshan, Mahipal and Vijay.

According to the villagers, six to seven cow smugglers were seen rushing to the village in a max open jeep late on Sunday night. When villagers wanted to know the reason, they could not give a satisfactory answer and started to flee from the village. In the meantime, on the doubt, two villagers followed them on a bike, and were hit by stones thrown from the jeep by the cow smugglers.

The villagers on the bike then took the help of a truck driver who was in a dhaba on the way. The truck driver helped them give chase in his truck but cops stopped the truck at the barrier and helped the cow smugglers escape with ease.

That enraged the villagers who went on the rampage and beat up the policemen. The rest of the police force fled the spot. Some hours after that, the villagers sat on a dharna on the Gurgaon-Badli road, causing a massive traffic jam.

When police reinforcements reached the spot and the ACP spoke to them, villagers agreed to end their blockade. Meanwhile, villagers also alleged that cattle theft had increased in the area and police were not lodging any complaint.

UP IPS Officer Shunted Out For Exposing Minister In Cow Smuggling

By Niticentral Staff on February 7, 2013

Gonda superintendent of police Navneet Kumar Rana, who exposed senior Samajwadi Party leader KC Pandey offering bribe for the release of culprits caught in trafficking cows for slaughter, has been shunted out by the Uttar Pradesh Government.

Pandey figured in a sting operation of cattle smuggling carried out by Rana.

But now, the many rascals heading the government allow animal slaughter. When Maharaja Pariksit saw a degraded man trying to kill a cow, he immediately drew his sword and said, "Who are you? Why are you trying to kill this cow?" He was a real king. Nowadays, unqualified men have taken the presidential post. And although they may pose themselves as very religious, they are simply rascals. Why? Because under their noses thousands of cows are being killed, while they collect a good salary. Any leader who is at all religious should resign his post in protest if cow slaughter goes on under his rule. Since people do not know that these administrators are rascals, they are suffering. And the people are also rascals because they are voting for these bigger rascals. It is Plato's view that the government should be ideal, and this is the ideal: The saintly philosophers should be at the head of the state; according to their advice the politicians should rule
~ Srila Prabhupada (Journey of Self Discovery 7.1)

On December 29, 2012, Gonda police seized a truck carrying a consignment of cows in Khargapur.

Rana had alleged that SP national secretary KC Pandey, who enjoys the status of a Minister of State as vice-chairman of UP Council of Sugarcane Research, had allegedly offered bribe for leaving the seized truck.

It is noted that Chief Minister Akhilesh Yadav had assured "proper inquiry" after the issue came to the light and promised action against the traffickers.

Meanwhile, the UP Government has transferred the probe into the cattle smuggling case to CB-CID.

Section-II

Desertification Of India

17.

Culture of Animal Killing And Meat Consumption

Lying At The Heart of Resource Depletion and Environmental Destruction

Most destructive aspect of industrial revolution was reflected in changes in dietary habits of whole nations. People steadily moved up the food chain, from a staple of bread, potato and cheese to beef, pork and lamb. But many did not care for the price tag attached to such extravagance, except for some sensible souls like Einstein who remarked, "Nothing will benefit human health and increase chances for survival of life on Earth as much as the evolution to a vegetarian diet." This wasn't coming from an old hat but from the most prominent scientist of modern era. Even in recent times, experts such as Dr. Neal Barnard duly warn us, "The beef industry has contributed to more American deaths than all the wars of this century, all natural disasters, and all automobile accidents combined. If beef is your idea of "real food for real people", you'd better live real close to a real good hospital."

Thus killing animals for food, fur, leather, and cosmetics is one of the most environmentally destructive practices taking place on the earth today.

The meat industry is linked to deforestation, desertification, water pollution, water shortages, air pollution, and soil erosion. Dr. Neal Barnard, president of the Physicians Committee for Responsible Medicine (USA), therefore says, "If you're a meat eater, you are contributing to the destruction of the environment, whether you know it or not. Clearly the best thing you can do for the Earth is to not support animal agriculture."

And Jeremy Rifkin warns in his widely read book Beyond Beef: "Today, millions of Americans, Europeans, and Japanese are consuming countless hamburgers, steaks, and roasts, oblivious to the impact their dietary habits are having on the biosphere and the very survivability of life on earth. Every pound of grain-fed flesh is secured at the expense of a burned forest, an eroded rangeland, a barren field, a dried-up river or stream, and the release of millions of tons of carbon dioxide, nitrous oxide, and methane into the skies."

When We Kill Animals, We Kill The Earth, We Kill Ourselves

Right now we raise about 40 billion animals for food. Animal based diet is leading to a global health crisis unparalleled in human history.

Dietary advice on the subject of global warming and environmental health was never as definitive as it is today. The United Nations has called on governments and individuals to open their eyes to climate change, calling it "the most serious challenge facing the human race." More than any other factor, how we meet that challenge will depend on what we eat.

Meat Eaters Devouring Forests, Destroying Ecosystems

A tree is our most intimate contact with nature and forests form the life line of Earth's atmosphere. In last two centuries, over 90% of the Earth's forests have been butchered and this is one of the most prominent feature of modern ecocidal policies.

You want to save forests? Just stop eating meat! Each person who becomes a vegetarian saves one acre of trees per year. According to Vegetarian Times, half of the annual destruction of tropical rain forests is caused by clearing land for beef cattle ranches. Each pound of hamburger made from Central American or South American beef costs about 55 square feet of rain forest vegetation. Forests all over the world are being cut so that Americans, Europeans and Japanese can have their hamburgers. Its a criminal waste of precious resources.

In the United States, about 260 million acres of forest have been cleared for a meat-centered diet. About 40% of the land in the western United States is used for grazing beef cattle. This has had a detrimental effect on wildlife.

About a fifth of the world's land is used for grazing meat animals -twice the area used for growing crops. Because of the deforestation, soil erosion and desertification meat industry causes, it is fundamentally unsustainable and has an extremely negative impact on the environment. Thirty percent of the earth's land is now occupied by livestock, with another 33 percent devoted to GMO feed crops, and this number is expanding every year. Seventy percent of previously forested land in the Amazon has been converted into cropland and pastures, destroying biodiversity, introducing carcinogenic pesticides, and playing a primary role in pushing species toward extinction at a rate 500 times of that we ought to be experiencing according to models based on fossil records.

Inevitably, intensive animal agriculture depletes valuable natural resources. Instead of being eaten by people, the vast majority of grains harvested is fed to farm animals. For this wasteful and inefficient practice, agribusinesses exploit vast stretches of land. Forests, wetlands, and other natural ecosystems and wildlife habitats have been decimated. Scarce fossil fuels, groundwater, and topsoil resources which took millenium to develop are now disappearing. Of all agricultural land in the United States, 80-87% is now used to raise animals for food.

The space equivalent to seven football fields is being destroyed in rainforests every minute; 50 million acres of tropical forest in Latin America alone have been cut down for livestock production since 1970. In Canada also, local wilderness is being destroyed for more and more grazing land for livestock.

Soil Erosion and Desertification

Bad soil is bad for global health, and the evidence is mounting that the world' soil is in trouble. We're dead without good soil. Soil holds minerals and organic compounds critical to life. Without good soil we have got nothing.

All over the world, more than seven and a half million acres of soil has been degraded. That's larger than the U.S. and Canada combined. What remains is ailing as a result of compaction, erosion and salination making it near impossible to plant and adding to greenhouse gases and air pollution. Soil degradation is putting the future of the global population is at risk according to a National Geographic article by Charles Mann.

Civil unrest in Latin America, Asia and Africa have been attributed to a lack of food and affordable food as a result of poor soil. Currently, only 11-percent of the world's land feeds six billion people.

Experts estimate that by 2030 the Earth's population will reach 8.3 billion. Farmers will need to increase food production by 40-percent. But not much soil remains.

Scientists don't know much and don't care either about this critical resource.

Overgrazing and the intensive production of feed grain for cattle and other meat animals results in high levels of soil erosion. According to Alan B. Durning of the Worldwatch Institute (1986), one pound of beef from cattle raised on feedlots represents the loss of 35 pounds of topsoil. Over the past few centuries, the United States has lost about two-thirds of its topsoil.

In other countries, such as Australia and the nations of Africa on the southern edge of the Sahara, cattle grazing and feed-crop production on marginal lands contribute substantially to desertification.

Increasing Animal Killings - Decreasing Survival Possibilities

Despite these horrifying statistics, global production of meat is projected to double in the next 10 years.

Viewing animals as commodities has had a profoundly negative impact on understanding the world we live in. There is no more important task at hand than combating the false notion that the entire natural world is economically quantifiable or exists simply for our purposes alone.

> *As we watch the sun go down, evening after evening, through the smog across the poisoned waters of our native earth, we must ask ourselves seriously whether we really wish some future universal historian on another planet to say about us: "With all their genius and with all their skill, they ran out of foresight and air and food and water and ideas," or, "They went on playing politics until their world collapsed around them."* ~ *U Thant*

An animal, an ocean, a forest, a species and humanity are not separate, but intimately connected in every way. The world consumes 240 billion kilos of meat each year. But more than 75 per cent of what is fed to an animal is lost through metabolism or inedible parts such as bones.

We have to make our choice now.... steak on our platter or our very survival.

18.

'32% Of Land Affected By Degradation In India'

And A Fourth Of India Turning Into Desert: ISRO Study

The United Nations Conference on Desertification, which popularized the word, defines it as "the reduction or destruction of the land's potential, finally resulting in the appearance of desert conditions" (United Nations, 1977). Gorse and Steeds (1987) write about a process of decline in the biological productivity of land that results in "desert, or skeletal soil that is irrecuperable".

The main on-farm effect of land degradation is a decline in yields or an increased need for inputs to maintain those yields: since "subsoils generally contain fewer nutrients than topsoils, more fertilizer is needed to maintain crop yields. This, in turn, increases production costs. Moreover, the addition of fertilizer alone cannot compensate for all the nutrients lost when topsoil erodes" (FAO, 1983). Where degradation is serious, the plots may be either abandoned temporarily or permanently, or converted to inferior value uses, e.g. cropland being converted to grazing land, or grazing land left to shrubs. So basically desertification is the degradation of formerly productive land.

The world's great deserts were formed by natural processes interacting over long intervals of time. During most of these times, deserts have grown and shrunk independent of human activities. Paleodeserts, large sand seas now inactive because they are stabilized by vegetation, extend well beyond the present margins of core deserts, such as the Sahara. In some regions, deserts are separated sharply from surrounding, less arid areas by mountains and other contrasting landforms that reflect basic structural differences in the regional geology. In other areas, desert fringes form a gradual transition from a dry to a more humid environment, making it more difficult to define the desert border.

Desertification is a complex process. It involves multiple causes, and it proceeds at varying rates in different climates. Desertification may intensify a general climatic trend toward greater aridity, or it may initiate a change in local climate. [Sources: Deserts: Geology and Resources by A.S. Walker, United States Geological Survey]

Desertification does not occur in linear, easily mappable patterns. Deserts advance erratically, forming patches on their borders. Areas far from natural deserts can degrade quickly to barren soil, rock, or sand through poor land management. The presence of a nearby desert has no direct relationship to desertification. Unfortunately, an area undergoing desertification is brought to public attention only after the process is well underway. Often little or no data are available to indicate the previous state of the ecosystem or the rate of degradation. Scientists still question whether desertification, as a process of global change, is permanent or how and when it can be halted or reversed. [Ibid]

Desertification became well known in the 1930's, when parts of the Great Plains in the United States turned into the "Dust Bowl" as a result of drought and poor practices in farming, although the term itself was not used until almost 1950. During the dust bowl period, millions of people were forced to abandon their farms and livelihoods. [Ibid]

Ministry of Environment & Forests Report On Land Degradation In India

June 21, 2011, Zee News, New Delhi

An estimated 32 per cent of India's total land area is affected by land degradation, most of which is undergoing desertification, which has severe implications for livelihood and food security, according to an Environment Ministry report.

About 69 per cent of the country is dry land, arid, semi-arid and dry sub-humid-- and "degradation has severe implications for livelihood and food security" for millions of people living in these heavily populated areas, said India's 4th National Report to United Nations Convention to Combat Desertification (UNCCD), 2010.

The UNCCD is a convention to combat desertification and mitigate the effects of drought through national action programmes.

"81.45 million hectares, or 24.8 per cent of the country's geographic area is undergoing desertification," (degradation is 32% of the land) said the report, which provides a holistic overview capturing comprehensively India's policies and programme related to desertification, land degradation and drought.

The report said water and soil erosion are major causes of land degradation and water erosion is most prominent in agricultural regions.

"The key anthropogenic factors resulting in degradation are unsustainable agricultural practices, diversion of land to development programmes, industrial effluents, mining and deforestation," it said.

The report said unsustainable resource management practices drive desertification, and accentuate the poverty of people affected by desertification.

"Land rehabilitation has been a major priority since Independence, and several policies and government agencies address desertification and degradation," it said

In his foreword note, Environment Minister Jairam Ramesh said poverty and environmental degradation are major problems in dry lands, where forests and trees contribute significantly to rural livelihoods.

If anyone wants to save the planet, all they have to do is just stop eating meat. That's the single most important thing you could do. It's staggering when you think about it. Vegetarianism takes care of so many things in one shot: ecology, famine, cruelty.

- Sir Paul McCartney

"In order to eradicate poverty in the dry lands, it is important to protect the land from deforestation, fragmentation, degradation and drought," he said.

The Minister said in order to tackle the issues of desertification, land degradation and droughts, 22 major programmes are being implemented in the country, including, the "Mission for Green India", which will address dry land forests, in addition to other ecosystems.

A Fourth Of India Turning Into Desert: ISRO Study

Divya Gandhi, The Hindu, November 27, 2009

No less than a fourth of India's geographical area, or 81 million hectares, is undergoing a process of desertification, reveals a first-of-its-kind 'desertification status map' of the country created by the Indian Space Research Organisation (ISRO) in collaboration with several scientific institutions across the country.

A host of reasons are responsible for this phenomenon, including changes in rainfall pattern and over-exploitation of natural resources, says a research paper based on this data and published in the latest issue of Current Science.

The spatial inventory, which uses satellite imagery from an Indian Remote Sensing Satellite, Resourcesat, also reveals that a third of the country's area (or 105.48 million hectares) is degraded.

At least eight processes were at work, of which water erosion is the most pronounced (affecting 10.21 per cent of the total geographical area), followed by reducing vegetation cover (9.63 per cent) and wind erosion (5.34 per cent). Together 32.07 per cent of the total geographic area is being transformed by land degradation.

State-wise, Rajasthan has the largest area (21.77 per cent of the total geographical area) undergoing land degradation, followed by Jammu and Kashmir (12.79 per cent), Maharashtra (12.66 per cent) and Gujarat (12.72 per cent).

"There is tremendous pressure on our land-based natural resources" say the authors of the paper, adding that this information could serve as baseline data to monitor and develop strategies to arrest desertification. "There has been a long-pending need for a scientific status mapping of desertification and land degradation of the entire country."

ISRO's Space Applications Centre in Ahmedabad served as the nodal coordinating organisation for the study.

The spatial inventory, at national and regional levels, will be integrated to generate a desertification status map of the world as envisaged by the United Nations Convention to Combat Desertification.

The research paper adds that about 15.8 per cent of the country's geographical area is arid, 37.6 per cent semi-arid and 16.5 per cent falls in the dry sub-humid region. Put together, about 228 million hectares, or 69 per cent of the country constitute 'dry land.'

The study noted that India accounted for 2.4% of the global land mass, but supported about 16.7% of the world's population and 18% of its cattle.

The Space Applications Centre study comes after research led by consulting firm McKinsey and Co. revealed this week that India's water needs were set to double by 2030, which could dry up its river basins.

Demand for rice, wheat and sugar will push India's huge agricultural sector to consume 1.5 trillion cubic metres (53 trillion cubic feet) of water by 2030, almost double that of China, the McKinsey study warned.

Surveys By National Bureau of Soil Survey and Land use Planning, National Remote Sensing Agency And The Forest Survey of India

In India, it is estimated that out of 329 million hectares of geographical area, 175 million hectors is suffering from various kind of degradation. The report of National Bureau of Soil Survey and Land use Planning describes that 57 per cent of the total geographical area of the country is suffering from different kinds of degradation of which a dominant part (45 per cent) is under water erosion and the rest 12 per cent is from wind, chemical and physical deterioration.

The top soil is very fragile, like an eggshell. If it is disturbed plants have a hard time to regain growth. Sometimes they never come back.

The extent of land degradation from one state to another depends upon topographical features, geological formations, soil characteristics, rainfall and other climatic parameters, land use, measures of soil conservation management practices etc. Rajasthan (37 mha) tops the list followed by Madhya Pradesh (20 mha), Maharashtra, Andhra Pradesh, Karnataka and Gujarat (more than 10 mha each).

According to the estimates of actual land-use and vegetation cover by the National Remote Sensing Agency and the Forest Survey of India based on satellite imagery, 80 mha out of 142 mha under cultivation is substantially degraded and about 40 mha out of 75 mha under the forest departments has a canopy cover of less than 40% (Gadgil 1993). Nearly 11 mha of pasturelands is also substantially degraded. Thus, a total of 131 mha, representing about 40% of the country's landmass, has a productivity well below its potential. According to Wastelands Atlas of India 2000 (1:50,000 scale map), the total wastelands area covered in 584 districts is 63.85 million which accounts 20.17% of the total geographical area.

19.

Report On Land Degradation

National Climate Center Research, India Meteorological Department, Pune

May 2011

Desertification has long been recognized as a major environmental problem affecting the livelihood of the people in the affected regions in many countries of the world. In 1977, a United Nations Conference on Desertification (UNCOD) was convened in Nairobi, Kenya to produce an effective, comprehensive and co-ordinated programme for addressing the problem of land degradation.

The UN Commission for Sustainable Development Report 1988 observed that desertification has become one of the most serious environmental and socio-economic problems of the world. The various assessments by UNEP continued to point out that desertification results from complex interactions among physical, chemical, biological, socio-economic and political problems that are local, national and global in nature.

1. Introduction

The studies of UNEP (United Nations Environmental Programme) indicated that over the preceding 20 years, the problem of land degradation had continued to worsen. The studies further indicated that over-cultivation, overgrazing, deforestation and poor irrigation practices are degrading dry land in every continent.

The major factors for this are population (human and livestock) pressures, inappropriate land use and agricultural practices, social conflicts and drought. There was also growing recognition of the part played by human activities and climate change such as prolonged or frequent droughts aggravating land degradation.

This led to formally defining desertification as "land degradation in Arid, Semi-Arid and Dry Sub-Humid areas resulting from various factors, including climatic variations and human activities" which is used as the basis of the UNCCD (United Nations Convention to Combat Desertification).

Aridity of a region is categorized by the ratio of P = Mean Annual Precipitation to PE = Mean Annual Potential Evapotranspiration, using Thornthwaite formula. The 'drylands' are defined as those regions where the ratio of the mean annual precipitation to the mean annual evapotranspiration is in the range of 0.05 to 0.65.

It is important to note that CCD considers Arid, Semi-Arid, and Dry Sub-Humid regions as dry land, but excluded Hyper-Arid region, where the P/PE ratio is less than 0.05, from the ambit of the Convention.

The Convention also excluded moist Sub-Humid, Humid and Per-Humid zones of various regions in the world. The most important objective of the Convention is to combat desertification occurring in the dryland regions of the world to mitigate the effects of drought.

Deserts have always spread over periodic intervals, of course, particularly during times of extreme drought. When adequate precipitation is available, however, a reversal automatically occurs; both are completely natural phenomena that have prevailed for as long as the deserts have existed. Still, desertification is a completely different phenomenon entirely. In this case totally new deserts and arid regions emerge through the desertification, whereby normally mostly dry, yet otherwise still productive semi-arid regions completely dry out and turn to sand etc.

Desertification is due to complex interactions among physical, biological, social, cultural and economic factors. Desertification impacts the economic growth of not only the affected region, but also of the country as a whole. It also affects the social and economic development.

Desertification and drought affect the sustainable development through their inter-relationships with important social problems such as poverty, poor health and nutrition, lack of food security and consequently results in migration, social conflicts and unrest. The Convention emphasizes the need to address these in an integrated manner.

India became a signatory to the UNCCD on 14 th October 1994 and it came into effect on 17th March 1997. One of the obligations of all developing country Parties to the Convention, including India, is to prepare the National Action Programme to Combat Desertification and to mitigate the effects of drought.

In the present study, land degradation has been examined with the help of soil moisture status in two different periods. Land degradation would lead to evolve a climate change, if any.

2. Methodology

The ratio of precipitation (P) to Potential Evapotranspiration (PE) provides a simple method of estimating the moisture status of a place. If ratio is less than one, it would mean that moisture content of soil in a place is not sufficient to cope with the needs of Evapotranspiration, i.e. the place has dry climate.

If the ratio is greater than one, the availability of soil moisture is greater and the climate is humid. Based on this Moisture Index, classification of the regions in different zones such as Arid, Semi Arid and Dry sub Humid etc., has been made.

In the present studies, an empirical criteria for the classification of different zones based upon P/PE ratio viz. Arid (P/PE=0.05-0.20), Semi Arid (P/PE=0.21-0.5) and Dry Sub Humid (P/PE = 0.51-0.65) is used.

The two sets of P/PE values have been calculated by considering rainfall normals for the period 1941-1990 for the recent period and the rainfall normals for the period 1901-1950 for the earlier period respectively for different stations in various states of the country.

Changes of P/PE values from the earlier period (1901-1950) to recent period (1941-1990) have been examined for the purpose of studying the climate change in different moisture conservation zones and its impact on the land.

For the purpose to demarcate the change in P/PE values in the two periods as significant, the difference in P/PE values in two different periods as mentioned above is taken as more than .05.

Considering this criteria, the significant change in the ratio P/PE for various stations in different states, in different climatic zones have been identified.

3. Data

The rainfall normals for the period 1901 to 1950 and 1941 to 1990 published by India Meteorological Department have been used for computation of P/PE (Precipitation/Potential Evapotranspiration) for various stations over India and PE values for those stations over India have been used from the publication entitled, 'Potential Evapotranspiration (PE) over India', IMD, Scientific Report No. 136.

4. Results

Based on the moisture index (P/PE) classification of the moisture index over the country has been made in Arid (P/PE = 0.05-0.20), Semi Arid (P/PE = 0.21-0.5) and Dry Sub Humid (P/PE = 0.51-0.65) regions by using rainfall normals for the periods 1901 to 1950 and 1941 - 1990.

In the state Rajasthan the districts are in Arid, Semi Arid and Dry Sub Humid regions. In Punjab, the districts are in Semi Arid and Dry Sub Humid region. In Haryana, the region is mostly Semi Arid.

In states Gujarat, Maharashtra, Uttar Pradesh, Karnataka, Andhra Pradesh and Tamil Nadu the districts are under Semi Arid and Dry Sub Humid regions. In Madhya Pradesh the region is mostly Dry Sub Humid.

The examination of increase or decrease in P/PE ratio in two periods viz. 1901 to 1950 and 1941 to 1990 shows the results as below:

In Rajasthan the districts Ganganagar, Anupgarh, Bikaner, Jodhpur and Jaisalmer (Arid region), the districts Jhunjhunu, Sikar, Jaipur, Ajmer, Tonk, Sirohi, Pali, Jalore and Churu (Semi

Arid region) and districts Sawai Madhopur and Bundi (Dry Sub Humid region) show increase in P/PE ratio.

The increase is significant in Sirohi, Jaipur and Sawai Madhopur districts. The districts Kota, Chittorgarh show decrease in P/PE ratio. The districts Barmer, Alwar, Bharatpur, Bhilwara, Udaipur from Semi Arid region show no change.

In Punjab the district Amritsar (Semi Arid region), Gurudaspur, Jalandhar, Ludhiana and Patiala (Dry Sub Humid region) show increase in ratio P/PE with significant increase at Amritsar, Jalandhar, Ludhiana and Patiala. The district Firozepur (Semi Arid region) show significant decrease in the ratio P/PE.

In Haryana the districts Rohtak, Hissar, Gurgaon, Karnal (Semi Arid region) and Ambala (Dry Sub Humid region) show increase in the ratio P/PE with significant increase for Gurgaon and Karnal.

Naturally, droughts and other climatic influences foster the formation of deserts and arid regions. And yet, the principal cause for the formation of deserts and arid regions in many areas of the world rests primarily and fundamentally with human beings themselves, for they criminally and carelessly destroy the land by forcibly increasing food production to feed the animals meant for meat production. In doing so, they completely leach the ground and deplete it of all its nutrients, without allowing the soil to revive itself or be regenerated artificially with the necessary energy that was also extracted, leaving the ground completely exhausted. The situation, therefore, is not remedied by artificially introducing new nutrients, because the soil also requires natural forces that Man cannot restore. In the long run, much more is extracted from the soil than can ever be replaced. The soil virtually dies, and this leads to the development of desert wastelands.

Behind the human crime of extensive desertification and destruction of nature lurks purely unscrupulous, irresponsible greed. This is especially evident in Argentina, for example, where vast areas are leased for short time periods to large-scale animal farming enterprises. To maximize their profits, they utilize, by hook and by crook, every possible means, including those forbidden in and harmful to nature, leaving the land a totally leached-out desert or arid wasteland only a few years later.

~Billy

In Delhi region (Semi Arid) significant increase in ratio P/PE is observed.

In Gujarat the Kachchh district (Arid region) shows increase in the ratio P/PE. The districts Mahesana, Sabarkantha, Ahmedabad, Jamnagar, Rajkot, Surendranagar, Bhavnagar and Amreli (Semi Arid region), the district Junagadh (Dry Sub Humid region) show increase in the ratio P/PE, with significant increase at Ahmedabad, Amreli, Junagadh and Jamnagar.

The district Banaskantha (Semi Arid region), the districts Vadodara, Surat and Panch Mahal (Dry Sub Humid region) show decrease in ratio P/PE. In district Surat significant decrease in ratio P/PE is noticed.

In state Maharashtra the districts Dhule, Jalgaon, Aurangabad, Ahmednagar, Beed, Solapur and Sangli (Semi Arid region), the districts Amravati, Yavatmal, Nanded, Parbhani and Buldhana (Dry Sub Humid region) show increase in the ratio P/PE.

The significant increase in ratio P/PE is noticed at Solapur, Sangli, Parbhani and Nanded. The significant decrease in ratio P/PE is observed at Pune. There is no change in the ratio P/PE at districts Akola and Osmanabad (Semi Arid region) and at Nashik (Dry Sub Humid region).

In Uttar Pradesh, the districts Aligarh, Mathura and Kanpur (Semi Arid region), the districts Meerut, Bulandshahar, Agra, Etawah and Jhansi (Dry Sub Humid region) show increase in the ratio P/PE. The significant increase is at Bulandshahar, Aligarh,

"That time is coming. It is predicted in the Srimad-Bhagavatam that anavrsti and kara-piditah. People gradually being godless, they will be suffering from these three principles. There will be no more rainfall. Therefore last time when I was in Europe -- I do not know what has happened now -- there was scarcity of rain, and England was making plan to import water. So this is scientist's program. There is enough water in the sea, but they cannot use it. So that is hand of God. Unless God helps, Krsna helps, mayadhyaksena prakrtih suyate sa-caracaram... [Bg. 9.10]. The vast ocean, although the water is there, you cannot use one drop. You are so controlled."

-Srila Prabhupada (Lecture on Srimad-Bhagavatam 5.5.1 -- Bombay, December 25, 1976)

Meerut, Agra and Etawah. The district Mainpuri (Semi Arid region) shows decrease in the ratio P/PE.

In state Madhya Pradesh the district Bhind (Semi Arid region) and the districts Morena, Gwalior, Datia, Shivpuri, Mandsaur, Jhabua, Dhar, Indore and Ujjain (Dry Sub Humid region) show increase in the ratio P/PE with significant increase at Gwalior, Datia, Bhind and Shivpuri.

In state Karnataka the districts Gulbarga, Bijapur, Raichur, Chitradurga and Mandya (Semi Arid region) and the districts Dharwad, Mysore, Bidar and Bangaluru (Dry Sub Humid region) show increase in P/PE ratio with significant increase at Gulbarga, Bijapur, Raichur and Bidar.

The districts Bellary, Tumkur (Semi Arid region) and Hassan (Dry Sub Humid region) show decrease in P/PE ratio with significant decrease at Hassan.

In Andhra Pradesh the districts Ananthapur, Cuddapah, Kurnool, Hyderabad and Nalgonda (Semi Arid region) and Chittoor, Nellore and Warangal (Dry Sub Humid region) show increase in the ratio P/PE with significant increase at Hyderabad, Cuddapah and Nellore. There is no change in P/PE ratio at Guntur (Semi Arid region) and Srikakulam (Dry Sub Humid region).

In Tamil Nadu the districts Madurai and Salem (Dry Sub Humid region) show increase in the ratio P/PE with significant increase at Salem. The district Coimbatore (Semi Arid region) and district

It is a misconception that droughts cause desertification. Droughts are common in arid and semiarid lands. Well-managed lands can recover from drought when the rains return. Continued land abuse during droughts, however, increases land degradation. By 1973, the drought that began in 1968 in the Sahel of West Africa and the land-use practices there had caused the deaths of more than 100,000 people and 12 million cattle, as well as the disruption of social organizations from villages to the national level.

Thanjavur (Dry Sub Humid region) show decrease in the ratio P/PE with significant decrease at Coimbatore.

The increase in the P/PE values from the earlier period (1901-1950) to the recent period (1941-1990) shows improvement in the soil moisture availability. There are 35 districts from Semi Arid and Dry Sub Humid region over the country which shows significant increase in soil moisture availability.

The decrease in P/PE values for the two periods as above indicates land degradation due to less soil moisture availability. There are total 18 districts from Semi Arid region (P/PE=0.21-0.5) and Dry Sub Humid region (P/PE=0.51-0.65), which show land degradation. Out of 18 districts, 5 districts show significant land degradation.

5. Conclusions

It can be concluded that based on the criteria of moisture index (P/PE) following land degraded districts have been identified in various regions.

i. In Arid region (P/PE=0.05-0.20) no more degradation is noticed.

ii. In Semi Arid Region (P/PE = 0.21-0.5) the districts Firozepur (Punjab), Banaskantha (Gujarat), Pune (Maharashtra), Mainpuri (Uttar Pradesh), Bellary and Tumkur (Karnataka), Coimbatore, Tiruchirappalli, Tirunelveli and Ramanathapuram (Tamil Nadu) show land degradation.

In India, land management has been largely unsystematic, arbitrary and, by no means, sustainable. So far the country has not implemented a well-defined integrated land use policy. This lacuna has largely been responsible for the current phase of land degradation.

To make things worse, there is no rural fuelwood as well as grazing and fodder policy also at the national level with the result, that grazing is far beyond the carrying capacity and extraction of fuel and fodder from forests is also far beyond the sustainable limits, creating enormous negative impacts on the forests and land.

Although land degradation is recognised as a serious problem, information available on the severity as also the area affected by various forms of degradation is limited, highly variable and sketchy.

iii. In Dry Sub-Humid region (P/PE = 0.51-0.65) the districts Kota and Chittorgarh (Rajasthan), districts Vadodara, Bharuch, Surat and Panch Mahal (Gujarat), Hassan and Thanjavur (Tamil Nadu) show land degradation.

iv. There are total 18 land degraded districts over the country from Semi Arid (P/PE = 0.21-0.5) and Dry Sub-Humid region (P/PE = 0.51-0.65). Most significant land degraded parts of the country based on moisture index (P/PE) criteria are Surat (Gujarat), Firozepur (Punjab), Hassan (Karnataka), Pune (Maharashtra) and Coimbatore (Tamil Nadu).

(Excerpts)

20.

India's Vanishing Groundwater

Two new studies suggest that India's aquifers are undergoing rapid depletion due, almost entirely, to water withdrawals for agricultural use. Satellite measurements indicate that the water table is sinking faster than anyone had previously estimated, with potentially dire implications for the 600 million people living regionally — nearly one-tenth of humanity — who rely on it.

One study appears in the journal Nature, the other in the journal Geophysical Research Letters.

From The Nature Study Press Release

Using satellite data, UC Irvine and NASA hydrologists have found that groundwater beneath northern India has been receding by as much as 1 foot per year over the past decade – and they believe human consumption is almost entirely to blame. More than 109 cubic kilometers (26 cubic miles) of groundwater disappeared from the region's aquifers between 2002 and 2008 – double the capacity of India's largest surface-water reservoir, the Upper Wainganga, and triple that of Lake Mead, the largest manmade reservoir in the U.S.

Surface water percolating down from rain, snow, lakes, and rivers recharges aquifers. Some aquifers contain water that's thousands to millions of years old. (According to New Scientist, the world's oldest aquifer lies beneath the Sahara — rain that fell perhaps 1 million years ago.)

How does this bode for India's agriculture? NASA's Matt Rodell, lead author on the Nature study, says: "If measures are not soon taken to ensure sustainable groundwater usage, consequences for the 114 million residents of the region may include a collapse of agricultural output, severe shortages of potable water, conflict, and suffering."

During the second half of the 20th century, water withdrawals increased dramatically. Beginning in the 1960s — the Green Revolution — the Indian government instituted policies meant to boost agricultural production. As a result, the amount of irrigated land in India nearly tripled between 1970 and 1999. In northern India, agriculture is responsible for up to 95 percent of groundwater use.

Science News says of the study reported in Geophysical Research Letters:

In the mid-1990s, India's Central Ground Water Board estimated that farmers pulled more than 172 cubic kilometers of water each year from aquifers in the study region of northeastern India, southern Nepal and western Bangladesh.... That's more than three times the volume of India's largest surface reservoir. New data gleaned from gravity-measuring satellites suggest that the annual rate of extraction in that region has jumped more than 60 percent since then.

The pace of groundwater depletion in northern India is greater than anyone expected and mirrors trends seen in many other regions, including China and the western United States, says Sandra Postel, director of the Global Water Policy Project, based in Los Lunas, N.M. When groundwater disappears or becomes too difficult to pump, people who now support themselves on the land will become economic refugees, she contends. In many parts of the world, Postel adds, "water problems are becoming very serious, very fast."

Bloomberg News gives some context to the issue of water groundwater withdrawals worldwide. Forecasts aren't cheery:

"A single person can save more water simply by not eating a pound of beef than they could by not showering for an entire year."

About a fifth of water used globally comes from under the ground, the Stockholm International Water Institute has said. Withdrawals are predicted to increase 50 percent by 2025 in developing countries, and 18 percent in developed countries, according to the policy group based in the Swedish capital.

But how do we know what's happening to India's underground water supply anyway? By definition, you can't see it, and we have little to no on-the-ground data.

The answer: Gravity. Scientists infer groundwater levels from variations in Earth's gravitational field measured by satellites.

Richard Kerr of Science Now explains how it works:

As the lead spacecraft passes over a patch of anomalously strong gravity, it accelerates ahead of the trailing spacecraft. Once past the anomaly, the lead satellite slows back down. Then the trailing spacecraft accelerates and again closes on the leader. By making repeated passes over the same spot, GRACE [the Gravity Recovery and Climate Experiment satellite mission] measures changes in Earth's gravity, which are mainly due to water moving on and under the surface. Most famously, GRACE has recorded the shrinking of ice sheets; it has also detected shifting ocean currents, the desiccation of droughts, and the draining of large lakes. Outside of wasting ice sheets, the world's largest broad-scale decline in gravity during GRACE's first 6 years came across a 2.7-million-square-kilometer, east-west swath centered on New Delhi.

The trouble with water—and there is trouble with water—is that they're not making any more of it. They're not making any less, mind, but no more either. There is the same amount of water in the planet now as there was in prehistoric times. People, however, they're making more of—many more, far more than is ecologically sensible—and all those people are utterly dependent on water for their lives (humans consist mostly of water), for their livelihoods, their food, and increasingly, their industry. Humans can live for a month without food but will die in less than a week without water. Humans consume water, discard it, poison it, waste it, and restlessly change the hydrological cycles, indifferent to the consequences: too many people, too little water, water in the wrong places and in the wrong amounts.

- Marq de Villiers

Of the gravity-measuring method, Jay Famiglietti, associate professor of earth system science at the University of California, Irvine, and co-author on the Nature study, tells Bloomberg:

"This is the first time that we have been able to go into the region with essentially no data on the ground and be able to come up with a pretty reasonable number for the rate of groundwater depletion."

(By Moises Velasquez-Manoff / August 13, 2009, The Christian Science Monitor)

Meat Production - Grave Threat To Water Supply

In the context of the global water supply, the impact of animal agriculture threatens utter catastrophe. Every kilo of beef requires 16,000 litres of water, according to the Institute for Water Education. This means a single person can save more water simply by not eating a pound of beef than they could by not showering for an entire year. Factory farming is responsible for 37 percent of pesticide contamination, 50 percent of antibiotic contamination and one-third of the nitrogen and phosphorus loads found in freshwater. Nearly half of all water consumed in the developed countries is used to raise animals for food.

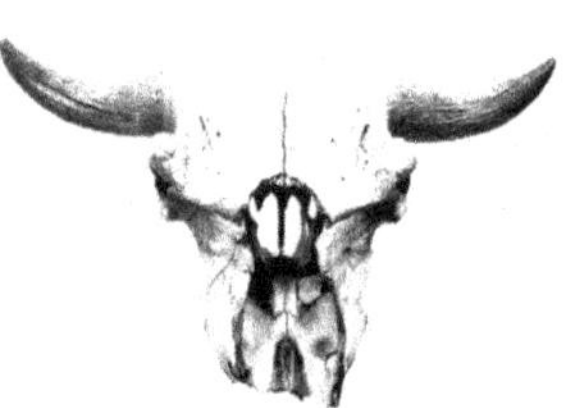

Poisoning water is bad enough, but depleting the supply is suicidal. The majority of the earth's water is now used to support animal agriculture, and much of it cannot be reclaimed.

About 50% of the water pollution is linked to livestock. Pesticides and fertilizers used in helping grow feed grains run off into lakes and rivers. They also pollute ground water. In the feedlots and stockyard holding pens, there is also a tremendous amount of pesticide runoff. Organic contaminants from huge concentrations of animal excrement and urine at feedlots and stockyards also pollute water. This waste is anywhere from ten

> *16 lakh litres of water is needed daily to keep ONE moderate sized slaughterhouse clean. That is drinking water for 10 lakh people. Can a water and energy starved country like India really afford to kill cattle anymore?*
>
> *~Maneka Gandhi*

to hundreds of times more concentrated than raw domestic sewage. According to a German documentary film (Fleisch Frisst Menschen [Flesh Devours Man] by Wolfgang Kharuna), nitrates evaporating from open tanks of concentrated livestock waste in the Netherlands have resulted in extremely high levels of forest-killing acid rain.

Feeding the average meat-eater requires about 4,200 gallons of water per day, versus 1,200 gallons per day for a person following a lacto-vegetarian diet. While it takes only 25 gallons of water to produce a pound of wheat, it takes 2,500 gallons of water to produce a pound of meat.

The animals raised for food in the US alone produce 130 times the excrement of the entire human population on Earth, at a rate of 86,600 pounds per second. Only a sixth of this excrement is used as fertilizer; the rest is just dumped into lakes and rivers, untreated. Slaughterhouse runoff is killing millions of fish, and is the main reason why 35% of Earth's rivers and streams are "impaired". In countries with concentrated animal agriculture, the waterways have become rife with a bacteria called pfiesteria. In addition to killing fish, pfiesteria causes open sores, nausea, memory loss, fatigue and disorientation in humans. Even groundwater, which takes thousands of years to restore, is being contaminated. For example, the aquifer under the San Bernadino Dairy Preserve in southern California contains more nitrates and other pollutants than water coming from sewage treatment plants.

Commenting on Srila Prabhupada's mood in Mayapur, Bhavananda Goswami said if a water tap on the land was dripping only once every three hours, then Srila Prabhupada would come at exactly the time it dripped, see it, and say, "Just see, Krsna's energy is being wasted."

In Bhaktivedanta Manor one time, Srila Prabhupada complained of a dripping water faucet that disturbed him. The devotees searched and searched, but found nothing. Finally, they found the offending faucet. It was outside his room, down the hall, down a small block of stairs, down another small hall, and inside a closet in a place from which water was hardly ever taken. No one knew how he could possibly have heard it drip.

-From Srila Prabhupada Nectar (by Satsvarupa dasa Goswami)

But it's not only fresh water sources that are at risk; ocean waters are also imperiled. Dead zones, vast stretches of coastal waters in which nothing can live, are created by untreated hormone, nitrate and antibiotic laden slaughterhouse waste seeping into the soil, groundwater and rivers before contaminating the ocean. According to the EPA, In USA, 35,000 miles of rivers in 22 states and groundwater in 17 states has been permanently contaminated by industrial farm waste.

One pig factory farm produces raw waste equivalent to that of a city of 120000 people -- except unlike a city, it doesn't have a waste treatment facility. Its raw wastes are dumped straight into surrounding rivers and lakes.

21.

Lessons From China

For India's Mao Zedongs

On The True Cost of Livestock Farming

Desertification is a major national issue in China and it is largely caused by bad policies. Situation is so serious that The Gobi desert has grown by 52,400 square kilometers, an area half the size of Pennsylvania, between 1994 and 1999, and continues to advance at a rate of two miles a year and is now only 240 kilometers or so from Beijing.

In western China the huge Taklimakan and Kumtag deserts are expanding at such a high rate they are expected to merge in the not too distant future. Two deserts in Inner Mongolia and Gansu Province are also in the process of reaching each other and merging.

The Chengdu plain, one of China's primary grain-growing areas, is threatened by sands from the Ruoergai grasslands. The grasslands were a rich grazing areas until a few decades ago when cows and goats began to multiply and overgraze the land. There is danger that a dust bowl situation could develop. Already wells have dried up and emergency grain supplies have to be brought in to keep people from starving. Many people are being encouraged to move to more hospitable lands.

The grassland has been likened to the thin skin on a bun. It can be destroyed if a couple of centimeters is disturbed. One Mongolian said, "Our elders used to say we should never cultivate the grassland."

Overgrazing

Poor land use and overgrazing are causing large areas of grasslands north of Beijing and in Inner Mongolia and Qinghai province to turn into a desert. One man who lived in a village on the eastern edge of the Qinghai-Tibet plateau that was being swallowed up by sand told the New York Times, "The pasture here used to be so green and rich. But now the grass is disappearing and the sand is coming."

Increased livestock pressure on marginal lands has accelerated desertification. In some areas, nomads moving to less arid areas disrupt the local ecosystem and increase the rate of erosion of the land. Nomads are trying to escape the desert, but because of their land-use practices, they are bringing the desert with them.

Huge flocks of sheep and goats strip the land of vegetation. In Xillinggol Prefecture in Inner Mongolia, for example, the livestock population increased from 2 million in 1977 to 18 million in 2000, turning one third of the grassland area to desert. Unless something is done the entire prefecture could be uninhabitable by 2020.

Overgrazing is exacerbated by a sociological phenomena called "the tragedy of the common." People share land but raise animals for themselves and try to enrich themselves by raising as many as they can. This leads to more animals than the land can support. One grassland in Qinghai that can support 3.7 million sheep had 5.5 million sheep in 1997

Animals remove the vegetation and winds finish the job by blowing away the top soil, transforming grasslands into desert.

To reduce the number of animals the government is encouraging herders to cut the size of their flocks by 40 percent, relocate and stall-feed their animals.

Now by your talent, you are producing nice food, but producing food, tilling the ground some way or other, by machine or by this way... But there must be rain, and so many other conditions. But time will come when there will be no rain. Then what you will do with your tractor and machine? You'll have to eat the tractor. (laughter) That's all.

-Prabhupada (Srimad-Bhagavatam 1.16.22 -- Hawaii, January 18, 1974)

Migration and Resettlement

Desertification is causing millions of rural Chinese to abandon unproductive land in Gansu, Inner Mongolia and Ningxia Provinces and migrate eastward. A study by the Asian Development Bank found 4,000 villages at risk of being swallowed up by drifting sand.

Already a migration on the scale of the Dust Bowl in the United States in the 1930 is taking place in China. The only problem is that in China there is no California to escape to. Many of those driven off land degreded by desertification have ended up in eastern cities as migrant workers.

In parts of the Ningxia Province, significant rain has not fallen for years and farming is impossible. Tens of thousands of people from villages mostly in poor southern Ningxia have been resettled.

Disastrous Policies

There are three events during the five-decade Communist rule in China that led to the severe desertification that we see today. These events all happened around the same time during the 60's, which were the dam projects on the Yellow River, the household irrigation system during the Cultural Revolution, and the most significantly, Mao's plan of turning grassland into farmland.

In the 1955, China's first National People's Congress approved the Soviet plan of 46 dam projects, and the Yellow River Dam was finished in 1960. The dam led to changing path of the Yellow River and disappearing of some of its tributaries, and then the grassland and farmland gradually dried up and turned into a desert.

Secondly, during the Cultural Revolution period in the late 60's, the engineers helped farmers build an irrigation system that enabled each household to divert water from the Yellow River to their individual farmland. This system helped farming; however, the more households adopted this system, the less water left to the

> *Lister Cheung Lai-ping said after digging "the land is then useless for growing anything else. By displacing the sand, it blows everywhere, covering houses, machinery, people... it covers everything. No other farming can be done; it's like living under snow - except it's not snow, it's sand." (BBC)*

downstream rivers. Gradually, the lands around these dried-out downstream rivers turned into desert.

The most significant cause of the desertification came from Mao's plan of farmland expansion, which turned out to be the most damaging. Mao saw these vast areas of grassland in the north and he came up with plans to put them to good use. He relocated farmers to these grasslands who removed all the grass to grow their crops. But the grassroots in these steppes were essential to retain rainwater and soil. The roots of the crops were unable to serve such functions. Gradually the soil lost its water retention capacity and wind and water erosion set in. In no time, the area turned into a vast desert. The actual amount of grassland lost is anyone's guess due to lack of reporting by the government controlled agencies.

The government has pledged $6.8 billion (56.8 billion Yuan) on an environmental program which includes planting multiple layers of green belt around the Gobi. In what has been described as the world's most ambitious reforestation project, the Chinese are planting a line of trees and shrubs, paralleling the Great Wall of China, to protect farmland in northern China from Gobi Desert sand blown by the fierce Mongolian winds. Stretching from Xinjiang to Heolongjang, this "Green Wall" will eventually cover strip of land 4,000 miles in length.

You have seen desert. Desert means it requires huge quantities of water. Nowadays, practically, in every country, especially in India, every land is just like desert for want of water. So you see in Vrndavana so much land lying vacant, no agriculture. Why? There is want of water. There is no sufficient supply of water. So in this way, if there is scarcity of water, then gradually these places will be converted into desert. Converted into desert. So the "desert" word is used because it requires huge quantity of water. Similarly, we are, in this material world, we are trying to be happy in the society, friendship and love. Suta-mita-ramani-samaje. But the happiness we are getting, that is compared with a drop of water in the desert. If in the vast desert, Arabian desert, if we say that "We want water," and somebody brings a drop of water and take it, it will be very insignificant, has no meaning. ~ Srila Prabhupada (Lecture, Bhagavad-gita 9.1 -- Vrndavana, April 17, 1975)

22.

Causes Of Land Degeneration

According to a new report published by the United Nations Food and Agriculture Organization, the livestock sector is a major source of land and water degradation.

Says Henning Steinfeld, Chief of FAO's Livestock Information and Policy Branch and senior author of the report: "Livestock are one of the most significant contributors to today's most serious environmental problems. Urgent action is required to remedy the situation."

United Nations scientists, in their 408-page indictment of the meat industry, point out that the meat industry is "one of the most significant contributors to the most serious environmental problems, at every scale from local to global," including "problems of land degradation, climate change and air pollution, water shortage and water pollution, and loss of biodiversity."

Meat in our diets takes its toll on Earth's surface in two main ways: over-grazing and use of land to grow feed for animals. As demand for animal products rise, demand on the lands that support grazing or feed production becomes overwhelming (that is, unsustainable).

Lester Brown, the founder of the Worldwatch Institute, calculated that the needs of 230 million cattle, 246 million sheep and 175 million goats grazing on the African continent exceed the lands' capacity by at least half. *In Africa, if current trends of soil degradation continue, the continent might be able to feed just 25%*

of its population by 2025, according to UNU's Ghana-based Institute for Natural Resources in Africa.

Clearing land to graze animals or to grow animal feed leads to erosion, food shortages (as land to grow other crops is reduced, and eventually left barren), and global warming (from loss of plant life that would otherwise absorb CO2). "Overgrazing of rangelands," notes Brown, "initially reduces their productivity but eventually it destroys them, leaving desert." Enter the term "desertification": the process whereby fertile and stable lands become — you got it — deserts. We lose billions of tons of topsoil every year to rising demands for meat and irresponsible growing and grazing practices — a rate that, putting it lightly, far outpaces the 100 to 500 years it takes to produce one inch of topsoil. (Industrial farming loses up to six inches of topsoil a year.)

Deforestation

In an undisturbed forest, the mineral soil is protected by a layer of leaf litter and an humus that cover the forest floor. These two layers form a protective mat over the soil that absorbs the impact of rain drops. They are porous and highly permeable to rainfall, and allow rainwater to slow percolate into the soil below, instead of flowing over the surface as runoff. The roots of the trees and plants hold together soil particles, preventing them from being washed away. The vegetative cover acts to reduce the velocity of the raindrops that strike the foliage and stems before hitting the ground, reducing their kinetic energy. However it is the forest floor, more than the canopy, that prevents surface erosion. The terminal velocity of rain drops is reached in about 8 meters. Because forest canopies are usually higher than this, rain drops can often regain terminal velocity even after striking the canopy. However, the intact

forest floor, with its layers of leaf litter and organic matter, is still able to absorb the impact of the rainfall.

Deforestation causes increased erosion rates due to exposure of mineral soil by removing the humus and litter layers from the soil surface, removing the vegetative cover that binds soil together, and causing heavy soil compaction from logging equipment. Once trees have been removed by fire or logging, infiltration rates become high and erosion low to the degree the forest floor remains intact.

Globally, we are using more and more land to make room for more and more animals and the crops needed to feed them. An estimated 30 percent of the earth's ice-free land is involved in livestock production, according to the U.N.'s Food and Agriculture Organization. Forests are a precious means of maintaining soil health and climate stability, but rain forests (Brazil) and ancient pine forests (China) — entire ecosystems worldwide — are being destroyed to feed the animals that feed us. The expanding use of land for grazing and growing animal feed crops is now a dominant reason for deforestation in most countries. Much of the prairies in central Canada have been lost.

Deforestation contributes to global warming, topsoil depletion, drought, plant and animal extinction, and loss of biodiversity. Basically, we are devouring trees to make way for an ever-increasing number of farmed animals. These animals, in turn, devour vast amounts of energy, natural resources and food calories, so that we can, in turn, devour their meat.

To give you some sense of the vast tracts of land needed to graze or otherwise feed the animals that feed us, scientists at the Smithsonian Institute figure that the equivalent of seven football fields of land is bulldozed every minute. *Every minute.* According to the U.S. General Accounting Office, more plant species are threatened or annihilated by livestock grazing than by any other cause.

In India not much forest cover remains. Tropical forest cover in India has been reduced to two major areas: the coastal hills of the Western Ghats (about 135,000 sq. km) and 34,500 sq. km in Northeastern India. Very little of India's forest cover is considered pristine. According to Forest Survey of India, the country has lost an alarming 3,762,000 ha of forest since 1990. That is 5.9% of the total forest area. At this rate, the country may become bald in next few decades.

Wind Erosion

Wind erosion in the study of geology and weather, pertain to wind activity and specifically to the wind's ability to shape the surface of the Earth. Winds may erode, transport, and deposit materials, and are effective agents in regions with sparse vegetation. Although water is a much more powerful eroding force than wind, wind erosion processes are more visible in arid environments such as deserts.

This type of erosion basically involves displacement of soil particles by the action of wind. Normally the soil is removed in thin layers as sheet erosion, but sometimes wind effect can carve out hollows and other features. Wind erosion is a function of wind velocity, soil characteristics and land use. Wind displaces fine to medium size sand particles.

Soil erosion due to growing livestock feed is estimated to be 40 billion tons per year (or 6 tons/year for every human being on the planet). About 60% of soil that is washed away ends up in rivers, streams and lakes, making waterways more prone to flooding and to contamination from soil's fertilizers and pesticides. Erosion increases the amount of dust carried by wind, polluting the air and carrying infection and disease.

In India the land degradation due to wind erosion is limited to arid regions. Experimental studies on wind erosion under different land uses were conducted by the Central Arid Zone Research Institute (CAZRI), Jodhpur, and different parameters have been standardized for wind erosion.

An area of 11 Million hectares is found suffering from wind erosion of various intensities. Very severe and severe wind erosion occur in 16% of the total geographical area (TGA) of the country. Moderate wind erosion occurs in 32% of TGA.

Wind erosion is more prominent in the hot arid region occupying 31.7 million hectares. Removal of vegetative cover and overgrazing enhance the intensity and extent of wind erosion and desertification. The sand movement causes calcine damage to the adjoining cultivated areas, roads, canals, buildings, etc.

Alarming Rise In Dust Storms

When surfaces are denuded either at high or low altitudes by grazing and intensive cultivation, the wind starts carving up the soil and starts blowing it across the country. These are known as dust storms.

Research shows that dust storms are increasing in certain parts of the world, including China and Africa. In parts of North Africa, annual dust production has increased tenfold in the last 50 years. According to Andrew Goudie, a professor of geography at Oxford University, in Mauritania alone there were just two dust storms a year in the early 1960s, but there are about 80 a year today. Levels of Saharan dust coming off the east coast of Africa in June 2007 were five times those observed in June 2006.

The huge amounts of dust blowing across the Earth may have serious consequences for the environment. Dust storms are transporting prodigious quantities of material for very long distances. Dust storms have also been shown to increase the spread of disease across the globe as they are now combining with airborne pollutants emitted by human activities.

Also, the virus spores in the ground are blown into the atmosphere by the storms with the minute particles. Their increasing frequency could affect the levels of carbon dioxide in the atmosphere, thus directly affecting temperatures and rainfall.

Using satellite imagery, scientists are able to monitor dust storms. Modern agricultural practices, deforestation, drought, winds and increased grazing etc. contribute to dust production.

The cross-boundary nature of dust makes it a truly global issue and one that is not receiving the attention it deserves.

Water Erosion

Water erosion is the process by which soil and rock are removed from the Earth's surface by water flow, and then transported and deposited in other locations.

While erosion is a natural process, human activities have increased by 10-40 times the rate at which erosion is occurring globally. Excessive erosion causes problems such as desertification, decreases in agricultural productivity due to land degradation, sedimentation of waterways, and ecological collapse due to loss of the nutrient rich upper soil layers. Water and wind erosion are now the two primary causes of land degradation; combined, they are responsible for 84% of degraded acreage, making excessive erosion one of the most significant global environmental problems.

Industrial agriculture, deforestation, roads, anthropogenic climate change and urban sprawl are amongst the most significant human activities in regard to their effect on stimulating erosion. However, there are many available alternative land use practices that can curtail or limit erosion, such as terrace-building, no-till agriculture, and revegetation of denuded soils.

In India, this is the most widespread form of degradation and occurs widely in all agroclimatic zones. Soil material displacement by water can result either in loss of top-soil or in terrain deformation or both through the processes of splash erosion, sheet erosion, rill erosion and gully erosion. Soil erosion starts with the falling of the raindrops onto the bare soil surface. The impact of raindrops breaks-up surface soil aggregates and splashes particles into the air.

Soil loss assessment for different states has been carried out under a collaborative project between the National Bureau of Soil Survey and Land-Use Planning (NBSS&LUP), Nagpur, and the Central Soil and Water Conservation Research and Training Institute (CSWCR&TI), Dehra Dun.

Soil loss values were categorized into five classes (moderate, moderately severe, severe, very severe and extremely severe), and statewise areas under different categories have been determined and mapped. An area of about 126 million hectares has been found suffering from various degrees of water erosion.

Out of 69 million hectares estimated to be 'critically' degraded in India approximately 43 million hectares are non-arable & barren, including 4 million hectares of ravine lands. The Himalayan Mountains with weak geological formation and poor physiographic conditions are under great stress and suffer from serious water erosion though water erosion is also rampant in the Western Ghats and other areas of high intensity rainfall. Water erosion not only removes the productive surface layer of soil but also reduces the storage capacity of reservoirs.

Acidic Soils

In India about 6.98 Million hectares are affected by acid soils; which is about 9.4% of the total geographical area of the country.

Acidification, which may occur either because of excessive application of acidifying fertilizer or because of drainage in particular types of soil. These soils develop in humid and per-humid areas, resulting in lowering of pH and loss of soil fertility, and can be partially reclaimed by addition of chemical amendments like lime.

For assessing area under acid soils, soil maps of different states on 1 : 250,000 scale were digitized in the GIS format. The non-spatial (attribute) data on pH values were linked to master soil layer to generate soil reaction (pH) map of India, which was reclassified to produce a soil acidity map of India.

The acidity map of India, thus produced, facilitates understanding of spatial distribution and pH status of soils in different parts of India. Based on the range of pH values, the map has been reclassified as strongly acidic (pH < 4.5); moderately acidic (pH 4.5–5.5); slightly acidic (pH 5.5–6.5) and non-acidic (pH > 6.5).

However, for the estimation of the degraded lands of India, only strongly acidic - pH < 4.5 and moderately acidic – pH 4.5–5.5 soils have been considered.

Salt-affected soils appear in different shades of white tone with fine to coarse texture on the False Colour Composite (FCC) prints of the satellite data, owing to presence of the salts, and are recognizable under normal crop growth.

For assessing these soils, India's National Remote Sensing Agency (NRSA) has prepared maps on 1 : 250,000 scale using satellite data. Information on the salt-affected soils provided by the Central Soil Salinity Research Institute (CSSRI), Karnal, was used for the harmonization of the degraded wasteland datasets of India. Salt-affected soils were regrouped into two classes namely saline and sodic soils in the GIS format.

Salt-affected Soils *(Salinization and Sodification)*

These soils contain excessive amount of either soluble salts or exchangeable sodium or both affecting crop yields and crop production. Depending upon the physiochemical properties and the nature of the salts, the soils are classified into saline, sodic and saline-sodic.

Continuous use of poor quality groundwater for irrigation is a major factor in the development of soil salinity or sodicity, particularly in the slowly permeable soils.

It is more serious in the Indo Gangetic Plain, black soil region, arid areas of Rajasthan and Gujarat and coastal areas.

The sodic soils possess high pH and exchangeable sodium percentage values, preponderance of carbonate and bicarbonate salts of sodium, deficient amount of organic matter, nitrogen, available calcium and zinc, presence of CaC03 (kankar) in the subsoil, impaired physical condition and poor moisture relations.

Addition of a suitable amendment like gypsum is essential for reclamation of these soils.

The saline soils, on the other hand have high concentration of neutral salts mainly of chlorides and sulphates, lower values of pH and exchangeable sodium, better physical conditions etc.

Many saline soils are often associated with high water table of poor groundwater quality. Provision of adequate drainage to lower the water table and leach out the soluble salts is imperative for amelioration of such saline soils.

In India about 7 million hectares is salt-affected, of which 2.5 million hectares represents the alkali soils in the Indo-Gangetic Plain and nearly 50% of the canal-irrigated areas are affected by salinisation and/or alkalisation due to inadequate drainage, inefficient use of available water resources, and socio-political reasons.

Typical examples of salinisation caused by the rise in ground water are observed in Uttar Pradesh, Haryana, Rajasthan, Maharashtra, and Karnataka. A recent study by Sehgal and Abrol (1994) shows that a total of 10.1 million hectares is affected by salinity-alkalinity, of which about 2.5 million hectares occurs in the Indo-Gangetic Plain.

Salinity/sodicity directly affects the productivity of soils by making the soil unfavourable for good crop growth. Indirectly, it lowers productivity through adverse effects on the availability of nutrients and on the beneficial activities of soil microflora.

According to Brandon, Hommann, and Kishor (1995), the loss in crop production due to salinity in India amounts to 6.2 million tonnes (FAO data) and 9.7 million tonnes (Indian data)

In extreme cases, "damage from salinization is so great that it is technically unfeasible or totally uneconomic to reverse the process" (FAO, 1983).

Physical Degradation

Land degradation by physical processes is classified as barren rock and stony wastelands, mining and industrial wastelands, snow-covered and ice-caps and waterlogged areas. This information has been generated by the NRSA using satellite data. An area of 13.8 Million hectares is affected by physical degradation in India.

The Loss Of Soil Nutrients

Soil nutrients (mainly nitrogen, phosphorus and potassium) or organic matter are lost through either erosion or by cultivating

Also in India, it was estimated in 1990-1991 that about 8 million hectares were damaged by waterlogging or salinity from irrigation and that as many as 1.5 million farmers had been displaced by those problems since Independence.

In Pakistan "irrigated land [was] going out of production at the rate of 100 hectares a day"; many displaced farmers moved to the newly irrigated areas in Western Punjab likely to face the same situation a few years later (Maloney, 1990). Others went to swell the numbers of urban slum dwellers.

on poor or moderately fertile soils, without sufficient application of manure or fertilizer. In addition, soils can be "depleted by the crops themselves, particularly if the same crops are grown on the same land year after year." (FAO, 1983)

In India the soil nutrient loss to the tune of 5.37 to 8.40 million tonnes occurs through erosion every year.

This aggravates the problem of soil fertility depletion. The transformation from high internal input agriculture in the past to the present day high external input (fertilizers, pesticides) agriculture causes this problem.

Here the removal of plant nutrients is sustainably higher than what is added through fertilizers, thereby, resulting in a negative soil nutrient balance.

Soil Pollution

Soil contamination or soil pollution is caused by the presence of man-made chemicals or other alteration in the natural soil environment. It is typically caused by industrial activity, agricultural chemicals, or improper disposal of waste. The most common chemicals involved are petroleum hydrocarbons, solvents, pesticides, lead, and other heavy metals. Contamination is correlated with the degree of industrialization and intensity of chemical usage.

The concern over soil contamination stems primarily from health risks, from direct contact with the contaminated soil, vapors from the contaminants, and from secondary contamination of water supplies within and underlying the soil. Mapping of contaminated soil sites and the resulting cleanup are time consuming and expensive tasks, requiring extensive amounts of geology, hydrology, chemistry and computer modeling skills.

These pollutions of various origins can strongly reduce the agricultural potential of lands.

Soil compaction

Another cause of soil degradation and erosion from cattle is their repeated trampling over the same areas. The result is compaction or "soil pugging" due to the impact of cattle hooves. Soil compaction can destroy soil structure and results in resistance to root penetration, reduced water infiltration, and reduced aeration. All of these impacts harm beneficial soil microorganisms.

Compaction is considered to be inevitable with cattle production. However, the severity varies with the soil type, and is worst on wet soil that has a high clay content. Severe compaction provides a site for surface runoff that can result in serious erosion and even the creation of deep trenches, a process called gullying.

Usage of heavy machinery like tractors, particularly in wet soils, is obviously another cause of soil compaction. In many areas, compaction is not easy to correct.

Waterlogging

Waterlogging is the rise of the water table to the root zone of plants, caused by an excessive input of water with respect to drainage capacities. It is typical of irrigated areas, but may also occur through river flooding. Waterlogging also increases salinity. As with salinization, the causes of waterlogging are in part physical and in part related to agricultural practices, namely inappropriate irrigation.

In India, roughly an area of 100,000 ha is estimated to be affected by water logging annually. Introduction of canal irrigation is the major reason for the once fertile lands to be affected by water logging (e.g., Hissar, Haryana). The menace of water logging has also taken place in the Indira Gandhi Nahar Project, which was initiated in 1961.

Such phenomena have occurred on a large scale in several parts of canal command areas such as the Indo-Gangetic plains and many other arid, semi-arid and sub-humid tracts of the country. Large areas have been rendered barren due to this.

Soil Poisoning

Farmland is occasionally poisoned with chemicals. While pesticides and even fertilizers are sometimes suspected of causing soil impairment, the damage in most cases is not permanent. However, some apple orchards sprayed with arsenic compounds in the 1930s were reported as still unproductive 30 years later. In recent years, there has been a general movement in many developed countries against using the more persistent insecticides, including a chemical group that includes DDT and chlordane. Radioactive fallout also caused public concern during the period of nuclear bomb tests.

Today a more serious problem is the indiscriminate dumping of chemical wastes, some of which are extremely toxic to plants, animals, and man and some of which contains dangerous heavy metals which can be taken up by plants.

Heavy metals

The pollution of soil with heavy metals due to improper disposal of industrial effluents, use of domestic and municipal wastes and pesticides, is becoming a major concern. Though no reliable estimates are available of the extent and degree of this type of soil degradation, it is believed that the problem is extensive and its effects are significant. Some commercial fertilisers also contain appreciable quantities of heavy metals, which have undesirable effects on the environment. The indiscriminate use of agro-chemicals such as fertilisers and pesticides is often responsible for land degradation.

Sheet Erosion

There are several types of man-made erosions but most of them are clearly recognizable. But one of the most insidious one is the

> *By God's arrangement one can have enough food grains, enough milk, enough fruits and vegetables, and nice clear river water. But now I have seen, while traveling in Europe, that all the rivers there have become nasty. In Germany, in France, and also in Russia and America I have seen that the rivers are nasty. By nature's way the water in the ocean is kept clear like crystal, and the same water is transferred to the rivers, but without salt, so that one may take nice water from the river. This is nature's way, and nature's way means Krsna's way.*
>
> *~ Srila Prabhupada (Teachings of Queen Kunti 23)*

invisible or sheet erosion. This occurs when a thin layer or "sheet" of soil from a field is removed. It is insidious because the amount of soil seen to be removed is usually so small in any given year that a farmer often fails to notice that erosion is occurring. Occasionally he becomes aware of sheet erosion only after he notices that a formerly buried object - a rock, the lower portion of a fence post, or root of a tree - is suddenly exposed.

However, sheet erosion removes great quantities of topsoil. Even a very thin layer of soil, only slightly thicker than a piece of wrapping paper, when transported down a slope, can weigh several tons per hectare. It does not take many years or many rainstorms for losses from sheet erosion to become significant.

23.

Agrochemical Degeneration Of Land

The use of cbemical fertilizers can reduce the natural nutrients on the soil surface. (Fred, 1991) Microorganisms decrease with the continued usage of the chemical fertilizers. (Katsunori, 2003) Chemical fertilizers are regarded as a non-point-source pollution for the environment. Because agriculture is heavily depended on the environmental resources, direct impacts are felt by local farmers with the loss of their ecological systems. (LIU Yu, et al., 2009)

Interestingly, if farmers apply chemical fertilizers or pesticides on their farms day in day out, this results in reduced pest control. Harmful organisms will become resistant and beneficial organisms which play a vital role in the improvement of the soil quality will decline. This also leads to land degradation. (Fred, 1991)

The chemical fertilizers used must annihilate both pests and other beneficial organisms that contribute high value functions in agricultural areas. (Preap, 2009)

Chemicals applied to soil take a heavy toll on earthworm which plays a vital role in maintaining soil fertility. (Richard, 2010)

According to Pierre A. Roger and Ian Simpson, 1991, chemical fertilizers are the greatest source of soil degradation and human activities are outweighing natural forces in degrading land resources.

Soil performs many important functions in the upkeep of the natural environment. It not only produces food but also acts as a carbon-sink, reducing the atmospheric pollution, protecting natural resource cycles and recovering nutrients. Chemical fertilizers and pesticides negatively impact soil's ability to perform these functions. (Sununtar, 2006)

Chemical fertilizers, by increasing the abundance of the crops without replacing all the exhausted elements of the soil, have indirectly contributed to change the nutritive value of cereal grains and vegetables.

India is the second largest consumption in the world after China, consuming about 26.5 million tonnes. It accounted for 15.3 % of the world's N consumption. 19% of phosphatic and 14.4 % of potassic nutrients in 2008(FAI, 2010)

Fertilizer consumption was around 78 thousand tonnes in 1965-66 and it picked up very fast during the late-1960s and 1970s. At the times of onset of green revolution in 1966-67 consumption of fertilizers was about 1 million tonnes. In 1970-71 total fertilizers consumption increased to 2.26 million tonnes which further increased to 12.73 million tonnes in 1991-92.

During 1990s total fertilization consumption fluctuated between 12.15 and 16.8 million tonnes. Total fertilization consumption reached record level of 26.5 million tonnes 2009-10.

By 2020 fertilizer demands in the country is projected to increase to about 41.6 million tones.

When the government neglects agriculture, which is necessary for the production of food, the land becomes covered with unnecessary trees. Of course, many trees are useful because they produce fruits and flowers, but many other trees are unnecessary. They could be used as fuel and the land cleared and used for agriculture. When the government is negligent, less grain is produced. As stated in Bhagavad-gita (18.44), krsi-go-raksya-vanijyam vaisya-karma svabhava jam: the proper engagements for vaisyas, according to their nature, are to farm and to protect cows. The duty of the government and the ksatriyas is to see that the members of the third class, the vaisyas, who are neither brahmanas nor ksatriyas, are thus properly engaged. Ksatriyas are meant to protect human beings, whereas vaisyas are meant to protect useful animals, especially cows.

Intensity of Fertilizer Use

In India, per hectare consumption of fertilizers has increased from 69.8 kg in 1991-92 to 113.3 kg in 2006-07, at an average rate of 3.3 percent.

On per hectare basis, fertilizer consumption was less than 2 kg during the 1950s and increased to about 5 kg in 1965-66. However, after introduction of green revolution in 1966-67, per hectare fertilizer consumption more than doubled in the next five years from about 7kg in 1966-67 to about 16 kg in 1971-72, which further increased and reached a level of 50kg in mid-1980s.

Average fertilizer consumption on per hectare basis crossed 100kg in 2005-06 and reached a record level of 135 kg in 2009-10. However, per hectare fertilizer consumption fell during 1973-74 and 1974-75 due to oil shock of 1973 when oil prices quadrupled almost overnight.

The next reversal in intensity of fertilizer use came in1992-93 when government decontrolled phosphatic and potassic fertilizers and increased fertilizer prices significantly. The total fertilizer consumption (N+P+K) fell by about 6 per cent from 69.84 kg per hectare to 65.45 kg per hectare.

However, during the last five years, intensity of fertilizer use has increased substantially (53%) from about 88 kg in 2005-06 to135 kg per hectare in 2009-10.

The intensity of fertilizer use varied greatly from about 48 kg per hectare in Rajasthan to as high as 237 kg per hectare in Punjab. The fertilizer use has generally been higher in northern (91.5 kg/ha average) and southern (85.3 kg/ha average) region and lower in the eastern (44.7kg/ha) and western region (40.7 kg/ha).

There was a time in ancient past when Sahara was green.

In 1999, a group of German scientists used computer simulation to create a model of the Earth's climate thousands of years ago. They concluded that the climatic transition of the Sahara took place abruptly, within a possible span of about 300 years.

24.

GE Crops Help Destroy Soil Fertility

Possibly Irreversibly

By Dr. Macola

The latest science seems to suggest genetically engineered plant cultivation may seriously disrupt soil ecology by reducing microbial diversity, which decreases soil fertility over time—possibly irreversibly.

As GE plants increasingly take over the major food-producing areas of the world, including the U.S., China, India, Argentina and Brazil, reduced soil fertility could lead to famine on a scale never previously seen. The mechanisms for this are just beginning to be understood, and what was recently only theory has inched closer to reality as science shines more light on the consequences of introducing genetically engineered organisms into the soil.

The mechanism goes something like this...

Special genetic elements (vector DNA) are present in all GE plants. This vector DNA enables unrelated microorganism species to mate, but can also be transferred to soil microorganisms. Soil fertility depends on the presence of a diverse blend of microorganisms, all serving different roles in balancing and optimizing the soil. But when unrelated species mate, the soil ecosystem loses diversity, which is proven to damage fertility.

Until recently, the transfer of genes between GE plants and soil bacteria was only theoretical. However, this mechanism has now been demonstrated by science, and it's our soil's worst nightmare. It should be noted that this same process of gene transfer has been shown to occur in your gastrointestinal tract when you eat GE foods—turning your intestines into a virtual pesticide factory.

Horizontal Gene Transfer Is Now Proven By Science

The following complications underscore the seriousness of the dangers introduced by cultivation of GE crops:

DNA from GE plants is not readily broken down in the soil and can be taken up by soil particles and microbes. The accumulation of foreign DNA may lead to a cumulative loss of soil diversity over repeated harvests.

Unlike the claims of Monsanto when it first approved GM crops, Bt genes (Bacillus thuringiensis) are not broken down, for the reasons already stated, so can accumulate in soil and potentially produce Bt toxins. These toxins may build up in the soil, further damaging the organisms crucial for soil fertility. Research from the New York University7 confirms that Bt toxins are not broken down by soil microbes and do indeed accumulate in soil; the toxins maintain their ability to kill insects, potentially creating superbugs that further endanger the ecosystem.

GE DNA is able to merge with the DNA of other organisms to create new varieties of soil microorganisms that disrupt the ecological balance. These new organisms, if virulent enough, could spread widely via wind erosion and ground water to compromise soil fertility on a broader scale.

A Swiss study8 showed that adult earthworms feeding on transgenic Bt corn lost 18 percent of their initial weight, suggesting GE DNA may have long-term toxic effects on earthworms. Earthworms are major decomposers of dead and organic matter in the soil and are major contributors to the recycling of nutrients. An earlier study9 showed that both earthworms and collembolans (another small soil-dwelling invertebrate) can be adversely affected by Bt crops.

Its also been shown that glyphosate can be toxic to rhizobia, a nitrogen-fixing bacterium10. Nitrogen fixing bacteria are important because nitrogen is the nutrient most commonly deficient in soil.

GE crops are adversely affecting our soil biology in numerous ways. There are differences observed in the bacteria occupying plant roots and changes in nutrient availability. Many studies show glyphosate can have toxic effects on microorganisms and can stimulate them to germinate spores and colonize root systems. Glyphosate has also been shown to immobilize manganese, an essential plant nutrient. Overall, glyphosate diminishes the health and nutritional value of the plants it's sprayed on, as well as the soil.

The two main types of GE foods—herbicide-tolerant crops and pesticide-producing crops—are both imprecise technologies riddled with unintended consequences, including hundreds to thousands of genetic mutations that have unknown effects on human health. Glyphosate and GE crops may be leading the human race over a cliff, as Dr. Don Huber explains in the following interview.

The so-called vaisyas -- the industrialists or businessmen -- are involved in big, big industrial enterprises, but they are not interested in food grains and milk. However, as indicated here, by digging for water, even in the desert, we can produce food grains; when we produce food grains and vegetables, we can give protection to the cows; while giving protection to the cows, we can draw from them abundant quantities of milk; and by getting enough milk and combining it with food grains and vegetables, we can prepare hundreds of nectarean foods. We can happily eat this food and thus avoid industrial enterprises and joblessness.

Agriculture and cow protection are the way to become sinless and thus be attracted to devotional service.

~ Srila Prabhupada (Srimad Bhagavatam 8.6.12)

25.

Global Soil Change

As Serious As Climate Change

Earth's climate and biodiversity aren't the only things being dramatically affected by humans—the world's soils are also shifting beneath our feet.

'Global soil change' due to human activities is a major component of what some experts say should be recognized as a new period of geologic time: the human-made age. This new era will be defined by the pervasiveness of human environmental impacts, including changes to Earth's soils and surface geology.

Daniel Richter of Duke University, in his report published in the December 2007 issue of the journal of Soil Science, warns that Earth's soils already show a reduced capacity to support biodiversity and agricultural production. As the amount of depleted and damaged soils increases, global cycles of water, carbon, nitrogen, and other materials are also being affected.

In another paper, Jan Zalaseiwicz of the University of Leicester in England and colleagues argue that the fossil and geologic record of our time will leave distinct signatures that will be apparent far into the future.

Overworked Earth

Today about 50 percent of the world's soils are subject to direct management by humans. Global soil change is also occurring in more remote areas due to the spread of contaminants and alterations in climate. Worldwide, soils are being transformed by human activities in ways that we poorly understand, with possibly dire implications.

The report warns that properties and processes in the soil are more dynamic and susceptible to change than previously thought. Only recently it has been documented that many aspects of soil chemistry and composition are highly responsive to human activities.

Report also warns that severe soil degradation is increasing globally at a rate of 12.4 million to 24.7 million acres (5 million to 10 million hectares) annually.

Soil Degradation And Climate Change - A Relationship

Soil degradation plays much a larger role in climate change than was previously suspected. That's because organic matter in soils store vast amounts of carbon—more than is present in the atmosphere and in all land vegetation combined.

According to the noted geologist Bruce Wilkinson of Syracuse University, heavily cultivated and degraded soils lose their carbon-storing ability as exposed organic matter breaks down.

Over the past half century or so, global soils have lost approximately a hundred billion tons of carbon [in the form of carbon dioxide] to the atmosphere through such exposure. Humans are now the predominant geological force operating on the planet.

Rates of sedimentation and erosion caused by human activities—mainly industrial agriculture—are ten times higher those attributable to natural processes. On agricultural land, soil is being lost ten times faster than it is being replaced. Humans are rapidly consuming the global soil reservoir. In light of the wasting grains to produce meat and biofuels, this is obviously a very serious change.

26.

World's Land Turning to Desert at Alarming Speed

United Nations Warns

by Chris Hawley, Associated Press, Published June 16, 2004

UNITED NATIONS -- The world is turning to dust, with lands the size of Rhode Island becoming desert wasteland every year and the problem threatening to send millions of people fleeing to greener countries, the United Nations says.

One-third of the Earth's surface is at risk, driving people into cities and destroying agriculture in vast swaths of Africa. Thirty-one percent of Spain is threatened, while China has lost 36,000 square miles to desert -- an area the size of Indiana -- since the 1950s.

This week the United Nations marks the 10th anniversary of the Convention to Combat Desertification, a plan aimed at stopping the phenomenon. Despite the efforts, the trend seems to be picking up speed -- doubling its pace since the 1970s.

"It's a creeping catastrophe," said Michel Smitall, a spokesman for the U.N. secretariat that oversees the 1994 accord. "Entire parts of the world might become uninhabitable."

Slash-and-burn agriculture, sloppy conservation, overtaxed water supplies and industrialization of agriculture are mostly to blame. But global warming is taking its toll, too.

I'm coming from London, Paris, and Tehran. All fields yellow. And Europe, so much scorching heat and sunshine, I never seen. Especially in London. This time I saw everything has become yellow. Greenness gone.
-Srila Prabhupada (Morning Walk — August 14, 1976, Bombay)

The United Nations is holding a ceremony in Bonn, Germany, to mark World Day to Combat Desertification, and will hold a meeting in Brazil to take stock of the problem.

The warning comes as a controversial movie, "The Day After Tomorrow" is whipping up interest in climate change, and as rivers and lakes dry up in the American West, giving Americans a taste of what's to come elsewhere.

The United Nations says:

* From the mid-1990s to 2000, 1,374 square miles have turned into deserts each year -- an area about the size of Rhode Island. That's up from 840 square miles in the 1980s, and 624 square miles during the 1970s.

* By 2025, two-thirds of arable land in Africa will disappear, along with one-third of Asia's and one-fifth of South America's.

* Some 135 million people -- equivalent to the populations of France and Germany combined -- are at risk of being displaced.

Most at risk are dry regions on the edges of deserts -- places like sub-Saharan Africa or the Gobi Desert in China, where people are already struggling to eke out a living from the land.

As consumption expands, those regions have become more stressed. Trees are cut for firewood, grasslands are overgrazed, fields are over-farmed and lose their nutrients, water becomes scarcer and dirtier.

Technology can make the problem worse. In parts of Australia, irrigation systems are pumping up salty water and slowly poisoning

nityam udvigna-manaso durbhiksa-kara-karsitah
niranne bhu-tale rajan anavrsti-bhayaturah

In the age of Kali, people's minds will always be agitated. They will become emaciated by famine and taxation, my dear King, and will always be disturbed by fear of drought.

-Srimad Bhagavatam 12.3.39

farms. In Saudi Arabia, herdsmen can use water trucks instead of taking their animals from oasis to oasis -- but by staying in one place, the herds are getting bigger and eating all the grass.

In Spain, Portugal, Italy and Greece, coastal resorts are swallowing up water that once moistened the wilderness. Many farmers in those countries still flood their fields instead of using more miserly "drip irrigation," and the resulting shortages are slowly baking the life out of the land.

The result is a patchy "rash" of dead areas, rather than an easy-to-see expansion of existing deserts, scientists say. These areas have their good times and bad times as the weather changes. But in general, they are getting bigger and worse-off.

"It's not as dramatic as a flood or a big disaster like an earthquake," said Richard Thomas of the International Center for Agricultural Research in the Dry Areas in Aleppo, Syria. "There are some bright spots and hot spots. But overall, there is a trend toward increasing degradation."

The trend is speeding up, but it has been going on for centuries, scientists say. Fossilized pollen and seeds, along with ancient tools like grinding stones, show that much of the Middle East, the Mediterranean and North Africa were once green. The Sahara itself was a savanna, and rock paintings show giraffes, elephants and cows once lived there.

Global warming contributes to the problem, making many dry areas drier, scientists say. In the last century, average temperatures

When I first went to Hyderabad they said that for three, four years there was no rain. Is it not? But since Hare Krsna mantra is being chanted, there is rainfall. So they do not know the secret of rainfall. Yajnad bhavanti parjanyah. If you perform yajna, then there will be cloud. Parjanyad anna-sambhavah. Annad bhavanti bhutani parjanyad anna-sambhavah [Bg. 3.14]. This prescription is there. As soon as you stop performing yajna -- you take pleasure in sporting, no yajna... Now big, big cities, they have got big, big Olympian sporting, but no yajna performance. So why there shall not be scarcity of rain? And as soon as there is scarcity of rain, there is scarcity of food grains.

- Srila Prabhupada (Srimad-Bhagavatam 7.12.5 -- Bombay, April 16, 1976)

have risen over 1 degree Fahrenheit worldwide, according to the U.S. Global Change Research Program.

As for the American Southwest, it is too early to tell whether its six-year drought could turn to something more permanent. But scientists note that reservoir levels are dropping as cities like Phoenix and Las Vegas expand.

"In some respects you may have greener vegetation showing up in people's yards, but you may be using water that was destined for the natural environment," said Stuart Marsh of the University of Arizona's Office of Arid Lands Studies. "That might have an effect on the biodiversity surrounding that city."

The Global Change Research Program says global warming could eventually make the Southwest wetter -- but it will also cause more extreme weather, meaning harsher droughts that could kill vegetation. Now, the Southwest drought has become so severe that even the sagebrush is dying.

"The lack of water and the overuse of water, that is going to be a threat to the United States," Thomas said. "In other parts of the world, the problem is poverty that causes people to overuse the land. Most of these ecological systems have tipping points, and once you go past them, things go downhill."

References:

United Nations Convention to Combat Desertification: www.unccd.int

International Center for Agricultural Research in the Dry Areas : www.icarda.org/

University of Arizona Office of Arid Lands Studies: ag.arizona.edu/OALS/oals/oals.html

annad bhavanti bhutani
parjanyad anna-sambhavah
yajnad bhavati parjanyo
yajnah karma-samudbhavah

All living bodies subsist on food grains, which are produced from rains. Rains are produced by performance of yajna [sacrifice], and yajna is born of prescribed duties. ~ Bhagavad-gita 3.14

27.

38% of World's Land in Danger of Turning into Desert

Brian Merchant, February 10, 2010

And now an analysis of the global desertification threat has revealed that 38% of surfaces around the world are vulnerable.

Science Daily reports:

"Researchers have measured the degradation of the planet's soil using the Life Cycle Assessment (LCA), a scientific methodology that analyses the environmental impact of human activities, and which now for the first time includes indicators on desertification. The results show that 38 percent of the world is made up of arid regions at risk of desertification."

Which is unfortunate news, to say the least. The study divided the world's land into "15 natural areas or "eco-regions" according to their degree of aridity." And 8 of those eco regions--that cover 38% of the planet--were deemed at risk of falling victim to desertification.

According to Science Daily, the 8 areas most prone to turn into desert are:

- coastal areas
- the Prairies
- the Mediterranean region

Fierce national competition over water resources has prompted fears that water issues contain the seeds of violent conflict.

- Kofi Annan (UN Chief)

- the savannah
- the temperate Steppes
- the temperate deserts
- tropical and subtropical Steppes
- the tropical and subtropical deserts

The areas at greatest risk are the subtropical deserts--areas in North Africa, Australia, and the Middle East were determined to have the highest desertification risk factor, a 7.6 out of 10. The Mediterranean region had the next highest risk. And bear in mind that while all of this sounds a little heavy on the doom and gloom side, it's very real: there are estimates that in China, for example, 1300 square miles of desert are created every year.

This sobering news means that an additional emphasis must be placed on land management and careful water conservation, especially in the most at-risk areas--unless we want to see a full third of the planet eventually get swallowed up in desert.

Travelling Spiritual Performers Bring Rain To Australia

For the last six years Australians have suffered the worst drought in a thousand years, say leading agriculturalists. As a result the price of food has nearly doubled in some areas. Water conservation schemes are mandated by local governments across the predominantly arid continent. Declared by politicians to be a national crisis, the situation is a recurring theme in the media and in citizens' minds.

Is it just coincidence that one of the longest uninterrupted streaks of wet weather broke at the same time Indradyumna Swami and his traveling spiritual festival team arrived on Australian shores?

Billed as 'Le Carnaval Spirituel' this vivid stage performance brings forth the timeless spiritual wisdom of ancient India's Vedic art and culture; culminating in a rousing full audience participation kirtana (call and response chanting of the Hare Krishna mantra). The European troupe of performing artists present eastern spirituality fused with a twist of the contemporary. Le Carnaval Spirituel, established in France in 1979, has for many years entertained audiences in Europe's largest music festival "Woodstock" which annually attracts crowds in excess of 250,000 people.

(From The West Australian)

28.

Soil Depletion

Plant, Animal And Human Health Deterioration

Soil and organic matter in the soil may be considered our most important national resource. Plant and animal health and subsequently human health depends on healthy soil. Unfortunately our current farm practices have enormously reduced the supply originally present in the soil and we must expect a permanently lower level of agricultural efficiency if we do not take corrective steps urgently. An adequate supply of organic matter in the soil is vital to the survival of life on the planet.

One of the factors responsible for the global health crisis today is soil deterioration. In the Museum of Natural History (New York), is an exhibit showing the effects of soil deficiency on plant life.

These plants, all of the same kind, were reared in soils lacking some element. The exhibit has to be seen to be fully appreciated. The plants range in size from about three inches to about eighteen inches in height. Their color ranges from pale yellow to dark green. The leaves of some are broad, of others narrow. Some of the leaves are kinky. All of the plants except one is defective both in size, color and features and all except that one were raised in soil lacking some food element. For example, one was raised in a soil lacking iron, (the plant has "anemia"), another in a soil lacking potassium, another in a soil lacking nitrogen, etc.

> *"Of all the social and natural crises we humans face, the water crisis is the one that lies at the heart of our survival and that of our planet Earth."*

Deficient soil means deficient food that grows on it. Humans and animals who consume such food also naturally become nutrient deficient. If essential food elements are lacking in their foods, they, like the plants in the experiments, fail and die. Ride along the highway with an experienced farmer and he will point out fertile soil and poor soil, by the vegetation growing thereon; sickly and stunted children (as well as the obese ones) are the result of poor soil.

Empty Foods, Hollow Lives

We've all heard and read it countless times - "the best way to maintain health is to eat a balanced diet including lots of fruit and vegetables". Of course, this is absolutely correct, so long as those fruits and vegetables are not grown on the mineral-depleted soils that necessitate todays ever-increasing range of chemical 'fertilizers'.

As long ago as in 1920s, the British and US Governments were warned by nutritional experts that the soils on which most crops were grown were so deficient in mineral content that the foods grown on them contained less than 10% of the vitamins and minerals they should normally have. The intention of these reports was to highlight the problem so that remedial action could be taken to remineralise the soils, leading once again to naturally healthy fruits and vegetables.

But in last one century, no remedial action has been taken and the problem has been intensified by modern intensive farming methods. The fruits and vegetables not only have little or no vitamin and mineral content, but they are routinely sprayed with such a broad selection of chemicals that they are actually poisonous.

How Can Plants Grow Without Vitamins And Minerals?

They can! Even when the soil is burnt out, farmers can still grow good looking fruits and vegetables. Most plants require only three nutrients to grow, namely nitrogen, phosphorus and water. In the presence of these nutrients, virtually all plants will grow into what appear to be healthy, nutritious adult specimens.

However, if the minerals found in their natural habitat are not present, such plants and their relevant fruits and vegetables will be nutritionally "empty".

As a result of this, these plants are less able to defend themselves against natural predators and are susceptible to insect attack and damage from viruses / bacteria. In order to control this, insecticides, antifungals, antibiotics, pesticides and dozens of other categories of chemicals have been designed to limit the damage done to plants by their natural enemies.

Unfortunately, many of these chemicals have not been properly tested to assess their effects on either plant or human health, and virtually none have been tested in combination to assess their combined effects. The result is that most fruits, vegetables and other plant-based foods are so contaminated with a huge variety of chemicals, and so deficient in nutrient content that they actually do more harm than good.

Section-III

Soil

The Earth's Fragile Skin That Anchors All Life

29.

Civilizations

Founded On Soil

Erosion Destroys Civilizations

Civilizations began where farming was most productive. When farm productivity declined, usually as a result of soil mismanagement, civilizations also declined - and occasionally vanished entirely.

Of the three requisites for a thriving civilization: fertile soil, a dependable water supply and relatively level land with reasonable rainfall which would not cause erosion, it is likely that the third factor was most important, and evidence is mounting that soil degradation has toppled civilizations as surely as military conquest. In countries bordering the Mediterranean, deforestation of slopes and the erosion that followed has created man-made deserts of once productive land. Ancient Romans survived on imported produce from North African regions that are desert today.

A recent study of the collapse in Guatemala around 900 AD of the 1700 year-old Mayan civilization suggests that it fell apart for similar reasons. Researchers have found evidence that population growth among the Mayans was followed by cutting trees on mountainsides to expand areas for farming. The soil erosion that resulted from growing crops on steeper and steeper slopes lowered soil productivity - both in the hills and in the valleys - to a point where the populations could no longer survive in that area. Today only empty ruins remain.

The same process of soil degradation which destroyed civilizations in the past are still at work today.

Firstly, billions of tons of soil are being physically lost each year through accelerated erosion from the action of water and wind and by undesirable changes in soil structure.

Secondly, many soils are being degraded by increases in their salt content, by waterlogging, or by pollution through the indiscriminate application of chemical and industrial wastes.

Thirdly, many soils are losing the minerals and organic matter that make them fertile, and in most cases, these materials are not being replaced nearly as fast as they are being depleted.

Finally, millions of hectares of good farmland are being lost each year to nonfarm purposes; they are being flooded for reservoirs or paved over for highways, airports, and parking lots. The result of all this mismanagement will be less productive agricultural land at a time when meat consumption is growing and expectations are rising among people everywhere for a better life.

30.

Soil Replenishment

And Survival of Civilization

The history of preceding civilizations and cultures indicate the imbalances that have developed when minerals have been permanently transferred from the soil. There are only a few localities in the world where great civilizations have continued to exist through long periods and these have very distinct characteristics.

It required only a few centuries, and in some profligated systems a few decades to produce so serious a mineral depletion of the soil that progressive plant and animal deterioration resulted. In such instances, regular and adequate replenishment was not taking place.

In nature's program, minerals are loaned temporarily to the plants and animals and their return to the soil is essential. In the case of a forest system, this replenishment is made by its plant and animal life automatically. But in case of agriculture, we have to make a conscious effort to do it. A few intelligent civilizations have done it but the balance of the cultures have largely failed at this point.

Another procedure for the replenishing of the depleted soils is by the annual overflow of great river systems which float enrichment from the highlands to the lower plains. This is illustrated by the history of the rivers like the Ganges or the Nile which have carried their generous blanket of fertilizing humus and rich soil over their long course and thus made it possible for the plains to sustain a very dense population. Where human beings have deforested vast mountainsides at the sources of these great waterways, the whole situation has reversed.

For example in China, its two great rivers, the Yangtze and the Yellow River have their source in the isolated vastness of the Himalayas in Tibet and through the centuries have provided the replenishment needed for supporting the vast population of the plains. Because of this natural replenishment, the Chinese have been exceedingly efficient in returning to the soil the minerals borrowed by the plant and animal life. Their efficiency as agriculturists has exceeded that of the residents of many other parts of the world.

But this is no longer so. Under the pressure of industrial progress, more and more of the highlands have been denuded. The forests have been ruthlessly cut down. Vast areas that nature had taken millenniums to forest have been denuded and the soil has been washed away in a few decades. These mountainsides have become a great menace instead of a great storehouse of plant food material for the plains.

The heavy rains now find little impediment and rush madly toward the plains, carrying with them not the rich vegetable matter of the previous era, but clay and rocks. This material is not good. Instead of replenishing the soil, it covers the plains with a layer of silt many feet deep, making it impossible to utilize the fertile soil underneath.

We have only to look over the departed civilizations of historic times to see the wreckage and devastation caused by these processes. The rise and fall in succession of such cultures as those of Greece, Rome, North Africa, Spain, and many districts of Europe, have followed the pattern which we are now pursuing with great pride, under the illusion of progress.

The complacency with which the mass of the people as well as the politicians view this trend is not unlike the drifting of a merry

The average age of the world's greatest civilizations has been two hundred years. These nations have progressed through this sequence: from bondage to spiritual faith; from spiritual faith to great courage; from great courage to liberty; from liberty to abundance; from abundance to selfishness; from selfishness to complacency; from complacency to apathy; from apathy to dependence; from dependency back again to bondage and into oblivion. *-Sir Alex Fraser Tytler* party in the rapids over a great water fall. There seems to be no sense of impending doom.

It is apparent that the present and past one or two generations have taken more than their share of the minerals and have done so without duly returning them back. Thus they have handicapped, to a serious extent, the succeeding generations. It is not easy to replenish the minerals in the soil and it practically takes many centuries to accumulate another layer of topsoil.

This constitutes one of the serious dilemmas. A program that does not include maintaining this balance between population and soil productivity must inevitably lead to disastrous degeneration. Over-population means strife and wars.

The history of many civilizations has recorded a progressive rise while civilizations were using the accumulated nutrition in the topsoil, and a progressive decline when these civilizations were destroying these essential sources of life. Their cycle of rise and fall is strikingly duplicated in our present industrial culture.

'The most successful and long lasting human cultures are those which have lived on nature's income rather than nature's capital.'

31.

Soil Conservation

Deserves The Highest National Priority

Why should the leaders of countries today commit their government and their people to a national programme of soil conservation?

The answer is that soil takes many years to create, but it can be destroyed in almost no time at all. With the loss of soil goes man's ability to grow food crops and graze animals, to produce fibre and forests. It is not enough to describe the soil as a country's greatest source of wealth; it is more than that; it is a country's life. And in one country after another today, the soil is washing or blowing away.

Soil Is A Complex Mixture

Soil covers most of the land surface of the earth in a thin layer, ranging from a few centimeters to several metres deep. It is composed of rock and mineral particles of many sizes mixed with water, air, and living things, both plant and animal, and their remains.

On our scale of time, soil formation is extremely slow. Where the climate is moist and warm, it takes thousands of years to form just a few centimetres of soil. In cold or dry climates, it takes even longer, or soil may not form at all. While soil is technically a renewable resource, its slow rate of formation makes it practically irreplaceable.

Soil is a dynamic mixture, forever changing as water comes and goes and plants and animals live and die. Wind, water, ice, and gravity move soil particles about, sometimes slowly, sometimes rapidly. But even though a soil changes, the layers of soil stay much the same during one human lifetime unless they are moved or scraped, or ploughed by man.

Soil Teems With Life

It is comprised of countless species that create a dynamic and complex ecosystem and is among the most precious resources to humans.

All soil is full of life, and good soils are teeming with it. Plants and animals help keep the soil fertile. Plant roots tunnel through the soil and break it up, and decaying plants form humus. Burrowing animals mix the soil; the excrete of animals contribute nutrients and improve soil structure.

Besides the soil's more obvious inhabitants, which include rodents, insects, mites, slugs and snails, spiders, and earthworms, there are countless microscopic residents, some helpful to man and his crops, some harmful.

Good soils seem to hold the greatest populations of bacteria. Almost without exception, bacteria are involved in basic enzyme transformations that make possible the growth of higher plants, including our food crops. From man's point of view, bacteria may well be the most valuable of the life forms in soil.

Chemical reactions occur in the soil as a result of exchange of positive ions, or cations. More exchanges take place in clay soils than in any other type. These chemical reactions are also essential to plant growth and development and are a good index of soil fertility.

32.

Soil

The Earth's Capital

By Sir Albert Howard, 1940

Since the Industrial Revolution the processes of growth have been speeded up to produce the food and raw materials needed by the population and the factory. Nothing effective has been done to replace the loss of fertility involved in this vast increase in crop and animal production. The consequences have been disastrous.

Half of the topsoil on the planet has been lost in the last 150 years. Agriculture has become unbalanced: the land is in revolt: diseases of all kinds are on the increase: in many parts of the world Nature is removing the worn-out soil by means of erosion.

We are destroying the earth's capital—the soil; we need to aware of the consequences of this.

The maintenance of the fertility of the soil is the first condition of any permanent system of agriculture. In the ordinary processes of crop production fertility is steadily lost: its continuous restoration by means of manuring and soil management is therefore imperative.

33.

Nature's Methods

Of Soil Management

By Sir Albert Howard, 1940

Little or no consideration is paid in the literature of agriculture to the means by which Nature manages land and conducts her water culture. Nevertheless, these natural methods of soil management must form the basis of all our studies of soil fertility.

What are the main principles underlying Nature's agriculture? These can most easily be seen in operation in our woods and forests. Mixed farming is the rule: plants are always found with animals: many species of plants and of animals all live together. In the forest every form of animal life, from mammals to the simplest invertebrates, occurs. The vegetable kingdom exhibits a similar range: there is never any attempt at monoculture: mixed crops and mixed farming are the rule.

The soil is always protected from the direct action of sun, rain, and wind. In this care of the soil strict economy is the watchword: nothing is lost. The whole of the energy of sunlight is made use of by the foliage of the forest canopy and of the undergrowth. The leaves also break up the rainfall into fine spray so that it can the more easily be dealt with by the litter of plant and animal remains which provide the last line of defence of the precious soil. These methods of protection, so effective in dealing with sun and rain, also reduce the power of the strongest winds to a gentle air current. The rainfall in particular is carefully conserved. A large portion is retained in the surface soil: the excess is gently transferred to the subsoil and in due course to the streams and rivers. The fine spray created by the foliage is transformed by the protective ground litter into thin films of water which move slowly downwards, first into the humus layer and then into the soil and subsoil. These latter have been made porous in two ways: by the creation of a wellmarked crumb structure and by a network of drainage and aeration channels made by earthworms and other burrowing animals. The pore space of the forest soil is at its maximum so that there is a large internal soil surface over which the thin films of water can creep.

There is also ample humus for the direct absorption of moisture. The excess drains away slowly by way of the subsoil. There is remarkably little run-off, even from the primeval rain forest. When this occurs it is practically clear water. Hardly any soil is removed.

Nothing in the nature of soil erosion occurs. The streams and rivers in forest areas are always perennial because of the vast quantity of water in slow transit between the rainstorms and the sea. There is therefore little or no drought in forest areas because so much of the rainfall is retained exactly where it is needed. There is no waste anywhere.

The forest manures itself. It makes its own humus and supplies itself with minerals. If we watch a piece of woodland we find that a gentle accumulation of mixed vegetable and animal residues is constantly taking place on the ground and that these wastes are being converted by fungi and bacteria into humus. The processes involved in the early stages of this transformation depend

throughout on oxidation: afterwards they take place in the absence of air. They are sanitary. There is no nuisance of any kind—no smell, no flies, no dustbins, no incinerators, no artificial sewage system, no water-borne diseases, no town councils, and no rates. On the contrary, the forest affords a place for the ideal summer holiday: sufficient shade and an abundance of pure fresh air.

The mineral matter needed by the trees and the undergrowth is obtained from the subsoil. This is collected in dilute solution in water by the deeper roots, which also help in anchoring the trees.

Even in soils markedly deficient in phosphorus trees have no difficulty in obtaining ample supplies of this element. Potash, phosphate, and other minerals are always collected in situ and carried by the transpiration current for use in the green leaves.

Afterwards they are either used in growth or deposited on the floor of the forest in the form of vegetable waste—one of the constituents needed in the synthesis of humus. This humus is again utilized by the roots of the trees. Nature's farming, as seen in the forest, is characterized by two things: (1) a constant circulation of the mineral matter absorbed by the trees; (2) a constant addition of new mineral matter from the vast reserves held in the subsoil. There is therefore no need to add phosphates: there is no necessity for more potash salts. No mineral deficiencies of any kind occur. The supply of all the manure needed is automatic and is provided either by humus or by the soil. There is a natural division of the subject into organic and inorganic. Humus provides the organic manure: the soil the mineral matter.

The soil always carries a large fertility reserve. There is no hand to mouth existence about Nature's farming. The reserves are carried in the upper layers of the soil in the form of humus. Yet any useless accumulation of humus is avoided because it is automatically mingled with the upper soil by the activities of burrowing animals such as earthworms and insects. The extent of this enormous reserve is only realized when the trees are cut down and the virgin land is used for agriculture. When plants like tea, coffee, rubber, and bananas are grown on recently cleared land, good crops can be raised without manure for ten years or more. Like all good administrators, therefore, Nature carries strong liquid reserves effectively invested. There is no squandering of these reserves to be seen anywhere.

The crops and live stock look after themselves. Nature has never found it necessary to design the equivalent of the spraying machine and the poison spray for the control of insect and fungous pests. There is nothing in the nature of vaccines and serums for the protection of the live stock. It is true that all kinds of diseases are to be found here and there among the plants and animals of the forest, but these never assume large proportions. The principle followed is that the plants and animals can very well protect themselves even when such things as parasites are to be found in their midst. Nature's rule in these matters is to live and let live.

If we study the prairie and the ocean we find that similar principles are followed. The grass carpet deals with the rainfall very much as the forest does. There is little or no soil erosion: the run-off is practically clear water. Humus is again stored in the upper soil.

The best of the grassland areas of North America carried a mixed herbage which maintained vast herds of bison. No veterinary service was in existence for keeping these animals alive. When brought into cultivation by the early settlers, so great was the store of fertility that these prairie soils yielded heavy crops of wheat for many years without live stock and without manure.

In lakes, rivers, and the sea, mixed farming is again the rule: a great variety of plants and animals are found living together: nowhere does one find monoculture. The vegetable and animal wastes are again dealt with by effective methods. Nothing is wasted. Humus again plays an important part and is found everywhere in solution, in suspension, and in the deposits of mud. The sea, like the forest and the prairie, manures itself.

The main characteristic of Nature's farming can therefore be summed up in a few words. *Mother earth never attempts to farm without livestock;* she always raises mixed crops; great pains are taken to preserve the soil and to prevent erosion; the mixed vegetable and animal wastes are converted into humus; there is no waste; the processes of growth and the processes of decay balance one another; ample provision is made to maintain large reserves of fertility; the greatest care is taken to store the rainfall; both plaints and animals are left to protect themselves against disease.

In considering the various man-made systems of agriculture, which so far have been devised, it will be interesting to see how far Nature's principles have been adopted, whether they have ever been improved upon, and what happens when they are disregarded.

(From An Agricultural Testament)

34.

Transformation Of A Farmer

Into A Bandit

By Sir Albert Howard, 1940

The wheel of life is made up of two processes—growth and decay. The one is the counterpart of the other. The processes of decay which round off and complete the wheel of life can be seen in operation on the floor of any woodland. It can be seen how the mixed animal and vegetable wastes are converted into humus and how the forest manures itself.

Such are the essential facts in the wheel of life. Growth on the one side: decay on the other. In Nature's farming a balance is struck and maintained between these two complementary processes.

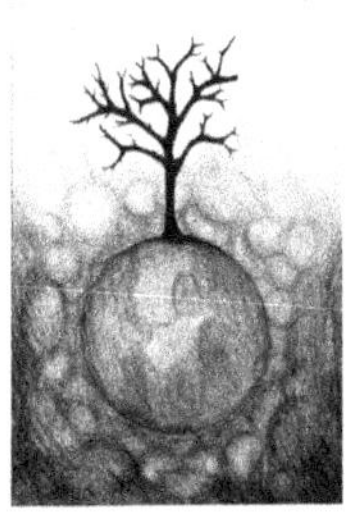

The only man-made systems of agriculture—those to be found in the East—which have stood the test of time have faithfully copied this rule in Nature. It follows therefore that the correct relation between the processes of growth and the processes of decay is the first principle of successful farming. Agriculture must always be balanced. If we speed up growth we must accelerate decay. If, on the other hand, the soil's reserves are squandered, crop production ceases to be good farming: it becomes something very different.

The farmer is transformed into a bandit.

35.

The Agriculture Of The Nations

Which Have Passed Away

By Sir Albert Howard, 1940

The difficulties inherent in the study of the agriculture of the nations which are no more are obvious. Unlike their buildings, where it is possible from a critical study of the buried remains of cities to reproduce a picture of bygone civilizations, the fields of the ancients have seldom been maintained. The land has either gone back to forest or has been used for one system of farming after another.

Peruvian Legacy

In one case, however, the actual fields of a bygone people have been preserved together with the irrigation methods by which these lands were made productive. No written records, alas, have come down to us of the staircase cultivation of the ancient Peruvians, perhaps one of the oldest forms of Stone Age agriculture.

This arose either in mountains or in the upland areas under grass because of the difficulty, before the discovery of iron, of removing the dense forest growth. In Peru irrigated staircase farming seems to have reached its highest known development. More than twenty years ago the National Geographical Society of the United States sent an expedition to study the relics of this ancient method of agriculture, an account of which was published by O. F. Cook in the Society's Magazine of May 1916, under the title: 'Staircase Farms of the Ancients.'

The system of the megalithic people of old Peru was to construct a stairway of terraced fields up the slopes of the mountains, tier upon tier, sometimes as many as fifty in number. The outer retaining walls of these terraces were made of large stones which fit into one another with such accuracy that even at the present day, like those of the Egyptian pyramids, a knife blade cannot be inserted between them.

After the retaining wall was built, the foundation of the future field was prepared by means of coarse stones covered with clay. On this basis layers of soil, several feet thick, originally imported from beyond the great mountains, were super-imposed and then levelled for irrigation. The final result was a small flat field with only just sufficient slope for artificial watering.

In other words, a series of huge flower pots, each provided with ample drainage below, was prepared with incredible labour by this ancient people for their crops. Such were the megalithic achievements in agriculture, beside which 'our undertakings sink into insignificance in face of what this vanished race accomplished. The narrow floors and steep walls of rocky valleys that would appear utterly worthless and hopeless to our engineers were transformed, literally made over, into fertile lands and were the homes of teeming populations in pre-historic days' (O. F. Cook).

The engineers of old Peru did what they did through necessity because iron, steel, reinforced concrete, and the modern power units had not been invented. The plunder of the forest soil was beyond their reach.

These terraced fields had to be irrigated. Water had to be led to them over immense distances by means of aqueducts. Prescott states that one which traversed the district of Condesuyu measured between four and five hundred miles. Cook gives a photograph of one of these channels as a thin dark line traversing a steep mountain wall many hundreds of feet above the valley.

Modern Day Semblance

These ancient methods of agriculture are represented at the present day by the terraced cultivation of the Himalayas, of the mountainous areas of China and Japan, and of the irrigated rice fields so common in the hills of South India, Ceylon, and the Malayan Archipelago.

Conway's description, published in 1894, of the terraces of Hunza on the North-West Frontier of India and of the canal, carried for long distances across the face of precipices to the one available supply of perennial water—the torrent from the Ultor glacier—tallies almost completely with what he found in 1901 in the Bolivian Andes.

This distinguished scholar and mountaineer considered that the native population of Hunza of the present day is living in a stage of civilization that must bear no little likeness to that of the Peruvians under Inca government. An example of this ancient method of farming has thus been preserved through the ages. This relic of the past is interesting from the point of view of quality in food as well as from its historical value.

Rome - The Sword And The Ploughshare

Some other systems of agriculture of the past have come down to us in the form of written records which have furnished ample material for constructive research.

In the case of Rome in particular a fairly complete account of the position of agriculture, from the period of the monarchy to the fall of the Roman Empire, is available; the facts can be conveniently followed in the writings of Mommsen, Heitland, and other scholars. In the case of Rome the Servian Reform (Servius Tullius, 578-534 B.C.) shows very clearly not only that the agricultural class originally preponderated in the State but also that an effort was made to maintain the collective body of freeholders as the pith and marrow of the community. The conception that the constitution itself rested on the freehold

system permeated the whole policy of Roman war and conquest. The aim of war was to increase the number of its freehold members.

'The vanquished community was either compelled to merge entirely into the yeomanry of Rome, or, if not reduced to this extremity, it was required, not to pay a war contribution or a fixed tribute, but to cede a portion, usually a third part, of its domain, which was thereupon regularly occupied by Roman farms.

Many nations have gained victories and made conquests as the Romans did; but none has equalled the Roman in thus making the ground he had won his own by the sweat of his brow, and in securing by the ploughshare what had been gained by the lance.

That which is gained by war may be wrested from the grasp by war again, but it is not so with the conquests made by the plough; whilst the Romans lost many battles, they scarcely ever on making peace ceded Roman soil, and for this result they were indebted to the tenacity with which the farmers clung to their fields and homesteads.

The strength of man and of the State lies in their dominion over the soil; the strength of Rome was built on the most extensive and immediate mastery of her citizens over the soil, and on the compact unity of the body which thus acquired so firm a hold.' (Mommsen)

Capitalist System Vs. Sound Agricultural Practices

Decay Sets In As Large Estates Takeover

These splendid ideals did not persist. During the period which elapsed between the union of Italy and the subjugation of Carthage, a gradual decay of the farmers set in; the small-holdings ceased to yield any substantial clear return; the cultivators one by one faced ruin; the moral tone and frugal habits of the earlier ages of the Republic were lost; the land of the Italian farmers became merged into the larger estates.

The farmland of India had remained fertile for hundreds of thousands of years by the application of cow dung. But now, because of cow slaughter, India has a shortage of cow dung for fertilizer, and chemical fertilizer has ruined the land, killing the soil. Venishakar M. Vasu says, "If we destroy our cattle wealth, not even God can save this country." ~ Lavangalatika Devi Dasi

The landlord capitalist became the centre of the subject. He not only produced at a cheaper rate than the farmer because he had more land, but he began to use slaves. The same space which in the olden time, when small-holdings prevailed, had supported from a hundred to a hundred and fifty families was now occupied by one family of free persons and about fifty, for the most part unmarried, slaves. 'If this was the remedy by which the decaying national economy was to be restored to vigour, it bore, unhappily, an aspect of extreme resemblance to disease' (Mommsen).

The main causes of this decline appear to have been fourfold: the constant drain on the manhood of the country-side by the legions, which culminated in the two long wars with Carthage; the operations of the Roman capitalist landlords which 'contributed quite as much as Hamilcar and Hannibal to the decline in the vigour and the number of the Italian people' (Mommsen); failure to work out a balanced agriculture between crops and live stock and to maintain the fertility of the soil; the employment of slaves instead of free labourers.

During this period the wholesale commerce of Latium passed into the hands of the large landed proprietors who at the same time were the speculators and capitalists. The natural consequence was the destruction of the middle classes, particularly of the small-holders, and the development of landed and moneyed lords on the one hand and of an agricultural proletariat on the other.

The power of capital was greatly enhanced by the growth of the class of tax-farmers and contractors to whom the State farmed out its indirect revenues for a fixed sum. Subsequent political and social conflicts did not give real relief to the agricultural community.

Colonies founded to secure Roman sovereignty over Italy provided farms for the agricultural proletariat, but the root causes

"Human society needs only sufficient grain and sufficient cows to solve its economic problems. All other things but these two are artificial necessities created by man to kill his valuable life at the human level and waste his time in things which are not needed."

~Srila Prabhupada

(Srimad Bhagavatam 3.2.29)

of the decline in agriculture were not removed in spite of the efforts of Cato and other reformers.

A capitalist system of which the apparent interests were fundamentally opposed to a sound agriculture remained supreme. The last half of the second century saw degradation and more and more decadence.

Then came Tiberius Gracchus and the Agrarian Law with the appointment of an official commission to counteract the diminution of the farmer class by the comprehensive establishment of new small-holdings from the whole Italian landed property at the disposal of the State: eighty thousand new Italian farmers were provided with land.

These efforts to restore agriculture to its rightful place in the State were accompanied by many improvements in Roman agriculture which, unfortunately, were most suitable for large estates.

Land no longer able to produce corn became pasture; cattle now roamed over large ranches; the vine and the olive were cultivated with commercial success. These systems of agriculture, however, had to be carried on with slave labour, the supply of which had to be maintained by constant importation.

Such extensive methods of farming naturally failed to supply sufficient food for the population of Italy. Other countries were called upon to furnish essential foodstuffs; province after province was conquered to feed the growing proletariat with corn. These areas in turn slowly yielded to the same decline which had taken place in Italy.

Finally the wealthy classes abandoned the depopulated remnants of the mother country and built themselves a new capital at Constantinople. The situation had to be saved by a migration to fresh lands. In their new capital the Romans relied on the unexhausted fertility of Egypt as well as on that of Asia Minor and the Balkan and Danubian provinces.

Judged by the ordinary standards of achievement the agricultural history of the Roman Empire ended in failure due to inability to realize the fundamental principle that the maintenance of soil fertility coupled with the legitimate claims of the agricultural population should never have been allowed to come in conflict with the operations of the capitalist.

The most important possession of a country is its population. If this is maintained in health and vigour everything else will follow; if this is allowed to decline nothing, not even great riches, can save the country from eventual ruin. It follows, therefore, that the strongest possible support of capital must always be a prosperous and contented country-side. *A working compromise between agriculture and finance should therefore have been evolved. Failure to achieve this naturally ended in the ruin of both.*

(From An Agricultural Testament)

36.

The Practices Of The Orient

By Sir Albert Howard, 1940

In the agriculture of Asia we find ourselves confronted with a system of peasant farming which in essentials soon became stabilized. What is happening to-day in the small fields of India and China took-place many centuries ago. There is here no need to study historical records or to pay a visit to the remains of the megalithic farming of the Andes.

The agricultural practices of the Orient have passed the supreme test—they are almost as permanent as those of the primeval forest, of the prairie or of the ocean. The small holdings of China, for example, are still maintaining a steady output and there is no loss of fertility after forty centuries of management.

What are the chief characteristics of this Eastern farming? The holdings are minute. Taking India as an example, the relation between man power and cultivated area is referred to in the Census Report of 1931 as follows: 'For every agriculturalist there is 2.9 acres of cropped land of which 0.65 of an acre is irrigated. The corresponding figures of 1921 are 2.7 and 0.61.'

In the seventh century, Hwen Thsang visited Mathura. "The people [of Mathura] are soft and easy-natured," wrote Hwen Thsang, "and take delight in performing meritorious works with a view to a future life." At that time, the soil was fertile, and grain grew abundantly. Cotton of a fine texture was cultivated, and there were great forests of mango trees. Hwen Thsang even described the two different types of mango: the large, which remains green, and the small, which turns yellow as it ripens.

These figures illustrate how intense is the struggle for existence in this portion of the tropics. These small-holdings are often cultivated by extensive methods (those suitable for large areas) which utilize neither the full energies of man or beast nor the potential fertility of the soil.

If we turn to the Far East, to China and Japan, a similar system of small-holdings is accompanied by an even more intense pressure of population both human and bovine.

In the introduction to Farmers of Forty Centuries, King states that the three main islands of Japan had in 1907 a population of 46,977,000, maintained on 20,000 square miles of cultivated fields. This is at the rate of 2,349 to the square mile or more than three people to each acre.

In addition, Japan fed on each square mile of cultivation a very large animal population—69 horses and 56 cattle, nearly all employed in labour; 825 poultry; 13 swine, goats, and sheep.

Although no accurate statistics are available in China, the examples quoted by King reveal a condition of affairs not unlike that in Japan. In the Shantung Province a farmer with a family of twelve kept one donkey, one cow, and two pigs on 2.5 acres of cultivated land—a density of population at the rate of 3,072 people, 256 donkeys, 256 cattle, and 512 pigs per square mile.

The average of seven Chinese holdings visited gave a maintenance capacity of 1,783 people, 212 cattle or donkeys, and 399 pigs—nearly 2,000 consumers and 400 rough food transformers per square mile of farmed land. In comparison with these remarkable figures, the corresponding statistics for 1900 in the case of the United States per square mile were: population 61, horses and mules 30.

Two Hungers–The Stomach And The Machine

Food and forage crops are predominant. *The primary function of Eastern agriculture is to supply the cultivators and their cattle with food.* This automatically follows because of the pressure of the population on the land: *the main hunger the soil has to appease is that of the stomach. A subsidiary hunger is that of the machine which needs raw materials for manufacture.*

This extra hunger is new but has developed considerably since the opening of the Suez Canal in 1869 (by which the small fields of the cultivator have been brought into effective contact with the markets of the West) and the establishment of local industries like cotton and jute. To both these hungers soil fertility has to respond. We know from long experience that the fields of India can respond to the hunger of the stomach.

Whether they can fulfil the added demands of the machine remains to be seen. The Suez Canal has only been in operation for seventy years. The first cotton mill in India was opened in 1818 at Fort Gloster, near Calcutta. The jute industry of Bengal has grown up within a century. Jute was first exported in 1838. The first jute mill on the Hoogly began operations in 1855.

These local industries as well as the export trade in raw products for the use of the factories of the West are an extra drain on soil fertility. Their future wellbeing and indeed their very existence is only possible provided adequate steps are taken to maintain this fertility.

There is obviously no point in establishing cotton and jute mills in India, in founding trading agencies like those of Calcutta and in building ships for the conveyance of raw products unless such enterprises are stable and permanent. It would be folly and an obvious waste of capital to pursue such activities if they are founded only on the existing store of soil fertility.

All concerned in the hunger of the machine— government, financiers, manufacturers, and distributors—must see to it that the

Human society's means of living is clearly mentioned here as 'visa', or agriculture and the business of distributing agricultural products, which involves transport, banking, etc. Industry is an artificial means of livelihood, and large-scale industry especially is the source of all the problems of society. In Bhagavad-gita also the duties of the vaisyas, who are engaged in 'visa', are stated as cow protection, agriculture and business. We have already discussed that the human being can safely depend on the cow and agricultural land for his livelihood.

~ Srila Prabhupada (Srimad Bhagavatam 3.6.32)

fields of India are equal to the new burden which has been thrust upon her during the last fifty years or so. The demands of commerce and industry on the one hand and the fertility of the soil on the other must be maintained in correct relation the one to the other.

The response of India to the two hungers—the stomach and the machine—will be evident from a study of Table 1, in which the area in acres under food and fodder crops is compared with that under money crops. The chief food crops in order of importance are rice, pulses, millets, wheat, and fodder crops. The money crops are more varied; cotton and oil seeds are the most important, followed by jute and other fibres, tobacco, tea, coffee, and opium. It will be seen that food and fodder crops comprise 86 percent of the total area under crops and that money crops, as far as extent is concerned, are less important, and constitute only one-seventh of the total cultivated area.

One interesting change in the production of Indian food crops has taken place during the last twenty-five years. The output of sugar used to be insufficient for the towns, and large quantities were imported from Java, Mauritius, and the continent of Europe. Today, thanks to the work at Shahjahanpur in the United Provinces, the new varieties of cane bred at Coimbatore and the protection now enjoyed by the sugar industry, India is almost self-supporting as far as sugar is concerned. The pre-war average amount of sugar imported was 634,000 tons; in 1937-8 the total had fallen to 14,000 tons.

TABLE I

Agricultural Statistics of British India, 1935-36 Area, in acres, under **food and fodder crops**

Rice	79,888,000
Millets	38,144,000
Wheat	25,150,000
Gram	14,897,000
Pulses and other food grains	29,792,000
Fodder crops	10,791,000
Condiments, spices, fruits, vegetables, and miscellaneous food crops	8,308,000
Barley	6,178,000

Maize	6,211,000
Sugar	4,038,000
Total, food and fodder crops	**223,397,000**
Area, in acres, under **money crops**	
Cotton	15,761,000
Oil seeds, chiefly ground-nuts, sesamum, rape, mustard, and linseed	15,662,000
Jute and other fibres	2,706,000
Dyes, tanning materials, drugs, narcotics, and miscellaneous money crops	1,458,000
Tobacco	1,230,000
Tea	787,000
Coffee	97,000
Indigo	40,000
Opium	10,000
Total, money crops	**37,751,000**

Following In Nature's Footsteps

Mixed crops are the rule. In this respect the cultivators of the Orient have followed Nature's method as seen in the primeval forest. Mixed cropping is perhaps most universal when the cereal crop is the main constituent. Crops like millets, wheat, barley, and maize are mixed with an appropriate subsidiary pulse, sometimes a species that ripens much later than the cereal.

The pigeon pea (Cajanus indicus Spreng.), perhaps the most important leguminous crop of the Gangetic alluvium, is grown either with millets or with maize. The mixing of cereals and pulses appears to help both crops. When the two grow together the character of the growth improves.

In Africa and Australia they have so much land -- and instead of relying on nature's bounty of crops, they are raising cattle to kill them. This is their intelligence. People are growing coffee and tea and tobacco, even though they know these things hurt their health. In some parts of the world people are dying for want of grain, and yet in other parts of the world people are growing tobacco, which will only bring disease and death. This is their intelligence.
~ Srila Prabhupada (Back To Godhead, #14-11, 1979)

Do the roots of these crops excrete materials useful to each other? Is the mycorrhizal association found in the roots of these tropical legumes and cereals the agent involved in this excretion? Science at the moment is unable to answer these questions: it is only now beginning to investigate them.

Here we have another instance where the peasants of the East have anticipated and acted upon the solution of one of the problems which Western science is only just beginning to recognize. Whatever may be the reason why crops thrive best when associated in suitable combinations, the fact remains that mixtures generally give better results than monoculture.

This is seen in Great Britain in the growth of dredge corn, in mixed crops of wheat and beans, vetches and rye, clover and rye-grass, and in intensive vegetable growing under glass. The produce raised under Dutch lights has noticeably increased since the mixed cropping of the Chinese vegetable growers of Australia has been copied. Mr. F. A. Secrett was, I believe, the first to introduce this system on a large scale into Great Britain. He informed me that he saw it for the first time at Melbourne.

A balance between live stock and crops is always maintained. Although crops are generally more important than animals in Eastern agriculture, we seldom or never find crops without animals. This is because oxen are required for cultivation and buffaloes for milk. Nevertheless, the waste products of the animal, as is often the case in other parts of the world, are not always fully utilized for the land.

The Chinese have for ages past recognized the importance of the urine of animals and the great value of animal wastes in the preparation of composts. In India far less attention is paid to these wastes and a large portion of the cattle dung available is burnt for fuel.

Although half a million examples of the connection between a fertile soil and a healthy plant exist in India alone, and these natural experiments have been in operation for centuries before experiment stations like Rothamsted were ever thought of, modern agricultural science takes no notice of the results and resolutely refuses to accept them as evidence, largely because they lack the support furnished by the higher mathematics.

Leguminous plants are common. Although it was not till 1888, after a protracted controversy lasting thirty years, that Western science finally accepted as proved the important part played by pulse crops in enriching the soil, centuries of experience had taught the peasants of the East the same lesson.

The leguminous crop in the rotation is everywhere one of their old fixed practices. In some areas, such as the Indo-Gangetic plain, one of these pulses—the pigeon pea—is also made use of as a subsoil cultivator. The deep spreading root system is used to promote the aeration of the closely packed silt soils, which so closely resemble those of the Holland Division of Lincolnshire in Great Britain.

Cultivation is generally superficial and is carried out by wooden ploughs furnished with an iron point. Soil-inverting ploughs, as used in the West for the destruction of weeds, have never been designed by Eastern peoples.

The reasons for this appear to be two: (1) soil inversion for the destruction of weeds is not necessary in a hot climate where the same work is done by the sun for nothing; (2) the preservation of the level of the fields is essential for surface drainage, for preventing local waterlogging, and for irrigation.

Another reason for this surface cultivation has recently been pointed out. The store of nitrogen in the soil in the form of organic matter has to be carefully conserved: it is part of the cultivator's working capital. Too much cultivation and deep ploughing would oxidize this reserve and the balance of soil fertility would soon be destroyed.

Rice is grown whenever possible. By far the most important crop in the East is rice. In India, as has already been pointed out, the production of rice exceeds that of any two food crops put together,

Whenever the soil and water supply permit, rice is invariably grown. A study of this crop is illuminating. At first sight rice appears to contradict one of the great principles of the agricultural science of the West, namely, the dependence of cereals on nitrogenous manures.

Large crops of rice are produced in many parts of India on the same land year after year without the addition of any manure whatever. The rice fields of the country export paddy in large quantities to the centres of population or abroad, but there is no corresponding import of combined nitrogen. Where does the rice crop obtain its nitrogen? One source in all probability is fixation from the atmosphere in the submerged algal film on the surface of the mud. Another is the rice nursery itself, where the seedlings are raised on land heavily manured with cattle dung.

Large quantities of nitrogen and other nutrients are stored in the seedling itself; this at transplanting time contains a veritable arsenal of reserves of all kinds which carry the plant successfully through this process and probably also furnish some of the nitrogen needed during subsequent growth. The manuring of the rice seedling illustrates a very general principle in agriculture, namely, the importance of starting a crop in a really fertile soil and so arranging matters that the plant can absorb a great deal of what it needs as early as possible in its development.

There is an adequate supply of labour. Labour is everywhere abundant, as would naturally follow from the great density of the rural population. Indeed, in India it is so great that if the leisure time of the cultivators and their cattle for a single year could be calculated as money at the local rates a perfectly colossal figure would be obtained. This leisure, however, is not altogether wasted.

It enables the cultivators and their oxen to recover from the periods of intensive work which precede the sowing of the crops and which are needed at harvest time. At these periods time is everything: everybody works from sunrise to sunset. The preparation of the land and the sowing of the crops need the greatest care and skill; the work must be completed in a very short time so that a large labour force is essential.

Taking Burma as an example of an area exporting rice beyond seas, during the twenty years ending 1924, about 25,000,000 tons of paddy have been exported from a tract roughly 10,000,000 acres in area. As unhusked rice contains about 1.2 percent of nitrogen the amount of this element, shipped overseas during twenty years or destroyed in the burning of the husk, is in the neighbourhood of 300,000 tons.

As this constant drain of nitrogen is not made up for by the import of manure, we should expect to find a gradual loss of fertility. Nevertheless, this does not take place either in Burma or in Bengal, where rice has been grown on the same land year after year for centuries. Clearly the soil must obtain fresh supplies of nitrogen from somewhere, otherwise the crop would cease to grow. The only likely source is fixation from the atmosphere, probably in the submerged algal film on the surface of the mud. This is one of the problems of tropical agriculture which is now being investigated.

It will be observed that in this peasant agriculture the great pressure of population on the soil results in poverty, most marked where, as in India, extensive methods are used on small-holdings which really need intensive farming. It is amazing that in spite of this unfavourable factor soil fertility should have been preserved for centuries: *this is because natural means have been used and not artificial manures. The crops are able to withstand the inroads of insects and fungi* without a thin film of protective poison.

Bibliography:

Agricultural Statistics Of India, I, Delhi, 1938.

Howard, A., And Howard, G. L. C. The Development Of Indian Agriculture, Oxford University Press, 1929.

King, F. H. Farmers Of Forty Centuries Or Permanent Agriculture In China, Korea, And Japan, London, 1926.

Agriculture is the noblest profession. It makes society happy, wealthy, healthy, honest, and spiritually advanced for a better life after death. The vaisya community, or the mercantile class of men, take to this profession. In Bhagavad-gita the vaisyas are described as the natural agriculturalists, the protectors of cows, and the general traders. When Lord Sri Krsna incarnated Himself at Vrndavana, He took pleasure in becoming a beloved son of such a vaisya family. Nanda Maharaja was a big protector of cows, and Lord Sri Krsna, as the most beloved son of Nanda Maharaja, used to tend His father's animals in the neighboring forest. By His personal example Lord Krsna wanted to teach us the value of protecting cows. Nanda Maharaja is said to have possessed nine hundred thousand cows, and at the time of Lord Sri Krsna (about five thousand years ago) the tract of land known as Vrndavana was flooded with milk and butter. Therefore God's gifted professions for mankind are agriculture and cow protection.

~ Srila Prabhupada (Light of Bhagavata, Verse 9)

37.

The Agricultural Methods Of The West

By Sir Albert Howard, 1940

If we take a wide survey of the contribution which is being made by the fields of the West, we find that they are engaged in trying to satisfy no less than three hungers: (1) the local hunger of the rural population, including the live stock; (2) the hunger of the growing urban areas, the population of which is unproductive from the point of view of soil fertility; and (3) the hunger of the machine avid for a constant stream of the raw materials required for manufacture.

The urban population during the last century has grown out of all knowledge; the needs of the machine increase as it becomes more and more efficient; falling profits are met by increasing the output of manufactured articles. All this adds to the burden on the land and to the calls on its fertility.

It will not be without interest to analyze critically the agriculture of the West and see how it is fitting itself for its growing task. This can be done by examining its main characteristics. These are as follows: The holding tends to increase in size. There is a great variation in the size of the agricultural holdings of the West from the small family units of France and Switzerland to the immense collective farms of Russia and the spacious ranches of the United States and Argentina.

Side by side with this growth in the size of the farm is the diminution of the number of men per square mile. In Canada, for example, the number of workers per 1,000 acres of cropped land fell from 26 in 1911 to 16 in 1926. Since these data were published the size of the working population has shrunk still further. This state of things has arisen from the scarcity and dearness of labour which has naturally led to the study of labour-saving devices.

Monoculture is the rule. Almost everywhere crops are grown in pure culture. Except in temporary leys, mixed crops are rare. On the rich prairie lands of North America even rotations are unknown: *crops of wheat follow one another and no attempt is made to convert the straw into humus by means of the urine and dung of cattle.* The straw is a tiresome encumbrance and is burnt off annually.

The machine is rapidly replacing the animal. Increasing mechanization is one of the main features of Western agriculture. Whenever a machine can be invented which saves human or animal labour its spread is rapid. Engines and motors of various kinds are the rule everywhere. The electrification of agriculture is beginning. The inevitable march of the combine harvester in all the wheat producing areas of the world is one of the latest examples of the mechanization of the agriculture of the West.

Cultivation tends to be quicker and deeper. There is a growing feeling that the more and the deeper the soil is stirred the better will be the crop. The invention of the gyrotiller, a heavy and expensive soil churn, is one of the answers to this demand. The slaves of the Roman Empire have been replaced by mechanical slaves.

The replacement of the horse and the ox by the internal combustion engine and the electric motor is, however, attended by one great disadvantage. *These machines do not produce urine and dung and so contribute nothing to the maintenance of soil fertility.* In this sense the slaves of Western agriculture are less efficient than those of ancient Rome.

Artificial manures are widely used. The feature of the manuring of the West is the use of artificial manures. The factories engaged during the Great War in the fixation of atmospheric nitrogen for the manufacture of explosives had to find other markets, the use of nitrogenous fertilizers in agriculture increased, until to-day the majority of farmers and market gardeners base their manurial programme on the cheapest forms of nitrogen (N), phosphorus (P), and potassium (K) on the market. What may be conveniently described as the NPK mentality dominates farming alike in the experimental stations and the country-side. Vested interests, entrenched in time of national emergency, have gained a stranglehold.

Artificial manures involve less labour and less trouble than farm-yard manure. The tractor is superior to the horse in power and in speed of work: it needs no food and no expensive care during its long hours of rest. These two agencies have made it easier to run a farm. A satisfactory profit and loss account has been obtained. For the moment farming has been made to pay. But there is another side to this picture. *These chemicals and these machines can do nothing to keep the soil in good heart.* By their use the processes of growth can never be balanced by the processes of decay. All that they can accomplish is the transfer of the soil's capital to current account.

That this is so will be much clearer when the attempts now being made to farm without any animals at all march to their inevitable failure.

Diseases are on the increase. With the spread of artificials and the exhaustion of the original supplies of humus, carried by every fertile soil, there has been a corresponding increase in the diseases of crops and of the animals which feed on them. If the spread of foot-and-mouth disease in Europe and its comparative insignificance among well fed animals in the East are compared, or if the comparison is made between certain areas in Europe, the conclusion is inevitable that there must be an intimate connection between faulty methods of agriculture and animal disease.

In crops like potatoes and fruit, the use of the poison spray has closely followed the reduction in the supplies of farm-yard manure and the diminution of fertility.

Food preservation processes are also on the increase. A feature of the agriculture of the West is the development of food preservation processes by which the journey of products like meat, milk, vegetables, and fruit between the soil and the stomach is prolonged. This is done by freezing, by the use of carbon dioxide, by drying, and by canning. Although food is preserved for a time in this way, what is the effect of these processes on the health of the community during a period of, say, twenty-five years? Is it possible to preserve the first freshness of food? If so then science will have made a very real contribution.

Science has been called in to help production. Another of the features of the agriculture of the West is the development of agricultural science. Efforts have been made to enlist the help of a number of separate sciences in studying the problems of agriculture and in increasing the production of the soil. This has entailed the foundation of numerous experiment stations which every year pour out a large volume of advice in the shape of printed matter.

These mushroom ideas of agriculture are failing; mother earth deprived of her ***manurial rights*** *is in revolt; the land is going on strike; the fertility of the soil is declining.* An examination of the areas which feed the population and the machines of a country like Great Britain leaves no doubt that the soil is no longer able to stand the strain. Soil fertility is rapidly diminishing, particularly in the United States, Canada, Africa, Australia, and New Zealand. In Great Britain itself real farming has already been given up except on the best lands.

The loss of fertility all over the world is indicated by the growing menace of soil erosion. The seriousness of the situation is proved by the attention now being paid to this matter in the press and by the various Administrations. In the United States, for example, the whole resources of government are being mobilized to save what is left of the good earth.

The agricultural record has been briefly reviewed from the standpoint of soil fertility. The main characteristics of the various methods of agriculture have been summarized. The most significant of these are the operations of Nature as seen in the forest. There the fullest use is made of sunlight and rainfall in raising heavy crops of produce and at the same time not only maintaining fertility but actually building up large reserves of humus.

The peasants of China, who pay great attention to the return of all wastes to the land, come nearest to the ideal set by Nature. They have maintained a large population on the land without any falling off in fertility.

The agriculture of ancient Rome failed because it was unable to maintain the soil in a fertile condition. The farmers of the West are repeating the mistakes made by Imperial Rome. The soils of the Roman Empire, however, were only called upon to assuage the hunger of a relatively small population. The demands of the machine were then almost non-existent. In the West there are relatively more stomachs to fill while the growing hunger of the machine is an additional burden on the soil. The Roman Empire lasted for eleven centuries.

How long will the supremacy of the West endure? The answer depends on the wisdom and courage of the population in dealing with the things that matter. Can mankind regulate its affairs so that its chief possession—the fertility of the soil—is preserved? On the answer to this question the future of civilization depends.

Bibliography

Lymington, Viscount. Famine In England, London, 1938.

Mommsen, Theodor. The History Of Rome, Transl. Dickson, London, 1894.

Wrench, G. T. The Wheel Of Health, London, 1938.

38.

Death Of Soil

A Result Of The Policy Failure

By Sir Albert Howard, 1940

Perhaps the most widespread and the most important disease of the soil at the present time is soil erosion, a phase of infertility to which great attention is now being paid. Soil erosion in the very mild form of denudation has been in operation since the beginning of time. It is one of the normal operations of Nature going on everywhere. The minute soil particles which result from the decay of rocks find their way sooner or later to the ocean, but many may linger on the way, often for centuries, in the form of one of the constituents of fertile fields.

This phenomenon can be observed in any river valley. The fringes of the catchment area are frequently uncultivated hills through the thin soils of which the underlying rocks protrude. These are constantly weathered and in the process yield a continuous supply of minute fragments in all stages of decomposition.

The slow rotting of exposed rock surfaces is only one of the forms of decay. The covering of soil is no protection to the underlying strata but rather the reverse, because the soil water, containing carbon dioxide in solution is constantly disintegrating the parent rock, first producing sub-soil and then actual soil. At the same time the remains of plants and animals are converted into humus. The fine soil particles of mineral origin, often mixed with fragments of humus, are then gradually removed by rain, wind, snow, or ice to lower regions. Ultimately the rich valley lands are reached where the accumulations may be many feet in thickness.

One of the main duties of the streams and rivers, which drain the valley, is to transport these soil particles into the sea where fresh land can be laid down. The process looked at as a whole is nothing more than Nature's method of the rotation, not of the crop, but of the soil itself.

When the time comes for the new land to be enclosed and brought into cultivation agriculture is born again. Such operations are well seen in England in Holbeach marsh and similar areas round the Wash. From the time of the Romans to the present day, new areas of fertile soil, which now fetch £100 an acre or even more, have been re-created from the uplands by the Welland, the Nen, and the Ouse. All this fertile land, perhaps the most valuable in England, is the result of two of the most widespread processes in Nature— weathering and denudation.

It is when the tempo of denudation is vastly accelerated by human agencies that a perfectly harmless natural process becomes transformed into a definite disease of the soil. The condition known as soil erosion—a man-made disease—is then established. It is, however, always preceded by infertility: the inefficient, overworked, dying soil is at once removed by the operations of Nature and hustled towards the ocean, so that new land can be created and the rugged individualists—the bandits of agriculture—whose cursed thirst for profit is at the root of the mischief can be given a second chance.

Nature is anxious to make a new and better start and naturally has no patience with the inefficient. Perhaps when the time comes for a new essay in farming, mankind will have learnt a great lesson—how to subordinate the profit motive to the sacred duty of handing over unimpaired to the next generation the heritage of a fertile soil. *Soil erosion is nothing less than the outward and visible sign of the complete failure of a policy.* The causes of this failure are to be found in ourselves.

The damage already done by soil erosion all over the world looked at in the mass is very great and is rapidly increasing. The regional contributions to this destruction, however, vary widely.

In some areas like north-western Europe, where most of the agricultural land is under a permanent or temporary cover crop (in the shape of grass or leys), and there is still a large area of woodland and forest, soil erosion is a minor factor in agriculture.

In other regions like parts of North America, Africa, Australia, and the countries bordering the Mediterranean, where extensive deforestation has been practised and where almost uninterrupted cultivation has been the rule, large tracts of land once fertile have been almost completely destroyed.

USA - Conservation As A National Agenda

The United States of America is perhaps the only country where anything in the nature of an accurate estimate of the damage done by erosion has been made. Theodore Roosevelt first warned the country as to its national importance. Then came the Great War with its high prices, which encouraged the wasteful exploitation of soil fertility on an unprecedented scale. A period of financial depression, a series of droughts and dust-storms, emphasized the urgency of the salvage of agriculture.

During Franklin Roosevelt's Presidency, soil conservation has become a political and social problem of the first importance. In 1937 the condition and needs of the agricultural land of the U.S.A. were appraised. No less than 253,000,000 acres, or 61 per cent. of the total area under crops, had either been completely or partly destroyed or had lost most of its fertility. Only 161,000,000 acres, or 39 percent of the cultivated area, could be safely farmed by present methods.

In less than a century the United States has therefore lost nearly three-fifths of its agricultural capital. If the whole of the potential resources of the country could be utilized and the best possible practices introduced everywhere, about 447,466,000 acres could be brought into use—an area somewhat greater than the present crop land area of 415,334,931 acres. The position therefore is not hopeless. It will, however, be very difficult, very expensive, and very time consuming to restore the vast areas of eroded land even if money is no object and large amounts of manure are used and green-manure crops are ploughed under.

The root of this soil erosion trouble in the United States is misuse of the land. The causes of this misuse include lack of individual knowledge of soil fertility on the part of the pioneers and their descendants; the traditional attitude which regarded the land as a source of profit; defects in farming systems, in tenancy, and finance—most mortgages contain no provisions for the maintenance of fertility; instability of agricultural production (as carried out by millions of individuals), prices and income in contrast to industrial production carried on by a few large corporations.

The need for maintaining a correct relation between industrial and agricultural production so that both can develop in full swing on the basis of abundance has only recently been understood. The country was so vast, its agricultural resources were so immense, that the profit seekers could operate undisturbed until soil fertility—the country's capital—began to vanish at an alarming rate.

The present position, although disquieting, is not impossible. The resources of the Government are being called up to put the land in order. The magnitude of the effort, the mobilization of all available knowledge, the practical steps that are being taken to save what is left of the soil of the country and to help Nature to repair the damage already done are graphically set out in *Soils and Men*, the Year Book of the United States Department of Agriculture of 1938. This is perhaps the best local account of soil erosion which has yet appeared.

Africa

The rapid agricultural development of Africa was soon followed by soil erosion. In South Africa, a pastoral country, some of the best grazing areas are already semi-desert. The Orange Free State in 1879 was covered with rich grass, interspersed with reedy pools, where now only useless gullies are found. Towards the end of the nineteenth century it began to be realized all over South Africa that serious over-stocking was taking place.

In 1928 the Drought Investigation Commission reported that soil erosion was extending rapidly over many parts of the Union, and that the eroded material was silting up reservoirs and rivers and causing a marked decrease in the underground water-supplies. The cause of erosion was considered to be the reduction of vegetal cover brought about by incorrect veld management—the concentration of stock in kraals, over-stocking, and indiscriminate burning to obtain fresh autumn or winter grazing.

In Basutoland, a normally well-watered country, soil erosion is now the most immediately pressing administrative problem. The pressure of population has brought large areas under the plough and has intensified over-stocking on the remaining pasture.

In Kenya the soil erosion problem has become serious during the last three years, both in the native reserves and in the European areas. In the former, wealth depends on the possession of large flocks and herds; barter is carried on in terms of live stock; the bride price is almost universally paid in animals; numbers rather than quality are the rule.

The natural consequence is over-stocking, over-grazing, and the destruction of the natural covering of the soil. Soil erosion is the inevitable result. In the European areas erosion is caused by long and continuous overcropping without the adoption of measures to prevent the loss of soil and to maintain the humus content. Locusts have of late been responsible for greatly accelerated erosion; examples are to be seen where the combined effect of locusts and goats has resulted in the loss of a foot of surface soil in a single rainy season.

The countries bordering the Mediterranean provide striking examples of soil erosion, accompanied by the formation of deserts which are considered to be due to one main cause—the slow and continuous deforestation. Originally well wooded, no forests are to be found in the Mediterranean region proper. Most of the original soil has been washed away by the sudden winter torrents.

In North Africa the fertile cornfields, which existed in Roman times, are now desert. Ferrari in his book on woods and pastures refers to the changes in the soil and climate of Persia after its numerous and majestic parks were destroyed; the soil was transformed into sand; the climate became arid and suffocating; springs first decreased and then disappeared.

Similar changes took place in Egypt when the forests were devastated; a decrease in rainfall and in soil fertility was accompanied by loss of uniformity in the climate. Palestine was once covered with valuable forests and fertile pastures and possessed a cool and moderate climate; to-day its mountains are denuded, its rivers are almost dry, and crop production is reduced to a minimum.

The above examples indicate the wide extent of soil erosion, the very serious damage that is being done, and the fundamental cause of the trouble—misuse of the land. In dealing with the remedies which have been suggested and which are now being tried out, it is essential to envisage the real nature of the problem. It is nothing less than the repair of Nature's drainage system—the river—and of Nature's method of providing the country-side with a regular water-supply. The catchment area of the river is the natural unit in erosion control. In devising this control we must restore the efficiency of the catchment area as a drain and also as a natural storage of water. Once this is accomplished we shall hear very little about soil erosion.

Japan - Preventing A National Disaster

Japan provides perhaps the best example of the control of soil erosion in a country with torrential rains, highly erodible soils, and a topography which renders the retention of the soil on steep slopes very difficult. Here erosion has been effectively held in check, by methods adopted regardless of cost, for the reason that the alternative to their execution would be national disaster.

The great danger from soil erosion in Japan is the deposition of soil debris from the steep mountain slopes on the rice-fields below. The texture of the rice soils must be maintained so that the fields will hold water and allow of the minimum of through drainage.

If such areas became covered with a deep layer of permeable soil, brought down by erosion from the hill-sides, they would no longer hold water, and rice cultivation—the mainstay of Japan's food-supply—would be out of the question.

For this reason the country has spent as much as ten times the capital value of eroding land on soil conservation work, mainly as an insurance for saving the valuable rice lands below. Thus in 1925 the

Tokyo Forestry Board spent 453 yen (£45) per acre in anti-erosion measures on a forest area, valued at 40 yen per acre, in order to save rice-fields lower down valued at 240 to 300 yen per acre.

The dangers from erosion have been recognized in Japan for centuries and an exemplary technique has been developed for preventing them. It is now a definite part of national policy to maintain the upper regions of each catchment area under forest, as the most economical and effective method of controlling flood waters and insuring the production of rice in the valleys. For many years erosion control measures have formed an important item in the national budget.

According to Lowdermilk, erosion control in Japan is like a game of chess. The forest engineer, after studying his eroding valley, makes his first move, locating and building one or more check dams. He waits to see what Nature's response is.

This determines the forest engineer's next move, which may be another dam or two, an increase in the former dam, or the construction of side retaining walls. After another pause for observation, the next move is made and so on until erosion is checkmated.

The operation of natural forces, such as sedimentation and re-vegetation, are guided and used to the best advantage to keep down costs and to obtain practical results. No more is attempted than Nature has already done in the region. By 1929 nearly 2,000,000 hectares of protection forests were used in erosion control. These forest areas do more than control erosion. They help the soil to absorb and maintain large volumes of rain-water and to release it slowly to the rivers and springs.

China - Callous Approach

China, on the other hand, presents a very striking example of the evils which result from the inability of the administration to deal with the whole of a great drainage unit. On the slopes of the upper reaches of the Yellow River extensive soil erosion is constantly going on.

Every year the river transports over 2,000 million tons of soil, sufficient to raise an area of 400 square miles by 5 feet. This is provided by the easily erodible loess soils of the upper reaches of the catchment area. The mud is deposited in the river bed lower down so that the embankments which contain the stream have constantly to be raised.

Periodically the great river wins in this unequal contest and destructive inundations result. The labour expended on the embankments is lost because the nature of the erosion problem as a whole has not been grasped, and the area drained by the Yellow River has not been studied and dealt with as a single organism.

The difficulty now is the over-population of the upper reaches of the catchment area, which prevents afforestation and laying down of grass. Had the Chinese maintained effective control of the upper reaches—the real cause of the trouble—the erosion problem in all probability would have been solved long ago at a lesser cost in labour than that which has been devoted to the embankment of the river.

China, unfortunately, does not stand alone in this matter. A number of other rivers, like the Mississippi, are suffering from overwork, followed by periodical floods as the result of the growth of soil erosion in the upper reaches.

Although the damage done by uncontrolled erosion all over the world is very great, and the case for action needs no argument, nevertheless there is one factor on the credit side which has been overlooked in the recent literature. A considerable amount of new soil is being constantly produced by natural weathering agencies from the sub-soil and the parent rock. This when suitably conserved will soon re-create large stretches of valuable land.

One of the best regions for the study of this question is the black cotton soil of Central India, which overlies the basalt. Here, although erosion is continuous, the soil does not often disappear altogether, for the reason that as the upper layers are removed by rain, fresh soil is reformed from below.

The large amount of earth so produced is well seen in the Gwalior State, where the late Ruler employed an irrigation officer, lent by the Government of India, to construct a number of embankments, each furnished with spillways, across many of the valleys, which had suffered so badly by uncontrolled rain-wash in the past that they appeared to have no soil at all, the scrub vegetation just managing to survive in the crevices of the bare rock. How great is the annual formation of new soil, even in such unpromising circumstances, must be seen to be believed.

In a very few years, the construction of embankments was followed by stretches of fertile land which soon carried fine crops of wheat. A brief illustrated account of the work done by the late Maharaja of Gwalior would be of great value at the moment for introducing a much needed note of optimism in the consideration of this soil erosion problem.

Why is the forest such an effective agent in the prevention of soil erosion and in feeding the springs and rivers? The forest does two things: (1) the trees and undergrowth break up the rainfall into fine spray and the litter on the ground protects the soil from erosion; (2) the residues of the trees and animal life met with in all woodlands are converted into humus, which is then absorbed by the soil underneath, increasing its porosity and water-holding power.

The soil cover and the soil humus together prevent erosion and at the same time store large volumes of water. These factors—soil protection, soil porosity, and water retention—conferred by the living forest cover, provide the key to the solution of the soil erosion problem.

All other purely mechanical remedies such as terracing and drainage are secondary matters, although of course important in their proper place. The soil must have as much cover as possible; it must be well stocked with humus so that it can drink in and retain the rainfall. It follows, therefore, that in the absence of trees there must be a grass cover, some cover-crop, and ample provision for keeping up the supply of humus. Each field so provided suffers little or no erosion.

This confirms the view of Williams (Timiriasev Academy, Moscow) who, before erosion became important in the Soviet Union, advanced an hypothesis that *the decay of past civilizations was due to a decline in soil fertility,* consequent on the destruction of the soil's crumb structure when the increasing demands of civilization necessitated the wholesale ploughing up of grass-land.

Williams regarded grass as the basis of all agricultural land utilization and the soil's chief weapon against the plundering instincts of humanity. His views are exerting a marked influence on soil conservation policy in the U.S.S.R. and indeed apply to many other countries.

Grass is a valuable factor in the correct design and construction of surface drains. Whenever possible these should be wide, very shallow, and completely grassed over. The run-off then drains away as a thin sheet of clear water, leaving all the soil particles behind.

The grass is thereby automatically manured and yields abundant fodder. This simple device was put into practice at the Shahjahanpur Sugar Experiment Station in India. The earth service roads and paths were excavated so that the level was a few inches below that of the cultivated area. They were then grassed over, becoming very effective drains in the rainy season, Carrying off the excess rainfalls clear water without any loss of soil.

If we regard erosion as the natural consequence of improper methods of agriculture, and the catchment area of the river as the natural unit for the application of soil conservation methods, the various remedies available fall into their proper place.

The upper reaches of each river system must be afforested; cover crops including grass and leys must be used to protect the arable surface whenever possible; the humus content of the soil must be increased and the crumb structure restored so that each field can drink in its own rainfall; over-stocking and over-grazing must be prevented; simple mechanical methods for conserving the soil and regulating the run-off, like terracing, contour cultivation and contour drains, must be utilized.

There is, of course, no single anti-erosion device which can be universally adopted. The problem must, in the nature of things, be a local one. Nevertheless, certain guiding principles exist which apply everywhere. First and foremost is the restoration and maintenance of soil fertility, so that each acre of the catchment area can do its duty by absorbing its share of the rainfall.

The Formation Of Alkali Lands

When the land is continuously deprived of oxygen the plant is soon unable to make use of it: a condition of permanent infertility results.

In many parts of the tropics and sub-tropics agriculture is interfered with by accumulations of soluble salts composed of various mixtures of the sulphate, chloride, and carbonate of sodium. Such areas are known as alkali lands.

When the alkali phase is still in the mild or incipient stage, crop production becomes difficult and care has to be taken to prevent matters from getting worse. When the condition is fully established, the soil dies; crop production is then out of the question. Alkali lands are common in Central Asia, India, Persia, Iraq, Egypt, North Africa, and the United States.

At one period it was supposed that alkali soils were the natural consequences of a light rainfall, insufficient to wash out of the land the salts which always form in it by progressive weathering of the rock powder of which all soils largely consist. Hence alkali lands were considered to be a natural feature of arid tracts, such as parts of north-west India, Iraq, and northern Africa, where the rainfall is very small.

Such ideas on the origin and occurrence of alkali lands do not correspond with the facts and are quite misleading. The rainfall of the Province of Oudh, in India, for example, where large stretches of alkali lands naturally occur, is certainly adequate to dissolve the comparatively small quantities of soluble salts found in these infertile areas, if their removal were a question of sufficient water only.

In North Bihar the average rainfall, in the sub-montane tracts where large alkali patches are common, is about 50 to 60 inches a year. Arid conditions, therefore, are not essential for the production of alkali soils; heavy rainfall does not always remove them. What is a necessary condition is impermeability.

In India whenever the land loses its porosity, by the constant surface irrigation of stiff soils with a tendency to impermeability, by the accumulation of stagnant subsoil water, or through some interference with the surface drainage, alkali salts sooner or later appear. Almost any agency, even over-cultivation and overstimulation by means of artificial manures, both of which oxidize the organic matter and slowly destroy the crumb structure, will produce alkali land.

In the neighbourhood of Pusa in North Bihar, old roads and the sites of bamboo clumps and of certain trees such as the tamarind (Tamarindus indica L.) and the pipul (Ficus religiosa L.), always give rise to alkali patches when they are brought into cultivation. The densely packed soil of such areas invariably shows the bluish-green markings which are associated with the activities of those soil organisms which live in badly aerated soils without a supply of free oxygen. A few inches below the alkali patches, which occur on the stiff loess soils of the Quetta Valley, similar bluish-green and brown markings always occur.

In the alkali zone in North Bihar, wells have always to be left open to the air, otherwise the water is contaminated by sulphuretted hydrogen, thereby indicating a well-marked reductive phase in the deeper layers. In a sub-soil drainage experiment on the black soils of the Nira valley in Bombay where perennial irrigation was followed by the formation of alkali land, Mann and Tamhane found that the salt water which ran out of these drains soon smelt strongly of sulphuretted hydrogen, and a white deposit of sulphur was formed at the mouth of each drain, proving how strong were the reducing actions in this soil.

Here the reductive phase in alkali formation was unconsciously demonstrated in an area where alkali salts were unknown until the land was water-logged by overirrigation and the oxygen-supply of the soil was restricted.

The view that the origin of alkali land is bound up with defective soil aeration is supported by the recent work on the origin of saltwater lakes in Siberia. In Lake Szira-Kul, between Bateni and the mountain range of Kizill Kaya, Ossendowski observed in the black ooze taken from the bottom of the lake and in the water a certain distance from the surface an immense network of colonies of sulphur bacilli which gave off large quantities of sulphuretted hydrogen and so destroyed practically all the fish in this lake.

The great water basins in Central Asia are being metamorphosed in a similar way into useless reservoirs of salt water, smelling strongly of hydrogen sulphide. In the limans near Odessa and in portions of the Black Sea, a similar process is taking place.

The fish, sensing the change, are slowly leaving this sea as the layers of water, poisoned by sulphuretted hydrogen, are gradually rising towards the surface. The death of the lakes scattered over the immense plains of Asia and the destruction of the impermeable soils of this continent from alkali salt formation are both due to the same primary cause— intense oxygen starvation. Often this oxygen starvation occurs naturally; in other cases it follows perennial irrigation.

The stages in the development of the alkali condition are somewhat as follows. The first condition is an impermeable soil. Such soils—the usar plains of northern India for example—occur naturally where the climatic conditions favour those biological and physical factors which destroy the soil structure by disintegrating the compound particles into their ultimate units. These latter are so extremely minute and so uniform in size that they form with water a mixture possessing some of the properties of colloids which, when dry, pack into a hard dry mass, practically impermeable to water and very difficult to break up.

Such soils are very old. They have always been impermeable and have never come into cultivation. In addition to the alkali tracts which occur naturally a number are in course of formation as the result of errors in soil management, the chief of which are:

(a) The excessive use of irrigation water. This gradually destroys the binding power of the organic cementing matter which glues the soil particles together, and displaces the soil air. Anaerobic changes, indicated by blue and brownish markings, first occur in the lower layers and finally lead to the death of the soil.

It is this slow destruction of the living soil that must be prevented if the existing schemes of perennial irrigation are to survive. The process is taking place before our eyes to-day in the Canal Colonies of India where irrigation is loosely controlled.

(b) Over-cultivation without due attention to the replenishment of humus. In those continental areas like the Indo-Gangetic plain, where the risk of alkali is greatest, the normal soils contain only a small reserve of humus, because the biological processes which consume organic matter are very intense at certain seasons due to sudden changes from low to very high temperatures and from intensely dry weather to periods of moist tropical conditions.

Accumulations of organic matter such as occur in temperate zones are impossible. There is, therefore, a very small margin of safety.

The *slightest errors in soil management* will not only destroy the small reserve of humus in the soil but also the organic cement on which the compound soil particles and the crumb structure depend.

The result is impermeability, the first stage in the formation of alkali salts.

(c) The use of artificial manures, particularly sulphate of ammonia. The presence of additional combined nitrogen in an easily assimilable form stimulates the growth of fungi and other organisms which, in the search for the organic matter needed for energy and for building up microbial tissue, use up first the reserve of soil humus and then the more resistant organic matter which cements the soil particles.

Ordinarily this glue is not affected by the processes going on in a normally cultivated soil, but it cannot withstand the same processes when stimulated by dressings of artificial manures.

Alkali land therefore starts with a soil in which the oxygen supply is permanently cut off. Matters then go from bad to worse very rapidly. All the oxidation factors which are essential for maintaining a healthy soil cease. A new soil flora—composed of anaerobic organisms which obtain their oxygen from the substratum—is established.

A reduction phase ensues. The easiest source of oxygen—the nitrates—is soon exhausted. The organic matter then undergoes anaerobic fermentation. Sulphuretted hydrogen is produced as the soil dies, just as in the lakes of Central Asia. The final result of the chemical changes that take place is the accumulation of the soluble salts of alkali land—the sulphate, chloride, and carbonate of sodium.

When these salts are present in injurious amounts they appear on the surface in the form of snowwhite and brownish-black incrustations. The former (white alkali) consists largely of the sulphate and chloride of sodium, and the latter (the dreaded black alkali) contains sodium carbonate in addition and owes its dark colour to the fact that this salt is able to dissolve the organic matter in the soil and produce physical conditions which render drainage impossible.

According to Hilgard, sodium carbonate is formed from the sulphate and chloride in the presence of carbon dioxide and water. The action is reversed in the presence of oxygen. Subsequent investigations have modified this view and have shown that the formation of sodium carbonate in soil takes place in stages. The appearance of this salt always marks the end of the chapter. The soil is dead.

Reclamation then becomes difficult on account of the physical conditions set up by these alkali salts and the dissolved organic matter.

The occurrence of alkali land, as would be expected from its origin, is extremely irregular. When ordinary alluvial soils like those of the Punjab and Sind are brought under perennial irrigation, small patches of alkali first appear where the soil is heavy; on stiffer areas the patches are large and tend to run together. On open permeable stretches, on the other hand, there is no alkali.

In tracts like the Western Districts of the United Provinces, where irrigation has been the rule for a long period, zones of well-aerated land carrying fine irrigated crops occur alongside the barren alkali tracts.

Iraq also furnishes interesting examples of the connection between alkali and poor soil aeration. Intensive cultivation under irrigation is only met with in that country where the soils are permeable and the natural drainage is good. Where the drainage and aeration are poor, the alkali condition at once becomes acute.

There are, of course, a number of irrigation schemes, such as the staircase cultivation of the Hunzas in northwest India and of Peru, where the land has been continually watered from time immemorial without any development of alkali salts. In Italy and Switzerland perennial irrigation has been practised for long periods without harm to the soil.

In all such cases, however, careful attention has been paid to drainage and aeration and to the maintenance of humus; the soil processes have been confined by Nature or by man to the oxidative phase; the cement of the compound particles has been protected by keeping up a sufficiency of organic matter. Every possible gradation in alkali land is met with.

Minute quantities of alkali salts in the soil have no injurious effect on crops or on the soil organisms. It is only when the proportion increases beyond a certain limit that they first interfere with growth and finally prevent it altogether. Leguminous crops are particularly sensitive to alkali especially when this contains carbonate of soda.

The action of alkali salts on the plant is a physical one and depends on the osmotic pressure of solutions, which increases with the amount of the dissolved substance. For water to pass readily from the soil into the roots of plants, the osmotic pressure of the cells of the root must be considerably greater than that of the soil solution outside. If the soil solution became stronger than that of the cells, water would pass backwards from the roots to the soil and the crops would dry up.

This state of affairs naturally occurs when the soil becomes charged with alkali salts beyond a certain point. The crops are then unable to take up water and death results. The roots behave like a plump strawberry when placed in a strong solution of sugar.

Like the strawberry they shrink in size because they have lost water to the stronger solution outside. Too much salt in the water therefore makes irrigation water useless and destroys the canal as a commercial proposition.

The reaction of the crop to the first stages in alkali production is interesting. For twenty years at Pusa and eight years in the Quetta Valley I had to farm land, some of which hovered, as it were, on the verge of alkali.

The first indication of the condition is a darkening of the foilage and the slowing down of growth. Attention to soil aeration, to the supply of organic matter, and to the use of deeprooting crops like lucerne and pigeon pea, which break up the subsoil, soon sets matters right.

Disregard of Nature's danger signals, however, leads to trouble—a definite alkali patch is formed. When cotton is grown under canal irrigation on the alluvial soils of the Punjab, the reaction of the plant to incipient alkali is first shown by the failure to set seed, on account of the fact that the anther, the most sensitive portion of the flower, fails to function and to liberate its pollen. The cotton plant naturally finds it difficult to obtain from mild alkali soil all the water it needs—this shortage is instantly reflected in the breakdown of the floral mechanism.

The theory of the reclamation of alkali land is very simple. All that is needed, after treating the soil with sufficient gypsum (which transforms the sodium clays into calcium clays), is to wash out the soluble salts, to add organic matter, and then to farm the land properly.

Such reclaimed soils are then exceedingly fertile and remain so. If sufficient water is available it is sometimes possible to reclaim alkali soils by washing only. I once confirmed this. The berm of a raised water channel at the Quetta Experiment Station was faced with rather heavy soil from an alkali patch. The constant passage of the irrigation water down the water channel soon removed the alkali salts. This soil then produced some of the heaviest crops of grass I have ever seen in the tropics.

When, however, the attempt is made to reclaim alkali areas on a field scale, by flooding and draining, difficulties at once arise unless steps are taken first to replace all the sodium in the soil complex by calcium and then to prevent the further formation of sodium clays.

Even when these reclamation methods succeed, the cost is always considerable; it soon becomes prohibitive; the game is not worth the candle. The removal of the alkali salts is only the first step; large quantities of organic matter are then needed; adequate soil aeration must be provided; the greatest care must be taken to preserve these reclaimed soils and to see that no reversion to the alkali condition occurs.

It is exceedingly easy under canal irrigation to create alkali salts on certain areas. It is exceedingly difficult to reverse the process and to transform alkali land back again into a fertile soil.

Nature has provided, in the shape of alkali salts, a very effective censorship for all schemes of perennial irrigation. The conquest of the desert, by means of the canal, by no means depends on the mere provision of water and arrangements for the periodical flooding of the surface. This is only one of the factors of the problem. The water must be used in such a manner and the soil management must be such that the fertility of the soil is maintained intact.

There is obviously no point in creating, at vast expense, a Canal Colony and producing crops for a generation or two, followed by a desert of alkali land. Such an achievement merely provides another example of agricultural banditry. It must always be remembered that the ancient irrigators never developed any efficient method of perennial irrigation, but were content with the basin system, a device by which irrigation and soil aeration can be combined. This system works like this: The land is embanked; watered once; when dry enough it is cultivated and sown. In this way water can be provided without any interference with soil aeration.

In his studies on irrigation and drainage, King concludes an interesting discussion of this question in the following words, which deserve the fullest consideration on the part of the irrigation authorities all over the world:

'It is a noteworthy fact that the excessive development of alkalis in India, as well as in Egypt and California, is the result of irrigation practices modern in their origin and modes and instituted by people lacking in the traditions of the ancient irrigators, who had worked these same lands thousands of years before. The alkali lands of today, in their intense form, are of modern origin, due to practices which are evidently inadmissible, and which in all probability were known to be so by the people whom our modern civilization has supplanted.'

Bibliography

Gorrie, R. M. 'The Problem Of Soil Erosion In The British Empire, With Special Reference To India', Journal Of The Royal Society Of Arts, Lxxxvi, 1938, P. 901.

Howard, Sir Albert. 'A Note On The Problem Of Soil Erosion', Journal Of The Royal Society Of Arts, Lxxxvi, 1938, P. 926.

Jacks, G. V., And Whyte, R. O. Erosion And Soil Conservation, Bulletin 25, Imperial Bureau Of Pastures And Forage Crops, Aberystwyth, 1938.

The Rape Of The Earth: A World Survey Of Soil Erosion, London, 1939.

Soils And Men, Year Book Of Agriculture, 1938, U.S. Dept. Of Agr., Washington, D.C., 1938.

Alkali Soils

Hilgard, E. W. Soils, New York, 1906.

Howard, A. Crop Production In India, Oxford University Press, 1924.

King, F. H. Irrigation And Drainage, London, 1900.

Ossendowski, F. Man And Mystery In Asia, London, 1924.

Russell, Sir John. Soil Conditions And Plant Growth, London, 1937.

39.

What Romans Could Teach Us

About Soils And Climate Change

Tom Hodgkinson, 2nd October, 2009

What have the Romans ever done for us? Well, they did at least try to warn us that intensive farming would render our soils and civilisation unviable.

I've been reading the old Roman husbandry writers like Columella and Cato. It's fascinating to note that the Romans, in the later period, had very similar problems to us today, in that they fretted about the depletion of the soil and climate change. Columella, who was a native of Cadiz in Southern Spain, then a Roman colony, wrote his books, very roughly speaking, in the years 50-70 AD, nearly 2,000 years ago. His De Re Rustica (On Agriculture), opens with the following comments:

> Again and again I hear leading men of our state condemning now the unfruitfulness of the soil, now the inclemency of the climate for some seasons past, as harmful to crops; and some I hear reconciling the aforesaid complaints, as if on well-founded reasoning, on the ground that, in their opinion, the soil was worn out and exhausted by overproduction of earlier days and can no longer furnish sustenance.

Columella argues that mother earth does not in actual fact become exhausted. It is really a problem of bad stewardship:

> For the matter of husbandry, which all the best of our ancestors had treated with the best of care, we have delivered over to all the worst of our slaves, as if to a hangman for punishment.

Then as now, farms had become enormous factories, with up to 80,000 slaves producing food for the Empire. Elegant Romans had removed themselves from the soil and actually looked down on farming and farmers. This was not the case, says Columella, in the old days, when keeping a smallholding was a noble pursuit:

> We think it beneath us to till our lands with our own hands... but it was a matter of pride with our forefathers to give their attention to farming, from which pursuit came Quinctius Cincinnatus [in 458 BC], summoned from the plough to the dictatorship to be the deliverer of a beleaguered consul and his army, and then, again laying down the power which he relinquished after victory more hastily than he had assumed it for command, to return to the same bullocks and his small ancestral inheritance of four iugera [one iugera was about three fifths of an acre].

Columella also mentions a Roman obesity problem, linked to lazy lifestyles, and criticises, rather like an outraged tabloid newspaper, an over-indulgence in 'drunkenness' and 'gaming':

> The consequence is that ill health attends so slothful a manner of living; for the bodies of our young men are so flabby and enervated that death seems likely to make no change to them.

So Columella, rather like Cobbett in the 19th century, John Seymour in the 20th, and Hugh Fearnley-Whittingstall in our own, sees that the answer to our agricultural problems is to return dignity to the art of husbandry and encourage more people to till the land. We should be doing something useful he says, and we make the mistake of 'plying our hands [ie clapping] in the circuses and theatres rather than in the grainfields and vineyards'.

To this end he wrote twelve books of farming and gardening advice, including many suggestions on how to improve the soil and keep it fertile. He also gives directions on how to look after bees, poultry, pigs, cattle and sheep. Columella's is a hopeful message because it returns power to the people, unlike the limp and ultimately profitless strategy of trying to persuade a capitalist government to change people's ways by force and persuasion. What is astonishing really is how close Columella's advice is to what you might find in a contemporary book about organic gardening or Permaculture. Climate change is clearly nothing new:

> I have found many authorities now worthy of remembrance were convinced that with the long wasting of the ages, weather and climate undergo a change... that regions which formerly, because of the unremitting severity of winter, could not safeguard any shoot of the vine or the olive planted in them, now that the earlier coldness has abated and the weather is becoming more clement, produce oil harvests and the vintages of Bacchus in the greatest abudnance.

The Roman Empire was to last another four hundred years or so after Columella was writing. It would seem that the answer to soil exhaustion and climate change is the same as it has ever been: simply to get back to the land.

Section-IV

Cow

The Life And Soul Of Soil

Vital Role Of Cow

In Soil And Fertility Preservation

40.

Living In Harmony

With The Web of Life

Human race does not exist in isolation on this planet but it's a minuscule link in a complex web of life. Human survival depends on the survival of life on this planet. The delicate web of life can not be disturbed without endangering the human survival itself. There are millions of species and trillions and quadrillions of other life forms. Fate of all these creatures is intimately connected with that of humanity. Its arrogance and ignorance to think that we can survive in isolation. We, like all other life forms, are products of our environment. Destroying our environment is like cutting off the branch we sit on.

Our present economics is anti-life. Our direct and indirect destruction of life has reached mammoth proportions. In the name of food, we kill over 60 billion animals and birds every year and in the name of economic development, we destroy forests and other species. In fact, It is estimated that a minimum of 54,000 species are becoming extinct each year, about 6 an hour, thanks to our 'developmental' efforts.

Even though the majority of mankind is happily entrenched in the electronic age and mostly prefers to live in a concrete jungle, the mysterious link between humans and other life forms continues to hold true. Most of our contact with other life forms these days is limited to the fleeting glimpse of a bird overhead, the scurry of a squirrel or chipmunk across our paths, or the companionship of a pet. Yet the role of these life forms in history is of such great importance that we would not be where we are today without them.

Every traditional society which flourished in the annals of history had their animals and were identified with them. You can not think of Native Americans without picturizing their buffalo herds. These buffaloes roaming the great plains shaped their lives and values. In the case of Laplanders, it was the reindeer and in the case of New England whaling villagers, it was the giant whale. Life of Tibetans revolved around their yaks and camel has been the mainstay of Middle East Asian life. For the people of India and Africa, their survival lay in the humble cow.

In each case, without a particular animal the culture of the people would be entirely different. Because of relations to that animal, whether by herding, shooting, or sailing after it, the society encourages attributes such as toughness, bravery, gentleness, or respect for nature.

Animals that did coexist with humans bore a hefty portion of the burden of transporting mankind toward civilization. One thing we do know is that the role of animals in history was crucial and their impact on our future is just as important. While we are spending billions to find life on Mars, animals on earth are going extinct right under our noses.

Any one with an intact brain would admit the obvious and commonplace fact that animals play a conspicuous part in the life of man. Animals affect everyone's life, whether you're an animal-lover, animal-hater, animal-eater or animal-saver.

Every traditional economy was based on its animals and land. That way, the human civilization survived for thousands of years. But in just last one hundred years, everything has been topsy turvied. Survival of humanity and planet itself has come into question. Some one rightly put it, "In the end, cockroaches would prove to be more intelligent than humans if humans destroy themselves. Intelligence is really a survival skill for the entire species and that which survives proves intelligent on a species level."

41.

Life With Animals

The Ultimate Survival Strategy

Every living being sustains life on the bounties offered by mother nature. The creator is the father and nature is the mother. Mother nature provides for all the necessities of all living beings and in this way every living being can live peacefully in this material world. The human beings, not satisfied with her generous gifts, are devouring the mother nature herself. Its like a child, not satisfied with the mother's milk, want to devour the mother herself.

We, as a society, have come to living off the nature's capital, being dissatisfied with its incomes. In economics, its called bad business. A business enterprise has to survive on its incomes and not on its capital. Capital depletion leads to bankruptcy. In human society, this is leading to our not only ecological but moral, social and economic bankruptcy as well.

At the dawn of the industrial age, we took this wrong turn. We started gorging upon resources that took nature millions of years to create and which were saved up by nature according to its own plan of functioning. Humanity has been squandering these assets at a quickening pace. In fact, we have treated many of these assets as if they had no value.

To check this suicidal drift, we need to seek the animals' cooperation once again. Living with our animals is living in harmony with life, nature and the universe. This is the way the life has been for thousands of years or for as long as one can remember.

Living in harmony and cooperation with our animal friends and with our natural world is the ultimate economic security, ultimate survival strategy.

UN biodiversity chief, Ahmed Djoghlaf says nations risk economic collapse and loss of culture if they do not protect the natural world

He rightly feels that what we are seeing today is a total disaster as we lose biodiversity at an unprecedented rate. If current levels of destruction go on we will reach a tipping point very soon. The future of the planet now depends on remedial measures taken very soon.

Our callous approach to life and nature is threatening the fundamentals of life itself.

According to the UN Environment Programme, the Earth is in the midst of a mass extinction of life. Scientists estimate that 150-200 species of plant, insect, bird and mammal become extinct every 24 hours. This is nearly 1,000 times the "natural" or "background" rate. Around 15% of mammal species and 11% of bird species are classified as threatened with extinction. UN is urging the governments to invest in nature. If they do not, they will pay very heavily later. They will be out of business if they miss the green train.

Mounting losses of ecosystems, species and genetic biodiversity is now threatening all life. In immediate danger are the two billion

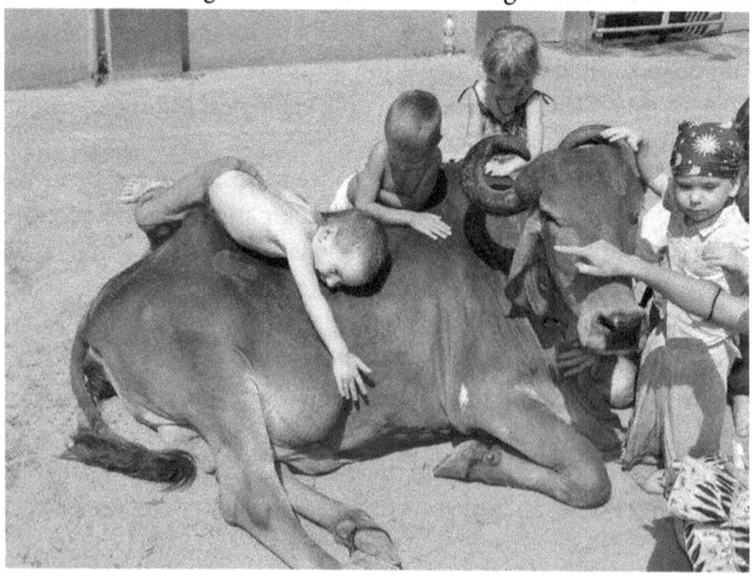

people who live in developing world and whose livelihood depends on their natural resources.

The loss of biodiversity is compounding poverty. By destroying our nature, we are increasing poverty and insecurity. Biodiversity is fundamental to social life, education and aesthetics. It's a human

The aborigines were in fact far better at maintaining and conserving the central Australian landscapes, the central Australian arid regions, than any Australian since European colonization.

The aborigines lived in almost perfect harmony with their environment for thirty thousand years, thirty to forty thousand recorded years -- that's how far our research can take us back -- whereas in a little over a hundred years, European man in Australia has done in places irreparable damage to not only the vegetation but also the soils of arid Australia. It's damage that will probably never, ever be repaired because the environment is so delicate in central Australia that as soon as our cloven-footed animals, our sheep and our cattle, for example, are brought into the arid areas, they eat, they trample, they remove vegetation. This loosens the soil; the soil is very thin. It's very unfertile, and it blows away. And virtually all you have left is rock. And nothing grows, of course, on rock. That's an over-simplification and perhaps an over-dramatization, but this has happened in Australia. It didn't happen when the aborigines lived here, undisturbed by us. It has happened since European man has come.

In Perth, in this city, around this city, since Europeans have come, we have removed forests, we've cut down trees, we've tilled the soil, we have changed the natural order of things, we have increased the amount of water from rain that flows through the soil. It's getting more and more salty. We are affecting our coastal wetlands, as we call them, the lagoons and the lakes and the marshes, so that they are becoming both more salty and more clogged with silt and soil and debris. Water birds can, in some areas, no longer live there. Fish are dying. A lot of migratory fish and crabs, for example, are no longer migrating to their traditional breeding grounds.

We're stuck with that... Whether we like it or not, we're stuck with our urban civilization. We're stuck with our Western way of doing things, unfortunately. ~Justin Murphy, Geographer (Conversation with Srila Prabhupada, May 14, 1975, Perth)

right to live in a healthy environment. Climate change cannot be solved without action on biodiversity, and vice versa.

Because of no contact with the animal world, children are losing contact with nature as they move to a more virtual world. Children today have no clue about nature. Most children in developed countries do not see a live cow or a live horse or an apple tree. How can they protect nature if they do not know it?

Nature has her own way; she better understands her own affairs than we. We have one planet to live on and all our needs have to be satisfied with whatever is in here. We can not import a thing from other planets for our survival, no matter how much we advertise our dubious moon missions. Outcome of such missions is few worthless rocks and sheer wastage of taxpayers' money.

This senseless exploitation of resources can not go on forever. This cradle to grave economics in which we turn every natural resource into a toxic waste is inherently self-destructive. In nature, there is no such thing as waste. So called waste generated by one living being is effectively utilized by another and so on until nothing is left over. This is called the cycle of life. But today our linear system of living which is immensely destructive has replaced this natural cyclical system.

This is where our animals come into picture. Living with animals and natural gifts of land is living on nature's income.

An agriculture and animals based economy is the only model which will stand the test of time. Its just a question of few years before this colossal industrial complex comes down crashing. The cracks are already quite visible and it is up to us to open our eyes.

42.

One Old Man With A Bucket Of Cow Dung

On A Mission To Save India's Soil

Can one man with a bucket of cow dung be a recipe to save the planet? No claim could be more preposterous and more insane. That is until you watch the international awards winning film, One Man One Cow One Planet!

This is the story of a New Zealander spearheading a silent revolution in some of the world's most destitute areas, all alone with a bucket of cow dung. This film is being claimed to be a blueprint for a post-industrial future. It takes you into the heart of the world's most important renaissance.

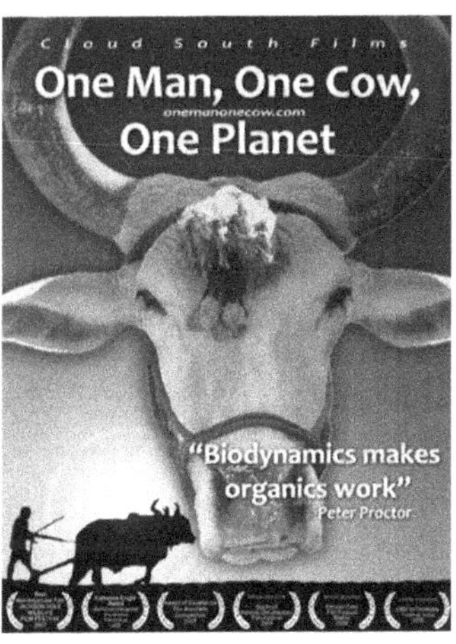

Cloud South Films
One Man, One Cow,
onemanonecow.com
One Planet
"Biodynamics makes organics work"
Peter Proctor

Hero of the film, Peter Proctar is an eighty year old gardener and soil expert from New Zealand. He comes with a vast experience of sixty years in his field.

His favourite animal is the cow because of all the dung she provides. Dung is something that Proctor prizes more highly than gold, jewels, fossil fuels, or many other natural resources. His favourite invertebrate is the earthworm, which he describes as "the unpaid servant of soil health."

In the film, his farm operates on human scale, and is self sustaining, ethical and biologically diverse. It is a blue print for future when fossil fuels will be scarce. World's most valuable commodity will be the knowledge of how to farm and the wisdom of how to grow food that is more than just stuff to fill our stomachs. Indeed what he is presenting may be the last chance this planet has.

His proposal assumes significance as our existence on this planet gets precarious and as modern industrial agriculture destroys the earth.

Desertification, water scarcity, toxic cocktails of agricultural chemicals are pervading our food chains as ocean ecosystems collapse and soil erosion and massive loss of soil fertility take place all over the world. Our ecosystems ore overwhelmed. Humanity's increasing demands are exceeding the Earth's carrying capacity. Modern agriculture causes topsoil to be eroded at 3 million tons per hour. (that's 26 billion tons a year)

Human mass is replacing biomass and other species. The carrying capacity of the earth is almost spent. To maintain our comfort zone lifestyles we will soon need five earths to sustain us in the style to which we have become accustomed.

Mainstay of any civilization is its agriculture. It thrives and survives on agriculture, because food is all that matters, first and foremost. Two other essential ingredients, water and air are of course free. Industries are artificial and they sap the vitality of human beings and nature. They deplete all resources, human, environmental and natural. Industries are a short run drama and a drama doesn't last very long. Next few decades will see the sad ending of this drama when the curtain of realities falls. Agriculture is real life. Drama is for few hours and real life is forever.

Modern industrial agriculture is a form of molesting earth. Humanity is set to pay a big price for this callousness, for this crime. Lesser and lesser number of people today are having an interest in agriculture. Unscrupulous profit crazy corporations are taking over small farms. These corporations have only one relationship with Earth - that of exploitation & profiteering. All this can not last forever. We are taking food for granted, we are taking God's nature for granted. Its not going to work. Something has to change and something will change, whether we like it or not.

Agriculture is still the occupation of almost 50% of the world's population, but the numbers vary from less than 3% in industrialized countries to over 60% in Third World countries.

What if the world were an apple? One quarter of the apple is land and the rest is water. Cut the one quarter of apple, that is land, into half and put aside that half which is deserts and mountains. Peel of what is left and that represents the topsoil that must feed the whole world. This analogy illustrates how important it is to get the best out of the available soil to provide abundant and nutritious food for everyone on the planet.

But modern agriculture couldn't care less for this precious resource. Modern agriculture is at war. It is at war with the mother Earth, with the environment. The weapons used in this war are massive agricultural machines, chemical fertilizers, herbicides, fungicides, pesticides and now genetic manipulation of the crops.

At the end of World War II, military industrial complex needed new markets for its surplus chemicals. It gave birth to Agriculture Industrial Complex. Decades of our addiction to these chemicals have led to toxic oceans, toxic water, toxic air and toxic food. From chemical deserts of factor farms to our inner life, our world as a place of nature is unrecognizable.

Most of us are far removed from the fields where our food is grown. Separating us from our food, our primary source of life, is a vast globalized distribution system, controlled my multinational corporations.

Fight against corporate control of our food is the fight for food sovereignty. When corporations dictate what farmers must grow, they are controlling what all of us must eat. The outcome of battle for agricultural control may dictate the future of the Earth.

India - A Case Study

Peter has been working with crisis-struck farmers in India for the past fifteen years and providing a strong grassroots alternative to industrialised conventional agriculture, which is failing on all counts.

India was one of the richest countries in the world, not because of its gold, diamonds or rubies, but because of its bio-mass. In India they could grow anything because of wonderful temperature, wonderful climate, the moisture and the warmth. That was the secret of India's legendary wealth.

India has been an agro-based economy since time immemorial. Cow has been an integral part (backbone) of its agriculture. But during industrial development and Green revolution, they switched over to chemical based and machine based farming, replacing age old methods involving cow dung, cow urine, and bull power.

Today chemical-based farming (Green Revolution) has rewarded India with degradation of soil, low yields of crops, emergence of new pests and diseases and percolation of toxic chemicals into the food chain.

This has resulted in more than 1.85 lakh farmers committing suicide all over India in the last 15 years. For millennia, organic cow based farming was practiced in India without any marked decline in soil fertility.

Green revolution was supposed to alleviate India's hunger. Viewed holistically, green revolution was a failure. Chemical agriculture destroyed India's natural abundance, farming communities and soil. High yielding plant varieties turned out to use far more water, growing significantly less crop per drop. Today in much of India, rivers have long since dried up. The only water is hundreds of meters down.

Just the thirty or forty years of chemical usage has destroyed the soil which was working flawlessly for thousands of years.

International Water Management Institute describes India's green revolution as 'living on borrowed water, and borrowed time'.

As an alternative to this destruction, the method Peter Proctar is proposing is called biodynamic farming. Cow which is venerated in India, is central to this biodynamic farming. With her 4 stomach, she is a unique animal of digestion. Cow dung forms the basis of many biodynamic preparations. Cow Pat Pit (CPP) is one way of processing cow dung. Proctors call is 'Muck And Magic' because the recipe contains mystical preparations.

A farmer who acquired a field six years ago was asked - how was the land when you started? He replied, "It was quite hard, like a rock." Why? "Because they were using chemicals at that time." How is it now? "In last six years, I have put compost and green manure, and it has become like cotton and even further it has become like butter. Its so smooth and easy to cultivate." Why are so many birds here while you are cultivating? "There is such a population of earth worms now, and as I cultivate they eat the earthworms and insects as they come out," came the reply. Healthy soil makes healthy plants, healthy animals and healthy people.

Cow Based Biodynamic Agriculture

Biodynamic agriculture is an advanced form of organic agriculture with an emphasis on food quality and soil health ; and as such, uses no synthetic fertilizers or pesticides. 'Biodynamic' originates from two Greek words, bios meaning life, and dynamos meaning energy. The pioneer of biodynamic agriculture was Rudolf Steiner (1861-1925) an Austrian scientist, philosopher, and educator. He identified the deleterious effects on the soil and the deterioration of the health and quality of crops and livestock that farmers experienced following the introduction of chemical fertilizers at the turn of the twentieth century. In a series of eight lectures known as the "Agricultural Course" made in 1924 Steiner taught the fundamental ecological principle that the farm is a living organism, an individual self-contained entity within a whole harmonious system. Bio-dynamics is a complete holistic outlook on agriculture. Though the Steiner theory of biodynamics might be a bit esoteric on reading, when it is put into practice, it becomes eminently practical.

Bio-dynamic agriculture is the oldest organic farming movement practiced in over 40 countries in the world. It includes the normal organic farming practices, such as the use of compost, green manures, and crop rotation. In addition, Bio-dynamic agriculture uses a series of Preparations numbered from 500 to 508 which are based on various mineral, plant, and animal substances. These enhance all the bacterial, fungal and mineral processes that are found in the organic farming system. Placing great importance on the auspicious positions of the moon, sun and planets, a Planting Calendar is used for applying the biodynamic preparations, sowing seeds, planting plants, applying liquid manures, spraying fruit trees and crops, and other farming activities. Experience has shown that use of the Bio-dynamic techniques can make all organic farming processes work more quickly and better.

A biodynamic farm is characterized by self-sufficiency and biological diversity where crops and livestock are integrated, nutrients are recycled, and the health of the soil, the crops and animals, and the farmer too, are maintained holistically. Consideration of the farm as an ecosystem feeds into holistic management practices that embrace the environmental, social and economic aspects of the farm.

Its objectives differ significantly from those of conventional agriculture, or agribusiness, which maximizes profit with mechanical and technological inputs for unlimited exploitation of the Earth's resources. The biodynamic model feeds family and farm workers first, and then trade surpluses to the local community. One main difference between organic and biodynamic farms is that organic farms often exclude animals for ethical reasons and monocrop production is common.

Movements like this may be the last chance this planet has for a healthy, secure, and ecologically efficient food supply.

An Emergent Agricultural Knowledge System Against The Corporate Takeover

Biodynamic farms have broad ecological implications as a blueprint for agriculture when fossil fuels are scarce. But they have cultural implications too. Today in India, biodynamic and organic farming methods represent a revolution, one farmer at a time, against the vested interests of agribusiness disguised as science and the global dominance of corporations such as Monsanto.

The advantage of a cow based biodynamic farming for Indian farmers is that they are practising a form of non-chemical, non-toxic farming that does not require the use of any hybrid or GM seeds. Monsanto is a company that's trying to monopolise seed production and its only objective is that every farmer in the world who buys seed should buy from Monsanto. As 60 percent of India's population depends on small and marginal farming, the impact of stopping traditional methods of seed saving and swapping, and taking farmers to court for patent infringement where they are fined 1-2 million rupees, is literally killing them. Indian farmers want freedom and independence from corporate control. They don't want any Monsanto or Syngenta to tell us what seed they grow and what crop they should harvest and what food to eat. This perspective reflects Gandhi's definition of food sovereignty or the right of all people to decide what they grow and eat free of international market forces.

Peter Proctor's book, Grasp The Nettle explains how it all works. The cow dung is used to create compost and it has to be prepared in a particular way. It involves CPP or Cow Pat Pits where the cow dung is layered in pits. One preparation involves the dung being put into cow horns and then being buried. It is left in these pits right through winter after which the crumbly textured mix it turns into is mixed with water and sprayed on the crops. This preparation enables the plant to hold on the moisture for longer and helps the roots go deeper. The experiments are a total success – farms that have adopted this method have healthier and juicier crops. Little wonder that Peter Proctor is almost venerated by the rural Indian farmer, many of whom have wiped out their debts and shed the yoke of corporate control thanks to following his 'back to Nature' philosophy. When they hear he's visiting, they come from miles around, sitting around him with their ubiquitous cell phones, waiting to hear the words of wisdom that fall from his mouth about the state of the soil. After all, it's because of him that thousands of Indian farmers have stopped using chemical fertilizers and pesticides and have adopted biodynamics as a way of life.

Maybe it was easier in India than anywhere else in the world. After all, the cow has always been worshipped and it was easy enough to make them see why this way was so much better. Cow dung has traditionally had a number of uses in India – made into cakes and burnt as fuel, mixed with water and applied on floors to prevent insects from coming into the home and to manufacture biogas. And maybe the typical small holding Indian farmer was in tune with his land – and his cow of course – to realize that the so called green revolution, ushered in by the global pesticide manufacturers, only resulted in polluting the soil, poisoning it as well as the ground water. Unlike many other places in the world, the harsh effects of chemical farming were much more visible here much sooner. With over half the population in India depending on agriculture, this was devastating!

Maybe that's why Peter Proctor can be seen working among the rural farmers of India - maybe it was so much easier to convince people who lived in close communion with the land rather than farmers in more westernized societies where it takes much longer for the ill effects of chemical farming to be felt. Maybe when the holdings are small and so much depends on it, there's a sensitivity to the soil and its needs – and an awareness of when things are good and in harmony with the rest of nature.

India's Organic Farms Work At Village Level

During the past fifteen years, Peter Proctor has visited India twenty five times to teach biodynamic farming methods to as many farmers as possible. Despite his eighty years, he visits ten villages a day. Proctor's involvement is part of a major campaign to promote and encourage alternative forms of agriculture that use no synthetic inputs in response to an epidemic of farmer suicides, most of whom were farming GM crops. This initiative has encouraged 4 million hectares under organic farming methods and 1000 officially supported training schemes for biodynamic and organic farms in the Maharastra region, a suicide hotspot. These farms work at village level and each village has formed an organic federation accredited at district level where farmers participate to solve their own problems. By building up their knowledge base, farmers gain independence from agribusinesses through reducing external inputs. By using biological practices such as green manures, cover cropping, companion planting, and natural insecticides, money is saved that would have been spent on costly pesticides and fertilizers, and is put back into their own communities to improve the quality of life of everyone. This great change in rural prosperity has brought whole communities back together again and enabled the integration of health education in local settings.

The good news about the benefits of this cow based farming has spread quickly and there are now in excess of 2,00,000 compost piles throughout India that recycles cow dung, paddy straw and almost anything else nature provides. Recycling local and freely available resources such as leaves and dung from the ubiquitous and revered cows provides an appropriate alternative technological strategy for Indian farmers and doesn't cost lives.

Alternatives To The "Green Revolution"

How to Save the World is an award winning independent film that documents the progress of Peter Proctor and his cow based biodynamic farming movement in India. Writer and director Barbara Burstyn treats us to visions of verdant biodynamic farms where colorfully dressed young men and women prepare the field preparations and spray them in spiral motions from large copper bowls onto the soil. The old ploughman driving two golden cows tells his story of how the soil has become soft and almost butter-like and alive with worms under biodynamic systems. Elsewhere, we see vast areas of land where the soil is so saturated with layer upon layer of chemicals that it has become great lumps of dry, dusty boulders where no life exists. Organic farmer Jaspal Singh explains that this is the result of the "Green Revolution", that has not only been a killer of farmers, but has made the soil unproductive, waterlogged, pest infested, depleted of nutrients, and has dried up rivers. Singh says that until he learned about chemical free organic and biodynamic farming systems that uses fifty percent less water, he had no alternative to the chemical and water intensive practices of the Green Revolution.

Despite the negative effects of chemicals on the soil, the use of pesticides is increasing and claims the lives of at least 2,00,000 people per year in India by direct poisoning.

In India, seed dealers get huge commission from chemical companies and Indian farmers are forced to take hybrid seeds and pesticides as part of credit packages from salesmen in order to continue to farm. Shantytowns of farmers evicted from their lands because of failed harvests and unpaid debts have sprung up by the rows of pesticide sellers set up in small roadside huts with shelves filled with packets of GM seeds and cans of pesticides. These seeds cost farmers four hundred percent more and yield thirty percent less. A 2006 report shows that 60 percent of farmers using GM seed could not cover their investment, let alone feed their families.

The film, How to Save the World captures the rhythmical movement and vitality of India, but cannot resist a cynical take on the corporate model that builds a market by forcing once independent farmers into debt and dependence on international aid for the very same grains and legumes they once grew successfully. It puts the blame for dependency and for world hunger fairly and squarely on the shoulders of industrial agriculture, genetic engineering, military dominance and trade liberalization, and not on food scarcity. The failure of the globalised free market is starkly symbolized by miles of empty toll roads, built as an infrastructure for corporate agriculture that many farmers in India cannot afford, or do not want.

How to Save The World leaves us in no doubt that one would be fortunate to find oneself connected to an idyllic rural biodynamic farm where pay and conditions for workers and their families are fair, food is of the highest quality and plentiful, the local economy thrives, the farm shop is a sell out, and the farmer and the local community is happy and content. And there is no reason why million more small to medium sized farming communities everywhere could not enjoy the same good life.

What Peter Proctor is doing however, is starting a revolution – quietly and effectively at the grassroots level of agricultural India. Why did this man come all the way from New Zealand braving the heat and dust of rural India to start a movement that would take on the might of multinationals and their juggernaut on its way to control everything we eat and drink? Why would a man who is partially deaf, with one glass eye, an opera buff, who doesn't particularly like spicy Indian curry come halfway across the world to try and save debt-ridden Indian farmers from the clutches of corporations like Monsanto?

Because he cares. Yes, Peter Proctor cares – and this caring goes beyond the farmers and their plight. He cares about the planet and what we as humans are doing to denigrate it. He cares enough to say, 'Enough!' and to do his bit to work in tandem with Nature, not against it. He cares enough to want to try and bring back the beauty of balance that Nature should ideally have. To repair the delicate web of interdependence that all creatures in the world should be connected with.

43.

Cow Represents Earth And Life

There are still parts of the world where people live a pre-industrial life. For example Indonesian Borneo. Daily life in Borneo's upcountry is usually pleasantly dull, as chickens scratch around, the women fan rice on mats to dry it, thunderstorms roll through, the sun dries the muddy paths, flowers riot into bloom, and it all starts over again the next day. Pastoral Mongolia partially fits the category too, with its world revolving around camels, cows and sheep rather than rice and bananas.

Preindustrial life was easy on resources - both human and natural. Before capitalism, most people did not work very long hours. The tempo of life was slow, even leisurely; the pace of work relaxed. People were at peace and so was Earth's environment.

As we have seen in earlier pages, in a vast number of ways and places, the biosphere of this planet is undergoing a great deal of damage. Parts of the environment have already been rendered uninhabitable through toxic wastes and nuclear power plant disasters, while systemic pollution, ozone holes, global warming, and other disasters are increasingly tearing the fabric on which all life depends. That such damage is wrought overwhelmingly by corporations in a competitive international market economy has never been clearer, while the need to replace the existing society with one such as social ecology advances has never been more urgent.

Modernization, the replacement of machines for muscle, is a universal social solvent. Even when resisted by traditional leaders, modernization erodes established social, economic patterns, and threatens ecosystems.

Peasants and tribal members ultimately succumb to mechanisms yielding enhanced productivity. They rapidly scrap traditional practices in favor of those more materially productive.

This modernization has taken a toll on our connection with nature and general web of life.

Gaia - The Earthly Deity

Gaia is the primal Greek goddess personifying the Earth. Gaia is a primordial deity in the ancient Greek pantheon and considered a Mother Goddess.

Etymologically Gaia is a compound word of two elements. Ge, meaning "Earth" and 'aia' is a derivative of an Indo-European stem meaning "Grandmother".

This epical name was revived in 1979 by James Lovelock, in 'Gaia: A New Look at Life on Earth' which proposed a Gaia hypothesis. The hypothesis proposes that living organisms and inorganic material are part of a dynamic system that shapes the Earth's biosphere, and maintains the Earth as a fit environment for life. In some Gaia theory approaches, the Earth itself is viewed as an organism with self-regulatory functions. Further books by Lovelock and others popularized the Gaia Hypothesis, which was widely embraced and passed into common usage as part of the heightened awareness of environmental concerns of the 1990s.

Gaia has been widely held throughout history and has been the basis of a belief which still coexists with the great religions. Today the very word 'Gaia' has come to mean ecology and sustainability. There is a thriving green community which runs the portal Gaia.com.

Interestingly, Vedic literatures have similar words, 'Gau' or 'Gava'. The word Gaia has been derived from these words. If we go to Nirukta, the earliest book of etymology from India, and look up its meaning, the two primary meanings of the word 'gau', from which 'gava' is derived, are given in the following order:

1. The planet earth
2. The animal cow.

By using interchangeable words for cow and Earth, Vedas, the oldest repository of knowledge, emphatically state that cow is a representation of the planet earth itself. In almost all Indian languages, cow is knows as 'gai'.

The cow is complete ecology, a gentle creature and a symbol of abundance. The cow represents life and the sustenance of life. It is so giving, taking nothing but grass. For thousands of years, mankind lived happily, depending on land and cows. To live with cows is to live in perfect cooperation with nature. In a society if you only had cows and agricultural pursuits, you wouldn't require anything else in the name of artificial luxuries.

Cow Protection - The Bottom Line In Sustainable Living

Knowing something of the current state of the environmental movements, we can say with amazing certainty that cow protection and ox power are the very epitome of the bottom line in sustainability. No matter how we look at the topic, there is nothing that comes as close to solving all the problems of the modern world as do cow protection and ox power. Just name an issue of the day: air and water pollution, crime, poverty, unemployment, war, famine, hunger, disease, pestilence, floods, earthquakes, over grazing, global warming, deforestation, etc. A society based on the Vedic principles of cow protection and ox power knows none of these issues.

Rama-rajya, or government by Lord Ramachandra, defines a society which is happy in all respects and where there exists perfect harmony between man, nature and other life forms. This is a society wherein no one even suffers from physical ailments or mental agony. In this society, the demigods or the controlling deities of nature are pleased to adjust universal affairs for the complete satisfaction of all the inhabitants, including even those lower than humans (the animals, birds, plants, fish, reptiles, and germs). And cow protection forms the backbone of such an ideal society. *(Sriman Vaninatha dasa)*

Cow & Environmental Protection

Vedic culture's concern for nature and life in general is reflected in an attitude of reverence for the cow. Cow represents the Vedic values of selfless service, strength, dignity, and non-violence. For these reasons, although not all Hindus are vegetarian, they traditionally abstain from eating beef.

As he [Lord Krsna] grew to be six or seven years old, the Lord was given charge of looking after the cows and bulls in the grazing grounds. He was the son of a well-to-do landholder who owned hundreds of thousands of cows, and according to Vedic economics, one is considered to be a rich man by the strength of his store of grains and cows. Human society needs only sufficient grain and sufficient cows to solve its economic problems. With these two things humanity can solve its eating problem. All other things but these two are artificial necessities created by man to kill his valuable life at the human level and waste his time in things which are not needed.

Lord Krsna, as the teacher of human society, personally showed by His acts that the mercantile community, or the vaisyas, should herd cows and bulls and give protection to the valuable animals. According to smrti regulations, the cow is the mother and the bull is the father of the human being. The cow is the mother because just as one sucks the breast of the mother, human society takes cow's milk. Similarly the bull is the father of human society because the father earns for the children just as the bull tills the ground to produce food grains. Human society will kill its spirit of life by killing the father and the mother.

It is mentioned herein that the beautiful cows and bulls were of various checkered colors -- red, black, blue, green, yellow, ash, etc. And because of their colors and healthy smiling features, the atmosphere was enlivening.
~ Srila Prabhupada (Srimad-Bhagavatam 3.2.29)

Vedic seers could see into the future... to our time when we would feed cows ground up cows and make mad cow disease... a time when mankind would be all bad... they saw us abusing everything...from our fellow creatures to nature all around us.

Africans for thousands of years used cow dung cakes as fuel. In 18th and 19th century missionaries taught them to give up this 'uncivilized' practice. People turned to forests for fuel and in no time the continent was bald.

The cow dung is an important source of producing non-conventional energy. It is a substitute for firewood and electricity. As a result, the forests can be conserved and their faunal wealth can be enriched.

Every single aspect of cow protection interweaves with protection of our environment. In fact, care for cow represents care for life and nature in general. The cow is central to our life and bio-diversity. Cow protection has a great potential in poverty alleviation and employment generation. It deserves full support at all levels.

Stop Killing The Cows, Stop Killing The Planet

We can safely conclude that reducing or eliminating meat consumption would have substantial positive effects on the environment. Fewer trees would be cut, less soil would be eroded, and desertification would be substantially slowed. A major source of air and water pollution would be removed, and scarce fresh water would be conserved. "To go beyond beef is to transform our very thinking about appropriate behavior toward nature," says Jeremy Rifkin. "We come to appreciate the source of our sustenance, the divinely inspired creation that deserves nurture and requires stewardship. Nature is no longer viewed as an enemy to be subdued and tamed."

44.

Vital Role Of Cattle Manure

In Maintaining Soil's Organic Matter

by William A. Albrecht, PhD

The use of "fossil" fuels in their various forms, like coal, kerosene, gasoline, and other volatile, readily combustible materials for agricultural power, to replace that of horses and mules, has brought about the highly exploitative attacks on the natural reserve organic matter of our surface soils.

This has resulted for two reasons: (a) more power and speed are applied to the tilling of the soil more deeply and vigorously to hasten the combustion of the reserves of microbial energy materials; (b) less organic matter is returned in the animal feed residues as manure, modified and improved as nutrition for the soil microbes and plants by the addition of the chemically more complex and varied waste products of the animal's physiology.

Reasons

The first of these reasons has been widely recognized as an unavoidable result of the high labor costs demanding such speed to raise the output per man.

The second reason has been generally disregarded. Manure handling has always been considered a distasteful sanitary chore incidental to keeping animals housed and penned, more than it has been appreciated as an essential, biochemical contribution to the nutritional quality of feeds and foods grown on manured soil. Also, it simultaneously does much to maintain the organic matter in its fertilizing services.

Striking Results . . . Farm manure (six tons per acre annually — right) demonstrated its effects (July, 1958) in the upkeep of soil productivity under corn continuously (69th successive crop) in contrast to that of the soil under similar cropping but no manure (left). The same noble hybrid seed on both plots didn't overcome the difference in the soils due to manure and no manure.

Chemical studies were made of the soils after 67 years of (a) no cattle manure on one set of plots, and (b) six tons per acre annually on another. Each set in such contrasting pairs had been under cropping to (a) wheat, (b) corn, (c) timothy annually, and also to (d) a four-year rotation of corn, oats, wheat, and clover, and (e) a six-year rotation of corn, oats, wheat, clover and timothy. From these data, it is clearly evident how much the use of barnyard manure (cow dung) has contributed to help in the upkeep of the organic matter supply in those soils. (See the table).

Results

Under cropping to wheat continuously, the manured plot of soil had 2.4 percent of organic matter, when the unmanured one had only 2.1 percent. The former was three parts richer over 21 parts, or higher by one-seventh. Under corn continuously, the manure plot was higher in organic matter after the 67 years by four-sevenths. Under timothy sod continuously, the increase figure was nearly one-third; under the four year rotation, it was over one-third; and in the six-year rotation, one-fourth, or next to the lowest, which was the soil under wheat. These were the effects from using manure when in all of these cases the entire crops had been removed and no crop residues were returned.

Soil Composition--Due to Barnyard Manure after 67 Years. Sanborn Field, Columbia, Missouri

Crop	Treatment	Organic Matter %	Phosphoric Acid, lbs/A	Essential M.E. Ca	Cations Exchangeable Mg	Cations Exchangeable K	Cation Exchange Capacity M.E.	Hydrogen M.E.
Wheat	Manure	2.4	189	2140	306	348	16	8.5
Wheat	None	2.1	77	1900	360	312	16	9.5
Corn	Manure	2.2	202	3350	565	414	17	6.0
Corn	None	1.4	62	2600	462	239	15	8.0
Timothy	Manure	3.0	201	2650	216	273	15	4.9
Timothy	None	2.3	15	2100	140	144	15	4.8
4-year Rotation	Manure	2.7	151	3850	245	307	18	4.8
4-year Rotation	None	2.0	38	3230	245	307	18	4.8
6-year Rotation	Manure	2.5	94	2600	210	233	16	4.5
6-year Rotation	None	2.0	22	2866	108	113	16	4.6

Help From Cattle Manure

As additional significance, there is the help from barnyard manure in the maintenance of the inorganic part of the soil fertility. This was shown by the ash analysis of the soil for phosphate (phosphoric acid, P2O5) and for some of the cationic essential elements, namely: calcium, Ca; magnesium, Mg; and potassium, K.

It is also significant to note the help from manure in keeping up the soil's exchange--absorption capacity (cation exchange capacity), in which the organic matter is more active than the clay. Also the lowered soil acidity resulting from the use of manure, as measured by the amount of exchangeable hydrogen, in the soil after 67 years, deserves attention as a modified soil condition not commonly appreciated in connection with this soil treatment.

Contrasting values in each of the above cases of the elements cited for manure and no manure (Table) show clearly that manure has fertility values we do not commonly emphasize.

Demonstration

After nearly three score and ten years of manuring, this treatment demonstrates that, in the matter of soil maintenance, cattle manure has values for:

(a) upkeep of the supply of reserve organic matter;

(b) holding up the soil's content of phosphorus even when manure is relatively low as a fertilizer for this essential element;

(c) preserving the supply of active potassium;

(d) maintaining the exchangeable magnesium;

(e) preserving the supply of active calcium; and

(f) helping to hold down the excessive concentration of acidity as hydrogen.

Manuring the soil has been doing these things for years under merely the belief in it as a good practice, and long before science gave us these few tabulations of what we can prove in favor of cattle manure. In the organic matter of the soil as part of the nutrition of microbes, plants, animals and man there is still much in the realm of good practice and much remains yet for science to prove and to explain.

Respect For Nature

The facts that have been outlined will be observed in nature by those who do not have preconceived ideas about plant growth. Unfortunately the professional agriculturalist often views the effects of soils on the plant's growth with a distant outlook, as if the only problems were those of industrial manipulation of dead materials, with emphasis on the various technologies for economic advantages only.

People who approach agricultural research in this way have lost sight of agriculture as a biological demonstration by the forces of nature, *where man is more spectator than manager in complete control of soil and produce.*

Such unrealistic views of agriculture have led to expressions and views by high government officials that soil is but a chemical and physical agent for the production of larger quantities of crops. They seem unaware that the soil of our planet is a complex material developed through many centuries, having the power of creation, not only for plants, but for everything that lives, moves and has its being upon the earth.

(William A. Albrecht, Phd, 1888–1974, was the Chairman of Department of Soils, College of Agriculture, University of Missouri, Columbia.)

45.

Organic Matter In Soil

Best Defense Against Erosion And Water Shortages

By Donald P. Hopkins

Organic matter in soil can absorb and store much more water than can inorganic fractions. It acts like a sponge, taking up water and releasing it as required by plants. It also helps bind soil particles into larger aggregates, or crumbs. Soils with this kind of structure are very resistant to erosion. Conversely, nearly all soils containing little or no organic matter are very susceptible to erosion.

Besides absorbing water readily, a good cropland soil should be able to dry out or warm up quickly when the rain is over. It should hold enough moisture to supply the needs of a crop between rains, yet permit water to pass through the soil. A good soil will not stay too wet or too dry.

There are other, less obvious relationships between soil erosion and crop selection and management. Many soils can be planted

"A governmental policy which results in impoverishing the natural fertility of land, no matter by what particular name it is called must have an end. It is only a question of time when this truly spendthrift course, this abuse of the goodness of Providence, shall meet its inevitable punishment.

Down to this day, great cities have ever been the worst desolators of the earth. It is for this that they have been so frequently buried many feet beneath the rubbish of their idols of brick, stone, and mortar, to be exhumed in after ages. . . . Their inhabitants violated the laws of nature which govern the health of man and secure the enduring productiveness of the soil.

with maize without much erosion risk if the maize crop is rotated with legumes and small grains. If maize is planted year after year, however, soil losses begin to mount.

46.

Earthworm - Our True Friend

Cattle Manure Is Earthworm Friendly And Chemical Fertilizers Destroy Them

Donald P. Hopkins (Chemicals, Humus And The Soil)

When we come to the larger soil organisms, and in particular to the earthworm, the humus school stands in a stronger position. For the earthworm's contribution to soil fertility has been sadly neglected by modern soil science. Even in the United States where official research facilities in agriculture are so liberally supported, even there most of the modern work upon the earthworm has been left in private hands.

The scientific estimation of the earthworm's contribution begins with Charles Darwin. Over a number of years he observed worms' habits and the many kinds of soil changes they brought about, and in 1881 he published a monograph, The Formation of Vegetable Mould Through the Action of Worms with Observations on Their Habits.

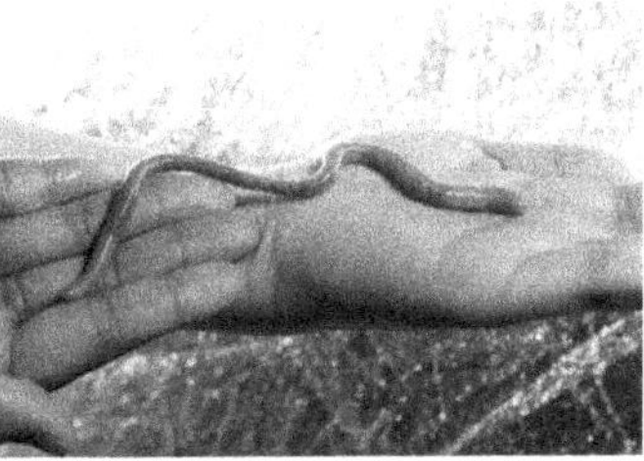

`This exhaustive study was no ordinary record of a naturalist's investigation, otherwise there might be more excuse for the scanty attention paid to it by contemporary and later science. Darwin was not content to present a 'purist' view of the worm—he went much beyond this and stressed the important consequences of worms' habits to the soil. But what should have been a classic in scientific literature caused practically no stir at all. Darwin's fame was to rest upon apes, not worms.

In 1945, however, and in no small measure due to the activity of the modern humus school, this book was republished under the neater title, Darwin on Humus and the Earthworm (Faber and Faber), with a preface by Sir Albert Howard. Not unnaturally Sir Albert tied up Darwin's neglected points with the humus school thesis. But before we inquire into this enrolment of Darwin as a member of the humus school—or should it be as a distinguished past-president?—it is best to see what Darwin himself said.

Apart from a large number of brilliant deductions about the way worms live, Darwin proved that they eat raw and half-decayed organic matter and also pass through their bodies considerable

The charge that chemical fertilizers are a prime cause of unhealthy growth is shown by the following quotations:

'Diseases are on the increase. With the spread of artificials and the exhaustion of the original supplies of humus carried by every fertile soil, there has been a corresponding increase in the diseases of crops and animals which feed upon them.'

~Sir Albert Howard, An Agricultural Testament.

'My canes (raspberry) have not had any chemical fertilizers, and in consequence have not required spraying. In this, as in other cases, no chemicals means no sprays.'

~F. C. King, article in The Market Grower, 18.3.44.

'The accelerated growth induced by chemical fertilizers has the effect, among others, of speeding up the rate at which humus is exhausted. As this depletion of humus proceeded, troubles began. Parasites and diseases appeared in the crops, and epidemics became rife among our livestock, so that poison sprays and sera had to be introduced to control these conditions.'

~E. B. Balfour, The Living Soil.

'Now sulphate of ammonia and many other artificial manures are likely to kill the earthworm and bacterial life of the soil, and so one gets ill-nourished plants which are liable to fatal attack by disease and insect pests. Disease, fungus, and insect pests are always with us, but they chiefly affect the unhealthy plant.'

~Lord Lymington, Famine in England.

quantities of earth. In this intermingling process they produce a rich vegetable mould or well-humified soil, and this is constantly being added to the upper surface of soils.

To quote the original monograph: 'Worms have played a more important part in the history of the world than most persons would at first suppose. In almost all humid countries they are extraordinarily numerous, and for their size possess great muscular power. In many parts of England a weight of more than ten tons of dry earth annually passes through their bodies and is brought to the surface of each acre of land; so that the whole superficial bed of vegetable mould passes through their bodies in the course of every few years. . . .'

And again: 'Worms prepare the ground in an excellent manner for the growth of fibrous-rooted plants and for seedlings of all kinds. They periodically expose the mould to the air, and sift it so that no stones larger than they can swallow are left in it. They mingle the whole together, like a gardener who prepares fine soil for his choicest plants.'

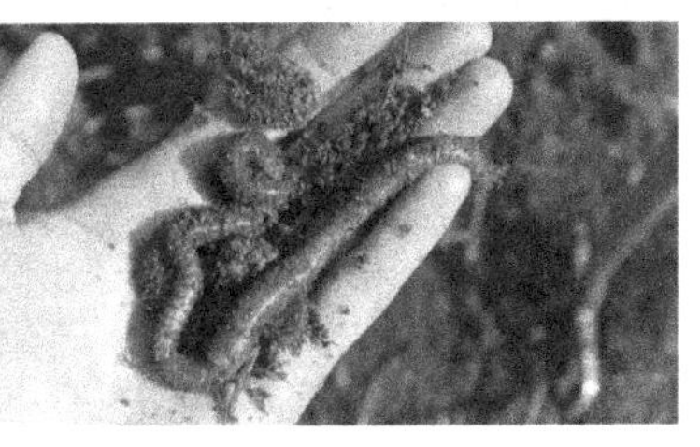

'In this state it is well fitted to retain moisture and to absorb all soluble substances, as well as for the process of nitrification. . . .'

As the figure of ten tons per year per acre may seem surprising, it might be as well to summarize the evidence upon which Darwin based this estimate. He was led to believe that the weight of soil normally brought to the surface by worms was fairly high from studying the rate at which large objects such as big stones or even old ruins were gradually buried in the land. He himself and one or two interested friends collected and weighed all the worm castings over timed periods on measured areas of land, on very small plots of about one square yard or so. If the areas were indeed rather tiny, on the other hand the time period was long; but in any case the run of various results was reasonably consistent.

Darwin was able to check the reliability of these figures by approaching the same problem in a different way.

An American measurement, quoted by Sir Albert Howard, shows that the soil of the castings is very much richer than the corresponding soil.

The point that Darwin made verbally in 1881 is thus well and truly confirmed by these 1942 figures from Connecticut Experiment Station.

There may have been other similar measurements in the interim but, if so, little attention has been paid to them. 1881 to 1942 is a long time, and the humus school can well claim in this matter that 'official' research has largely ignored a known biological factor in soil fertility - earthworms.

The Cattle Compost Factory

The compost factory at Indore adjoins the cattle shed. This latter has been constructed for forty oxen and is provided with a cubicle, in which a supply of powdered urine earth can conveniently be stored. The cattle stand on earth. A paved floor is undesirable as the animals rest better, are more comfortable and are warmer on an earthen floor. The earth on which the cattle stand absorbs the urine, and is replaced by new earth to a depth of six inches every three or four months. The compost factory itself is a very simple arrangement. It consists of thirty-three pits, each 30 ft. by 14 ft. and 2 ft. deep with sloping sides, arranged in three rows with sufficient space between the lines of pits for the easy passage of loaded carts. The pits themselves are in pairs, with a space 12 ft. wide between each pair. This arrangement enables carts to be brought up to any particular pit. Ample access from the compost factory to the main roads is also necessary, so that during the carting of the compost to the fields, loaded and empty carts can easily pass one another, and also leave room for the standing carts which are being filled.

Manurial Value Of Indore Compost

One-cart load of Indore compost is equivalent, as regards nitrogen content, to two cart-loads of ordinary farmyard manure. Properly made compost has another great advantage over ordinary manure, namely its fine powdery character which enables it to be uniformly incorporated with the soil and to be rapidly converted into food materials for the crop. Taking everything into consideration, Indore compost has about three times the value of ordinary manure.

~ By Sir Albert Howard, (An Agricultural Testament)

With this point behind them the humus school has launched a strong attack at chemical fertilizers on the grounds that these materials discourage earthworms, drive them away and thus greatly diminish their powerful contributions. Where chemical fertilizers are used the earthworm populations are low or nil; additional supplies of chemical NPK are then needed to make up for the supplies from the soil's store that would otherwise have been made available by the worms.

47.

The Importance Of Farmyard Dung

In The Beginning Days, Even Fertilizer Companies Admitted It

Donald P. Hopkins (Chemicals Humus, And The Soil)

It is often said that those who have chemicals to sell have harnessed science to their own interests rather than to the interests of the soil.

That is to say, they have paid chemists to concentrate upon the kinds of research that deal with the effects of chemicals whilst nobody else has been very ready or able to foot the bill for scientific inquiries in other directions. It is also often said that the advertising pressure of large chemical firms over-accentuates the favourable claims of chemicals, and this has in a long period led to an unbalanced fashion for chemicals even among scientists themselves.

A kind of fixed-idea-mentality has been built up. From my own contacts with people who directly live by the soil and its produce, I very much doubt whether there could be any kind of humanity less susceptible either to subtle or crude advertising.

Suspicion and scepticism go hand in hand with the plough and the harvester.

Here are extracts from pre-war literature issued for sales-purposes by one of the largest chemical companies and fertilizer manufacturers in Britain.

When writing the original edition of this book, I made a survey of the sales-literature this company had issued, though it was admittedly limited to the amount that still remained intact and could be gathered together during the war period. I was anxious to check whether charges of chemical bias, and in particular the advocating of using fertilizers to the exclusion of manures, could be substantiated. I found that on the contrary the complementary use of manure and fertilizers had often been strongly advised.

'The most successful potato growers manure their crops with dung and complete fertilizers.'

'Fertilizers will help to restore exhausted grasses to vigour, but cannot give their full effect unless the pasture is rested at the right time and is therefore in a fit condition to respond.'

'In every country where sugar beet is cultivated, it has been found both essential and profitable to manure the land well with dung and a complete fertilizer.'

'The best rule for the amateur to follow is to apply as much dung as he can get in order to improve the physical condition of his soil, and to make up for any lack of plant-food by the use of other organic and artificial fertilizers.'

'It is not possible to grow well-developed healthy plants with the aid of nitrogen exclusively, whether it be applied in the form of sulphate of ammonia or any other purely nitrogenous fertilizer . . . sulphate of ammonia should be used in conjunction with fertilizers supplying

The prosecution states that plants raised with chemicals are less robust, less able to withstand the attacks of fungi, pests, and viruses; so that epidemic ill health results. This being so, extra yields are short-term and illusory benefits, quantity and not quality, and quantity in any case that must be frequently discounted by severe loss.

The humus school have suggested why this happens, and we have already analysed some of their evidence for specific charges against chemicals in chapter eleven. But details hardly matter—a fact is still a fact whether it can be explained or not. And we should be able to decide whether the use of fertilizers has increased diseases and attacks by pests—it is the kind of thing that can be assessed reasonably well by observation and measurement; in the widest sense, indeed, by mass observation and statistics. ~ Donald P. Hopkins phosphates and potash. . . . Supplement your work of cultivation by conserving all the trimmings from your garden, all lawn mowings, hedge clippings, dead plants, and the like, in a compost heap.'

'Fertility depends on light and air; on methods of cultivation; on the presence in the soil of water; organic matter (humus); of bacteria; of nitrogen, phosphates, potash, calcium; and of small quantities of what are known as the minor elements. All these factors are interrelated so that all must be maintained at the right level if fertility is not to suffer.'

None of these quotations was printed in any lesser type than the type in the rest of the general statement. By way of history, here are extracts from a very old-established fertilizer manufacturers' guide for farmers issued as long ago as 1857.

'Judiciously applied, in agriculture, artificial manures meet the natural deficiency of valuable fertilizing constituents in farmyard manures, and when both kinds are used conjointly (which we always recommend when practicable) the value of dung is greatly enhanced.'

'And it should always be borne in mind that these (artificial) manures are intended to supply any deficiency in quantity or quality of farmyard dung, and not to supersede its use.'

A good deal of compost has been made on tea-estates in North India, where the necessary vegetable matter is easily collected from the uncultivated land near the estates. The collection of this material has, however, in places led to bad soil erosion.

'It is stated that the results are best when sufficient quantities of cattle or other animal manure are available; they are said to be less satisfactory where the animal manure has been deficient. Attempts to run tea estates on compost alone, however, proved unsatisfactory; it was necessary to provide the proper artificials where ever sufficient cattle manure was lacking. ~ Sir Albert Howard

48.

Importance Of Humus In Soil Preservation

And Role Of Farmyard Dung In Humus creation

Humus is a word that was invented before the days of Liebig to cover up a large number of complexities that could not be simplified, and the word remains because the situation also remains. We are still very much in the dark about the precise composition of humus and exactly why it is so important.

However, evidence that comes from observing effects must not be rated lower in value than evidence that can explain the effects. To take up again the analogy of the trial for murder; if a witness is produced who saw the accused stick a knife into the victim, that evidence—provided the witness is reliable—outweighs all the circumstantial evidence that tries to show why the accused had reason to commit the murder or how he had the opportunity and so on.

Humus is the dark brown or black decomposed organic matter invariably noticeable in what are called rich soils. Farmyard manure, stable manure, vegetable waste matter, these in their fresh forms are not humus but rather the raw materials that can be turned into humus.

Its Properties

By far the simplest way to interpret humus is to list the things it can do. Its properties—from the point of view of soil fertility—can be divided into three classes; mechanical or physical, biological, and chemical.

The physical or mechanical effects are as follows. It can bind together a light, crumbling soil; but it can also make a sticky, heavy soil more friable.

The erosion disasters in the United States, in which thousands of crop-producing acres became a desert or 'dust-bowl', are now generally admitted to have been caused by humus deficiency. The soils were originally very rich; they were farmed without attention to humus replacement—the top-soils became more and more friable, crumbled into dry dust; then, once a certain level in deterioration was reached, nothing could save the soils from being swept away by rough weather.

Humus keeps the soil particles apart and so keeps air moving through the soil. It holds water better than soil so that plants in a humus-rich soil are less affected by drought conditions.

Sir John Russell has reported that plots at Rothamsted regularly treated with farmyard manures contain 3 to 4 per cent more water than plots under similar cropping conditions but which receive non-humus containing manures. And, of course, every gardener knows how much better are his moisture-needing summer crops like beans, peas, tomatoes, marrows, etc., if rotted organic matter is trenched in underneath them.

A minor physical effect comes from its colour, for by tending to darken the soil it increases the absorption capacity of the soil for warm sun rays and thus can keep the soil temperature a little higher.

Its biological properties are vital. It increases the activities of so many organisms whose work is a favourable factor to soil fertility. From the earthworm to the invisible earth bacteria, the life of the soil population is stimulated by the presence of humus. This is an

'Humus is a natural body; it is a composite entity, just as are plant, animal, and microbial substances; it is even more complex chemically, since all these materials contribute to its formation.'

~ S. A. Waksman

important matter that we shall have to consider in much more detail later—for the moment let it be left at that.

Chemically, humus—or at any rate the manures that contain humus—will contain supplies of the elements of plant-growth. This is obvious for the manures have been produced by the 'rotting' of plant material-—whether a cow has eaten, digested, and expelled grass or mangolds or whether waste green material has been directly composted in a heap.

At this preliminary and general stage, we need not go into the question of how much of the original minerals etc. taken from the soil by the plants will still remain in the humus type manures which are later put back into the soil; but clearly the manures will have some definite value of this kind.

Also, in this plant food department of soil fertility, humus plays an indirect role; for it can increase the soil's capacity for retaining soluble (and therefore active) kinds of these plant-foods. As we shall see later, there is always a tendency for immediate fertility in soils to be lost through the soil's inability to hold all its active plant-food supply indefinitely. So that the help of humus in compensating for this adverse factor is important.

Humus Creation

How can the humus content of the soil be kept up? By the digging or ploughing in of animal manures—farmyard, stable, or sewage manures. By composting all organic wastes. By the deliberate growing of what are called 'green manure' crops, e.g. mustard, for digging in.

And by the digging in of all crop wastes left after harvesting, e.g. stubble, mangold tops, and so on. When grassland is converted to arable land, as has happened so widely in wartime, the turned-in turf provides valuable humus as it slowly rots down in the soil.

It will be noted that the application of fertilizers has not been given as a direct method of providing humus, but the application of bulky organic manures is. This is a fundamental distinction.

Larger crops mean bigger residues for ploughing-back, and also bigger root systems left in the soil to rot down into humus. The extent to which the below-ground parts of crops provide humus is much under-estimated. When a ley is ploughed in, we realize obviously enough that its green stem and foliage matter must make a big contribution to the soil's humus; but the thick mass of root systems underneath may well make an even bigger one.

Farmyard Manure Vs Fertilizer

The difference between farmyard manures and fertilizers is confused by the fact that the manures contain not only humus but also supplies of the fertility elements. In this latter sense, therefore, they overlap the function of fertilizers. We must neither exaggerate the value of this overlap, nor underestimate it.

Important questions affecting the whole argument about fertilizers are: (1) how much 'chemical' plant-food do these natural manures provide; (2) how much natural manure of all kinds is, or can be made, available; (3) how much plant-food must be added to the soil to maintain fertility at the level necessary for our requirements?

It is the chemical plant-foods with which fertilizers are more concerned. Liebig made the point that any element found by analysis in the composition of a healthy plant was ipso facto an element necessary to its proper growth. (It is not so true in a quantitative sense, for an element that is present in large quantities in a plant may not be any more important than one present only in very much smaller quantities. The different elements have different functions. One element may function as a direct food; another may be needed only in traces in order to allow the plant to digest the first element.)

If your energy is all engaged in manufacturing tires and wheels, then who will go to the farm...So gradually farming will be reduced, and the city residents, they are satisfied if they can eat meat. And the farmer means keeping the, raising the cattle and killing them, send to the city, and they will think that "We are eating. What is the use of going to..." But these rascals have no brain that "If there is no food grain or grass, how these cattle will be...?" Actually it is happening. They are eating swiftly.

-Srila Prabhupada (Room Conversation with Dr. Theodore Kneupper — November 6, 1976, Vrndavana)

The elements found in plants generally are: carbon, nitrogen, hydrogen, oxygen, phosphorus, potassium, calcium, magnesium, sulphur, iron, manganese, chlorine, boron. Even this is not a complete list but it contains the main ones and some minor ones.

Now of these elements there are three important ones that the soil itself does not seem able to supply sufficiently for our cropping needs—nitrogen, phosphorus, and potassium. Each harvested crop takes away supplies of these elements that have come from the soil and, after a time, these losses reduce the soil's ability to go on feeding crops.

By sampling and analysis it is a simple matter for a chemist to measure just how much of these elements is removed, say, per acre by a crop.

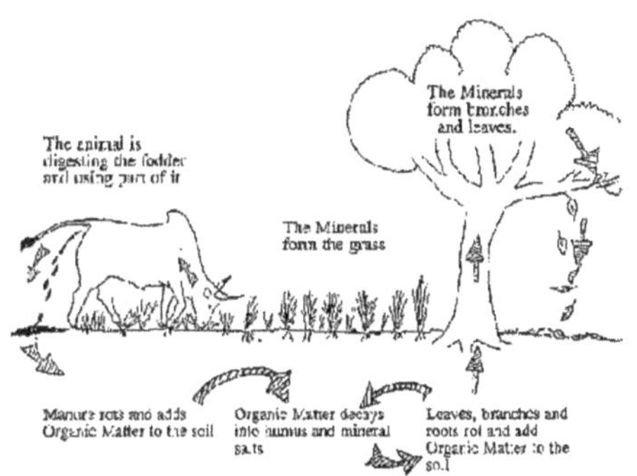

Thus, a good crop of potatoes might take from the soil about 150 pounds of potash (oxide of potassium) per acre. What happens to this 150 pounds? The potatoes are eaten, digested, expelled from the human system into the sewage system. In a modern city this usually means that the sewage is treated and then conducted into a river or sea as quietly and unobtrusively as possible. That part of the potash in the discarded peelings may go on to a compost heap or be fed to pigs or poultry in which case a fraction of the potash will eventually find its way back to the soil. But, in sewage disposal, most of the potash is lost completely.

'The fixation of nitrogen is vital to the progress of civilized humanity, and unless we can class it among the certainties to come, the great Caucasian race will cease to be foremost in the world, and will be squeezed out of existence by the races to whom wheaten bread is not the staff of life.'

~ Sir William Crookes, 1898.

Admitted, there is some sewage reclamation carried on, but it must be remembered that sewage in modern sanitation is heavily diluted with water and this means that the active plant-food—the kind that can dissolve in water-must pass into the liquid fraction of sewage. And it is this liquid fraction that is discarded in most systems—the sludges that are reclaimed at some works are composed of the solid, insoluble parts of sewage. There is, therefore, continuous loss. In less civilized countries—or perhaps it is fairer to say less industrialized countries— the sewage is disposed of by putting it directly back on to and into the soil.

In cattle farming, the nitrogen, phosphorus, and potash consumed when the cattle eat grass or fodder crops returns to the farm as manure. That is why the farmyard manures have been valued so much in traditional farming.

49.

Land Restoration

In India's Conflict Zones

India has a total of 671 districts and out of these, 82 districts are severely affected by Maoist insurgency. These insurgents practically control these vast swathes of territories and even security forces have a hard time accessing some of these areas.

Collapsed agriculture and soil erosion is responsible, in no small measure, for the rise of inurgency in these areas. The youth often have no means of livelihood other than joining the rebel ranks.

One such district in Central India's Chhattisgarh state is Kanker. Most of the land here is degraded and agriculture is in shambles.

Government Projects Facing Reistance

In 2010, the government launched an 820 crore rupee ($150 million) initiative to develop the district. This included building roads, supplying electricity and drinking water, building schools and community health centres and implementing the Mahatma Gandhi National Rural Employment Guarantee Act (MNREGA), a programme designed to end rural poverty by giving 100 days' employment a year to the rural poor.

The plan faced stiff opposition from Maoist activists, who said it would only lead to displacement of local tribal people and fill up the pockets of corrupt government officials.

Kalavati Salam, a resident, recalls how Maoists disrupted a government project in 2010. "We brought in trucks full of stone chips, cement and sand to build a tar road. But when the bulldozers came, they set them afire. We had to stop the work and couldn't spend the budget allocated for the project."

A half-built archway at the village entrance, together with heaps of stone and concrete on the roadsides, back up her testimony.

Maya Kavde, head of Makdi Khuna, another village in the same district, says suspected Maoist activists recently vandalised a mobile phone tower in her village by cutting wires and pulling apart the antennas.

Four years after Kalavati Salam was elected to lead the Nangarbeda village council in Central India's Chhattisgarh state, she has finally got her first development plan rolling.

The plan, focused on reversing land degradation and boosting crop yields, benefits from a generous budget and a dedicated work force. Equally important, it has the support of the Communist Party of India (Maoist), a banned political organisation that has blocked many previous development efforts.

"Now we are taking up works like restoring village land. We are trying to change the definition of development," she adds, visibly relieved.

The process includes levelling the land, clearing it of stones, and then covering it with cow dung.

"Most of the farm plots here are uneven, lifeless. We remove layers of soil from those plots that are higher, until the entire farm

When we examine the facts, we must put the Northern Indian cultivator down as the most economical farmer in the world as far as the utilization of the potent element of fertility—nitrogen—goes. In this respect he is more skilful than his Canadian brother. He cannot take a heavy overdraft of nitrogen from the soil. He has only the small current account provided by the few pounds annually added by nature, yet he raises a crop of wheat on irrigated land in the United Provinces that is not far removed from the Canadian average. He does more with a little nitrogen than any farmer I ever heard of. We need not concern ourselves with soil deterioration in these provinces. The present standard of fertility can be maintained indefinitely.

~ Sir Albert Howard (The Waste Products Of Agriculture And Their Utilization As Humus)

is at the same level," says villager Sonkumari Bai, 42. "We also remove big and small stones. Sometimes we winnow the top soil before putting it back into the land. *Finally, we till the land and cover it with dried cow dung and gypsum.*"

The inhabitants of Nangarbeda, which has a population of 2,700, hope this will help improve their harvests.

"The temperature here is increasing day by day. Earlier in the summer, we would grow vegetables like cucumbers and cow beans. But now the land is so dry, we can grow nothing," says Bhagobai Pradhan, who has a three-acre farm. "This treatment has made some difference. When the rain comes, the once-tilled land will get soaked easily and the cow dung will mix with it well."

Nanak Baghel, a senior Maoist leader in Kanker, says his party fully supports the land restoration project.

"We are against the government-backed so called development projects that are just tools to systematically destroy the tribal people. But we never oppose people's right to better land, water or forest," says Baghel, an area commander.

Sukhanti Bai, head of Handitola village in another conflict-affected district, Rajnandgaon, describes how soil degradation and falling yields have pushed villagers to restore their land too.

"There are many companies here mining for iron ore and limestone. They have caused a lot of deforestation. Also security forces cut many trees to build their camps inside forests. Now, we have less rain and a lot of dust coming from the mines and damaging our fields," she explains.

"Everyone in my village is experiencing a 10 to 20 percent drop in rice yield. Last year, we held a meeting to discuss what work we must make a priority, and everyone said it should be land restoration," she adds.

The majority of the local people are landless, marginal farmers who own less than 2.5 acres of land.

According to Luc Gnacadja, executive secretary of the United Nations Convention to Combat Desertification (UNCCD), including land in development plans will help nations fight food insecurity. "Avoiding land degradation and restoring degraded land should be a centrepiece to every state's development plans," Gnacadja said in a recent interview.

For local people, the land restoration projects in these villages are not only a step towards ensuring food supplies. They also create a more secure working environment.

Ramulu Amma, a 32-year-old villager in Peda Bandirevu, says she feels safer now. We are working to improve our own fields and there are no feelings of fear or insecurity now.

(Source: Report by Stella Paul, Reuters, 7 May 2013. Stella Paul is a multimedia journalist based in Hyderabad, India.)

"We have got experience. Sometimes we find in mango season profuse mango supply. People cannot end it by eating. And sometimes there is no mango. Why? The supply is in the hand of God through His agent, the material nature, this earth. The earth can produce profusely if people are honest, God conscious. There cannot be any scarcity. Therefore it is said that kamam vavarsa parjanyah [SB 1.10.4]. God gives. Eko yo bahunam vidadhati kaman. Nityo nityanam cetanas cetananam (Katha Upanisad 2.2.13). So God, Krsna, fulfills all our desires."

-Srila Prabhupada (Srimad-Bhagavatam 1.10.4, Mayapur, June 19, 1973)

50.

Grazing

A Time-Honored Agricultural Practice

And Its Far-Reaching Benefits In Maintaining The Health And Vitality Of A Landscape.

Excessive pressure on the vegetal cover by animals can be a crucial problem, especially in developing countries where rangelands usually are much more crowded than in the developed world (FAO,1983). While livestock does not necessarily cause environmental problems, overgrazing can be a major factor in land degradation, causing half of the damage assessed in Africa and one-fourth in other developing regions.

Cases such as the damage caused by goats in the Mediterranean area and elsewhere are well known. In Africa, the increase in cattle numbers and the decline in the quality of rangelands have been significant during the recent decades (FAO,1986). These two trends are obviously incompatible in the long run, and local crises are likely in the future.

Nomadic grazing in semi-arid areas is an environmentally compatible, effective land use system developed over the centuries by pastoralists; but local collapses of such systems are being noted with increasing frequency. *Human greed, rather than human need is to be blamed for much of the damage inflicted.*

Cows - The Art Of Living In Perfect Harmony With Other Life Forms

By Morgan Kelly, February 21, 2012

In August, the Princeton researchers reported in the journal Evolutionary Ecology Research that cows paired with wildlife gained 60 percent more weight than those left to graze only with other cows.

Princeton University researchers are leading an effort to put to pasture the long-held convention of cattle ranching that wild animals compete with cows for food.

Two recently published papers — including one in the journal Science — offer the first experimental evidence that allowing cattle to graze on the same land as wild animals can result in healthier, fattier bovines by enhancing the cows' diet. The findings suggest a new approach to raising cattle that could help spare wildlife from encroaching ranches.

The reports stem from large-scale studies conducted in Kenya wherein cows shared grazing land with donkeys in one study and, for the other, grazed with a variety of wild herbivorous animals, including zebras, buffalo and elephants. The lead author on both papers was Wilfred Odadi, a postdoctoral research associate in the lab of Dan Rubenstein, the Class of 1877 Professor of Zoology and chair of Princeton's Department of Ecology and Evolutionary Biology.

In August, Rubenstein and Odadi reported in the journal Evolutionary Ecology Research that cows paired with donkeys gained 60 percent more weight than those left to graze only with other cows. The researchers proposed that the donkeys — which were chosen as tamer stand-ins for zebras and other wild horses — ate the rough upper-portion of grass that cows have difficulty digesting, leaving behind the lush lower vegetation on which cattle thrive.

In September, Odadi and his co-authors on the Science paper reported that other grazers, especially zebras, did remove the dead-stem grass layer and that cattle indeed seemed to benefit from sharing land with wild animals. Cows in mixed grazing pastures took in a more nutritious diet and experienced greater daily weight gain. — but this effect was limited to the wet season.

Nonetheless, the Princeton studies help counter an enduring perception that wildlife is an inherent threat to the food supply of livestock, Rubenstein explained.

These results could prove crucial to preserving animals that are increasingly threatened as the human demand for food drives the expansion of land used to raise cattle. Zebras and wild horses are especially vulnerable to the spread of pastures because of their abundance.

"Grazing competition from other animals has been an issue throughout history," Rubenstein said.

"There's a fear that if some other animal is eating grass meant for livestock, that hurts the rancher. Those perceived competitors were seen as vermin and exterminated," he said. "These experiments suggest that in certain cases cows can actually experience considerable advantages in terms of growth when allowed to graze with other species."

The Benefits Of Grazing

By Kate Campbell, July/August 2009 California Country magazine

Cattle grazing, and other good range management practices, can add greatly to the health and vitality of any landscape.

In the spring, California rangeland is carpeted with wildflowers and dotted with grazing cattle. In the fall, the grassy meadows look like brown velvet and wildlife rattles the chaparral.

Monterey County rancher George Work says the beauty of this ever-changing landscape is one of his greatest pleasures because he knows cattle grazing, and other good range management practices, can add greatly to the health and vitality of this important native landscape.

Through a variety of wildlife management techniques, the Work Family Ranch has more than 300 different species thriving there, including tule elk, which at one time were nearly extinct. Along with that, there are several hundred head of cattle and a small herd of horses.

"I grew up here and took over management from my father in the 1950s," Work said. "We've run cattle and farmed dryland grain and hay since the 1800s. In those days, exotic annual grasses began to take over, creating a significant impact on the land. And there were other forces—erosion, invasive plants and animals, as well as grazing practices—that left their marks."

Today the family manages the ranch using techniques very different than the ones employed by early California ranchers. These days the Works focus on a "whole system approach" that takes into consideration the needs of a complex environment.

To ensure a healthy environment in the future, the Works make decisions about the land based on how it exists today.

"Our family uses a holistic decision-making process that aims for outcomes that are ecologically sound, socially just and economically viable," Work said.

The cattle part of the family operation has undergone a dramatic transformation with the adoption of holistic management techniques, he says, explaining that seeing how all parts of the landscape work together aids in managing for a healthier environment.

Rather than raising cattle as an end in itself, the Work family, and many like them, now view cattle as a tool for good range management.

"Some years back we realized that we're not really in the cattle business," Work said with a chuckle. "That was a surprise. What we found is that we're really grass farmers. The cattle are just a way to harvest it and make a living."

To improve the grasses on his ranch, Work says they've combined herds to makes it easier to use the cattle in ways that benefit the range. This also provides recovery periods for the plants.

"But grazing isn't the only thing that impacts the range. A big problem we have in California is invasive species," he said. "Grazing is probably one of the most important tools we have for controlling things like yellow starthistle. Cows, sheep and goats all eat it."

A native of Eurasia, yellow starthistle was introduced accidentally sometime around 1849. Alvarez says it is by far the fastest-spreading and most-invasive nonnative plant the state has ever seen.

Work offers another example of how cattle improve the rangeland. To begin a habitat restoration project, the family used their cattle to knock down invasive, fire-prone brush and allow a greater variety of native plants to return. They tossed some alfalfa hay into the area they wanted cleared and turned the cattle in.

"In two feedings of about 15 minutes each, the hungry cattle crushed the brush with their excited behavior," he said. The trampled brush provided ground cover to prevent winter erosion from runoff and spring brought a resurgence of perennial grasses and tender sprouts, which was wonderful deer feed."

Ranchers agree that there's a change in the way people think about grazing, a growing recognition that, when done properly, there can be far-reaching benefits from this time-honored agricultural practice. But, they also understand that past practices have done damage to the environment and created public concerns.

"Managed grazing, when it's done well, actually enhances the organic matter in the soil, improving its ability to store carbon," said Shasta County rancher Henry Giacomini, who is chairman of California Farm Bureau Federation's Public Lands Advisory Committee. "And, it improves the water and mineral cycles and allows the whole ecosystem to function in a way that's healthier.

"At our ranch we use irrigated pastures and concentrate the cattle, moving them every day. We monitor the condition of residual

"The philosophy for improving or restoring the environment used to be, remove humans, leave it alone and the land will go back to nature," said environmental activist and author Dan Dagget.

The problem with removing people and their food-producing activities from the land, he says, is that "humans are an important part of the very ecosystems we're trying to restore.

"Removing ourselves from (the landscape) dooms us," he said. "It's like trying to put back together an extremely complex puzzle with a very important piece missing—us."

grass after we move them and watch to see how well the grasses recover after a rest.

"We use buffers along our creeks, ungrazed strips of grasses that can filter material running off the fields," he added. "That technique protects the stream banks from erosion and improves water quality.

Noting that grazing animals, including great herds of elk and deer, have been a vital part of the state's grassland ecology for thousands of years, Giacomini said Farm Bureau policy recognizes that grazing is the most practical and environmentally acceptable way to prevent the buildup of excessive, dry vegetation that can lead to catastrophic wildfires.

Grazing Offers A Bounty Of Benefits

Grazing animals can be an important factor in maintaining balanced and diverse ecosystems. Researchers say there are a number of very important environmental benefits from responsible grazing of public and private lands. Those benefits include:

Benefits To Plant Life

Open grasslands and woodlands are generally dominated by non-native and/or invasive annual grasses and herbs.

The vegetation, when left unmanaged, tends to inhibit the germination and growth of other plants by using up most of the available water and mineral resources in the soil and by producing large amounts of thatch.

Livestock grazing controls the growth of the non-native grasses and herbs so that other desirable plants (wildflowers and native grasses) can regenerate and coexist with them. Many plants, including several endangered species, require grazing to maintain viable populations.

Benefits To Wildlife

Well-managed livestock grazing increases the diversity of habitats available to wildlife species. Many species, including several endangered species, benefit form the vegetation management performed by livestock.

Ground squirrel colonies in grazed areas support the foraging needs of predators like bobcats and golden eagles and at the same time, recreate underground tunnels that are used by insects, reptiles, amphibians, and many small mammals. Burrowing owls, kit fox, and badgers occupy them as well.

Biomass Production

Hoofed animals play a major role in regulating primary production (energy produced by photosynthesis) in grazing ecosystems (Huntly 1991). Defoliation can promote shoot growth and enhance light levels, soil moisture, and nutrient availability (Frank et al. 1998). Overgrazing, however, can significantly reduce biomass production.

Seed Production, Dispersal, and Germination

Grazing animals can decrease flower and seed production directly by consuming reproductive structures, or indirectly by stressing the plant and reducing energy available to develop seeds. Grazing animals can also disperse seeds by transporting seed in their coats (fur, fleece, or hair), feet, or digestive tracts (Wallander et al. 1995, Lacey et al. 1992). For some plant species, grazing animals may facilitate seed germination by trampling seed into the soil.

Protection From Erosion

Organic components of feces and urine from grazing animals can build soil organic matter reserves, resulting in soils having increased water-holding capacity, increased water-infiltration rates, and improved structural stability. These changes can decrease soil loss by wind and water erosion (Hubbard et al. 2004).

Incorporating Organic Matter

The hoof-action of large grazing ungulates can incorporate plant material into soils and increase organic matter.

Ecosystem Processes

Grazing contributes to nutrient cycling and the food web.

Fire Hazard Reduction

Properly managed livestock grazing helps to reduce fire hazards by controlling the amount and distribution of grasses and other potential fuel.

Ponds developed for livestock watering support large numbers of breeding amphibians, which also feed on the abundant insect life found in the grasslands. Proper utilization of livestock grazing promotes healthier, diverse wildlife populations in parks.

Herbivores consume plant leaves, stems, flowers, seeds, and sometimes roots. Patterns of herbivory largely determine plant community composition, structure, and productivity.

Through hoof action, pawing, and wallowing, grazing animals trample plants, break up soil surfaces, incorporate seed into the soil, and compact soils.

Grazing animals contribute to nutrient cycling by depositing nitrogen-rich urine and dung, and their carcasses can provide an important contribution to the food web.

In human-controlled grazing systems, the detrimental or beneficial effects of grazing are largely determined by how and where grazing is used. The negative impacts of livestock grazing are often the result of misuse.

Grazers enhance mineral availability by increasing nutrient cycling within patches of their waste and increasing nitrogen availability to plants (Holland et al. 1992). In natural grazing systems, the decomposing carcasses of wild animals provide feasts for decomposers and scavengers, constituting a central node in the food web (Dunne et al. 2002). However, in grazing systems managed by humans, livestock carcasses are often removed from the environment.

Grazing Can Alter Fire Regimes

Fire frequency, intensity, and behavior are dictated largely by type, condition, and quantity of vegetation (DiTomaso and Johnson 2006). Grazing alters fuel-load characteristics by changing plant community composition, structure, and biomass.

51.

Zero Budget Farming

All You Need Is One Cow

Zero Budget Natural Farming (ZBNF) or holistic agriculture is a method of agriculture that counters the commercial expenditure and market dependency of farmers for the inputs like fertilisers and pesticides.

The method involves locally obtainable natural bio-degradable materials like cow dung and urine and combine scientific knowledge of ecology and modern technology with traditional farming practices based on naturally occurring biological processes.

Zero budget farming methods are promoted by agri-scientists like Subash Palekar and Masanobu Fukuoka.

It requires absolutely no monetary investment for purchase of key inputs like seeds, fertilizers and plant protection chemicals from the market. The farmer can grow hardy local varieties of crops without application of fertilizers and pesticides. Since it is a zero budget farming, no institutional credit would be required and dependence on hired labour is also reduced to bare minimum.

The whole philosophy behind this system is to make the farmer self-reliant so that he is not subjected to volatile market forces.

All that the system requires is a native breed of cow which in any case forms an integral part of farming in India's rural areas. It is claimed that one cow is sufficient to take up this method of farming on thirty acres of land.

Soil Is A Prefect And Complete System

Zero Budget Farming works on the premise that soil is a complete system in itself, independent and self-sustaining. Soil is perfectly capable of supporting life without any need for artificial inputs or technologies.

How much nutrients the crops takes from the soil? Only 1.5 to 2.0 % Remaining 98 to 98.5% nutrients are taken from air, water and Sun. Every green leaf is a food producing factory. It takes carbon dioxide & nitrogen from the air, water from the clouds and light from the Sun. Every green leaf produces 4.5 gram carbohydrates per square feet surface, from which we get 1.5 gram grains or 2.25 gram fruits. Neither air, nor cloud or Sun send us any bill for their contribution. All these inputs are available free of cost.

Green leaves do not use the technology of the Agriculture Universities or multinational food companies. Neither do the Sun, Moon, cloud and air depend on our technological inventions.

All these natural elements that go in our food production are available for free. Earth, water, air and light are freely available in all parts of the world. Where is the question of farming becoming a colossal industry, requiring billions of dollars in investment.

If this is all true, then what is the role of agricultural universities and multi-trillion dollar agribusinesses? What is the role of government subsidies and international trade agreements. Why people have to starve when they can grow their own food with simple efforts in any part of the world.

om purnam adah purnam idam
purnat purnam udacyate
purnasya purnam adaya
purnam evavasisyate

"The Personality of Godhead is perfect and complete, and because He is completely perfect, all emanations from Him, such as this phenomenal world, are perfectly equipped as complete wholes. Whatever is produced of the complete whole is also complete in itself. Because He is the complete whole, even though so many complete units emanate from Him, He remains the complete balance." ~ Sri Isopanisad

A Forest is a proof of nature's prefect and complete system. Since time immemorial, forest eco-systems have existed, producing fruits, flowers, herbs and honey. No agricultural scientist was ever required to maintain these delicate system. Neither there was any need for chemical or organic fertilizers, insecticides, cultivation by tractor, irrigation or GMO seeds. Nature, when left to itself, takes care of everything. Even trees in our countryside produce fruits year after year without any attention on our part.

Experts admit that natural soils are rich in nutrients but they emphasize chemical fertilizers because these nutrients in their natural form can not be utilized by the plant roots. The plant roots can not make use of them in spite of their abundant availability. The soil testing report may say that there is enough Potash in the soil but it is in an unavailable form. So we have to add it from outside.

That is where micro-organisms and friendly creatures like earthworms come into picture. They convert soil nutrients from their non-available form to available form. Just like we can not eat wheat unless it is converted into a bread.

In a forest system, soil is teeming with micro-organisms and therefore their is no necessity of any external input.

However, in our modern farms these nutrients (in acceptable format) are not available because the micro-organisms who convert these non-available nutrients are destroyed by poisonous chemical fertilizers, insecticides, fungicides, herbicides etc. It's like if you don't cook at home, you have to get your dinner from a restaurant. When soil's innate capacity to generate nutrients is impaired, we have to add artificial nutrients from outside.

If we want to avoid unhealthy restaurant food, we have to establish home cooking. Same way if we have to facilitate generation of nutrients within farm soil, then there will be no necessity of adding fertilizers externally.

How can we re-establish these micro-organisms in the soil? This is done by applying the cow dung of local cow. The cow dung of the local cow is a miraculous culture. As we add a spoonful of curd (culture) to a pot of milk , likewise the local cow dung is a culture for the whole field. One gram of cow dung contains about 3000 to 5000 million beneficial microbes.

How much cow dung is needed for one acre of land? Subash Palekar researched this subject for six years. He studied all Indian cow breeds like Gaulao, Lal Kandhari, Khilar, Deoni, Dangi, Nimari from Maharashtra; Gir, Tharparkar, Sahiwal, Redsindhi from West India; Amrutmahal, Krishna kathi from South India and Hariyana from North India. He tested the dung and urine of all these breeds on every crop, in each moon phase and constellation.

His first conclusion was that only dung from traditional local cows is effective, not from Holstein-Friesian breeds. We can mix half cow dung and half the dung of bullock or buffalo, but not of Jersey or Holstein at any cost.

Secondly, the cow dung and urine of black colored Kapila cow is most effective. Thirdly, the cow dung should be used as fresh as possible and the urine as old as possible. Fourthly, only one cow is needed for thirty acres of land. Farmer need not use any compost, vermi-compost for farmyard manure.

For one acre land, only ten kilogram of local cow dung is sufficient per month. One local cow gives on an average about 11 Kg of cow dung, one bullock about 13 Kg of dung and one buffalo about 15 Kg dung per day. For one acre one day's cow dung is enough. That means thirty days cow dung for thirty acres.

You can not imagine a forest without its fauna. To continually regenerate itself, a forest needs the excreta of the animals, birds, earthworms and insects. These inputs are necessary in any self-developing, self-nourishing system. That means the use of cow dung and urine is very natural and hence scientific.

Similar principal applies to this system of farming. Micro-organisms present in cow dung decompose the dried biomass in the soil and make the nutrients available to the plants. There is complete symbiosis in the nature. Jaggery is added in the mix to facilitate biological reaction.

The cow that gives more milk, its dung and urine are less effective and the cow that gives less milk, its dung and urine are more effective. *(Subash Palekar)*

Zero Budget Farming Preparations

Seed Treatment with Beejamrita

Composition:

a) Water 20 litres

b) Desi cow dung 5 kg

c) Desi cow urine 5 Litres

d) One handful of soil from the surface of field

e) Lime 50 grams

The above mixture termed as 'Beejamrita' can be used to treat seeds, seedlings or any planting material. The planting material has to be simply dipped in 'Beejamrita, taken out and planted. Beejamrita protects the crop from harmful soil borne and seed borne pathogens during the initial stages of germination and establishment.

Jeevamritam

Composition:

1) Water 200 litres

2) Desi cow dung 10 kg

3) Desi cow urine 5 to 10 litres

4) Jaggery 2 kg

5) Flour of any pulse 2 kg

6) Handful of soil from farm or forest -

The above mixture will suffice for one time application on one acre crop. 'Jeevamritam' is to be provided once in a fortnight or at least once in a month. It promotes immense biological activity in the soil and makes the nutrients available to the crop. Jeevamritam is not to be considered as nutrient for the crop but only a catalytic agent to promote biological activity in the soil.

Mulching

Mulching with organic residues or live mulching reduces tillage and consequently labour requirements, suppresses weeds, promotes humus formation and enhances the water holding capacity of the soil. Mulching enhances the biological activity and replenishes the nutrient base of the soil. Adequate mulching keeps the top and sub soil moist and enhances the water holding capacity of the soil and also reduces water loss due to evaporation so that the crop will be better equipped to tide over drought conditions.

Plant Protection

In the event of outbreak of insects and diseases the farmer can himself prepare home made pesticides and use it on the crops.

Fungicide-I

a) Butter milk fermented for five days 5 litres

b) Water 50 litres

Fungicide –II

a) Desi cow milk 5 litres

b) Black Pepper Powder 200 grams

c) Water 200 litres Insecticide- I

a) Powder of neem seed or Neem leaves 20 kg

b) Water 200 litres

Insecticide- II

a) Cow dung 5 kg

b) Cow urine 10 litres

c) Neem leaves 10 kg

d) Water 200 litres

This mixture is particularly effective against aphids, jassids, mealy bugs and white flies.

Insecticide – III

a) Neem leaves 10 kg

b) Tobacco powder 3 kg

c) Garlic paste 3 kg

d) Green chillies paste 4 kg

The above ingredients should be soaked in cow urine for ten days. About 3 litres of this mixture can be mixed with 100 litres of water and sprayed on crops.

The above mentioned fungicides and insecticides can be prepared by the farmer himself and used either as prophylactic or as curative measure for control of crop pests. If the economic injury to crops due to pests is less than five percent, it should be deemed to be 'return to nature' and no plant protection measures should be taken.

Mixed Cropping and Crop Rotation

Zero Budget Natural Farming advocates cultivation of diverse species of crops depending on site specific agro climatic conditions. Mixed cropping provides buffer against total failure of single crop and also widens the income source of farmers. There is stress on inclusion of leguminous crops to ensure replenishment of soil fertility. Crop rotation is also emphasized to discourage build up of endemic pests. In the scheme of mixed cropping, cereals, millets, leguminous crops, horticulture crops particularly vegetables and even medicinal plants can be included to make farming more lucrative.

The system also advocates wider spacing of crops to facilitate inter cropping. Palekar has repeatedly stressed that just as diversity is the rule of nature, the farm should also have diverse species.

Observations And Inferences

By R.Yogananda Babu

Visit to fields where Palekar's Zero Budget Natural Farming has been adopted and interaction with farmers whose profiles have been collected, revealed that all of them were raising crops using modern technology of improved seeds, fertilizers and plant protection chemicals before adopting this new method. They found the old method to be very cost intensive and by their own estimates the cost of cultivation of one acre of paddy was Rs.5000/- to Rs. 6000/- and that of sugarcane Rs. 15000/- to Rs. 20000/-.

Similarly the cost of cultivation of one acre of banana was Rs. 25,000/- to 30,000/-. This often compelled them to raise loan from conventional and institutional sources. However, the returns were not commensurate with the investments made for raising crops. The produce from field crops generally met the requirements of the family and the marketable surplus was not sufficient to repay the loan. Market forces were also some times detrimental to the interests of the farmers resulting in low price realization. It was evident from interaction with the selected farmers that they practiced a form of subsistence farming.

In this bleak scenario all the farmers selected for study attended orientation courses conducted by Subhash Palekar at different places of Karnataka. They were convinced that zero budget natural farming is farmer friendly, eco-friendly and above all extremely cost effective. These reasons were cogent enough for them to give this method a fair trial and hence they switched over to this new method. The experience of the practicing farmers and field observations over a period of time lends credence to the following conclusions.

a) The system of zero budget natural farming is eminently suited to the farmers, particularly small and marginal farmers because of its simplicity, adoptability and drastic cut in cost of cultivation of crops. The appeal to the farming community lies in the fact that maintaining optimum levels of production and keeping the cost of cultivation to the bare minimum will substantially enlarge the profit margin.

All the sample farmers acknowledged it as farmer friendly and financially viable. However during the initial period of transition to new system, the results may not be encouraging because of the lingering effects of chemical farming. The results will become evident only after adequate mulching and restoration of biological activity in the soil. Hence, patience and perseverance are required on the part of farmers.

b) Treatment with Beejamrita and Jeevamrita has given extremely encouraging results for successful cultivation of crops. Beejamrita does provide adequate protection to crops from insects and diseases during the initial stages of germination and establishment. Mortality in case of treated crop is reported to be almost negligible.

The experience of the farmers bears ample testimony to the fact that Jeevamrita promotes rapid and enormous biological activity in the soil. However, it should be coupled with adequate mulching so that the soil is transformed into humus rich reservoir of nutrients. It is also observed that providing Jeevamrita once in a fortnight is better than providing it once in a month. It has been the experience of farmers that dispensing with the use of fertilizers has not adversely affected crop yields. The use of home made pesticides has also been found to be effective in managing the crop pests without economic injury to crops.

c) Experience with this method of farming corroborates the fact that adequate mulching promotes humus formation, suppresses weeds and greatly reduces the water requirement of the crops. Live mulching particularly with leguminous crops has been found to be not only a subsidiary source of income but also a safeguard against depletion of nutrients by crops.

d) Mixed cropping particularly with short duration legumes, vegetables and even medicinal plants has certainly expanded the income source of farmers.

Vegetables rich in vitamins and minerals are generally marketed after adequately providing for home consumption and this certainly augurs well for overcoming malnutrition which is widespread in rural areas. Mr. Bannur Krishnappa obtained an additional income of more than Rs. 15,000/- by planting Ashwagandha and Coleus in one acre as intercrop with sugarcane.

e) All the farmers selected for study have expressed satisfaction that switching over to the new method from chemical agriculture has paid them good dividends.

Savings on cost of seeds, fertilizers and plant protection chemicals has been substantial. Almost all the farmers have stopped borrowing crop loan. They are also not depending on hired labour as the family labour is sufficient to carry out all the farming operations. The yields have been optimal with possibly no decline in future, because of continuous incorporation of organic residues and replenishment of soil fertility. The new system of farming has freed the farmers from the debt trap and it has instilled in them a renewed sense of confidence to make farming an economically viable venture. This is a noteworthy feature in an era marked with farmers committing suicide across the country.

Following reports on the success of zero budget farming were published in India's national newspapers.

Zero Budget Farming A Success

The Hindu, April 30, 2010

For A.C. Joshykumar of Muttukad in Bison Valley grama panchayat employing zero budget natural farming methods in his seven-acre multi-crops land has proved successful with considerable increase in yield.

Joshykumar is one of around 45 farmers in the district who have already shifted to zero budget farming, devised by Subhash Palekar of Amaravathy in Maharashtra.

Mr. Joshykumar said he could easily shift to zero budget farming since he had always practised organic farming methods. He said that full dedication and keen efforts were needed to shift to zero budget farming .

> *"Modern agriculture is the use of land to convert petroleum into food. Without Petroleum we will not be able to feed the global population."*
> *-Professor Albert Bartlett*

Zero budget farming proposes that only a single cow is needed to cultivate 30 acres of land. It employs scientific methods to rejuvenate the micro organisms in the soil with the help of earthworms. Fertilizers or pesticides are not used in the method. The focus of the cultivation is through the activation of micro organisms in the soil.

Mr. Joshyjkumar said that his main cultivation, pepper, is completely resisting pest attack even though he was not using any pesticides and production has increased considerably. He bought an indigenous variety of cow- Jaboo - from Kasargod when he shifted to this farming method.

Cow dung is the main component used for revitalising soil with the help of dried plants, which is used to cover the ground around the cultivated plants.

Besides pepper, he also cultivates vegetables, nutmeg and clove. "An exporting agent from Marayur who markets organic produce bought clove from me at Rs.400 a kg when the market price was Rs.310," he said.

Another farmer, Sunny Kudankavil of Panamkutty said he got an yield of 400 kg from 5 kg of ginger rizhome since he shifted to zero budget farming. "If you follow the guidelines suggested by Mr. Palekar, you will get the result," Mr. Kudankavil, who had attended a three-day workshop organised by Mr. Palekar said.

Though the Kerala Agriculture Development Society procures organic produce at 10 to 30 percent higher price, lack of a regular procurement scheme for organic produce is one problem faced by farmers, he said.

Jose Ammencheri, a cardamom farmer in Vandanmedu, said yield had not fallen when he shifted his 14-acre plantation to the new farming method. "There will not be a sudden increase in yield, but it sustains. Also, organic pest control methods are used," he said. Cardamom plantation is known for its high usage of pesticides.

V.C. Devasia said his cocoa plants and rubber plantation have shown higher yield since he shifted to zero budget farming three years ago.

Shaji Thundathil, who is co-ordinating the farmers engaged in zero budget farming, said that thousands of farmers were keen to shift to the farming method. He said that 300 acres of fallow grass land in Muttukadu would be cultivated using zero budget farming methods jointly by farmers, who have found success employing the method.

Zero-Budget Farming In Vithura, Kerala

The Hindu, Thiruvananthapuram, May 31, 2013

Farming is no 'hobby' for Abu Dhabi-based businessman Rohini Vijayan Nair from Vithura. Realising that the rooftop garden at his flat in Abu Dhabi is just too small for his experiments, this agri-enthusiast has now taken up farming in 100 acres of land at his hometown here.

"I needed to do a little more than terrace cultivation and thus took to farming in 100 acres of rubber plantation last year," says Mr. Nair, who manages to juggle farming in Kerala and business abroad.

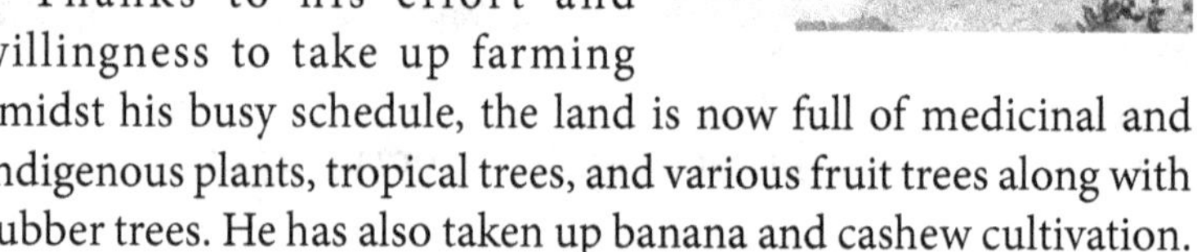

Thanks to his effort and willingness to take up farming amidst his busy schedule, the land is now full of medicinal and indigenous plants, tropical trees, and various fruit trees along with rubber trees. He has also taken up banana and cashew cultivation.

> *India's civilization was based on village residence. They would live very peacefully in the villages. In the evening there would be bhagavata-katha. They will hear. That was Indian culture. They had no artificial way of living, drinking tea, and meat-eating and wine and illicit sex. No. Everyone was religious and satisfied by hearing -- what we are just introducing -- Bhagavatam, Bhagavad-gita, Puranas, and live simple life, keeping cows, village life as it is exhibited by Krsna in Vrndavana.*
> *-Srila Prabhupada (Morning Walk -- Durban, October 13, 1975)*

But unlike other farmers, this man wanted to make sure that his farming techniques did not, in anyway, affect the natural pattern of the soil and land. The search for a suitable farming method finally ended with the zero-budget natural farming advocated by noted agricultural scientist Subhash Palekar.

"The method involves using locally obtainable natural bio-degradable materials and traditional techniques to improve fertility. Though it is not 'zero-budget' here as many other factors such as the State's climate and the labour cost have to be taken into account, it is a highly successful model," Mr. Nair says.

Test Farm

And for those who need proof of how beneficial and environment-friendly the method is, Mr. Nair has a test farm. In three sections of this land, he has been using bio-fertilisers, chemical fertilisers, and 'Jeevamritam' (fertilizer used for zero-budget farming), separately.

"When visitors ask me how nature-friendly the technique is, I want to show them the results of the three types of farming, their pros and cons. When they see the test farm and the produce, they themselves will understand how profitable budget farming is," Mr. Nair says. He has now joined hands with the Krishi Bhavan and has dedicated 25 acres of his land for vegetable cultivation, expecting to reap the harvest during Onam.

His date with farming does not end here. He takes classes for school children and organises field trips to his farm for them.

He says that many people have land but are not willing to cultivate. "But the younger generation is willing to listen and if we inculcate an interest in them, may be we can bring back what we have lost," Mr. Nair says.

52.

The Fragrance Of Nature In Balance

Jon Morgan - Businessday, November 11, 2010

Ms Heather Smith, an American from the verdant eastern state of Vermont has made a home in New Zealand for the past 14 years. She lives at her picturesque farm in the shadow of Hawke's Bay's craggy Te Mata Peak.

She first heard about New Zealand as a university student in the 1980s.

She arrived in New Zealand in 1997, after working with groups in Vietnam, Taiwan, Hawaii and Alaska fighting to save endangered species, such as tigers and bears, and on habitat restoration projects.

Now, on her 275-hectare farm, she has a similar mission.

It is to help revive a way of life that she fears has been almost submerged by the drive for greater productivity at any cost.

She is concerned that farming is becoming too industrialised at the expense of the small family unit, of environmental and animal health and of urban shoppers' knowledge of where their food comes from and what goes into the making of it.

Her farm is an eclectic mix of sheep, cattle, chickens, feijoas, grain crops and truffle trees, all grown organically using the principles of early 20th-century philosopher Rudolf Steiner.

Known as biodynamics, the farming methods shun all synthetic chemicals, replacing them with compost and manure fertiliser nurtured in buried cow horns, and follow the phases of the moon and planets in planting crops.

"I know it sounds wacky," Ms Smith says, "but it works for me. *There's a feeling here of nature in balance. It's hard to explain, but there's a fragrance in the air - the trees, the soil, the animals, everything just smells right. People who come here tell me their souls feel so much better."*

She was travelling by train from Napier to Wellington when she first encountered biodynamics. Seated near her was a family with a bucket of worms. The worms were a gift from pioneering Kiwi biodynamics soil scientist Peter Proctor to the family. "I sat there with them for the whole five-hour trip, talking and learning. They were so smart, really into it."

Inspired by her encounter with the family, she began to learn more about biodynamics by reading and talking to practitioners.

With the help of farm manager Nick Radly, she gradually began to change the farm over to the new regime.

An essential part is the use of Steiner's Preparation 500, made by filling a cow horn with cow dung and burying it in autumn to be dug up in spring.

The cow horn is a keratin-rich container and it is filled with beneficial material from one of nature's most complex digestive systems. She describes the contents of the retrieved horn as fine, silky dirt. "It doesn't look like manure any more. It's full of beneficial fungi and bacteria."

A teaspoon of the preparation is stirred into 40 to 60 litres of warm water and sprayed on pasture to "kick the soil organisms into activity".

She calls on a science analogy to explain it. "It's like taking a swab from a strep throat and making a culture of the bugs in agar in a petri dish. On the farm, that's the cow horn of manure. In the dish, you can see the bacteria expand rapidly. And on the farm the same thing is happening when we've sprayed the bugs around. The difference is we're using good bugs."

The spray stimulates the soil biology, which leads to the growth of more nutrient-rich pastures, crops and garden vegetables and fruit, she says.

On her farm, this is seen in healthier animals and pastures. "The cows and sheep are more fertile, the sheep have less flystrike, I don't need to worm the horses, thistle numbers have plummeted and the pastures hold on to water longer and stay greener longer in summer."

It meant they coped better in the recent droughts, not being forced to sell stock. A low stocking rate and more than 7000 trees for shade and shelter also helped.

This Solution Could Make Paddy More Resistant To Pests

The following was taken from the daily, The Hindu, October 22, 2009.

"Dilute one litre of cow's urine in about 5 litres of water, take paddy seeds required for an acre and tie them into several small bundles and dip them in the solution for half an hour then dry the seeds under shade before sowing. Using this method several farmers have been successful and able to record that the seeds have become more resistant to infestations from pest attacks!"

With a mindful application the farmers, may be able to avoid the cost of pesticides, delivering a less harmful product to the consumer at a cheaper cost!

The soil is dark, crumbly and full of worms. Grass roots go deep and a clay pan is gradually being broken up. "People who come here, curious about what's happening, dig a hole, look at my soil and go, 'Ooh, aah'," she says.

Other fertilisers are lime, a worm-based compost tea and a variety of composts made from horse, cow and sheep manure, food scraps, basalt dust and Steiner preparations using camomile to stop nitrogen from leaching, yarrow to help the absorption of potassium and sulphur, nettles to promote iron and magnesium, dandelion for silica and valerian for phosphorus.

She has 300 ewes and 220 cattle of varying ages and takes 150 dairy grazers at a time.

At weaning, the cattle are given a black walnut remedy to reduce stress. "Every year, it gets easier," Ms Smith says and adds with a laugh, "and this year I swear the calves ran from their mothers."

The feijoas are a big future hope. She sells them to a juicer and an ice-cream maker, getting $1.30 a kilogram for her organically grown fruit, as against 70 cents for conventionally grown.

"It's a gem of a fruit," she says. "It's made into juice and pulp and all through the process retains its unique taste character, much more than other fruits."

However, the local market is saturated and export sales are needed to grow the industry.

She has seen the demand for organic food grow enormously and is frustrated that more is not being done to encourage organic farming. "It's crazy," she says. "The Government is allowing the science institutes to spend money on genetic engineering research when there's no demand for it. Why can't that money go into organics, which is in hot demand?"

She has a favourite saying: "We don't photosynthesise - we are what we eat. More and more people are coming to realise that. They don't want chemicals in their food. They want natural goodness."

Thirteen years on from her first experiments with biodynamics, she feels she is still learning.

"We're still in an establishment phase and I don't know how long that will last, but every year it is a little easier. There is a cost to it, though, and it can be difficult some years to keep your head above water."

An endless stream of wwoofers (Willing Workers on Organic Farms) flock her farm. "They're fabulous workers, so keen. They care so much for the planet and they come here to get back to nature, learn how to milk a cow, make cheese and bake bread - and hopefully spread the word as they travel. It's really inspiring."

53.

Story Of Life And Death

A Tale Of Two Farmers

Here we narrate the story of two farmers who live in the same area in south India. One is happy and prosperous and the other is broke and dead. This may shed some light on the satanic forces responsible for farmers genocide in India. These reports were published in the newspapers on the same day.

Lankan Farmers Take Lessons In Cow Based Farming

Decca Herald, February 11 2012

A delegation of farmers from Sri Lanka visited farm of natural farmer Ramesh Raju at Kurahatti, Karnataka India last week.

Raju has succeeded in reaping good yield by adopting natural farming. Instead of fertiliser and other stimulants, Raju uses cow urine, cow dung cakes and jaggery to increase productivity of crops like banana and sugarcane.

Sharing his success story with his Sri Lankan counterparts - led by Jayant Tilak on a study tour, Raju said he cultivated 50 tonnes of sugarcane on one acre of land, spending Rs. 30,000. He has already earned Rs. 50,000 by growing sub-crops like brinjal, chilly and others.

The sugarcane expected to be harvested in five months will help produce 50 quintals of jaggery. According to the prevailing price jaggery costs Rs 3,500 per quintal.

He advised the delegates to adopt natural farming as propagated by Subhash Palekar - invest less and earn more without depending on fertilisers or pesticides. "Already five workshops have been conducted in Sri Lanka. It was the workshop that aroused the curiosity of farmers and hence we are on a study tour. We will also urge the government to adopt natural farming to increase food production to meet the growing demand," he said.

The delegation included Sri Lanka Farmers' Association president Darshan de Silva and Subramanya Pillai among others.

Two Farmers Commit Suicide In State

Deccan Herald, February 11 2012

Two farmers, unable to repay debts, commit suicide in separate incidents on Saturday.

Venkate Gowda, 65, a resident of Hosakote village in Pandavapura taluk of Mandya district, committed suicide by consuming insecticide at his field in the morning. The villagers, who saw him writhing in pain, rushed him to the district hospital.

In India with small holdings and small scale farming, there is no better alternative to employing cattle in farming.

While ploughing, the oxen stride with gentle gait, not harming the surface of the earth, unlike tractors.

Even as they plough the land, the oxen defecate and urinate, fertilising the land.

Cattle Manure : organic manure, green leaf manure, earth-worms, and slurry manure with cattle manure bond with the nature and make the land fertile. They do not create the challenge of chemical waste.

99% of the pests in nature are beneficial to the system. Insecticides prepared from cow urine or well fermented butter milk do not affect these helpful pests.

Dung from one cow is adequate to fertilise upto 30 acres of land and its urine can protect upto 10 acres of crops from insects.

However, the treatment was ineffective and Gowda was declared dead in the afternoon.

The farmer grew sugar cane, paddy and ragi on his three-acre field. He was depressed due to repeated crop failures, despite purchasing seeds from reputed companies.

He had availed a loan of more than Rs. one lakh from State Bank of Mysore. In addition to this, he had borrowed Rs two lakh from private moneylenders.

In Sira

Eeranna, 45, committed suicide by consuming insecticide at his farm at M Dasarahalli village of Sira taluk.

He died while being taken to the hospital. The number of suicides by farmers has risen to 12, following the drought in the taluk.

Disappointed after repeated crop failure, Eeranna set up a petty shop, availing a loan of Rs 15,000 from Canara Bank. Losses in business led him to try his hand at manure business.

He had availed loans from private moneylenders also.

Both Ramesh Raju and Venkate Gowda's villages are about 6 kilometers distance.

Now what is the differences between these two farmers?

The difference is in their methods of farming. And these methods make a difference of life and death.

Joys of Cow Based Farming

Indian agriculture has variety. There is no farm-product that Indians don't cultivate. This land grows all kinds of grains, pulses, vegetables, fruits, flowers, cotton and silk.

About 70% of Indian population depend on agriculture for their livelihood. Majority of them are small farmers, owning one or two acres of land.

Indian agricultural landscape is diverse and vivid – in land topology, soil type and quality, irrigation method and frequency of harvesting.

Cattle are integral part of this huge canvas of agriculture. We use oxen to plough, to pick and move harvested crops and in irrigation. Cow manure is used as fertiliser, and cow urine as insecticide.

54.

Cow Dung

On The Face Of Monsanto And Its Agents In The National Capital

In November 2012, Indian government told the Supreme Court in an affidavit that it could not achieve the goal of reducing the number of hungry people by half without taking recourse to genetically modified (GM) crops, which could herald the second green revolution in the country. The central government said GM crops would not only lead to increased food security but would also reduce pressure on land use.

The central government pronounced its position backing field trials of GM crops while junking the interim report of the court-appointed Technical Expert Committee (TEC) report, which had recommended a 10-year moratorium on GM crops field trials.

But what about the farmers who are growing much more per acre than Mosanto or its forefathers can ever imagine? They are being conveniently ignored by the mainstream agricultural establishment. Why not make their techniques available to the masses?

G. Nagarathanam Naidu is one such farmer, based in South India, in Hyathnagar mandal near Hyderabad. He is producing 15.5 tons of rice per hectare by using indigenous cow based inputs in his field. His consumption of seeds, water, labour and other inputs is also much lower compared to other farmers.

Cropping System

- A combination of Zero Budget Natural Farming (ZBNF) and System of Rice Intensification (SRI)

- Application of farmyard manure (cow, sheep and goat manure) @ 5 tons/acre.

- Incorporation of Green manure and green leaf manure (Neem).

- Application of jeevamritham directly or along with farmyard manure to soil twice as top dressing.

- Using 2 kg seed for transplanting one acre, instead of 30 kg normally used.

- Planting 12 day old seedlings.

- Planting at 25x25cm spacing.

- Running three Row Cono weeder four times.

- Adopting alternate wetting and drying

- Controlling pests and diseases with bio-dynamic formulations, neem kernel

- Formation of irrigation channels round the field and for every 2 meters which are interconnected to save on irrigation water.

Jeevamritham Composition:

10kg cow dung

10 lit of cow Urine

0.5kg cow ghee

1kg jaggery

200g virgin red soil

Mixed in 200 lit of water

Application of bio-fertilizers (Azospirillum, Azotobacter, Phosphorus Solubilising bacteria) along with farmyard manure as top dressing.

Benefits

- Radical improvement in the soil health.

- Saving larger quantities of seeds i.e., 28kg seeds per acre

- Saving of irrigation water by 40% compared to conventional practice

- Higher yields for national food security.

- Overall cost of cultivation reduced by 25 percent.

- Increases yields by 30 percent over conventional practices.

G. Nagarathanam Naidu hails from a remote village Balakrishnapuram in Chittoor district, Andhra Pradesh. After obtaining his diploma in electronics, he was settled in a job. But that could not satisfy his innate desire to be connected with the land. It was then he and his wife decided to acquire 17 acres of barren and rocky land on the outskirts of Hyderabad. They could not afford better land.

The couple converted their new land into a gold mine by sheer hard work. They now have a mini forest with its own micro-climate. They also practice floriculture and grow varieties of exotic fruits and other crops.

He travels to different parts of India to train other farmers. Students from various schools and colleges also visit his farm to learn something about natural farming.

Awards And Appreciations

Various dignitaries have visited his farm which include scientists from various countries and Chief Minister of Andhra Pradesh.

When the former US President George Bush visited India, he was allowed to interact with him as a farmers' representative.

In 2005, he received appreciation from the WWF international Project. In 2007, he was given a certificate of appreciation by Association for Land reforms and Development, Dhaka, Bangladesh. In 2008, he was give a letter of honor by ICRISAT for implementing organic farming practices in groundnut cultivation and generating a record yield.

Also he received a Letter of Appreciation from Jara Agro Industrial PLC, Ethiopia, in the year 2011 for his sincere efforts in educating the local farming community on high yield strategies and innovative techniques.

Recently he was honored as the "Best SRI Farmer" by WWF Netherlands in collaboration with ICRISAT.

Section-V

Government As A Corporate Agent

Serving Western Interests As Its Foremost Priority

Gradual Corporate Takeover Of India

55.

National Policies

Made In Boardrooms As Parliament Takes A Backseat

Modern Imperialism - The Corporate Takeover of the World

According to Noreena Hertz, over the last three decades the balance of power between politics and commerce has shifted radically, leaving politicians increasingly subordinate to the colossal economic power of big business. Unleashed by the Thatcher-Reagan axis, and accelerated by the end of the Cold War, this process has grown Hydra-like over the last two decades and now manifests itself in diverse forms. Whichever way we look at it, corporations are taking on the responsibilities of government.

And as business has extended its role, it has actually come to define the public realm. The political state has become the corporate state. Governments are shattering the implicit contract between state and citizen that lies at the heart of a democratic society.

Pursuing a policy of neo-colonialism, the multinational corporations infringe up on the sovereignty of the Third World

> *All over the world, concerns are being raised about governments' loyalties and corporations' objectives. Concerns that the pendulum of capitalism may have swung just a bit too far; that our love affair with the free market may have obscured harsh truths; that too many are losing out. That the state cannot be trusted to look after our interests; and that we are paying too high a price for our increased economic growth. They are worried that the sound of business is drowning out the voices of the people. ~ Noreena Hertz (Global Capitalism and the Death of Democracy)*

countries, seek to gain control over their natural resources, impose unequal agreements upon them and impede the development of their independent national economies.

Imperialists, like everyone else, have always sought to justify their actions. In the latter 19th Century and the early decades of the 20th Century, imperialism was more direct than it is today, and it was called imperialism. The basic concept was rather simple. A militarily strong country from Europe would enter a militarily weak third world country and take control of it. The natural resources and human labor of the weaker country were put in the service of the stronger country.

'White Man's Burden'

The justification of this process has been captured by the phrase "white man's burden". Under this theme, imperialism was justified on the basis that the dominated countries were inhabited by culturally backwards savages who were in need of being "civilized". Dominating them was not something that the imperialists did in order to enrich themselves, but rather it was a burden that they carried out for strictly 'altruistic purposes'.

Numerous successful rebellions by the colonized countries in the first half of the 20th Century eventually discredited the concept, so that imperialism went out of favor. The new anti-imperialist world attitude towards imperialism is captured in the preamble to the United Nations Charter, which came into existence in 1945:

We the people of the United Nations determined:

> *"I have traveled across the length and breath of India and I have not seen one person who is a beggar, who is a thief, such wealth I have seen in this country, such high moral values, people of such caliber (of noble character), that I do not think we would ever conquer this country..........unless we break the very backbone of this nation which is her spiritual and cultural heritage."*
>
> *-Lord MCLau, British colonial, on February 2, 1835*

To save succeeding generations from the scourge of war, which twice in our lifetime has brought untold sorrow to mankind, and

To reaffirm faith in fundamental human rights, in the dignity and worth of the human person, in the equal rights of men and women and of nations large and small, and

To establish conditions under which justice and respect for the obligations arising from treaties and other sources of international law can be maintained, and

To promote social progress and better standards of life in larger freedom.

But progress has never followed a straight line. Imperialism is alive and well in the world today, but it goes under different names, such as "free trade", "foreign investment", or "structural adjustment".

Naomi Klein, in her book, "The Shock Doctrine – The Rise of Disaster Capitalism", uses another name for it: Shock therapy. As always has been the case, its practitioners and proponents provide justifications for the new imperialism, just as they did for the old imperialism. But of course they use different justifications than the old ones, in order to conform to the new ideologies.

One of the ideologies at the root of all these policies is supplied by Milton Friedman's economic theories, developed at the University of Chicago. These theories, when put into practice in several countries over more than three decades, have served primarily to increase the wealth and power of the wealthy, at the expense of everyone else.

Invading The World - One Economy At A Time

Antonia Juhasz, in her book, "The Bush Agenda – Invading the World One Economy at a Time", describes how force and violence are used by third world governments to protect corporate interests:

"Cochabamba is the 3rd largest city in Bolivia. In late 1999, the World Bank required that Bolivia privatize Cochabamba's water in return for reduction of its debts. Bechtel – one of the top ten water privatization companies in the world – won the contract.

Immediately after Bechtel took over the Cochabamba water system, and before any of the promised investments in infrastructure were made to improve or expand services, the company raised the price of water by 100%... Many were simply forced to do without running water. The same law that privatized the water system also privatized any collected water, including rainwater collected in barrels.

The majority of the people voted for the cancellation of the contract with Bechtel. When this demand was met with silence from government officials, the citizens went on a citywide strike. The Bolivian government defended Bechtel's right to privatize by sending armed military troops into the streets to disperse the crowds. At least one 17-year-old boy was shot and killed and hundreds more were injured."

Petras describes the role of the U.S. military as the ultimate guarantee that their preferred policies will be realized:

'The responsibility of the US for the growth of Latin American billionaires and mass poverty is several-fold and involves a very wide gamut of political institutions, business elites and academic and media moguls. First and foremost the US backed the military dictators and Neoliberal politicians who set up the billionaire economic models.'

The New Imperialism

Under the new imperialism, various strict and related conditions are imposed upon a country in return for a loan, usually structured by international financial institutions that are largely under the control of the United States. In addition to a strict schedule for repaying of the loan, the conditions generally include: opening the country to private investment; the privatization of national resources, services, and industries; various favors towards those industries, like selling off state assets at bargain prices, tax breaks, subsidies, a paucity of regulation, and laws that greatly favor capital over labor; and drastic cuts in social services for the country's inhabitants.

The primary result is that the foreign corporations and investors make vast profits while the country's inhabitants become even more impoverished than they were. The process is something akin to loan sharking.

The rationalization used to justify this process is that the privatized industries, through the process of the unfettered "free market", will be far more efficient and productive than they were when they were under government ownership. This will result in improved goods and services for the country's inhabitants, and will provide tons of jobs as well. However, it rarely works like that.

The bottom line is that rather than serving as a financial asset to the country, profits accrue to the MNC and its investors while draining the country of its financial and other resources.

Foreign investors have successfully secured control over some of the most lucrative oil and gas fields from compliant rulers. The obvious result has been a huge transfer of wealth from the national economy to the MNCs under the assumption that the new investments will provide compensatory benefits. The problem is that energy corporations are notorious for not fulfilling their investment obligations.

Why Do Countries Allow This To Happen To Them?

Payoffs

These corporations have given rise to a big question mark whether political freedom will continue to exist when economic power is getting more and more concentrated in fewer and fewer hands.

They lobby for a particular interest. They finance individual members of a political party and parties themselves in elections. These days money plays a major role in elections. Any party that can manipulate funds has better chances of victory. Naturally they get political control of the developing countries.

In this context we can mention Lockheed scandal in which top officials in Western European countries and Japan were involved. When the facts came to light, the Japanese Prime Minister had to resign on corruption charges in the aeroplanes deal.

Dr. V. Gauri Shanker makes startling disclosures in his research thesis, "Taming the Giants: Transnational Corporation" which he wrote under the auspices of Jawaharlal Nehru University.

> *"The liberty of a democracy is not safe if the people tolerate the growth of private power to a point where it becomes stronger than the democratic state itself. That in its essence is fascism: ownership of government by an individual, by a group or any controlling private power." ~President Franklin D. Roosevelt.*

He writes how the Multinationals operating in India and Indonesia set apart secret funds for bribing officials and making political contributions. Sometimes the Multinationals act as fronts for their governments and interfere in the internal affairs of the host countries and cause political destabilization.

Persuasion

Persuasion is often the preferred initial method to convince countries to accept the conditions required by international lending institutions. Persuasion of course is apt to be more effective when countries are desperate for money. And it can take many forms.

First there are the ideological arguments about the wonders of the "free market". Such arguments may have held some sway with well meaning people in the past. However, by now the fallacy of these arguments has become well known, as least among those who have studied their effects on developing countries.

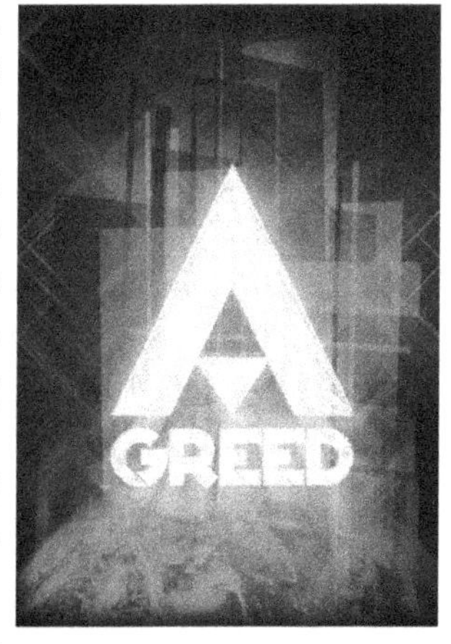

John Perkins, in "Confessions of an Economic Hit Man", explains how persuasion is often used, from the perspective of an insider who formerly did the dirty work that he describes in his book. Perkins explains that economic hit men (EHM) are paid by multinational corporations to develop economic projections for major development projects in third world countries. Their projections are supposed to predict substantial economic growth and thereby justify huge loans from

The Multinationals concerned with food have succeeded in weaning the developing countries away from grain production so that they could make profitable grain exports to them.

On the land so released from food, the Multinationals themselves set up frontal vegetable growing business, earning big profits by exporting these items back to the West.

Mexico, which once grow a variety of local food grains, has been converted into an exporter of fruits and vegetables.

international lending institutions. The money from the loan then is immediately funneled into U.S. oil, engineering or construction companies (which is a precondition of the loan) to develop their projects.

Sometimes there are darker aspects to persuasion, for which we will probably never know the full extent. Perkins describes these aspects in his second book, "The Secret History of the American Empire – Economic Hit Men, Jackals, and the Truth about Global Corruption", quoting an anonymous source, who was a fellow EHM:

> "I walked into El Presidente's office two days after he was elected and congratulated him. I said "Mr. President, in here I got a couple of hundred million dollars for you and your family, if you play the game – you know, be kind to my friends who run the oil companies, treat your Uncle Sam good." Then I stepped closer, reached my right hand into the other pocket, bent down next to his face, and whispered, "In here I got a gun and a bullet with your name on it – in case you decide to keep your campaign promises." I stepped back, sat down, and recited a little list for him, of presidents who were assassinated or overthrown because they defied their Uncle Sam: from Diem to Torrijos – you know the routine. He got the message."

Financial Manipulation Or Indifference

Naomi Klein explains in her book that countries are much more susceptible to requests to alter their laws and economic policies to benefit foreign corporations when they are in shock. The shock can result from war, assassination or overthrow of a head-of-state, natural disaster, or financial calamity. In any of these cases, the shock can provide great opportunities for opportunistic foreign scavengers.

The Southeast Asian financial crisis of 1997 – the economic collapse of the so-called Asian Tigers – provides a good example of how international financial institutions have used their financial powers to facilitate a financial crisis to benefit powerful corporations. Just prior to their collapse, the Asian Tigers were

'The business of America is business.'
~1920s US President Calvin Coolidge's dictum

being held up as great success stories of globalization. Klein explains the role of international financial institutions in the crisis.

In the mid-nineties, under pressure from the IMF and the newly created World Trade Organization, Asian governments agreed to lift barriers to their financial sectors, allowing a surge of paper investing and currency trading.

As for the IMF, the world body created to prevent crashes like this one, it took the 'do-nothing approach' that had become its trademark since Russia. It did eventually respond – but not with the sort of fast, emergency stabilization loan that a purely financial crisis demanded. Instead, it came up with a long list of demands, pumped up by the Chicago School certainty that Asia's catastrophe was an opportunity in disguise.

Klein also explains in great detail the motivation for the financial elites wanting the Asian economies to fail. Here is part of that explanation:

> If the crisis was left to worsen, all foreign currency would be drained from the region and Asian-owned companies would have either to close down or to sell themselves to Western firms.

The IMF was exclusively focused on how the crisis could be used as leverage. The meltdown had forced a group of strong-willed countries to beg for mercy; to fail to take advantage of that window of opportunity was, for the Chicago School economists running the IMF, tantamount to professional negligence.

Multinationals have been exploiting the Third World countries in the field of pharmaceuticals.

This is particularly the in case of India. Such Multinationals have been propagating the use of non-essential drugs and making large profits through over-pricing. An expert committee insists that of the 43,600 drugs registered and sold in India, three-fourths are non-essential.

A survey conducted by the Indian Council of Medical Research points out that seven out of every ten purchases of antibiotics made in India are uncalled for.

Recently, there was a controversy over the multinationals marking and selling non-essential baby foods in India.

To 'take advantage of the opportunity' the IMF required the Asian countries to adopt a host of Milton Friedman's Chicago School economic 'reforms':

> The IMF also demanded that the governments make deep budget cuts, leading to mass layoffs of public sector workers in countries where people were already taking their own lives in record numbers. They were now ready to be reborn, Chicago-style: privatized basic services, independent central banks, low social spending and, of course, total free trade. Indonesia would cut food subsidies.

Government Overthrow

John Perkins explains that if the EHMs are unsuccessful in their efforts to convince a government to play ball, then the "jackals" are sent in to assassinate or overthrow the uncooperative government officials in question, as was done for example in Iran in 1953, Guatemala in 1954, inChile in 1973, or in Indonesia in 1965.

Naomi Klein describes how Milton Freidman's economic theories and policies worked in tandem with U.S. covert assistance to destroy the economic functioning of several South American countries in the 1970s, following the overthrow of Salvador Allende

In line with historic conflicts all over the world, the current battle is between the global public and the corporate and political elite over the control of government. Who decides how people organize and live their lives? Who decides if people go with or without water, food, healthcare or education? These rights must rest with the global public and their representative bodies, and not with a tiny minority who directly benefit from an ideology that shrinks public involvement in these central decisions.

Corporations are not people. They do not exist without shareholders and they exist only for profit. They are incapable of demonstrating the same values that people hold and express within their communities. The national constitution was never meant to represent the rights of economic entities; there is no mention of corporations or other such entities in the constitution of any country. The corporation must not enjoy the protection of the Bill of Rights. In a true democracy, corporations must exist at the pleasure of the people and under their sovereignty, not the other way round .

and his replacement by the brutal dictator Augusto Pinochet in 1973:

'The Chicago School counterrevolution quickly spread. Brazil was already under the control of a U.S. supported junta. Friedman traveled to Brazil in 1973, at the height of that regime's brutality, and declared the economic experiment a "miracle". In Uruguay the military had staged a coup in 1973 and the following year decided to go the Chicago route. The effect on Uruguay's previously egalitarian society was immediate: real wages decreased by 28% and hordes of scavengers appeared on the streets. Next to join the experiment was Argentina in 1976, when a junta seized power from Isabel Peron. That meant that Argentina, Chile, Uruguay and Brazil – the countries that had been showcases of developmentalism – were now all run by U.S. backed military governments and were living laboratories of Chicago School economics.'

Violence And War

Violence and war blend with government overthrow as a means of getting countries to go along with their wishes. Perkins explains that when other methods don't work, then they send in the military, as they did in Panama in 1989 or in Iraq in 1991 and 2003.

Klein explains that the preferred economic policies are often so painful to a country's population, that peaceful means are not enough to maintain them. She describes the role of systematic violence in persuading Chileans to accept new economic policies following the installation of Pinoche's regime:

'The generals knew that their hold on power depended on Chileans being truly terrified. The trail of blood left behind over those four days came to be known as the Caravan of Death. In short order the entire country had gotten the message: resistance is deadly. In all, more than 3,200 people disappeared or were executed, at least 80,000 were imprisoned, and 200,000 fled the country.'

Examples Of The Consequences Of New Imperialism

The books described above provide numerous examples of the consequences of new imperialism in a wide range of countries. Here are just a few of them:

Russia 1991

Following the break-up of the Soviet Union, Russia was in dire financial straights as it attempted to convert to capitalism. Under pressure from the United States and international financial institutions, Boris Yeltsin decided to go the economic shock therapy route:

> After only one year, shock therapy had taken a devastating toll: millions of middle-class Russians had lost their life savings when money lost its value, and abrupt cuts to subsidies meant millions of workers had not been paid in months. The average Russian consumed 40% less in 1992 than in 1991, and a third of the population fell below the poverty line. The middle class was forced to sell personal belongings from card tables on the streets.

Chile 1973

As described in Klein's book, following the overthrow of Allende and his replacement by Pinochet:

> In 1974, inflation reached 375%. The cost of basics such as bread went through the roof. At the same time, Chileans were being thrown out of work because Pinochet's experiment with "free trade" was flooding the country with cheap imports. Unemployment hit record levels and hunger became rampant. Chicago boys argued that the problem didn't lie with their theory but with the fact that it wasn't being applied with sufficient strictness.

Poland – 1988

Poland won its independence from the Soviet Union in 1988, and it was in dire financial straights at that time. It was made clear to them that they could expect little or no help unless they agreed to economic shock therapy. Klein describes how that worked out:

Shock therapy in Poland did not cause "momentary dislocations," as predicted. It caused a full-blown depression: a 30% reduction in industrial production, unemployment skyrocketed, and in 1993 it reached 25% in some areas – a wrenching change in a country that, under Communism, for all its many abuses and hardships, had no open joblessness.

In 1989, 15% of Poland's population was living below the poverty line; in 2003, 59% of Poles had fallen below the line. Shock therapy, which eroded job protection and made daily life far more expensive, was not the route to Poland's becoming one of Europe's "normal" countries.

The Asian Tigers – 1997

Klein describes what happened to the Asian people following the financial crisis described above:

24 million people lost their jobs in this period. What disappeared in these parts of Asia was what was so remarkable about the region's "miracle" in the first place: its large and growing middle class. 20 million Asians were thrown into poverty in this period of what Rodolfo Walsh would have called "planned misery". Women and children suffered the worst of the crisis. Many rural families in the Philippines and South Korea sold their daughters to human traffickers who took them to work in the sex trade. The crisis saw a 20 percent increase in child prostitution.

Iraq – 2003

Antonia Juhasz explains in her book that economic plunder was one of the chief reasons, and probably the chief reason, for the

Three hundred multinational corporations now account for 25 per cent of the world's assets. The annual values of sales of each of the six largest transnational corporations, varying between \$111 and \$126 billion, are now exceeded by the GDPs of only twenty-one nation states.

Corporate sales account for two thirds of world trade and a third of world output (Coca-Cola, Toyota and Ford derive nearly half of their revenues outside their base in the USA), while as much as 40 per cent of world trade now occurs within multinational corporations. ~ Noreena Hertz

U.S. invasion and occupation of Iraq. In that sense, it was a great success, not the failure that it is often made out to be.

The Foreign Investment Order provided the legal framework for the invasion of U.S. corporations into Iraq. It provided for the privatization of Iraq's state-owned enterprises, foreign ownership of Iraqi businesses, tax-free remittance of all profits, immunity of foreign businesses from Iraqi courts, and much else. As with everything else about the U.S. occupation, these provisions did great damage to the Iraqi people, for the benefit of U.S. corporations. Juhasz describes the effects of privatization of Iraqi industries:

> In Bremer's own words, "Restructuring inefficient state enterprises requires laying off workers.". Even those workers who still had jobs in Iraq at the time only received about half of what they made before the war. At the same time, prices skyrocketed.

And with respect to the lack of any constraints on foreign corporations:

> U.S. corporations are therefore invited to enter the Iraqi economy, exploit a nation at its most vulnerable point, with no obligation to reinvest in the country at a time when rebuilding Iraq is professed to be the Bush administration's most vital assignment. U.S. corporations have reaped staggering revenues from their Iraqi operations. Chevron, Bechtel, and Halliburton have each experienced skyrocketing returns to their Iraqi endeavors.

In the hands of U.S. corporations, the effort to rebuild Iraq was a miserable failure:

> The Bush administration failed in this mission because it did not focus its efforts on the immediate provision of needs, but rather on the opening of Iraq to private foreign corporations. Iraqis have continually pointed to the lack of electricity as a primary source of unrest.

Human civilizations should depend on the production of material nature without artificially attempting economic development to turn the world into a chaos of artificial greed and power only for the purpose of artificial luxuries and sense gratification. This is but the life of dogs and hogs.

~ Srila Prabhupada (Srimad Bhagavatam 1.10.4)

Electricity has remained far below prewar levels and significantly below U.S. stated goals.

The result was frequent blackouts and the availability of electricity for only a few hours a day, with air conditioning unavailable much of the time in the face of outside temperatures of 130 degrees. Lack of potable water and sewage treatment has been another continuing and major problem:

> The full failure of the reconstruction was revealed in a January 2006 U.S. government audit. Although more than 93% of the U.S. appropriation has been spent or committed to specific companies and projects, as much as 60% of all water and sewer projects will not be completed.

Why So Much Concern About Multinationals?

Big business elicits strong reactions. In his book The Corporation, now a successful television series and film, the Canadian academic Joel Bakan argues that the corporation is 'a pathological institution, a dangerous possessor of the great power it wields over people and societies'. The multinational corporation, because of its apparent mobility and assumed lack of loyalty to any one jurisdiction, is particularly mistrusted. But how did this mistrust come about?

In Europe, the controversy surrounding multinationals can be traced back to the post-war years. This was a time of huge expansion for corporations, particularly those originating in the USA. Many Europeans were beginning to resent the level of reliance by local industry on US foreign investment and worried, too, about the 'Americanisation' of culture, tastes and management methods. By the late 1960s, opposition to US-owned multinationals was high, as evidenced by the popularity of books critical of the 'American invasion'.

In the USA, on the other hand, multinationals appear to have been regarded relatively benignly by the public until the 1960s. But by this time the reputation of corporate America had begun to wane, as Hood vividly describes:

> Investigative journalism became a heroic, even romantic, calling, with the name of the game being to catch greedy corporations in the act of polluting the water, selling shoddy and overpriced products, exploiting workers and families, and sacrificing the public's health,

safety and welfare to make a quick buck. On television and in the movies, business executives increasingly became villains, to be challenged by heroic lawyers, policemen, reporters and activists.

By the 1970s, the multinational had become synonymous, around the world, with power and wealth and, to many, a potent symbol of the economic and political dominance of the USA. What is striking about much of the literature on multinationals from that time, compared with today, is the extent to which the interests of the multinational are identified with the interests of its state of origin, or 'home state'. Multinationals were viewed, perhaps simplistically, as economic agents of their home states, with no particular allegiances to the states in which they chose to invest. With this mindset, the nationality of the foreign investor was of crucial importance. Foreign-owned multinationals were regarded as a threat to the sovereignty of their host states in two ways: first, because of fears that they might exercise undue influence over the host state's national policies and, second, because they helped

The privilege of influencing policy is one that rightly belongs to the public, not the corporate elite who make up less than 1% of the population. But since political influence increases with economic and financial power, the corporate influence in national and global governance structures far outweighs public influence. Thus, democratic process has been the battle ground whereupon the pubic good has fought the corporate agenda. Only when the global public seize back the democratic process and implement appropriate measures to curb corporate influence on the democratic process will the global economy reflect the needs of the majority.

The public's attention in many western countries has turned away from government - a fact born out by the very low turnouts during recent elections in the UK and US. Such national apathy to government is to a large extent the result of the failure of political leadership to sincerely represent the public or to convince the public that they are on their side, fighting for public issues. The resulting consensus within society adds momentum to the private sector's ambitions to roll back government control in favour of market forces. It has also contributed to the strengthening of the 'partnership' between the government and the business sector, and this has made it even easier for corporations to successfully lobby governmental to loosen their hold on the economy.

to perpetuate inequalities between states. But while foreign ownership of local industry was a concern for all host states, these issues had particular significance for less developed countries.

Legal Jurisdiction Of Multinationals

Multinationals are not traditional subjects of international law. Historically, the role of international law in relation to multinationals has primarily been to define the rights and obligations of states with respect to international investment issues. International law has been used to regulate the jurisdiction of states over multinationals, and their rights of diplomatic protection and, through treaties, has provided states with a means by which investment conditions for multinationals could be stabilised, harmonised, and generally enhanced.

But the world is changing fast. Concern about the social and environmental impacts of 'globalisation' means that new demands are now being made of international law. Can international law respond to these demands? Does international law provide an adequate framework for the regulation of the social and environmental impacts of multinationals on a global scale? Many people think not. Some have doubted that international law is even 'conceptually equipped' to perform such a role.

Public opinion, too, is generally sceptical as to the extent to which multinationals can be regulated effectively. Critics point out the ease with which multinationals can avoid national regulation through their mobility and flexibility of structure and organisation. While each state is entitled to regulate those parts of a multinational incorporated or operating within its territory, many states may not have the resources or political will to do so effectively, giving rise to differences in social and environmental standards between states. These differences, it is argued, are exploited by some multinationals for commercial advantage; that is, multinationals will tend to gravitate to regions in which production costs are lowest because of low regulatory standards and expectations.

56.

Dynamics Of World Hunger

A recent article in The Nation, titled "Manufacturing a Food Crisis", by Walden Bello, explains much of the dynamics of world hunger in today's world:

The apostles of the free market and the defenders of dumping - the policies they advocate are bringing about a globalized capitalist industrial agriculture. Developing countries are being integrated into a system where export-oriented production of meat and grain is dominated by large industrial farms. The elimination of tariff and nontariff barriers is facilitating a global agricultural supermarket of elite and middle-class consumers.

There is little room for the hundreds of millions of rural and urban poor in this integrated global market. They are confined to giant suburban slums, where they contend with high food prices or to rural reservations, where they are trapped in marginal agricultural activities and increasingly vulnerable to hunger. Indeed, within the same country, famine in the marginalized sector sometimes coexists with prosperity in the globalized sector.

This transformation is a traumatic one for hundreds of millions of people, since *peasant production is not simply an economic activity. It is an ancient way of life, a culture.*

Such is, and has always been, the results of imperialism – war, misery, and the repression of the many, so that a small minority may live in luxury beyond the imagination of most normal people.

57.

Rush To Control India's Food Supply

A disturbing trend in the food sector is accelerating worldwide with the emergence of the new "food barons". There is no better way to control a country than to control its food supply.

Indian government is brazenly siding with these demoniac forces and putting the country's food supply up for grabs. Following reports may testify to this fact.

Clinton Gives GM Crops A Push

Though Hillary Avoided The Emotive Word GM, She Waxed Eloquent On Agri Tech

Rumu Banerjee | Times of India, Jul 20, 2009

New Delhi: Days after the government said it was planning to introduce genetically modified food crops in the country in three years, US secretary of state Hillary Clinton gave a clear indication of the US administration's approval of deploying 'cutting-edge technology' to raise crop yields.

During her first visit to India as secretary of state,which included a strategic stop at the country's premier agriculture institute, Indian Agricultural Research Institute, Clinton was vocal about the need to address the "root" of the problem of world hunger: Crop productivity. And helping increase crop yield would be cutting-edge technology, she claimed.

"India's leadership in agriculture is absolutely crucial,"Clinton said as she spoke at length on the US administration's focus on global hunger and malnutrition. Pledging to "work and support"

Indian initiatives, Clinton added,"We have to work together. It is imperative that we invest in science that increases crop yield."

The remarks comes in the face of continued opposition to genetically modified food crops in India.

Clinton's statement at the Pusa institute, however, was clear about where the US administration stood on the issue. Talking about the Green Revolution that took place in India in the 1960s, she emphasized the need for close cooperation between the two countries again: This time, in agriculture and the use of technology in this field.

"India has 3% of the world's crop land but feeds 17% of the world's population. Its leadership in agriculture is crucial... we are looking at ways to accelerate in a short period of time the growth of productivity," Clinton said.

Food For Thought: Agriculture minister Sharad Pawar with US Secretary of State Hillary Clinton at IARI in New Delhi

Asked about the US's commitment to GM crops, as opposed to the cautious stand taken by the EU, Clinton admitted,"We're looking at it in a holistic way, by being very vigilant about how we do it. "Interestingly, while the emphasis on technology in agriculture was more than apparent, Clinton avoided using the emotive word 'GM' throughout.

However, Clinton's visit -- which was to learn more about research done by IARI, helped by US funding, to develop seeds that give better productivity and crops that use less water as well as farm equipment that reduce production costs -- was indicative of the thrust on technology that US plans to give in the collaboration agreement that will be signed on Monday.

Speaking about the "five pillars of collaboration that India and US would be redefining", Clinton said agriculture was one of the "strongest pillars". Giving support to Clinton's statement was agriculture minister Sharad Pawar. "For India,a key priority is to trigger the next generation of reforms in the agrarian economy ... Our joint collaboration in frontier areas of research including biotechnology could make a significant contribution to the world," he said.

Accompanying Clinton was new US ambassador to India Timothy Roemer and special envoy on climate change Todd Stern as well as other senior officials. Also present were Dr Mangala Rai,DG,ICAR; Indian ambassador to US Meera Shankar, A K Upadhyay, special secretary, department of agriculture and education and H S Gupta, director, IARI.

Agriculture To Be Pillar Of Us-India Cooperation: Clinton

Zeenews, July 19, 2009

New Delhi: Stating that India was well positioned to help it lead the fight against hunger, the US on Sunday said agriculture will be the strongest of the five pillars of cooperation the Obama administration was seeking with New Delhi.

"We will be announcing the five pillars of our cooperation (after talks tomorrow). And one of the strongest and most important will be agriculture," US Secretary of State Hillary Clinton told reporters after a visit to the Indian Agriculture Research Institute (IARI), where she toured the agriculture research site.

Recalling 50 years of US-Indo partnership in agriculture, Clinton said, "We have to work together because it is imperative that we invest in science that will increase crop yields."

"We have collaborated over more than 50 years and today we called to collaborate once again," she said.

Areas of collaboration she highlighted included linking farms and markets so that farmers can sell their products, expanding the export of technology and training to bring more assistance to farmers, and strengthening the response to climate change, which

Government Of The Criminals, By The Criminals, For The Criminals

Latest reports state that 162 members of parliament in India (out of 545) have legal charges levied against them and are being investigated. There is a high level of criminalization in politics, which is now getting regularly exposed. A number of members of parliament were implicated in scams last year. This has put the government on a back foot and political parties are losing ground. In nutshell, Indian politics is tough and dirty.

threatens the waterways that sustain agriculture in many parts of the world including South Asia.

Stating that hunger persists and affects the entire human conditions as well as peace, she said, "It would be a signature issue of the Obama administration to do what we can to fight hunger and extend food security. And India is well positioned to help us lead this fight."

"The work has already begun clearly here, when I just saw scientists are developing seeds that produce higher yields, crops that require less water, farm equipment that conserve energy. All this is part of meeting the challenge we face with global hunger," she said.

On possible areas of partnerships, Clinton said the two nations are working together to produce better seeds, hybrids that can grow with less water and new farming techniques.

"We have no limits on what we are going to be exploring together. But our goal is the same -- we want to improve agriculture productivity. We want to get more of agriculture dollar into the hands of the farmer. We want India to do more food processing and value added agriculture.

The so-called political leaders are busy making plans to advance the material prosperity of their nation, but factually these political leaders only want an exalted position for themselves. Due to their greed for material position, they falsely present themselves as leaders before the people and collect their votes, although they are completely under the grip of the laws of material nature. These are some of the faults of modern civilization. Without taking to God consciousness and accepting the authority of the Lord, the living entities become ultimately confused and frustrated in their planmaking attempts. Due to their unauthorized plans for economic development, the price of commodities is rising daily all over the world, so much so that is has become difficult for the poorer classes, and they are suffering the consequences. And due to lack of Krsna consciousness, people are being fooled by so-called leaders and planmakers. Consequently, the sufferings of the people are increasing. According to the laws of nature, which are backed by the Lord, nothing can be permanent within this material world; therefore everyone should be allowed to take shelter of the Absolute in order to be saved.

~ Srila Prabhupada (Srimad Bhagavatam 4.24.66)

"We are going to be working with India very closely. And I am excited about the potential that holds," she said.

"So as we look at strengthening agriculture and fighting hunger particularly in South Asia, but also in Africa and elsewhere, India's leadership is absolutely crucial. And the United States is today just as proud to work with and support India's efforts as we were 50 years ago," Clinton said.

Stating that the world has the resources to feed everyone, Clinton said, "Nonetheless, hunger persists; that is why the G-8 and other countries committed USD 20 billion to end global hunger." The US has committed USD 3.5 billion to this effort. Clinton noted that research is a critical component in improving agriculture.

58.

Too Powerful

For Being Just A Firm

Of the world's 100 largest economic entities, 51 are multinational companies and 49 are nation states. Sales and net profit figures for some multinationals are higher than GNPs of developing countries, like for example the annual sales of Shell are roughly £68billion, which is two and half times the income of Nigeria's 110 million people. In 1989, more than 18 per cent of all share trading was in the shares of the major multinationals.

In 1993 the combined assets of the top 300 MNCs would make up roughly a quarter of the worlds $20trillion productive assets and there was an accusation by Jack Behrman that several American companies could "buy out" some European countries. Coca-Cola advertisements are being shown 560 million times a day, everyday in 160 countries, while majority of world population does not know where Fiji is.

These facts and figures undoubtfully may lead to the conclusion that indeed the MNCs do possess distinctive economical superiority over some nation states, and therefore are too powerful for being just a firm with such cynical target as profit maximisation and not welfare of the citizens.

Since MNCs dominate media production and distribution - just six corporations sell 80 percent of all the recorded music worldwide - they introduce ideas and images that some governments and religious groups fear may destabilize their societies.

Government As A Corporate Agent

Accelerated process of Globalisation is one of the main features of twentieth century world politics and is "one of the most dramatic developments of the period and has more than just economical and industrial significance". Professor Sakamoto has identified the globalisation of capitalism as the "...key element in the changing world order". Accordingly, the notion of the nation state becomes less vivid, while new actors, such as multinational companies are being spotted on the international stage. Multinationals(MNCs) by their virtue are direct creations of globalisation, however, the humanity is still in doubt whether the sudden "mushrooming" of these institutions bodes good for the new global order or whether they are going to turn into 'mutant monsters' causing major economic disasters. Bill Emott argued that Multinationals do not dominate the world market and 'are not even global', while others strongly feel that "multinationals are increasingly going global" and call them "powerful beasts".

MNCs have emerged because of 'structural' and 'inherent' market imperfections, such as restrictions on imports, excise duties, subsidies, unstable exchange rates, distribution and marketing

> *"Human prosperity flourishes by natural gifts and not by gigantic industrial enterprises. The gigantic industrial enterprises are products of a godless civilization, and they cause the destruction of the noble aims of human life. The more we go on increasing such troublesome industries to squeeze out the vital energy of the human being, the more there will be unrest and dissatisfaction of the people in general, although a few only can live lavishly by exploitation. The natural gifts such as grains and vegetables, fruits, rivers, the hills of jewels and minerals, and the seas full of pearls are supplied by the order of the Supreme, and as He desires, material nature produces them in abundance or restricts them at times."*
>
> *-Srila Prabhupada (Srimad Bhagavatam 1.8.40)*

costs and have grown rapidly because of economies of scale and particularly due to their burst through national boundaries, customs and ideologies.

The primary target of promotional policies of multinationals is to create one customer culture, so that people around the globe purchase identical basket of goods: "watch Hollywood films on Phillips television set, while smoking Marlboro and drinking Coke". During the 1970s largest number out of 7000 MNCs was based in USA. By the early 1990s there were 35000 multinationals, however USA still maintained its leadership. These companies aim at promoting same goods around the globe in order to create one identical consumer culture, which is very much influenced by that of American.

Historically, public opposition to multinationals has arisen mainly from concerns about undue concentrations of power, and their implications for national sovereignty and cultures. In recent years, however, there has been a shift in emphasis away from these 'state-centred' concerns towards more 'people-centred' concerns, such as the environment and human rights.

"The dinosaur's eloquent lesson is that if some bigness is good, an overabundance of bigness is not necessarily better."

- Eric Johnston.

59.

Profit

The Only Thing That Matters

A corporation has its own life; it lives for profit, at all costs. It only shares humane concerns for social and environmental issues insofar as it is profitable to do so. Actions deemed to be cooperative with environmental, health, safety or social concerns, are motivated primarily by self interest, the wider interests of society are a distant second. Legally there is nothing wrong with this; it is what a corporation is designed to do, and what it is bound by through its charter. As such we should not expect anything more from these profit making economic entities, and we should certainly not expect them to harbour any significant environmental or social concern.

A profit oriented private enterprise can never look after the citizens' welfare the way a government can. For example, crop insurance is not an area where any private insurance company would be interested, but the government can go beyond the concern for profitability in the insurance business and subsidise crop insurance in order to stabilise agricultural earnings and make investment in agriculture less risky and more attractive.

Similarly, no private electricity company would be even remotely interested in distributing power to widely diffused rural settlements. This is a task that only a state enterprise would undertake, maybe at a loss initially, and with a generous subsidy; but if it helps the local economy to bloom, maybe in the long run, it will help make profit.

There is also the question of the interests of future generations. A private company motivated only by profit and discounting the present value of future earnings at the current rate of interest, would not see anything beyond 15 years, as the present value of earnings beyond that period would be nearly zero. Only the government can protect the interests of future generations and save the environment from degradation that is not discernible at one point of time but accumulates over decades - for example, the depletion of the ozone shield.

For a corporation, environmental concerns are secondary to securing profit, and environmental catastrophes are common 'externalities' of the business economy. At a time when many of our resources are depleting globally- in particular our fossil fuels, and even regionally-such as water supplies, the profit motive does not encourage restraint or conservation. Logically, a profit making company cannot advise its customers to consume less, as this

santustasya nirihasya
atmaramasya yat sukham
kutas tat kama-lobhena
dhavato 'rthehaya disah

One who is content and satisfied and who links his activities with the Supreme Personality of Godhead residing in everyone's heart enjoys transcendental happiness without endeavoring for his livelihood. Where is such happiness for a materialistic man who is impelled by lust and greed and who therefore wanders in all directions with a desire to accumulate wealth?

sada santusta-manasah
sarvah sivamaya disah
sarkara-kantakadibhyo
yathopanat-padah sivam

For a person who has suitable shoes on his feet, there is no danger even when he walks on pebbles and thorns. For him, everything is auspicious. Similarly, for one who is always self-satisfied there is no distress; indeed, he feels happiness everywhere.

~ Srila Prabhupada (Srimad Bhagavatam 7.15.16-17)

directly undermines business revenues. In the case of fossil fuels, this simple fact has seen the continual increase in oil consumption that is so dangerously poisoning our biosphere. It is unlikely that alternative energy production will prove more profitable in the near future, and thus quite unlikely that alternatives will be vigorously pursued by profit making companies.

In the UK, despite current drought conditions and water usage restrictions imposed upon the general public, Thames Water PLC has declared record pre-tax profits. Meanwhile it has neglected to reduce the 894 million litres a day that is lost through faulty pipes and leakage. A publicly owned and managed water supplier would not be under financial pressure by shareholders and would be able to reinvest profits into infrastructure and conservation.

60.

Countries On Sale

Gold Rush For The Lands In The Third World

The 'Neo-Colonial' Food Grab

In the 1800s, European colonial powers divided up the Third World in their quest for primary agricultural and mineral commodities. In post-colonial times, oil corporations have gained oil concessions in these nations through questionable dealings with local elites, enriching the elites and leaving the vast majority in these countries desperately poor. Recently, a new scramble has begun: the attempt by food-deficit countries, primarily in the Middle East, to buy or rent hundreds of thousands of hectares of prime agricultural land in the poor countries. In the meantime, millions in these countries are starving and are in desperate need of food aid.

What is spurring this attempt to secure agricultural land in other countries is the global food crisis and price volatility. Saudi Arabia and other oil exporting Middle Eastern countries have decided to use their oil wealth to buy land in poorer nations, including Ukraine, Kazakhstan, Pakistan, Uganda, Ethiopia and Sudan. China is also trying to buy lands abroad, but is concentrating on Kazakhstan.

In August, Andrew England reported in The Financial Times that "Saudi Arabia plans to set up large-scale projects overseas that will later involve the private sector in growing crops such as corn, wheat and rice. Once a country has been selected, each project could be in excess of 100,000 hectares – about ten times the size of Manhattan Island – and the majority of the crop would be exported directly to Saudi Arabia. This is not trade, but direct shipment of food crops to the land-owners.

"While Saudi Arabia's plans are among the grandest, they reflect growing interest in such projects among capital-rich countries that import most of their food. The United Arab Emirates is looking into Kazakhstan and Sudan. Libya is hoping to lease farms in Ukraine, and South Korea has hinted at plans in Mongolia."

Joachim von Braun, director of the International Food Policy Research Institute, says, "This is a new trend within the global food crisis. The dominant force today is security of food supplies."

England wrote, "Alarmed by exporting countries' trade restrictions – such as India's curbs on exports of rice, Ukraine's halt to wheat shipments, and Argentina's imposition of heavy taxes on overseas sales of soya – importing countries have realized that their dependence on the international food market makes them vulnerable not only to an abrupt surge in prices but, more crucially, to an interruption in supplies. As a result, food security is at the top of the political agenda for the first time since the 1970s."

For poor countries rich in cultivable land and water but short of capital, such plans could also make a lot of sense. Lennart Bage, of the UN's International Fund for Agriculture Development in Rome, says that "land was long thought less important than oil or mineral deposits. But now fertile land with access to water has become a strategic asset."

Sudan is seeking to attract at least one billion dollars of capital for its agricultural sector from Arab and Asian investment groups. The investment ministry is marketing 17 large-scale projects that would cover an area of 880,000 hectares.

Ethiopia's Prime Minister Meles Zenawi is also enthusiastic. He welcomed the Saudi agriculture delegation with the following words: "We would be very eager to provide hundreds of thousands of hectares of agricultural land for investment."

Jacques Diouf, director general of the U.N. Food and Agriculture Organization, has warned that the headlong drive by rich food-importing countries to buy up vast tracts of farmland in the world's poorer states risks "creating a neo-colonial" agricultural system.

The food-producing countries need to be wary of these deals, warns England. "Through secretive bilateral agreements, the investors hope to be able to bypass any potential trade restriction that the host country might impose during a crisis."

Maryknoll Father Ken Thesing, who is working with the Jesuit Refugee Service in Juba, Southern Sudan, offers further insight and caution, "In Southern Sudan we have vast tracts of land that can be very productive, without irrigation. But we need infrastructure, inputs, and expertise to positively 'harvest' the potential of the land. It is going to be a challenge to do that without Southern Sudan ending up either missing the opportunity to move ahead and use its natural advantage at this time of food shortage/crisis or ending up exploited by other 'rich' countries and entrepreneurs using the resources for their private benefit."

For some policymakers this evokes the nightmare scenario of crops being transported out of fortified farms as hungry locals look on. Jacques Diouf, director general of the UN Food and Agriculture Organization (FAO), says he dreads "the emergence of a neocolonial pact for the supply of raw materials with no value added for the producer countries. We are deliberating on land policy tools that we can use to counsel the governments involved. The idea is not to renounce such a potential godsend, but to avoid expropriations of small producers and speculation."

Lennart Bage, president of the U.N. International Fund for Agriculture Development in Rome, says that land was long considered less important than oil or mineral resources.

But now, with food prices having doubled on average from a year ago, "fertile land with access to water has become a strategic asset."

But many of the countries whose farmland is being snapped up are already unable to feed their own people, and it may be just a matter of time before that triggers anti-government unrest and the resource wars that many fear will erupt in the coming decades.

Alain Karsenty, a researcher in agronomics, claims that there will be another devastating impact of the headlong rush into these agricultural schemes – deforestation. "As the price of agricultural land increases, land with forest values will lose profitability. Maintaining forests, whether for environmental purposes or for economic purposes, will be abandoned as a national objective."

In his new book, Rising Powers, Shrinking Planet: The New Geopolitics of Energy, Michael T. Klare writes that we are now seeing the resurrection of a mercantilist form of global economy, similar to the colonial era of the 19th century, when national states took control of resources in colonial territories. As essential to the global economy as are corporations, the effort to lock in foreign sources of energy and strategic resources is now "statist," rather than corporate. Examples in the energy sector are President Bush's two trips to Saudi Arabia to plead for increased oil production in order to stabilize prices, and China's dealings with Sudan (also Congo and Zimbabwe).

These state efforts to insure that energy, strategic metals and food will go to rich countries is further marginalizing the poor countries, where many of these resources are found. To sum up his analysis: the first quarter of the 21st century is characterized by a statist effort to lock in foreign sources of strategic resources, in a planet now running out of these resources, increasing the possibility of military confrontations between nuclear powers.

George Monbiot of the Guardian concludes with this harsh outlook. "None of this is to suggest that the poor nations should not sell food to the rich. To escape from famine, countries must enhance their purchasing power. This often means selling farm products and increasing their value by processing them locally. But there is nothing fair about the deals described above. Where once they used gunboats and sepoys, the rich nations now use checkbooks and lawyers to seize food from the hungry. The scramble for resources has begun, but in the short term, at any rate, we will hardly notice. The rich world's governments will protect themselves from the political cost of shortages, even if it means that other people must starve."

In 2008, the South Korean multinational Daewoo Logistics secured 1.3 million hectares of farmland in Madagascar, half the size of Belgium, to grow maize and crops for biofuels. Roughly half of the country's arable land, as well as rainforests of rich and unique biodiversity, were to be converted into palm and corn monocultures, producing food for export from a country where a third of the population and 50 percent of children under 5 are malnourished, using workers imported from South Africa instead of locals. Those living on the land were never consulted or informed, despite being dependent on the land for food and income. The controversial deal played a major part in prolonged anti-government protests on the island that resulted in over a hundred deaths. Shortly after the Madagascar deal, Tanzania announced that South Korea was in talks to develop 100,000 hectares for food production and processing for 700 to 800 billion won. Scheduled to be completed in 2010, it will be the largest single piece of agricultural infrastructure South Korea has ever built overseas.

In 2009, Hyundai Heavy Industries acquired a majority stake in a company cultivating 10,000 hectares of farmland in the Russian Far East and a wealthy South Korean provincial government secured 95,000 hectares of farmland in Oriental Mindoro, central Philippines, to grow corn. The South Jeolla province became the first provincial government to benefit from a newly created central government fund to develop farmland overseas, receiving a cheap loan of $1.9 million for the Mindoro project. The feedstock is expected to produce 10,000 tonnes of feed in the first year for South Korea. South Korean multinationals and provincial governments have also purchased land in Sulawesi, Indonesia, Cambodia and Bulgan, Mongolia. The South Korean government itself announced its intention to invest 30 billion won in land in Paraguay and Uruguay. Discussions with Laos, Myanmar and Senegal are also currently underway.

(Source: NewsNotes, November-December 2008)

61.

Making A 'Banana Republic' Of India

Monsanto And Others Following In The Footsteps Of United Fruit Co.

History Is Repeating Itself

The United Fruit Company was an American corporation that traded in tropical fruit (primarily bananas) grown on Central and South American plantations and sold in the United States and Europe. The company was formed in 1899.

It flourished in the early and mid-20th century and came to control vast territories and transportation networks in Central America, the Caribbean coast of Colombia, Ecuador, and the West Indies. Though it competed with the Standard Fruit Company for dominance in the international banana trade, it maintained a virtual monopoly in certain regions, some of which came to be called banana republics.

It had a deep and long-lasting impact on the economic and political development of several Latin American countries. Critics often accused it of exploitative neocolonialism and described it as the archetypal example of the influence of a multinational corporation on the internal politics of the banana republics.

At its founding in 1899, United Fruit was capitalized at US$11,230,000. The company proceeded to buy a share in 14 competitors, assuring them of 80% of the banana import business in the United States, then their main source of income.

In 1901, the government of Guatemala hired the United Fruit Company to manage the country's postal service and in 1913 the United Fruit Company created the Tropical Radio and Telegraph Company. By 1930 it had absorbed more than 20 rival firms, acquiring a capital of US$215,000,000 and becoming the largest employer in Central America.

Throughout most of its history, United Fruit's main competitor was the Standard Fruit Company, now the Dole Food Company.

Reputation

The United Fruit Company was frequently accused of bribing government officials in exchange for preferential treatment, exploiting its workers, paying little by way of taxes to the governments of the countries in which it operated, and working ruthlessly to consolidate monopolies. Latin American journalists sometimes referred to the company as el pulpo ("the octopus"), and leftist parties in Central and South America encouraged the company's workers to strike.

Criticism of the United Fruit Company became a staple of the discourse of the communist parties in several Latin American countries, where its activities were often interpreted as illustrating Vladimir Lenin's theory of capitalist imperialism. Major left-wing writers in Latin America, such as Carlos Luis Fallas of Costa Rica, Ramón Amaya Amador of Honduras, Miguel Ángel Asturias and Augusto Monterroso of Guatemala, Gabriel García Márquez of Colombia, and Pablo Neruda of Chile, denounced the company in their literature.

The business practices of United Fruit were also frequently criticized by journalists, politicians, and artists in the United States. Little Steven released a song called "Bitter Fruit" in 1987 in which lyrics referred to a hard life for a company "far away" and whose accompanying video, depicted orange groves worked by peasants overseen by wealthy managers. Although the lyrics and scenery are generic, United Fruit (or its successor Chiquita) was reputed to be the target. In 1950, Gore Vidal published a novel "Dark Green, Bright Red", in which a thinly fictionalized version of United Fruit supports a military coup in a thinly fictionalized Guatemala.

History in Central America

The United Fruit Company (UFCO) owned vast tracts of land in the Caribbean lowlands. UFCO's policies of acquiring tax breaks and other benefits from host governments led to it building enclave economies in the regions, in which a company's investment is largely self-contained for its employees and overseas investors and the benefits of the export earnings are not shared with the host country.

One of the company's primary tactics for maintaining market dominance was to control the distribution of banana lands. UFCO claimed that hurricanes, blight and other natural threats required them to hold extra land or reserve land. In practice, what this meant was that UFCO was able to prevent the government from distributing banana lands to peasants who wanted a share of the banana trade.

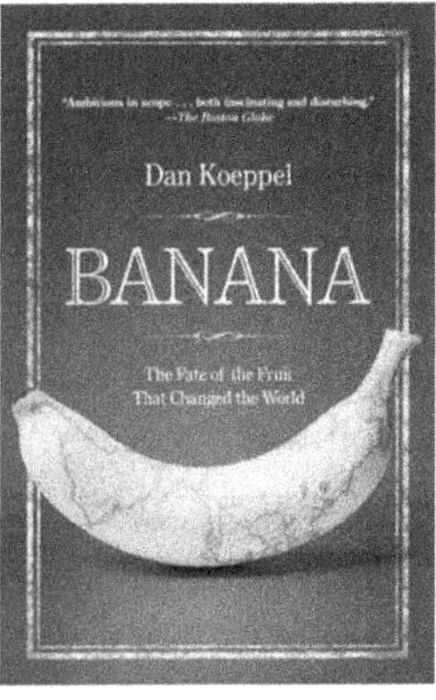

The fact that the UFCO relied so heavily on manipulation of land use rights in order to maintain their market dominance had a number of long-term consequences for the region. For the company to maintain its unequal land holdings it often required government concessions. And this in turn meant that the company had to be politically involved in the region even though it was an American company. In fact, the heavy-handed involvement of the company in governments which often were or became corrupt created the term "Banana republic" representing a "servile dictatorship".

It allowed vast tracts of land under its ownership to remain uncultivated and, in Guatemala and elsewhere, it discouraged the government from building highways, which would lessen the profitable transportation monopoly of the railroads under its control. UFCO had also destroyed at least one of those railroads upon leaving its area of operation.

In 1954, the democratically elected Guatemalan government of Colonel Jacobo Arbenz Guzmán was toppled by U.S.-backed forces led by Colonel Carlos Castillo Armas who invaded from Honduras. Assigned by the Eisenhower administration, this military opposition was armed, trained and organized by the U.S. Central Intelligence Agency.

The directors of United Fruit Company (UFCO) had lobbied to convince the Truman and Eisenhower administrations that Colonel Arbenz intended to align Guatemala with the Soviet Bloc. Besides the disputed issue of Arbenz's allegiance to Communism, UFCO was being threatened by the Arbenz government's agrarian reform legislation and new Labor Code.

Vested Interests In High Places

United States Secretary of State was John Foster Dulles whose law firm Sullivan and Cromwell had represented United Fruit. His brother Allen Dulles was the director of the CIA, and a board member of United Fruit.

Ed Whitman, who was United Fruit's principal lobbyist, was married to President Eisenhower's personal secretary,Ann C. Whitman. Many individuals who directly influenced U.S. policy towards Guatemala in the 1950s also had direct ties to UFCO.

Company holdings in Cuba, which included sugar mills in the Oriente region of the island, were expropriated by the 1959 revolutionary government led by Fidel Castro. By April 1960 Castro was accusing the company of aiding Cuban exiles and supporters of former leader Fulgencio Batista in initiating a seaborn invasion of Cuba directed from the United States. Castro warned the U.S. that "Cuba is not another Guatemala" in one of many combative diplomatic exchanges before the failed Bay of Pigs invasion of 1961.

PR Pioneers

Finally, United Fruit are notable for pioneering PR. They were clients of Edward Bernays, Freud's nephew and not coincidentally the godfather of public relations. Applying the principles of Freudian psychology to advertising, Bernays developed the ideas of product placement, celebrity endorsement, and selling things with sex.

For United Fruit, he publicized their (occasional) philanthropic endeavours in Central America, made educational films and radio programmes, and set up a Middle America Information Bureau to inform journalists about the realities of life in the growing regions. He encouraged United Fruit to donate to the exploration of the archaeological ruins that had been uncovered in the course of their jungle-clearing.

Bananagate

In 1975, the U.S. Securities and Exchange Commission exposed a scheme by United Brands (dubbed Bananagate) to bribe Honduran President Oswaldo López Arellano with US$1.25 million, plus the promise of another US$1.25 million upon the reduction of certain export taxes. Trading in United Brands stock was halted and López was ousted in a military coup.

Banana Massacre

One of the most notorious strikes by United Fruit workers broke out on 12 November 1928 on the Caribbean coast of Colombia, near Santa Marta.

On December 6, Colombian Army troops allegedly under the command of General Cortés Vargas, opened fire on a crowd of strikers gathered in the central square of the town of Ciénaga. Estimates of the number of casualties vary from 400 to 2000.

The military justified this action by claiming that the strike was subversive and its organizers were Communist revolutionaries. Congressman Jorge Eliécer Gaitán claimed that the army had acted under instructions from the United Fruit Company. The ensuing scandal contributed to President Miguel Abadía Méndez's Conservative Party being voted out of office in 1930, putting an end to 44 years of Conservative rule in Colombia.

The Columbian government claimed that they had to resort to the military action on the innocent strikers as they feared a US invasion.

There may be a grain of truth in this claim as US military was used in Mexico, the Caribbean, and Central America close to 30 times prior to the 1929 massacre for the purposes of putting down strikes and generally making large areas of land in other countries "safe for bananas". Howard Zinn wrote quite a bit about US military interventions on behalf of United Fruit in his People's History of the United States.

The telegram from Bogotá Embassy to the U.S. Secretary of State, dated December 5, 1928, stated:

"I have been following Santa Marta fruit strike through United Fruit Company representative here; also through Minister of Foreign Affairs who on Saturday told me government would send additional troops and would arrest all strike leaders and transport them to prison at Cartagena; that government would give adequate protection to American interests involved."

The telegram from Bogotá Embassy to Secretary of State, date December 7, 1928, stated:

"Situation outside Santa Marta City unquestionably very serious: outside zone is in revolt; military who have orders "not to spare ammunition" have already killed and wounded about fifty strikers. Government now talks of general offensive against strikers as soon as all troopships now on the way arrive early next week."

The Dispatch from US Bogotá Embassy to the US Secretary of State, dated December 29, 1928, stated:

"I have the honor to report that the legal advisor of the United Fruit Company here in Bogotá stated yesterday that the total number of strikers killed by the Colombian military authorities during the recent disturbance reached between five and six hundred; while the number of soldiers killed was one."

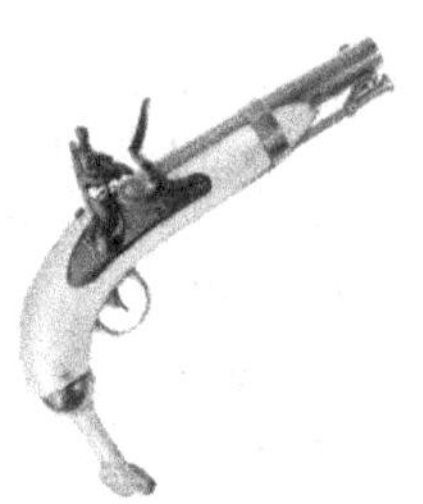

The Dispatch from US Bogotá Embassy to the US Secretary of State, dated January 16, 1929, stated:

"I have the honor to report that the Bogotá representative of the United Fruit Company told me yesterday that the total number of strikers killed by the Colombian military exceeded one thousand."

The surviving strikers of the massacre were immediately put in jail and executed. There were many other small strikes that were inspired by the one that caused the banana massacre.

The Banana massacre is said to be one of the main events that preceded the Bogotazo, the subsequent era of violence known as La Violencia, and the guerrillas who developed during the bipartisan National Front period, creating the ongoing armed conflict in Colombia.

That day marked a turning point, the end of a hopeful age of reform and the beginning of a bloody age of revolution and reaction. Over the next four decades, hundreds of thousands of people —

200,000 in Guatemala alone — were killed in guerrilla attacks, government crackdowns and civil wars across Latin America.

A resident of Bogota provides an epitaph: "Look at the mess we've got ourselves into just because we invited a gringo to eat some bananas."

The GM Genocide In India

Thousands Of Indian Farmers Are Committing Suicide After Using Genetically Modified Crops

History is repeating itself. Only the players have changed. Instead of South America, it is South Asia and instead of UFCO, it is Monsanto and others.

When Prince Charles claimed thousands of Indian farmers were killing themselves after using GM crops, he was branded a scaremonger. In fact, situation is even worse than he feared. Beguiled by the promise of future riches, thousands of farmers are borrowing money in order to buy the GM seeds. But when the harvests fail, they are left with spiralling debts - and no income.

Thousands of farmers have taken their own life as a result of the ruthless drive to use India as a testing ground for genetically modified crops. The crisis, branded the 'GM Genocide' by

> *The more self-reliant people become in third world countries, the less they need the products of the global economy. If they replace the export crops that have been foisted on them and grow locally adapted food crops, they won't need to import American grain. In the history of the world, every place where humans have prospered has provided them with the food and fiber and building materials that they needed, for if food wouldn't grow (like in Antarctica and the Sahara), people didn't stick around long.*
>
> *People are naturally self-reliant and it takes quite a social derangement to keep them from building adequate shelters and growing adequate food. Corporate imperialists are exporters of social derangement. They build a pipeline to the resources of an area and hook it up to a vacuum, pulling out things of value and leaving only pollution behind. The sooner that indigenous peoples take up arms against the visiting corporatist who is casing the joint, the better off they will be.*
>
> *~ Daniel Rodriguez*

campaigners, was highlighted when Prince Charles claimed that the issue of GM had become a 'global moral question' - and the time had come to end its unstoppable march.

The price difference is staggering: £10 for 100 grams of GM seed, compared with less than £10 for 1,000 times more traditional seeds.

But GM salesmen and government officials had promised farmers that these were 'magic seeds' - with better crops that would be free from parasites and insects. Indeed, in a bid to promote the uptake of GM seeds, traditional varieties were banned from many government seed banks.

India's economic boom means cities such as Mumbai and Delhi have flourished, while the farmers' lives have slid back into the dark ages. When crops failed in the past, farmers could still save seeds and replant them the following year.

But with GM seeds they cannot do this. GM seeds contain 'terminator technology', so that the resulting crops do not produce viable seeds of their own.

As a result, farmers have to buy new seeds each year at the same punitive prices. For some, that means the difference between life and death. Thus the cost of the genetically modified future is murderously high.

Official figures from the Indian Ministry of Agriculture do indeed confirm that it is a huge humanitarian crisis, more than 1,000 farmers are killing themselves each month. According to the National Crime Records Bureau (NCRB), between 1995 and 2009, more than a quarter-million farmers committed suicide.

When civilization is disconnected from the loving relation of the Supreme Personality of Godhead, symptoms like changes of seasonal regulations, foul means of livelihood, greed, anger and fraudulence become rampant. The change of seasonal regulations refers to one season's atmosphere becoming manifest in another season -- for example the rainy season's being transferred to autumn, or the fructification of fruits and flowers from one season in another season. A godless man is invariably greedy, angry and fraudulent.

~ Srila Prabhupada (Srimad Bhagavatam 1.14.3)

In 2009 alone, more than 17,000 farmers committed suicide just in the state of Uttar Pradesh.

Some experts believe the actual number of farmer suicides is much higher than official data indicates.

"The official statistics in India rely on the National Crime Records Bureau -- basically what are police reports of suicide," says Professor Prabhat Jha of the Center for Global Health Research in Toronto, according to BBC.

"Suicide is a taboo subject," he adds, suggesting that some deaths have likely been attributed by their families to other causes, like serious illness.

Indian agriculture is in such dire straits that everyday 2000 farmers are quitting agriculture to join the swelling ranks of coolies in urban slums. This fact was reported by International Business Times in a report dated May 02, 2013.

(Source: Wikipedia and others)

62.

Why Fears Of A Foreign Hand Are Real

Arun Kumar, The Hindu, June 22, 2012

There are enough reasons to suspect that companies overseas influence Indian politics.

Pranab Mukherjee is likely to be India's next President. It seemed to be touch and go until the tide turned in his favour. It has been suggested that the corporates swung it for him not because he is one of the most seasoned Indian politicians but because they wanted him out of the Ministry of Finance. He has acted tough on retrospective taxation and GAAR – the measures in his recent budget to tackle black income generation. But it would not be surprising if the real pressure was from foreign shores. Indian corporates are sensitive to what their foreign counterparts think. So is our political leadership. Britain and Netherlands exerted strong influence on the Vodafone case. How much of our politics is being determined by such pressures?

Pressure On Polity

Several recent events testify that pressure is certainly being exerted on the polity: Hillary Clinton's visit to India to influence the government's policies on trade with Iran and on FDI in retail, the S&P downgrade of India and the Aircel Maxis deal. There are also less visible cases of foreign pressure as in defence purchases (the British were upset at our rejection of the Eurofighter), energy sector investments (oil, gas and nuclear), opening of markets and so on.

The Bofors scam has had a continuing impact on politics since 1987. Sten Lindstrom, the former head of the Swedish police who led the investigations into the Bofors-India howitzer deal, recently underlined that there was conclusive evidence that Ottavio Quattarocchi, a close friend of the Nehru-Gandhi family, was one of the recipients of kickbacks. His role in swinging the Bofors deal at the last minute was known. It is not in doubt that payoffs were made or that the Bofors guns are good. The only unsettled issue is who got the money.

That Mr. Quattrochi had powerful friends was confirmed when he was allowed to escape the country. The case was apparently deliberately spoilt by the investigative agencies, including the CBI and, therefore, lost in the courts — in Malaysia, Britain and Argentina. The red corner notice against him "could not be executed" since our police agencies could not "find" him even though journalists could interview him.

Evidence points to a high level cover up. M.S. Solanki, then the External Affairs Minister, sacrificed his Cabinet berth rather than reveal what he wrote in the paper he passed on to the Swiss counterpart at a meeting. At that point of time, the Swiss bank accounts were being investigated by the Indian agencies to trace the Bofors payoff trail. Could such a sacrifice of a political career be for an ordinary leader?

Culture Of Kickbacks

Kickbacks are common globally. Sweden is one of the least corrupt countries in the world but its corporations have bribed to get contracts as the Bofors case shows. U.S.-based multinational corporations have resorted to bribes in spite of their being illegal under that country's law.

Recently, Walmart admitted to having bribed its way through in Mexico. When the top management learnt of it, rather than exposing corruption, the internal probe was closed. The same Walmart has been trying to enter India. Ms Clinton's agenda included "persuading" India to open its doors to foreign retail.

The only Chief Minister she visited was Mamata Banerjee, the important UPA partner opposing FDI in retail. It is reminiscent of Henry Kissinger and the Secretaries of Energy and Defence flying to India to lobby for Enron in the mid-1990s. Enron admitted to spending $60 million in India, to "educate" policymakers.

It is not just a few MNCs that indulge in corruption or use their governments to apply pressure on policies. MNC banks are known to help Indians take their capital out of India. UBS bank, the largest Swiss bank, was fined $750 million by the U.S. for helping its citizens to keep secret bank accounts. The same UBS bank was allowed entry into India in spite of its known role; was it a reward for helping some powerful people?

Executives of Siemens, a supposedly honest MNC and an important player in India, were indicted in the U.S. in December 2011 for bribery in Argentina. Investigations revealed that the company also made illegal payments to the tune of $1.4 billion from 2001 to 2007 in Bangladesh, China, Russia, Venezuela and other countries. These were often routed via 'consultants'. The company paid fines and fees of $1.6 billion to the U.S. and German governments for the bribes it paid across the globe.

Siemens started bribing soon after the end of World War II to get contracts under the Marshall Plan which were mostly going to the Americans. Since its prosecution, Siemens claims to have appointed Compliance Officers to check bribery. But, with the prevalence of a high degree of illegality internationally, can one company be honest while others are not? How would it win contracts when those in charge expect to be bribed? Since non-transparent processes are set up, at every step, decisions need to be influenced, as seen in the Bofors case or the 2G spectrum allocation.

The Vodafone case is significant. MNCs (Indian and foreign) have used tax havens and tax planning to avoid paying taxes in India. They create a web of holdings to hide the identity of the real owners of a company or who it is being transferred to.

A man becomes too greedy for wealth and power when he has no higher objective in life and when he thinks that this earthly life of a few years is all in all. Ignorance is the cause for all these anomalies in human society, and to remove this ignorance, especially in this age of degradation, the powerful sun is there to distribute light in the shape of Srimad-Bhagavatam.

~ Srila Prabhupada (Srimad Bhagavatam 1.14.3)

In 1985, in the Mcdowell case, the Supreme Court bench observed, "Colourable devices cannot be part of tax planning and it is wrong to encourage or entertain the belief that it is honourable to avoid the payment of tax by resorting to dubious methods".

This judgment was overturned in 2003 in Union of India vs Azadi Bachao Andolan on the use of the Mauritius route to avoid paying tax in India. Vodafone took advantage of this judgment to successfully argue against having to pay capital gains tax in India on transfer of a company in a tax haven which owned the Indian assets. Mr. Mukherjee was trying to recover lost ground.

Dominant Interests

Indian policies have been subject to foreign pressures since the days of the Cold War in the 1950s. But until the mid-1980s, the decisions were accepted as being in the "long-term national interest." There were accusations in the procurement of the Jaguar aircraft also but these did not create the furore that the Bofors scam did. Since the late 1980s, as in the case of Bofors or the new economic policies in 1991 or the Indo-U.S. nuclear deal, sectional or individual interests have become dominant. These have played havoc with national politics. Pressures and counter pressures are mounted through political parties and their leaders and big business.

The lesson is that foreign pressures tend to damage processes that national politics cannot undo. The public is left bewildered by the goings on, as in the present case of selection of the presidential candidate.

(The writer is Chairperson, Centre for Economic Studies and Planning, School of Social Sciences, Jawaharlal Nehru University.)

63.

India's Tryst

With Multinational Corporations

The existence of Multinational Corporations (MNCs) in India is approximately three centuries old. As such, the historical background of MNCs in India can be traced back to as early as 1600s whereby the British capital came to dominate the Indian scene through their Multinational Corporation known as East India Company. However, demarcation of the clear boundary lines of this history is hampered by the lack of abundant and authentic data. Moreover, such outlining is also obstructed by the discontinuity in the nature of the data relating to these MNCs. Furthermore, the data available with regard to such FDI in one secondary source do not match with that of another source (Nayak, 2006).

As a result of this, researchers could not portray the complete history of Multinational Corporations and FDI pouring in India even during the post independence era.

To discuss the historical background and policy framework for the MNCs, the analsysis has been divided into two periods i.e. pre and post independence era:

Pre Independence Era Policy

According to Nayak (2006), the period from 1900s-1918 can be called as the first phase of FDI in India when there were no restrictions on the nature as well as type of FDI pouring into India.

Majority of these investments at those times were exploitative in nature and were just concentrating in the sectors such as mining and extractive industries to suit the general British economic interest.

It is a noticeable fact that even in the post independence era, a major pie of the FDI source of India continued to come from the same source. It is interesting to note that despite of allowance of this free flow of FDI, no other country was interested in investing in India other than UK and all FDI coming to India during that period were sourced through the Managing Agents from UK

However, the period from 1919-1947 is considered to be more important when the FDI actually originated in India. This phase can be called as second phase of pre-independence FDI history in India. Import duties were introduced during this period to stimulate various British companies to invest in the manufacturing sector in order to protect their businesses in India. Though some Japanese companies also enhanced their trade share with India, yet UK maintained its position as most dominant investor in India during this period.

Post Independence Era Policy

After independence, various issues relating to foreign capital and its accompanying expertise sought attention of the policy makers. With the changing times, the policy of Indian governments kept on changing as per economic and political exigencies prevailing at the time. Accordingly, it can be spilt into four phases (Kumar, 1998 and Chopra, 2003). Whereas in 1960s, these policies were quite liberal, yet these became very stringent in 1970s. However, these were again liberalized in 1980s and real liberalization occurred in 1990s.

But inspite of these changes and modifications in the policies, the underlying principal remained the same - exploitation and plunder. The colonial plunder went on for two centuries but it was not limited to that. They plundered the internal resources of the populace as well by the process of 'mind colonization'.

The slavery was not only physical and financial but intellectual as well. So much so that after India gained independence, post-independence leaders, coloured by the ideas and institutions of Western colonialism largely ignored what were seen as the idiosyncratic views of Mahatma Gandhi, the revered father figure of the Indian independence movement. They preferred the familiar structures of the British Raj. The sad result was the continuation of colonial legacy, at times in its more hideous form. The brown British were to prove worse than the original white British.

And this brings us to the biggest loot ever in mankind's history, the looting of India by her leaders in the post independence era. Trillions of dollars were siphoned off and deposited in the safe heavens of Swiss banking systems while millions died of malnutrition and hunger back home.

Swiss Banking Association report. 2008, gives a break up of countrywise deposits. Here are the top 5 countries.

India—- $1,456 billion
Russia —$ 470 billion
UK ——-$390 billion
Ukraine – $100 billion
China —-$ 96 billion

Source: Swiss Banking Association report 2008

This is more money than all the money in all the banks in India taken together. There is more Indian money in Swiss banks than rest of the world combined.

Is India a poor country? An amount 13 times larger than the country's foreign debt stashed away in secret Swiss accounts, one needs to rethink if India is a poor country. This ill-begotten wealth is even higher than India's GDP and three times that of market capitalisation on national stock exchange.

Corrupt industrialists, politicians, bureaucrats, cricketers, film actors, sex trade and protected wildlife operators, to name just a few,

"In an era rife with globalization, transparent business practices and zero tolerance to fraud and misconduct are key concerns for companies doing business in India," according to a recent KPMG India fraud survey report. The global professional services firm found that top-level executives in India were reluctant to discuss the topics of bribery and corruption. Some 71% of survey respondents felt fraud was an inevitable cost of doing business. A global survey by Ernst & Young is equally blunt about the country: "Seventy percent of India respondents to our survey think that bribery and corruption are widespread in the country."

are the accomplices in this historical heist. But this is just the story of Swiss bank accounts. What about other international banks?

By allowing the proliferation of tax havens in the twentieth century, the Western world explicitly encourages the movement of scarce capital from the developing countries.

Often corporations target new markets in developing countries as Nestle did in the 80's and more recently, the tobacco industry. In these and many other cases, corporations deny any health risks to their products, even in the face of overwhelming scientific evidence, in order to maximize profit. Nestlé's fierce marketing of powdered milk in the 80's caused the deaths of an estimated 1.5 million children through the contaminated water used to make the infant formula.

Nor are human rights observed. Chevron and Coca Cola have been indirectly involved in the violent killings of workers and union officials in developing countries in attempts to suppress workers rights. Instances of kidnappings, torture, discrimination, health violations, fuelling conflicts, privatizing and contaminating local water sources, using child labour and even sex trafficking have all been documented as occurring under the responsibility of the largest corporations. Sweatshops are often used in developing countries by the apparel industry which usually pay negligible wages to under age workers who often work long hours in terrible conditions.

~Rajesh Makwana

64.

MNCs

Bigger Than Their Assets

The reach and influence of multinationals, large and small, is far greater than the official statistics suggest. Policymakers can, therefore, seriously underestimate the extent to which national economies have become intertwined with others. There are at least two sources for this misconception: the way in which cross-border investments are estimated and the manner in which the "boundary" of a firm is defined.

The official figures for the flow of FDI - the historical cost-accounting basis for the asset base of multinational corporations - show an annual flow of nearly $400 billion. The United Nations, however, has recently begun to question these figures and has estimated that if one includes the capital mobilized by local borrowings and the equity shares of partners, the "real" figure is closer to $1.4 trillion per year. In other words, a corporation's "presence" in a country goes beyond the assets that it chooses to locate there.

From a mere three thousand in 1990 the number of multinationals has grown to over 63,000 today. Along with their 821,000 subsidiaries spread all over the world, these multinational corporations directly employ 90 million people (of whom some 20 million in the developing countries) and produce 25 per cent of the world's gross product. The top 1,000 of these multinationals account for 80 percent of the world's industrial output. With its $210 billion in revenues, ExxonMobil is ranked number 21 among the world's 100 largest economies, just behind Sweden and above Turkey.

The influence of a multinational can also be gauged by its effect on local suppliers as it creates new demand and sets new standards of quality. All these elements are part of a world where the local production of MNCs in overseas markets now greatly exceeds the sum of world trade. The resulting deep integration of national economies is growing so fast that any suggestion in developed economies that the domestic-policy agenda can be isolated from the global economy seems antediluvian.

Perhaps even more seriously, the explosion of strategic alliances among firms is transforming the competitive landscape. One estimate is that more than 20,000 alliances have been formed within the last two years alone. How, then, should one now think about where economic power is located? As one executive observed some years ago: "The electronics business in Europe is not the same as the European electronics business." Competition is no longer defined solely by the ownership of assets; it is also a matter of who is in league with whom.

The global economy is in a very precarious state, relying on volatile financial markets and driven increasingly by commercial pressures. Many economists and analysts are predicting a global economic failure sparked by a stock market or financial collapse. This possibility is strengthened by the current conflicts over resources, political instability in many parts of world and the declining strength and influence of the US dollar.

65.

Globalisation Of Corruption

Further Case Studies

Today, often on a daily basis, television and newspaper headlines are filled with corporate corruption scandals that range, from minor cases of individual corruption to multi-billion dollar corporate collapses that shock the conscience of society.

Corruption is a corrosive drain on public trust and on the legitimacy of public and private sector institutions. Its toll can be devastating to a national economy, particularly at a time when open global markets can rapidly reverse investment and capital flows if confidence and trust are compromised by revelations of systemic corruption.

According to a report Sue Hawley and published by the NGO, The Corner House, the growth of corruption across the globe is largely the result of rapid privatization of public enterprises, along with 'reforms' to downsize and undervalue civil services, pushed on developing countries by the World Bank, the IMF and western governments supporting their transnational corporations.

The report estimates that western businesses pay bribes to the tune of $80 billion a year - roughly the amount that the United Nations believes is needed to eradicate global poverty.

"There is seldom just one cockroach in the kitchen"
~Warren Buffet (Stanford Business Magazine, August 2008)

SGS And Hubco, Pakistan

In April 1999, Benazir Bhutto and her husband were found guilty of accepting bribes worth US$ 9m from SGS, were sentenced to five years in prison, and banned from holding seats in parliament for seven years (the defendants appealed against this judgement) (Australian Business Intelligence, 26 April 1999). However, the multinational escaped with no punishment. A group in Pakistan had to apply to the Lahore High Court complaining that SGS 'was still operating in the country despite the fact that the court had convicted one party as being the guilty of the corruption'; and obtained a ruling barring the government from 'allocating any business to SGS' (Business Recorder, 17 May 1999 and 30 May 1999).

Hubco Case

The government of Pakistan has been pursuing cases of alleged bribery of members of the previous regime, especially in energy. Two contracts - one involving Southern Company (USA) (reported in the South China Morning Post, 7 July 1997), and one involving National Grid (UK) (Financial Times, 24 April 1997) were cancelled on the grounds that they had been improperly obtained. The government also took proceedings against existing contracts, investigating alleged corruption, and stating that it would cut the price of electricity agreed under these contracts. The main target of these investigations was Hubco, the largest stock exchange quoted company in Pakistan, which is 26 per cent owned by National Power, a UK energy multinational.

World Bank: No Loan Unless Contracts Left Alone

When the Pakistan government insisted that power tariffs should be reduced because of the evidence that corruption had led to

Under the spell of ignorance, one cannot understand a thing as it is. For example, everyone can see that his grandfather has died and therefore he will also die; man is mortal. The children that he conceives will also die. So death is sure. Still, people are madly accumulating money and working very hard all day and night, not caring for the eternal spirit. This is madness. In their madness, they are very reluctant to make advancement in spiritual understanding.

~ Srila Prabhupada (Bhagavad Gita 14.8)

inflated prices, this 'drew anxious reactions' from many, including the World Bank. Senior government officials say the Bank has urged Pakistan to keep its so-called investigations into alleged corruption in Hubco's contract separate from the future of the company's tariff. The future of an International Monetary Fund agreement, currently under negotiation in Islamabad, is also partly tied to the extent to which Pakistan resolves its dispute with the power companies' (Financial Times, 18 November 1998).

At the end of 1998, the Bank authorised the IMF to proceed with a US$1.3 billion bailout package for Pakistan, 'as it was satisfied with the government assurances for out of court settlement of two-year long row with the Independent Power Producers' (The Nation, 31 December 1998).

At no stage did the UK government appear to have supported the Pakistan government's decision to prosecute Hubco for corruption. The company's chief executive is now living in the 'safe haven' of Cheshire, having 'fled Pakistan following threats that he might be arrested' (Financial Times, 27 October 1998).

The British and other governments actively supported the World Bank's position that Pakistan had to resolve Hubco impasse before it can expect any financial help. (The Nation, 30 December 1998).

In February 1999, a UK government minister emphasised that the action against Hubco was a step backwards for 'investor confidence', rather than a step forward in the fight against corruption:

'Minister of State for Foreign and Commonwealth Affairs Derek Fatchett told a news conference in Karachi that the longer the

Indian officials have raided the offices of Vodafone India, a subsidiary of Vodafone Plc of the U.K., in connection with the massive irregularities in 2G spectrum allocation and following close on the heels of a renewed US$2.54 billion tax demand on the company.

row continued the more it would damage Pakistan's prospects for attracting foreign investment. "Let me say this is an issue in my opinion that has gone on for much too long. It is an issue that needs to be resolved. It is an issue that is damaging investor confidence in Pakistan," he said at the end of a three-day trip' (Reuters, 10 February 1999).

French-Canadian Consortium, Mexico

The 1997 local elections in Mexico City resulted in a landslide victory for the opposition, which had campaigned on an anti-corruption platform. The party promised to review all contracts awarded by the outgoing administration, and cancel those in which irregularities were detected.

One casualty was a US$400m contract for rolling stock for the Mexico City metro, which had been awarded to a French-Canadian consortium. The response of the French and Canadian governments, at the highest possible level, showed little interest in the question of corruption:

> President Jacques Chirac of France and Jean Chretien, the Canadian prime minister, have sent strongly worded letters to Ernesto Zedillo, the Mexican president, protesting at the way a French-Canadian consortium was disqualified from a US$400m tender to provide rolling stock for the Mexico City metro. A new tender for the metro rolling stock is expected only after Cuauhtémoc Cardenas, the mayor-elect, takes office in December and appoints a new management for the Mexico City metro. In his letter to President Zedillo, Mr Chretien lamented Mexico's inadequate legal safeguards for foreign investors'. (Financial Times, 3 October 1997)

One of the most scandalous cases was in the 1980s where the US chemical business Union Carbide tolerated very poor safety standards at a factory in Bhopal, India. The result was an explosion which released clouds of toxic gas and killed thousands. Many more thousands are still alive and very ill because of this. What was particularly irresponsible was the long years it took to force Union Carbide to accept responsibility and pay compensation.

EDS In Czech Republic

In the Czech Republic in 1998, in the case of a US computer firm EDS, the US embassy responded to public accusations of corruption not with encouragement to investigate but with a bland statement:

> The US embassy told CTK today that it had no information to suggest that the US computer firm EDS had bribed the former Christian Democrat (KDU-CSL) government in order to win lucrative defence contracts for the new army command information system. The embassy also said that it could not confirm claims that EDS had been warned on at least two occasions by embassy officials that it was under suspicion of corruption. (Czech News Agency, 24 July 1998)

Indeed, the embassy invoked the existence of the FCPA (Foreign Corrupt Practices Act) as evidence that a US company would not be corrupt:

> The embassy added that US firms operating abroad were bound by the 1977 Foreign Corrupt Practices Act, which clearly bans offering of bribes in order to win contracts. If an American firm was found guilty of offering bribes in the Czech Republic it would also have to face responsibility back home in the US, and would at least lose the right to compete for US government orders, it went on. (ibid.)

AES, Norpak Hydroelectric Schemes, Uganda

There were two proposals to build private hydroelectric power schemes in Uganda - one at Bugali Falls, by a consortium led by US multinational AES - and one at Owen Falls to be built by the Norwegian company Norpak. Corruption allegations arose in respect to both.

The failure of the global economy and the existing aid and development programs to address poverty and inequality is apparent. At the heart of this failure is the competitive, profit driven, self interest of economically dominant nations. Modern, multinational corporations are the embodiments of these traits, and they play a key role in sustaining the status quo through their economic and political influence.

Ugandan MPs repeatedly refused to authorise the schemes because they believed them to be against Uganda's interests; but the World Bank's intervention focused on providing financial support and guarantees to AES, while insisting on yet more privatisation.

In April 1999, six MPs were allegedly compromised by accepting a week's trip to Norway, arranged by Norpak. The politicians denied that they had been compromised:

> 'Six MPs who have just returned from a one-week trip to Norway to inspect Norpak projects yesterday said they have no apologies to offer over the trip. They defended their trip saying, "We were duly nominated by Parliament Speaker, Mr. Francis Ayume, following an invitation by Norpak"' (New Vision, 28 April 1999).

The cost of the trip was reportedly not paid by the company, but by the Norwegian state:

> 'The bills, that include: first class accommodation, air tickets and shopping in Norway, were reportedly paid by the Norwegian embassy' (New Vision, 21 April 1998).

Undermining The Judicial Authority

The lack of enthusiasm for anti-corruption investigations echoes the readiness of the multinationals and their business associations

Walmart has been in the news in India because it was perceived as one of the principal beneficiaries of the contentious new foreign direct investment (FDI) policy in multi-brand retail. Then the company revealed that its joint venture in India -- Bharti Walmart -- had suspended its chief financial officer and some members of its legal team after an anti-corruption probe.

The scrutiny facing Walmart intensified when newspapers claimed that the company had been lobbying in India to woo Members of Parliament to its side in the FDI vote. The Lok Sabha (the lower house of Parliament) was totally paralyzed for a couple of days and, on January 24, 2013, the government appointed a one-man panel to probe the charges. Walmart says the lobbying was done in Washington, where it is legal, and not in New Delhi, where it is not.

The Walmart inquiry started from a New York Times report about bribery by the retail giant in Mexico. Further investigation uncovered that the corruption charges spread to India, China and Brazil.

to undermine the authority of judicial institutions when they rule against the companies' interests.

Early in 1997, for example, trade unionists and environmentalists in the Philippines brought court cases against the proposed water privatisation in Manila. Formal protests by the entire business community of OECD countries were used to insist that the courts should not rule against western business interests.

The courts had already displeased the government with rulings which went against their privatisation policies. The reported reaction of the multinationals and their governments showed little respect for the due process of law:

'Loud complaints about "terrorists in robes" have resonated in government and business circles in the past month as the courts delivered a series of blows to investor confidence with controversial rulings against the state's privatisation programme.' (Bangkok Post, 14 February 1997)

This is part of a general unwillingness by multinationals to accept the authority of courts in developing countries. When the government of Maharashtra in India decided to end or renegotiate

Corruption like other forms of entrepreneurship has evolved considerably. A few years after liberalization, Enron admitted to a U.S. Congressional committee that it had spent US$20 million to "educate Indians" on the benefits of its power project in Maharashtra. Today, the money moves more subtly. In telecommunications, for instance, Indian companies acquired licenses at a knock-down price from the government with the aid of corrupt ministers. They then sold stakes in the companies that held these licenses to foreign telecom majors seeking an entry into India. The foreign companies paid several times what the Indian entities had shelled out for the licenses. On paper, they look foolish, but not criminal. All the players would have been happy if the Supreme Court hadn't stepped in and cancelled the process. The art of graft has advanced fast.

With new scams and scandals vying for attention, the older ones often fall by the wayside. The politicians shrug off the allegations and are back in positions of power in no time.

~S. Raghunath, Professor Of Corporate Strategy And Policy, Indian Institute Of Management, Bangalore

an energy deal with Enron, the company sought arbitration in London; when the province of Tucuman in Argentina terminated the water concession that had been awarded to Générale des Eaux, the company referred its dispute to the World Bank for arbitration.

In some cases, governments of OECD countries act as 'official channels' for payments which could be considered corrupt.

Water Privatisation, Indonesia

In 1997, while Jakarta was still under the control of president Suharto, its water supply was privatised, under the auspices of the World Bank. One concession went to a consortium led by Thames Water (UK), another to a consortium led by Lyonnaise des Eaux (France). Both consortia included partners which were owned by friends of the president. After Suharto's fall, even the consortia accepted that these concessions were no longer defensible. The multinationals moved rapidly with new 'clean' companies to negotiate new contracts with Jakarta City Council, to run from February 1999.

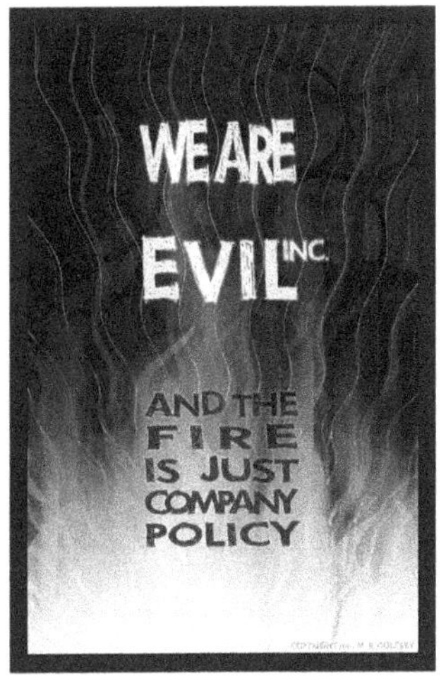

But these contracts have been subject to bitter criticism on the grounds that they were never properly advertised, that the prices contained in them are excessive, and that Suharto's son continued

If all else fails, financial accounts can be adjusted to create the impression of profit and growth. This was the case in numerous corporate scandals and the collapse of corporations such as Enron. Its case simultaneously implicated many other sectors of the accounting and banking industry, such as Arthur Andersen and the National Westminster Bank, who were taken in by and facilitated Enron's false accounting, financing and fraudulent activities. Of course the big losers were the 21,000 employees who not only lost their jobs, but their pension plans and savings which were all tied to Enron stock.

~ Rajesh Makwana

to hold five per cent equity in the new Thames Water venture. Court action has been taken to have the contracts declared void, and a trade union of water workers has demanded that the contracts be rescinded (Asia Pulse, 29 April 1999).

The original concession awards under the Suharto regime had been made under the auspices of a World Bank-supported tendering procedure, yet the Bank made no public statement calling for investigation of the alleged corruption. On the contrary, three weeks before the June 1999 general election, it announced new loans of US$400m-US$300m for the water sector.

66.

Manipulating Public Opinion

Public Relations, Marketing and Advertising

The revolutionary shift that we are witnessing at the beginning of the 21st Century from democracy to corporate rule is as significant as the shift from monarchy to democracy, which ushered in the modern age of nation states. It represents a wholesale change in cultural values and aspirations.[1]

This eclipse of democratic values by corporate values is not a natural evolution but the consequence of a deliberate strategy employed by corporate executives who have combined their financial and political resources to spread free market ideology. Corporations, individually and in concert, have utilised all the major communication institutions of a modern society – including the media and education – to shape community beliefs, values and behaviour. This has enabled corporations 'to enthral and becloud the understanding' of large numbers of citizens so that it is commonly believed that large corporations are benevolent institutions that should be minimally regulated because what is good for them is good for society as a whole.[2]

Throughout the 20th Century business associations and coalitions coordinated mass propaganda campaigns that combined sophisticated public relations techniques developed in 20th Century America with revitalised free market ideology originating in 18th Century Europe. The purpose of this propaganda onslaught has been to persuade a majority of people that it is in their interests to eschew their own power as workers and citizens, and forego their democratic right to restrain and regulate business activity. As a result the political agenda is now largely confined to policies aimed at furthering business interests.[3]

The public relations industry has basically compromised the integrity of the opinion expressed in the public domain by giving the illusion of independence to arguments that are essentially self serving. This is done primarily by a kind of ideological ventriloquism — putting the arguments into the mouths of people/institutions/authorities with important sounding titles that appear to be independent of those forwarding the arguments. PR in this sense is nothing short of an attempt by those that can afford it to buy credibility, integrity, and/or independence for arguments that stem from self interests — essentially an attempt to hide the self serving nature of the arguments.

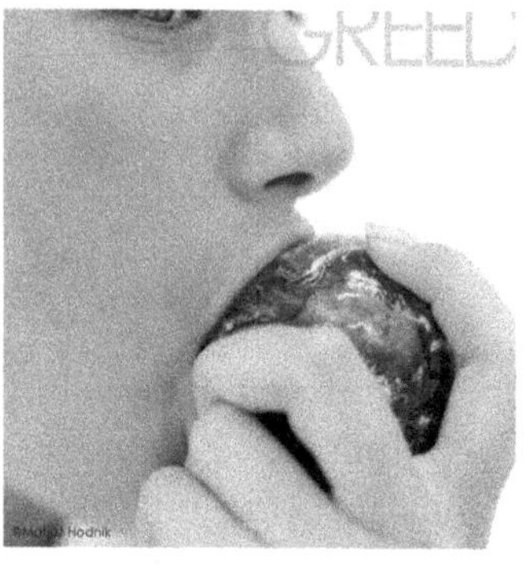

Since the 70's, as public objection to corporate rule and environmental degradation increased, corporations have mounted a successful campaign to increase corporate rights and win back public opinion. This initiative saw the rise of corporate sponsored law firms who fiercely defended corporate interests by, for example, opposing environmental and social standards and regulations. Such organizations were presented as 'public interest' groups in an attempt to equate public and corporate interests whilst masking corporate involvement. They included environmental and consumer groups that are nothing more than extensions of corporate lobbying in disguise, promoting environmental and commercial deregulation. The academic world was also targeted as corporations funded programs and research in economics and law

All major corporations, particularly those which have the greatest negative impact upon the environment, have repackaged themselves recently as having 'green' credentials to great effect. The oil giant BP's new green, flower-like logo and recent PR campaign is an excellent example. As a result, BP has successfully managed to shift public focus away from the fact that it is one of the world's foremost polluters of the environment and considered by many as one of the top 10 corporate criminals.

that favoured neo-liberal ideals. The success of the public relations campaign was guaranteed by their huge financial resources and broad coalition across business groups.[4]

In order to influence policy more directly, conservative policy think tanks were established, such as the Heritage Foundation, the American Enterprise institute and the Cato institute. Influential Business Roundtables made up of CEOs were also established in the 70's, enabling representatives from broad spectrums of industry to actively campaign for the common agenda of economic globalization. Currently almost 200,000 public relations employees in the US actively manipulate public opinion to the advantage of their corporate sponsors.[5]

Far from supplying public demand, corporations actively dictate cultural habits and create demand by influencing the public mind through a sophisticated and well funded combination of research, marketing, advertising and media manipulation. The result is the subtle, but quite apparent, alignment of public and corporate interest. This cultural homogenization of society both nationally and globally is fertile ground for maximizing profit. Whilst levels of unnecessary and unsustainable consumption increase globally, corporate longevity is secured. This non consensual capitalization of the public by the wealthy few is another example of an undemocratic process resulting from excessive financial capability and political influence. The sophistication and effectiveness of advertising and marketing methods is well understood. The ubiquity of the television and the increasing number of hours it is watched, especially by children, is particularly disturbing. In the US, watching TV is the 3rd most time consuming pastime, after sleeping and working. In the US, 75% of commercial television time and 50% of public television time is paid for by the 100 largest corporations.

At present, the battle for control of the democratic process is being won by the corporate elite. The phenomenon of market forces is becoming more entrenched in every aspect of public life, even influencing our subconscious minds, conscious attitudes and behaviour. As many industrialized nations call for democracy to be spread globally, the economic ideologies they have vested our future in are cancerous to these same democratic principles.

Projected global advertising expenditure for corporations in 2006 is over $427 billion dollars.[6]

As traditional markets are saturated, or public opinion turns against a particular product, corporations, using the same aggressive marketing, shift their attention to developing countries with devastating effect. Nestle is notorious for its aggressive marketing of infant formula in poor countries in the 1980s. Because of this practice, Nestle is still one of the most boycotted corporations in the world, and its infant formula is still controversial. In Italy in 2005, police seized more than two million litres of Nestle infant formula that was contaminated with the chemical isopropylthioxanthone (ITX). In recent years, as public awareness of dire health consequences of smoking tobacco have come to light in industrialized nations, tobacco giants have had to shift their focus to increasing demand in developing countries. The WHO has reported that 84% of the estimated 1.3 billion smokers live in developing and transitional economy countries. A 1994 WHO report estimated that the use of tobacco resulted in an annual global net loss of US$ 200 billion, a third of this loss being in developing countries, stumping development efforts.[7]

COMMUNITY

NOT CORPORATION

Education

The education system provides arguably the most fertile ground on which to influence public opinion. In the US, corporations are making significant in-roads by sponsoring teaching materials

kamasyantam hi ksut-trdbhyam
krodhasyaitat phalodayat
jano yati na lobhasya
jitva bhuktva diso bhuvah

The strong bodily desires and needs of a person disturbed by hunger and thirst are certainly satisfied when he eats. Similarly, if one becomes very angry, that anger is satisfied by chastisement and its reaction. But as for greed, even if a greedy person has conquered all the directions of the world or has enjoyed everything in the world, still he will not be satisfied.

~ Srila Prabhupada (Srimad Bhagavatam 7.15.20)

and aggressively marketing and supplying junk foods through vending machines and lunch programs. Of greatest concern are corporate sponsored curriculum modules, public education propaganda videos, and grants and sponsorship programs that refocus education to pro-corporate aspects of law and economics. Competition, economic growth and profitability are emphasized-qualities that secure future corporate opportunity. There is a simultaneous shift away from learning the benefits of cooperation, community endeavor and goodwill. Together such tactics effectively skew public opinion from an early age and further enshrine the neo-liberal, corporate agenda. Unsurprisingly there is a trend in the US, the EU and developing countries for corporations to operate public schools for profit, capitalizing on yet another market opportunity.[8]

References:

[1][2][3], The Corporate Assault on Democracy, Sharon Beder

[4][5][6][7][8], Rajesh Makwana, October 2006

67.

Corporations

The Centrally Planned Economies

The argument is that centrally planned economies are less efficient and are unresponsive to consumer demand. They argue that to achieve efficiency, government intervention needs to be reduced to a minimum and the democratic, public control of the economy minimized. Thus, free trade and neoliberal policies are being actively promoted through international bodies such as the WTO, World Bank and IMF.

However, this argument is flawed. For a start, corporations are themselves centrally planned economies. Decisions are not open to question within a corporation and absolute control is exercised over production and distribution networks by management. Also, whereas public companies are required to be transparent to public scrutiny, the contracts that corporations have with respect to resource management or service delivery remain a commercial secret, removing an important level of accountability.

Many of these unaccountable corporations now have a greater turnover than the GDP of most countries. Of the 100 largest economies in the world, 52 are corporations and 48 are countries, and these corporations have sales figures between $51 billion and $247 billion.

68.

Corporations

Bringing About Inequality And Unemployment

Seventy percent of world trade is controlled by just 500 of the largest industrial corporations, and in 2002, the top 200 had combined sales equivalent to 28% of world GDP. However, these 200 corporations only employed 0.82% of the global work force, highlighting the reduction in employment created by excessive economies of scale.

In the US, ninety-eight percent of all companies account for only 25 percent of business activity; the remaining two percent account for nearly 75 percent of the remaining activity.

The top 500 industrial corporations, which represent only one-tenth of one percent of all US companies, control over two-thirds of the business resources in the US and collect over 70 percent of all US profits. Thus there is also a disproportionate distribution of financial benefit from economic activity, which clearly does not pass to local communities through opportunity or wages. It is retained instead by a small number of major shareholders of an even smaller number of corporations.

Whereas corporations are based mainly in affluent countries such as the US, the EU, Japan, Canada and Australia, their key markets, productive facilities and many of their resources are based in or extracted from developing countries. According to the International Finance Corporation (IFC), inflows of foreign direct investment to the emerging markets have grown by an average of 23 percent per year between 1990 and 2000. The combined value of stock markets in emerging economies is set to exceed $5 trillion in 2006, and has more than doubled in the past decade.

As corporations grow, they find it economically beneficial (profitable) to operate in multiple countries, seeking out favourable conditions such as low labour costs, fewer regulations and other financial or tax incentives. Many of these multinational corporations can now be described as 'transnational', as they have 'globalized' their operations and retain no particular affiliation to any country. This allows them greater flexibility in operative structure and greater leverage over governments who compete for their business.

The convergence of economic power has created a concentration of political influence in society which is reflected nationally and globally. The resulting influence of the private sector has manipulated global economic, political and public thinking and established an unsustainable, consumerist culture.

As a result of mergers, acquisitions and jobs being transferred abroad (in line with globalized market forces), job losses even in affluent countries are common. Between 1980 and 1993, over four million jobs were shed by the largest 500 industrial corporations in the US. Since President Bush took office, two million lost their jobs and in 2004 nearly one in ten could not find a full time job.

The International Labor Organization (ILO) calculates that global unemployment rates are at an all time high. Of the 2.8 billion workers in the world in 2005, nearly 1.4 billion still did not earn

Extensive legislation now exists internationally and within countries to protect corporate rights. Therefore, wide-ranging structural and regulatory changes are essential if we are to transform the corporate led economy into one centered on communities that actively participate in political and economic life. The prioritization of community based enterprise and the curtailing of mega corporate entities will inevitably create greater social equity in both the East and West.

enough to lift themselves and their families above the two dollars a day poverty line - the same proportion as ten years ago.

The substantial benefits gained from streamlining operations serve mainly to increase profits, and are channelled into bonuses for directors and CEOs. Chevron's CEO received $37 million in total compensation in 2005, whilst Exxon's CEO received a $400 million pay and retirement package. In the meanwhile the minimum wage in a country like America (£5.15 per hour) is at a 50 year low.

Sadly, the prevalence in recent years, of huge corporations has significantly impacted on small businesses and communities, and is creating a homogenization of culture throughout the world. These corporations have created huge economies of scale which result in a downward levelling of job numbers, wages and employment standards. The most visible culprits are agri-business, giant fast food chains and retail outlets such as supermarkets. The goods supplied by these companies have quickly replaced local businesses who often supply the same goods with greater levels of nutrition and with negligible social and environmental consequences.

The effects are visible and measurable in society. For example, in the 10 years that Wal-Mart moved to Iowa, in the USA, 7326 local business closed as a direct result. In the UK, the supermarket giant, Tesco, currently opens one new 'Tesco Express' (a smaller, local version of their larger stores) each day. This results in a local grocer going out of business each day, and 50 local specialist stores close each week. The impact on the developing world is also stark as corporations move steadily into emerging markets. India has recently experienced a surge in contracts to large agri-business firms as the government pursues the high output agricultural policies of the US and EU. This has resulted in entire villages being put up for sale in some states and, according to the National Sample Survey Organization (NSSO), more than 40 per cent of Indian farmers are keen to quit agriculture altogether as a result of these market pressures. In addition, the competitive activity of multinationals has helped to sustain an unfair international trading regime that increases global inequality through biased trade rules and increases global warming through inefficient import and export networks.

It is imperative that these trends are reversed, and that community involvement in economic life is strengthened and safeguarded.

Whilst global economic growth remains slow, at around three percent, corporate growth is around four times as high, again reflecting the concentration of financial gain from a global economy led by corporations. In the year 2005, the number of millionaires globally swelled to a phenomenal 8.7 million, 5.7 million of whom are based in North America and Europe. In addition, Forbes reported a 15% rise in the number of billionaires since last year alone, virtually all have made their fortune from their involvement in various sectors of industry and are now worth a combined $2.6 trillion.

(Source: Rajesh Makwana, October 2006)

> *"There is a spiritual hunger in the world today - and it cannot be satisfied by better cars on longer credit terms" - Adlai E. Stevenson*

69.

Corporate Welfare

Publicly Funded

Corporate profit is exaggerated by what is effectively publicly funded corporate welfare. The package of corporate welfare begins with governments who offer incentives to corporations in order to attract their business, increase their GDP and compete with other nations. National resources that rightfully belong to the public are the first carrots on the stick, and are offered at highly discounted prices to corporations without public consent. Governments even give away valuable common assets at no cost to corporations, such as oil and mineral rights, saving corporations billions of dollars in costs.

In addition, affluent governments pay out huge subsidies to the largest corporations. Government support to farmers in OECD countries totalled $283 billion in 2005, representing 29% of total farm income. Unfortunately, the majority of farmers who own small to medium sized farms do not benefit from these subsidies. 30% of farmers in the US do not receive any of the $26 billion of US subsidies, and over 85% go to only 20% of the largest farms, a pattern repeated in the EU.

Industrialized countries also subsidize corporate exports and agri-business inputs such as energy, pesticides and chemical fertilizers. This encourages energy and chemical intensive production methods that only large scale agri-business can sustain. As a direct result, the number of small farms in the US has decreased from 6.8 million in 1935 to 1.5 million in 1998. In global commodity markets these subsidies mean that producers in developing countries, many of whom produce their goods with more efficiency and less cost than the US and EU, cannot compete with agri-business suppliers. Their livelihoods are destroyed. Market competition is cut throat, valued higher than life itself. Individual cows in Japan receive $8 a day in subsidies alone, whilst half of India's 1.2 billion people live on less than $2 a day. These actions strengthen the market dominance of corporations, whilst marginalizing smaller, community based producers.

In addition, corporations pay much less tax than ordinary people, often registering their headquarters in tax havens. According to the Centre for American Progress "At a time of rising corporate profits, the US Government Accountability Office (GAO) reports that 95 percent of corporations paid less than 5 percent of their income in taxes, and 6 in 10 paid nothing at all in federal taxes from 1996 through to 2000". The corporate share of taxes paid fell from 33 percent in the 1940's to 15 percent in the 1990's. The individual's share of taxes has risen from 44 to 73 percent. At a time of record corporate revenues, the American public is making up the loss in tax revenue through the government's biased tax regime.

The effect of corporate welfare upon the poorest nations is most disastrous. When local resources and basic goods are controlled by corporations and absentee owners, local industry is curbed, essential services are often unaffordable and profits are repatriated in wealthy countries, bypassing the local economy. Although privatization in developing countries does prove beneficial in certain cases, overall the process resembles economic mercantilism as it is ultimately fuelled by selfish, commercial interest. What is needed is a significant transfer of resources to the global south, not to multinational corporations.

When governments give away public resources, subsidize the largest industries and provide tax incentives to corporations, it usually occurs without the public's knowledge and proves detrimental to their local communities. The price we pay for goods does not include the cost we have already paid through our taxes, the cost to the poorest producers around the world, or the cost to the environment.

Cost Externalization

Classical economic thinking and accounting procedures are heavily biased against local communities and the environment, as they only reflect financial profit and loss. Maximizing profit means passing more immaterial or long-term costs on to society for them to deal with. This process is known as externalization, and externalities are typically negative social or environmental costs to a community, region or the planet which corporations do not have to account for in anyway. Corporations are compelled to externalize costs wherever possible so that they can increase their profits.

For example, export-oriented industrial agriculture is a major contributor to climate change. Agricultural externalities poison our soil, waterways and atmosphere. And corporations are learning to externalize more efficiently - they may, for example, relocate to countries with lower labour or environmental standards. The negative effect upon society and the environment of these externalities and lower standards are unaccounted for in the cost of their products or their financial reports. In the meantime, consumers are taken in by the illusion of low cost goods and services and they seek out ever cheaper suppliers. However, as the true environmental and social costs of corporate activity are becoming apparent, consumers must realize that they cannot avoid paying for them in one way or another. For example, these costs are paid through aid sent to developing countries (often after climate-change aggravated disasters); through the public money spent on tackling climate change; through the millions spent nationally tackling poverty, inequality, unemployment and other social issues; and through the detrimental effect upon quality of life that results from lower working standards and conditions.

Every year corporations are fined hundreds of millions of dollars as their externalities create serious environmental catastrophes, neglect employee rights and even cause deaths. Examples are plentiful and well documented by countless NGO and civil society groups, and usually concern the most well known and largest corporations. However, mainstream media coverage of these issues is virtually non existent. Take for example Chevron. The majority are unaware that it is guilty of some of the worst environmental and human rights abuses in the world such as the dumping of 18 billion gallons of toxic waste into rivers used for bathing water in the Amazon, devastating the health of the local community.

However, fines for these corporate crimes are negligible in relation to a company's turnover. The likelihood of being fined is often accounted for well before the event. Given the potential financial savings to be gained by violating environmental protection laws and workers rights, the decision to ignore these laws constitute a simple cost-benefit calculation. Worryingly, shareholders cannot be held accountable for these violations as they are protected by their limited liability, and directors and executives successfully plea that they have no direct involvement with the corporate crime committed. Thus the corporate 'entity' itself is fined, and little incentive to change irresponsible corporate behaviour is provided.

Taking the cost of these externalities into account, Ralph Estes estimated that the public cost of private corporations was over $3 trillion in 1995. His externalities included "workplace injuries, pollution, employment discrimination, consumer rip-offs, corporate white collar crime, tax abatements and all the other instances of corporate welfare, government contracting fraud and creative accounting" all of which have carry an equivalent financial cost to the public. Estes calculations reveal that the corporate claim to efficiency is clearly false - most corporations would not be able to continue without major changes if they bore the full costs of their of their product or service.

Conclusion

Clearly a corporation's pressing need for increased profits comes at too high a cost to the global public. When corporate welfare and the public cost of externalities are taken into account, corporate profit is a meaningless term. Within the current framework, corporate profit must be viewed alongside the social and environmental consequences of corporate activity. This more balanced approach calls into question the global economic system that perpetuates this state of affairs.

(Source: Multinational Corporations, STWR)

70.

Patenting The Life

Under the WTO's Agreement on Trade-Related Aspects of Intellectual Property Rights (TRIPS) agreement, the most insidious corporate victories to date have been the granting of patent protections to all genetic material. In 1980, the US Supreme Court ruled that a particular genetically engineered micro-organism could be patented. This patent right was extended by the US patent Office in 1985 to cover all genetically-engineered plants, seeds and plant tissue, and was further extended to cover all animals in 1987. In 1998 EU countries extended patent laws to cover patents on plants, humans and life forms.

Biotech companies are being snapped up by giant 'Life Science' corporations in a race to consolidate the food and seeds industry which tripled in size between 1992 and 2002. It was worth around $2,000 billion a year in 2001. By May 2002, there were 1,457 biotechnology companies in the US with a total value

Discussions regarding economic systems should not be based on ideologies of socialism or capitalism, but on the practicalities and realities of our modern world. Today, the reality is that thousands will die from a lack of food, water and medicine, because of the failure of the global economy to allow them to have access to these basics. At the same time, a few business people will have earned millions of dollars in wages, thanks to the same economic system. These extremes must be reconciled urgently.

of $224 billion. Market consolidation is acute, 70% of patents on staple food crops are held by six multinational corporations who can set the market price for them and block competition for 20 years, thereby monopolizing the market.

Patenting costs can be up to $1 million, ensuring that those in the developing countries cannot possibly compete with the wealthy corporations. The developing world, where 75% of people's livelihoods depend upon agriculture, is the source of 90 per cent of all biological resources. Yet transnational companies based in developed counties hold 97 percent of global patents. Since 1985 there have been 10,778 patents on plants registered in the US. Overall, patent applications at the World Intellectual Property Organization have soared from 3,000 in 1979 to 67,000 in 1997.

Commercially owned genetic varieties of such staples as cotton and soya beans have devastated farming communities in developing countries, who can no longer store seeds without paying corporations for the privilege. There has been widespread opposition to what has been deemed 'bio piracy'. This is when biotechnology corporations, in their haste to secure financial advantages, patent varieties of plants, seeds and applications that already exist and remain in use by indigenous communities. The patenting of life goes against the sharing of traditional knowledge

The Global Economy

Corporations should exist as an integral component of a global economy that prioritizes the provision of basic needs for the global public - economic, social, political and spiritual. The primary objective of the global economy should not be commerce, trade liberalization or economic growth, but the production and distribution of all resources that are essential to life. International consensus must eventually lead to a clear demarcation with regards to what can be commoditized and what cannot be.

and the preservation of biodiversity and culture. This precedent is a major victory for corporations. The potential for future profit is almost limitless.
(Source: Rajesh Makwana, STWR, October 2006)

71.

Lobbying

The Prime Corporate Pastime

In his exhaustive book, 'When Corporations Rule the World', David Korten identifies the Council of Foreign Relations, the Bilderberg and the Trilateral Commission as key historical institutions that shaped modern economic globalization.

These well funded, highly influential and often rather secretive institutions, brought together key government ministers, business leaders, educators and media representatives as early as 1939.

Together they created the necessary consensus for economic globalization and shaped public opinion to support the policies that were essential to their goal.

Eighty percent of all corporations reside in the US and EU, and through their lobbyists they enjoy privileged access to the government policy makers who partake in trade talks. Over 30,000 corporate lobbyists are based in Washington and Brussels, vastly outnumbering the US Congress and European Commission staff that they lobby.

The vast majority of lobby groups represent business interests who spend billions of dollars annually advocating their main cause,

> *The result of association with the qualities of passion and ignorance is that one becomes lusty and greedy. But when one is elevated to the platform of goodness, he is satisfied in any condition of life and is without lust and greed. This mentality indicates one's situation on the platform of goodness.*
>
> *~ Srila Prabhupada (Srimad Bhagavatam 4.21.52)*

which is currently market access in emerging economies. In the US, corporations and their agencies spent $9.7 billion lobbying Congress between 1997 and 2000, about $4.5 million per year per member of Congress.

On the other hand, many developing countries do not have the resources to send enough, if any, representatives to argue for fairer trade practices that would benefit their own economic development. In addition, WTO negotiations are undemocratic, with the public denied access to, or information about, the discussions. The same is not true of corporate lobby groups such as the European Services Forum (ESF) and many US corporations who can directly affect and have access to Trade Committees.

Unsurprisingly then, the interests of rich nations and their corporations form the basis of WTO agreements and directly influence the global political and economic architecture. The corporate bottom line, espoused by the WTO, is to open market access in all countries to resources, services and intellectual property in an endless drive for greater profits.

Corporate Links to Government

In his book Captive State (2000), George Monbiot lists 43 individuals who, since the 1997 elections in the UK, have been appointed as ministers, heads, chairmen, and advisors to as many government departments and independent committees. In each case their previous corporate positions (mostly as directors, chairmen or chief executives) and existing links to industry present a direct conflict of interest with their governmental roles.

To take a random example, Lord Simon of Highbury, the previous chairman of oil giant BP and vice chairman of the European Roundtable of industrialists (a powerful corporate lobby

Large swathes of Africa, Asia and South America do not have the resources to compete internationally even if the terms of trade were rendered fair and their debts forgiven. Within a system of sharing, resources that are considered essential to life would not be commoditized or controlled by business interests.

group) was appointed minister for Trade and Competitiveness in Europe at the Department of Trade and Industry.

As expected, the same conflict of interest exists at the highest levels in the US government, only more openly and to greater detriment. The majority of President Bush's cabinet were multimillionaires. The President, Vice-President, Commerce Secretary and National Security Adviser all had strong ties to the oil industry. The Bush family had strong ties to Enron-which was President G. W. Bush's largest corporate source of funding.

Condoleezza Rice was a director of Chevron. Secretary of Commerce Donald Evans held stock valued between $5m and $25m in Tom Brown Inc, the oil and gas exploration company he headed, and the list goes on, highlighting in particular a pronounced concentration of energy connections.

Unsurprisingly, US domestic and foreign policies are highly biased. The securing of Iraqi oil fields is a pertinent recent example. Since the beginning of the Iraq war, Halliburton, the Texas energy giant once headed by Vice President Dick Cheney, has seen its stock price more than triple in value. According to Halliburton Watch, Halliburton's contracts under the Bush administration grew by 600%.

To take a key aspect of the administration's tax plan, Bush's cabinet members, according to one estimate, saved between $5 million and $19 million each as the Bush administration repealed the Estate Tax. This will come at the cost of an estimated $1 trillion dollars over the first 10 years to the public.

tvam vartamanam nara-deva-dehesv
anupravrtto 'yam adharma-pugah
lobho 'nrtam cauryam anaryam amho
jyestha ca maya kalahas ca dambhah

If the personality of Kali, irreligion, is allowed to act as a man-god or an executive head, certainly irreligious principles like greed, falsehood, robbery, incivility, treachery, misfortune, cheating, quarrel and vanity will abound. This kind of government cannot check the resultant actions of sinful life, namely war, pestilence, famine, earthquakes and similar other disturbances.

~ Srila Prabhupada (Srimad Bhagavatam 1.17.32)

Those who benefited from the tax cuts represent a fraction of 1% of the American public. It is this same elite section of US citizens that dominate and manipulate the entire political system. As such, a symbiotic relationship is established, with both the government and the corporate elite sustaining each others legitimacy.

Winning Elections

Money is equated with political influence within global governance structures. Raising massive contributions for campaign spending is only open to those with very strong connections to wealthy individuals. Civil society simply cannot compete financially, and the current state of politics reflects this situation. This misused financial leverage and influence is also at the heart of global governance injustice. The IMF and World Bank operate on a 'one dollar, one vote' basis, denying the democratic rights of the majority of the world simply because they are not wealthy enough.

In US, corporations were allowed to finance elections in the mid 1970's when the US Supreme Court extended First Amendment Constitutional Rights to corporations, allowing them an extension of 'free speech' rights originally intended for people. The 2004 US

Is it not the desire to uphold outmoded systems of commerce and economy, based on competition and selfish, nationalistic foreign policy objectives, which is truly reactionary and conservative?

The need for far reaching reform of business structure and activity is apparent, as is the need for democratic participation to be re-established at the community level. Economic development must be a process which is not imposed from above, but secured locally, and then regionally. For this to occur, all necessary resources should be made available to the majority world who mainly live in isolated, rural communities in developing countries. We have a United Nations General Assembly, the only world body with the potential to bring about these reforms. We also have the technology to implement complex systems that can span the globe, and we have the infrastructure and capability to distribute resources anywhere. All this is required is a shift in priorities; the political will to share what we have.

presidential elections were the most expensive ever; total campaign contributions were $880,500,000.

Even in the 2002 Congressional races, where money was much less a determinant of the victors than the 2000 elections, 95% of all House seats and 75% of Senate seats were won by the higher-spending candidate.

The coal industry donated $1.5 million during the 2002 election cycle, mostly to the Republicans, Enron gave $2 million between 1999 and 2002, and Eli Lilly and Company gave over $1 million. In return for these and countless other contributions, President Bush's policies during his administration clearly favoured the wealthy and corporate interests by awarding lucrative contracts and by adjusting policy and laws.

Section-VI

Devastation Of A Continent

Lessons From Africa

72.

Food Emergency

How The World Bank And IMF Have Made African Famine Inevitable

By Rania Khalek, September 8, 2011

Lending policies pushed by the World Bank and IMF have transformed a self-sufficient, food-producing Africa into a continent vulnerable to food emergencies and famine.

Famine is spreading like wildfire throughout the horn of Africa. As 12 million people battle hunger, the UN warns that 750,000 people in Somalia face imminent death from starvation over the next four months, in the absence of outside intervention. Over the course of just 90 days, an estimated 29,000 children under the age of five died in Southern Somalia, with another 640,000 children suffering from acute malnourishment.

In the rush to find a culprit to blame for the tragedy unfolding in East Africa, the mainstream news outlets attributed the cause to record droughts, a rise in food prices, biofuel production and land grabs by foreign investors with an added emphasis on the role of the Somali terrorist group Al-Shabaab.

Yet these factors alone are not responsible for the famine; instead they have intensified an already dire hunger crisis that has persisted in Sub-Saharan Africa for decades, thanks to lending policies pushed by the World Bank and International Monetary Fund

> *"Why, in a world that produces more than enough food to feed everybody, do so many – one in seven of us – go hungry?"* -- Oxfam

(IMF) that transformed a self-sufficient, food-producing Africa into a continent dependent on imports and food aid, leaving the continent vulnerable to food emergencies and famine.

Since 1981, when these lending policies were first implemented, Oxfam found that the amount of sub-Saharan Africans surviving on less than one dollar a day doubled to 313 million by 2001, which is 46 percent of the population. Since the mid-1980s, the number of food emergencies per year on the continent has tripled.

According to Oxfam International spokesperson Caroline Pearce, the IMF and World Bank structural adjustment programs of the '80s and '90s led to "huge disinvestments in the agricultural sector." Pearce concludes, "What we're seeing now in poor agricultural systems partly relates to those kind of policies. In many cases, we're actually calling for things to be reestablished that were dismantled under structural adjustment programs in the past."

Yet the impoverished countries of Africa, imperiled by mass starvation, continue to pay for a "free market" agenda, and it's costing them their lives.

From Food Abundance To Mass Starvation

Walden Bello, reporting for Foreign Policy in Focus, observes that Africa was self-sufficient in food production after declaring independence from its colonial rulers in the 1960s. Yet today, hunger and famine in Africa have "become recurrent phenomena" across the continent.

According to BBC analyst Martin Plaut, Africa was also a food net exporter between 1966 and 1970, with an average of 1.3 million tons of food exported each year. In stark contrast, almost all of today's African countries are dependent on imports and food aid, a dramatic shift that took less than 40 years to transpire.

Which begs the question: how did an entire continent go from being a net food exporter to a net food importer, from food abundance to mass starvation, in such a short period of time?

In her book The Shock Doctrine: The Rise of Disaster Capitalism, Naomi Klein details how global power players use times of crisis and chaos as a pretext for imposing destructive free-market policies that advance the interests of the wealthy. As far back as the 1970s, economists inspired by free-market guru Milton

Friedman were inspiring U.S.-backed coups and military juntas to push an unpopular radical free-market agenda onto the unwilling populations of countries like Chile, Brazil and Argentina.

But Klein highlights a significant shift in strategy that took place in the mid-1980s, when economists recognized that a financial crisis "simulates the effects of a military war—spreading fear and confusion, creating refugees and causing large loss of life" -- the same shock-inducing conditions that left societies ripe for disaster capitalism.

Throughout the '60s and '70s, Western financial institutions went on a lending spree at extremely low interest rates, mostly to developing countries that were encouraged to borrow. By the late '70s and early '80s, U.S. interest rates soared to levels as high as 21 percent, devastating the fragile economies of developing nations that had taken on massive debt.

Klein compares the impact of this "debt shock" to "a giant Taser gun fired from Washington, sending the developing world into convulsions." African countries could barely afford the sky-high interest payments, let alone the actual debt and were thrown into a downward spiral of financial crises. This is where the story of Africa's famine truly begins.

'The Dictatorship Of Debt'

The erosion of African agriculture is due in large part to policies imposed on debt-ridden African countries by the World Bank and the IMF—financial institutions set up in the aftermath of World War II with the stated aim of deterring financial crises like the ones that pushed Weimer Germany toward fascism.

The donor nations of the IMF and World Bank divvy up power within each institution based on the size of a country's economy, allowing a handful of privileged nations, led by the U.S., to dominate decision making. As a result, Klein explains that the pro-corporatist administrations of Reagan and Thatcher in the '70s and '80s were "able to harness the two institutions for their own ends, rapidly increasing their power and turning them into primary vehicles for the advancement of the corporatist crusade."

Driven by the ideology of the so-called free market, the IMF and World Bank attached conditions to desperately needed debt relief that required developing nations to implement Structural Adjustment Programs (SAPs), what Naomi Klein calls "the dictatorship of debt."

SAPs forced governments to impose a neoliberal package of austerity, privatization and massive deregulation. For Africa, this meant cutting government subsidies to small farmers, eliminating tariffs and price controls, selling off food and grain reserves (which kept countries from starving in cases of drought or crop failure), increasing cash crop exports of raw materials to the west, and allowing foreign imports from the US and Europe to flood their markets.

Although the IMF and World Bank argued that restructuring was necessary to reduce Africa's debt and foster economic growth, their policies produced the opposite effects: soaring debt and economic stagnation.

In a 2004 study commissioned by the Halifax Initiative, writer Asad Ismi meticulously documents the consequences of SAPs on the African continent. Between 1980 and 1993, he found a total of 566 structural adjustment programs were forced onto 70 developing countries, including 36 of Africa's 47 Sub-Saharan nations. Since the implementation of SAPs in the 1980s, Africa's debt soared more than 500 percent, with an estimated $229 billion worth of debt payments transferred from Sub-Saharan Africa to the west, four times the original debt owed.

According to the IMF's World Economic Outlook Database, African debt still stands at $324.7 billion, with the overwhelming majority, $278.5 billion, owed by Sub-Saharan Africa, demonstrating that SAPs have pushed Africa into perpetual debt, with no end in sight.

What does this have to do with famine? Well, perpetual debt forces governments to divert spending to debt repayment, rather than investing in basic infrastructure like healthcare and education, which is relatively non-existent in Sub-Saharan Africa. With only 10 percent of the world's population, the Sub-Saharan region comprises 68 percent of all people living with HIV. Yet, according to Ismi, "Africa spends four times more on debt interest payments than on health care."

The same holds true for the agricultural sector. SAPs initiated the collapse of African food security, diverting land, water and labor away from small-scale farming toward the production of cash crops, whose earnings were used to pay off debt.

Ironically, as they demanded that African states eliminate subsidies for small-scale farmers, the United States and Europe continued to provide their agricultural sectors with billions of dollars in subsidies, forcing peasant farmers to compete with an influx of cheap, subsidized commercial staples from the west—clearly a losing battle.

In 2004, Project Censored described this U.S. practice as "underselling starving nations," a process that ensures U.S. commodities cost less than their small-scale counterparts, essentially pricing local farmers out of the market.

Walden Bello points out that the World Trade Organization's (WTO) Agreement on Agriculture cemented these lopsided policies, making developing countries the permanent dumping grounds for cheap surplus production from the global north. Thus, between 1995 and 2004, agriculture subsidies in developed countries went from $367 billion to $388 per year.

The few subsidies the IMF did permit were strictly reserved for African commercial agriculture goods for export to Europe and America. For Kenya, where a quarter of the population lives on less than a dollar a day, this meant ditching government support for subsistence farmers and diverting resources to the production of raw exports (cash crops) for the west, like tea, coffee, tobacco and cut flowers. Earnings from exports were then used to service the country's massive debt.

After investigating the impacts of SAPs on Kenya's struggle with malnutrition, Catherine Mezzacappa concludes, "Through their role in agricultural policy and social spending, structural adjustment policies imposed by the IMF and World Bank have contributed to the deepening of poverty and perpetuation of malnutrition in Kenya," a country where "the leading causes of death among children are preventable and can be linked to malnutrition."

As environmental activist Vandana Shiva put it in her book Stolen Harvest, "The hungry starve as scarce land and water are diverted to provide luxuries for rich consumers in Northern countries."

Somalia's Road To Famine

But for Somalia, the outcome was far worse, because the application of these neoliberal policies coincided with U.S. meddling and military intervention.

Michel Chossudovsky, author of The Globalization of Poverty, explains that despite frequent droughts, Somalia's economy, led by small-scale farmers and pastoralists or "nomadic herdsmen," was self-sufficient in food well into the 1970s.

The pastoralists proved quite successful as livestock produced 80 percent of Somalia's export earnings through 1983. But under SAPs, veterinarian services for livestock were privatized, making it difficult and unaffordable for herders in rural grazing areas to access animal healthcare, ultimately devastating pastoralists who made up half of the population.

As for agriculture, the cheap imports of rice and wheat displaced small farmers, and resources were diverted to grow export commodities. Worst of all, "Water points and boreholes dried up due to lack of maintenance, or were privatized by local merchants and rich farmers," due to the privatization of water resources.

The impact of structural adjustment on Somalia's food security was compounded by American and Soviet meddling during the Cold War. Stephen Zunes, professor of politics at the University of San Francisco, explains that Somalia was initially a client state of the Soviet Union in the early '70s until Somali dictator Said Barre switched sides following a military coup in Ethiopia that replaced the U.S.-backed Ethiopian monarchy with a Soviet-backed "Marxist-Leninist" government.

The U.S. proceeded to prop up the Barre regime with $50 million worth of weapons a year for access to strategic military bases, despite warnings that Somalia's authoritarian leader was committing atrocious human rights violations.

Eventually, repression and social unrest led to the outbreak of civil war in 1988 between rival factions, fought with weapons provided by the United States. When Barre was overthrown in 1991, he left behind a chaotic "power vacuum," with rival factions vying for control in a country lacking any centralized structure capable of alleviating the food insecurity to come.

The neoliberal dismantling of Somalia's agro-pastoralist economy combined with U.S.-fed sectarian violence left Somalia extremely vulnerable to famine when faced with a drought in 1992, causing the mass starvation of 300,000 people.

Fast forward to 2011, and conditions in Somalia remain relatively unchanged. Civil war continues unabated, food insecurity persists, and recurring U.S. intervention endures in the name of "fighting terror" as journalist Michelle Chen recently highlighted at Colorlines. Only this time, Somalia and its neighbors are battling this lethal combination after having spent decades living just above starvation levels.

While economic policies from the '80s and '90s are not solely responsible for Somalia's current famine, Chossudovsky asserts, it's impossible to ignore that "ten years of IMF economic medicine laid the foundations for the country's transition towards economic dislocation and social chaos."

Malawi Starves

In one of most outrageous episodes of neoliberal incompetence, Walden Bello described the role of structural adjustment on Malawi in the late 1990s, when subsistence farmers were provided with "starter packs" of free fertilizers and seeds. The program yielded a surplus of corn. But then the World Bank and IMF stepped in to dismantle the program and compelled the government to sell the majority of its grain reserves in order to service its debt. Bello explains the fallout:

When the crisis in food production turned into a famine in 2001-2002, there were hardly any reserves left to rush to the countryside. About 1,500 people perished. The IMF, however, was unrepentant;

in fact, it suspended its disbursements on an adjustment program with the government on the grounds that "the parastatal sector will continue to pose risks to the successful implementation of the 2002/03 budget."

According to Bello, when the next food crisis hit in 2005, the Malawian government gave up on the "institutionalized stupidity" of the IMF and the World Bank. Bello writes:

A new president reintroduced the fertilizer subsidy program, enabling two million households to buy fertilizer at a third of the retail price and seeds at a discount. The results: bumper harvests for two years in a row, a surplus of one million tons of maize, and the country transformed into a supplier of corn to other countries in Southern Africa.

In the 2008 World Development Report, the World Bank shocked many when it acknowledged that structural adjustment from the 1980s was a failure that "dismantled the elaborate system of public agencies that provided farmers with access to land, credit, insurance inputs, and cooperative organization."

The Bank insists the intention was to "free up the market" so the supposed more efficient and less costly private sector could take over, but "that didn't happen," the report admits. It goes on to confess that the beneficiaries of privatization were "commercial farmers," which left "smallholders exposed to extensive market failures, high transaction costs and risks, and service gaps" that threatened "their survival."

Nevertheless, when asked whether structural adjustments increased food insecurity and vulnerability to famine in Sub-Saharan Africa, a World Bank spokesperson responded with the following statement:

> "The famine that has now been declared in six regions of Somalia and the food insecurity that has affected other neighboring countries in the Horn of Africa is the result of climate-related hazards in a context of political instability and conflict. It would be inaccurate to blame it on structural adjustment programs implemented three decades ago."

Recognizing Economic Violence

As tragic images of starving Africans in underdeveloped countries riddled with seemingly neverending violence and conflict fill the airwaves, a narrative emerges depicting Africa as a bottomless pit of charity and aid—one that ignores the historical context essential to understanding Africa's impoverishment.

Writing for Al Jazeera English, David Nally, the author of Human Encumbrances: Political Violence and the Great Irish Famine, concludes, "The portrayal of the passive victim enables NGOs and Western governments to assume the role of rescuer without having to ask uncomfortable questions about their own complicity in the suffering that is unfolding."

It's time the West faced up to the reality that this famine is the inevitable consequence of a broken food system that prioritizes the hefty pockets of the privileged above the empty stomachs of the vulnerable, draining Africa of its resources and essentially stripping Africans of their right to food and life.

David Nally quotes Susan Sontag, reminding us that, "The more it's shown that 'the sort of thing which happens in that place' is partly an outcome of policies designed in this place, the more responsibility we have to do something about it. When viewing images of starving children or reading about deaths from malnutrition in the daily newspapers, we ought to consider critically the architecture of violence behind the picture or story, not merely the sad abjection of the victim."

(Rania Khalek is a progressive activist. She runs a blog called Missing Pieces. She can be reached at raniakhalek@gmail.com)

As human society is presently structured, there is sufficient production of grains all over the world. Therefore the opening of slaughterhouses cannot be supported. In some nations there is so much surplus grain that sometimes extra grain is thrown into the sea, and sometimes the government forbids further production of grain. The conclusion is that the earth produces sufficient grain to feed the entire population, but the distribution of this grain is restricted due to trade regulations and a desire for profit. Consequently in some places there is scarcity of grain and in others profuse production. If there were one government on the surface of the earth to handle the distribution of grain, there would be no question of scarcity, no necessity to open slaughterhouses, and no need to present false theories about over-population.
~ Srila Prabhuapda (Srimad Bhagavatam 4.17.25)

73.

Africa

Food Crisis Is A Policy Crisis

By James Tulloch, July 28, 2011

Bad policies, not just bad weather, have created the East African famine. That's the message from experts battling the hunger.

Starving people appear to most of us as an indistinct mass of human misery. Their pain is what moves us. Their needs compel us to help. They look and suffer alike. Who they are is not really important.

But to understand why East Africans are starving, and to really help them, we need to know who they are and where they came from, says Karol Boudreaux, a poverty economist with USAID.

Then we'll see that it's not just drought that has caused the East African famine, it is bad governance. The food crisis is a policy crisis. Unless policies are changed, she warned the TEDGlobal 2011 conference in Edinburgh, Scotland, "the same thing is going to happen over and over again".

So who are these people? And what are the policies that have pushed them to the brink?

Pastoralists In Peril

"The people most affected are pastoralists who live in these arid regions of northern Kenya, Somalia and eastern Ethiopia," explained Boudreaux afterwards. "They rely for almost all their needs on their livestock."

They have been dealing with drought for centuries, moving their livestock between pastures, their nomadic existence a strategy to keep one step ahead of hunger. But their capacity to live this way has been crippled by the gradual loss of their grazing lands, lands held under traditional custody rights, lands that may at times appear unoccupied.

Governments moved in, ignoring those communal rights, created national parks and sold land and water sources to farmers. They also tightened border controls and so blocked pastoralists' movement between wet and dry season pastures.

"For decades they have tried to get pastoralists to settle down. And in the development community there was a sense that pastoralism was not as viable a production system as we now know it is," Boudreaux explains.

The result was too many farmers settling in places with too little rainfall and so squeezing pastoralists into smaller areas. This all makes it harder for people to find food when times are tough. The ongoing conflict in Somalia has made things much, much worse.

"In conflict-prone South and Central Somalia, a stable government and peace are the only solutions," to the immediate crisis, says Christoph Mueller, Head of the German Red Cross in Eastern Africa.

But what should be done in the medium to long term to prevent the endlessly repeating cycle Boudreaux warns about?

Power Back To Communities

Karol Boudreaux thinks pastoralism should be supported as it is often "more sustainable than farming" in arid areas. "They need

> *"Those who live off their livestock have a very, very difficult time now."*
> *~Ali Abdi, a former herder*

help restocking their herds, they need secure land and water rights, and they need access to livestock markets," she says.

Her model is Community Based Natural Resource Management (CBNRM). The poster-child for this approach is Namibia.

Since 1996 black Namibians have had robust rights to manage the lands they live on and the wildlife that shares those lands. Communities organized themselves into 'conservancies' and now about 10 percent of Namibians are members of the 59 conservancies that in 2009 earned about 5.5 million dollars. Wildlife numbers recovered too– between 2004 and 2009 buffalo and elephant numbers tripled.

"This is considered the gold standard worldwide for handing power back to communities," says Boudreaux, "and the impact on the wildlife has been nothing short of astonishing".

Also these countries lack food storage and transport facilities. Up to 40 percent of wheat grown in sub-Saharan African countries is lost to rodents or rot because it doesn't get to market quickly enough.

Warehousing food securely for the bad times is also essential to help "get over the boom and bust cycle," said Sheeran.

Considering that hunger costs poor countries an average of 6 percent of GDP, fighting food insecurity is clearly an economic imperative. "If a child doesn't get adequate nutrition in its first 1000 days the damage is irreversible... we see brain volumes of 40 percent less than normal. The earnings potential of children can be cut in half," Sheeran explained.

And fighting hunger is perfectly affordable. The World Bank says it would cost 10.3bn dollars to deal with malnutrition in the worst-affected countries. India, home to the highest numbers of malnourished children in the world, this year plans to spend 11bn dollars on 126 fighter planes.

Bad policies, unlike bad climate changes, can be quickly reversed.

> *The right time to eat is: for a rich man when he is hungry, for a poor man when he has something to eat.*
>
> *-Mexican Proverb*

74.

Financial Terrorism

Americans Milk Africa To Death

By Bob Astles

Vulture funds buy up the debt of poor countries cheaply when it is about to be written off and then use a variety of devices to force the debtor nations to pay out.

They often recover 10 times what the speculator paid for the debt and it is poor countries in Africa or Latin America who are being targeted.

These companies are run by Americans through a maze of companies registered in offshore tax havens and they pursue legal actions in jurisdictions around the world. They have been condemned by the British chancellor, Gordon Brown, as "morally outrageous", and also by the International Monetary Fund and the World Bank. But no action is taken and they are still in business.

BBC TV's Newsnight team tracked down some of these vultures. Recently they have targeted Zambia and the Republic of Congo amongst others. Their bosses are coy about publicity. The biggest, Elliott Associates, told the BBC, "We have nothing to hide-we just don't do interviews."

The BBC Newsnight team caught up with one of them outside his house near Washington DC. Michael Sheehan runs an organization called Debt Advisory International which is linked to a web of British Virgin Islands companies including Donegal International which sued Zambia. He also sometimes appears to communicate under the name of Goldfinger - a bond speculator using the name of a villain from a James Bond movie.

On Thursday February 15, 2007 he won a case against the Zambian government in London which will probably net his company US$20 million.

A BBC Newsnight reporter asked Sheehan, "Why are you squeezing the poor nation of Zambia for US$40 million-doesn't that make you a vulture?"

He replied, "No comment. I'm in litigation. It's not my debt".

Sheehan claims to act on behalf of a consortium of anonymous investors. The Newsnight reporter asked him if he felt guilty about freeloading on the backs of the countries and institutions who have given US$100 billion to relieve third world debt. "Aren't you just profiteering from the work of good people who are trying to save lives by cutting the debt of these poor nations?" he was asked.

Sheehan's reply was, "Well there was a proposal for investment. That's all I can talk about right now."

Tractors Of Doom

The Zambia case shines a light on the way vulture funds operate. Back in 1979 Romania sold Zambia tractors and gave them a US$15 million loan to finance the deal. The tractors were not of the highest quality. The tractors— and Zambia — were soon broke and the debt was not paid off.

By the mid 1990s various governments were beginning the process of debt forgiveness to the poorest nations with the multi millionaire Bob Geldof doing most of the shouting. Zambia was one of these Highly Indebted Poor Countries.

In 1999, Zambia negotiated with Romania to settle the debt for around US$3 million. Somehow Sheehan and his agents persuaded Romania to sell the debt to them instead. They then made payments to a number of Zambian officials and persuaded them to sign a document promising to pay US$15 million to Sheehan's company. A key figure was Fisho Mwale, an ex-mayor of Lusaka who was paid US$270,000 and made payments to others.

Sheehan told the BBC Newsnight the money was not an offer of a bribe but "a charitable initiative" before adding, "You're contorting the facts; you're on my property and I would ask you to step off."

Zambia paid US$2 million to Donegal International but when a new president was elected he launched a corruption investigation which raised suspicions about the deal and the payments were stopped. This left Sheehan's firm US$1 million out of pocket - they had paid US$3 million and were paid only US$2 million. So they sued in the British courts for US$43 million plus a further US$12 million in interest.

Judge Smith said Sheehan was "deliberately evasive and even dishonest"; that he "deliberately gave false evidence" and misled courts around the world in pursuit of this claim. The judge thought US$55 million was too much but the law required him to rule in favor of the vulture fund and Zambia will have to pay around US$20 million — or half the annual savings to the Zambian budget of international debt relief.

An ex-adviser to current Zambian President Levy Mwanawasa is Martin Kalunga-Banda. He estimates that US$20 million could pay for free education for 150,000 children.

Sheehan is also suing Congo along with other speculators such as FG Hemisphere and Elliott Associates. Elliott virtually invented vulture funds. They are owned by a reclusive billionaire called Paul Singer. In 1996 Elliott paid US$11 million for some discounted Peruvian debt and then threatened to bankrupt the country unless they paid him US$58 million. They got their US$58 million. Then Singer bought some discounted debt from Congo for about US$10 million.

Now, Singer's company has been awarded US$127 million in a British court but they want more. The British court accepted that Congo set up a system of front companies to try to keep oil earnings out of the hands of the vultures. These arrangements inevitably made it easier for corrupt government officials to take a cut as well.

saka-mulamisa-ksaudra-
phala-puspasti-bhojanah
anavrstya vinanksyanti
durbhiksa-kara-piditah

Harassed by famine and excessive taxes, people will resort to eating leaves, roots, flesh, wild honey, fruits, flowers and seeds. Struck by drought, they will become completely ruined.

-Srimad Bhagavatam 12.2.9

Using the British judgment about concealing earnings through front companies Elliott have now taken the case to the US where they can claim triple damages using the Racketeer Influenced and Corrupt Organizations (RICO) law.

This was brought in to combat Mafia money laundering by imposing massive damages but Elliott is now exploiting it to make US$400 million profit on a US$10 million investment. The funds comb the world looking for courts which will legally recognize their claims such as London, Brussels, Paris or wherever. Then they take those judgments back to the US and get court orders to seize the assets of those countries or any company which does business with them. FG Hemisphere even tried to take Congo's diplomatic buildings in Washington.

There is a potential problem about suing in the US though, and this is where President George Bush could come to the rescue. Lee Buchheit is a partner at a New York law firm which defends countries when they are sued. Buchheit says the president has the power to "intervene, when appropriate, in maverick lawsuits commenced in US courts against foreign sovereigns". This principle is called international comity. In other words a stroke of the presidential pen could stop these actions. Traditionally the funds have spent a fortune on lobbying in Washington. Elliott's Paul Singer is very well connected. He is the biggest donor to Bush and the Republican cause in New York City, giving around US$2 million since Bush first ran for president. Elliott also uses lobbyists.

When Congo's (Brazzaville) President Denis Sassou-Nguesso visited Washington to meet Bush the press were somehow supplied with Sassou-Nguesso's extravagant hotel bills and the story became what Elliott call "Sassou's lavish lifestyle" rather than the US$400 million which they were trying to extract from his country.

Debt Advisory International also has Washington lobbyists. Michael Sheehan's firm paid Greenberg Traurig US$240, a year until their chief lobbyist-Jack Abramoff was jailed for bribing

"Plenty sits still, hunger is a wanderer"
- Proverb

politicians on behalf of other clients. Many campaigners assumed the funds had political protection from Bush's administration.

Congressman John Conyers saw the BBC Newsnight film before a scheduled meeting with the president and decided to speak out. He said, "It was my job, I felt, to raise the whole question of this bond speculation that goes on at the expense of poor debtor countries, in which their debt is bought up and then they're sued for the full amount. It's bought up at pennies on the dollar, and then they're sued."

Conyers heads the House Judiciary Committee and he wants to investigate vulture funds. He says he asked Bush two questions "one, about Paul Singer and Michael Sheehan; and two, whether he would be willing to stop this incredible misuse of our government's charity toward funding aid to our poorer nations". Bush put one of his White House staff on to the issue immediately and indicated that he wanted to curb the excesses of vulture funds.

"Profiteering doesn't get any more cynical than this," says Caroline Pearce of the Jubilee Debt Campaign which calls for debt cancellation. "Zambia has been planning to spend the money released from debt cancellation on much-needed nurses, teachers and infrastructure."

Sheehan (aka Goldfinger) may face an investigation from Congressman Conyers' House Judiciary Committee and his email linking the Zambian deal to a donation may cause him problems. The BBC Newsnight went to Greenberg Traurig, Sheehan's former lobbyists.

They have a beautiful office overlooking the White House. Frederick Shaheen is a regular visitor there and he told the BBC News night that these were the "places we have to go to help our clients get what they want". Africa is being made to suffer by many Vultures, but who cares right? Cynicism abounds.

(Columnist Bob Astles is based in Portugal)

75.

A Heartbreaking Journey

Through The Famine-Stricken Territories

By Lisa, Oxfam News, July 27th, 2011

Jim Clarken, chief executive of Oxfam Ireland, spent a week in the Horn of Africa in 2011. He travelled as part of a group of NGOs sent to assess the devastating situation and hear the stories of some of those directly affected by the famine. Former UN High Commissioner Mary Robinson, who is the Honorary President of Oxfam International, also took part in the visit.

Here, Mr Clarken describes for the Irish Daily Mail his heartbreaking journey through the famine-stricken territories.

Someone once said to me that the worst sight in the world was a hungry mother trying to feed a hungry, crying baby from an empty breast. In East Africa, and particularly Somalia, this is the scenario being played out each day now.

Mothers and fathers, having literally run out of options when it comes to providing the basics for their children, are burying them instead of being able to nurture them.

As a parent myself, I could imagine the despair to which parents were driven in this terrible struggle to survive.

But this week I got to meet some of those parents, during a visit to Kenya and Somalia with former Irish President Mary Robinson – who is now the president of Oxfam International – and other Irish aid agencies.

We saw first hand the trauma experienced by exhausted people who were pouring into Kenya across the Somali border. They had been walking for days in some cases, supporting elderly parents, coaxing young children along and carrying young babies. Some had been forced to leave the weaker, older people behind, others had left infant children.

When families were lucky enough to reach the safety of Dadaab refugee camp, they were able to get food, water and shelter, along with medical attention for the severely malnourished. Thousands of people are now arriving in this camp each day.

Every single coping mechanism they might have had is gone. They have typically sold their livestock, eaten or sold any crops and run out of money to buy food if it was available.

Tears Of Blood

Eyes Are Too Parched To Shed Tears

Driving across the Chalbi Desert,on our way to Marsabit Town in Northern Kenya, we came across two herders, an old man and young boy. Jarosyl Adi was in his 70s and told us how he had lived in the area all of his life. He spoke about how much things have changed in his lifetime, about how much further they have to bring their cattle to try to find food and water. He told us that he has never seen things as bad as this.

The people here mainly live off their animals – everything you own is your cattle or your goats – but it's been so dry that the animals are weak and dying.

The only livestock we saw on our journey were camels, and even they were weak. We were told that they are dying of thirst and keeling over –things are severe if a camel can't survive. We travelled on and passed through a small village of about 1,700 women, children and old men.

They that die by famine die by inches.-Matthew Henry

All of the other men had gone to find food for their livestock. Those left behind were on the brink, waiting and hoping that the men would return with something, or that someone would come and help.

Already 40 of them had died, mostly children. On the outskirts of Marsabit, we met people who had traveled huge distances on very little food or water, all their cattle had died and they needed help. There was a great sense of frustration. These were people willing to work and help themselves. They had tried everything, planting different crops, mixing their herds, but this savage drought has had such a huge impact.

But as bad as things were in Marsabit, we had a huge sense of foreboding that we were about to see a lot worse. The following day we traveled to Dolo in Somalia.

The Death Roads

Our first stop was on the side of the road where a large group of exhausted women and children were settled under some trees. We spoke with Sadia Abdul who had walked most of the way from Birbwell – 200km away! She had left behind conflict and any means of earning an income was gone.

The group was hungry and in desperate need of food and water. Many had the listless look of people who have gone through so much and were nearly too weak to travel further. We saw some truly awful scenes of severely malnourished children, babies with arms no thicker than your finger.

As we entered the village of Dolo there was a reception party of boys and girls singing to welcome Mary Robinson and signs saying how much they appreciated the Irish focus on their plight and hoping that we can make a difference for them.

At the clinic, we saw babies being weighed, measured and checked for malnutrition. Too many babies were small and underweight for their age.

The real worry now is that this is still early in the 'hunger' season. Hunger won't peak until around October and the head of the clinic believed that it could be worse this time around than it was in 1992.

The clinic is overwhelmed. Up to 2,000 people are passing through that clinic every day. Staff work from early in the morning until late at night and people are already queuing when they open. The staff members give high-nutrition food known as plumpy-nut to those children who are most malnourished. But because families have nothing else they share this among themselves. This means no-one gets the proper nutrition.

Sodo Abdulahi Nuh, 25, was having her 14-month-old malnourished baby boy weighed. He registered just 7 kgs on the scale. She has three other children to care for too. Around six children die each week at this very clinic – because they have no food.

I met a woman who had a little baby in her arms – she had eight children and had traveled 50km on foot. Her husband had been killed in fighting in Mogadishu. She had arrived into Dolo not knowing anybody. A local family, who were desperate themselves, brought her in and were doing their best to feed her and her children, sharing the little bit they had. That's the kind of extraordinary people they are.

Amina had walked 50 kms from Luk with three-year-old daughter, Asha. She had already lost two children. All of her cattle died too.

In Kenya too, families are running out of options. Karagi village, in Turkana, Kenya has buried 40 of its people in the recent past, most of them children, and all due to hunger.

The most striking thing about Karagi is that we didn't see one man of working age. These men have travelled very long distances to try and find water for their livestock – the only source of income they have. They send back money when they can. The village is entirely comprised of women, children and elderly men who are on the brink of disaster. The sense of foreboding was palpable.

In Marsabit, we heard from 65-year-old Tabich Galgal. He simply said that they have no food. Some members of the community are receiving food aid but they share what they have with others, so everyone is trying to survive on rations.

The right time to eat is: for a rich man when he is hungry, for a poor man when he has something to eat.

-Mexican Proverb

The frustration in Tabich's voice was evident as he described how they had tried everything. It's not that they are not doing all they can to eke out a living, it's just that the drought has really placed such a huge burden on them, he said.

Then Elena Boru explained how the lack of water is having a devastating effect on women, who have to spend most of the day collecting it.

She explained that there are plenty of people in the village more than willing and able to work, to do anything where they can provide for their families and she stressed that the elderly must be taken care of. Along our travels we saw very feeble and clearly malnourished older people – a shocking prospect considering all they have contributed to their communities during their lives.

Famine has now gripped parts of Somalia. This is the inevitable consequence of drought, climate change, conflict, entrenched poverty and lack of investment in development.

Dadaab - The Biggest Refugee Camp In The World

Our next stop was Dadaab in Kenya, the biggest refugee camp in the world.

Flying in you can see the vastness of it. It goes on for miles and miles. It was originally built for 90,000 people but now there's upwards of 400,000 living there. It's completely overflowing. Up to 80,000 people are living on the outskirts of the camp.

At one point I was right beside a woman who was hiding her baby who had just died. She was sitting there, just privately mourning. What an extraordinarily terrible thing for any mother to go through.

Her father told us how things had been so very bad for them and the awful thing was, that they had survived their long journey from Somalia but the child died just as they arrived at the camp. It was shockingly sad.

The atmosphere at Dadaab is very hot, dirty, with all these desperate people continuing to stream in, about 9,000 a week. The worst thing that could happen now, in these very built up camps, is that there would be cholera or an outbreak such as that.

Up to 1.75million people are displaced within Somalia itself. The war has been going on for several years and the fact that Somalia doesn't have a stable, democratic government is a major factor in the current hardship.

We met a woman who had travelled from Luk in Somalia, 50 km away from the camp. She just had one of her daughters with her, her other two children died on the way. As we were leaving, an old man with a very weak infant came up to me with his hand out. I've spent a lot of time in many different countries in Africa, I used to live and work running a health program in South Sudan, in Kenya, The Congo, Rwanda and other places. Nobody ever came up to me with a hand out, it's not what people here do.

Those are questions that must be addressed, in time, but first we have to deal with this humanitarian crisis. 12 million lives are on the line but if we act right now we can prevent further large-scale loss of life.

Oxfam is working right through the region, providing food, clean water, and shelter, and helping people to earn a living again. Through our programmes we intend to reach three million people.

At the moment, Oxfam is implementing the single largest nutrition programme in the capital city, Mogadishu, treating more than 12,000 severely malnourished children, pregnant women and those who are breastfeeding. We are also providing water and sanitation for 300,000 internally displaced people and giving life-saving equipment to Somalia's only functioning children's hospital.

In Kenya and Ethiopia, we are giving people money through cash for work schemes to build water tanks and reservoirs. We are trucking in water supplies for 32,000 people in Ethiopia and treating the water for drinking, cooking, washing and keeping animals alive. We are helping people who have livestock to keep them healthy and vaccinated. We are digging and repairing wells and boreholes, and providing sanitation and latrines.

But we can't do it alone. We need the help of governments and the public to stop this human catastrophe spreading and claiming greater numbers of lives. Otherwise we are condemning countless thousands of people to a needless death.

"Hunger is the best pickle."
-Benjamin Franklin

The total amount required to resolve this crisis is estimated to be €1.9billion. It sounds like a lot of money but it isn't, not from the whole world. We have spent thousands of billions on shoring up banks and fighting useless wars. Just the Iraq war cost us more than a thousand billion in direct costs. But this is the biggest crisis in the world right now and the world needs to pay attention. I think the most ominous and most frightening thing is that local people believe things are worse than they were in 1992 when hundreds of thousands of people died.

It was my first time in Somalia and it was only afterwards, when I got home and had time to reflect, that I fully realised how desperate things are there and how sad it was witnessing it. I hope to return again and I hope it will be better. Some of the people I met and some of the images I saw will stay with me forever.

It's just so shocking that this can happen in 2011 – the word famine should have been eradicated because it should be something that happened in our past. The idea it can happen today is abhorrent.

Section-VII

Depopulation Agenda

The Great Plan

76.

India

A Genocide In Progress

Genocide is "the deliberate and systematic destruction, in whole or in part, of an ethnic, racial, religious, or national group". While a precise definition varies among genocide scholars, a legal definition is found in the 1948 United Nations Convention on the Prevention and Punishment of the Crime of Genocide (CPPCG).

Article 2 of the Convention defines genocide as any of the following acts committed with intent to destroy, in whole or in part, a national, ethnic, racial or religious group, as such:

(a) Killing members of the group;

(b) Causing serious bodily or mental harm to members of the group;

(c) Deliberately inflicting on the group conditions of life calculated to bring about its physical destruction in whole or in part;

(d) Imposing measures intended to prevent births within the group;

(e) Forcibly transferring children of the group to another group.

Raphael Lemkin, in his work Axis Rule in Occupied Europe (1944), coined the term "genocide" by combining Greek genos (race, people) and Latin cīdere (to kill).

Lemkin defined genocide as follows: "Generally speaking, genocide *does not necessarily mean the immediate destruction of a nation, except when accomplished by mass killings of all members of a nation. It is intended rather to signify a coordinated plan of different actions aiming at the destruction of essential foundations of the life of national groups,* with the aim of annihilating the groups themselves.

The objectives of such a plan would be the disintegration of the political and social institutions, of culture, language, national feelings, religion, and the economic existence of national groups, and the destruction of the personal security, liberty, health, dignity, and even the lives of the individuals belonging to such groups." The preamble to the CPPCG states that instances of genocide have taken place throughout history,[3] but it was not until Raphael Lemkin coined the term and the prosecution of perpetrators of the Holocaust at the Nuremberg trials that the United Nations agreed to the CPPCG which defined the crime of genocide under international law.

According to this definition, in India, there is a genocide in progress. The food supply of 1.2 billion people is being systematically

Great Scarcity of Soil Nutrients

It is estimated that every year, 20.2 million tonnes of the three major nutrients – nitrogen, phosphorus, and potassium – is removed by growing crops (Tandon 1992) but the corresponding addition through chemical fertilisers and organic manures falls short of this figure. It was determined that only 23% of the applied fertiliser is consumed by plants; the remaining 77% is either leached out beyond the root zone or lost by volatilisation, etc. Thus, out of 20.2 million tonnes of nutrients removed by plants, only 2.66 million tonnes comes from fertilisers and nearly 3 million tonnes from organic sources. This leaves a little less than 14 million tonnes, which is obviously contributed by soil. If the loss of nutrients due to soil erosion is included the loss of nutrients from the top soil is 43 million tonnes, which amounts to 0.24% of the nutrient reserves of the soils.

According to Brandon, Hommann, and Kishor (1995), the annual loss in production of eleven major crops in India due to depletion of nutrient as a result of unsuitable agricultural practices amounts to 0.5 to 1.3 million tonnes. This estimate, however, does not take into account the loss due to erosion.

The problem of maintaining the nutrient balance and preventive the consequent nutrient deficiencies will be a major concern in most cultivated areas.

destroyed. Gradual handing over of food sector to unscrupulous corporations is a bold step in that direction.

It is happening at a rather fast pace. Agriculture, the livelihood of 70% of the Indian population, is being turned into an untenable occupation. Every day 2000 farmers are calling it quits and heading for urban shanty towns. Out of those who dare to stay on, one is committing suicide every fifteen minutes.

Indian agriculture is a fragile system which had withstood the test of time. India supports approximately 16% of the world's human population and 20% of the world's livestock population on merely 2.5% of the world's geographical area. Any tinkering in this sensitive area will have disastrous impact on the nation's food security.

Already the widespread incidence of poverty, and the current phase of economic and trade liberalisation are exerting heavy pressures on India's limited land resources for competing uses in forestry, agriculture, pastures, human settlements and industries.

This has led to very significant land degradation. According to the latest estimates (Sehgal and Abrol 1994), about 187.8 mha (57% approximately) out of 328.73 mha of land area has been degraded in one way or the other. It appears therefore, that most of our land is degraded, is undergoing degradation or is at the risk of getting degraded.

Modern word for unscrupulous colonials is corporations. Corporatisation is the modern way of colonizing the world. Today's world is getting ground under the corporate jackboot. These huge corporations make obscene profits from human misery and they want the world to remain in misery.

They run our health care industry. They run our oil and gas companies. They run our bloated weapons industry. They run Wall Street and the major investment firms. They run our manufacturing firms. They also, ominously, run our government.

World is simply not a safe place in the shadows of these greedy monsters. They want profits - when economy thrives and they want profits - when economy dies. Profits in a dying economy means war, death and destruction. That's the only way to go about it.

The negative effects of land degradation are telling very heavily on India's environment and economy, which are causes of grave concern.

Indian government, in tandem with the vested interests is applying the same policies that have destroyed Africa's agriculture. In just three decades Africa has gone from a net food exporter to become a net food importer.

> *Formerly, men worked in the open air only as much as they liked. Now thousands of workmen meet together and for the sake of maintenance work in factories or mines. Their condition is worse than that of beasts. They are obliged to work, at the risk of their lives, at most dangerous occupations, for the sake of millionaires.* -*Gandhi*

77.

Displacing Farmers

India Will Have 400 million Agricultural Refugees

Devinder Sharma, STWR, 22nd June 07,

It was on the cards. With the Prime Minister announcing the formation of a new rehabilitation policy for farmers displaced from land acquisitions, it is now official -- farmers have to quit agriculture.

Ever since the present coalition assumed power in May 2004, the Prime Minister initiated a plethora of new policies for the spread of industrialization. After having laid the policy framework that allows private control over community resources – water, biodiversity, forests, seeds, agriculture markets, and mineral resources -- the UPA government finally looked at the possibility of divesting the poor people of their only economic security – a meagre piece of land holding.

"Special Economic Zone (SEZ) is an idea whose time has come," the Prime Minister said at an award ceremony in Mumbai sometime back. Supported by all political parties, including the Left Front, he has actually officiated a nationwide campaign to displace farmers. Almost 500 special economic zones are being carved out. What is however less known is that successive governments are actually following a policy prescription that had been laid out by the World Bank as early as in 1995.

A former vice-president of the World Bank and a former chairman of Consultative Group on International Agricultural Research (CGIAR), a body that governs the 16 international agricultural research centers, Dr Ismail Serageldin, had forewarned a number of years ago. At a conference organised by the M S Swaminathan Research Foundation in Chennai, he quoted the World Bank saying the number of people estimated to migrate from rural to urban India by the year 2015 is expected to be equal to twice the combined population of UK, France and Germany.

The combined population of UK, France and Germany is 200 million. The World Bank had therefore estimated that some 400 million people would be willingly or unwillingly moving from the rural to urban centres by 2015.

Subsequent studies have shown that massive distress migration will result in the years to come. For instance, 70 per cent of Tamil Nadu, 65 per cent of Punjab, and nearly 55 per cent of Uttar Pradesh is expected to migrate to urban centres by the year 2020.

These 400 million displaced will constitute the new class of migrants – agricultural refugees.

Acerbating the crisis are the policy initiatives that promote privatization of natural resources, take over of farm lands, integration of Indian agriculture with the global economy, and moving farmers out of agriculture – in essence the hallmark of the neo-liberal economic growth model.

Agricultural reforms that are being introduced in the name of increasing food production and minimizing the price risks that the farmers continue to be faced with, are actually aimed at destroying the production capacity of the farm lands and would lead to further marginalisation of the farming communities. Encouraging contract farming, future trading in agriculture commodities, land leasing, forming land-sharing companies, direct procurement of farm commodities by amending the APMC Act will only drive out a majority of farmers out of subsistence agriculture.

"Innocent men, women, they are kept in that factory simply for livelihood. A little work will provide their needs. Nature has given so much facility. They can grow a little food anywhere. The cows are there in the pasturing ground. Take milk and live peacefully. Why you open factories?"

— Srila Prabhupada (New Vrindavan, June 26, 1976)

Although the land holding size is diminishing, the answer does not lie in allowing the private companies to replace farmers. *Somehow the entire effort of the policy makers is to establish that Indian agriculture has become a burden on the nation and the sooner the country offloads the farming class the better it will be for economic growth.*

Contract farming therefore has become the new agricultural mantra. Not realising that private companies enter agriculture with the specific objective of garnering more profits from the same piece of land. These companies, if the global experience is any indication, bank upon very intensive farming practices which drain the soil of nutrients and use up the ground water and render the fertile lands barren in a few years. It is estimated that the crops that are contracted by the private companies require on an average 20 times more chemical inputs and water than the staple foods.

Sugarcane farmers, for instance, who follow a system of cane bonding with the mills, actually were drawing 240 cm of water every year, which is three times more than what wheat and rice require on an average. Rose cultivation, introduced a few years back, requires 212 inches of groundwater consumption in every acre.

Contract farming will therefore further exploit whatever remains of the ground water resources. After it's all over, these companies would terminate the lease and hand over the barren land back to the farmers, and move on to other fertile areas. This has been the global experience so far.

Allowing direct procurement of farm commodities, setting up special markets for the private companies to mop up the produce, and to set up land share companies, are all directed at the uncontrolled entry of the multinational corporations in the farm sector. Coupled with the introduction of the genetically modified crops, and the unlimited credit support for the agribusiness companies, the focus is to strengthen the ability of the companies to take over the food chain.

I have always warned that agribusiness companies in reality hate farmers. Nowhere in the world have they worked in tandem with farmers. Even in North America and Europe, agribusiness companies have pushed farmers out of agriculture. As a result, only 7,00,000 farming families are left on the farms in the United States. Despite massive subsidies in European Union, one farmer quits agriculture every minute. Knowing well that the markets will displace farmers, the same agriculture prescription is being applied in India.

A Planning Commission study has shown that 73 per cent of the cultivable land in the country is owned by 23.6 per cent of the population. With more and more farmers being displaced through land acquisitions, either for SEZ or for food processing and technology parks or for real estate purposes, land is further getting accumulated in the hands of the elite and resourceful. With chief ministers acting as property dealers, farmers are being lured to divest control over cultivable land. Food security and food self-sufficiency is no longer the country's political priority.

LOANS
At least once in your life
you'll need a doctor,
a lawyer,
an architect,
but every day
three times a day
you'll need a farmer!
Save FARMERs ....
save INDIA

Gandhi wanted it ... Village organization. He started that Wardha Ashram. But you have rejected. What Gandhi can do? That was good proposal -- to remain satisfied in one's own place. That was Gandhi's proposal. That "Don't go to the city, town, for so-called better advantage of life. Remain in your own home, produce your food, and be satisfied there." That was Gandhi's policy. The economic problem he wanted to solve by keeping cows, by agriculture, by spinning thread. "You want food, shelter and cloth? Produce here, and remain here. Don't be allured by the capitalists and go to cities and engage in industries." But Jawaharlal Nehru wanted, overnight, to Americanize the whole India. That is the folly.

-Srila Prabhupada (Room Conversation with Reporter from Researchers Magazine -- July 24, 1973, London)

The government has very conveniently taken refuge behind an NSSO study (National Sample Survey Organisation) that says some 40 per cent of the farmers have expressed the desire to quit farming. After all, what the government is facilitating is to make it easier for the farmers to abandon their land. It believes that a rehabilitation policy for the farmers therefore is the need of the hour. What is however not being seen through is that an agrarian economy like India cannot afford large-scale displacement of farmers. It will lead to social unrest the kind of which has not been witnessed so far. What India needs desperately is a policy paradigm that restores pride in agriculture, stops take-over of agricultural lands, and ensures sustainable livelihoods for 600 million farmers.

78.

Eugenics

And Foul Smelling Government Policies

Eugenics is a social philosophy advocating the improvement of human hereditary traits through the promotion of higher reproduction of more desired people and traits, and reduced reproduction of less desired people and traits.[1]

The American Journal of Eugenics (1906) defined it as "the science of good generation" and "the doctrine of Progress, or Evolution, especially in the human race, through improved conditions in the relations of the sexes."

In 1970, I. Gottesman, a director of the American Eugenics Society, defined it in this way: "The essence of evolution is natural selection; the essence of eugenics is the replacement of 'natural' selection by conscious, premeditated, or artificial selection in the hope of speeding up the evolution of 'desirable' characteristics and the elimination of undesirable ones."

Eugenics in the first part of the 20th century was not just an academic exercise. Eugenicists were organizing, particularly in England and the United States, to implement policies consistent with their theories. The work of the eugenicists included: racism and white supremacy, promoting birth control among the dysgenic, restricting immigration, sterilizing the handicapped, promoting euthanasia, and seeking for ways to increase the number of genetically well-endowed individuals.

History

Eugenics, as a modern concept, was originally developed by Francis Galton. Galton had read his cousin Charles Darwin's theory of evolution, which sought to explain the development of plant and animal species, and desired to apply it to humans. In 1883, one year after Darwin's death, Galton gave his research a name, Eugenics.[2] Throughout its recent history, eugenics remains a controversial concept.[3] Many countries enacted various eugenics policies and programs, including: genetic screening, birth control, promoting differential birth rates, marriage restrictions, segregation (both racial segregation and segregation of the mentally ill from the rest of the population), compulsory sterilization, forced abortions or forced pregnancies and genocide. Most of these policies were later regarded as coercive and/or restrictive.

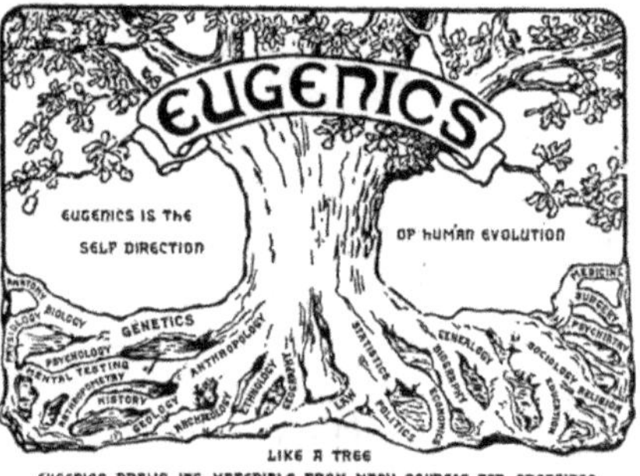

The methods of implementing eugenics varied by country; however, some of the early 20th century methods were identifying and classifying individuals and their families, including the poor, mentally ill, blind, deaf, developmentally disabled, promiscuous women, homosexuals and entire racial groups — such as the Roma and Jews — as "degenerate" or "unfit"; the segregation or institutionalisation of such individuals and groups, their sterilization, euthanasia, and in the case of Nazi Germany, their mass murder.[4]

Eugenics became an academic discipline at many colleges and universities, and received funding from many sources.[5] Three International Eugenics Conferences presented a global venue for eugenicists with meetings in 1912 in London, and in 1921 and 1932 in New York. Eugenic policies were first implemented in the early 1900s in the United States.[6] Later, in the 1920s and 30s, the eugenic policy of sterilizing certain mental patients was implemented in a variety of other countries, including Belgium,[7] Brazil,[11] Canada,[12] and Sweden,[8] among others.

In addition to being practiced in a number of countries, eugenics was internationally organized through the International Federation of Eugenic Organizations. (Black 2003, p. 240) Its scientific aspects were carried on through research bodies such as the Kaiser Wilhelm Institute of Anthropology, Human Heredity and the Eugenics Record Office (Black 2003, p. 45).

Its moral aspects included rejection of the doctrine that all human beings are born equal and redefining morality purely in terms of genetic fitness (Black 2003, p. 237). Its racist elements included pursuit of a pure "Nordic race" or "Aryan" genetic pool and the eventual elimination of less fit races (see Black, Chapter 5 Legitimizing Raceology and Chapter 9 Mongrelization).

Both the public and some elements of the scientific community have associated eugenics with Nazi abuses, such as enforced "racial hygiene", human experimentation, and the extermination of "undesired" population groups. However, developments in genetic and reproductive technologies at the end of the 20th century are, as per some, raising for some people numerous new questions regarding the ethical status of eugenics, effectively creating a resurgence of interest in the subject.

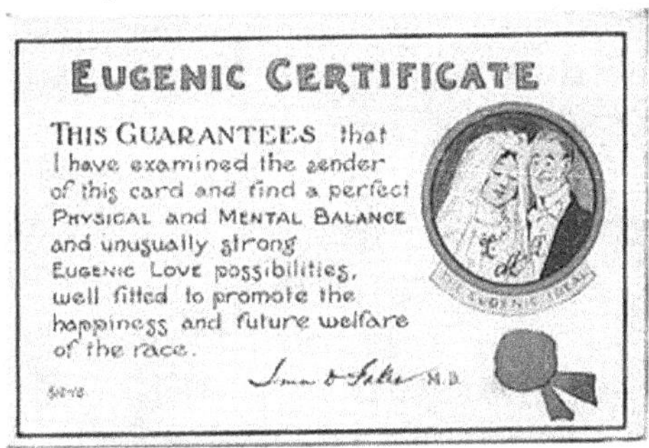

EUGENIC CERTIFICATE
THIS GUARANTEES that
I have examined the sender
of this card and find a perfect
PHYSICAL and MENTAL BALANCE
and unusually strong
EUGENIC LOVE possibilities,
well fitted to promote the
happiness and future welfare
of the race.
M.D.

Today it is still regarded by some as a brutal movement which inflicted massive human rights violations on millions of people.[9] Some practices engaged in by people in the name of eugenics involving violations of privacy, violations of reproductive rights, attacks on reputation, violations of the right to life, to found a family, to freedom from discrimination are all today classified as violations of human rights.

The practice of negative racial aspects of eugenics, after World War II, fell within the definition of the new international crime of genocide, set out in the Convention on the Prevention and Punishment of the Crime of Genocide.[10]

International Federation of Eugenics Organizations

The International Federation of Eugenic Organizations (IFEO) was founded in 1925. Most members of this organization united eugenics with racism with political propaganda for the enhancement of the 'white race.'" Charles Davenport founded the International Federation of Eugenic Organizations (IFEO) and was its first president. Charles Davenport was using the information gathered by other workers in the field of bastard studies to construct a 'World Institute for Miscegenations' and was working on a 'world map' of the 'mixed-race areas,' which he introduced for the first time at a meeting of the IFEO in Munich in 1928." [11,12] Ernst Rüdin was director of the Deutsche Forschungsanstalt für Psychiatrie (DFA) or the German Research Institute for Psychiatry (a Kaiser Wilhelm Institute). His expertise was in sterilization, and he wrote in his field of expertise. Rüdin was the second president of the International Federation of Eugenic Organizations (IFEO), by 1933.[13]

"Nobody's perfect, but we're working on it."

References:

Source: Wikipedia and others.

1. Currell, Susan; Christina Cogdell (2006). Popular Eugenics: National Efficiency and American Mass Culture in The 1930s. Athens, OH: Ohio University Press. p. 203. ISBN 0-8214-1691-X.

2. http://www.amazon.com/DNA-The-Secret-Life-ebook/dp/B001PSEQAG

3.Blom 2008, p. 336

4.See for example, Black 2003

5.Allen, Garland E. (2004). "Was Nazi eugenics created in the US?". EMBO Rep. 5 (5): 451–2. doi:10.1038/sj.embor.7400158.

6. Barrett, Deborah; Kurzman, Charles (October 2004). "Globalizing Social Movement Theory: The Case of Eugenics". Theory and Society 33 (5): 505.

7. "The National OFfice of Eugenics in Belgium" (PDF). Science 57 (1463): 46. 12 January 1923. Bibcode:1923Sci....57R..46.. doi:10.1126/science.57.1463.46.

8. a b Social Democrats implemented measures to forcibly sterilise 62,000 people. World Socialist Web Site

9. See for example Weigmann K (October 2001). "In the name of science. The role of biologists in Nazi atrocities: lessons for today's scientists". EMBO Rep. (European Molecular Biology Organization) 2 (10): 871–5. doi:10.1093/embo-reports/kve217. PMC 1084095. PMID 11600445. It concludes, "It was scientists who interpreted racial differences as the justification to murder ... It is the responsibility of today's scientists to prevent this from happening again."

10.Charter of Fundamental Rights of the European Union, Article 3, 2

11. Galton, Francis (1883). Inquiries into Human Faculty and its Development. London: Macmillan Publishers. p. 199.

12. "Correspondence between Francis Galton and Charles Darwin". Galton.org. Retrieved 2011-11-28.

13. "Darwin Correspondence Project » The correspondence of Charles Darwin, volume 17: 1869". Darwinproject.ac.uk. Retrieved 2011-11-28.

79.

Eugenics in the United States

A Dark Chapter Of Corporate History

Eugenics, the social movement claiming to improve the genetic features of human populations through selective breeding and sterilization,[1] based on the idea that it is possible to distinguish between superior and inferior elements of society,[2] played a significant role in the history and culture of the United States prior to its involvement in World War II.[3]

Eugenics was practised in the United States many years before eugenics programs in Nazi Germany[4] and actually, U.S. programs provided much of the inspiration for the latter.[5,6,7] Stefan Kühl has documented the consensus between Nazi race policies and those of eugenicists in other countries, including the United States, and points out that eugenicists understood Nazi policies and measures as the realization of their goals and demands.[5]

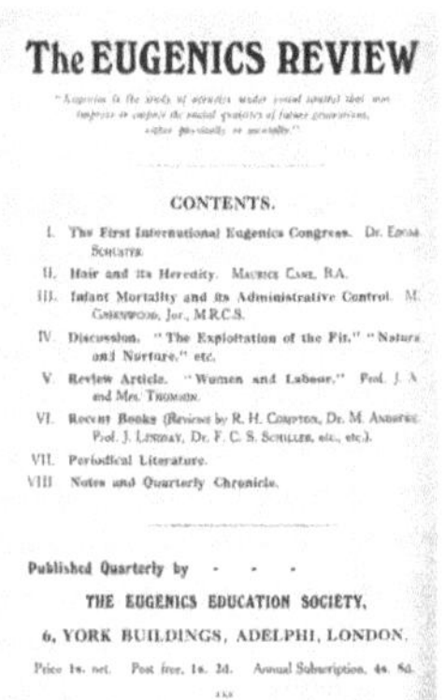
The EUGENICS REVIEW

CONTENTS.

I. The First International Eugenics Congress. Dr. Edgar Schuster.
II. Hair and its Heredity. Maurice Cane, B.A.
III. Infant Mortality and its Administrative Control. M. Greenwood, Jnr., M.R.C.S.
IV. Discussion. "The Exploitation of the Fit." "Nature and Nurture," etc.
V. Review Article. "Women and Labour." Prof. J. A. and Mrs. Thomson.
VI. Recent Books (Reviews by R. H. Compton, Dr. M. Andrews, Prof. J. Lindsay, Dr. F. C. S. Schiller, etc., etc.).
VII. Periodical Literature.
VIII. Notes and Quarterly Chronicle.

Published Quarterly by - - -

THE EUGENICS EDUCATION SOCIETY,

6, YORK BUILDINGS, ADELPHI, LONDON.

Price 1s. net. Post free, 1s. 2d. Annual Subscription, 4s. 8d.

Early Proponents

The American eugenics movement was rooted in the biological determinist ideas of Sir Francis Galton, which originated in the 1880s. Galton studied the upper classes of Britain, and arrived at the conclusion that their social positions were due to a superior genetic makeup.[8]

Early proponents of eugenics believed that, through selective breeding, the human species should direct its own evolution. They tended to believe in the genetic superiority of Nordic, Germanic and Anglo-Saxon peoples; supported strict immigration and anti-miscegenation laws; and supported the forcible sterilization of the poor, disabled and "immoral".[9]

The American eugenics movement received extensive funding from various corporate foundations including the Carnegie Institution, Rockefeller Foundation, and the Harriman railroad fortune.[6] In 1906 J.H. Kellogg provided funding to help found the Race Betterment Foundation in Battle Creek, Michigan.[8] The Eugenics Record Office (ERO) was founded in Cold Spring Harbor, New York in 1911 by the renowned biologist Charles B. Davenport, using money from both the Harriman railroad fortune and the Carnegie Institution.

As late as the 1920s, the ERO was one of the leading organizations in the American eugenics movement.[8,10] In years to come, the ERO collected a mass of family pedigrees and concluded that those who were unfit came from economically and socially poor backgrounds.

Eugenicists such as Davenport, the psychologist Henry H. Goddard, and the conservationist Madison Grant (all well respected in their time) began to lobby for various solutions to the problem

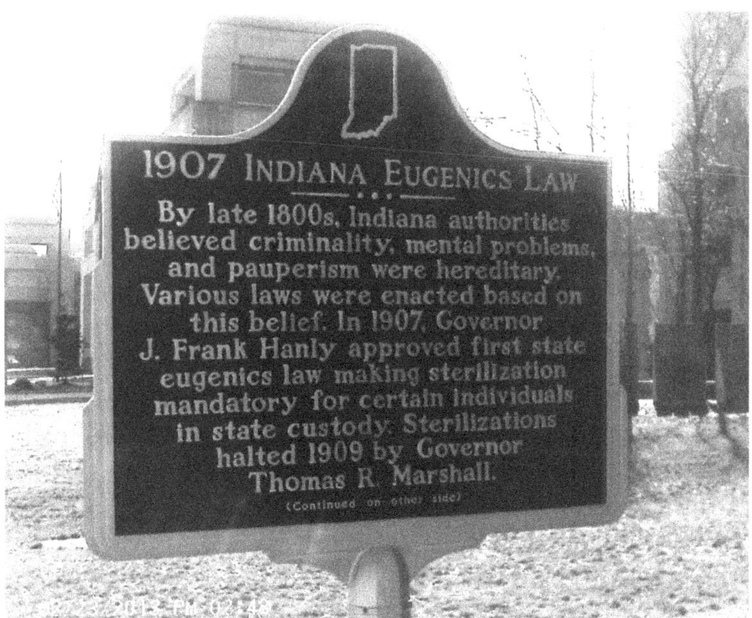
1907 INDIANA EUGENICS LAW
By late 1800s, Indiana authorities
believed criminality, mental problems,
and pauperism were hereditary.
Various laws were enacted based on
this belief. In 1907, Governor
J. Frank Hanly approved first state
eugenics law making sterilization
mandatory for certain individuals
in state custody. Sterilizations
halted 1909 by Governor
Thomas R. Marshall.
(Continued on other side)

of the "unfit". Davenport favored immigration restriction and sterilization as primary methods; Goddard favored segregation; Grant favored all of the above and more, even entertaining the idea of extermination.[11] The Eugenics Record Office (ERO) later became the Cold Spring Harbor Laboratory.

Eugenics was widely accepted in the U.S. academic community.[6] By 1928 there were 376 separate university courses in some of the United States' leading schools, enrolling more than 20,000 students, which included eugenics in the curriculum.[12]

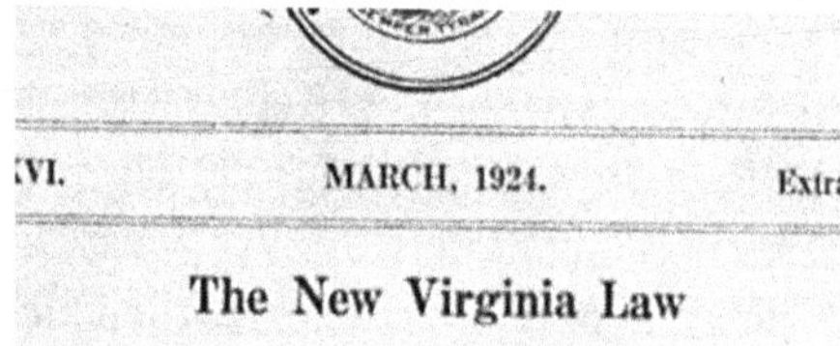

ΧVI. MARCH, 1924. Extra

The New Virginia Law

To Preserve Racial Integrity

PLECKER, M. D., *State Registrar of Vital Statistics, Richmon*

enate Bill 219, To preserve racial integrity, passed the
8, 1924, and is now a law of the State.
his bill aims at correcting a condition which only the more th
ople of Virginia know the existence of.
is estimated that there are in the State from 10,000 to
ly more, near white people, who are known to possess an
re of colored blood, in some cases to a slight extent it is tr
ough to prevent them from being white.
the past it has been possible for these people to declare
as white, or even to have the Court so declare them. The

It did, however, have scientific detractors (notably, Thomas Hunt Morgan, one of the few to explicitly criticize eugenics), though most of these focused more on what they considered the crude methodology of eugenicists.[13]

By 1910, there was a large and dynamic network of scientists, reformers and professionals engaged in national eugenics projects and actively promoting eugenic legislation. The American Breeder's Association (ABA) was the first eugenic body in the U.S., established in 1906 under the direction of biologist Charles B. Davenport.

The ABA was formed specifically to "investigate and report on heredity in the human race, and emphasize the value of superior blood and the menace to society of inferior blood." Membership included Alexander Graham Bell, Stanford president David Starr Jordan and Luther Burbank.[14,15]

Several feminist reformers advocated an agenda of eugenic legal reform. The National Federation of Women's Clubs, the Woman's Christian Temperance Union, and the National League of Women Voters were among the variety of state and local feminist organization that at some point lobbied for eugenic reforms.[16,17,18]

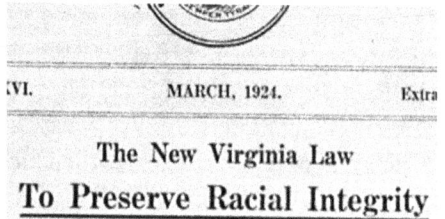

One of the most prominent feminists to champion the eugenic agenda was Margaret Sanger, the leader of the American birth control movement. Margaret Sanger saw birth control as a means to prevent unwanted children from being born into a disadvantaged life, and incorporated the language of eugenics to advance the movement.[19,20]

Sanger also sought to discourage the reproduction of persons who, it was believed, would pass on mental disease or serious physical defect. She advocated sterilization in cases where the subject was unable to use birth control.[19] Unlike other eugenicists, she rejected euthanasia.[21,22,23]

In the Deep South, women's associations played an important role in rallying support for eugenic legal reform. Eugenicists recognized the political and social influence of southern clubwomen in their communities, and used them to help implement eugenics across the region.[24]

For example, the Legislative Committee of the Florida State Federation of Women's Clubs successfully lobbied to institute a eugenic institution for the mentally retarded that was segregated by sex.[26] Their aim was to separate mentally retarded men and women to prevent them from breeding more "feebleminded" individuals.

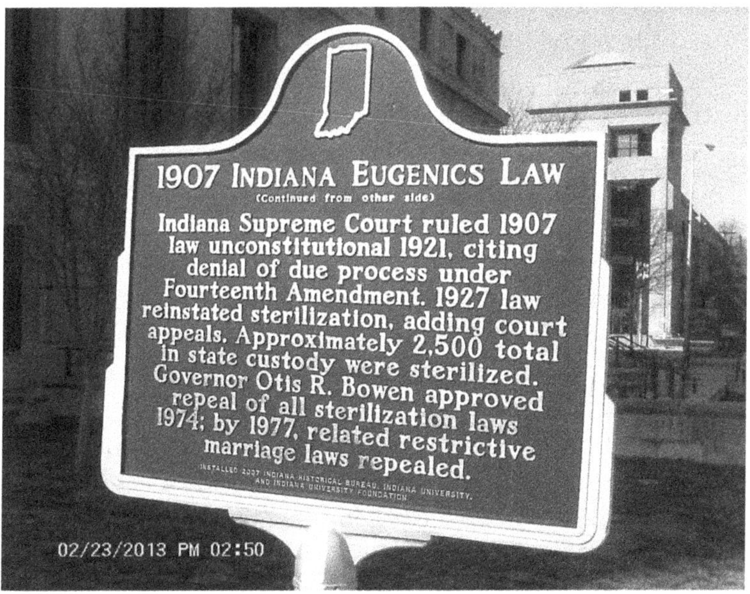

Public acceptance in the U.S. was the reason eugenic legislation was passed. Almost 19 million people attended the Panama-Pacific International Exposition (PPIE) in San Francisco, open for 10 months from February 20 to December 4, 1915.[27,28,29]

The PPIE was a fair devoted to extolling the virtues of a rapidly progressing nation, featuring new developments in science, agriculture, manufacturing and technology. A subject that received a large amount of time and space was that of the developments concerning health and disease, particularly the areas of tropical medicine and race betterment (tropical medicine being the combined study of bacteriology, parasitology and entomology while racial betterment being the promotion of eugenic studies).

Having these areas so closely intertwined, it seemed that they were both categorized in the main theme of the fair, the advancement of civilization. Thus in the public eye, the seemingly contradictory areas of study were both represented under progressive banners of improvement and were made to seem like plausible courses of action to better American society.[30]

> *truth revealed:*
>
> **"We do not want word to go out that we want to exterminate the Negro population..."**
>
> **-Margaret Sanger**
>
> *Sanger, Margaret. Letter to Clarence J. Gamble, M.D. December 10, 1939. Sanger manuscripts, Sophia Smith Collection, Smith College, North Hampton, Massachusetts.*

Beginning with Connecticut in 1896, many states enacted marriage laws with eugenic criteria, prohibiting anyone who was "epileptic, imbecile or feeble-minded"[31] from marrying.

The first state to introduce a compulsory sterilization bill was Michigan in 1897 but the proposed law failed to garner enough votes by legislators to be adopted. Eight years later Pennsylvania's state legislators passed a sterilization bill that was vetoed by the governor. Indiana became the first state to enact sterilization legislation in 1907,[32] followed closely by Washington and California in 1909.

Sterilization rates across the country were relatively low (California being the sole exception) until the 1927 Supreme Court case Buck v. Bell which legitimized the forced sterilization of patients at a Virginia home for the mentally retarded. The number of sterilizations performed per year increased until another Supreme Court case, Skinner v. Oklahoma, 1942, complicated the legal situation by ruling against sterilization of criminals if the equal protection clause of the constitution was violated. That is, if sterilization was to be performed, then it could not exempt white-collar criminals.[33]

While California had the highest number of sterilizations, North Carolina's eugenics program which operated from 1933 to 1977, was the most aggressive of the 32 states that had eugenics programs.[35]

An IQ of 70 or lower meant sterilization was appropriate in North Carolina.[36] The North Carolina Eugenics Board almost always approved proposals brought before them by local welfare boards.[36] Of all states, only North Carolina gave social workers the power to designate people for sterilization.[35]

"Here, at last, was a method of preventing unwanted pregnancies by an acceptable, practical, and inexpensive method," wrote Wallace Kuralt in the March 1967 journal of the N.C. Board of Public Welfare. "The poor readily adopted the new techniques for birth control."[36]

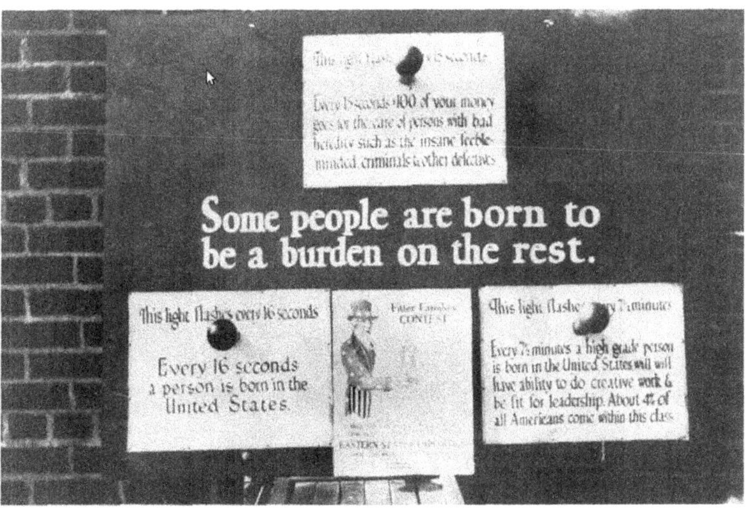

U.S. eugenics poster advocating for the removal of genetic "defectives" such as the insane, "feeble-minded" and criminals, and supporting the selective breeding of "high-grade" individuals, c. 1926

Immigration Restrictions

The Immigration Restriction League was the first American entity associated officially with eugenics. Founded in 1894 by three recent Harvard University graduates, the League sought to bar what it considered "inferior races" from entering America and diluting what it saw as the superior American racial stock (upper class Northerners of Anglo-Saxon heritage).

They felt that social and sexual involvement with these less-evolved and less-civilized races would pose a biological threat to the American population. The League lobbied for a literacy test for immigrants, based on the belief that literacy rates were low among "inferior races". Literacy test bills were vetoed by Presidents in 1897, 1913 and 1915; eventually, President Wilson's second veto was overruled by Congress in 1917. Membership in the League included: A. Lawrence Lowell, president of Harvard, William DeWitt Hyde, president of Bowdoin College, James T. Young, director of Wharton School and David Starr Jordan, president of Stanford University.[37]

The League allied themselves with the American Breeder's Association (ABA) to gain influence and further its goals and in 1909 established a Committee on Eugenics. In their mission statement, they wrote:

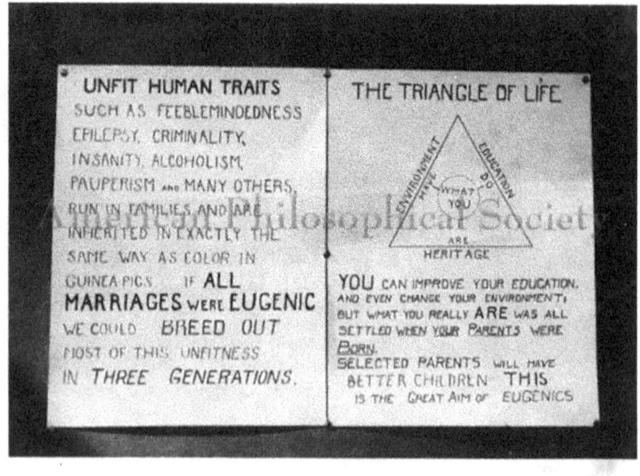

Society must protect itself; as it claims the right to deprive the murderer of his life so it may also annihilate the hideous serpent of hopelessly vicious protoplasm. Here is where appropriate legislation will aid in eugenics and creating a healthier, saner society in the future."[38]

Money from the Harriman railroad fortune was also given to local charities, in order to find immigrants from specific ethnic groups and deport, confine, or forcibly sterilize them.[6] With the passage of the Immigration Act of 1924, eugenicists for the first time played an important role in the Congressional debate as expert advisers on the threat of "inferior stock" from eastern and southern Europe.[39]

The new act, inspired by the eugenic belief in the racial superiority of "old stock" white Americans as members of the "Nordic race" (a form of white supremacy), strengthened the position of existing laws prohibiting race-mixing.[40]

"The most merciful
thing that a
large family
does to one of its
infant members
is to kill it."
-Margaret Sanger
Founder of Planned Parenthood
From her book, Women and the New Race,

During the early 20th century, the United States and Canada began to receive far higher numbers of Southern and Eastern European immigrants. Influential eugenicists like Lothrop Stoddard and Harry Laughlin (who was appointed as an expert witness for the House Committee on Immigration and Naturalization in 1920) presented arguments they would pollute the national gene pool if their numbers went unrestricted.

It has been argued that this stirred both Canada and the United States into passing laws creating a hierarchy of nationalities, rating them from the most desirable Anglo-Saxon and Nordic peoples to the Chinese and Japanese immigrants, who were almost completely banned from entering the country.[40,42]

Unfit Vs. Fit Individuals

Both class and race factored in to eugenic definitions of "fit" and "unfit." By using intelligence testing, American eugenicists asserted that social mobility was indicative of one's genetic fitness.[43] This reaffirmed the existing class and racial hierarchies and explained why the upper-to-middle class was predominately white. Middle-to-upper class status was a marker of "superior strains."[26] In contrast, eugenicists believed poverty to be a characteristic of genetic inferiority, which meant that that those deemed "unfit" were predominately of the lower classes.[26]

Because class status designated some more fit than others, eugenicists treated upper and lower class women differently. Positive eugenicists, who promoted procreation among the fittest in society, encouraged middle class women to bear more children. Between 1900 and 1960, Eugenicists appealed to middle class white women to become more "family minded," and to help better the race.[44] To this end, eugenicists often denied middle and upper class women sterilization and birth control.[45]

Since 'poverty was associated with prostitution' and "mental idiocy," women of the lower classes were the first to be deemed "unfit" and "promiscuous."[26] These women, who were predominately immigrants or women of color, were discouraged from bearing children, and were encouraged to use birth control.

Compulsory Sterilization

In 1907, Indiana passed the first eugenics-based compulsory sterilization law in the world. Thirty U.S. states would soon follow their lead.[46,47] Although the law was overturned by the Indiana Supreme Court in 1921,[48] the U.S. Supreme Court upheld the constitutionality of a Virginia law allowing for the compulsory sterilization of patients of state mental institutions in 1927.[49]

Eugenics supporters hold signs criticizing various "genetically inferior" groups. Wall Street, New York, c. 1915.

Some states sterilized "imbeciles" for much of the 20th century. The U.S. Supreme Court ruled in the 1927 Buck v. Bell case that the state of Virginia could sterilize those it thought unfit. Although compulsory sterilization is now considered an abuse of human rights, Buck v. Bell was never overturned, and Virginia did not repeal its sterilization law until 1974.[50]

Beginning around 1930, there was a steady increase in the percentage of women sterilized, and in a few states only young women were sterilized. From 1930 to the 1960s, sterilizations were performed on many more institutionalized women than men.[26] By 1961, 61 percent of the 62,162 total eugenic sterilizations in the United States were performed on women.[26]

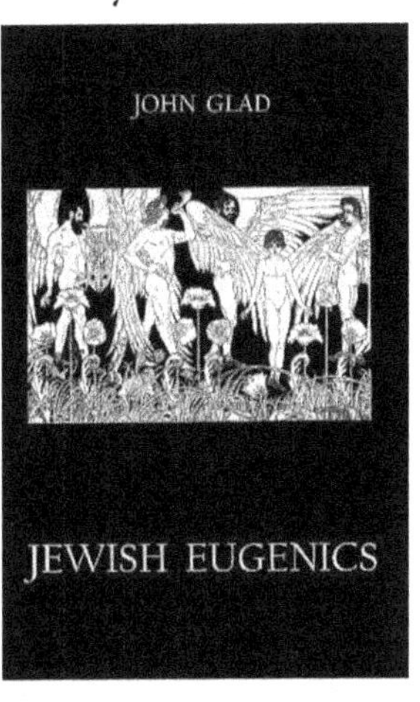

A favorable report on the results of sterilization in California, the state with the most sterilizations by far, was published in book form by the biologist Paul Popenoe and was widely cited by the Nazi government as evidence that wide-reaching sterilization programs were feasible and humane.[52,53]

Men and women were compulsorily sterilized for different reasons. Men were sterilized to treat their aggression and to eliminate their criminal behavior, while women were sterilized to control the results of their sexuality.[54] Since women bore children, eugenicists held women more accountable than men for the reproduction of the less "desirable" members of society.[26] Eugenicists therefore predominately targeted women in their efforts to regulate the birth rate, to "protect" white racial health, and weed out the "defectives" of society.[26]

Although the following events were not explicitly justified through the by-now-discredited eugenics movement, they certainly fit the older pattern.

In 1970's, several activists and women's rights groups discovered several physicians to be performing coerced sterilizations of specific ethnic groups of society. All were abuses of poor, nonwhite, or mentally retarded women, while no abuses against white or middle-class women were recorded.[56]

For example, in 1972, United States Senate committee testimony brought to light that at least 2,000 involuntary sterilizations had been performed on poor black women without their consent or knowledge. An investigation revealed that the surgeries were all performed in the South, and were all performed on black welfare mothers with multiple children. Testimony revealed that many of these women were threatened with an end to their welfare benefits until they consented to sterilization.[57]

These surgeries were instances of sterilization abuse, a term applied to any sterilization performed without the consent or knowledge of the recipient, or in which the recipient is pressured into accepting the surgery. Because the funds used to carry out the surgeries came from the U.S. Office of Economic Opportunity, the sterilization abuse raised older suspicions, especially amongst the black community, that "federal programs were underwriting eugenicists who wanted to impose their views about population quality on minorities and poor women."[26]

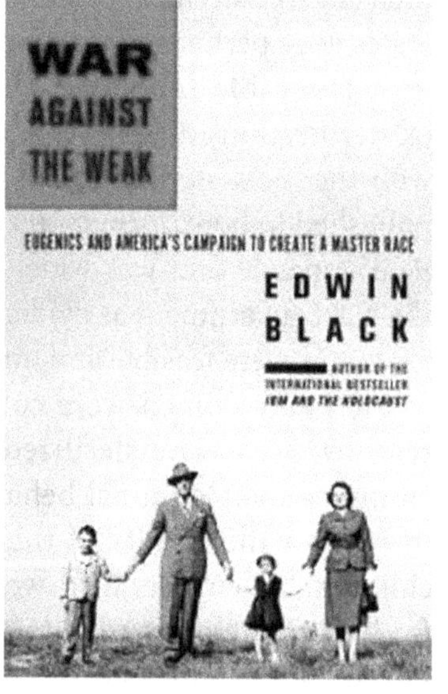

WAR
AGAINST
THE WEAK
EUGENICS AND AMERICA'S CAMPAIGN TO CREATE A MASTER RACE
EDWIN
BLACK

Native American women were also victims of sterilization abuse up into the 1970s.[58] The organization WARN (Women of All Red Nations) publicized that Native American women were threatened that, if they had more children, they would be denied welfare benefits.

The Indian Health Service also repeatedly refused to deliver Native American babies until their mothers, in labor, consented to sterilization. Many Native American women unknowingly gave consent, since directions were not given in their native language.

According to the General Accounting Office, an estimate of 3,406 Indian women were sterilized.[58] The General Accounting Office stated that the Indian Health Service had not followed the necessary regulations, and that the "informed consent forms did not adhere to the standards set by the United States Department of Health, Education, and Welfare (HEW)."[59]

Euthanasia (Mercy Killing) Programs

One of the methods that was commonly suggested to get rid of "inferior" populations was euthanasia. A 1911 Carnegie Institute report mentioned euthanasia as one of its recommended "solutions" to the problem of cleansing society of unfit genetic attributes. *The most commonly suggested method was to set up local gas chambers.*

However, many in the eugenics movement did not believe that Americans were ready to implement a large-scale euthanasia program, so many doctors had to find clever ways of subtly implementing eugenic euthanasia in various medical institutions. For example, a mental institution in Lincoln, Illinois fed its incoming patients milk infected with tuberculosis (reasoning that genetically fit individuals would be resistant), resulting in 30-40% annual death rates. Other doctors practiced eugenicide through various forms of lethal neglect.[60]

Wir stehen nicht allein: "We do not stand alone". Nazi propaganda poster from 1936. The woman is holding a baby and the man is holding a shield inscribed with the title of Nazi Germany's 1933 Law for the Prevention of Hereditarily Diseased Offspring (their compulsory sterilization law). The couple is in front of a map of Germany, surrounded by the flags of nations which had enacted (to the left) or were considering (bottom and to the right) similar legislation.

In the 1930s, there was a wave of portrayals of eugenic "mercy killings" in American film, newspapers, and magazines. In 1931, the Illinois Homeopathic Medicine Association began lobbying for the right to euthanize "imbeciles" and other defectives. The Euthanasia Society of America was founded in 1938.[61]

Better Baby Contests

Mary deGormo, a former classroom teacher was the first person to combine ideas about health and intelligence standards with competitions at state fairs, in the form of "better baby" contests.

She developed the first such contest, the "Scientific Baby Contest" for the Louisiana State Fair in Shreveport, in 1908. She saw these contests as a contribution to the "social efficiency" movement, which was advocating for the standardization of all aspects of American life as a means of increasing efficiency.[16]

deGarmo was assisted by the pediatrician Dr. Jacob Bodenheimer, who helped her develop grading sheets for contestants, which combined physical measurements with standardized measurements of intelligence.[63] Scoring was based on a deduction system, in that every child started at 1000 points and then was deducted points for having measurements that were below a designated average. The child with the most points (and the least defections) was ideal.[64]

The topic of standardization through scientific judgment was a topic that was very serious in the eyes of the scientific community. A lot of time, effort, and money were put into these contests and their scientific backing, which would influence cultural ideas as well as local and state government practices.[65]

Fitter Family for Future

First appearing in 1920 at the Kansas Free Fair, Fitter Family competitions, continued all the way until WWII. Mary T. Watts and Florence Brown Sherbon, both initiators of the Better Baby Contests in Iowa, took the idea of positive eugenics for babies and combined it with a determinist concept of biology to come up with fitter family competitions.[66]

There were several different categories that families were judged in: Size of the family, overall attractiveness, and health of the family, all of which helped to determine the likelihood of having healthy children. These competitions were simply a continuation of the Better Baby contests that promoted certain physical and mental qualities.[67]

Doctors and specialists from the community would offer their time to judge these competitions, which were originally sponsored by the Red Cross.[27] The winners of these competitions were given a Bronze Medal as well as champion cups called "Capper Medals." The cups were named after then Governor and Senator, Arthur Capper and he would present them to "Grade A individuals".[68]

The perks of entering into the contests were that the competitions provided a way for families to get a free health check up by a doctor as well as some of the pride and prestige that came from winning the competitions.[27]

By 1925 the Eugenics Records Office was distributing standardized forms for judging eugenically fit families, which were used in contests in several U.S. states.[69]

After the eugenics movement was well established in the United States, it spread to Germany.

After 1945, however, historians began to attempt to portray the US eugenics movement as distinct and distant from Nazi eugenics.[70]

Notes

Source: Wikipedia and others.

1. Pilgrim, David (2009-12-01). Key Concepts in Mental Health. p. 141.ISBN 9781848608801.

2. Kühl, Stefan (2002-02-14). The Nazi Connection: Eugenics, American Racism, and German National Socialism. p. 70. ISBN 9780195348781.

3. Susan Currell (2006). Popular eugenics: national efficiency and American mass culture in the 1930s. Ohio University Press. pp. 2–3. ISBN 9780821416914. Retrieved July 18, 2011.

4. Lombardo, 2011: p. 1

5. a b Kühl, Stefan (2002-02-14). The Nazi Connection: Eugenics, American Racism, and German National Socialism. p. 86. ISBN 9780195348781.

6. a b c d e Black, 2003: p. 1

7. a b Murphy & Lappé, 1994: p. 18

8. a b c Selden, 2005: p. 202

9. Ordover, 2003: p. xii

10. Bender, 2009: p. 192

11. Kevles, 1986: p. 133-135

12. Selden, 2005: p. 204

13. Hamilton Cravens, The triumph of evolution: American scientists and the heredity-environment controversy, 1900–1941 (Philadelphia: University of Pennsylvania Press, 1978): 179.

14. Stern, 2005: pp. 82–91

15. Elof Axel Carlson (2001). The unfit: a history of a bad idea. p. 193.ISBN 9780879695873. Retrieved July 14, 2011.

16. a b Selden, 2005: p. 206

17. Cameron, M. E. "Book Reviews ." The American Journal of Nursing 13.1 (1912):75-77. JSTOR. Web. 10 April 2010. [1]

18. Ziegler, Mary (2008). "Eugenic Feminism: Mental Hygiene, The Women's Movement, And The Campaign For Eugenic Legal Reform, 1900-1935". Harvard Journal of Law & Gender 31 (1): 211–236.

19. a b "The Sanger-Hitler Equation", Margaret Sanger Papers Project Newsletter, #32, Winter 2002/3. New York University Department of History

20. Carole Ruth McCann. Birth control politics in the United States, 1916-1945.. Cornell University Press. pp. 100.

21. Sanger, Margaret (1922). The Pivot of Civilization. Brentano's. pp. 100–101. "Nor do we believe that the community could or should send to the lethal chamber the defective progeny resulting from irresponsible and unintelligent breeding."

22. Sanger, Margaret (1919). Birth Control and Racial Betterment. Birth Control Review. p. 11. "We maintain that a woman possessing an adequate knowledge of her reproductive functions is the best judge of time and conditions under which her child should be brought into the world. We maintain that it is her right, regardless of all other considerations, to determine whether she shall bear children or not, and how many children she shall bear if she chooses to become a mother."

23. Sanger, Margaret (1920). Woman and the New Race. Brentano. p. 100.

24. Larson, Edward J. (1995). Sex, Race, and Science: Eugenics in the Deep South. Baltimore: Johns Hopkins University Press. p. 74.

25. Larson, Edward J. (1995). Sex, Race, and Science: Eugenics in the Deep South. Baltimore: Johns Hopkins University Press. p. 75.

26. a b c d e f g h i Kluchin, Rebecca M. (2009). Fit to Be Tied: Sterilization and Reproductive Rights in America 1950-1980. New Brunswick: Rutgers University Press. pp. 17–20.

27. a b c d Stern, 2005:[page needed]

28. "1915 San Francisco Panama-Pacific International Exposition: In color!". National Museum American History. February 11, 2011. Retrieved July 14, 2011.

29."The Panama Pacific Exposition". Retrieved July 14, 2011.

30. Stern, 2005: pp. 27–31

31. JAMA.: the Journal of the American Medical Association (American Medical Association.): 1138. June 6, 1896.

32. The Indiana Supreme Court overturned the law in 1921 in Williams v. Smith, 131 NE 2 (Ind.), 1921, text at [2]

33. On the legal history of eugenic sterilization in the U.S., see Paul Lombardo, "Eugenic Sterilization Laws", essay in the Eugenics Archive, available online athttp://www.eugenicsarchive.org/html/eugenics/essay8text.html.

34. Stern, 2005: pp.84, 144

35. a b Severson, Kim (9 December 2011). "Thousands Sterilized, a State Weighs Restitution". New York Times. Retrieved 10 December 2011.

36. a b c Helms, Ann Doss and Tomlinson, Tommy (26 September 2011). "Wallace Kuralt's era of sterilization: Mecklenburg's impoverished had few, if any, rights in the 1950s and 1960s as he oversaw one of the most aggressive efforts to sterilize certain populations". Charlotte Observer. Retrieved 10 December 2011.

37. McWhorter, 2009: p. 204

38. a b McWhorter, 2009: p. 205

39. Watson, James D.; Berry, Andrew (2003). DNA: The Secret of Life. Alfred A. Knopf. pp. 29–31. ISBN 0-375-41546-7.

40. a b Lombardo, Paul; "Eugenics Laws Restricting Immigration,", Eugenics Archive

41. Lombardo, Paul; "Eugenic Laws Against Race-Mixing", Eugenics Archive

42. Gould, Stephen J. (1981) The mismeasure of man. Norton:[page needed]

43. Dorr, Gregory (2008). Segregation's Science. Charlottesville: University of Virginia Press. p. 10.

44. Kline, Wendy (2005). Building a Better Race: Gender, Sexuality, and Eugenics From the Turn of the Century to the Baby Boom. University of California Press. p. 4.

45. Critchlow, Donald T. (1999). Intended Consequences: Birth Control, Abortion, and the Federal Government in Modern America. New York: Oxford University Press. p. 15.

46. Lombardo, 2011: p. ix

47. Indiana Supreme Court Legal History Lecture Series, "Three Generations of Imbeciles are Enough:"Reflections on 100 Years of Eugenics in Indiana, at In.gov

48. Williams v. Smith, 131 NE 2 (Ind.), 1921, text at

49. Larson 2004, pp. 194–195 Citing Buck v. Bell 274 U.S. 200, 205 (1927)

50. Dorr, Gregory Michael. "Encyclopedia Virginia: Buck v Bell". Retrieved May 3, 2011.

51. Lombardo, Paul; "Eugenic Sterilization Laws", Eugenics Archive

52. J. Mitchell Miller (2009-08-06). 21st Century Criminology: A Reference Handbook, Volumen 1. p. 193. ISBN 9781412960199. Retrieved July 15, 2011.

53. Tukufu Zuberi (2001). Thicker than blood: how racial statistics lie. University of Minesotta Press. p. 69. ISBN 9780816639090. Retrieved July 15, 2011.

54. Kluchin. Missing or empty |title= (help)

55. McWhorter, 2009: p. 377

56. Gordon, Linda (2003). The Moral Property of Women: A History of Birth Control Politics in America. Urbana: University of Illinois Press. p. 345. ISBN ISBN 0-252-07459-9.

57. Ward, Martha C. (1986). Poor Women, Powerful Men: America's Great Experiment in Family Planning. Boulder: Westview Press. p. 95.

58. a b Lawrence, Jane (2000). "he Indian Health Service and the Sterilization of Native American Women". The American Indian Quarterly. 3 24 (3): 400–419.doi:10.1353/aiq.2000.0008.

59. Johansen, Bruce E. (September 1998). "Sterilization of Native American Women". Native Americas.

60. Black, 2003: p. 2

61. Pernick, 2009: p. 161

62. a b Black, 2003: p. 3

63. Selden 2005: p. 207

64. Crnic, Meghan. "Better babies: social engineering for 'a better nation, a better world.'" ScienceDirect 33.1 (2008): Web. [3]

65. Pernick, 2002

66. "Fitter Family Contests." Eugenics Archive. Web. 2 March 2010. [4].

67. Boudreau 2005:[page needed]

68. Selden, 2005: p. 211

69. Bender, 2009: p. 207

70. Kühl 2001: p. xiv

80.

Nazi Eugenics

Under The Able Tutelage of Uncle Sam

After the eugenics movement was well established in the United States, it was spread to Germany. California eugenicists began producing literature promoting eugenics and sterilization and sending it overseas to German scientists and medical professionals.[3]

By 1933, California had subjected more people to forceful sterilization than all other U.S. states combined. The forced sterilization program engineered by the Nazis was mostly inspired by California's.[4]

The Rockefeller Foundation helped develop and fund various German eugenics programs, including the one that Josef Mengele worked in before he went to Auschwitz.[35]

Upon returning from Germany in 1934, where more than 5,000 people per month were being forcibly sterilized, the California eugenics leader C. M. Goethe bragged to a colleague:

> "You will be interested to know that your work has played a powerful part in shaping the opinions of the group of intellectuals who are behind Hitler in this epoch-making program. Everywhere I sensed that their opinions have been tremendously stimulated by American thought. I want you, my dear friend, to carry this thought with you for the rest of your life, that you have really jolted into action a great government of 60 million people."[6]

Eugenics researcher Harry H. Laughlin often bragged that his Model Eugenic Sterilization laws had been implemented in the 1935 Nuremberg racial hygiene laws.[7] In 1936, Laughlin was invited to an award ceremony at Heidelberg University in Germany (scheduled on the anniversary of Hitler's 1934 purge of Jews from the Heidelberg faculty), to receive an honorary doctorate for his work on the "science of racial cleansing".

Due to financial limitations, Laughlin was unable to attend the ceremony and had to pick it up from the Rockefeller Institute. Afterwards, he proudly shared the award with his colleagues, remarking that he felt that it symbolized the "common understanding of German and American scientists of the nature of eugenics."[8]

Hitler's Views On Eugenics

Adolf Hitler read racial hygiene tracts during his imprisonment in Landsberg Prison.[9] He thought that Germany could become strong again only if the state applied the principles of racial hygiene and eugenics to German society.

Hitler believed the nation had become weak, corrupted by the infusion of degenerate elements into its bloodstream.[10] These had to be removed quickly. He also believed that the strong and the racially pure should be encouraged to have more children, and that the weak and the racially impure should be neutralized by one means or another.

The racialism and idea of competition, termed social Darwinism in 1944, were discussed by European scientists and also in the Vienna press during the 1920s. Where Hitler picked up the ideas is uncertain.

The theory of evolution had been generally accepted in Germany at the time but this sort of extremism was rare.[11] In 1876, Ernst Haeckel

Propaganda for Nazi Germany's T-4 Euthanasia Program: "This person suffering from hereditary defects costs the community 60,000 Reichsmark during his lifetime. Fellow German, that is your money, too." from the Office of Racial Policy's Neues Volk.

had discussed the selective infanticide policy of the Greek city of ancient Sparta.[12]

In his Second Book, which was unpublished during the Nazi era, Hitler praised Sparta, "The exposure of the sick, weak, deformed children, in short, their destruction, was more decent and in truth a thousand times more humane than the wretched insanity of our day which preserves the most pathological subject, and indeed at any price, and yet takes the life of a hundred thousand healthy children in consequence of birth control or through abortions, in order subsequently to breed a race of degenerates burdened with illnesses."[13,14]

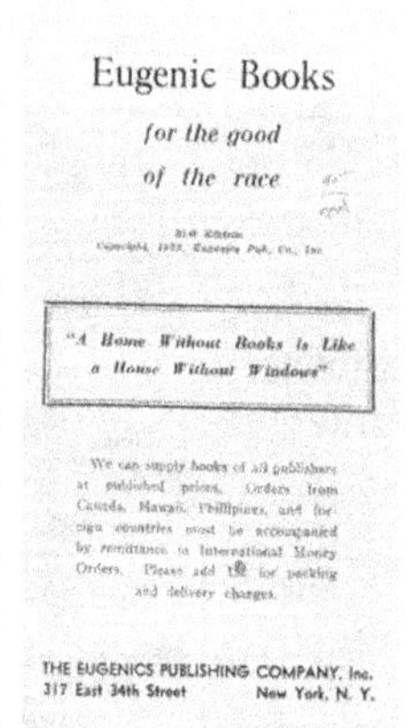

Nazi Eugenics Program

The Law for the Prevention of Hereditarily Diseased Offspring, proclaimed on July 14, 1933, required physicians to register every case of hereditary illness known to them, except in women over 45 years of age.[16] Physicians could be fined for failing to comply.

In 1934, the first year of the Law's operation, nearly 4,000 people appealed against the decisions of sterilization authorities. A total of 3,559 of the appeals failed.

Ladies and gentlemen, thank you very much for kindly participating in this Krsna consciousness movement. This movement is very important. It is the movement to save human society from spiritual death. At the present moment human society is being misled by blind leaders. The situation is like that of a blind man helping other blind men to cross the street. There is blind following in the sense that we do not know what the real aim of human life is.

The aim of human life is to achieve self-realization and reestablish our lost relationship with the Supreme Personality of Godhead. That relationship is the missing point in today's society. The Krsna consciousness movement is trying to enlighten human society on this important point.

~ Srila Prabhupada (Paris, 1973)

By the end of the Nazi regime, over 200 Hereditary Health Courts (Erbgesundheitsgerichte) were created, and under their rulings over 400,000 people were sterilized against their will.[17] 70,000 were killed under Action T4, a "euthanasia" program. [12]

Nazi Eugenics Institutions

The Hadamar Clinic was a mental hospital in the German town of Hadamar used by the Nazi-controlled German government as the site of Action T4. The Kaiser Wilhelm Institute of Anthropology, Human Heredity, and Eugenics was founded in 1927.

Hartheim Euthanasia Centre was also part of the euthanasia programme where allegedly disabled individuals were murdered by the Nazis.

The first method used involved transporting patients by buses in which the exhaust gases were passed into the interior of the buses, and so killed the passengers. Gas chambers were developed later and used pure carbon monoxide gas to kill the patients.

Grafeneck Castle was one of Nazi Germany's killing centers, and today it is a memorial place dedicated to the victims of the Action T4.

Identification

The Law for Simplification of the Health System of July 1934 created Information Centers for Genetic and Racial Hygenie, as well as Health Offices. The law also described procedures for 'denunciation' and 'evaluation' of people, who were then sent to a Genetic Health Court where sterilization was decided.[18]

Collection bus for killing patients

Information to determine who was considered 'genetically sick' was gathered from routine information supplied by people to doctor's offices and welfare departments. Standardized questionnaires had been designed by Nazi officials with the help of Dehomag (a subsidiary of IBM in the 1930s), so that the information could be encoded easily onto Hollerith punch cards for fast sorting and counting.[19]

In Hamburg, doctors gave information into a Central Health Passport Archive (circa 1934), under something called the 'Health-Related Total Observation of Life'. This file was to contain reports from doctors, but also courts, insurance companies, sports clubs, the Hitler Youth, the military, the labor service, colleges, etc. Any institution that gave information would get information back in return.[20]

Nazi Eugenics Policies Regarding Marriage

Nazi Germany had strict marriage laws in which marriage partners had to be tested for any hereditary diseases. Everyone was encouraged to carefully evaluate their prospective marriage partners eugenically during courtship. Members of the SS were cautioned to carefully interview prospective marriage partners to make sure they had no family history of hereditary disease or insanity.

Reference

Source: Wikipedia and others.

1. "Close-up of Richard Jenne, the last child killed by the head nurse at the Kaufbeuren-Irsee euthanasia facility.". United States Holocaust Memorial Museum. Retrieved July 29, 2011.
2. Ian Kershaw, Hitler: A Profile in Power, Chapter VI, first section (London, 1991, rev. 2001)
3. a b Black, 2003: p. 1
4. Murphy & Lappé, 1994: p. 18
5. Black, 2003: p. 5
6. Black, 2003: p. 4
7. Jackson, John P. & Weidman, Nadine M. (2005). Race, racism, and science: social impact and interaction. Rutgers University Press. p. 123.ISBN 978-0-8135-3736-8.
8. Lombardo, Paul A. (2008). Three Generations, No Imbeciles: Eugenics, the Supreme Court, and "Buck v. Bell". JHU Press. pp. 211–213.ISBN 9780801890109.

9. Friedman, Jonathan C. (2011). The Routledge History of the Holocaust. Taylor & Francis. p. 49. ISBN 978-0-415-77956-2. Retrieved 1 August 2011.

10. Evans, Richard J. (2005). The Third Reich in Power. Penguin Press. p. 429. ISBN 978-1-59420-074-8. Retrieved 1 August 2011.

11. Dónal P O'Mathúna: "Human dignity in the Nazi era: implications for contemporary bioethics", BMC Med Ethics 2006. online March 14, 2006(English)

12. Haeckel, Ernst (1876). "The History of Creation, vol. I". New York: D. Appleton. p. 170. "Among the Spartans all newly born children were subject to a careful examination or selection. All those that were weak, sickly, or affected with any bodily infirmity, were killed. Only the perfectly healthy and strong children were allowed to live, and they alone afterwards propagated the race."

13. Hitler, Adolf (1961). Hitler's Secret Book. New York: Grove Press. pp. 17–18.ISBN 0-394-62003-8. OCLC 9830111.

14. Hawkins, Mike (1997). Social Darwinism in European and American Thought, 1860-1945: nature as model and nature as threat. Cambridge University Press. p. 276. ISBN 0-521-57434-X. OCLC 34705047.

15. San Francisco Chronicle Sunday, November 9, 2003--"Eugenics and the Nazis - the California connection" by Edwin Black:

16. facinghistorycampus.org – The Law for the Prevention of Hereditarily Diseased

17. Robert Proctor, Racial Hygiene: Medicine Under the Nazis (Cambridge, Massachusetts: Harvard University Press, 1988): 108.

18. The Nazi census: identification and control in the Third Reich, By Götz Aly, Karl Heinz Roth, Edwin Black, Assenka Oksiloff , 2004, Temple University Press, p104

19. Please see IBM and the Holocaust by Edwin Black, 2001, Crown / Random House, pg 93-96 and elsewhere

20. The Nazi census: identification and control in the Third Reich, By Götz Aly, Karl Heinz Roth, Edwin Black, Assenka Oksiloff , 2004, Temple University Press, p104-108

21. Padfield, Peter Himmler New York:1990--Henry Holt

81.

Life Unworthy Of Life

The phrase "life unworthy of life" (in German: „Lebensunwertes Leben") was a Nazi designation for the segments of populace which had no right to live and thus were to be "euthanized". The term included people with serious medical problems and those considered grossly inferior according to the racial policy of the Third Reich. This concept formed an important component of the ideology of Nazism and eventually helped lead to the Holocaust[1] The euthanasia program was known as Action T4.

History

The expression first occurs in the title of a book, Die Freigabe der Vernichtung Lebensunwerten Lebens (Allowing the Destruction of Life Unworthy of Life) by jurist Karl Binding, retired from the University of Leipzig, and psychiatrist Alfred Hoche from the University of Freiburg, both professors.

Nature's Secrets Revealed
SCIENTIFIC KNOWLEDGE OF
THE LAWS OF SEX LIFE and HEREDITY
OR
EUGENICS
SOCIAL PURITY, HEREDITY,
PHYSICAL MANHOOD AND WOMANHOOD

According to Hoche, some living people who were brain damaged, mentally retarded, psychiatrically ill were "mentally dead", "human ballast" and "empty shells of human beings". Hoche felt killing such people was useful. Some people were simply considered disposable.[2] Later the killing was extended to people considered 'racially impure' or 'racially inferior' according to Nazi thinking.[3]

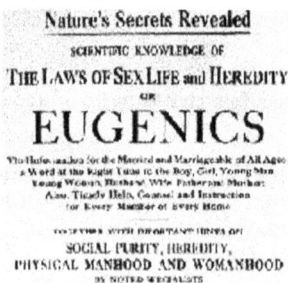

Nazi Categorization

Those considered to be "deviant" or a "source of social turmoil" in Nazi Germany and the occupied Europe fell under this designation. The "deviant" category included the mentally ill, people with disabilities, political dissidents, homosexuals, interracial couples, and criminals.

The "social turmoil" category included Communists, Jews, Romani people, Jehovah's Witnesses, "non-white" or non-Caucasian peoples, and some clergy. More than any other of these groups, the Jews soon became the primary focus of this genocidal policy.

The concept culminated in Nazi extermination camps, instituted to systematically kill those who were unworthy to live according to Nazi ideologists. It also justified various human experimentation and eugenics programs, as well as Nazi racial policies.

Development Of The Concept

According to the author of Medical Killing and the Psychology of Genocide psychiatrist Robert Jay Lifton, the policy went through a number of iterations and modifications:

Of the five identifiable steps by which the Nazis carried out the principle of "life unworthy of life," coercive sterilization was the first. There followed the killing of "impaired" children in hospitals; and then the killing of "impaired" adults, mostly collected from mental hospitals, in centers especially equipped with carbon monoxide gas. This project was extended (in the same killing centers) to "impaired" inmates of concentration and extermination camps and, finally, to mass killings in the extermination camps themselves.[1]

Reference

1. The Nazi Doctors: Medical Killing and the Psychology of Genocide by Dr. Robert Jay Lifton (holocaust-history.org)

2. "Life Unworthy of Life" and other Medical Killing Programmes

3. Robert Jay Lifton (September 21, 1986). "German Doctors and the Final Solution". The New York Times.

82.

Eugenics After World War II

John Cavanaugh-O'Keefe, January, 1995

Most people have never heard of eugenics, and most of those who have heard of it think it died with Hitler. Of the few people who are aware that eugenics was still a force after World War II, many believe that its remnants were reformed. In fact, the eugenics movement continued to thrive, without reform.

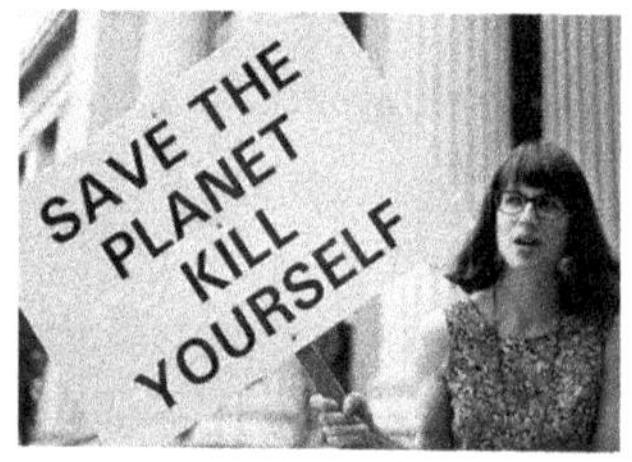

The development and promotion of birth control was a major eugenic success. The discovery of the population explosion and the hysteria about the need to control it was a major eugenic success. The field of genetics grew faster than fruit flies in the 1950s, and although the accumulating knowledge was valuable, the field was dominated by eugenicists, who could use their knowledge for eugenic purposes.

UNESCO, founded in 1948, was directed by Julian Huxley, a determined eugenicist who used his global platform very effectively. The welfare state in Britain was based largely of the work of Richard Titmuss, John Maynard Keynes and William Henry Beveridge, members of the Eugenics Society.

Historians who rely too heavily on the eugenicists themselves will overlook a great deal. Daniel Kevles, for example, makes the post-war eugenics movement sound like a group of dusty academics. But one of their activities in Britain beginning in the 1960s was running a flourishing abortion business.

Beginning in the 1960s, a few members of the Eugenics Society built and controlled almost the entire private abortion industry. Whether you think abortion is killing a child or exercising a fundamental liberty, this activity is not the work of dusty academics: at least some of the eugenicists were activists.

The influence on the eugenicists on abortion in America is perhaps best seen by comparing Roe v. Wade and a book by Professor Glanville Williams, The Sanctity of Life and the Criminal Law. The book is cited repeatedly in the 1973 abortion decision, but the numerous citations do not reveal the full extent of the influence.

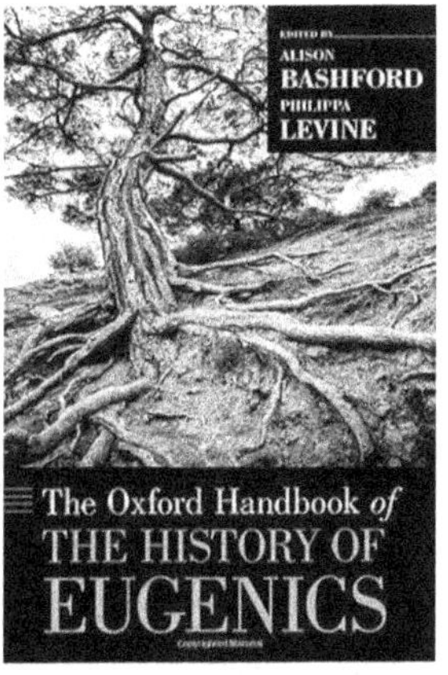

Justice Blackmun lifted his whole argument from Williams, including the history of abortion, ancient attitudes, the influence of Christianity, common law, Augustine's and Aquinas' teaching, canon law and English statutory law. And Williams was a member of the Eugenics Society. Roe v. Wade was based on eugenics.

Crypto-Eugenics

In 1968, the Eugenics Review ran an article summarizing some of the activities of the Eugenics Society. The article quoted a proposal made by in the late 1950s by Dr. Carlos Paton Blacker, who had been an officer in the Eugenics Society since 1931 (Secretary, then General Secretary, then Director, then Chairman):

> "That the Society should pursue eugenic ends by less obvious means, that is by a policy of crypto-eugenics, which was apparently proving successful in the US Eugenics Society."

In 1960, Blacker's proposal was adopted by the Eugenics Society. A resolution which was accepted stated (in part):

> "The Society's activities in crypto-eugenics should be pursued vigorously, and specifically that the Society should increase its monetary support of the FPA [Family Planning Association, the English branch of Planned Parenthood] and the IPPF [International Planned

Parenthood Federation] and should make contact with the Society for the Study of Human Biology, which already has a strong and active membership, to find out if any relevant projects are contemplated with which the Eugenics Society could assist."

At the time this resolution was adopted by the Eugenics Society, Blacker was the Administrative Chairman of IPPF. When IPPF was founded in 1952, it was housed in the offices of the Eugenics Society.

The dominant figure in the eugenics movement in the United States, considered by the English to be a model of crypto-eugenics, was Major General Frederick Osborn, a master propagandist. In 1956, he said people "won't accept the idea that they are in general, second rate. We must rely on other motivation."

Favored Races

He called the new motivation "a system of voluntary unconscious selection." The way to persuade people to exercise this voluntary unconscious selection was to appeal to the idea of "wanted" children. Osborn said, "Let's base our proposals on the desirability of having children born in homes where they will get affectionate and responsible care." In this way, the eugenics movement "will move at last towards the high goal which Galton set for it."

Osborn stated the public relations problem bluntly: *"Eugenic goals are most likely to be attained under a name other than eugenics."* He pointed to genetic counseling as a prime example: "Heredity clinics are the first eugenic proposals that have been adopted in a practical form and accepted by the public. ... The word eugenics is not associated with them."

Osborn is often credited with reforming the eugenics movement after World War II, and purging the racism. However, during the time of this reform, he was President of the Pioneer Fund, holding that office secretly from 1947 to 1956. The Pioneer Fund is a notorious white supremacist organization. A secret racist might not purge racism; he would purge open racism, leaving a policy that critics might call "crypto-racism."

In 1960, a member of the Eugenics Society, Reginald Ruggles Gates, founded a new periodical to advance racist ideas. The Advisory Council of the new journal, Mankind Quarterly, included yet another member of the Darwin family, Charles Galton Darwin.

One idea advanced in the journal is the belief that anthropology, if it is understood honestly, shows that mankind is divided into four species. The first issue stated that desegregation happened because "American anthropologists were responsible for introducing equalitarianism into anthropology, ignoring the hereditary differences between races, ...until the uninstructed public were gradually misled. Equality of opportunity, which everyone supports, was replaced by a doctrine of genetic and social equality, which is something quite different."

Even in Germany, the eugenics movement did not die out. The most offensive example of its resurgence after Hitler was the rehabilitation of Professor Dr. Otmar Freiherr von Verschuer.

In 1935, von Verschuer said that he was "responsible for ensuring that the care of genes and race, which Germany is leading worldwide, has such a strong base that it will withstand any attacks from outside." In 1937, he was Director of the Third Reich Institute for Heredity, Biology and Racial Purity.

Von Verschuer was Josef Mengele's mentor before the Nazi holocaust, and his collaborator during the holocaust. Mengele's horrific experiments at Auschwitz have put his name alongside those of Hitler and Eichmann. And yet, a few years after the war, von Verschuer founded the Institute of Human Genetics in Munster, where he worked educating another generation until his death in 1969. He had not turned away from his old ideas: was an adviser for the Mankind Quarterly, and a member of the American Eugenics Society.

The first, a review of his book Erbpathologie, said: "Race culture, the selection of proposed cases for sterilization or marriage advice [i.e., genetic counseling] are impossible without the earnest collaboration of the entire medical profession.

In this book the author clearly outlines the duties of the physician to the nation. *The word 'nation' no longer means a number of citizens living within certain boundaries, but a biological entity.* This point of view also changes the obligation of the physician.

The Shift To Genetics

Before the war, the American Eugenics Society laid out its research aims, including many investigations in sociology, psychology, anthropology and biology. But they noted especially the important new fields: population study and genetics.

After the war, research in genetics was led by one of the German eugenicist besides von Verschuer who had continued his work, Dr. Franz J. Kallmann. He had been "associated with Dr. Ernst Rdin, investigating in genetic psychiatry."

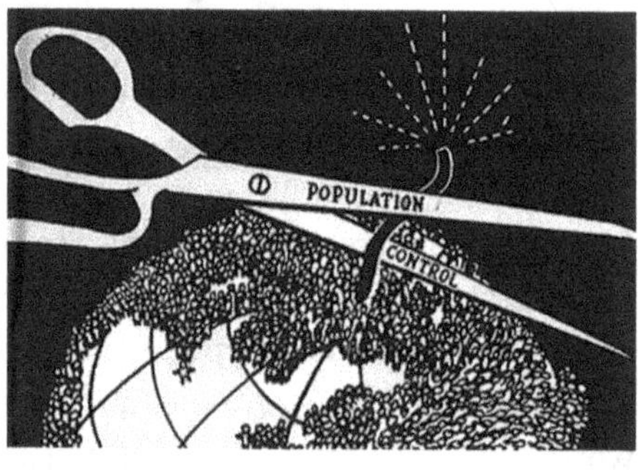

He was half Jewish, so he was driven out of Germany in 1936 by Hitler. Nonetheless, he testified on behalf of von Verschuer after the war. Kallmann taught psychiatry at Columbia, and in 1948 he founded the American Society of Human Genetics. He became a member of the American Eugenics Society. This Society developed hundreds of prenatal tests but did not look for cures, although every test was hyped as a potential lead towards a cure.

Over the next years, at least 124 people were members of both Kallmann's American Society of Human Genetics and the American Eugenics Society. The overwhelming evidence of a commitment to eugenics at the American Society of Human Genetics is especially troubling when you note that members of this society promoted, developed and now lead the multi-billion dollar Human Genome Project.

Negative eugenics, or ending the over-production of the "unfit," is obviously well underway with widespread contraception, sterilization and abortion. But positive eugenics, or the increased production of the "fit," can be advanced through artificial insemination, in vitro fertilization and genetic engineering. The Human Genome Project would certainly help in a scheme of positive eugenics.

Second New Field: Population Control

After World War II, the eugenics movement discovered (or invented) the population explosion, and whipped up global hysteria about it. From 1952 on, a major part of the eugenics movement

Eko bahunam vidadhati kaman. The meaning is that one living force is supplying all the demands of all other living entities. Just like in a family the father is supplying the necessities of the wife, the children, the servant, a small family. Similarly, you expand it: the government or the state or the king is supplying the necessities of all the citizens. But everything is incomplete. Everything is incomplete. You can supply your family, you can supply your society, you can supply your country, but you cannot supply everyone. But there are millions and trillions of living entities. Who is supplying food? Who is supplying hundreds and thousands of ants within the hole in your room? Who is supplying food? When you go to the green lake there are thousands of ducks. Who is taking care of them? But they are living. There are millions of sparrows, birds, beasts, elephants. At one time he eats hundred pounds. Who is supplying food? Not only here, but there are many millions and trillions of planets and universes everywhere. That is God. Nityo nityanam eko bahunam vidadhati kaman. Everyone is dependent on Him, and He is supplying all the necessities, all the necessities. Everything complete. Just like this planet, everything is complete.

purnam idam purnam adah
purnat purnam udacyate
[Iso Invocation]

Every planet is so made that it is complete in itself. The water is there, reserved in the seas and oceans. That water is taken away by the sunshine. Not only here, in other planets also, the same process is going on. It is transformed into cloud, then distributed all over the land, and there is growing of vegetables, fruits and plants, everything. So everything is complete arrangement. That we have to understand, that who has made this complete arrangement everywhere. The sun is rising in due time, the moon is rising in due time, the seasons are changing in due time. So how you can say? There is evidence in the Vedas there is God. In every scripture, every great personality, devotee, representative of God... Just like Lord Jesus Christ, he gave information of God. Although he was crucified, he never changed his opinion.
~ Srila Prabhupada (Lecture, Seattle, October 4, 1968)

was the population control movement. The population explosion made it possible for eugenics movement to continue its work more from the fit, less from the unfit *with the same people to do the same things, but with a new public rationale.*

The transformation from open eugenics to population planning is described well by Germaine Greer:

> "It now seems strange that men who had been conspicuous in the eugenics movement were able to move quite painlessly into the population establishment at the highest level, but if we reflect that the paymasters were the same Ford, Mellon, Du Pont, Standard Oil, Rockefeller and Shell are still the same, we can only assume that people like Kingsley Davis, Frank W. Notestein, C. C. Little, E. A. Ross, the Osborns Frederick and Fairfield, Philip M. Hauser, Alan Guttmacher and Sheldon Segal were being rewarded for past services."

That is, the population control movement was the same money, the same leaders, the same activities with a new excuse.

One of the organizations that promoted eugenics under the new population rubric was the Population Council. It was founded in 1952 by John D. Rockefeller 3rd, and spent $173,621,654 in its first 25 years. That is not a bad budget for one of the organizations in a dead movement! Clearly, the people who think the eugenics movement died in the rubble in Berlin do not understand crypto-eugenics, genetics or population control!

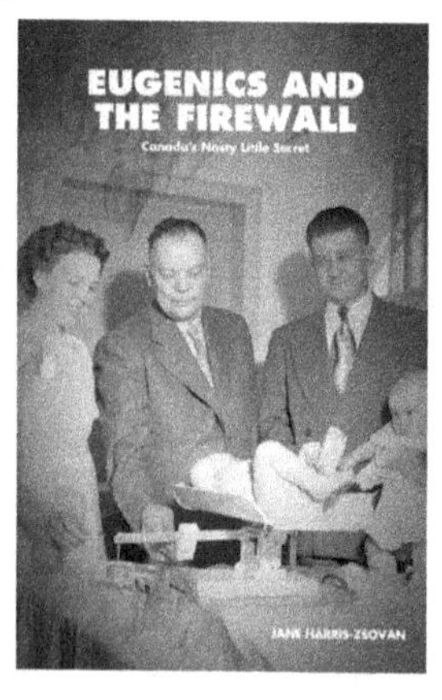

The extent of the population control movement is hard to imagine, and harder to exaggerate. *During the past 25 years, there have been approximately 1.5 billion surgical abortions globally.* The United Nations Population Fund has sponsored three meetings

> *In ancient Egypt, Carthage, Greece and Rome, the collapse of society began each time with a period of obvious moral decay. Every one of the symptoms of decline are present in this nation today... to ignore such lessons is to court disaster*
>
> *-Black*

bringing together the heads of state from most of the world to develop a global population strategy, in Bucharest in 1974, Mexico City in 1984, and in Cairo in 1994.

No other global problem has been the occasion for meetings comparable to these three. The World Bank, the U.S. Agency for International Development, and governmental agencies from nearly all the industrialized nations have contributed billions of dollars to campaigns designed to decrease population growth.

The population control movement has not been noted for respect for human rights. In 1972, for example, essays by members of the American Eugenics Society appeared in Readings in Population. Kingsley Davis explained the need for genetic control, and examined the obstacles, including a widespread attachment to the ideal of family life. But he saw some hope of developing a more effective program of improving the human race, although improvement would be slow:

> "Under the circumstances, we shall probably struggle along with small measures at a time, with the remote possibility that these may eventually evolve into a genetic control system. The morality of specific techniques of applied genetics artificial insemination, selective sterilization, ovular transplantation, eugenic abortion, genetic record keeping, genetic testing will be thunderously debated in theological and Marxian terms dating from ages past. Possibly, within half a century or so, this may add up to a comprehensive program."

What he wanted, though was "the deliberate alteration of the species for sociological purposes," which would be "a more fateful step than any previously taken by mankind. When man has conquered his own biological evolution he will have laid the basis for conquering everything else. The universe will be his, at last."

In the same book, Philip M. Hauser, also a member of the American Eugenics Society, explained the difference between family planning, which relies on the voluntary decisions of individuals or couples, and population control, which would include abortion, a commitment to zero population growth, coercion, euthanasia and restrictions on international migration.

Perhaps the clearest example of the power of the eugenics movement today is in China, with its one-child-only family policy.

This policy is an assault on prenatal life and on women's privacy, both. The program was described and praised in 16 articles in a remarkable issue of IPPF's quarterly journal, People, in 1989, on the eve of the massacre in Tiananmen Square. But this anti-life, anti-choice policy is not unique to China; most of the nations of Asia have some coercive elements in their population policies.

The coercive Chinese policy has a great deal of acceptance and support in the United States, including from feminist leaders like Eleanor Smeal and Molly Yard. When the Reagan administration cut off funds for the United Nations Population Fund (UNFPA) because of its support for the Chinese population program, two American organizations sued to restore funds: Rockefeller's Population Council and the Population Institute in Washington. A 1978 survey of members of the Population Association of America found that 34 percent of members agreed that "coercive birth control programs should be initiated in at least some countries immediately."

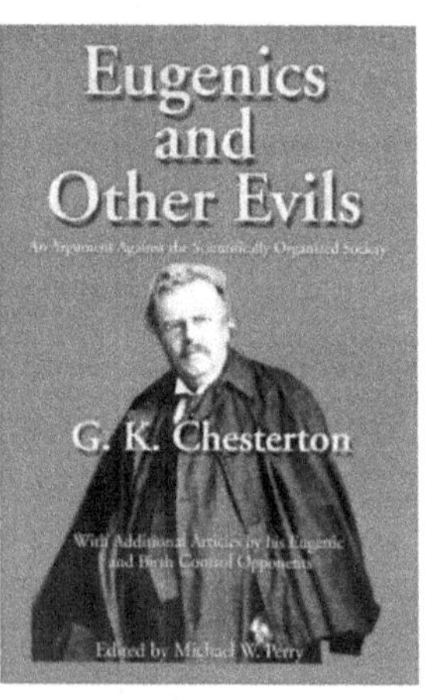

The United States government is said to be responsible for much of the global population control. In 1976, a formal definition of national security interests, NSSM 200, described the major threats to the United States. Some of these are obvious.

The first, of course, was Communism in Europe, with the military charged with principal responsibility for defending American national security from this threat. In the Pacific, the threat was the possibility of losing bases; the military was charged with the principal responsibility for defending this national interest. In Latin America, there was the threat of incipient Communism; the CIA had principal responsibility for the country's defense.

Technological revolution that we witnessed in the last century has gone so far for our human moral to catch up with.
~Hun Sen

In Africa, according to the American government in 1976 and ever since, the threat to American national security interests is population growth. The Agency for International Development was given the responsibility of defending America from this grave threat. This document was classified until 1992; when it was declassified, the Information project for Africa distributed it, and the covert depopulation policy tucked into the American foreign aid program caused a great deal of resentment.

Current Development

In late 1994, the publication of The Bell Curve made the word "eugenics" known again. The research quoted in the book is drawn overwhelmingly from members of the American Eugenics Society and other eugenic groups.

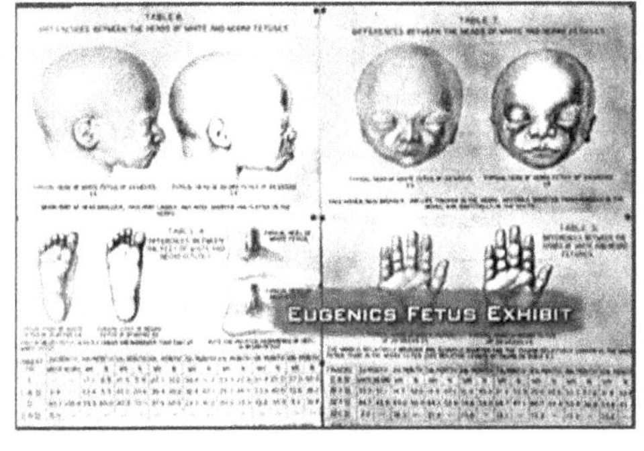

Curiously, most commentators focused on one chapter in the lengthy book, and debated whether it was racist. The conclusion of the book is that men are not equal, and that the Declaration of Independence is badly worded. This lengthy restatement of eugenics was on the bestseller list for weeks.

The book was generally praised by conservatives (The National Review, December 5, 1994, an issue devoted to The Bell Curve) and attacked by liberals (The New Republic, October 31, 1994, which included a lengthy defense of the book by its authors and 21 critical or hostile responses).

Systematic Response

One excellent way to understand the eugenics movement in our time is to read through a list of the members of the Eugenics Society and its successor, the Society for the Study of Social Biology.

Eugenics is not a conspiracy, it is a movement and an ideology. But the pieces of it are often considered in isolation, perhaps because of the success of the strategy of crypto-eugenics. Reading through the list of members helps to see the whole picture. (A list of members of the American Eugenics Society, with notes, is available from American Life League.)

In 1925, John Thomas Scopes was charged with teaching evolution in a public school in Tennessee, in violation of state law. The trial became a highly visible confrontation between Fundamentalist views of Scripture and the theory of evolution. Shaping the debate this way allowed the proponents of evolution to score a tremendous public relations victory.

Nonetheless, the questions, then and now, are theological and moral, not just scientific. Darwin and the evolutionists and eugenicists had indeed precipitated a religious crisis, and were debating the existence of God and the meaning of human life.

From the beginning, the great obstacle to the eugenics movement has been the Roman Catholic Church, and the Church's position has been repeatedly distorted. A sketch of the Church's position can be found in:

Gaudium et Spes or The Church in the Modern World the Vatican II document explaining to all people of good will why the Church wants to be involved in discussions of the problems facing the world and what she thinks she offers;

- Humanae Vitae: Pope Paul VI's letter on human life, best known for his re-statement of the Church's unwavering assertion that contraception is objectively and cannot be made moral, but also contains a sharp warning about the threat of coercive population control;

- Populorum Progressio: Pope Paul VI's powerful letter on development, urging the wealthy nations to help the poor generously, and calling development the "new name for peace"; Laborem Exercens Pope John Paul II's letter on work, offering a radically new approach to the place of work in the life of an individual and a society;

- Familiaris Consortio: Pope John Paul II's letter on family life, best known for re-stating opposition to contraception, but defends the rights of families, including the right to migrate in search of a better economic life;

- Sollicitudo Rei Socialis: one of Pope John Paul II's letters on the crises facing the modern world, stating that the measure of a social program is its impact on the dignity of the individual, and stating that the route to freedom from social evil is solidarity with the victims of the evil.

The social sciences in our time are thoroughly imbued with eugenic theory. It would be a noble work to rescue them, to work through the basic texts and theories of each field, identifying the eugenic taint and replacing it with an unswerving devotion to the dignity of the individual, including the poor.

Bibliography

History of Eugenics

Adams, Mark, ed. The Wellborn Science: Eugenics in Germany, France, Brazil and Russia (New York, Oxford: Oxford University Press, 1990)

Bajema, Carl L., ed. Eugenics, Then and Now (Stroudsburg,: Hutchinson & Ross, 1976)

Baker-Benfield, G. J. The Horrors of the Half-Known Life: Male Attitudes Toward Women and Sexuality in Nineteenth Century America (New York: Harper Colophon, 1976

Bigelow, Maurice A. "Brief History of the American Eugenics Society," Eugenic News, 31 (1946): 49-51.

Chase, Allen. The Legacy of Malthus: The Social Costs of the New Scientific Racism (New York: Alfred A. Knopf, 1977).

Degler, Carl N. In Search of Human Nature: The Decline and Revival of Darwinism in American Social Thought (New York: Oxford University Press, 1991)

Haller, Mark H. Eugenics: Hereditarian Attitudes in American Thought (New Brunswick: Rutgers University Press, 1963)

Kevles, Daniel J. In the Name of Eugenics: Genetics and the Uses of Human Heredity (Berkeley and Los Angeles: University of California Press, 1986)

Kuhl, Stefan. The Nazi Connection, (New York, Oxford: Oxford University Press, 1994)

Lifton, Robert. The Nazi Doctors: Medical Killing and the Psychology of Genocide (New York: Basic Books, 1986)

Ludmerer, Kenneth M. Genetics and American Society (Baltimore and London: Johns Hopkins University Press, 1972)

Mehler, Barry. "A History of the American Eugenics Society, 1921-1940," dissertation, University of Illinois, 1988.

Pernick, Martin S. The Black Stork: Eugenics and the Death of Defective Babies in American Medicine and Motion Pictures since 1915 (New York: Oxford University Press, 1992)

Pickens, Donald K. Eugenics and the Progressives (Nashville: Vanderbilt University Press, 1968)

Rosenberg, Charles E. No Other Gods: On Science and American Social Thought (Baltimore: Johns Hopkins University Press, 1976)

Shapiro, Thomas M. Population Control Politics: Women, Sterilization and Reproductive Choice(Philadelphia: Temple University Press, 1985)

Stepan, Nancy. The Idea of Race in Science: Great Britain 1800-1960 (London: Macmillan, 1982), The Hour of Eugenics: Race, Gender and Nation in Latin America (Ithaca: Cornell University Press, 1991)

Trombley, Stephen. The Right to Reproduce: A History of Coercive Sterilization (London:Weidenfeld & Nicolson, 1988)

Weinreich, Max. Hitler's Professors: The Part of Scholarship in Germany's Crimes Against the Jewish People (New York: Yiddish Scientific Institute, 1946)

Weiss, Sheila F. Race Hygiene and National Efficiency: The Eugenics of Wilhelm Schallmayer (Berkeley, Los Angeles, London: University of California Press, 1987)

Reproductive Technology

Corea, G., The Mother Machine (New York: Harper and Row, 1985)

Congregation for the Doctrine of the Faith, Instruction on Respect for Human Life in Its Origins and on the Dignity of Procreation (Vatican City: 1987)

De Marco, Don, Biotechnology and the Assault on Parenthood (San Francisco: Ignatius Press, 1991)

Fletcher, Joseph, Morals and Medicine (Boston: Bacon Press, 1960)

Frank, Diana, and Vogel, Marta, The Baby Makers (New York: Carroll & Graf, 1988)

Howard, Ted, and Rifkin, Jeremy, Who Should Play God? (New York: Dell Publishing, 1987)

Lejeune, Jerome; Ramsey, Paul; and Wright, Gerard, The Question of In Vitro Fertilization (London: SPUC Educational Trust, 1984)

McLaughlin, Loretta, The Pill, John Rock, and the Church (Boston: Little,Brown and Co, 1982)

Rini, Suzanne M. Beyond Abortion: A Chronicle of Fetal Experimentation (Rockford, IL: Tan Books, 1988)

U.S. Congress, Office of Technology Assessment, Infertility: Medical and Social Choices (Washington: U.S. Government Printing Office, 1988)

Population Control

Aird, John S., Slaughter of the Innocents: Coercive Birth Control in China (Washington: AEI Press, 1990)

Greer, Germaine, Sex and Destiny (New York: Harper & Row, 1984)

Hartmann, Betsy, Reproductive Rights and Wrongs (New York: Harper & Row, 1987)

Information Project for Africa, Population Control and National Security (Washington, 1991). IPFA has four other studies that have also been used by opponents of population imperialism throughout the developing world.

Fiction

H. G. Wells and Isaac Asimov were eugenicists, and much science fiction follows their lead. It is, therefore, good to know there is some excellent science fiction that challenges eugenics:

Huxley, Aldous, Brave New World

Lewis, C.S., That Hideous Strength

Miller, Walter M., A Canticle for Liebowitz (New York: Bantam Books, 1969)

Percy, Walker, The Thanatos Syndrome (New York: Farrar, Straus, Giroux, 1987)

Recent Eugenic Theory

Gore, Al, Earth in the Balance (Boston, New York and London: Houghton Mifflin, 1992)

Herrnstein, Richard J. and Murray, Charles, The Bell Curve (New York: Free Press, 1994)

Odom, Guy R., Mothers, Leadership, and Success (Houston: Polybius Press, 1990)

Rushton, J. Philippe, Race, Evolution, and Behavior (New Brunswick, NJ: Transaction Publishers, 1995)

83.

The 'Problematic' Countries

In 1952 John D. Rockefeller III established the 'Population Council' and in doing so, brought the issue of overpopulation into the public arena. In 1972, at the request of President Nixon, another commission, 'The Rockefeller Commission on Population Growth,' completed a two year study on the subject. The commission concluded:

"After two years of concentrated effort, we have concluded that, in the long run, no substantial benefits will result from further growth of the Nation's population, rather that the gradual stabilization of our population through voluntary means would contribute significantly to the Nation's ability to solve its problems. We have looked for, and have not found, any convincing economic argument for continued population growth. The health of our country does not depend on it, nor does the vitality of business nor the welfare of the average person. By its very nature, population is a continuing concern and should receive continuing attention. Later generations, and later commissions, will be able to see the right path into the future. In any case, no generation needs to know the ultimate goal or the final means, only the direction in which they will be found." ~John D. Rockefeller 1972.

National Security Study Memorandum 200

Implications of Worldwide Population Growth for U.S. Security and Overseas Interests (NSSM200)

Only two years later, came the `National Security Study Memorandum 200,` which was completed on December 10, 1974 by the United States National Security Council under the direction of Henry Kissinger. It was adopted as official U.S. policy by President Gerald Ford in November 1975. It was originally classified, but was later declassified and obtained by researchers in the early 1990s.

The basic thesis of the memorandum was that population growth in the least developed countries is a concern to U.S. national security, because it would tend to risk civil unrest and political instability in countries that had a high potential for economic development.

Thirteen countries are named in the report as particularly problematic with respect to U.S. security interests: India, Bangladesh, Pakistan, Indonesia, Thailand, Philippines, Turkey, Nigeria, Egypt, Ethiopia, Mexico, Colombia, and Brazil. These countries are projected to create 47 percent of all world population growth by 2050 and beyond. The report advocates the promotion of contraception and other population reduction measures.

It also raises the question of whether the U.S. should consider preferential allocation of surplus food supplies to countries that are deemed constructive in use of population control measures. The report advises, "In these sensitive relations, however, it is important in style as well as substance to avoid the appearance of coercion."

The Memorandum recommended that the below goals were necessary to safeguard US Interests:

· Zero rate population growth in the developed countries by 1985

· Zero rate population growth in Lesser Developed Countries by 2000.

So it is not that because there is overpopulation there is scarcity of food. No. That is not the cause. The cause is that as soon as people will become godless, the supply will be stopped. That time is coming.

-Srila Prabhupada (Srimad-Bhagavatam 5.5.1 — Bombay, December 25, 1976)

84.

USDA Funded Project

To Create A GM Corn That Sterilizes People

William Engdahl, March, 2010

One long-standing project of the US Government has been to perfect a genetically-modified variety of corn, the diet staple in Mexico and many other Latin American countries. The corn has been field tested in tests financed by the US Department of Agriculture along with a small California bio-tech company named Epicyte. Announcing his success at a 2001 press conference, the president of Epicyte, Mitch Hein, pointing to his GMO corn plants, announced, "We have a hothouse filled with corn plants that make anti-sperm antibodies."

The Pregnancy Prevention Plants

Hein explained that they had taken antibodies from women with a rare condition known as immune infertility, isolated the genes that regulated the manufacture of those infertility antibodies, and, using genetic engineering techniques, had inserted the genes into ordinary corn seeds used to produce corn plants.

The birds and beasts have no such problem. In the morning they are immediately chirping, "Jee, jee, jee, jee." They know that they will have their food. No one is dying, and there is no such thing as overpopulation because everyone is provided for by God's arrangement.

~ Srila Prabhupada (Eeasy Journey To Other Planets 2: Varieties of Planetary Systems)

In this manner, in reality they produced a concealed contraceptive embedded in corn meant for human consumption. "Essentially, the antibodies are attracted to surface receptors on the sperm," said Hein. "They latch on and make each sperm so heavy it cannot move forward. It just shakes about as if it was doing the lambada." Hein claimed it was a possible solution to world "over-population."

The moral and ethical issues of feeding it to humans in Third World poor countries without their knowing it, he left out of his remarks.

Normally, biologists use bacteria to grow human proteins. However, Epicyte decided to use corn because plants have cellular structures that are much more like those of humans, making them easier to manipulate.

The questions raised by "spermicides hidden in GMO corn provided to starving Third World populations through the generosity of the Gates' foundation, Rockefeller Foundation and Kofi Annan's AGRA" are many and profound.

1. Isn't GM technology directed beyond third world countries but at all countries in the world, and first and most heavily in the US?

2. Is there a relationship, since the introduction of GM-crops in the US, of how steeply birthrates in the US have fallen?

U.S. birthrates overall are at an all time low. Continuing a 12-year decline, the U.S. birth rate has dropped to the lowest level since national data have been available ...

Bt-corn was introduced in the US in 1996, three years before the dramatic decline began. "Some seven million acres were planted to Bt corn in 1997 with hybrids primarily from Mycogen, Novartis (formerly Ciba), and Northrup King. Mycogen and Novartis both produce pharmaceutical contraceptives.

(Source: http://www.guardian.co.uk/science/2001/sep/09/gm.food)

Research Indicates That GMO Could Be a Cause of Infertility

Hethir Rodriguez C.H., C.M.T.

Is it possible that the foods you eat are actually affecting your fertility and inhibiting your chances of getting pregnant? The answer is a resounding, "Yes," according to dozens of research groups worldwide who have been studying the effects of Genetically Modified Organisms found in many of today's most common foods.

Genetically Modified foods, according to researchers, are becoming a real problem when it comes to fertility, causing an influx in worldwide infertility rates. Since the 1970's alone, sperm counts among the world's male population have declined as much as 40-50%, according to some studies. GMO foods may be just one of the reasons, warn those studying the phenomenon.

Despite alerts being published by the world's most renowned scientists, manufacturers continue to use these products in their products fed to both livestock and humans.

The problem has become so great that the EU has actually banned the use of GMO products throughout Europe. While some of the top food manufacturers like Kellogg, Heinz, Pepsi, Coke and Kraft, have changed their recipes in Europe, no longer using GMO ingredients in their products, those same products sold in the States continue to use these dangerous ingredients.

So, why do genetically modified foods present such a danger for animal and human fertility? According to a report published last spring by the American Academy of Environmental Medicine (AAEM), "there is more than a casual association between GM foods and adverse health effects." These findings have caused the AAEM to encourage all physicians to "educate their patients, the medical community and the public top avoid all genetically modified foods."

Risks Most Associated with GMO Foods

The Austrian Health Ministers reported in 2008, that their own research indicated that fertility rates have suffered dramatically due

And whatever produce they get, sometimes they dump tons of it into the ocean to keep the prices high. And I have heard here in Geneva that when there was excess milk production, some of the people wanted to slaughter twenty thousand cows just to reduce the milk production.

This is what is going on in people's brains. Actually, they have no brains.

~ Srila Prabhupada

to GMO exposure, as have the health of the human immune system. Those who regularly ingest GMO foods are more likely to be sick, age faster and have a harder time getting (and staying) pregnant.

In study after study, the effects of fertility were alarming, claim researchers. In one report, the testicles of some animals actually changed colors from a normal pink to an alarming blue after being fed GMO produced feed. In addition, sperm was shown to be altered, resulting in fewer pregnancies overall. DNA too has shown alterations after ingesting even the smallest amount of GMO foods.

But, males are not the only ones being affected by GMOs. Female fertility too is under attack. Female animals being studied showed an alarming increase in an inability to get pregnant as well as a spike in premature births; low birth weight babies and infant moralities after being fed a regular diet of GMO. Rats given GMO feed in Europe were shown to give birth to babies that regularly died within weeks of their birth (sometimes as many as 99%), compared to only a 10% mortality rate for those fed regular feed.

One of the few long-terms studies (there are not many long-term studies done on GMO foods) showed that mice fed GMO corn over a period of 20 weeks had greatly impaired fertility compared to the mice fed non-GMO corn. In addition the offspring of the GMO mice also suffered from lower fertility rates.

In the U.S., pig farmers in the Midwest reported that more than 1,000 pigs on their farms became sterile after being fed a regular diet of GMO feed over several months.

This has left some food manufacturers scrambling to change their ingredients in Europe, while continuing to use these same dangerous products in U.S. foodstuffs.

To make matters worse, the FDA has yet to require food manufacturers to list the use of GMO foods on their packages, leaving many consumers unaware of what they are really eating. This can make it even harder to make the wisest and healthiest food choices while shopping.

Which Foods are Most Likely GMO?

The highest GMO food grown is soy. In the U.S., approximately 54% of all soybeans cultivated in 2000 were genetically-modified, in 2010, 93% of soybeans are genetically modified. Yet another reason to avoid soy foods.

While soy, corn and potatoes are the most prevalent GMO foods, there are many others that you should be aware about as well, such as:

Salmon

Canola oil

High fructose corn syrup/corn sugar (one of the reasons there is so much GMO corn being grown. The other reason for so much corn is that it is readily fed to livestock)

Dairy (conventional cows are injected with the genetically engineered hormone rBGH/rBST and are frequently fed GMO corn and grains.)

Processed foods (many processed foods have been tested and shown to contain some GMO ingredients.)

References:

1. Seeds of Deception by Dr. Jeffrey M. Smith
2. Austrian Health Ministers Report 2008
3. Organic Consumers Organization (website)
4. American Academy of Environmental Medicine

The Infertility Timebomb: Are Men Facing Rapid Extinction?

By Tamara Sturtz, Daily Mail, UK, 10 May 2010

One in five men could suffer from fertility problems. And scientists have warned that it's just going to get worse...

There's a crisis brewing, but it has nothing to do with the economic deficit or the current political uncertainty. Scientists are warning that rising levels of male infertility have become so perilous that it is a serious 'public health issue'. And some go even further.

Professor Niels Skakkebaek, of the University of Copenhagen, describes the issue 'as important as global warming'. Last week, one science writer even suggested, in starkly terrifying terms, that if scientists from Mars were to study the male reproductive system, they would possibly conclude that man was destined for rapid extinction.

And if it continues, this trend could indicate men are on a path to becoming completely infertile within a few generations.

Reports claim that as many as one in five healthy young men between the ages of 18 and 25 produce abnormal sperm counts.

Only 5 to 15 per cent of their sperm is good enough to be classed as 'normal' under World Health Organisation rules - proving that infertility is not just a female problem. Indeed, among those experiencing difficulty with conception, a male fertility problem is considered important in about 40 per cent of couples.

But women trying to get pregnant are facing another astonishing claim: that the core problems of male fertility - while they may be exacerbated by environmental issues - start in the womb.

'Sperm counts are declining and there is mounting evidence that the problem starts even before birth,' says Dr Gillian Lockwood, medical director of Midland Fertility Services.

She cites growing evidence that although the process of sperm production - known as spermatogenesis - starts in adolescence, the crucial preparations are made in the few months before and after birth.

Experts talk of a 'window' of testicular development that begins in the growing foetus and ends in the first six months of life. Problems in this period mean that the baby boy may never be able to produce babies of his own.

It's a theory that Karl Tonks, a clinical skills trainer, is particularly interested in. Karl, 47, and his teaching assistant wife Lorraine, 41, consider themselves among the lucky ones: they have two healthy

Srimad-Bhagavatam instructs us solely on this subject from the very beginning to the end. Human life is simply meant for self-realization. The civilization which aims at this utmost perfection never indulges in creating unwanted things, and such a perfect civilization prepares men only to accept the bare necessities of life or to follow the principle of the best use of a bad bargain. Our material bodies and our lives in that connection are bad bargains because the living entity is actually spirit, and spiritual advancement of the living entity is absolutely necessary. Human life is intended for the realization of this important factor, and one should act accordingly, accepting only the bare necessities of life and depending more on God's gift without diversion of human energy for any other purpose, such as being mad for material enjoyment. The materialistic advancement of civilization is called "the civilization of the demons," which ultimately ends in wars and scarcity.

- Srila Prabhupada (Srimad Bhagavatam 2.2.3 Purport)

children, despite Karl's low sperm count. Their twins Ben and Kira, now 12, were born as a result of arduous and expensive IVF.

85.

Unethical Human Experimentation

In The United States

This chapter deals with U.S. medical experiments that are alleged to be unethical, non-consensual, or illegal. There have been numerous experiments performed on human test subjects in the United States that have been considered unethical, and were often performed illegally, without the knowledge, consent, or informed consent of the test subjects.

The experiments include: the deliberate infection of people with deadly or debilitating diseases, exposure of people to biological and chemical weapons, human radiation experiments, injection of people with toxic and radioactive chemicals, surgical experiments, interrogation/torture experiments, tests involving mind-altering substances, and a wide variety of others. Many of these tests were performed on children, the sick, and mentally disabled individuals, often under the guise of "medical treatment". In many of the studies, a large portion of the subjects were poor, racial minorities, or prisoners.

Funding for many of the experiments was provided by United States government, especially the Central Intelligence Agency, United States military and federal or military corporations. The human research programs were usually highly secretive, and in many cases information about them was not released until many years after the studies had been performed.

The ethical, professional, and legal implications of this in the United States medical and scientific community were quite significant, and led to many institutions and policies that attempted to ensure that future human subject research in the United States would be ethical and legal. Public outcry over the discovery of government experiments on human subjects led to numerous congressional investigations and hearings, including the Church Committee, Rockefeller Commission, and Advisory Committee on Human Radiation Experiments, amongst others.

Surgical Experiments

Throughout the 1840s, J. Marion Sims, who is often referred to as "the father of gynecology", performed surgical experiments on enslaved African women and other poor women, without anaesthesia. The women regularly died from infections resulting from the experiments.[1] One of the women was experimented on 30 times.

His first operation performed after leaving medical school, was on the infant son of a farm wife. The baby had an infection in his gums and high fever, which Sims had no idea how to treat, so he decided to use whatever tool he had available, which happened to be an icepick. He jabbed the baby's gums with it and left. The next day he returned to the farm and found that the baby had died. In order to test one of his theories about the causes of trismus in infants, Sims performed experiments where he used a shoemaker's awl to move around the skull bones of the babies of enslaved women.[23]

U.S. troops being used to measure the effects of radiation exposure from tactical nuclear weapons, during Exercise Desert Rock I (November 1, 1951)

Later in his career, Dr. Sims found it more lucrative to treat the wives of wealthier men using the same ruthless approach in a more practiced phase.

In 1874, Mary Rafferty, an Irish servant woman, came to Dr. Roberts Bartholow of the Good Samaritan Hospital in Cincinnati for treatment of her cancer. Seeing a research opportunity, he cut open her head, and inserted needle electrodes into her exposed brain matter.[4] He described the experiment as follows:

> When the needle entered the brain substance, she complained of acute pain in the neck. In order to develop more decided reactions, the strength of the current was increased ... her countenance exhibited great distress, and she began to cry. Very soon, the left hand was extended as if in the act of taking hold of some object in front of her; the arm presently was agitated with clonic spasm; her eyes became fixed, with pupils widely dilated; lips were blue, and she frothed at the mouth; her breathing became stertorous; she lost consciousness and was violently convulsed on the left side. The convulsion lasted five minutes, and was succeeded by a coma. She returned to consciousness in twenty minutes from the beginning of the attack, and complained of some weakness and vertigo. —Dr. Bartholow's research report[4]

In 1896, Dr. Arthur Wentworth performed spinal taps on 29 young children, without the knowledge or consent of their parents, at the Children's Hospital in Boston, Massachusetts to discover whether doing so would be harmful.[5]

From 1913 to 1951, Dr. Leo Stanley, chief surgeon at the San Quentin Prison, performed a wide variety of experiments on hundreds of prisoners at San Quentin. Many of the experiments involved testicular implants, where Stanley would take the testicles out of executed prisoners and surgically implant them into living prisoners.

In other experiments, he attempted to implant the testicles of rams, goats, and boars into living prisoners. Stanley also performed various eugenics experiments, and forced sterilizations on San Quentin prisoners.[6] Stanley believed that his experiments would rejuvenate old men, control crime (which he believed had biological causes), and prevent the "unfit" from reproducing.[6,7]

"America is the only country that went from barbarism to decadence without civilization in between."

-Oscar Wilde

Pathogens, Disease, And Biological Warfare Agents

In the 1880s, in Hawaii, a Californian physician working at a hospital for lepers injected twelve girls under the age of 12 with syphilis.[5]

In 1895, the New York pediatrician Henry Heiman intentionally infected two "idiots" (mentally disabled boys)—one four-year-old and one sixteen-year old—with gonorrhea as part of a medical experiment. A review of the medical literature of the late 19th and early 20th centuries found that there were more than 40 reports of experimental infections with gonorrheal culture, including some where gonorrheal organisms were applied to the eyes of sick children.[5,8,9]

In 1900, U.S Army doctors in the Philippines infected five prisoners with bubonic plague and induced beriberi in 29 prisoners; four of the test subjects died as a result.[10,11] In 1906, Professor Richard Strong of Harvard University intentionally infected 24 Filipino prisoners with cholera, which had somehow become contaminated with plague. He did this without the consent of the patients, and without informing them of what he was doing. All of the subjects became sick and 13 died.[11,12]

In 1908, three Philadelphia researchers infected dozens of children with tuberculin at the St. Vincent's House orphanage in Philadelphia, causing permanent blindness in some of the children and painful lesions and inflammation of the eyes in many of the others. In the study they refer to the children as "material used".[13]

In 1909, F. C. Knowles released a study describing how he had deliberately infected two children in an orphanage with Molluscum contagiosum after an outbreak in the orphanage, in order to study the disease.[5]

In 1911, Dr. Hideyo Noguchi of the Rockefeller Institute for Medical Research injected 146 hospital patients (some of whom were children) with syphilis. He was later sued by the parents of some of the child subjects, who allegedly contracted syphilis as a result of his experiments.[14]

In 1931 Cornelius Rhoads, also of the Rockefeller Institute, claimed to have injected cancer cells into Puerto Ricans. He later claimed he was joking and was acquitted.

The Tuskegee Syphilis Experiment

The Tuskegee syphilis experiment[15] was a clinical study conducted between 1932 and 1972 in Tuskegee, Alabama, by the U.S. Public Health Service. In the experiment, 400 impoverished black males who had syphilis were offered "treatment" by the researchers, who did not tell the test subjects that they had syphilis and did not give them treatment for the disease.

By 1947, penicillin became available as treatment, but those running the study prevented study participants from receiving treatment elsewhere, lying to them about their true condition, so that they could observe the effects of syphilis on the human body. By the end of the study in 1972, only 74 of the test subjects were alive.

A subject of the Tuskegee syphilis experiment has his blood drawn, c. 1953

28 of the original 399 men had died of syphilis, 100 were dead of related complications, 40 of their wives had been infected, and 19 of their children were born with congenital syphilis. The study was not shut down until 1972, when its existence was leaked to the press, forcing the researchers to stop in the face of a public outcry.[16]

In 1941, at the University of Michigan, doctors Francis and Jonas Salk and other researchers deliberately infected patients at several Michigan mental institutions with the influenza virus by spraying the virus into their nasal passages.[17] Francis Rous, editor of the Journal of Experimental Medicine wrote the following to Francis regarding the experiments:

> "It may save you much trouble if you publish your paper ... elsewhere than in the Journal of Experimental Medicine. The Journal is under constant scrutiny by the anti-vivisectionists who would not hesitate to play up the fact that you used for your tests human beings of a state institution. That the tests were wholly justified goes without saying."[18]

In 1941 Dr. William C. Black inoculated a twelve month old baby "offered as a volunteer" with herpes. He submitted his research to The Journal of Experimental Medicine and it was rejected on ethical grounds.

The editor of the Journal of Experimental Medicine, Francis Payton Rous, called the experiment "an abuse of power, an infringement of the rights of an individual, and not excusable because the illness which followed had implications for science."[19,20,21] It was later published in the Journal of Pediatrics.[22]

The Stateville Penitentiary Malaria Study

The Stateville Penitentiary Malaria Study was the site of a controlled study of the effects of malaria on the prisoners of Stateville Penitentiary near Joliet, Illinois beginning in the 1940s.

The study was conducted by the Department of Medicine at the University of Chicago in conjunction with the United States Army and the State Department. At the Nuremberg trials, Nazi doctors cited the malaria experiments as part of their defense.[23,24]

The study continued at Stateville Penitentiary for 29 years. In related studies from 1944 to 1946, Dr. Alf Alving, a professor at the University of Chicago Medical School, purposely infected psychiatric patients at the Illinois State Hospital with malaria, so that he could test experimental malaria treatments on them.[25]

Guatemala Penicillin Study

In a 1946 to 1948 study in Guatemala, U.S. researchers used prostitutes to infect prison inmates, insane asylum patients, and Guatemalan soldiers with syphilis and other sexually transmitted diseases, in order to test the effectiveness of penicillin in treating sexually transmitted diseases. They later tried infecting people with "direct inoculations made from syphilis bacteria poured into the men's penises and on forearms and faces that were slightly abraded ...or in a few cases through spinal punctures".

Approximately 700 people were infected as part of the study (including orphan children). The study was sponsored by the

Surely the only sound foundation for a civilization is a sound state of mind.

~E. M. Forster

Public Health Service, the National Institutes of Health and the Pan American Health Sanitary Bureau (now the World Health Organization's Pan American Health Organization) and the Guatemalan government.

The team was led by John Charles Cutler, who later participated in the Tuskegee syphilis experiments. Cutler chose to do the study in Guatemala because he would not have been permitted to do it in the United States.[26,27,28,29]

Serratia Tests

In 1950, in order to conduct a simulation of a biological warfare attack, the U.S. Navy used airplanes to spray large quantities of the bacteria Serratia marcescens - considered harmless at this time - over the city of San Francisco, which caused numerous citizens to contract pneumonia-like illnesses, and killed at least one person.[30,31,32,33,34,35] The family of the man who was killed sued for gross negligence, but a federal judge ruled in favor of the government in 1981.[36] Serratia tests were continued until at least 1969.[37]

Also in 1950, Dr. Joseph Stokes of the University of Pennsylvania deliberately infected 200 female prisoners with viral hepatitis.[38]

From the 1950s to 1972, mentally disabled children at the Willowbrook State School in Staten Island, New York were intentionally infected with viral hepatitis, in research whose purpose was to help discover a vaccine.[39]

From 1963 to 1966, Saul Krugman of New York University promised the parents of mentally disabled children that their children would be enrolled into Willowbrook in exchange for signing a consent form for procedures that he claimed were "vaccinations." In reality, the procedures involved deliberately infecting children with viral hepatitis by feeding them an extract made from the feces of patients infected with the disease.[40,41]

In 1952, Sloan-Kettering Institute researcher Chester M. Southam injected live cancer cells into prisoners at the Ohio State Prison. Half of the prisoners in this NIH-sponsored study were black. Also at Sloan-Kettering, 300 healthy women were injected with live cancer cells without being told. The doctors stated that they knew at the time that it might cause cancer.[42]

In 1955, the CIA conducted a biological warfare experiment where they released whooping cough bacteria from boats outside of Tampa Bay, Florida, causing a whooping cough epidemic in the city, and killing at least 12 people.[43,44,45]

In 1956 and 1957, several U.S. Army biological warfare experiments were conducted on the cities of Savannah, Georgia and Avon Park, Florida. In the experiments, Army bio-warfare researchers released millions of infected mosquitoes on the two towns, in order to see if the insects could potentially spread yellow fever and dengue fever.

Hundreds of residents contracted a wide array of illnesses, including fevers, respiratory problems, stillbirths, encephalitis, and typhoid. Army researchers pretended to be public health workers, so that they could photograph and perform medical tests on the victims. Several people died as a result of the experiments.[10,46]

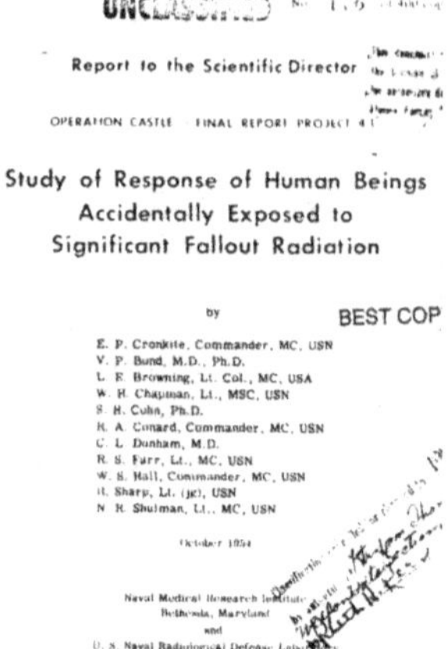

UNCLASSIFIED

Report to the Scientific Director

OPERATION CASTLE — FINAL REPORT PROJECT 4.1

Study of Response of Human Beings Accidentally Exposed to Significant Fallout Radiation

by

BEST COP

E. P. Cronkite, Commander, MC, USN
V. P. Bond, M.D., Ph.D.
L. E. Browning, Lt. Col., MC, USA
W. H. Chapman, Lt., MSC, USN
S. H. Cohn, Ph.D.
R. A. Conard, Commander, MC, USN
C. L. Dunham, M.D.
R. S. Farr, Lt., MC, USN
W. S. Hall, Commander, MC, USN
R. Sharp, Lt. (jg), USN
N. R. Shulman, Lt., MC, USN

October 1954

Naval Medical Research Institute
Bethesda, Maryland
and
U. S. Naval Radiological Defense Laboratory
San Francisco, California

Cover of the final report of Project 4.1, which examined the effects of radioactive fallout on the natives of the Marshall Islands

In 1962, twenty-two elderly patients at the Jewish Chronic Disease Hospital in Brooklyn, New York were injected with live cancer cells by Chester M. Southam, who in 1952 had done the same to prisoners at the Ohio State Prison, in order to "discover the secret of how healthy bodies fight the invasion of malignant cells".

The administration of the hospital attempted to cover the study up, but the New York State medical licensing board ultimately placed Southam on probation for one year. Two years later, the American Cancer Society elected him as their Vice President.[47]

In 1966, the U.S. Army released the harmless Bacillus globigii into the tunnels of the New York subway system as part of a field study called A Study of the Vulnerability of Subway Passengers in New York City to Covert Attack with Biological Agents.[43,48,49,50,51] The

Chicago subway system was also subject to a similar experiment by the Army.[43]

Human Radiation Experiments

Researchers in the United States have performed thousands of human radiation experiments to determine the effects of atomic radiation and radioactive contamination on the human body, generally on people who were poor, sick, or powerless.[52]

Most of these tests were performed, funded, or supervised by the United States military, Atomic Energy Commission, or various other US federal government agencies.

The experiments included a wide array of studies, involving things like feeding radioactive food to mentally disabled children or conscientious objectors, inserting radium rods into the noses of schoolchildren, deliberately releasing radioactive chemicals over U.S. and Canadian cities, measuring the health effects of radioactive fallout from nuclear bomb tests, injecting pregnant women and babies with radioactive chemicals, and irradiating the testicles of prison inmates, amongst other things.

Much information about these programs was classified and kept secret. In 1986 the United States House Committee on Energy and Commerce released a report entitled "American Nuclear Guinea Pigs : Three Decades Of Radiation Experiments On U.S. Citizens".[53]

In the 1990s Eileen Welsome's reports for The Albuquerque Tribune prompted the Advisory Committee on Human Radiation Experiments, created by executive order of president Bill Clinton. It published results in 1995. Welsome later wrote a book called The Plutonium Files.

Radioactive Iodine Experiments

In 1953, the U.S. Atomic Energy Commission (AEC) ran several studies on the health effects of radioactive iodine in newborns and pregnant women at the University of Iowa. In one study, researchers

> *"There are many humorous things in the world; among them, the white man's notion that he is less savage than the other savages."*
> *~ Mark Twain*

gave pregnant women from 100 to 200 microcuries (3.7 to 7.4 MBq) of iodine-131, in order to study the women's aborted embryos in an attempt to discover at what stage, and to what extent, radioactive iodine crosses the placental barrier.

In another study, they gave 25 newborn babies (who were under 36 hours old and weighed from 5.5 to 8.5 pounds (2.5 to 3.9 kg)) iodine-131, either by oral administration or through an injection, so that they could measure the amount of iodine in their thyroid glands.[54]

In another AEC study, researchers at the University of Nebraska College of Medicine fed iodine-131 to 28 healthy infants through a gastric tube to test the concentration of iodine in the infants' thyroid glands.[54]

In a 1949 operation called the "Green Run," the AEC released iodine-131 and xenon-133 to the atmosphere which contaminated a 500,000-acre (2,000 km2) area containing three small towns near the Hanford site in Washington.[55]

In 1953, the AEC sponsored a study to discover if radioactive iodine affected premature babies differently from full-term babies. In the experiment, researchers from Harper Hospital in Detroit orally administered iodine-131 to 65 premature and full-term infants who weighed from 2.1 to 5.5 pounds (0.95 to 2.5 kg).[54]

People everywhere are suffering on account of being led by blind leaders who are devoid of all knowledge of the soul. Such foolish men lead other foolish men and all concerned suffer. Andha yathandhair upaniyamana, when one blind man leads another, the result is that both of them fall into the ditch. Therefore there is a requirement for a section of society to become first class men, free of the influence of the modes of material nature, who can understand the mission of this human form of life and who can teach it to others. I am trying to create these men, but it is hard, for people have become lost of all intelligence due to the coverings of the three modes of material nature. So I am one man alone, yet now there are so many nice boys and girls like you to help me push on this movement in my old age.

~Srila Prabhupada (Letter to: Jagajivana -- New Delhi 1 September, 1976)

From 1955 to 1960 Sonoma State Hospital in northern California served as a permanent drop off location for mentally handicapped children diagnosed with cerebral palsy or lesser disorders. The children subsequently underwent painful experimentation without adult consent.

Many were given irradiated milk, some spinal taps "for which they received no direct benefit."[60] Minutes Wednesday learned that in these fifteen years, the brain of every cerebral palsy child who died at Sonoma State was removed and studied without parental consent. According to the CBS story, over 1,400 patients died at the clinic.[56]

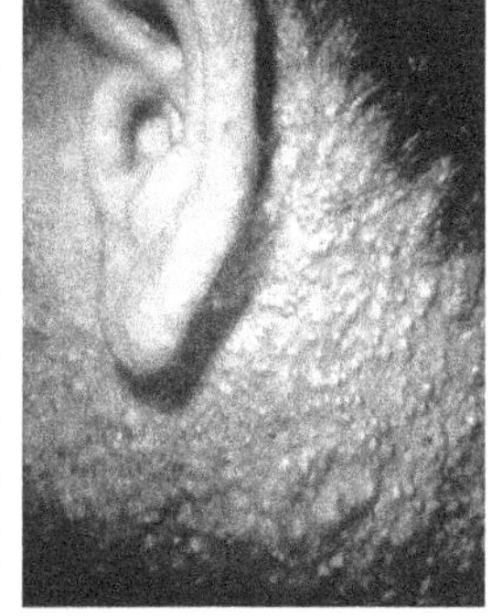

Chloracne resulting from exposure to dioxins, such as those that Albert Kligman injected into prisoners at the Holmesburg Prison

In 1962, the Hanford site again released I-131, stationing test subjects along its path to record its effect on them. The AEC also recruited Hanford volunteers to ingest milk contaminated with I-131 during this time.[54]

Uranium Experiments

Following is an Atomic Energy Commission memo from Colonel O.G. Haywood, Jr. to Dr. Fidler at the Oak Ridge Laboratory in Tennessee, dated April 17, 1947.[57]

> "It is desired that no document be released which refers to experiments with humans and might have adverse effect on public opinion or result in legal suits. Documents covering such work should be classified secret."

Between 1946 and 1947, researchers at the University of Rochester injected uranium-234 and uranium-235 in dosages ranging from 6.4 to 70.7 micrograms per kilogram of body weight into several people to study how much uranium their kidneys could tolerate before becoming damaged.[58]

Between 1953 and 1957, at the Massachusetts General Hospital, Dr. William Sweet injected eleven terminally ill, comatose and semi-comatose patients with uranium in an experiment to determine, among other things, its viability as a chemotherapy treatment against brain tumors, which all but one of the patients had (one being a mis-diagnosis). Dr. Sweet, who died in 2001, maintained that consent had been obtained from the patients and next of kin.[59,60]

Plutonium Experiments

In 1945, as part of the Manhattan Project, three patients at Billings Hospital of the University of Chicago, Oak Ridge, and the University of California Hospital in San Francisco were injected with plutonium.[63] One of these, Albert Stevens accumulated the highest known radiation dose to a human as a result of this experiment.

In 1946, six employees of a Chicago metallurgical lab were given water that was contaminated with plutonium-239, so that researchers could study how plutonium is absorbed into the digestive tract.[58]

An eighteen-year-old woman at an upstate New York hospital, expecting to be treated for a pituitary gland disorder, was injected with plutonium.[64]

Experiments Involving Other Radioactive Materials

Immediately after World War II, researchers at Vanderbilt University gave 829 pregnant mothers in Tennessee what they were told were "vitamin drinks" that would improve the health of their babies, but were, in fact, mixtures containing radioactive iron, to determine how fast the radioisotope crossed into the placenta.

At least three children are known to have died from the experiments, from cancers and leukemias.[65,66] Four of the women's babies died from cancers as a result of the experiments, and the women experienced rashes, bruises, anemia, hair/tooth loss, and cancer.[52]

From 1946 to 1953, at the Walter E. Fernald State School in Massachusetts, in an experiment sponsored by the U.S. Atomic Energy Commission and the Quaker Oats corporation, 73 mentally disabled children were fed oatmeal containing radioactive calcium and other radioisotopes, in order to track "how nutrients were digested". The children were not told that they were being fed radioactive chemicals and were told by hospital staff and researchers that they were joining a "science club".[65,67,68,69]

Experiment On Burn Victims

In the 1950s, researchers at the Medical College of Virginia performed experiments on severe burn victims, most of them poor and black, without their knowledge or consent, with funding from the Army and in collaboration with the AEC.

In the experiments, the subjects were exposed to additional burning, experimental antibiotic treatment, and injections of radioactive isotopes. The amount of radioactive phosphorus-32 injected into some of the patients, 500 microcuries (19 MBq), was 50 times the "acceptable" dose for a healthy individual; for people with severe burns, this likely led to significantly increased death rates.[70,71]

Between 1948 and 1954, funded by the federal government, researchers at the Johns Hopkins Hospital inserted radium rods into the noses of 582 Baltimore, Maryland schoolchildren as an alternative to adenoidectomy.[72,73,74]

Similar experiments were performed on over 7,000 U.S. Army and Navy personnel during World War II.[72]

In another study at the Walter E. Fernald State School, in 1956, researchers gave mentally disabled children radioactive calcium orally and intravenously. They also injected radioactive chemicals into malnourished babies and then pushed needles through their skulls, into their brains, through their necks, and into their spines to collect cerebrospinal fluid for analysis.[69,75]

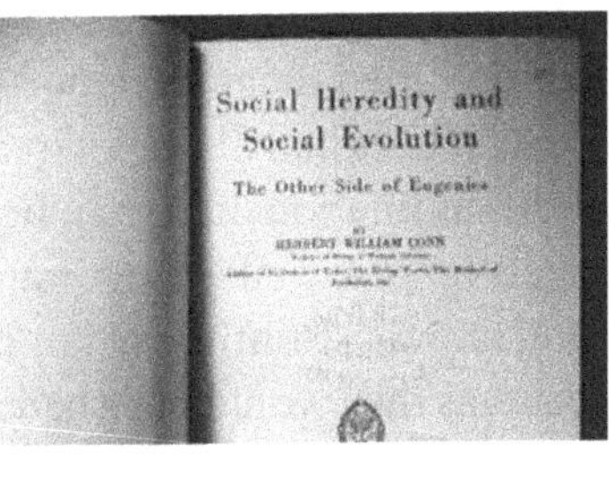
Social Heredity and Social Evolution

The Other Side of Eugenics

In 1961 and 1962, ten Utah State Prison inmates had blood samples taken which were then mixed with radioactive chemicals and reinjected back into their bodies.[76]

In a 1967 study that was published in the Journal of Clinical Investigation, pregnant women were injected with radioactive cortisol to see if it would cross the placental barrier and affect the fetuses.[77]

Fallout Research

In 1954, American scientists conducted fallout exposure research on the citizens of the Marshall Islands after they were inadvertently irradiated[78] by the Castle Bravo nuclear test in Project 4.1. The Bravo test was detonated upwind of Rongelap Atoll and the residents were exposed to serious radiation levels, up to 180 rads (1.8 Gy).

Of the 236 Marshallese exposed, some developed severe radiation sickness and one died, and long term effects included birth defects, "jellyfish" babies, and thyroid problems.[79]

In 1957, atmospheric nuclear explosions in Nevada, which were part of Operation Plumbbob were later determined to have released enough radiation to have caused from 11,000 to 212,000 excess cases of thyroid cancer amongst U.S. citizens who were exposed to fallout from the explosions, leading to between 1,100 and 21,000 deaths.[80]

Early in the Cold War, in studies known as Project Gabriel and Project Sunshine, researchers in the United States, the United Kingdom, and Australia attempted to determine just how much nuclear fallout would be required to make the Earth uninhabitable.[81,82] They realized that atmospheric nuclear testing had provided them an opportunity to investigate this.

Such tests had dispersed radioactive contamination worldwide, and examination of human bodies could reveal how readily it was taken up and hence how much damage it caused. Of particular interest was strontium-90 in the bones. Infants were the primary focus, as they would have had a full opportunity to absorb the new contaminants.[83]

As a result of this conclusion, researchers began a program to collect human bodies and bones from all over the world, with a particular focus on infants. The bones were cremated and the ashes analyzed for radioisotopes. This project was kept secret primarily because it would be a public relations disaster; as a result parents and family were not told what was being done with the body parts of their relatives.[84]

Irradiation Experiments

Between 1960 and 1971, the Department of Defense funded non-consensual whole body radiation experiments on poor, black cancer patients, who were not told what was being done to them.

Patients were told that they were receiving a "treatment" that might cure their cancer, but in reality the Pentagon was attempting to determine the effects of high levels of radiation on the human body.

One of the doctors involved in the experiments, Robert Stone, was worried about litigation by the patients, so he only referred to them by their initials on the medical reports. He did this so that, in his words, "there will be no means by which the patients can ever connect themselves up with the report", in order to prevent "either adverse publicity or litigation".[85]

From 1960 to 1971, Dr. Eugene Saenger, funded by the Defense Atomic Support Agency, performed whole body radiation experiments on more than 90 poor, black, cancer patients with inoperable tumors at the University of Cincinnati Medical Center.

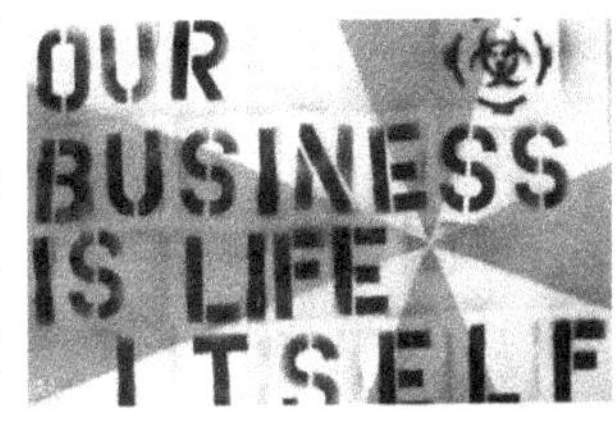

He forged consent forms, and did not inform them of the risks of irradiation. The patients were given 100 or more rads (1 Gy) of whole-body radiation, which in many caused intense pain and vomiting. Critics have questioned the medical rationale for this study, and contend that the main purpose of the research was to study the acute effects of radiation exposure.[86,87]

From 1963 to 1973, a leading endocrinologist, Dr. Carl Heller, irradiated the testicles of Oregon and Washington prisoners. In

Unfortunately, our modern materialistic civilization is filled with so-called leaders who are devoid of spiritual knowledge and who refuse to take guidance from genuine spiritual authorities. Such leaders are blind in the truest sense, and therefore both they and their blind followers waste their time in a hopeless, meaningless struggle to be happy by gratifying the senses of the temporary material body. In defiance of God's laws for spiritual life in harmony with the laws of nature, such leaders encourage all sorts of sinful activities, such as gambling, intoxication, meat eating, and illicit sex. As a result they make civilization hellish, and in their next lives both they and their followers are thrown into hellish planets. Such leaders should certainly be known as demons.

~ Srila Prabhupada

return for their participation, he gave them $5 a month, and $100 when they had to receive a vasectomy upon conclusion of the trial.

The surgeon who sterilized the men said that it was necessary to "keep from contaminating the general population with radiation-induced mutants". One of the researchers who had worked with Heller on the experiments, Dr. Joseph Hamilton, said that the experiments "had a little of the Buchenwald touch".[88]

In 1963, University of Washington researchers irradiated the testes of 232 prisoners to determine the effects of radiation on testicular function. When these inmates later left prison and had children, at least four of them had offspring born with birth defects.

The exact number is unknown because researchers never followed up on the status of the subjects.[89]

Chemical Experiments

From 1942 to 1944, the U.S. Chemical Warfare Service conducted experiments which exposed thousands of U.S. military personnel to mustard gas, in order to test the effectiveness of gas masks and protective clothing.[90,91,92,93]

From 1950 through 1953, the U.S. Army sprayed toxic chemicals over six cities in the United States and Canada, in order to test dispersal patterns of chemical weapons. Army records stated that the chemicals which were sprayed on the city of Winnipeg, Canada, included zinc cadmium sulfide.[94]

To test whether or not sulfuric acid, which is used in making molasses, was harmful as a food additive, the Louisiana State Board of Health commissioned a study to feed "Negro prisoners" nothing but molasses for five weeks. One report stated that prisoners didn't "object to submitting themselves to the test, because it would not do any good if they did".[12]

A 1953 article in the medical/scientific journal Clinical Science[95] described a medical experiment in which researchers intentionally blistered the skin on the abdomens of 41 children, who ranged in age from 8 to 14, using cantharide. The study was performed to determine how severely the substance injures/irritates the skin of children. After the studies, the children's blistered skin was removed with scissors and swabbed with peroxide.[77]

Dermatological Research

From approximately 1951 to 1974, the Holmesburg Prison in Pennsylvania was the site of extensive dermatological research operations, using prisoners as subjects. Led by Dr. Albert M. Kligman of the University of Pennsylvania, the studies were performed on behalf of Dow Chemical Company, the U.S. Army, and Johnson & Johnson.[96,97,98]

In one of the studies, for which Dow Chemical paid Kligman $10,000, Kligman injected dioxin — a highly toxic, carcinogenic compound found in Agent Orange, which Dow was manufacturing for use in Vietnam at the time — into 70 prisoners (most of them black).

The prisoners developed severe lesions which went untreated for seven months.[10] Dow Chemical wanted to study the health effects of dioxin and other herbicides, and how they affect human skin, because workers at their chemical plants were developing chloracne.

In the study, Kligman applied roughly the amount of dioxin Dow employees were being exposed to. In 1980 and 1981, some of the people who were used in this study sued Professor Kligman for a variety of health problems, including lupus and psychological damage.[99]

Kligman later continued his dioxin studies, increasing the dosage of dioxin he applied to 10 prisoners' skin to 7,500 micrograms of dioxin, which is 468 times the dosage that the Dow Chemical official Gerald K. Rowe had authorized him to administer. As a result, the prisoners developed inflammatory pustules and papules.[99]

The Holmesburg program also paid hundreds of inmates a nominal stipend to test a wide range of cosmetic products and

> *If because of excessive greed for one's own pleasure one commits violence against living beings. He is also attacking Lord Sri Hari, who is present in the bodies of all living entities as the Supersoul.*
> *~ Srila Prabhupada (Srimad Bhagavatam 11.5 Summary)*

chemical compounds, whose health effects were unknown at the time.[100,101]

Upon his arrival at Holmesberg, Kligman is claimed to have said "All I saw before me were acres of skin ... It was like a farmer seeing a fertile field for the first time".[102] It was reported in a 1964 issue of Medical News that 9 out of 10 prisoners at Holmesburg Prison were medical test subjects.[103]

In 1967, the U.S. Army paid Kligman to apply skin-blistering chemicals to the faces and backs of inmates at Holmesburg to, in Kligman's words, "learn how the skin protects itself against chronic assault from toxic chemicals, the so-called hardening process."[99]

Psychological And Torture Experiments

The United States government funded and performed numerous psychological experiments, especially during the Cold War era. Many of these experiments were performed to help develop more effective torture and interrogation techniques for the U.S. military and intelligence agencies, and to develop techniques for resisting torture at the hands of enemy nations and organizations.

In studies running from 1947 to 1953, which were known as Project Chatter, the U.S. Navy began identifying and testing truth serums, which they hoped could be used during interrogations of Soviet spies. Some of the chemicals tested on human subjects included mescaline and the anticholinergic drug scopolamine.[104]

Shortly thereafter, in 1950, the CIA initiated Project Bluebird, later renamed Project Artichoke, whose stated purpose was to develop "the means to control individuals through special interrogation techniques", "ways to prevent the extraction of information from CIA agents", and "offensive uses of unconventional techniques, such as hypnosis and drugs".[104,105,106]

The purpose of the project was outlined in a memo dated January 1952 that stated, "Can we get control of an individual to

> *... it was fun, fun, fun. Where else could a red-blooded American boy lie, kill, cheat, steal, rape and pillage with the sanction and bidding of the All-highest?*
>
> *~George Hunter White, who oversaw drug experiments for the CIA as part of Operation Midnight Climax*[120]

the point where he will do our bidding against his will and even against fundamental laws of nature, such as self preservation?" The project studied the use of hypnosis, forced morphine addiction and subsequent forced withdrawal, and the use of other chemicals, among other methods, to produce amnesia and other vulnerable states in subjects.[107,108,109,110,111]

Project Bluebird

In order to "perfect techniques for the abstraction of information from individuals, whether willing or not", Project Bluebird researchers experimented with a wide variety of psychoactive substances, including LSD, heroin, marijuana, cocaine, PCP, mescaline, and ether.[112]

Project Bluebird researchers dosed over 7,000 U.S. military personnel with LSD, without their knowledge or consent, at the Edgewood Arsenal in Maryland. More than 1,000 of these soldiers suffered from several psychiatric illnesses, including depression and epilepsy. Many of them committed or tried to commit suicide.[113]

In 1952, professional tennis player Harold Blauer died when injected with a fatal dose of a mescaline derivative at the New York State Psychiatric Institute of Columbia University, by Dr. James Cattell.

The United States Department of Defense, which sponsored the injection, worked in collusion with the Department of Justice, and the New York State Attorney General to conceal evidence of its involvement for 23 years. Cattell claimed that he did not know what the army had given him to inject into Blauer, saying: "We didn't know whether it was dog piss or what we were giving him."[114,115]

In 1953, the CIA placed several of its interrogation and mind-control programs under the direction of a single program, known by the code name MKULTRA, after CIA director Allen Dulles

The frequent screams of the patients that echoed through the hospital did not deter Cameron or most of his associates in their attempts to depattern their subjects completely

~John D. Marks, The Search for the Manchurian Candidate, Chapter-8[124]

complained about not having enough "human guinea pigs to try these extraordinary techniques".[116]

The MKULTRA project was under the direct command of Dr. Sidney Gottlieb of the Technical Services Division.[116] The project received over $25 million, and involved hundreds of experiments on human subjects at eighty different institutions.

In a memo describing the purpose of one MKULTRA program subprogram, Richard Helms said:

> We intend to investigate the development of a chemical material which causes a reversible, nontoxic aberrant mental state, the specific nature of which can be reasonably well predicted for each individual. This material could potentially aid in discrediting individuals, eliciting information, and implanting suggestions and other forms of mental control.
>
> —Richard Helms, internal CIA memo117

In 1954, the CIA's Project QKHILLTOP was created to study Chinese brainwashing techniques, and to develop effective methods of interrogation. Most of the early studies are believed to have been performed by the Cornell University Medical School's

The Bhagavad-gita explains:

pravrttim ca nivrttim ca
jana na vidur asurah
na saucam napi cacaro
na satyam tesu vidyate

"Those who are demonic do not know what is to be done and what is not to be done. Neither cleanliness nor proper behavior nor truth is found in them" (Bhagavad-gita 16.7).

Because demons do not know what to do and what not to do, they become involved in unclean dealings. For example, the highest elected official in the world's most influential country was recently implicated in all sorts of dirty dealings intended to increase his own wealth and power. And even after his dirty tricks were brought to light, he refused to admit the truth. As clearly indicated in the Bhagavad-gita, these are classic symptoms of a demonic personality. As long as such demons falsely occupy responsible government posts, the people in general will not be peaceful, prosperous, or happy.

~ Srila Prabhupada

human ecology study programs, under the direction of Dr. Harold Wolff.[104,118,119]

Wolff requested that the CIA provide him any information they could find regarding "threats, coercion, imprisonment, deprivation, humiliation, torture, 'brainwashing', 'black psychiatry', and hypnosis, or any combination of these, with or without chemical agents". According to Wolff, the research team would then:

> ...assemble, collate, analyze and assimilate this information and will then undertake experimental investigations designed to develop new techniques of offensive/defensive intelligence use ... Potentially useful secret drugs (and various brain damaging procedures) will be similarly tested in order to ascertain the fundamental effect upon human brain function and upon the subject's mood ... Where any of the studies involve potential harm of the subject, we expect the Agency to make available suitable subjects and a proper place for the performance of the necessary experiments.
>
> —Dr. Harold Wolff, Cornell University Medical School[119]

Operation Midnight Climax

Another of the MKULTRA subprojects, Operation Midnight Climax, consisted of a web of CIA-run safehouses in San Francisco, Marin, and New York which were established in order to study the effects of LSD on unconsenting individuals.

Prostitutes on the CIA payroll were instructed to lure clients back to the safehouses, where they were surreptitiously plied with a wide range of substances, including LSD, and monitored behind one-way glass. Several significant operational techniques were developed in this theater, including extensive research into sexual blackmail, surveillance technology, and the possible use of mind-altering drugs in field operations.[120]

In 1957, with funding from a CIA front organization, Dr. Ewan Cameron of the Allan Memorial Institute in Montreal, Canada began MKULTRA Subproject 68.[121]

His experiments were designed to first "depattern" individuals, erasing their minds and memories—reducing them to the mental level of an infant—and then to "rebuild" their personality in a manner of his choosing.[122]

To achieve this, Cameron placed patients under his "care" into drug-induced comas for up to 88 days, and applied numerous high voltage electric shocks to them over the course of weeks or months, often administering up to 360 shocks per person.

He would then perform what he called "psychic driving" experiments on the subjects, where he would repetitively play recorded statements, such as "You are a good wife and mother and people enjoy your company", through speakers he had implanted into blacked-out football helmets that he bound to the heads of the test subjects (for sensory deprivation purposes). The patients could do nothing but listen to these messages, played for 16–20 hours a day, for weeks at a time.

In one case, Cameron forced a person to listen to a message non-stop for 101 days.[122] Using CIA funding, Cameron converted the horse stables behind Allen Memorial into an elaborate isolation and sensory deprivation chamber which he kept patients locked in for weeks at a time.[122]

Cameron also induced insulin comas in his subjects by giving them large injections of insulin, twice a day for up to two months at a time.[104] Several of the children who Cameron experimented on were sexually abused, often by several men. One of the children was filmed numerous times performing sexual acts with high-ranking federal government officials, in a scheme set up by Cameron and other MKULTRA researchers, to blackmail the officials to ensure further funding for the experiments.[123]

The CIA leadership had serious concerns about their unethical and illegal behavior, as evidenced in a 1957 Inspector General Report, which stated:

> Precautions must be taken not only to protect operations from exposure to enemy forces but also to conceal these activities from the American public in general. The knowledge that the agency is engaging in unethical and illicit activities would have serious repercussions in political and diplomatic circles ...
>
> —1957 CIA Inspector General Report[125]

The Tulane Electrical Brain Stimulation Program.

Starting in the early 1950s, Dr. Robert Heath of Tulane University performed experiments on various mentally ill patients, most of whom had schizophrenia. The experiments were funded by the U.S. Army.

The program implanted electrodes deep into the patients brains to electrically stimulate and take recordings. In addition to the deep brain electrodes, cannulas were surgically placed to allow injections, a direct chemical stimulation of the brain. In some of the studies, he dosed the patients with LSD, mescaline, acetylcholine, and/or norepinephrine. In the early 1970s the Tulane program began to be criticized when homosexuality was no longer considered a mental illness.[126,127]

MKULTRA activities continued until 1973 when CIA director Richard Helms, fearing that they would be exposed to the public, ordered the project terminated, and all of the files destroyed.[116]

However, a clerical error had sent many of the documents to the wrong office, so when CIA workers were destroying the files, some of them remained, and were later released under a Freedom of Information Act request by investigative journalist John Marks.

Many people in the American public were outraged when they learned of the experiments, and several congressional investigations took place including the Church Committee and the Rockefeller Commission.

On April 26, 1976, the Church Committee of the United States Senate issued a report, "Final Report of the Select Committee to Study Governmental Operation with Respect to Intelligence Activities".[128]

In Book I, Chapter XVII, p 389 this report states:

> LSD was one the materials tested in the MKULTRA program. The final phase of LSD testing involved surreptitious administration to unwitting non-volunteer subjects in normal life settings by undercover officers of the Bureau of Narcotics acting for the CIA.
>
> A special procedure, designated MKDELTA, was established to govern the use of MKULTRA materials abroad. Such materials were used on a number of occasions. Because MKULTRA records were destroyed, it is impossible to reconstruct the operational use of MKULTRA materials by the CIA overseas; it has been determined that the use of these materials abroad began in 1953, and possibly as early as 1950.[107,129,130,131,132]

> Drugs were used primarily as an aid to interrogations, but MKULTRA/MKDELTA materials were also used for harassment, discrediting, or disabling purposes. [107,129,130,131,132]

In 1963, CIA had synthesized many of the findings from its psychological research into what became known as the KUBARK Counterintelligence Interrogation handbook,[133] which cited the MKULTRA studies and other secret research programs as the scientific basis for their interrogation methods.[122]

Cameron regularly traveled around the U.S. teaching military personnel about his techniques (hooding of prisoners for sensory deprivation, prolonged isolation, humiliation, etc.), and how they could be used in interrogations.

Latin American paramilitary groups working for the CIA and U.S. military received training in these psychological techniques at places like the School of the Americas, and even today, many of the torture techniques developed in the MKULTRA studies and other programs are being used at U.S. military and CIA prisons such as Guantanamo Bay and Abu Ghraib.[122,134]

In the aftermath of the Congressional hearings, major news media mainly focused on sensationalistic stories related to LSD, "mind-control", and "brainwashing", and rarely used the word "torture". This propagated the image that CIA researchers were, as one author put it "a bunch of bumbling sci-fi buffoons", rather than a rational group of men who had run torture laboratories and medical experiments in major U.S. universities, and who had tortured, raped, and psychologically abused young children, driving many of them permanently insane.[122]

From 1964 to 1968, the U.S. Army paid $386,486 to professors Albert Kligman and Herbert W. Copelan to perform experiments with mind-altering drugs on 320 inmates of Holmesburg Prison. The goal of the study was to determine the minimum effective dose of each drug needed to disable 50 percent of any given population. Kligman and Copelan initially claimed that they were unaware of any long-term health effects the drugs could have on prisoners, however, documents later revealed that this was not the case.[99]

Medical professionals gathered and collected data on the CIA's use of torture techniques on detainees, in order to refine those techniques, and "to provide legal cover for torture, as well as to help justify and shape future procedures and policies", according to a report by Physicians for Human Rights.

The report stated that: "Research and medical experimentation on detainees was used to measure the effects of large-volume waterboarding and adjust the procedure according to the results." As a result of the waterboarding experiments, doctors recommended adding saline to the water "to prevent putting detainees in a coma or killing them through over-ingestion of large amounts of plain water."

Sleep deprivation tests were performed on over a dozen prisoners, in 48-, 96- and 180-hour increments. Doctors also collected data intended to help them judge the emotional and physical impact of the techniques so as to "calibrate the level of pain

Cleanliness and truthfulness are basic principles of proper behavior. Unless one is clean and truthful, how can he qualify as a political, religious, or intellectual leader? And this purity must be more than just skin deep. Anyone who bathes regularly with soap and water may be considered superficially clean, but one must also be clean within. In other words, one's heart must be free from the dirt of lust, greed, envy, false pride, anger, and so on. Because of these material contaminations, one thinks that his body is his self and that temporary material possessions and arrangements for bodily comfort will actually satisfy him. This spiritual blindness disqualifies one for leadership of any kind.

To cleanse the heart of all misconceptions, the Vedic authorities recommend that one chant the holy names of the Supreme Personality of Godhead, especially as found in the maha-mantra -- Hare Krsna, Hare Krsna, Krsna Krsna, Hare Hare/ Hare Rama, Hare Rama, Rama Rama, Hare Hare. Also, one should live in accordance with Lord Krsna's instructions in the Bhagavad-gita. Krsna, the Supreme Personality of Godhead, is the Absolute Truth, and therefore one who follows His instructions is truthful in the deepest sense. Thus, by avoiding the four great sins (meat eating, illicit sex, intoxication, and gambling), by chanting God's names, and by following the Bhagavad-gita's instructions, a God conscious leader can fulfill his responsibility to the general mass of people, who are his wards.

~ Srila Prabhupada

experienced by detainees during interrogation" and to determine if using certain types of techniques would increase a subject's "susceptibility to severe pain.". The CIA denied the allegations, claiming they never performed any experiments, and saying "The report is just wrong"; however, the U.S. government never investigated the claims.[135,136,137,138,139,140]

In August 2010, the U.S. weapons manufacturer Raytheon announced that it had partnered with a jail in Castaic, California in order to use prisoners as test subjects for a new non-lethal weapon system that "fires an invisible heat beam capable of causing unbearable pain."[141]

Academic Research

In 1939, at the Iowa Soldiers' Orphans' Home in Davenport, Iowa, twenty-two children were the subjects of the so-called "monster" experiment. This experiment attempted to use psychological abuse to induce stuttering in children who spoke normally. The experiment was designed by Dr. Wendell Johnson, one of the nation's most prominent speech pathologists, for the purpose of testing one of his theories on the cause of stuttering.[142]

In 1961, in response to the Nuremberg Trials, the Yale psychologist Stanley Milgram performed his "Obedience to Authority Study", also known as the Milgram Experiment, in order to determine if it was possible that the Nazi genocide could have resulted from millions of people who were "just following orders".

The Milgram Experiment raised questions about the ethics of scientific experimentation because of the extreme emotional stress suffered by the participants, who were told, as part of the experiment, to apply electric shocks to test subjects.

Pharmacological Research

At Harvard University, in the late 1940s, researchers began performing experiments where they tested diethylstilbestrol, a synthetic estrogen, on pregnant women at the Lying-In Hospital of the University of Chicago. The women experienced an abnormally high number of miscarriages and babies with low birth weight. None of the women were told that they were being experimented on.[143]

In 1962, researchers at the Laurel Children's Center in Maryland tested experimental acne medications on children, and continued their tests even after half of the children developed severe liver damage from the medications.[77]

From 1988 to 2008, the number of overseas clinical trials for drugs intended for American consumption increased by 2,000%, to approximately 6,500 trials. These trials are often conducted in areas with large numbers of poor and illiterate people who grant their consent by signing an "X" or making a thumb print on a form.

These tests are rarely monitored by the FDA, and have in some cases proved deadly, such as a case where 49 babies died in New Delhi, India during a 30-month trial. The cost of testing in countries without safety regulations is much lower; and, due to lax or nonexistent oversight, pharmaceutical corporations (or research companies they've contracted out to) are able to more easily suppress research that demonstrates harmful effects and only report positive results.[144,145]

In May 2004, a young man named Dan Markingson committed suicide in a controversial AstraZeneca-funded study of atypical antipsychotics conducted by the University of Minnesota Department of Psychiatry. Markingson had been recruited into the study while acutely psychotic after he had been placed under an involuntary commitment order, the terms of which instructed him to obey the treatment orders of his psychiatrist.

His mother, Mary Weiss, had objected to his recruitment into the study and attempted for months to have him released, warning

6. [redacted] - (W) - Resident Buncombe County

Proceedings instituted by George H. Lawrence, SPW

Medical history by H. C. Whems, M. D.

Sterilization recommended by Dr. Whems

Social history:
Married woman, [redacted] years of age, who is the mother of 3 children ranging in ages from [redacted] to [redacted] years. On a psychological examination given by Dorothy Hamilton she was found to have an I. Q. of 56. The family has been financially dependent for many years and there is a history of inter-marriage with Indian and Negro.

Diagnosis: Feeblemindedness

Operation will be performed by surgeon on staff of Biltmore Hospital at time of delivery.

Consents: Consent is signed by [redacted], patient, and by [redacted], husband.

that his condition was deteriorating and that he was in danger of committing suicide.[146]

In 2010 a group of University of Minnesota faculty members wrote a public letter to the Board of Regents requesting an investigation of Markingson's death. The letter outlined a series of ethical violations, including financial conflicts of interest on the part of the researchers, the inability of Markingson to give informed consent, improper financial incentives for enrolling subjects, and the questionable scientific value of the study.[147] University of Minnesota officials have denied any wrongdoing.

Other Experiments

The 1846 journals of Dr. Walter F. Jones of Petersburg, Virginia, describe how he poured boiling water onto the backs of naked slaves afflicted with typhoid pneumonia, at four-hour intervals, because he thought that this might "cure" the disease by "stimulating the capillaries".[148,149,150]

In 1914, Joseph Goldberger restricted prisoner diets to induce pellagra, which he suspected were caused by vitamin deficiencies, not infectious diseases, as was believed at the time. He was nominated for the Nobel Prize for his work.

From early 1940 until 1953, Dr. Lauretta Bender, a highly respected pediatric neuropsychiatrist who practiced at Bellevue Hospital in New York City, performed electroshock experiments on at least 100 children. The children's ages ranged from 3–12 years. Some reports indicate that she may have performed such experiments on more than 200.

Electroconvulsive treatment was used on more than 500 children at Bellevue Hospital from 1942 to 1956, including Bender's experiments, and then at Creedmoor State Hospital Children's Service from 1956 to 1969.

Publicly, Bender claimed that the results of the "therapy" were positive, but in private memos, she expressed frustration over mental health issues caused by the treatments.[151]

Bender would sometimes shock schizophrenic children (some less than 3 years old) twice per day, for 20 consecutive days. Several of the children later became violent and suicidal as a result of the treatments.[152]

At Willowbrook State School for the mentally disabled in Staten Island, NY, a highly controversial medical study was carried out there between 1963 and 1966 by medical researchers Saul Krugman and Robert W. McCollum.

Dr. Saul Krugman injected disabled children with live hepatitis virus in experiments for the U.S. Army. After infecting the children, Krugman would then experiment with developing a vaccine to be used to protect United States military personnel from the chronic and often fatal disease.

In addition, feces were taken from institutionalized children with hepatitis and put it in milkshakes which were then fed to newly admitted children. This, despite the morbidity and mortality of this disease, which causes cirrhosis of the liver more frequently than from excessive consumption of alcohol.

Poor families were often coerced into allowing their children to be included in these "treatments" as a prerequisite for admission into the state school which was the only option for working-class families needing care for a child suffering from mental retardation or other disability.

Staff at Willowbrook, who later quit in disagreement or disgust over the experiments, testified to the pressure put on families and the false reassurances they got from the doctors. When the school was finally closed, the children who once resided there were often refused entry to regular school's programs for Special Needs because they were infected with the hepatitis virus.

Krugman was not only never censured for these abuses, but was awarded the Lasker Prize for Medicine.[3] A public outcry forced the study to be discontinued after it was exposed and condemnend by Senator Robert F. Kennedy.[153] New York Senator Robert Kennedy and a television crew visit Willowbrook State school in Staten Island NY.

"He likens the conditions at Willowbrook to that of a "snake pit," and states that the residents of these institutions were "denied access to education and are deprived of their civil liberties." Later that same year, he addressed a joint session of the NYS Legislature on the "dehumanizing conditions" of the State's institutions. Dr Krugman was appointed head of the Pediatrics Academy in 1972.[154]

In 1942, the Harvard University biochemist Edward Cohn injected 64 Massachusetts prisoners with cow blood, as part of an experiment sponsored by the U.S. Navy.[155,156,157]

In 1950, researchers at the Cleveland City Hospital ran experiments to study changes in cerebral blood flow where they injected people with spinal anesthesia, and inserted needles into their jugular veins and brachial arteries to extract large quantities of blood, and after massive blood loss which caused paralysis and fainting, measured their blood pressure. The experiment was often performed multiple times on the same subject.[77]

In a series of studies which were published in the medical journal Pediatrics, researchers from the University of California Department of Pediatrics performed experiments on 113 newborns ranging in age from 1-hour to 3 days, where they studied changes in blood pressure and blood flow.

In one of the studies, researchers forced a catheter through the babies' umbilical arteries and into their aortas, and then submerged their feet in ice water. In another of the studies, they strapped 50 newborn babies to a circumcision board, and then turned them upside down so that all of their blood rushed into their heads.[77]

From 1963 to 1969 as part of Project Shipboard Hazard and Defense (SHAD), the U.S. Army performed tests which involved spraying several U.S. ships with various biological and chemical warfare agents, while thousands of U.S. military personnel were

The real duty of a government leader is to govern in such a way that everyone has both proper employment and the opportunity to advance spiritually. Without favoring one religious sect over another, the government must nevertheless foster God consciousness as vigorously as possible. That will make for a happy and contented citizenry, free from the degrading activities of meat eating, illicit sex, intoxication, and gambling. Unfortunately, because demonic leaders reject the principles of God consciousness put forth in the revealed scriptures, the world must bear the burden of corrupt governments in which self-interested politicians exploit the populace.

~ Srila Prabhupada (The Blind Leaders)

aboard the ships. The personnel were not notified of the tests, and were not given any protective clothing. Chemicals tested on the U.S. military personnel included the nerve gases VX and Sarin, toxic chemicals such as zinc cadmium sulfide and sulfur dioxide, and a variety of biological agents.[158]

The San Antonio Contraceptive Study was a clinical research study about the side effects of oral contraceptives published in 1971. Women came to a clinic in San Antonio for preventing pregnancies and were not told they were participating in a research study or receiving placebos. Many of the women became pregnant while on placebos.[159,160,161]

In the 2000s (decade), artificial blood was transfused into research subjects across the United States without their consent by Northfield Labs.[162] Later studies showed the artificial blood caused a significant increase in the risk of heart attacks and death.[163]

Legal, Academic And Professional Policy

During the Nuremberg trials, several of the Nazi doctors and scientists who were being tried for their human experiments claimed that the inspiration for their studies had come from studies that they had seen performed in the United States.[10,47]

In 1945, as part of Operation Paperclip, the United States government recruited 1,600 Nazi scientists, many of whom had performed human experimentation in Nazi concentration camps. The scientists were offered immunity from any war crimes they had committed during the course of their work for the Nazi government, in return for doing similar research for the United States government. Many of the Nazi scientists continued their human experimentation when they arrived in the United States.[164]

A secret AEC document dated April 17, 1947, titled Medical Experiments in Humans stated: "It is desired that no document be released which refers to experiments with humans that might have an adverse reaction on public opinion or result in legal suits. Documents covering such fieldwork should be classified Secret."[54]

At the same time, the Public Health Service was instructed to tell citizens downwind from bomb tests that the increases in cancers were due to neurosis, and that women with radiation sickness, hair loss, and burned skin were suffering from "housewife syndrome".[54]

In 1964, the World Medical Association passed the Declaration of Helsinki, a set of ethical principles for the medical community regarding human experimentation.

In 1969, Kentucky Court of Appeals Judge Samuel Steinfeld dissented in Strunk v. Strunk, and made the first judicial suggestion that the Nuremberg Code should be applied to American jurisprudence.

Project MK-ULTRA was first brought to wide public attention in 1975 by the U.S. Congress, through investigations by the Church Committee, and by a presidential commission known as the Rockefeller Commission.[165,166]

In 1987 the United States Supreme Court ruled in United States v. Stanley, that a U.S. serviceman who was given LSD without his consent, as part of military experiments, could not sue the U.S. Army for damages.

Dissenting the verdict in U.S. v. Stanley, Justice Sandra Day O'Connor stated:

> No judicially crafted rule should insulate from liability the involuntary and unknowing human experimentation alleged to have occurred in this case. Indeed, as Justice Brennan observes, the United States played an instrumental role in the criminal prosecution of Nazi scientists who experimented with human subjects during the Second World War, and the standards that the Nuremberg Military Tribunals developed to judge the behavior of the defendants stated that the 'voluntary consent of the human subject is absolutely essential ... to satisfy moral, ethical, and legal concepts.' If this principle is violated, the very least that society can do is to see that the victims are compensated, as best they can be, by the perpetrators.

On January 15, 1994, President Bill Clinton formed the Advisory Committee on Human Radiation Experiments (ACHRE). This committee was created to investigate and report the use of human beings as test subjects in experiments involving the effects of ionizing radiation in federally funded research.

The committee attempted to determine the causes of the experiments, and reasons why the proper oversight did not exist, and made several recommendations to help prevent future occurrences of similar events.167

As of 2007, not a single U.S. government researcher had been prosecuted for human experimentation, and most of the victims of U.S. government experiments have not received compensation, or in many cases, acknowledgment of what was done to them.[168]

Notes

Source: Wikipedia and others.

1. Some defend 'father of gynecology' by Barron H. Lerner, The Tuscaloosa News, October 30, 2003 (Retrieved February 17, 2010)
2. Washington, 2008: pp. 62–63
3. Cina & Perper, 2010: p. 88
4. a b Lederer, 1997: pp. 7–8
5. a b c d Grodin & Glantz, 1994: pp. 7–11
6. a b The Strange Career of Leo Stanley: Remaking Manhood and Medicine at San Quentin State Penitentiary, 1913–1951, Ethan Blue, Pacific Historical Review, May 2009, Vol. 78, No. 2, pp. 210–241, DOI 10.1525/phr.2009.78.2.210
7. Hornblum, 1998: p. 79
8. Lederer, 1997: p. 3
9. Shamoo & Resnick, 2009: pp. 238–239
10. a b c d Germ War: The US Record – Alexander Cockburn, Counterpunch
11. a b Cina & Perper, 2010: p. 89
12. a b Hornblum, 1998: pp. 76–77
13. Roger Cooter (1992). In the Name of the Child. Routledge. pp. 104–105. ISBN 978-0-203-41223-7.
14. Reviews and Notes: History of Medicine: Subjected to Science: Human Experimentation in America before the Second World War, Annals of Internal Medicine, American College of Physicians, July 15, 1995 vol. 123 no. 2 159
15. "Tuskegee Study – Timeline". NCHHSTP. CDC. June 25, 2008. Retrieved 2008-12-04.
16. The Tuskegee Syphilis Experiment Borgna Brunner. Retrieved 2010-03-25
17. Meiklejohn, Gordon N., M.D. "Commission on Influenza." in Histories' of the Commissions Ed. Theodore E. Woodward, M.D., The Armed Forced Epidemiological Board, 1994

18. Halpern, 2006: p. 199

19. Grodin & Glantz, 1994: p. 14

20. Brody, 1998: p. 120

21. Cina & Perper, 2010: p. 94

22. Black WC (February 1942). "The etiology of acute infectious gingivostomatitis (Vincent's stomatitis)". The Journal of Pediatrics 20 (2): 145–60. doi:10.1016/S0022-3476(42)80125-0.

23. George Annas & Michael Grodin, 1995: p. 267

24. Hornblum, 1999: p. 76

25. Rothman, 1992: p.36

26. "U.S. sorry for Guatemala syphilis experiment". CBC News. October 1, 2010.

27. Rob Stein (October 1, 2010). "U.S. apologizes for newly revealed syphilis experiments done in Guatemala". The Washington Post.

28. "US sorry over deliberate sex infections in Guatemala". BBC News. October 1, 2010.

29. Chris McGreal (October 1, 2010). "US says sorry for 'outrageous and abhorrent' Guatemalan syphilis tests". The Guardian (London).

30. Moreno, 2001: pp. 233–234

31. Blum, William (2006). Rogue state: a guide to the world's only superpower. Zed Books. pp. 147–149. ISBN 978-1-84277-827-2.

32. "How the U.S. Government Exposed Thousands of Americans to Lethal Bacteria to Test Biological Warfare", Democracy Now!, July 13, 2005

33. Howard Gordon Wilshire, Jane E. Nielson, Richard W. Hazlett (2008). The American West at risk: science, myths, and politics of land abuse and recovery. Oxford University Press. p. 176. ISBN 978-0-19-514205-1.

34. Tansey, Bernadette (October 31, 2004). "Serratia has dark history in region: Army test in 1950 may have changed microbial ecology". San Francisco Chronicle.

35. Anía BJ (October 1, 2008). "Serratia: Overview". eMedicine. WebMD. Retrieved November 23, 2011.

36. Cole, 1996: p. 17

37. Melnick, Alan L. (2008). Biological, Chemical, and Radiological Terrorism: Emergency Preparedness and Response for the Primary Care Physician. Springer. p. 2. ISBN 978-0-387-47231-7.

38. Hornblum, 1998: p. 91

39. Frederick Adolf Paola, Robert Walker, Lois Lacivita Nixon, ed. (2009). Medical Ethics and Humanities. Jones & Bartlett Publishers. pp. 185–186. ISBN 978-0-7637-6063-2.

40. Hammer Breslow, Lauren. "The Best Pharmaceuticals for Children Act of 2002: The Rise of the Voluntary Incentive Structure and Congressional Refusal to Require Pediatric Testing", Harvard Journal of Legislation, Vol. 40

41. Offit, Paul A. (2007). The Cutter Incident: How America's First Polio Vaccine Led to the Growing Vaccine Crisis. Yale University Press. p. 37. ISBN 978-0-300-12605-1.

42. Goliszek, 2003: p. 228

43. a b c Blum, William (2006). Rogue state: a guide to the world's only superpower. Zed Books. pp. 150–151. ISBN 978-1-84277-827-2.

44. Michael Parenti, The Sword and the Dollar: Imperialism, Revolution, and the Arms Race, St. Martins Press, 1989, pp.74–81, Excerpt available online at:1 (Retrieved February 18, 2010)

45. Biological Warfare and the National Security State: A Chronology, Tom Burghardt

46. Cole, 1996: pp. 28–30

47. a b Loue, 2000: pp. 26–29

48. Moreno, 2001: p. 234

49. Cina & Perper, 2010: p. 95

50. Wheelis, Mark;Rózsa, Lajos; Dando, Malcolm (2006). Deadly cultures: biological weapons since 1945. Harvard University Press. pp. 27–28. ISBN 978-0-674-01699-6.

51. "How the U.S. Government Exposed Thousands of Americans to Lethal Bacteria to Test Biological Warfare". Democracynow.org. 2005-07-13. Retrieved 2012-12-16.

52. a b Loue, 2000: pp. 19–23

53. a b c American nuclear guinea pigs : three decades of radiation experiments on U.S. citizens. United States. Congress. House. of the Committee on Energy and Commerce. Subcommittee on Energy Conservation and Power, published by U.S. Government Printing Office, 1986, Identifier Y 4.En 2/3:99-NN, Electronic Publication Date 2010, at the University of Nevada, Reno, unr.edu

54. a b c d e f Goliszek, 2003: pp. 132–134

55. Goliszek, 2003: pp. 130–131

56. Rebecca Leung. "A Dark Chapter In Medical History". CBS News, February 11, 2009.

57. Atomic Energy Commission's Declassification Review of Reports on Human Experiments and the Public Relations and Legal Liability Consequences, presented as evidence during the 1994 ACHRE hearings.

58. a b Goliszek, 2003: pp. 136–137

59. Moreno, 2001: p. 132

60. LeBaron, Wayne D. (1998). America's nuclear legacy. Nova Publishers. pp. 109–111. ISBN 978-1-56072-556-5.

61. Studies of polonium metabolism in human subjects, Chapter 3 of Biological Studies with Polonium, Radium, and Plutonium, National, Nuclear Energy Series, Volume VI-3, McGraw-Hill, New York, 1950., cited in "American Nuclear Guinea Pigs...", 1986 House Energy and Commerce committee report

62. "The Human Plutonium Injection Experiments" (pdf) by William Moss and Roger Eckhardt, Los Alamos Science, Number 23, 1995. retrieved from fas. org on 2012 9 30

63. Eileen Welsome (1999). The Plutonium Files: America's Secret Medical Experiments in the Cold War. New York: Dial Press. pp. 146–148. ISBN 0-385-31402-7.

64. "Plutonium Files: How the U.S. Secretly Fed Radioactivity to Thousands of Americans", Democracy Now!, May 5, 2004

65. a b LeBaron, Wayne D. (1998). America's nuclear legacy. Nova Publishers. pp. 97–98. ISBN 978-1-56072-556-5.

66. Pacchioli, David, (March 1996) "Subjected to Science", Research/Penn State, Vol. 17, no. 1

67. Goliszek, 2003: p. 139

68. "America's Deep, Dark Secret". CBS News. April 29, 2004. Retrieved February 18, 2010.

69. a b Abhilash R. Vaishnav (1994). The Tech online edition. The Tech.

70. "Transcript – February 15, 1995", Eleventh Meeting, February 19–20, 1995 – Washington D.C., Advisory Committee on Human Radiation Experiments (Retrieved February 19, 2010) – see testimony of Honicker

71. Eckart, 2006: p. 263

72. a b c Cherbonnier, Alice (October 1, 1997) "Nasal Radium Irradiation of Children Has Health Fallout", Baltimore Chronicle and Sentinel (Retrieved February 19, 2010)

73. Danielle Gordon (January 1996). "The Verdict: No harm, no foul". Bulletin of the Atomic Scientists 52 (1).

74. Stewart A. Farber (March 12, 1996). "Nasal Radium Irradiation: Bad Science, Bad Medicine, Bad Ethics". Testimony to U.S. Senate Committee on Governmental Affairs (ACHRE hearings).

75. Goliszek, 2003: p. 253

76. LeBaron, Wayne D. (1998). America's nuclear legacy. Nova Publishers. p. 105.ISBN 978-1-56072-556-5.

77. a b c d e Goliszek, 2003: pp. 223–225

78. "Operation Castle". Operation Castle. Retrieved June 11, 2011.

79. "Nuclear Issues". Rmiembassyus.org. Retrieved 2012-12-16.

80. Institute of Medicine (U.S.). Committee on Thyroid Screening Related to I-131 Exposure, National Research Council (U.S.). Committee on Exposure of the American People to I-131 from the Nevada Atomic Bomb Tests, ed. (1999). Exposure of the American people to Iodine-131 from Nevada nuclear-bomb tests: review of the National Cancer Institute report and public health implications. National Academies Press. pp. 113–114. ISBN 978-0-309-06175-9. – deaths taken from 90% survival rate, applied to # of cases

81. ACHRE Report:New Ethical Questions for Medical Researchers

"In 1949, the AEC undertook Project GABRIEL, a secret effort to study the question of whether the tests could threaten the viability of life on earth. In 1953, Gabriel led to Project Sunshine..."

82. U.S. Department of Energy, "Report on Project Gabriel", July 1954

83. Goncalves, Eddie (June 3, 2001). "Britain snatched babies' bodies for nuclear labs". The Guardian (London).

84. "Dundee University Medical School; PDF" (PDF). Retrieved 2012-12-16.

85. LeBaron, Wayne D. (1998). America's nuclear legacy. Nova Publishers. pp. 99–100. ISBN 978-1-56072-556-5.

86. Thomas H. Maugh II, "Eugene Saenger, 90; physician conducted pivotal studies on effects of radiation exposure", Los Angeles Times, October 6, 2007 (Retrieved February 18, 2010)

87. "Human Experiments". Netti.fi. Retrieved 2012-12-16.

88. Cockburn, Alexander; Jeffrey St. Clair (1998). Whiteout: The CIA, Drugs and the Press. New York: Verso. pp. 157–159. ISBN 1-85984-258-5.

89. Goliszek, 2003: Ch. 4

90. Moreno, 2001: pp. 40–43

91. Freeman, Karen (December 1991). "The Unfought Chemical War". Bulletin of the Atomic Scientists: 30–39.

92. Pechura, Constance M. & Rall, David P., ed. (1993). Veterans at Risk: the health effects of mustard gas and Lewisite. National Academies Press. p. 31. ISBN 978-0-309-04832-3.

93. Cina & Perper, 2010: p. 96

94. Mangold, Tom; Goldberg, Jeff (2000). Plague wars: a true story of biological warfare. Macmillan. p. 37. ISBN 978-0-312-20353-5.

95. B.M. Ansell, F. Antonini, L.E. Glynn: "Cantharides blisters in children with rheumatic fever". Clinical Science, November 1953, 12 (4): 367–373.

96. Hornblum, 1998: p. 216

97. Cina & Perper, 2010: pp. 92–93

98. Washington, 2008: pp. 249–262

99. a b c d Kaye, Jonathan. "Retin-A's Wrinkled Past", Pennsylvania History Review, Spring 1997.

100. Hornblum, 1998: p. 320

101. "Ex-Inmates Sue Penn and Kligman over Research". The Pennsylvania Gazette(The University of Pennsylvania). January/February 2001. Retrieved November 9, 2009.

102. Hornblum, 2007: p. 52

103. Goliszek, 2003: p. 226

104. a b c d Goliszek, 2003: pp. 152–154

105. Michael Evans. "Science, Technology and the CIA". Gwu.edu. Retrieved 2012-12-16.

106. Church Committee; p. 390 "MKULTRA was approved by the DCI Director of Central Intelligence on April 13, 1953"

107. a b c Estabrooks, G.H. "Hypnosis comes of age". Science Digest, 44–50, April 1971

108. Gillmor, D. I Swear by Apollo: Dr. Ewen Cameron and the CIA-Brainwashing Experiments. Montreal: Eden press, 1987.

109. Scheflin, A.W., & Opton, E.M. The Mind manipulators. New York: Paddington Press, 1978.

110. Thomas, G. Journey into Madness: The Secret Story of Secret CIA Mind Control and Medical Abuse. New York: Bantam, 1989 (paperback 1990).

111. Weinstein, H. Psychiatry and the CIA: Victims of Mind Control. Washington, DC: American Psychiatric Press, 1990.

112. Otterman, 2007: p. 23

113. Otterman, 2007: pp. 21–22

114. John S. Friedman, ed. (2005). The secret histories: hidden truths that challenged the past and changed the world. Macmillan. p. 146. ISBN 978-0-312-42517-3.

115. Cole, 1996: pp. 31–32

116. a b c McCoy, 2006: pp. 28–30

117. Goliszek, 2003: p. 155

118. APPENDIX C: Documents Referring To Subprojects – 1977 Senate MKULTRA Hearing (Retrieved February 18, 2010)

119. a b Otterman, 2007: pp. 24–25

120. a b Cockburn, Alexander; Jeffrey St. Clair (1998). Whiteout: The CIA, Drugs and the Press. New York: Verso. pp. 206–209. ISBN 1-85984-258-5.

121. Otterman, 2007: pp. 45–47

122. a b c d e f Naomi Klein (2007). "1". The Shock Doctrine: The Rise of Disaster Capitalism. New York: Metropolitan Books. ISBN 0-8050-7983-1.

123. Goliszek, 2003: pp. 170–171

124. Marks, John D., Chapter 8, The Search for the Manchurian Candidate

125. Otterman, 2007: p. 27

126. Baumeister, Alan A. (2000). "The Tulane Electrical Brain Stimulation Program. A historical Case Study in Medical Ethics". Journal of the History of the Neurosciences 9 (3): 262–278.

127. Mohr, Clarence L.; Joseph E. Gordon (2001). Tulane: the emergence of a modern university, 1945–1980. LSU Press. p. 123. ISBN 978-0-8071-2553-3.

128. "Final report of the Select Committee to Study Governmental Operations with Respect to Intelligence Activities, United States Senate : together with additional, supplemental, and separate views". Archive.org. Retrieved 2012-12-16.

129. a b Gillmor, D. I Swear by Apollo. Dr. Ewen Cameron and the CIA-Brainwashing Experiments. Montreal: Eden press, 1987.

130. a b Scheflin, A.W., & Opton, E.M. The Mind manipulators. New York: Paddington Press, 1978.

131. a b Thomas, G. Journey into Madness. The Secret Story of Secret CIA Mind Control and Medical Abuse. New York: Bantam, 1989 (paperback 1990).

132. a b Weinstein, H. Psychiatry and the CIA: Victims of Mind Control. Washington, DC: American Psychiatric Press, 1990.

133. McCoy, 2006: pp. 50–53

134. U.S. Has a History of Using Torture – Alfred W. McCoy, Z Magazine.

135. Sheldon Richman (June 23, 2010). "Did the CIA Conduct Medical Experiments on Detainees?". Counterpunch.

136. Experiments in Torture: Human Subject Research and Experimentation in the "Enhanced" Interrogation Program, Physicians for Human Rights, June 2010

See also:

*Related Publications

*Outside Academic Experts Respond to Experiments in Torture

*Complaint to Office of Human Research Protections Regarding Evidence of CIA Violations of Common Rule

*Experiments in Torture (video)

137. Experiments in Torture: Medical Group Accuses CIA of Carrying Out Illegal Human Experimentation, Democracy Now!, June 8, 2010

138. Accounting for Torture: Being Faithful to our Values, (video) National Religious Campaign Against Torture (cited by PHR)

139. Risen, James (June 6, 2010). "Medical Ethics Lapses Cited in Interrogations".The New York Times.

140. ICRC Report on the Treatment of Fourteen "High Value Detainees" in CIA Custody, International Committee of the Red Cross, February 14, 2007

141. "California Jail to Test Ray Gun on Prisoners". Democracy Now!. August 23, 2010.

142. Theory improved treatment and understanding of stuttering: Ethics concerns led researchers to conceal the experiment Decades later, the experiment's victims struggle to make sense of their past, Jim Dyer, San Jose Mercury News, Monday, June 11, 2001 (Retrieved February 17, 2010)

143. Loue, 2000: p. 30

144. Deadly Medicine: FDA Fails to Regulate Rapidly Growing Industry of Overseas Drug Testing, Democracy Now!, December 17, 2010

145. Barlett, Donald L. & Steele, James B. (January 2011). "Deadly Medicine". Vanity Fair.

146. Elliott, Carl (September–October 2012). "The Deadly Corruption of Clinical Trials". Mother Jones. Retrieved 2 December 2012.

147. Perry, Susan (December 6, 2010). "Bioethicists ask U of M Regents to appoint outside panel to review ethics of 2004 Dan Markingson case". MinnPost. Retrieved 2 December 2012.

148. Washington, 2008: pp. 60–63

149. Savitt, Todd Lee (2002). Medicine and slavery: the diseases and health care of Blacks in antebellum Virginia. University of Illinois Press. p. 299. ISBN 978-0-252-00874-0.

150. Shamoo & Resnick, 2009: p. 239

151. Albarelli Jr., H.P.; Kaye, Jeffrey S.; "The Hidden Tragedy of the CIA's Experiments on Children", Truthout, Wednesday August 11, 2010

152. Whitaker, Robert (2010). Mad in America: Bad Science, Bad Medicine, and the Enduring Mistreatment of the Mentally Ill. Basic Books. p. 315. ISBN 978-0-465-02014-0.

153. The Bryant Park Project. "Remembering an Infamous New York Institution". NPR. Retrieved 2012-12-16.

154. http://philosophy.tamucc.edu/print/583

155. Cina & Perper, 2010: p. 92

156. Hornblum, 1999: p. 80

157. Dober, Gregory "Cheaper than Chimpanzees: Expanding the Use of Prisoners in Medical Experiments", Prison Legal News, VOL. 19 No. 3, March 2008

158. Blum, William (2006). Rogue state: a guide to the world's only superpower. Zed Books. pp. 152–154. ISBN 978-1-84277-827-2.

159. Goldzieher JW, Moses LE, Averkin E, Scheel C, Taber BZ. A placebo-controlled double-blind crossover investigation of the side effects attributed to oral contraceptives. Fertil Steril. 1971 Sep;22(9):609-23. "PMID4105854"

160. Levine, Robert J. "Ethics and regulation of clinical research, 2nd ed". Yale University Press, 1986, p.71-72. ISBN Special:BookSources/0806711124

161. Veatch RM. "Experimental pregnancy: the ethical complexities of experimentation with oral contraceptives". Hastings Cent Rep. 1971 Jun; (1):2–3. "PMID4137658"

162. Brian Ross (May 23, 2007). "Test of Controversial Artificial Blood Product a Failure". ABC News, "The Blotter".

163. Ed Edelson (April 28, 2008when?). "Experimental Blood Substitutes Unsafe, Study Finds". ABC News.

164. Goliszek, 2003: pp. 108–109

165. Science, Technology, and the CIA, National Security Archive Electronic Briefing Book, Jeffrey T. Richelson, Editor, September 10, 2001 (Retrieved February 18, 2010)

166. "U.S. Senate: Joint Hearing before The Select Committee on Intelligence and The Subcommittee on Health and Scientific Research of the Committee on Human Resources", 95th Cong., 1st Sess. August 3, 1977.

167. "Final report of ACHRE". Eh.doe.gov. Retrieved 2012-12-16.

168. Henry N. Pontell, Gilbert Geis, ed. (2007). International handbook of white-collar and corporate crime. Springer. p. 62. ISBN 978-0-387-34110-1.

86.

U.N.

Complicit in Forced Sterilizations

By Wendy McElroy, December 23, 2002

There is compelling evidence that the United Nations collaborated in the forced sterilization of poor, rural women in countries like Peru.

The controversy revolves around Peru's National Program for Family Planning, which received funding from both the United Nations Population Fund and U.S. Agency for International Development. The Program included a campaign entitled Voluntary Surgical Contraception—that is, sterilization. An estimated 100,000 to 300,000 people, mostly women, were sterilized.

Some Peruvian health workers reportedly received bonuses ranging variously from $4 to $12 U.S. for each woman they "persuaded" to have a tubal ligation. Doctors and hospitals were pressured to meet sterilization quotas. It's not surprising that reports and testimonials of forced sterilizations abound.

Felipa Cusi went to a rural clinic because she was suffering from symptoms of the flu. After being anesthetized, she was sterilized

> *Actually, there is no scarcity of food. Krsna is so kind that he is providing food for everyone (eko bahunam yo vidadhati kaman). He is feeding millions and trillions of living entities. Throughout the world there are billions of birds. Who is feeding them? Krsna is feeding them. So the real problems in the world are not overpopulation or a scarcity of food. The problem is a scarcity of God consciousness. That is why people are suffering.*
>
> ~ *Srila Prabhupada* (Dharma: The Way of Transcendence 2)

without her knowledge. Some women died as a result of such surgery. Magna Morales was kidnapped by health workers and sterilized at a makeshift clinic. Without follow-up medical care, she died 10 days later.

On Jan. 11, 1998, the Miami Herald introduced Magna Morales' story to its readership and accused the Peruvian government, then under President Alberto Fujimori, of forced sterilizations. In February, both the New York Times and the Washington Post ran articles repeating the charges.

That same month, Grover Joseph Rees, Staff Director of the U.S. House of Representatives Subcommittee on International Operations and Human Rights, released a personal account of his visit to Peru. Rees confirmed the presence of forced sterilization.

His report recommended that the U.S. discontinue funding to Peru's family planning programs and disassociate itself from them. Rees went so far as to caution against expressing support of a billboard campaign that encouraged Peruvians to have small families. He worried that such support could be misconstrued as an endorsement of sterilization policies.

Inspite of these reports, the US government continued to fund the UNFPA despite the stories of forced sterilization coming out of Peru and of forced abortions emerging from China.

The U.N. assumed no responsibility for these incidents. A July 26 press release captures the agency's response. It denies all charges and claims that the allegations are "being disseminated through the media by PRI [Population Research Institute], a fringe group that engages in a campaign against UNFPA in pursuit of its ideological opposition to family planning."

The Peruvian parliamentarian and medical doctor, Hector Chavez told a subcommittee investigating the forced sterilizations, "The United Nations was aware of this policy; U.N. personnel worked in the health ministry."

In a June 2002 report entitled "Anticoncepcion Quirurgica Voluntaria" the Peruvian Congress added that, in the early 1990s, "National Population Program established demographic strategies and methods explicitly restrictive and controlling; in this line, the United Nations Population Fund, known for its support of population control in developing countries, took charge. For that end, the United Nations Population Fund acted as Technical Secretary, working in coordination with the National Population Council."

The report concludes that the "UNFPA increased their support and even participation in the task during the government of the ex-president Alberto Fujimori, especially in the period 1995-2000."

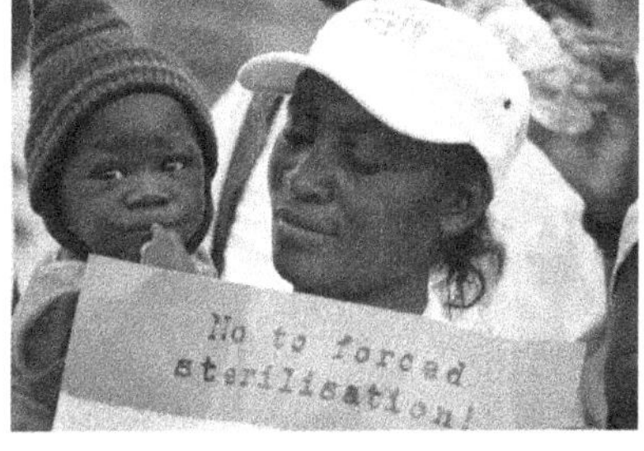

Abubakar Dungus, a spokesperson for the UNFPA, contends that the U.N. did not "learn" of the involuntary sterilization until "late 1997" even though reports of the abuse had been circulating in international and human rights circles long before. Upon hearing of the agonized testimony of brutalized women, the U.N. allegedly expressed "concern" to the Peruvian Ministry of Health. Unlike the U.S., it conducted no public investigation.

In Bhagavad-gita the Lord says that He is the seed-giving father of all living entities (aham bija-pradah pita [Bg. 14.4]), and therefore He is responsible for maintaining them. This is also confirmed in the Vedas. Eko bahunam yo vidadhati kaman: although God is one, He maintains all living entities with their necessities for life. The living entities in different forms are sons of the Lord, and therefore the father, the Supreme Lord, supplies them food according to their different bodies. The small ant is supplied a grain of sugar, and the elephant is supplied tons of food, but everyone is able to eat. Therefore there is no question of overpopulation. Because the father, Krsna, is fully opulent, there is no scarcity of food, and because there is no scarcity, the propaganda of overpopulation is only a myth.
~ Srila Prabhupada (Srimad Bhagavatam 9.20.21)

The Bush administration chose to play safe and backed away from the UNFPA and its controversial policies and withholding $34 million dollars from the agency at the same time. The proximate cause was the administration's concern over U.N. complicity in China's one-child policy, under which women have been forced to abort. Now other nations are coming forward with tales of atrocities committed with the U.N.'s complicity.

Policies of these people are wrong. They are pursuing the sort of bureaucratic control over women's bodies that led to the death of Magna Morales, who was as much as murdered because she

We cannot maintain even a small family, our capacity is so limited. At the present moment especially, in this age, a man does not like to marry because he's unable to maintain even a family, wife and children. He cannot maintain them, even a family consisting of four or five living entities.

But God is the whole family. Eko yo bahunam vidadhati. He's supplying food to the elephants. We are, we are so much advanced in civilization that because we cannot take care of a child, therefore we are killing child even within the womb of mother, abortion. We are so unfit. But God, you see, He's feeding millions of elephants in the Africa. Not only elephants, there are so many. Out of 8,400,000 species of life, there are 8,000,000 species of life nonhuman being, the majority -- the birds, beasts, reptiles, trees, so many other living entities. But they have no business. They have no occupation, profession, to maintain themselves. So who is maintaining them? Who is there? Eko yo bahunam vidadhati kaman. Even if within your room, there is a little hole, sometimes you'll find thousands of ants coming out. Have you got this experience? And who is feeding them? Who is supplying them food? They are living within that hole, millions, and hundreds and thousands of ants, but they're also eating, they're also sleeping, they have got their wife, they have got their children. But who is supplying food? So in this way, if you analyze that everything is being maintained by the Supreme Personality of Godhead, that is real understanding of Krsna consciousness, how Krsna is great, or God is great. So that is a real civilization of life, to understand, to appreciate, to appreciate the greatness of God. That is real civilization. ~ Srila Prabhupada (Lecture, Srimad-Bhagavatam 1.16.21 -- Hawaii, January 17, 1974) wanted to have children. No country should participate in the family planning of other nations.

(Wendy McElroy is a Research Fellow at The Independent Institute, Oakland, California.)

87.

Social Darwinism

Social Darwinism is an ideology of society that seeks to apply biological concepts of Darwinism or of evolutionary theory to sociology and politics, often with the assumption that conflict between groups in society leads to social progress as superior groups outcompete inferior ones.

The name social Darwinism is a modern name given to the various theories of society that emerged in England and the United States in the 1870s, which, it is alleged, sought to apply biological concepts to sociology and politics.[1,2]

The term social Darwinism gained widespread currency when used in 1944 to oppose these earlier concepts. Today, because of the negative connotations of the theory of social Darwinism, especially after the atrocities of the Second World War (including the Holocaust), few people would describe themselves as social Darwinists and the term is generally seen as pejorative.[3]

Social Darwinism is generally understood to use the concepts of struggle for existence and survival of the fittest to justify social policies which make no distinction between those able to support themselves and those unable to support themselves.

Thie ideology has also motivated ideas of eugenics, scientific racism, imperialism,[4] fascism, Nazism and struggle between national or racial groups.[5,6]

Opponents of evolution theory have often maintained that social Darwinism is a logical entailment of a belief in evolutionary theory as it provides a justification for policies of inequality. In The Descent of Man, and Selection in Relation to Sex, Darwin described how medical advances meant that the weaker were able to survive and have families, and as he commented on the effects of this, he cautioned that hard reason should not override sympathy and considered how other factors might reduce the effect:

> Thus the weak members of civilized societies propagate their kind. No one who has attended to the breeding of domestic animals will doubt that this must be highly injurious to the race of man. It is surprising how soon a want of care, or care wrongly directed, leads to the degeneration of a domestic race; but excepting in the case of man himself, hardly any one is so ignorant as to allow his worst animals to breed.
>
> The aid which we feel impelled to give to the helpless is mainly an incidental result of the instinct of sympathy, which was originally acquired as part of the social instincts, but subsequently rendered, in the manner previously indicated, more tender and more widely diffused. Nor could we check our sympathy, even at the urging of hard reason, without deterioration in the noblest part of our nature. The surgeon may harden himself whilst performing an operation, for he knows that he is acting for the good of his patient; but if we were intentionally to neglect the weak and helpless, it could only be for a contingent benefit, with an overwhelming present evil. ... We must therefore bear the undoubtedly bad effects of the weak surviving and propagating their kind; but there appears to be at least one check in

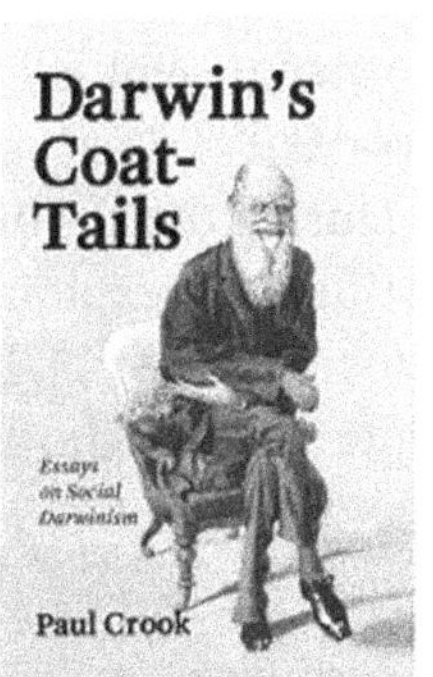

Our father is rich. He's not poor. God is not poor. Sad-aisvarya-purna. Six kinds of opulence fully. So why are you talking of this over-population, scarcity of food? Why? Actually the father is God. He's maintaining. And factually we see how many human beings, civilized human beings, are there. The other living beings are many hundred thousand times bigger quantity. If they can be maintained by God, what we have done, that He'll not maintain us? ~ Srila Prabhupada (Room Conversation with Indian Ambassador -- September 5, 1973, Stockholm)

steady action, namely that the weaker and inferior members of society do not marry so freely; and this check might be indefinitely increased by the weak in body or mind refraining from marriage, though this is more to be hoped for than expected.[19]

Nazism, Eugenics, Fascism, Imperialism

Some followers of the ideology advocated racial and national struggle where the state planned and controlled human breeding through science and eugenics.[37]

Critics have frequently linked evolution, Charles Darwin and social Darwinism with racialism, nationalism, imperialism and eugenics, contending that social Darwinism became one of the pillars of fascism and Nazi ideology, and that the consequences of the application of policies of "survival of the fittest" by Nazi Germany eventually created a very strong backlash against the theory.[38,39]

During the age of New Imperialism, the concepts of evolution justified the exploitation of "lesser breeds without the law" by "superior races."[40] To elitists, strong nations were composed of white people who were successful at expanding their empires,

"The most extreme ideological expression of nationalism and imperialism was Social Darwinism. In the popular mind, the concepts of evolution justified the exploitation of "lesser breeds without the law" by superior races. This language of race and conflict, of superior and inferior people, had wide currency in the Western states. Social Darwinists vigorously advocated the acquisition of empires, saying that strong nations-by definition, those that were successful at expanding industry and empire-would survive and that others would not. To these elitists, all white men were more fit than non-whites to prevail in the struggle for dominance. Even among Europeans, some nations were deemed more fit than others for the competition. Usually, Social Darwinists thought their own nation the best, an attitude that sparked their competitive enthusiasm. In the nineteenth century, in contrast to the seventeenth and eighteenth centuries, Europeans, except for missionaries, rarely adopted the customs or learned the languages of local people. They had little sense that other cultures and other people had merit or deserved respect."

~ From 'Western Civilization: Ideas, Politics, and Society'

and as such, these strong nations would survive in the struggle for dominance.[40] With this attitude, Europeans, except for Christian missionaries, seldom adopted the customs and languages of local people under their empires.[40]

Nazi Germany's justification for its aggression was regularly promoted in Nazi propaganda films depicting scenes such as beetles fighting in a lab setting to demonstrate the principles of "survival of the fittest" as depicted in Alles Leben ist Kampf (English translation: All Life is Struggle).

Hitler often refused to intervene in the promotion of officers and staff members, preferring instead to have them fight amongst themselves to force the "stronger" person to prevail.[43]

The argument that Nazi ideology was strongly influenced by social Darwinist ideas is often found in historical and social science literature.[44]

References

Source: Wikipedia and others.

1. a b c d Riggenbach, Jeff (2011-04-24) The Real William Graham Sumner, Mises Institute

2. Williams, Raymond. 2000. Social Darwinism. in Herbert Spencer's Critical Assessment. John Offer. (ed). pp. 186 -199

3. a b Hodgson 2004, pp. 428–430

4. a b c d Leonard, Thomas C. (2009) Origins of the Myth of Social Darwinism: The Ambiguous Legacy of Richard Hofstadter's Social Darwinism in American Thought Journal of Economic Behavior & Organization 71, p.37–51

5. Gregory Claeys (2000). The "Survival of the Fittest" and the Origins of Social Darwinism. Journal of the History of Ideas 61 (2):223-240.

6. Bowler 2003, pp. 298–299

7. a b "CA002.1: Social Darwinism.". TalkOrigins Archive. 2003-09-26. Retrieved 25 April 2012.

8. Paul, Diane B. 2003. Darwin, Social Darwinism and Eugenics. in The Cambridge companion to Darwin. Cambridge University Press, 2003 ISBN 0-521-77730-5 p.

9. http://www.pbs.org/wgbh/evolution/darwin/nameof/

10. a b Fisher, Joseph (1877). "The History of Landholding in Ireland". Transactions of the Royal Historical Society (London) V: 250., quoted in the Oxford English Dictionary

11. Ward, Lester F (1907). "Social Darwinism". American Journal of Sociology(Chicago) 12: 709–10.

12. Hodgson 2004, pp. 445–446

13. Bannister, 1979; Hodgson, 2004

14. Huxley, T.H. (April 1860). "ART. VIII.- Darwin on the origin of Species". Westminster Review. pp. 541–70. Retrieved 2008-06-19. "What if the orbit of Darwinism should be a little too circular?"

15. Bowler 2003, p. 197

16. a b Fisher 1877, pp. 249–250

17. Hodgson

18. Desmond & Moore 1991, p. 598

19. Darwin 1882, p. 134

20. Spencer, Herbert. 1860. 'The Social Organism', originally published in The Westminster Review. Reprinted in Spencer's (1892) Essays: Scientific, Political and Speculative. London and New York.

21. Barbara Stiegler, Nietzsche et la biologie, PUF, 2001, p.90. ISBN 2-13-050742-5. See, for ex., Genealogy of Morals, III, 13 here 1

22. Friedrich Nietzsche, Human, All Too Human, §224 here 2

23. Scott F Gilbert (2006). "Ernst Haeckel and the Biogenetic Law". Developmental Biology, 8th edition. Sinauer Associates. Retrieved 2008-05-03. "Eventually, the Biogenetic Law had become scientifically untenable."

24. Schmidt, Oscar; J. Fitzgerald (translator) (March 1879). "Science and Socialism".Popular Science Monthly (New York) 14: 577–591. ISSN 0161-7370. "Darwinism is the scientific establishment of inequality"

25. but see:Wells, D. Collin. 1907. "Social Darwinism". American Journal of Sociology. Vol. 12, No. 5, pp. 695-716

26. Descent of Man, chapter 4 ISBN 1-57392-176-9

27. http://www.gutenberg.org/files/18603/18603-h/18603-h.htm

28. "A careful reading of the theories of Sumner and Spencer exonerates them from the century-old charge of social Darwinism in the strict sense of the word. They did not themselves advocate the application of Darwin's theory of natural selection." The Social Meaning of Modern Biology: From Social Darwinism to Sociobiology

29. "At least a part--and sometimes a generous part" of the great fortunes went back to the community through many kinds of philanthropic endeavor, says Robert H. Bremner, American Philanthropy (1988) p. 86 online at Amazon.com

30. "Borrowing from Charles Darwin's theory of evolution, social Darwinists believed that societies, as do organisms evolve over time. Nature then determined that the strong survive and the weak perish. In Jack London's case, he thought that certain favored races were destined for survival, mainly those that could preserve themselves while supplanting others, as in the case of the White race." The philosophy of Jack London

31. Eugenics in Japan: some ironies of modernity, 1883-1945 by Otsubo S, Bartholomew JR. Sci Context. 1998 Autumn-Winter;11(3-4):545-65.

32. http://sitemaker.umich.edu/jennifer.robertson/files/blood_talks__eugenic_modernity_anthro___hist_2002.pdf

33. Jonathan D. Spence. The Search for Modern China." W.W. Norton, 1990, p. 301.

34. Ibid.

35. Ibid., 414-15.

36. McLean, Iain (2009). The Concise Oxford Dictionary of Politics. Oxford University: Oxford University Press. p. 490.ISBN Special:BookSources/9780199 20780|978019920780Category:Articles with invalid ISBNs Check |isbn= value (help).

37. Leonard, Thomas C. (2005) Mistaking Eugenics for Social Darwinism: Why Eugenics is Missing from the History of American Economics History of Political Economy, Vol. 37 supplement: 200-233

38. a b "Hitler & Eugenics". Expelled Exposed. National Center for Science Education. National Center for Science Education. Retrieved 2008-06-09.

39. a b "Senior Fellow Richard Weikart responds to Sander Gliboff". Center for Science and Culture. October 10, 2004. Retrieved 2008-05-17.

40. a b c d Western Civilization: Ideas, Politics, and Society. Houghton Mifflin Harcourt Publishing Company. 2008-10. ISBN 978-0-547-14701-7. Retrieved 2007–03–25.

41. Kropotkin, kniaz' Petr Alekseevich. "Mutual Aid: A Factor of Evolution".

42. Chomsky, Noam (July 8, 2011). "Noam Chomsky - on Darwinism".

43. cf. 1997 BBC documentary: "The Nazis: A Warning from History"

44. E.g. Weingart, P., J. Kroll, and K. Bayertz, Rasse, Blut, und Gene. Geschichte der Eugenik und Rassenhygiene in Deutschland (Frankfurt: Suhrkamp, 1988).

45. Arendt, H.: Elements of Totalitarianism, Harcourt Brace Jovanovich: New York 1951. pp. 178-179

46. Jonathan Sarfati (2002) "Nazis planned to exterminate Christianity" Creation24:3 p27ff.

47. Jonathan Sarfati (1999) "The Holocaust and evolution" Creation 22:1 p4ff.

48. Zimmerman, Andrew Zimmerman (Volume 110, Issue 2, Page 566–567, April 2005). "Richard Weikart. From Darwin to Hitler". The American Historical Review(American Historical Review) 110 (2): 566. doi:10.1086/531468.

49. "Richard Weikart: From Darwin to Hitler". Isis. Volume 96, Issue 4, Page 669–671, December 2005. Retrieved 2007-05-17.

50. "Review: Richard Weikart, From Darwin to Hitler". H-German. September, 2004. Retrieved 2007-05-17.

51. a b "Review: Richard Weikart, From Darwin to Hitler". H-Ideas. June, 2005. Retrieved 2007-05-17.

52. "Book Review of From Darwin to Hitler". The Journal of Modern History. (March 2006): 255–257. Retrieved 2007-05-17.

53. "Creationists for Genocide". Talk Reason. 2007. Retrieved 2007-05-17.

54. Weikart, Richard (2002). ""Evolutionäre Aufklärung"? Zur Geschichte des Monistenbundes". Wissenschaft, Politik und Öffentlichkeit: von der Wiener Moderne bis zur Gegenwart. Wien: WUV-Universitätsverlag. pp. 131–48. ISBN 3-85114-664-6.

88.

Vaccines

Can Help Reduce World Population: Bill Gates

by Mike Adams, Editor, Natural News, October 01, 2010

In a recent TED conference presentation, Microsoft billionaire Bill Gates, who has donated hundreds of millions of dollars to new vaccine efforts, speaks on the issue of CO2 emissions and its effects on climate change. He presents a formula for tracking CO2 emissions as follows: CO2 = P x S x E x C.

P = People

S = Services per person

E = Energy per service

C = CO2 per energy unit

Then he adds that in order to get CO2 to zero, "probably one of these numbers is going to have to get pretty close to zero."

Following that, Bill Gates begins to describe how the first number - P (for People) - might be reduced. He says:

> "The world today has 6.8 billion people... that's headed up to about 9 billion. Now if we do a really great job on new vaccines, health care, reproductive health services, we could lower that by perhaps 10 or 15 percent."

He can be watched saying this at:

http://www.naturalnews.tv/v.asp?v=A155D113455FAC882A3290536575C723

This statement by Bill Gates was not made with any hesitation, stuttering or other indication that it might have been a mistake. It appears to have been a deliberate, calculated part of a well developed and coherent presentation.

So what does it mean when Bill Gates says "if we do a really great job on new vaccines... we could lower [world population] by 10 or 15 percent?"

Clearly, this statement implies that vaccines are a method of population reduction. So is "health care," which all NaturalNews readers already know to be more of a "sick care" system that actually harms more people than it helps.

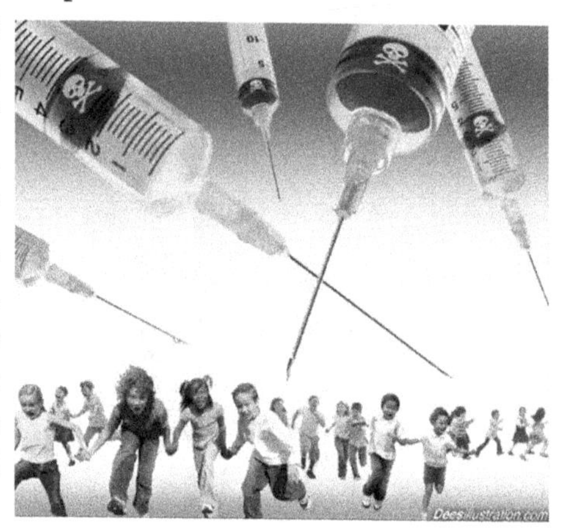

Perhaps that's the whole point of it. Given that vaccines technology help almost no one from a scientific point of view (http://www.naturalnews.com/029641_vaccines_junk_science.html), it raises the question: For what purpose are vaccines being so heavily pushed in the first place?

Bill Gates seems to be saying that one of the primary purposes is to reduce the global population as a mechanism by which we can reduce CO2 emissions. Once again, watch the video yourself to hear him say it in his own words:

http://www.naturalnews.tv/v.asp?v=A155D113455FAC882A3290536575C723

How Can Vaccines Actually Be Used To Reduce World Population?

Let's conduct a mental experiment on this issue. If vaccines are to be used to reduce world population, they obviously need to be

> *Why you have occupied so much land? Others, they are not allowed to enter; where there is overpopulation? How you can expect peace? Just like in China and India and other places they're overpopulation. Why don't you allow them, that "In Africa there is no sufficient population. Please come and toil and grow your food and live peacefully"? Where is that formula? Rascals, they are wanting peace. And why they have become rascal, rogues? For want of God consciousness. They do not know that it is God's property, falsely thinking, "My property."*
>
> *~ Srila Prabhupada (Vedic versus modern...good and bad work...)*

accepted by the majority of the people. Otherwise the population reduction effort wouldn't be very effective.

And in order for them to be accepted by the majority of the people, they obviously can't just kill people outright. If everybody

Formerly, they used to have one hundred sons. Now the fathers have no such power. But in the, up to five thousand years ago, King Dhrtarastra gave birth to one hundred sons. Now we are... We say, we are saying that we are overpopulated. But that's not the fact. At the present moment, where there is the question of overpopulation? Now how many of us giving birth hundreds of children? No. Nobody. But formerly, a father could give birth to one hundred children. So there is no question of overpopulation. And even there is overpopulation, we get information from the Vedas: eko bahunam yo vidadhati kaman. That one chief living entity, God, He can maintain innumerable living entities.

There is no question of overpopulation. This is a false theory. If God can create, He can maintain also. And actually, this is the fact. I am travelling all over the world. There are so much vacant places upon the surface of the globe that, that ten times more than the present population can be easily maintained. But we, we do not know how to use it. In Africa, in Australia, in your America, enough land still lying. But because we have encroached upon the land of Krsna, the difficulty's there. China is overpopulated. India is overpopulated. But we, if we take to Krsna consciousness, these difficulties will be over within a second.

Krsna consciousness means to take everything Krsna's. I am also Krsna's. That is Krsna consciousness. Actually, that is the fact. Everything... Krsna means God. Everything belongs to God. I also belong to God. Isavasyam idam sarvam [Iso mantra 1]. Everything belongs to God. That's a fact. But we do not not accept the fact. We take something illusory. Therefore, it is called maya.

Just like the Americans. They are claiming this land is for the American group. Similarly, other nations, they're... but the land actually belongs to God. The land, the sky, the water, and the products in the land, in the sky, in the water, everything belongs to God. And we are children of God. We have got the right to live at the expense of father. Just like we live, small children. They live at the cost of father. Similarly, we also live by the arrangement of God. Why should we claim that this is our property?

~ Srila Prabhupada (Lecture, Bhagavad-gita 4.13 -- New York, April 8, 1973)

started dropping dead within 24 hours of receiving the flu shot, the danger of vaccines would become obvious rather quickly and the vaccines would be recalled.

Thus, if vaccines are to be used as an effective population reduction effort, there are really only three ways in which they might theoretically be "effective" from the point of view of those who wish to reduce world population:

1) They might kill people slowly in a way that's unnoticeable, taking effect over perhaps 10 - 30 years by accelerating degenerative diseases.

2) They might reduce fertility and therefore dramatically lower birth rates around the world, thereby reducing the world population over successive generations. This "soft kill" method might seem more acceptable to scientists who want to see the world population fall but don't quite have the stomach to outright kill people with conventional medicine. There is already evidence that vaccines may promote miscarriages (http://www.naturalnews.com/027512_vaccines_miscarriage.html).

3) They might increase the death rate from a future pandemic. Theoretically, widespread vaccination efforts could be followed by a deliberate release of a highly virulent flu strain with a high fatality rate. This "bioweapon" approach could kill millions of people whose immune systems have been weakened by previous vaccine injections.

This is a known side effect of some vaccines, by the way. A study documenting this was published in PLoS. Read the story here: http://www.naturalnews.com/028538_seasonal_flu_shot_vaccines.html

Here's the study title and citation:

Viboud C, Simonsen L (2010) Does Seasonal Influenza Vaccination Increase the Risk of Illness with the 2009 A/H1N1 Pandemic Virus? PLoS Med 7(4): e1000259. doi:10.1371/journal.pmed.1000259

It's true, seasonal flu vaccines do cause increased susceptibility to the H1N1 pandemic virus. In other words, seasonal flu vaccines could set up the population for a "hard kill" pandemic that could wipe out a significant portion of the global population (perhaps 10 to 15 percent, as Bill Gates suggested).

Conveniently, their deaths could be blamed on the pandemic, thereby diverting blame from those who were really responsible for the plot. As yet another beneficial side effect for the global population killers, the widespread deaths could be used as a fear tool to urge more people to get vaccinated yet again, and the entire cycle could be repeated until world population was brought down to whatever manageable level was desired... all in the name of health care!

The more people around the world are vaccinated before the release of the "hard kill" pandemic virus, the more powerful the effect of this approach.

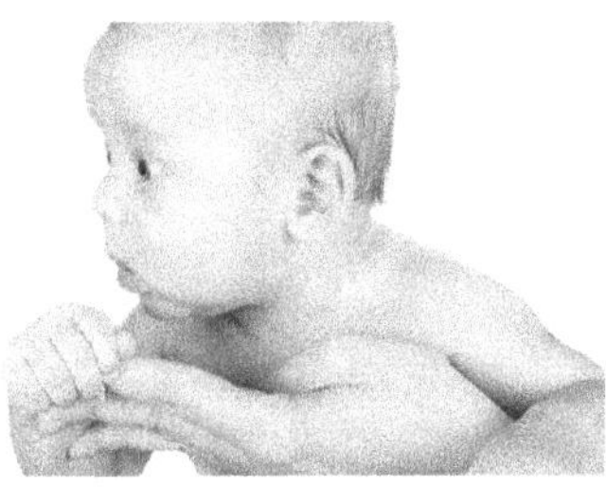

Perhaps not coincidentally, the Bill and Melinda Gates Foundation has funneled hundreds of millions of dollars into vaccine programs targeting people all over the world. One such program is researching the development of "sweat-triggered vaccines" that could use specially-coated nano-materials to deliver vaccines to people without using injections.

More interestingly, his foundation has also invested millions in sterilization technologies that have been called a "temporary castration" solution. (http://www.naturalnews.com/028887_vaccines_Bill_Gates.html)

It seems that the actions of the Gates foundation are entirely consistent with the formula for CO2 reduction that Bill Gates eluded to in his TED conference speech: CO2 = P x S x E x C.

By reducing birth rates (through sterilization technologies) and increasing vaccine penetration throughout the world population (by using sweat-triggered nano-vaccines), his stated goal of reducing the world population by 10 to 15 percent could be reached within just a few years.

Who Will Be Left Alive? The Smart People

The interesting thing about all this is that this campaign to reduce global population through vaccines will obviously not impact people who consciously avoid vaccines. And those people, by and large, tend to be the more intelligent, capable people who actually have an improved ability to move human civilization forward with thoughtful consideration.

I can only imagine that those people designing this vaccine-induced population control measure might be sitting around a table chuckling to themselves and saying, "It's only the stupid people that are going to be killed off anyway, so this is actually helping the future of humankind!" (Their words, not mine.)

In a weird world government kind of way, this effort might actually be based on some distorted vision of philanthropy where some of the most powerful people in the world quite literally believe the way to save humanity is to kill off as many of the gullible people as possible.

Vaccines are, in effect, an "evil genius" kind of way to conduct an IQ test on the population at large: If you go get vaccinated every flu season, you're not too bright and probably don't engage the kind of strong mental faculties that humanity will no doubt need if it is to face a future.

My Guru Maharaja used to say that "I don't find any scarcity within this world, except Krsna consciousness." ... Actually, that is the fact. There is no scarcity all over the world. In India there may be scarcity, but outside India still there are so much vacant places, especially in Africa, in America, in Australia, in New Zealand, that ten times of the population of the whole world can be fed. Still. There is so much potency of producing food grains, milk, and other things. Profusely. In America, they throw away so many grains and vegetables daily. It is simply mismanagement. Otherwise, there is no question of scarcity or poverty. There is no question. It is simply propaganda. Because they cannot manage, the foolish people, they present the population has increased and the foodstuff is not properly supplied. Foodstuff is always sufficient. But when there are demons, the supply is restricted by nature.

-Srila Prabhupada (Srimad-Bhagavatam 1.2.10 -- Vrndavana, October 21, 1972)

If humanity is to save itself from its own destruction, killing off the least intelligent members of society (or making them infertile) may appear to the world controllers to be a perfectly reasonable approach. I disagree with that approach, but it may be precisely what they are thinking.

In any case, choosing to receive a seasonal flu shot is undoubtedly an admission that you have failed some sort of universal IQ test, whether or not this is the intention of world influencers such as Bill Gates. More importantly, it is also a betrayal of your own biology, because it indicates you don't believe in the ability of your own immune system to protect you even from mild infections.

Perhaps the world vaccine conspirators figure that if people are willing to betray themselves anyway, it's not much different for governments and institutions to betray them as well. In other words, if you don't even care enough about your own health, why should any government care about protecting your health, either?

As you ponder this, also consider something else: The U.S. is going broke due to sick-care costs which are rising dramatically under the new federal health care reform guidelines. Can you guess the fastest and easiest way to reduce those health care costs? If you guessed, "unleash a hard-kill pandemic that takes out a significant portion of the weak or sick people" then you guessed right.

Sadly, killing off those most vulnerable to sickness could save the U.S. government literally billions of dollars in sick-care expenditures. Plus, it would save Social Security yet more billions by avoiding ongoing monthly payouts. (Again, I am completely against such an approach because I value human life, but I also know we live in a world where the people in charge have little or no respect for human life and will readily sacrifice human lives to achieve their aims.)

As far as Bill Gates goes, consider his statement in the context of what we've discussed here: "The world today has 6.8 billion people... that's headed up to about 9 billion. Now if we do a really great job on new vaccines, health care, reproductive health services, we could lower that by perhaps 10 or 15 percent."

It suddenly seems to make a lot of sense when you understand that reducing the population reduces CO2 emissions, and using more vaccines on more people increases the death rate of the population.

My advice? Try to avoid being among those 10 to 15 percent who get culled through global vaccine programs. You will not only save your life, you'll also pass the "universal IQ test" which determines whether you're smart enough to know that injecting your body with chemicals and viral fragments in order to stop "seasonal flu" is a foolish endeavor.

Be healthy and wise, and you'll survive the world depopulation effort that victimizes conventional thinkers who don't have the intelligence to question what they're being told to do by their own corrupt governments.

89.

The Population Control Agenda

Stanley K. Monteith, M.D.

One of the most difficult concepts for many of us to accept is that there are human beings dedicated to coercive population control and genocide. Many readers will acknowledge that our government is helping to finance the Red Chinese program of forced abortion, forced sterilization, infanticide, and control of the numbers of live births. Most readers will accept the fact that our nation is helping to finance the United Nations' world-wide "family planning program," a form of population control. Most rational men and women, however, find it impossible to believe that such programs are really part of a "master plan" to kill off large segments of the world's population.

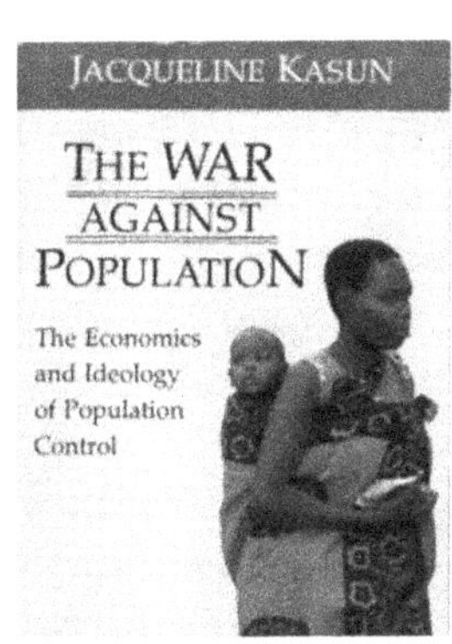

I shall have to admit that I studied the politics of AIDS (HIV disease) for over a decade before I finally came to a horrifying conclusion. The real motivation behind efforts to block utilization of standard public health measures to control further spread of the HIV epidemic was "population control." That was not an easy concept for me to acknowledge, despite the fact that I had long recognized that the twentieth century has been the bloodiest hundred-year period in all recorded human history.

Before you scoff, and reject my suggestion as some sort of madness, check out my references, then try to disprove my conclusions. If my allegations are unfounded, you will soon recognize the deception and return to your daily activities, certain that there is no cause for concern. On the other hand, should you determine that my assessment is correct, or even partially correct, then you have a moral obligation to decide just what part you intend to play in response to the unfolding world genocide - how you will protect yourself, your loved ones, and the countless millions of helpless human beings throughout the world.

You must never forget the warning recorded for posterity by Martin Niemoeller, the Lutheran minister who lived in Hitler's Germany during the 1930s and 1940s. His words echo down to us over succeeding decades:

> "In Germany they came first for the Communists, and I didn't speak up because I wasn't a Communist. Then they came for the Jews, and I didn't speak up because I wasn't a Jew. Then they came for the trade unionists, and I didn't speak up because I wasn't a trade unionist. Then they came for the Catholics, and I didn't speak up because I was a Protestant. Then they came for me, and by that time no one was left to speak up." [2]

The question that I am most frequently asked is, "How can you possibly believe that there are people who intend to kill off

He is the maintainer. You cannot get anything without His mercy. There may be ample supply of necessities of life by the grace of Krsna, and there may be scarcity. So they are now complaining about overpopulation. There is no question of overpopulation. Krsna is quite competent, able to maintain everyone. But as you become godless, as you become disobedient to the laws of God, there will be restriction. You cannot have full supply of necessities of life. That time has already come. All these rascals, godless rascals, they are now suffering.

The only remedy is to become devotee. He is bharta. He can maintain many millions. There is no question of overpopulation. He can maintain. Bharta. But nature will not supply. Nature will restrict supply if you become godless. Therefore nature is very strong, strict. Daivi hy esa gunamayi mama maya duratyaya [Bg. 7.14]. He'll restrict supply.

~ Srila Prabhupada (Lecture, Bhagavad-gita 13.23 -- Bombay, October 22, 1973)

large segments of the world's population?" My answer is really quite simple. I hold that belief because I have read their writings. I believe they are telling the truth. Just as Adolf Hitler wrote of his plans for Europe in "Mein Kampf" (My Plan), so too, those who intend to depopulate large segments of the earth have written of the necessity of limiting the world's population. They fully intend to "exterminate" a significant portion of the world's population.

Margaret Sanger And Planned Parenthood

As you read on you will soon discover that I have primarily relied on material which can be readily found in books, audio-taped interviews, and public news sources. If you take the time to check my references, you will soon discover that there really are those who have publicly advocated the elimination of "human weeds" and "the cleansing of society." Indeed, to this very day your tax money is used to finance Planned Parenthood, an organization founded by Margaret Sanger. During the 1930s Margaret Sanger openly supported the Nazi plan for

nityo nityanam cetanas cetananam
eko bahunam yo vidadhati kaman
(Katha Upanisad 2.2.13)

The one is singular number, nitya, cetana. The others are plural number. So we living entities, we are many, asankhya. There is no limit how many living entities are there. That you have got experience. Even within your room, from a small hole, thousands and thousands of ants may come out. Just imagine. Even within a drop of water there are thousands of microbes. They are all living entities under different condition of life. So living entities are many, but God is one, not God many. God cannot be many. Therefore it is singular number. Nityo nityanam cetanas cetananam (Katha Upanisad 2.2.13). Then what is the distinction between this singular number and plural number? The distinction is also stated, eko bahunam yo vidadhati kaman: "That one single number living entity is supplying all the necessities of these plural number living entities." That is the distinction between God and living entity. ~Srila Prabhupada (Lecture, Srimad-Bhagavatam 1.2.5 -- New Vrindaban, September 4, 1972) genetic engineering of the German population, and the propagation of a "super race."

In Planned Parenthood's 1985 "Annual Report" leaders of that organization proclaimed that they were, "Proud of our past, and planning for our future." [3]

How could anyone possibly claim to be proud of the organization founded by Margaret Sanger when history records that she wrote of the necessity of: "the extermination of 'human weeds' ...the 'cessation of charity,' ... the segregation of 'morons, misfits, and the maladjusted,' and ... the sterilization of 'genetically inferior races."[4]

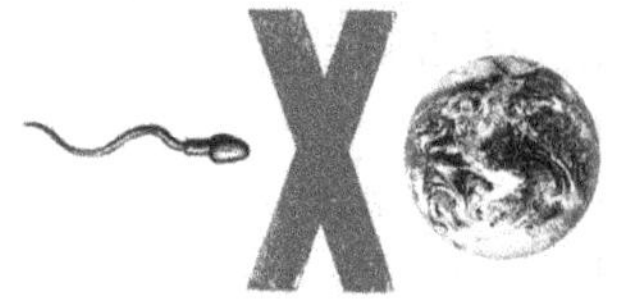

Margaret Sanger published "The Birth Control Review." In that magazine she openly supported the "infanticide program" promoted by Nazi Germany in the 1930s, and publicly championed Adolf Hitler's goal of Aryan white supremacy. In the years prior to World War II Margaret Sanger commissioned Ernst Rudin, a member of the Nazi Party, and director of the dreaded German Medical Experimentation Programs, to serve as an advisor to her organization.

In his excellent book "Killer Angel," George Grant chronicles the life and writings of Margaret Sanger, and painstakingly documents Sanger's plans for the genetic engineering of the human race. George Grant noted that in the 1920s Margaret Sanger wrote "The Pivot of Civilization" in which she called for:

> "The 'elimination of 'human weeds,' for the 'cessation of charity' because it prolonged the lives of the unfit, for the segregation of 'morons, misfits, and the maladjusted,' and for the sterilization of genetically inferior races.'"[5]

According to George Grant, Margaret Sanger believed that the unfit should not be allowed to reproduce. Accordingly, she opened a birth control clinic in "The Brownsville section of New York, an area populated by newly immigrated Slavs, Latins, Italians, and Jews. She targeted the 'unfit' for her crusade to 'save the planet.'" [6]

Nineteen years later, in 1939, Margaret Sanger organized her "Negro project," a program designed to eliminate members of what she believed to be an "inferior race." Margaret Sanger justified her proposal because she believed that: "The masses of Negroes ...particularly in the South, still breed carelessly and disastrously, with the result that the increase among Negroes, even more than among whites, is from that portion of the population least intelligent and fit..." [7]

Margaret Sanger then went on to reveal that she intended to hire three or four Colored Ministers "to travel to various black enclaves to propagandize for birth control." She wrote: "The most successful educational approach to the Negro is through a religious appeal. We do not want word to go out that we want to exterminate the Negro population, and the Minister is the man who can straighten out that idea if it ever occurs to any of their more rebellious members."[8]

As Margaret Sanger's organization grew in power, influence, and acceptance, she began to write of the necessity of targeting religious groups for destruction as well, believing that the "dysgenic races" should include "Fundamentalists and Catholics" in addition to "blacks, Hispanics, (and) American Indians." [9]

How many times have you been told that Adolf Hitler killed 6 million Jews in the Holocaust? What you probably have never been told, however, is the segment of the Holocaust tragedy recorded by Professor Norman Cohn in his historical account of the Jewish Holocaust, "Warrant for Genocide." Professor Cohn chronicled the dark days of World War II, noting:

> Only about a third of the civilians killed by the Nazis and their accomplices were Jews ...Other peoples were marked out for decimation, subjugation, and enslavement, and the civilian losses of some of these countries amounted to 11 per cent to 12 per cent of the total population." [12]

If Professor Cohn's figures are accurate - then why haven't we been allowed to learn the fact that in addition to the 6 million Jews murdered by the Nazis, somewhere between 7 and 12 million non-Jews were also ruthlessly liquidated in Hitler's Germany?

A full discussion on the subjects of population control beyond the scope of this short monograph. At this point let me simply offer a few examples of the views expressed by those who publicly advocate population reduction and/or genocide.

David Graber, a research biologist with the National Park Service, was quoted in the Los Angeles Times Book Review Section, October 22, 1989, as saying:

> "Human happiness and certainly human fecundity are not as important as a wild and healthy planet. I know social scientists who remind me that people are part of nature, but it isn't true ... We have become a plague upon ourselves and upon the Earth ...Until such time as homo sapiens should decide to rejoin nature, some of us can only hope for the right virus to come along." [14]

Michael Fox, when he was the vice-president of The Humane Society of the United States wrote, "Mankind is the most dangerous, destructive, selfish and unethical animal on the earth." [15]

In "The First Global Revolution," published by The Council of the Club of Rome, an international elitist organization, the authors note that: "In searching for a new enemy to unite us, we came up with the idea that pollution, the threat of global warming, water shortages, famine, and the like would fit the bill. All these dangers are caused by human intervention ...The real enemy, then, is humanity itself." [16]

The Los Angeles Times of April 5, 1994 quoted Cornell University Professor David Pimentel, speaking before the American Association for the Advancement of Science, as saying that, "The total world population should be no more than 2 billion rather than the current 5.6 billion."

In the UNESCO Courier (magazine) of November 1991, Jacques Cousteau wrote: "The damage people cause to the planet is a function of demographics - it is equal to the degree of development. One American burdens the earth much more than twenty Bangladeshes ... This is a terrible thing to say. In order to stabilize world population, we must eliminate 350,000 people per day. It is a horrible thing to say, but it's just as bad not to say it."[17]

Bertrand Russell, in his book, "The Impact of Science on Society," wrote:

> "At present the population of the world is increasing ... War so far has had no great effect on this increase ... I do not pretend that birth control is the only way in which population can be kept from increasing. There are others ... If a Black Death could be spread throughout the world once in every generation, survivors could procreate freely without making the world too full ... the state of affairs might be somewhat unpleasant, but what of it? Really high-minded people are indifferent to suffering, especially that of others." [18]

Negative Population Growth Inc. of Teaneck, New Jersey recently circulated a letter stating their long-range goal.

sarva-yonisu kaunteya
murtayah sambhavanti yah
tasam brahma mahad yonir
aham bija-pradah pita
[Bhagavad-gita. 14.4]

God is father, supreme father of everyone. If we simply study this verse from the Bhagavad-gita, that the mother nature is the mother of all living entities and God is the supreme father of everyone... We can study these two lines very carefully. On the earth we can see so many living entities are coming out, beginning from the grass, then so many insects, reptiles, big trees, then animals, birds, beasts, then human beings. They are all coming from the earth, and they are living at the expense of earth. The earth is supplying food to everyone. As the mother gives life or maintains the child by the milk of her breast, similarly, the earth mother is maintaining all different types of living entities. There are 8,400,000 different forms of life, and the earth, mother earth is supplying food. There are thousands of elephants in the African jungle, they are also being supplied with food. And within your room in a hole there are thousands of ants, they are also being supplied food by the mercy of the Supreme Personality of Godhead. So the philosophy is that we should not be disturbed by the so-called theory of over-population. If God can feed elephants, why he cannot feed you? You do not eat like the elephant. So this theory, that there is a shortage of food or overpopulation, we do not accept it. God is so powerful that He can feed everyone without any difficulty. Simply we are mismanaging. Otherwise there is no difficulty.
~ Srila Prabhupada (Lecture, Ratha-yatra -- New York, July 18, 1976)

"We believe that our goal for the United States should be no more than 150 million, our size in 1950. For the world, we believe our goal should be a population of not more than two billion, its size shortly after the turn of the century." [19]

In the Global Assessment Report of UNEP (a United Nations sponsored study group), Phase One Draft, Section 9, the authors quoted an expert who suggested that:

"A reasonable estimate for an industrialized world society at the present North American material standard of living would be 1 billion. At the more frugal European standard of living, 2 to 3 billion would be possible." [20]

More New Age Influence

Speaking at a round-table discussion group at the Gorbachev Conference held in San Francisco in the fall of 1996, Dr. Sam Keen, a New Age writer and philosopher stated that there was strong agreement that religious institutions have to take a primary responsibility for the population explosion. He went on to say that, "We must speak far more clearly about sexuality, contraception, about abortion, about values that control the population, because the ecological crisis, in short, is the population crisis. Cut the population by 90% and there aren't enough people left to do a great deal of ecological damage."

Mr. Keen's remarks were met with applause from the assembled audience made up largely of New Age adherents, Socialists, Internationalists and occultists. Many of the leading occultists of our modern world attended that meeting in San Francisco, a meeting organized by Mikhail Gorbachev, former Director of the Soviet KGB, and later President of Russia. [21]

The Relationship Between Abortion, Breast Carcinoma, and Population Control

Let me offer another example of a population control program which is being promoted here in the United States today. Many physicians have expressed their concern about the dramatic increase in breast carcinoma seen in women in recent years.

Despite the fact that 18 scientific studies published in both domestic and foreign medical journals have clearly demonstrated the direct causal relationship between first-trimester abortion and breast cancer, all efforts to disseminate that information here in the United States have been consistently blocked by those who favor abortion and population control. In the fall of 1996 a new scientific paper dealing with a meta-analysis of 23 different scientific studies on the relationship between first-trimester abortions and breast cancer was published in a British medical journal.

That study clearly demonstrated a higher incidence of breast cancer in women who had had first-trimester abortions. In response to that publication, the American Medical Association (AMA), the American Cancer Society (ACS), and pro-abortion/population-control advocates joined together in an unholy alliance to attack the conclusions of the authors, and to block all efforts to disseminate that information to American physicians.

All of the organizations mentioned above continue to oppose efforts to have physicians warn women of the risk they face when they submit themselves to first-trimester abortions. Before carrying out all surgical procedures in America "advised consent" is required, except for abortion.

The AMA, the ACS, and the pro-death lobby continue to insist that women must not be advised of the risk they incur when they destroy the life of their unborn child. Why is there such inconsistency? Current abortion policies in America are absolutely necessary to reduce our population. That is why a minor child can be taken from school to an abortion clinic without parental notification, yet that same child cannot be given an aspirin without parental consent. It all has to do with population control. [28]

There are literally dozens of other examples of population-control programs which have been implemented throughout our world by modern-day "Malthusians" in their effort to ensure that the world population is dramatically curtailed.

To date it is estimated that far more than 1.5 billion human lives have been terminated as a result of the world-wide abortion programs.

In addition, we are beginning to see the devastating effects of the AIDS epidemic as this modern-day plague begins to depopulate large areas of both Asia and Africa. Because of the influence of population controllers, however, all logical efforts to address the HIV epidemic throughout the world continue to be blocked.

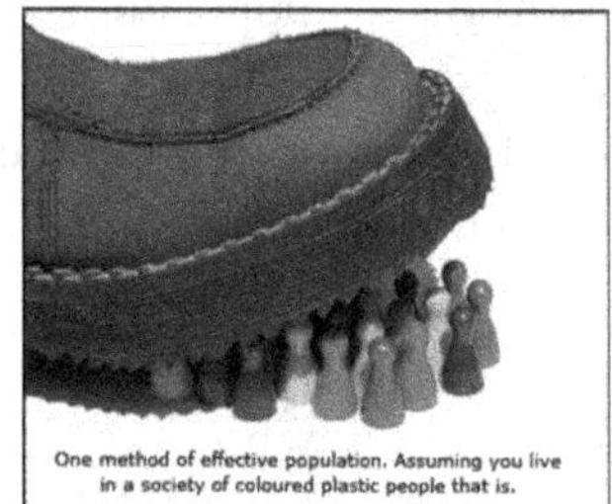

One method of effective population. Assuming you live in a society of coloured plastic people that is.

Rather than utilizing the proven public health methods used with all other illnesses, advocates of population control continue to promote both hedonistic sex education and condom distribution.

I will conclude this monograph by quoting from the writings of the English Churchman, Thomas Robert Malthus (1766-1834). In his "An Essay on the Principle of Population," Malthus wrote:

> "All children born, beyond what would be required to keep up the population to a desired level, must necessarily perish, unless room may be made for them by the deaths of grown persons ...Therefore ...we should facilitate, instead of foolishly and vainly endeavoring to impede, the operations of nature in producing this mortality..." [32]

References:

1) The Population Controllers: New American Magazine: May 21, 1993

2) Bartlett's Familiar Quotations: Fifteenth Edition: Little, Brown, and Company: p. 824.

3) Killer Angel: George Grant: Reformer Press: p 105: available from Radio Liberty: P.O. Box 13, Santa Cruz, CA, 95063.

4) ibid: page 65

5) ibid p 65, 71-72, 92: see also Pivot of Civilization: Sanger: New York: Bretano's: pp 101,108,123:

6) Woman's Body, Woman's Right: Linda Gordon: New York: Penguin Press: p 204: see also: Killer Angel: p 64

7) Woman's Body, Woman's Right: p 332: see also Killer Angel: p 73

8) Killer Angel: p 74: see also: Woman's Body, Woman's Right: Linda Gordon: New York: Penguin Press: pp 229-334.

9) Woman's Body, Woman's Right: pp 229-334: see also Killer Angel: p 73

10) Killer Angel: p 104

11) Killer Angel: p 90: see also The Dark Side of Freemasonry: Decker: Huntington House: p 71: equating Satan with the "white deity": see also: The Hidden Dangers of the Rainbow:

Cumbey: Huntington House: available from Radio Liberty.

12) Warrant for Genocide: Cohn: Harper and Rowe: 1966: p 15.

13) Killer Angel: op cited: p 90: see also: Hitler and the New Age: Rosio: Huntington House: Available from Radio Liberty. P.O. Box 13, Santa Cruz, CA, 95063: see also the Radio Liberty interview with Aaron Zellman: see also The Pagan Agenda: tape series available from Radio Liberty: See also The Aquarian Conspiracy by Marylin Ferguson: see also The Hidden Dangers of the Rainbow: Constance Cumbey: available from Radio Liberty.

14) Los Angeles Times: Book Review Section: October 22, 1989: p 9.

15) Animal Rights: A New Species of Egalitarianism: The Intellectual Activist: September 14, 1983: p 3: Also quoted in The War on the West: William Perry Pendley: Henry Regnery: p 15.

16) The First Global Revolution: Club of Rome, Alexander King and Bertrand Schneider, 1991: Pantheon Books, New York, p 115

17) The Population Controllers: New American Magazine: June 27, 1994: p 7.

18) The Impact of Science on Society: Bertrand Russell: 1953: p xv.

19) Material is available from Radio Liberty, P.O. Box 13, Santa Cruz, CA, 95063.

20) The World Conservative Union: Rue Mauverney 28, CH-1196 Gland, Switzerland.

21) Copies of the text of Dr. Keen's remarks are available from Radio Liberty.

22) A copy of the letter quoted from The Lucis Trust is available from Radio Liberty for researchers.

23) Quotation from Yoko Ono was found on the web site: http:www.odysee.net%7Ericjoly/geostone.htlm#francisco. Copies available from Radio Liberty for researchers.

24) AIDS and the Doctors of Death: Aries Rising Press: Los Angeles: pp 168-170.

25) Remembering Silent Spring and its Consequences: J. Gordon Edwards: a monograph: p 7: available from Radio Liberty, or from Dr. Edwards at San Jose State University in San Jose, CA.

26) Reported by Chairman John Rarick: House Hearings on the Federal Pesticide Control Act of 1971, pp 266-267, in Serial No 92-A: quoted in a treatise by Dr. J. Gordon Edwards: A taped interview with Dr. Edwards is available from Radio Liberty, as is his treatise: see also Environmental Overkill: Dixy Lee Ray: Regnery: p 77.

27) Environmental Overkill: op cited: pp 76-77 and 192: see also my 2-hour interview with Dr. Dixy Lee Ray: see also Dr. Edwards' treatise on DDT, available from Radio Liberty.

28) Strong Abortion-Breast Cancer Link Revealed: Washington Times: October 12, 1996: A1.

29) Russia Strives to Reverse Population Shrinkage: Washington Times: September 22, 1996: p A8.

30) An audio-taped interview with Peter Hammond of Front Line Ministries is available from Radio Liberty: also see Holocaust in Rwanda: Peter Hammond: available from In Touch Mission Int'l (ITMI), P.O. Box 28240, Tempe, AZ, 85285.

31) Special Warfare: May 1996: PB 80-96-2: Special Operations and LIC in the 21st Century: The Joint Strategic Perspective: Brian Sullivan: p 2.

32) Killer Angel: op cited: pp 50-51.

90.

India

Poisoning of A Nation

1.2 Billion Lives At Stake

India has become a dumping ground for dangerous pesticides. According to a Times of India report dated Oct 30, 2010, the amount of pesticides used in eatables in India is as much as 750 times the European standards.

The report portrays an alarming picture of how the rampant use of banned pesticides in fruits and vegetables is putting at risk the life of the common man. Farmers apply pesticides such as chlordane, endrin and heptachor that can cause serious neurological problems, kidney damage and skin diseases. A documentary on the subject reveals how *an indian consumes pesticides that are more than forty times what an average American would consume.*

Several studies conducted so far confirm to these facts. One such study was a Delhi-based NGO Consumer-Voice. They collected sample data from various wholesale and retail shops in Delhi, Bangalore and Kolkata.

"Out of five internationally-banned pesticides, four were found to be common in vegetables sold in the Indian markets. Banned pesticides were found in bitter gourd and spinach," says Sisir Ghosh, head of Consumer-Voice. The banned chemicals included chlordane, a potent central nervous system toxin, endrin, which can cause headache nausea and dizziness, and heptachor that can damage the liver and decrease fertility.

Tests conducted on vegetables at the government-approved and NABL-accredited laboratory, Arbro Analytical Division, revealed that the Indian ladies finger contained captan, a toxic pesticide, up to 15,000 parts per billion (ppb) whereas ladies finger in the EU has captan only up to 20 ppb. "Indian cauliflower can have malathion pesticide up to 150 times higher than the European standards," says an official.

The vegetables studied included potato, tomato, snake gourd, pumpkin, cabbage, cucumber and bottle gourd, among others. "We have informed the Food Safety and Standards Authority of India about the excessive use of pesticides in fruits and vegetables that pose serious health hazards," says Ghosh. He adds that strict monitoring from government agencies is required to check manufacture, import and use of banned pesticides. The pesticide residue limits have not been reviewed for the past 30 years.

In another survey, the consumer organisation conducted tests on fruits sold in Indian markets which again showed that 12 fruits, including bananas, apple and grapes, had high quantity of pesticides, violating both Indian and European Union standards. The chemical contents found in fruits were endosuplhan, captan, thiacloprid, parathion and DDT residues.

The Slow Poisoning of India - A Film

The Slow Poisoning of India is a 26-minute documentary film directed by Ramesh Menon and produced by the New Delhi-based The Energy and Resources Institute (TERI). It deals with the dangers of excessive use of pesticide in agriculture. India is one of the largest users of pesticide in Asia and also one of the largest importers and manufactures. The toxins have entered into the food chain and into our breakfast, lunch and dinner.

The film showcases startling case studies from Kerala where villagers in Kasaragod district are paying a heavy price as it has been exposed to pesticide spraying for many years. It talks of the health impacts in other parts of India and also on how the magic of the green revolution in Punjab is fading as land and water bodies are poisoned.

Farmers use pesticides carelessly. Some use the wrong chemical, while others overuse. Many harvest immediately after spraying. Annunal consumption is nearly 90,000 tonnes and it's rising rapidly.

But some farmers are bouncing back into better practices, and this is a silver lining shown towards the end. "Many farmers are now switching from chemcial to organic farming as they see that it is the only way out of getting into a spiralling whirlpool of debt created by the high cost of pesticides. Farmers like Tokia Modu in Warangal are waging a silent biological war against pests and are winning.

(The film can be ordered at outreach@teri.res.in)

Indian Government - Putting 1.2 Billion Lives On The Line

Present Indian government is completely ignoring the indigenous agricultural methods and techniques which have been in practice in India for more than 50 centuries. These have been proven suitable to the climate and conditions on the sub-continent. This deliberate neglect reeks of foul play and is nothing less than a criminal act.

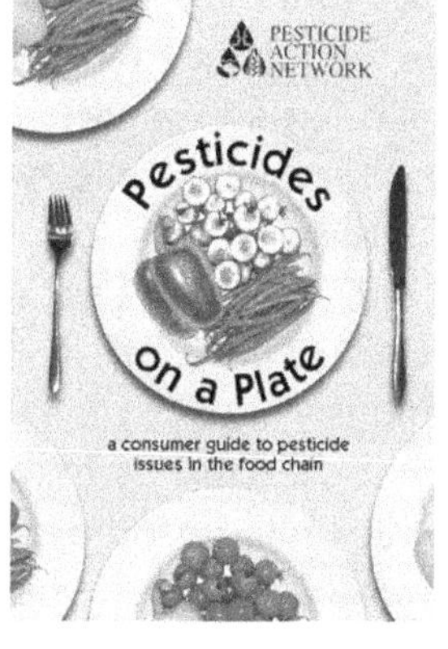

Hundreds of thousands of farmers are successfully practicing organic farming and outproducing farmers who use synthetic pesticides. But the government is turning a blind eye to all these eco-friendly technologies and brazenly promoting pesticide use.

Cow is farmer's best friend and corporation is his worst enemy. The government is killing cows and befriending corporations. The sorry outcome of this is a farmer's suicide every 15 minutes. Cow dung and urine are the best fertilizer and pesticide. Countless rich and happy farmers will testify to this fact.

But the government's agenda is anything but welfare of the common man. Following news report shows the government's complicity in this regard.

National Conference To Promote Pesticides

Latha Jishnu, Down To Earth, Jan 15, 2011

The timing and the message of the conference could not have been more stark. At a time when the endosulfan problem is in the limelight, sparking calls for a nationwide ban on the pesticide, its manufacturers staged a remarkable feat.

They held a three-day conference on rural prosperity at Delhi's Vigyan Bhavan, venue for high-power official meetings, and put across the message that the hazardous chemicals are safe. Their biggest coup: roping in President Pratibha Patil to inaugurate the event.

Organised by Crop Care Federation of India (CCFI), formerly Pesticides Association of India, the association of the 45 leading pesticides manufacturers, the conference had both the Ministry of Agriculture and the Ministry of Chemicals and Fertilizers as partners for the three-day conference.

The high-profile event also roped in related industries: seed, fertiliser and processed food. It was a powerful showing with leading sponsors such as Monsanto India, Excel Crop Care and United Phosphorus (UPL) along with the association of the biotech industry (ABLE) and the National Seeds Association of India.

Excel Crop Care is a subsidiary of Excel Industries, the leading endosulfan producer, and a sister concern of UPL. With the campaign against endosulfan gaining momentum in Kerala, it is obvious why the pesticides lobby was keen to organise such a seminar.

It claimed "rural prosperity through better agriculture" as its theme but the conference had minimal participation from the farmers: just Sharad Joshi, president of Shetkari Sanghatana of Pune.

Krishi Bhavan, headquarters of the agriculture ministry, had no convincing argument to justify its partnership with CCFI, which is chaired by Raju D Shroff, chairman and managing director of UPL.

Agriculture minister Sharad Pawar, the main speaker, focused on the pet theme of the ministry: increasing private sector participation in agriculture services. He said the new momentum in Indian agriculture meant "the private sector has a critical role in meeting the demand of higher investment, inputs and services in agriculture". Kerala, though, was incensed by the open display of cosiness between the endosulfan lobby and the government.

The strongest criticism came from Congress stalwart V M Sudheeran who has been in the forefront of the campaign against endosulfan. "When the country is asking for a ban on the hazardous pesticide, I am completely at a loss to hear the Ministry of Agriculture had organised an agricultural development seminar sponsored by none other than the producers of endosulfan," he wrote to Pawar.

Sudheeran, a former member of Parliament, is a highly regarded member of the Kerala Pradesh Congress Committee. His letter summed up the shock and anger such an event has occasioned, more so since it was used to promote endosulfan. "The irony is that when thousands have been killed by this chemical and many more seriously impacted in the villages of Kasaragod, the pesticides industry has used the good offices of the ministry to unleash its propaganda that endosulfan is a safe chemical."

He was referring to the fact that Arun V Dhuri, vice-president (registration & business development) of Excel Crop Care, had facilitated the discussion on the "truth and falsehoods and remedies" regarding pesticides and had used the occasion to depict endosulfan as harmless.

CCFI, formerly Pesticides Association of India, puts the total value of agro-chemicals produced in the country at Rs 13,000 crore, of which exports account Rs 7,000 crore. A recent report by Rabobank, which pegs the production of pesticides at Rs 7,000 crore, says 50 percent of the domestic market is controlled by multinational corporations.

The event was also used for pushing genetically modified (GM) crops. According to CCFI, one of the key aims of the conference was to promote technological innovation. "If a second Green Revolution is to ramp up food production, quicker green signals are needed on GM," it said.

91.

Food Fascism

When It Is A Crime To Produce Your Own Food

Waging A War Against Humanity - Using Seeds In Place Of Bullets

Corporations like Monsanto are seeking total global domination (and corporate ownership) over the entire food supply. This concept is called "food fascism," and it would allow corporations and governments to determine who eats and who starves.

Genetically modified organisms have nothing to do with higher yields or disease resistance. They're a trojan horse designed to turn farmers (and the rest of us) into 21st century serfs.

They intend not only to steal our wealth, but also our ability to feed ourselves without total dependence on their "products." This is all part of the food fascism assault that's already underway in our world.

Food Fascism In The Land Of The Free

Eric Blair, Activist Post, September 21, 2010

The food industry is no longer a free market. In fact, I'd go as far as saying it's becoming the most glaring example of corporate-government fascism in the world.

Actual monopolies fully control the basic building blocks of the food that makes up the majority of our diet -- and no one seems to care. Simply put, those who control the corn, wheat, and soybeans control all food, since all livestock and all processed foods are dependent on those food resources.

These monopolies place their cronies in government regulatory agencies like the FDA and USDA to weed out their competition through excessive regulation. Currently proposed legislation are textbook examples of their methods.

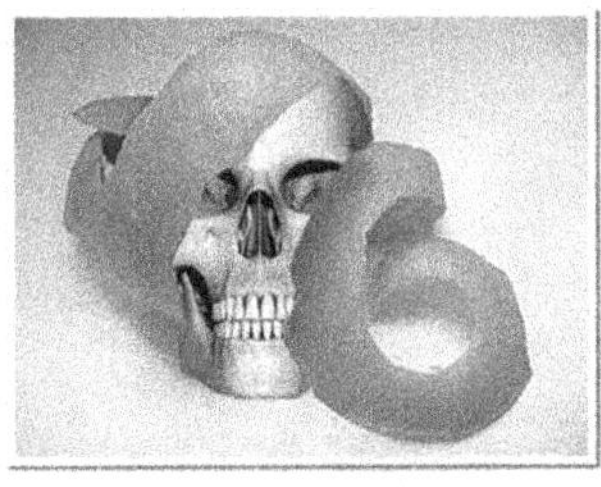

There once was a time when free markets existed for food. Back when local food ruled the day, if a farmer sold milk that was bad, he would not get return customers unless he adjusted his practices to make a healthier product. This free market was self-regulating. In other words, in a truly free market we shouldn't need the FDA. However, as mentioned before, we are light years from a free market.

Subsidies rain down on big agribusinesses that grow what the government tells them to grow. Industry leaders like Cargill, Monsanto, and Tyson essentially turn farmers into indentured sharecroppers. The food engineers at General Mills and others weave corn, wheat, and soybeans into chemical concoctions that end up in brightly colored packages -- some even come with free Chinese-made toys. The finished product develops from a Genetically Modified base, using multiple poisons to glue it together, demonstrating that the monopolies and their regulatory lapdogs care not for our health.

But what about voting with our pocketbooks, isn't that a free market? Surely that is what we have been taught. Yet, all 16 flavors of Cheerios -- which give the appearance of free choice -- are all made by General Mills from a genetically modified corn base. This illusion of choice hides the monopolistic nature of food.

Enter Senate bill S. 510 Food Safety Modernization Act, already passed in the House as HR 2749. Some have demonized the bill as ultimate food fascism where the FDA will micromanage even small farms and co-ops to the point where it will become illegal to grow, share, trade or

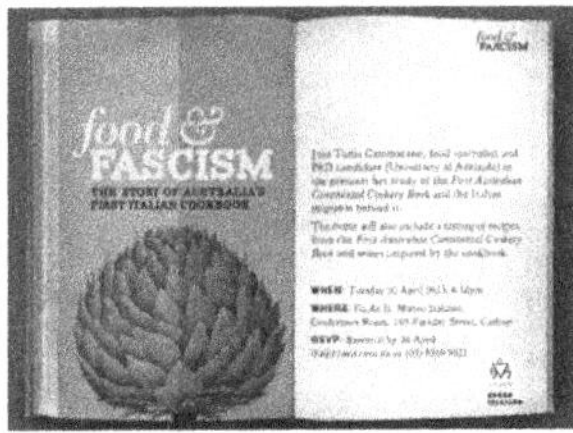

sell homegrown food. While others see it as a measured way to control the health and quality of factory farms. One thing is for sure, S.510 gives more power to the corrupt FDA to regulate our food.

This bill does nothing to change the actual practices of factory farming and the way the food for animals is grown and delivered. It does give the FDA draconian powers to force inspections to be paid for by the farmers themselves. This can be an effective tool for the big multinational agri-corporations to further squeeze out their competition and gain near complete control of food resources in America. Furthermore, S.510 essentially hands much of the FDA's duties over to the liberty-smashing Department of Homeland Security -- which is mentioned 41 times in the bill.

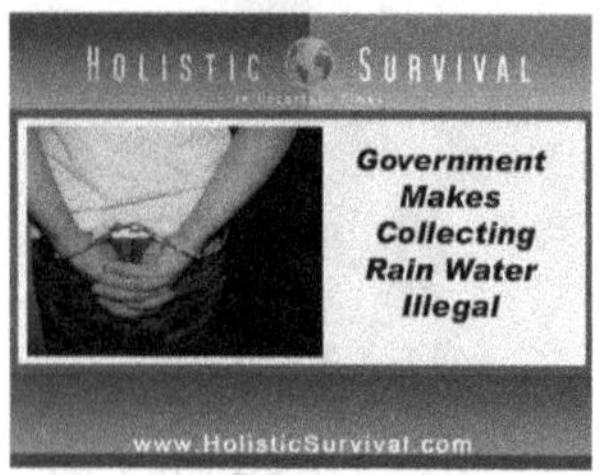

All 273 pages of the bill contain legal jargon that can be difficult to decode, but one of the easiest ways to determine if it is good for average Americans is to view who is supporting the bill, versus who opposes the bill. Monsanto and other agri-monopolies support the bill with full force. Indeed, some speculate that they even wrote the bill themselves.

Sadly, this bill is gaining momentum because of the recent food recalls. One way or another, our corrupt politicians and their corporate overlords will see to it that there is more regulation over our food. If this bill passes, we can expect more consolidation in agriculture and more police-state raids of private health-food cooperatives.

Worse yet, this bill may just be the primer for the even more egregious bill HR.759 Food and Drug Administration Globalization Act, which fully restricts local food producers and natural health remedies.

WARNING
DUE TO AN EVER-EXPANDING TYRANNICAL GOVERNMENT GROWING YOUR OWN FOOD ON YOUR OWN PROPERTY MAY RESULT IN FINES.

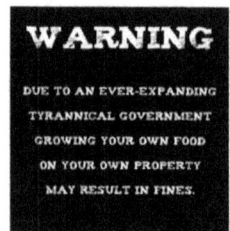

Food freedom starts at home with the individual choices that we make. However, exposing the corrupt regulatory system and educating the powers that be about healthier ways to produce food is also vital to maintaining our food freedom. It's time we tell the corporate government to back off our food.

Senate Bill S510 Makes It Illegal To Grow, Share, Trade Or Sell Homegrown Food

S 510, the Food Safety Modernization Act of 2010, may be the most dangerous bill in the history of the US.

Dr. Shiv Chopra, "If accepted [S 510] would preclude the public's right to grow, own, trade, transport, share, feed and eat each and every food that nature makes. It will become the most offensive authority against the cultivation, trade and consumption of food and agricultural products of one's choice. It will be unconstitutional and contrary to natural law or, if you like, the will of God."

OCCUPY
THE
FOOD
SUPPLY!
END CORPORATE EXPLOITATION OF OUR FOOD SYSTEMS.

It is similar to what India faced with imposition of the salt tax during British rule, only S 510 extends control over all food in the US, violating the fundamental human right to food.

Monsanto says it has no interest in the bill and would not benefit from it, but Monsanto's Michael Taylor who gave us rBGH and unregulated genetically modified (GM) organisms, appears to have designed it and is waiting as an appointed Food Czar to the FDA to administer the agency it would create — without judicial review — if it passes. S510 would give Monsanto unlimited power over all US seed, food supplements, food and farming.

Couple Fined For Having Garden: Florida To Impose $500 A Day Fine For Growing Vegetables

By Jessica Rodriguez, Christian Post, January 9, 2013

Jason and Jennifer Helvenston, from Florida, have been warned they could face a fine of up to $500 a day if they have not removed their vegetable garden by Thursday. It has been found that they are violating a local Orlando City Code that says people are prohibited from using their front gardens to grow vegetables.

However, the Helvenstons are refusing to back down and have started a protest against the restrictions, saying it violates their right to grow their own food, according to Click Orlando.

The couple have launched the "Plant a Seed, Change the Law" initiative, which is a formal protest against the local gardening restrictions they have been found to be breaking.

The Helvenstons were told back in November by Florida officials that they were violating the rules. However, news of the couple's plight spread quickly and the city was flooded with letters and emails protesting, demanding that they be allowed to grow vegetables in their front garden if they wished.

That wave of protests moved city officials to postpone any move against the Helvenstons temporarily. However, it now appears they are moving on the violations again and have given the couple until Thursday to remove their vegetable garden.

Jason Helvenston has said, "The greatest freedom you can give someone is the freedom to know they will not go hungry. Our Patriot Garden pays for all of its costs in healthy food and lifestyle while having the lowest possible carbon footprint. It supplies valuable food while being attractive. I really do not understand why there is even a discussion. They will take our house before they take our Patriot Garden."

Ari Bargil, an attorney for the Institute of Justice, has confirmed that the couple can be fined up to $500 a day from Thursday if the garden is not dug up and destroyed. He has offered his assistance to the couple, saying: "We are seriously interested in taking a look

at this. We're focused on helping the Helvenstons get the word out, encouraging the city to reach a sensible compromise here."

Government Threatens Jail Time For Growing Produce In Front-Yard Garden

Elizabeth Renter, Infowars.com, Sept 3, 2012

It seems like every month a few more stories hit the social media grapevines, where home owners are being punished for growing food. Some of these front-yard gardeners have created landscapes that rival those created by high-paid landscaping companies. The difference—all of this greenery is edible.

When we can't trust what we find at the grocery store, and farmer's markets are limited and not always within driving distance, growing our own food doesn't just make sense, it makes perfect sense.

And once you've begun growing your own, you will likely begin to wonder why Americans ever moved away from self-sustaining gardens.

It may sound crazy that a city government would spend (waste) resources to target gardeners, but it actually happens more often than you would think.

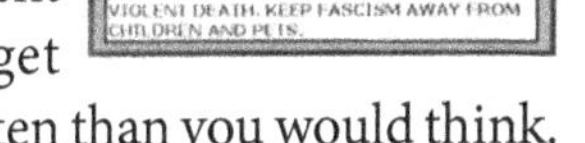

As reported by Dr. Mercola:

In 2011, Julie Bass of Oak Park, Michigan was charged with a misdemeanor and threatened with jail time for planting a vegetable garden in her front yard.

In British Columbia, Dirk Becker was threatened with six months in jail for converting an acre of his 2.5-acre lot into an organic farm. What's even more unsettling about the charges in this case is that the lot was literally stripped bare down to a gravel pit before this. The owner spent over a decade healing the land and converting it into a self-contained ecosystem that is now home to thriving vegetable crops, fruit trees, bees, butterflies, birds, frogs, dragonflies and more. But because the area is zoned a "residential" lot, the local government is calling on him to "cease all agricultural activity" or pay the consequences.

Earlier this year, city inspectors bulldozed more than 100 types of plants, including garlic chives, strawberry and apple mint, being grown by Denise Morrison in Tulsa, Oklahoma. The inspectors said her plants were too tall, but city code allows for plants over 12 inches if they're meant for human consumption, which hers were. Morrison is now suing the city for violating her civil rights.

Steve Miller was fined $5,200 for growing vegetables in his Clarkston, Georgia backyard, which he not only consumed but also sold at farmers markets and shared with friends.

Illegal Gardens In The News

Global wars continue, food and water shortages are eminent and climate change threatens land and growing ability everywhere. Faced with these challenges, city and suburban dwellers across the country are digging into the dirt to reconnect with their food, helping their homes and cities become more food self-sufficient in the process.

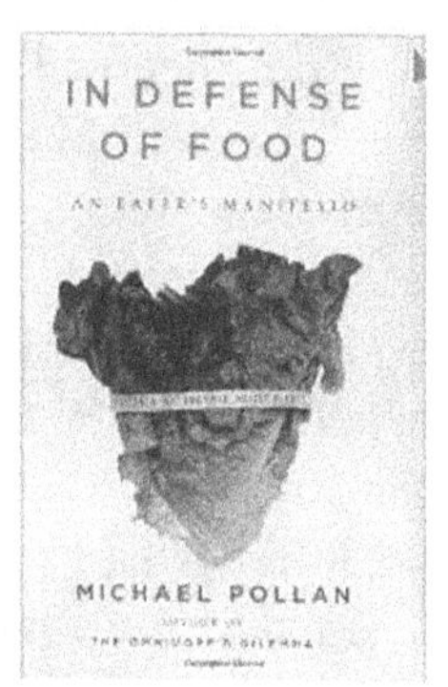

The "defiant" gardens profiled in the articles listed here are sparking a national debate, challenging our perception of subversive plots and recasting the image of the modern victory garden.

- Orlando, Fla. Illegal Front Yard Vegetable Garden Dispute Heard by Orlando Planning Board, By Bob Ewing. Mother Earth News, Jan. 18, 2013.

- Orlando. Fla. Continuing Fight for the Right to Grow Food: Orlando's War on Gardens, By Kale Roberts. Mother Earth News, Nov. 29, 2012.

- Orlando, Fla. Homeowners Cited for Illegal Gardening: Orlando Couple Fight forthe Right to Grow Food, By David Yener Goodman. Mother Earth News, Nov. 15, 2012.

- New South Wales, Australia. Bondi Woman's 'Illegal' Community Garden Gets Locals' Support, By Shane McDonald. Wentworth Courier, Nov. 14, 2012.

- Orlando, Fla. College Park Man Fights to Keep Vegetable Garden in Front Yard, By Kristin Giannas. WKMG Local 6 News, Nov. 7, 2012.

- Drummondville, Quebec.Illegal Front Yard Garden: Canadian Couple's Kitchen Garden Targeted by Authorities, Huffington Post, Jul. 19, 2012.

- Ferguson, Mo. City Officials in Ferguson Attempt to Bulldoze Citizens' Rights, Gardens, By Dave Roland. Freedom Center of Missouri, Jul. 3, 2012.

- Tulsa, Okla. Woman Sues City of Tulsa for Cutting Down Her Edible Garden, By Lori Fullbright. News on 6, Jun. 15, 2012.

- Newton, Mass. Newton Officials Call Tomato Display Illegal, By Deirdre Fernandes. The Boston Globe, May 22, 2012.

- Los Angeles, Calif. An Illegal Curbside Garden Flourishes in L.A., By Nate Berg. The Atlantic Cities, Apr. 10, 2012

- Oak Park, Mich. Oak Park Drops Charges Against Homeowner Julie Bass, but Hits Her with Two Other Misdemeanor Crime Charges, By Mike Adams. NaturalNews.com, Jul. 15, 2011.

- See related blog at OakParkHatesVeggies.Wordpress.com

- Washington Heights, N.Y. Rogue Farm Ripped Up Because Gardener Broke Rules, Says Parks Dept., By Carla Zanoni. DNAinfo, Jun. 22, 2011

- Chatham Township, N.J. Young Organic Farmer Fighting Rebuke of Chatham Twp. Law, By Aaron Morrison. Cornicopia Institute, Jun. 3, 2011.

- Los Angeles, Calif. Is a Balcony Garden Against the Fire Code? By Mike Lieberman. Urban Organic Gardener, May 26, 2011.

- Boulder, Co. Home Garden Laws: Weeding in the Nude and Other No-Nos, By Jennifer Kongs. Mother Earth News, Aug. 18, 2010.

- Clarkston, Ga. 'Cabbagegate': Man Fined $5k for Home Garden, By Dave Their. Huffington Post, Sep. 15, 2010

92.

You Can Be Jailed

For Selling And Drinking Farm Fresh Milk

One hundred years ago milk came from the cow to your doorstep. Other than bottling, there was little processing involved and you basically knew which farm your milk came from.

Today the process isn't as simple. With dairy, it's more complicated. Each bottle has at least three different companies associated with it – the farm that raised the cow, the cooperative that bought and transports the milk, and the processor that bottles and distributes it. Bottled milk on your grocer's shelf is "commingled" – meaning it doesn't come from one farm, but a combination of different places. With vegetables and poultry one company often oversees the entire process, but with milk it's not so easy to know exactly where your food came from.

But it hardly matters where it comes from because milk from factory farms can only be described as white blood. Cows in these 'farms' are artificially inseminated, fed feed that they are not designed to digest and given hormones to produce 100 pounds of watery milk a day.

This is several times more than they would produce naturally. As a result, a huge percentage of dairy cows suffer from mastitis, a bacterial infection of the udders. Since this milk is still considered drinkable, the blood and pus from their infections, along with massive quantities of antibiotics, ends up in the milk on supermarket shelves.

Injecting cows with Monsanto's rBGH growth harmone only worsens the already sad picture.

And even milk processing plants are big, big factories where visitors are not allowed. Here milk shipped from the farm is completely remade. First it is separated in centrifuges into fat, protein and various other solids and liquids. Once segregated, these are reconstituted to set levels for whole, low-fat and no-fat milks; in other words, the milk is reconstituted to be completely uniform.

The butterfat left over will go into butter, cream, cheese, toppings and ice cream. The dairy industry loves to sell low fat milk and skim milk because they can make a lot more money from the butterfat when consumers buy it as ice cream. When they remove the fat to make reduced fat milks, they replace the fat with powdered milk concentrate, which is formed by high temperature spray drying.

All reduced-fat milks have dried skim milk added to give them body, although this ingredient is not usually on the labels. The result is a very high-protein, low fat product.

The milk is then pasteurized at 161 degrees F by rushing it past superheated stainless steel plates. If the temperature is 200 degrees the milk is called ultrapasteurized. This will have a distinct cooked milk taste but it is sterile and can be sold on the grocery shelf. In other words, they don't even have to keep it cool. The bugs won't touch it. Once processed, the milk will last for weeks and months, not just days.

Many people, particularly our children, cannot tolerate the stuff that we are calling milk that is sold in the grocery shelves. Milk is nature's perfect life-giving food which builds strong bone, healthy organs and a strong nervous system. Industrial processing transforms this miracle food into an allergen and carcinogen.

What If You Want To Enjoy Natural, Farm Fresh Milk?

Sorry, you can not! It's a criminal offence in countries like US, Canada and Australia. And with the spread of food fascism, it will become so in more and more countries. Even in India, the land of holy cow, pure milk is hard to find. 70% of the milk sold in the country is adulterated with synthetic ingredients.

The sale of fresh, raw milk directly to consumers is prohibited in Canada under the Food and Drug Regulations since 1991.

> No person shall sell the normal lacteal secretion obtained from the mammary gland of the cow, genus Bos, or of any other animal, or sell a dairy product made with any such secretion, unless the secretion or dairy product has been pasteurized by being held at a temperature and for a period that ensure the reduction of the alkaline phosphatase activity so as to meet the tolerances specified in official method MFO-3, Determination of Phosphatase Activity in Dairy Products, dated November 30, 1981.
>
> —Section B.08.002.2

How many deputies does it take
to suppress raw milk freedom?

Provincial laws also forbid the sale and distribution of raw milk. For instance, Ontario's Health Protection and Promotion Act, subsection 18 reads:

> "No person shall sell, offer for sale, deliver or distribute milk or cream that has not been pasteurized or sterilized in a plant that is licensed under the Milk Act or in a plant outside Ontario that meets the standards for plants licensed under the Milk Act."

In Australia, the sale of raw milk for drinking purposes is illegal in all states and territories, as is all raw milk cheese. This has been circumvented somewhat by selling raw milk as bath milk. There is some indication of share owning cows, allowing the "owners" to consume the raw milk, but also evidence that the government is trying to close this loophole.

In United States most states impose restrictions on raw milk suppliers due to concerns about safety. Mostly it is illegal to sell farm fresh raw milk. People try to circumvent these provisions by opening cow shares where the buyer owns a cow in the farm. But the noose is tightening on these marginal farmers. Big agribusiness is going after them as evidenced by the following incidents.

Multi-Agency Armed Raid Hits Rawesome Foods, Healthy Family Farms For Selling Raw Milk And Cheese

Mike Adams, Natural News, August 3, 2011

A multi-agency SWAT-style armed raid was conducted this morning by helmet-wearing, gun-carrying enforcement agents from the LA County Sheriff's Office, the FDA, the Dept. of Agriculture and the CDC (Centers for Disease Control).

Rawesome Foods, a private buying club offering wholesome, natural raw milk and raw cheese products (among other wholesome foods) is founded by James Stewart, a pioneer in bringing wholesome raw foods directly to consumers through a buying club. James was followed from his private residence by law enforcement, and when he entered his store, the raid was launched.

Law enforcement demanded that all customers (members) of the store vacate the premises, then they demanded to know how much cash James had at the store. When James explained the amount of cash he had at the store — which is used to purchase product for selling there — agents demanded to know why he had such an

> *As the twenty-first century dawns, American culture is in a mess... the system has lost its moorings, and, like ancient Rome is drifting into a dysfunctional situation.*
>
> *~Morris Berman (The Twilight of American Culture)*

amount of cash and where it came from. The raid was conducted like a terrorist operation.

Feds not only seized cash and raw milk supplies (much of which was also dumped out) but also mangos and other fresh, organic produce.

James was handcuffed, was never read his rights and was stuffed into an unmarked car. While agents said they would leave behind a warrant, no one has yet had any opportunity to even see if such a warrant exists or if it is a complete warrant.

This was an ILLEGAL raid being conducted mob-style by government thugs who respect no law and no rights. This is an all-out war by the government against people who try to promote healthy raw and living foods. Later they raided his home too.

James is now being held at the Pacific division police department at Centinela and Culver in Los Angeles. He is being held at $123,000 bail with no possibility of using bail bonds. Law enforcement has demanded that if he comes up with the money to cover bail, he must disclose to them all the sources of that money. (This is an illegal demand!)

Sharon Palmer, a mom and owner of Healthy Family Farms was also arrested and taken to jail. A third woman, Victoria Bloch, the LA County liaison for the Weston A Price Foundation, was also reportedly arrested.

All three are reportedly being charged with conspiracy to commit a crime. What crime? The "crime" of advocating raw milk for consumers!

This raid was an act of economic terrorism against a legitimate, ethical business selling wholesome, healthful products to a very happy group of members.

Massive public protests are needed to teach these criminal law enforcement agencies that they cannot illegally arrest and persecute individuals merely for buying and selling raw milk and cheese. We are organizing a public protest day in cooperation with James.

See this video of James Stewart talking about his farm:

http://www.youtube.com/watch?v=foKg-oShJP0

Video of the raid:

http://www.youtube.com/watch?v=lI1gvPmA_c8

Here's background on Healthy Family Farms which was also targeted in the raid:

Healthy Family Farms in Santa Paula, California:

"Healthy Family Farms is a sustainable, pasture-based farming operation. We raise all our livestock on pasture. We raise all of our animals from birth. We do not feed any of our animals soy, choosing instead to feed animals as they are designed to be fed. This results in healthy, sturdy animals needing no hormones, antibiotics, or other artificial "enhancements." We harvest our animals humanely by hand before they are delivered to the farmers markets. We never freeze our products. In addition to farmer's markets sales, we have an active Community Supported Agriculture (CSA), which offers discounts to our valued members."

There is need to send a message to the law enforcement tyrants that we will not tolerate our health food stores being terrorized by criminal cops and rogue federal agencies.

Spread the word, folks. Enough is enough! We must take a stand against this government-run campaign of terror against health food retailers. It is time to stop government-run terrorism against health food stores.

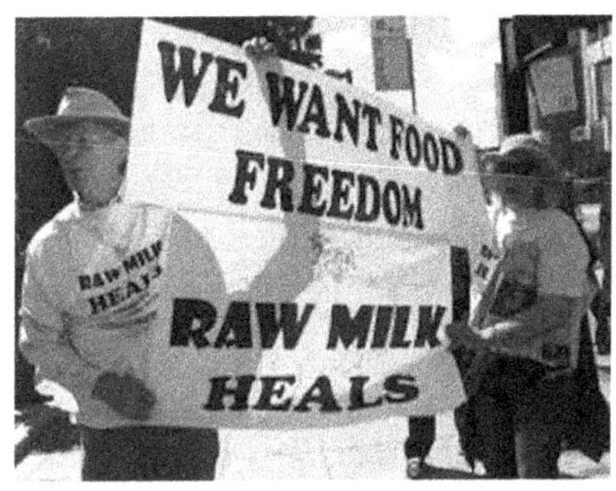

It's time we fought back and let these criminals know we will not be treated like food slaves by a corrupt, criminally-run government that wishes to force everyone to drink DEAD MILK and DEAD CHEESE (which they know cause disease).

This is it, friends! Big Government has declared war on the innocent. The administration, which has already gone out of its way to promote yet more GMOs in the food supply, is now overseeing government-sponsored terrorism against the health food movement. If you don't take a stand against this, you might as well lay down, surrender to Big Brother, and eat your soylent green.

We are fighting for our basic rights and freedoms against a police state cabal of criminals who now run our federal government and will stop at nothing to turn innocent citizens into gulag prisoners.

'Raw Milk' Farmer Fined $9,150 And Put On Year Probation

By Linda Nguyen, Postmedia News, Nov 25, 2011

An Ontario dairy farmer was fined $9,150 and placed on a year's probation for making and providing raw milk and cheese through a cow-share business.

Michael Schmidt was found guilty on appeal last September on 13 charges related to the production, sale and distribution of unpasteurized milk under the province's Health Protection and Promotion Act.

Have some small cottage, and grow your own food grains, vegetables, and have your cow's milk. Get nice foodstuff, save time. Why should you go in the city, hundred miles in car and again hundred miles come back and take unnecessary trouble? Stick to this spot and grow your own food, your own cloth, and live peacefully, save time, chant Hare Krsna. Very nice program. This is actual life. What is this nonsense life, big, big cities and always people busy? If he wants to see one friend, he has to go thirty miles. If he has to see a physician, he has to go fifty miles. If he has to go to work, another hundred miles. So what is this life? This is not life. Be satisfied. The devotee's life should be yavad artha-prayojanam. We require material necessities as much as it is required, no artificial life. That is spiritual life. Simply increasing artificial life, even for shaving, a big machine is required. What is this? Simply wasting time. Devil's workshop. Make life very simple. And simple living, high thinking, and always conscious to go back to home, back to Krsna. That is life. Not this life, that simply machine, machine, machine, machine.

-Srila Prabhupada (Srimad-Bhagavatam 6.1.49 -- New Orleans Farm, August 1, 1975)

An earlier court decision in January 2010 had acquitted Schmidt of all the charges.

In Canada, it is illegal to market, sell, distribute or deliver unpasteurized milk or cream. Schmidt admitted he supplied raw milk to 150 families through a cow-share business in which he sold $300 memberships for partial shares in 26 cows he keeps at Glencolton Farms, about 2 1/2 hours northwest of Toronto.

He argued raw milk has greater health benefits than pasteurized milk and that consumers should have a right to decide what to put in their bodies.

Ontario Justice Peter Tetley acknowledged the more than 60 people in the courtroom Friday were a testament to Schmidt's character.

"(Mr. Schmidt) is a man of principle," Tetley told the court. "He's willing to fight for his principles. There's a lot to admire about Mr. Schmidt."

Despite this, Tetley said he had no choice but to hand down the sentence. He also acknowledged there are many people in the province, the country and even in his own family who consume unpasteurized milk to no ill health effect, but said there was still a "public health component" to the case.

"The present legislation is inconsistent, at best," said Tetley, explaining that it is not up to the courts but the government to change current laws.

Schmidt also took the stand. When asked if he wanted a glass of water, he replied "No, milk please" to laughter in the courtroom.

Schmidt was charged in 2006 following an undercover police operation and armed raid of his farm. In 1994, he was fined $3,500 on similar charges.

Earlier this month, the outspoken farmer ended a month-long hunger strike following an impromptu meeting with Ontario Premier Dalton McGuinty.

A Peaceful Farmer On Trial For Feeding His Community

The Wisconsin Department of Agriculture, Trade and Consumer Protection (DATCP), encouraged by the FDA, is spending tens of thousands of dollars to prevent Wisconsin citizens from having access to the foods of their choice.

"The gigantic industrial enterprises are products of a godless civilization." Godless civilization, they no more can depend on the natural gifts. They think by industrial enterprises, they will get more money and they'll be happy. And to remain satisfied with the food grains, vegetables and natural gifts, that is primitive idea. They say, "It is primitive." When men were not civilized, they would depend on nature, but when they are advanced in civilization, they must discover industrial enterprises.

They do not know what is spiritual life, what is ultimate goal. Simply like cats and dogs. The dog jumps over with four legs, and if a man can jump over with four wheels, then that is advance. Just see. They think, "Now we are advanced. We have got four-wheel car to jump over. And the dog is jumping with legs. Therefore this is advanced." They do not know this is also the same dog's business. They do not know it.

...again they have made this car, coming from miles away, but the business is fishing. Just see. Bambharambhe laghu-kriya. "Advancement of civilization, we have got car, we are nicely dressed, we are human being, ev..." But what is your business? Fishing. Bambharambhe... Arambha, gorgeous arrangement — the business is the same. The skylark, what is called? Skylark? These birds?

Devotee (1): Oh, the seagulls. Seagull.

Prabhupada: Oh, seagull. They are doing the same business, and after his much advancement of civilization, he is doing the same business. The tiger is also eating flesh and blood, and human being — a scientific slaughterhouse. The same business, but they have got scientific instrument how to cut the throat quickly. This is the advance, advancement of civilization. The dog and cat they are having sex on the open street, and now they are talking of homosex in the school, colleges for education. This is their position. They do not know even what is the standard of human civilization. If you are doing the same business like ordinary animals, then where is the advancement of civilization?

—Srila Prabhupada (Lecture, Srimad-Bhagavatam, Mayapura, October 20, 1974)

They have used two methods; the "Fielder ruling", and to prosecute peaceful farmers like Vernon Hershberger, who have contracted directly with individuals who actively seek fresh farm foods, including raw milk and other raw dairy products from his farm known as "Grazin' Acres".

He has rejected a plea bargain that could have kept him out of jail. He was told he could plead guilty to two of four misdemeanors. In exchange, he would have had to pay a fine, been placed on probation, and would have had to agree to never sell or distribute raw milk products in future.

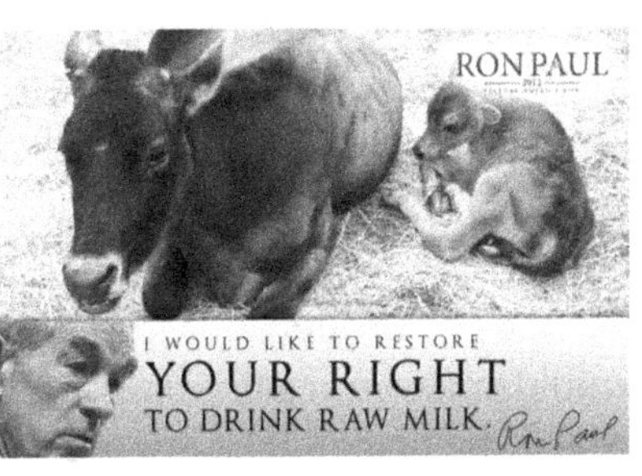

It is specifically because Vernon Hershberger provides raw milk for his members that he is facing a week long jury trial with over 70 witnesses. 70 witnesses... for allegedly violating dairy licensing regulations, and defying a DATCP hold order allowing the 200 some people in his private food club access to their own food. A week long jury trial for misdemeanor charges is an incredible waste of tax payer dollars, and an abuse of power.

At the center of this case is the billion dollar conventional dairy industry. Dairy is a global commodity, Wisconsin ranks 2nd in the nation behind California for milk production. Also a player in this is Monsanto, maker of rBGH growth hormones and producer of GM feed corn.

In a separate case in 2011, Judge Patrick J.Fiedler ruled ..."no, plaintiffs do not have a fundamental right to produce and consume the foods of your choice... no right to contract with a farmer... no right to own a cow..." Three weeks later he resigned from the bench and joined a law firm that represents Monsanto. Google Fiedler Ruling, then http://axley.com/patrick-j-fiedler. Coincidence? Or erosion of our basic human rights and freedoms?

FASCISM
Any Movement, Ideology, Or Attitude That Favors Dictatorial Government, Centralized Control Of Private Enterprise, And Repression Of All Opposition.

The point is we all need to get involved. We need to support ethical forward thinking and really hard working organic farmers. Our health, our kids health, the health of the planet depends on it.

We need to establish our own – Local Food Rules. And we need to not be bullied by our own government when we opt out of the commercial food supply system. To feed ourselves is a basic human right. To choose what we eat and who raised and grew it is a constitutional freedom. These rights and freedoms are being meticulously eroded by rulings like Fiedler's.

Many think the outcome of this trial has international significance. DATCP has been working with the FDA since at least 2009 to outlaw raw milk distribution, and kill any legislation introduced across the country that would make it legal. Vernon Hershberger's trial is the first judicial test of Fielder's ruling.

I don't drink raw milk and I'm not a Hershberger Farm member. Does this effect me?

Yes! The reason this case is so important politically is that it isn't just about whether Vernon has the right to distribute food privately, it is about whether all of us have this right on either end of the equation- to distribute food privately or to contract with producers to obtain food privately.

If Vernon is acquitted by the jury of his peers, the shock effects will reverberate throughout the country, and regulators will be forced to re-examine their crackdown on private food distribution. If Vernon loses, not only could he go to jail for more than a year, but regulators everywhere will be emboldened to go after private food more aggressively than ever. We owe it to our children to preserve their inherent right to make private food choices.

Who is Vernon Hershberger?

He is a 41 year old father of 10 children who is committed to his family and to serving the 200 or so members of his food club. He was raised as an Amish farm boy and even though his family left the Amish community a number of years ago, the family remains very conservative Christians who love to work together as a family.

Why is Vernon on trial?

Vernon refuses to stop feeding his food club community as the Government has ordered him to do. He feels he has the right, used by people for hundreds of years in this country and other countries, to distribute food under private contract to members of his community. He also feels it is his calling from the Lord to feed his brethren as the Bible teaches (John 3:16 & 17).

What is Vernon being accused of?

He is being accused of being a criminal for producing and distributing raw milk and other foods. The State, however, refuses to give him a license covering raw milk because it has no such license.

Is Vernon above the law?

Absolutely not. He is following the law to the best of his knowledge and has tried his best to work with the State for the last 10 years. But he has been unable to keep up with all the varying interpretation and definition changes that have been applied to him and other Wisconsin farmers during that time. As a result, he decided several years ago that he should not be part of the state's permit system, but should instead distribute milk and other foods his farm produces on a private basis to members of his farm.

Is raw dairy safe?

Like any food, raw dairy can make people sick if it isn't properly produced and handled. If it is handled properly, it is as safe as any other food. Please see; http://www.westonaprice.org/press/flawed-government-report-thwarts-state-raw-milk-initiatives

This seems crazy! Has any other farmer gone through this?

Unfortunately, many owners of small farms have gone through this in the last 20 years, all over the country. The crackdown on small farms seems to be a result of government policies designed to aid large factory farms. The crackdown seems to have intensified as growing numbers of people have come to question the safety and nutritional quality of factory farm food and highly processed food produced by big food companies, and have organized food clubs and herd shares to acquire food directly from traditional small farms.

This attack on Vernon Hershberger is about milk as a global commodity. Sales of fluid milk are down nationwide which puts a strain on the profits of agricultural, chemical and pharmaceutical giants. Demand for raw milk and other whole nutrient dense foods is growing which cuts into the market share of these powerful industries. Now for the vicious circle... Elected officials appoint agency secretaries who establish and direct food regulations. Industry giants contribute to campaigns of elected officials who also appoint judges. And suddenly an organic small family farmer feeding his community is a crime.

93.

Judge: Americans Don't Have Right to Drink Cow Milk

No "Fundamental Right to Produce and Consume Foods"

By Raven Clabough, New American, 29 September 2011

In a court case sure to go down in history for one of the most bizarre rulings, a Wisconsin judge has held that American citizens do not have a "fundamental right to produce or consume foods of their choice." The decision was so shocking that the Farm-to-Consumer Legal Defense Fund asked the judge to issue a clarification of the ruling.

Judge Fiedler went on to clarify his ruling further:

"no, Plaintiffs do not have a fundamental right to own and use a dairy cow or a dairy herd;

"no, Plaintiffs do not have a fundamental right to consume the milk from their own cow;

"no, Plaintiffs do not have a fundamental right to board their cow at the farm of a farmer;

"no, the ... Plaintiffs' private contract does not fall outside the scope of the State's police power;

"no, Plaintiffs do not have a fundamental right to produce and consume the foods of their choice."

The case involved people who owned cows and sought to board them at a farm. As noted by Foolocracy.com, "Although the commercial relationship between the owner of the cow and owner of the land gives cause for the state to intervene, Fiedler took his ruling into a more personal and troubling direction."

The plaintiffs in the case argued that their right to privacy should also translate into the right to "consume food of his/her own choice."

Judge Patrick Fiedler remained unconvinced, claiming that the constitutionality of food rights is "wholly without merit." He added that the plaintiffs' use of the Roe v Wade case as a precedent does "not explain why a woman's right to have an abortion translates to a right to consume unpasteurized milk.... This court is unwilling to declare that there is a fundamental right to consume the food of one's choice without first being presented with significantly more developed arguments on both sides of the issue."

While some of the points put forward by the judge are reasonable to an extent, points two and five are particularly disturbing to constitutionalists, as they propose severe limitations on personal rights.

A person growing a tomato plant in his or her home and choosing to eat that tomato would seem to have that right. Frighteningly, Fiedler thinks otherwise.

It seems Judge Fiedler believes that food consumption is one of those rights that are not God-given but rather granted by the state.

Some analysts believe that such increased food regulations are being proposed because big agriculture fears competition from little producers, and therefore uses lobbyists to virtually eliminate small family farms that have been successful outside of the mainstream. Interestingly, those involved in large-scale agriculture are already the beneficiaries of massive government subsidies.

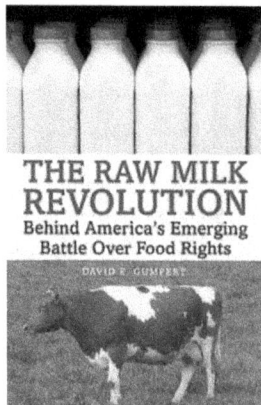

Evidence of federal government pressure that will affect small family farms more than large-scale agriculture can be found in recent regulations from the Federal Motor Carrier Safety Administration, an arm of the Department of Transportation. The regulations reclassify farm vehicles and implements, and require all farm workers to meet the same set of requirements that over-the-road truck drivers do. Such a regulatory burden would be felt much more significantly by small family farms than by large ones.

GRADE A
RETAIL RAW MILK
DAISY BELLE
DAIRY FARM
9311 State Hwy 125 • Fair Grove, MO 65648 • Plant # 29-033

Regulations are beginning to have an impact on nearly every aspect of food consumption in the United States. In Oregon, for example, Multnomah County inspectors recently targeted a lemonade

Driving at breakneck speed. And then what is the business? Searching out some means of food, exactly like the hog, he is loitering here and there, "Where is stool? Where is stool? Where is stool?" And this is going on in the polished way as civilization. There is so much risk, as running these cars so many people are dying. There is record, it is very dangerous. At least I feel as soon as I go to the street, it is dangerous. The motorcar are running so speedy, and what is the business? The business is where to find out food. So therefore it is condemned that this kind of civilization is hoggish civilization. This hog is running after, "Where is stool? And you are running in a car. Purpose is the same: Therefore this is not advancement of civilization. Advancement of civilization is, as Krsna advises, that you require food, so produce food grain. Remain wherever you are. You can produce food grain anywhere, a little labor. And keep cows, go-raksya, krsi-go-raksya vanijyam vaisya-karma svabhava-jam [Bg. 18.44]. Solve your problem like... Produce your food wherever you are there. Till little, little labor, and you will get your whole year's food. And distribute the food to the animal, cow, and eat yourself. The cow will eat the refuse. You take the rice, and the skin you give to the cow. From dahl you take the grain, and the skin you give to the... And fruit, you take the fruit, and the skin you give to the cow, and he will give you milk. So why should you kill her? Milk is the miraculous food; therefore Krsna says cow protection. Give protection to the cow, take milk from it, and eat food grains -- your food problem is solved. Where is food problem? Why should you invent such civilization always full of anxieties, running the car here and there, and fight with other nation, and economic development? What is this civilization?

— Srila Prabhupada (Philosophical discussion)

stand for operating without a license and threatened to fine the "seven-year-old" operator $500.

Likewise, the Food and Drug Administration has turned its attention to Amish milk, setting up a sting operation to stop Rainbow Acres Farm from selling unpasteurized milk in the Washington area.

The Obama administration signed the FDA Food Safety Modernization Act, which, as noted by the Heritage Foundation, would "authorize the FDA to dictate how farmers grow fruits and vegetables, including rules governing soil, water, hygiene, packing, temperatures, and even what animals may roam which fields and when." The act also "increases inspections of food facilities and taxes them to do so ... and grants the FDA unilateral authority to order recalls."

Now, Fiedler's ruling opens the door for the need for "plant police" to help enforce restrictions on the personal use and growing of vegetables.

Groups of citizens around the country are beginning to recognize how federal government regulations are infringing on their personal rights, and as a result, have launched a counter-attack.

In Sedgwick, Maine, for example, approximately 100 residents unanimously approved a food sovereignty initiative at a March 5 town meeting, which permits food producers in the town to sell food without federal and state regulatory interference. Entitled "The Ordinance to Protect the Health and Integrity of the Local Food System," the four-page document invoked the town's right to self-governance and states that local producers and processors may sell food to consumers without licensing.

A number of other towns in Hancock County have elected to follow Sedgwick's example.

Still, there is more to be done for Americans to shake the shackles of federal regulations. Prison Planet asserts that citizens should be more vigilant and publicize the issues in blogs, on the web, and via letters to their representatives and local newspapers, even calling for an end to subsidies to all industries. It adds that Americans should be supporting their local farmers.

However, given that humans have farmed, and drunk the milk from their dairy animals, for more than 5,000 years, the breadth of the court's ruling has astonished many.

I THINK
THEREFORE I AM
DEFIANT

As the Ninth Amendment to the U.S. Constitution concedes, not all the rights of people are written out, providing that the "enumeration in the Constitution, of certain rights, shall not be construed to deny or disparage others retained by the people."

In spite of this, Judge Fiedler has made several blanket denials of civil rights, based on his argument that the Plaintiffs' "reasoning behind why the court should declare that there is a fundamental right to consume the food of one's choice" is "underdeveloped."

Indeed, it is an emphatic decision, with its point-by-point denial of all of the rights asserted by the farmers and their shareholders.

Judge On His Way Out

Even before his ruling, Judge Fiedler was scheduled to step down from his post. "I wanted to go back to being an advocate and being a lawyer," he said. He is slated to work as a trial lawyer with the Axley Brynelson law firm.

Incidently this firm also represents Monsanto.

94.

'GM Crops Only Answer To Nation's Food Security'

Indian Government's Affidavit To Supreme Court

IANS, November 12, 2012

The central government has told the Supreme Court that it could not achieve the goal of reducing the number of hungry people by half without taking recourse to genetically modified (GM) crops, which could herald the second green revolution in the country.

"Despite rapid economic growth in the past two decades, India is unlikely to meet the target of cutting the proportion of hungry people by half if recourse to advanced and safe biotechnology tools are not adopted," the central government told the apex court in an affidavit.

The central government said GM crops would not only lead to increased food security but would also reduce pressure on land use. While the population had increased by 181 million in the last decade, the land under sowing remained static at 140-143 million hectares since 1970.

The central government pronounced its position backing field trials of GM crops while junking the interim report of the court-appointed Technical Expert Committee (TEC) report, which had recommended a 10-year moratorium on GM crops field trials.

The TEC was appointed by the apex court while hearing a petition by Aruna Rodrigues seeking a mechanism mandating scientific examination of all the aspects of biosafety before GM crops are released for commercial cultivation.

Pitching for field trials of GM crops, the government said: "Genetic engineering promises remarkable advances in medicine, agriculture and other fields."

"Ban on GM crop field trials will be highly detrimental and not in national interest," the central government said in its affidavit.

In an attempt to persuade the apex court to reject the recommendation of the TEC, the central government's affidavit said: "In biotechnology and genetics, the principle sciences behind the GM crops, India has done exceedingly well in investing in HRD, education and training since 1986 with the establishment of department of biotechnology, the first country to do so globally."

It added that the success of the green revolution was driven by sufficient human resources available.

Making a strong plea for field trials of GM crops, the government said that "a 10-year moratorium would have a "cascading effect" of putting all the related research fields which thus far on the upswing into a decline".

It added that it would be a "blow to Indian science as it would put the country 20 years back in scientific research in comparison to fast growing economies who are developing GM crops like Brazil, China etc".

Government Ignores Adverse Technical Expert Committee (TEC) Report

Neha Saigal, India Together, 26 February 2013

The Ministry of Agriculture moves to introduce adoption of genetically modified crops in India, in the name of food security. Scientists, however, are critical of this move.

Three years ago, the then Minister of Environment and Forests, Jairam Ramesh declared a moratorium on Bt Brinjal, adopting a precautionary approach to the introduction of genetically modified foods in India. More importantly, he cited among his reasons for the moratorium the need to be "responsive to society and responsible to science."

The decision to impose a moratorium was an important one in many ways. It re-instated the growing evidence by the scientific community on the health and environmental impacts of Genetically Modified (GM) crops, and - perhaps even more importantly - the inadequacies in our own regulatory mechanism to regulate this controversial technology. The most valued lesson from this milestone decision was the coming together of sound science and public opinion, which resulted in democratic decision making.

This year, to mark the importance of 9 February (the date on which the moratorium was issued in 2010), diverse groups from around the country celebrated 'National Safe Food Day.'

A variety of events from different states around the country displayed the strength and diversity of the opposition to GM crops in India. From the organic mela organised by farmers in Karnataka, to the initiative by young people in Kerala to spread awareness about the risks of switching to GM crops, and a rally of 300 people

At least in India, say, hundred years before, there was no problem for eating, even for the lower class or any... No, there was no... The society was so made, there was no problem. Why fifty years? In 1933 or '36 in Vrndavana somebody wanted milk, some pilgrims amongst ourselves. So went to a house. "Can you supply us some milk?" "Ah, how much you want?" So it was about ten pounds. So she supplied immediately, one woman, and when she was offered price, "Oh, why shall I take a price for ten or twenty pounds of milk? Oh, you can take it." That is my practical experience. Milk was so freely available. So simply we are creating problems by godless civilization. That is a fact.

— Srila Prabhupada (Room Conversation, December 21, 1970, Surat, India)

in Gujarat, the day saw strong voices of opposition to GM crops echo throughout the country.

In Bangalore, Greenpeace volunteers created the image of happy brinjals walking down a traffic signal, imitating the famous Beatle's Abbey Road album cover. The message that these smiling brinjals carried was one of hope - that the people of India can imagine a GM-Free future due to the moratorium on Bt Brinjal and can only hope that the current Minister of Environment, Jayanthi Natrajan will also uphold the precedent set by Jairam Ramesh.

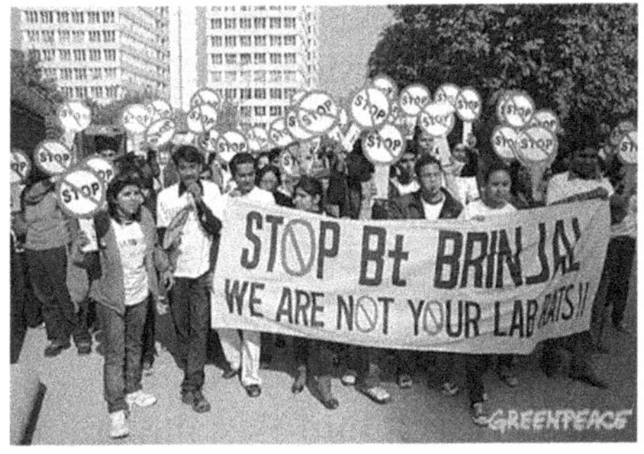

The most valued lesson from the moratorium decision was the coming together of sound science and public opinion, which resulted in democratic decision making.

While the debate around GM crops in India has always shown the voices of dissent from civil society, the past few months have also established that science is divided on the need for and the safety of GM crops. One recent example was the scientific interim report by the Technical Expert Committee (TEC) of the Supreme Court in October 2012. The report highlighted the potential impact of GM crops on human health, biodiversity and our socio-economic conditions, and has recommended a precautionary approach

The Kali-yuga people will forget performing yajna. They will be busy in ghora-rupa activities, horrible and fierceful activities, not yajna. They will neglect yajna. So then how your these bolts and nuts and rubber tires will help you? Therefore there is scarcity of anna, food grains. That will increase more and more. It will so increase that now you are getting anna by paying high price, but time will come when even if you are prepared to pay price, there will be no more grains. That time is coming. Naturally, what people will eat? They will eat mamsa (meat) and roots and seeds. No milk. No sugar. No wheat.

-Srila Prabhupada, (Lecture, Srimad-Bhagavatam 3.26.26 — Bombay, January 3, 1975)

towards the adoption of GM crops, including those being released for open field trials.

The Government, however, has decided to ignore this warning. The Ministry of Agriculture, on behalf of the Government of India, has filed an affidavit to the effect that we need GM crops in order to achieve food security in this country. This is the same argument that is used by global biotech companies to promote GM crops. This is also an argument made very casually and loosely - exactly what food security the government seeks, while it has no capacity for storing and transporting the produce that is already grown, is never spelled out properly.

It is very absurd that the Ministry of Agriculture, under Minister Sharad Pawar, seeks to lead the country down the path of GM crops while scientists from around the nation have roundly criticised the illogic of GM crops being linked to food security.

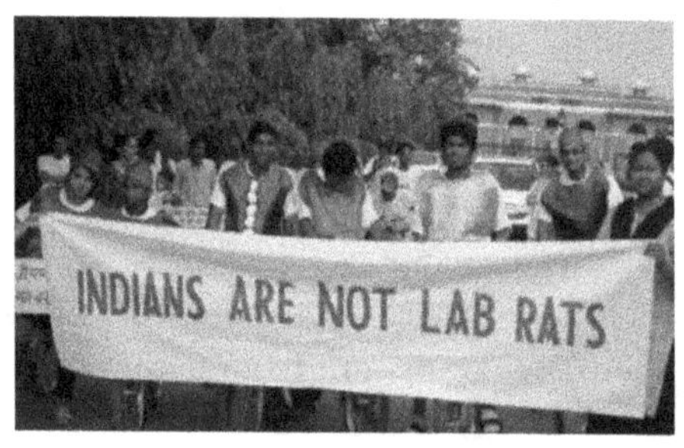

While civil society celebrated the moratorium on BT Brinjal on 9 February, a letter addressed to Jayanthi Natrajan, signed by 150 scientists, was made public. The letter highlights that GM crops are only grown in 3 per cent of the world's agricultural lands, and in countries like the USA, which is the largest cultivator of GM crops, food insecurity has actually increased. The scientists finally urge the Ministry of Environment and Forests (MoEF) to come forward to accept the recommendations of the TEC, so that the MoA does not misdirect the debate on GM crops and food security in the country.

The sounds and colours of the celebrations of the National Safe Food Day have a serious message for our decision makers. There has been enough and more evidence in the last year pointing to the inefficiency in our regulatory system and the risk to human/animal health and biodiversity. This was also emphasised in the report by the Parliamentary Standing Committee on Agriculture, which was tabled in August 2012; its recommendations were unanimously agreed across party lines.

What further evidence does the Government need? If the MoEF is not going to act on the recommendations of the Committee, it must explain to the public why not. For the moment, the problem appears to be that the only 'explanations' it can offer don't find favour with the scientific community. *Such deliberate ignorance of informed input only adds fuel to the fire of suspicion that the Government's actions reflect the agenda of vested interests in corporate agriculture, rather than the public interest.*

Food Rights Organisations Flay Agriculture Minister's Pitch For GM Crops

Bureau, The Hindu Business Line, February 19, 2013

Food rights organisations, under the aegis of the Right to Food Campaign (RFC), have written to Agriculture Minister Sharad Pawar urging him to tackle food security in more 'fundamental ways' rather than link it with genetically modified (GM) crops.

At a press conference here, RFC released the letter signed by hundreds of organisations, including National Advisory Council member Aruna Roy criticising the Agriculture Ministry's stance in an affidavit to the Supreme Court calling it a "*trivialisation and mockery* of the grave situation of hunger and malnutrition that exists in India".

"We need innovation to move beyond an agriculture shaped by the war industry. After the war, the chemical warfare industry mutated into the agri-chemicals industry, saying that without chemical fertilisers and pesticides, we would have no food security. Today, that same industry is bringing us GMOS to sell more herbicides through pushing herbicide-resistant crops like Monsanto's Roundup Ready soya and corn."

THE NATURAL INDEPENDENT --Vandana Shiva

"In this affidavit, your Ministry argued that GM crops and their field trials were needed for India's food security, in addition to wilfully choosing to misinterpret the sound recommendations of the Technical Expert Committee set up by the Supreme Court," says the letter.

Maintaining that food security was not "a simplistic supply-related matter, as our paradox of overflowing godowns, record buffer stocks and the hungry millions showcases", the letter said it was unfortunate that while the discourse around food security and hunger had become more nuanced the world over, the Indian Government chooses to be "unscientific" in its outlook.

It urged the Agriculture Ministry not to "come in the way of much-needed improvements in the transgenics scene in India," reminding it of the recommendations made by the Technical Expert Committee.

The letter said it did not make sense that the Ministry, instead of focusing on strengthening local food production and distribution, was diverting valuable investments towards "controversial, unproven techno-fixes."

Pushing for the GM crops to boost farm output, Pawar on Monday had said scientists should not be denied the right to conduct field trials of such crops. In August last year, the Parliamentary Standing Committee on Agriculture had recommended discontinuation of that all field trials in GM crops. Three years earlier, the Government had placed a moratorium on the commercial release of Bt brinjal.

Some Urgent Considerations On Genetically Modified Crops And Food Security

Neha Saigal, March 4, 2013

maharha-vastrabharana-
kancukosnisa-bhusitah
gopah samayayu rajan
nanopayana-panayah

O King Pariksit, the cowherd men dressed very opulently with valuable ornaments and garments such as coats and turbans. Decorated in this way and carrying various presentations in their hands, they approached the house of Nanda Maharaja.

When we consider the past condition of the agriculturalist in the village, we can see how opulent he was, simply because of agricultural produce and protection of cows. At the present, however, agriculture having been neglected and cow protection given up, the agriculturalist is suffering pitiably and is dressed in a niggardly torn cloth. This is the distinction between the India of history and the India of the present day. By the atrocious activities of ugra-karma, how we are killing the opportunity of human civilization!

~ Srila Prabhupada (Srimad Bhagavatam 10.5.8)

The Budget Session is upon us and we might be witness to one of UPA's most ambitious flagship programmes, the National Food Security Bill (NFSB), becoming a reality. So it seems like Food Security is the flavour of this session with President, Mr Pranab Mukherjee, reiterating UPA's commitment to food security in his maiden speech at the start of the Budget Session.

But this commitment comes under serious question when one of the responsible agencies of the Government dilutes the issue of food security and further misleads the debate on an important issue like hunger and malnutrition. I am referring to the Ministry of Agriculture (MoA) under Sharad Pawar mindlessly promoting GM crops as a solution to food security.

Sharad Pawar has, on more than one occasion, voiced the faulty argument that GM is needed to feed India's growing population. This was overly emphasised by the Ministry on behalf of the Union of India in its affidavit to the Supreme Court in the PIL of GMOs.[1] This narrow minded and false argument put forth by the Ministry of Agriculture (MoA) is unfortunately the same approach put forward by global biotech companies and their cronies to promote controversial GM technology in food and farming, overlooking the obvious risks with Genetically Modified (GM) crops and at the same time trivialising the debate on food security in India.

Indian Paradox Of Excess Production And Increasing Starvation

A logical understanding of what constitutes food security and the food production situation in India will paint a clearer picture as to why GM is no silver bullet to food security and not much more than a very expensive distraction.

The MoA along with the promoters of GM crops have advocated the need for GM crops to increase production and feed India's

growing population. But an analysis of the food grain production confirms the Indian paradox of excess production and increasing starvation.

The Economic Survey 2013 presented a day before the budget suggests that production has improved remarkably growing twice as fast as the population. It has also noted that the food grain production was at a record high of 259.32 million tonnes in 2011-12. Apart from food grain production India is also ranked 1st in the world in fresh fruit, milk and pulses production and 2nd in terms of production of fresh vegetables.

So clearly India need not be in a hurry to adopt risky technology like GM crops to increase production and this was also pointed out by the recommendations of the Parliamentary Standing Committee on Agriculture.

GM Crops Do Not Fit The Bill Of Food Security

If one were insistent to go down the path of the need for increased production through increased yield, one would find again that GM

ime jana-padah svrddhah supakvausadhi-virudhah
vanadri-nady-udanvanto hy edhante tava viksitaih

"All these cities and villages are flourishing in all respects because the herbs and grains are in abundance, the trees are full of fruits, the rivers are flowing, the hills are full of minerals and the oceans full of wealth. And this is all due to Your glancing over them."

This is Vedic civilization. There is mention of so many things, that "The grains are in abundance and the trees are full of fruits. The rivers are flowing nicely. The hills are full of minerals and the ocean full of wealth." So where is the scarcity? There is no mention that slaughterhouse is flourishing, industry is flourishing. No such mention. There are all nonsense things they have created. Therefore problems are there. If you depend on God's creation, then there is no scarcity, simply ananda. If the trees are full of fruits, if you have got sufficient grains and... Because there is sufficient grains, there is sufficient grass also. The animals, the cows, they will eat the grass. You'll eat the grains, the fruits. And the animal will help you, the bulls will help you to produce grains. And he will partake little, what you throw away.

-Srila Prabhupada (Srimad-Bhagavatam 1.8.40 -- Los Angeles, May 2, 1973)

crops have failed to show any increase in yield in the nearly two decades of their existence. There has been no GM crop developed anywhere in the world to increase yield. The Bt cotton experience back home and a look at government statistics only confirms this and further raises many a question on the sustainability to Indian farming. The insignificant increase in yield when Bt cotton area touched 96% was also accepted by the Planning Commission of India in its draft of the 12th year plan. Further, Bt cotton has only added to the burden of agrarian distress of the small, marginal and landless farm families who also are highly food insecure.

GM crops are controversial world over and do not fit the pillars of food security defined by credible agencies like the WHO. Apart from the monopolistic control of seeds, control of our food systems by seed companies and cost of high cultivation for farmers, there is growing scientific evidence on the health and environmental risks of GM crops. Therefore GM crops do not pass the food safety criterion which is very vital to food security.

Mockery Of Food Security And Ignorance To Public Opposition Of GM Crops

Hunger and malnutrition is a vital issue for a country like India and every citizen is concerned that half the children in this country are underweight and a third of them are born malnourished. What is worrying is a mockery of such an important and complex issue by Sharad Pawar and the biotech giants by offering simplistic techno-fixes like GM crops.

"On the eve of the budget session to voice their opposition, 17 Greenpeace activists occupied the FCI godown in Delhi to challenge Sharad Pawar on this mindless, unfounded promotion of GM crops for food security. While 12 of these young activists were detained for 12 hours by the police, as are many activists in this country for expressing dissent with the State on several issues."

The Government's effort to ignore public opposition has been ongoing with the debate on GM crops in the country; it cannot be the case anymore as the opposition has become stronger and diverse over the last few months.

From the Parliamentary Standing Committee on Agriculture to the high profile scientific Technical Expert Committee[2] appointed by the Supreme Court, all have recommended to tread cautiously down the path of GM crops. Very recently 150 scientists from around the country have also expressed their displeasure at the unscientific advocacy of GM crops by the MoA for food security[3].

Can The Common Man Pin His Hope On The Government?

There is enough evidence and many alternatives if one wants to seriously consider India's farming to be sustainable and to ensure that every Indian has the access to available food. But the Agriculture Minister's relentless attitude to introduce GM into food and farming can make anyone wonder whether this is due to vested interests and not public interest. Unfortunately this attitude seems to be the representation of the Government of India in important judicial arenas like in the PIL filed in the Supreme Court on GMOs.

It is only obvious that the common man is left confused and angry by the cruel joke played the Government where on one hand they talk about their commitment to bring in a National Food Security Bill and on the other they want to open the flood gates to risky GM crops and allow multi-national biotech companies to take over our food and farming system, destroying the livelihood of the poorest farmer in this country and paving the path for food insecurity for the next many future generations.

Now in black market you can get things, means eatables, rice, wheat. But if you don't take to Bhagavad-gita, there will be no more even if you pay black price. Just time it... That time is coming. There will be no more available. There will be no milk. There will be no more sugar. There will be no more rice. There will be no more wheat. No more fruits. Then you have to eat meat. Oh, beef shop. Then that will go on. Then human shop also. Gradually it will come. You have to eat the human being also. Cannibals. So it is therefore a great necessity that rajarsayo viduh, raja, those who are government men, they must study Bhagavad-gita. Otherwise don't give them vote.

-Srila Prabhupada (Lecture, Bhagavad-gita 4.2 — Bombay, March 22, 1974)

In this situation with a schizophrenic government and profit hungry biotech companies, is there anyone that the common man can pin his hope on? The history of GM crops has shown the Ministry of Environment under Mr Jairam Ramesh stand up for public interest and declared a moratorium on Bt Brinjal at that time.

Can we expect the same from Smt Jayanthi Natrajan, the current Minister of Environment and also the decision maker on GM crops in India to intervene so that the Ministry of Agriculture does not lead the country down the dangerous path of GM crops under the fallacy that it is a need for food security?

References:

[1] http://www.thehindubusinessline.com/industry-and-economy/agri-biz/food-rights-organisations-flay-sharad-pawars-pitch-for-gm-crops/article4432415.ece

[2] http://indiagminfo.org/wp-content/uploads/2012/10/SC-TEC-interim-report-oct17th-2012-GMO-PIL.pdf

[3] http://indiagminfo.org/?p=540

Biodiversity Is Key In The Road Map To Food Security With No Role For GM Crops

By Neha Saigal, 18 October, 2012, Countercurrents.org

There has been much talk around biological diversity and biosafety in the country as India was host to the eleventh meeting of the Conference of Parties to the Convention of Biological Diversity (COP-11) and the sixth meeting of the Conference of the Parties serving as the Meeting of the Parties to the Cartagena Protocol on Biosafety (COP-MOP6) in Hyderabad. During these conventions there are also elaborate speeches made by our political

> *As we watch the sun go down, evening after evening, through the smog across the poisoned waters of our native earth, we must ask ourselves seriously whether we really wish some future universal historian on another planet to say about us: "With all their genius and with all their skill, they ran out of foresight and air and food and water and ideas," or, "They went on playing politics until their world collapsed around them."* ~ U Thant

leaders that bring in a new ray of hope to the environment & nature which always seems to take a back seat when we talk of a country's development.

One such recent speech was that of the Indian Prime Minister's at the inauguration of the high level segment of the 11th CoP, where he stated all the right things, but the question that lingers is whether he meant all of what he said and whether it will reflect in policy making from now on.

If one were to focus on part of the speech around food security, one would be left thoroughly confused as the government's policies in agriculture are in a different direction. I also choose to focus on the food security bit of the PM's speech as it was made on 16th of October which was marked as World Food Day.

Quoting a part of the PM's speech:

> "We know that food security is a key challenge for the world, particularly in an increasingly climate vulnerable world. Biodiversity, found in our forests and our fields, could provide us keys to the solutions of the future. So we need to build a movement to conserve traditional varieties of crops."

But on the contrary the Prime Minister has been strongly advocating that Genetically Modified (GM) crops are key to increasing productivity in agriculture and also his government strongly asserts that they are essential for food security. It is clear from these contradicting lines of thought that there is a huge lack of understanding within the Manmohan Singh's Government on the issue of food security, though it has been one of the supposed main agenda's of the UPA government.

On one hand there is an understanding that agro-biodiversity systems are essential to food security especially in the face of climate change. In India farmers for many years have developed locally diverse crop systems with traditional seeds which have been sustainable and this has also played an important role in fulfilling their nutritional requirements. On the other hand the government is advocating for GM crops which is in conflict to encouraging biodiversity in fields.

It's no secret that GM crops encourage monocultures and are also known to contaminate other non-GM crops, there have been instances in our own backyard of contamination. So, in the context of food security we need to decide whether we want GM crops or biodiversity in our farms as both cannot co-exist. Added to this there is growing scientific evidence that GM crops are not safe for human and animal consumption and this does not fit into the ambit of food security which is also about access to safe food.

There is an increasing consensus around the world that food security is going to be more and more dependent on agro-biodiversity and not on chemical intensive agricultural practices or GM technology in agriculture.

A very exhaustive and comprehensive report was produced in our own country by the Parliamentary Standing Committee on Agriculture headed by Shri Basudev Achariya. The report which was unanimously accepted by 31 MPs across party lines was tabled in Parliament on the 9th of August 2012. The Committee has recommended the government to come up with a fresh road map to ensure food security that involves sustainable agricultural practices and excludes technologies like GM in agriculture that jeopardize biodiversity and human health.

So respected Prime Minister you got one thing right that biodiversity in our forests and fields is essential for achieving food security especially in these vulnerable times, but if you are going down that road, you have to realize that GM crops play no role.

95.

Organic Farmers' Kick On Big Ag's Face

And Government's Deliberate And Criminal Ignorance Of Indigenous Technologies

In a village in India's poorest state, Bihar, farmers are growing world record amounts of rice – with no GM, no herbicide and using only cow dung as fertilzer. Why is Indian government deliberately ignoring these developments in its own backyard? Why is it still harping on the GM string inspite of it's repeated failures in the country and elsewhere. This is nothing but a deliberate and criminal attempt to sell off the country to big Agribusinesses. Why did the Indian government's affidavit on GMO to the Supreme Court not mention the following report? This clearly reeks of a hidden agenda. There is no considerations for teeming masses, poor and malnourished.

Following is the report published by the UK weekly, The Observer.

India's Rice Revolution

John Vidal, The Observer, 16 February 2013

Sumant Kumar was overjoyed when he harvested his rice last year. There had been good rains in his village of Darveshpura in north-east India and he knew he could improve on the four or five tonnes per hectare that he usually managed. But every stalk he cut on his paddy field near the bank of the Sakri river seemed to weigh heavier than usual, every grain of rice was bigger and when his crop was weighed on the old village scales, even Kumar was shocked.

This was not six or even 10 or 20 tonnes. Kumar, a shy young farmer in Nalanda district of India's poorest state Bihar, had – using only farmyard manure and without any herbicides – grown an astonishing 22.4 tonnes of rice on one hectare of land. This was a world record and with rice the staple food of more than half the world's population of seven billion, big news.

It beat not just the 19.4 tonnes achieved by the "father of rice", the Chinese agricultural scientist Yuan Longping, but the World Bank-funded scientists at the International Rice Research Institute in the Philippines, and anything achieved by the biggest European and American seed and GM companies.

And it was not just Sumant Kumar. Krishna, Nitish, Sanjay and Bijay, his friends and rivals in Darveshpura, all recorded over 17 tonnes, and many others in the villages around claimed to have more than doubled their usual yields.

The villagers, at the mercy of erratic weather and used to going without food in bad years, celebrated. But the Bihar state agricultural universities didn't believe them at first, while India's leading rice scientists muttered about freak results.

The Nalanda farmers were accused of cheating. Only when the state's head of agriculture, a rice farmer himself, came to the village with his own men and personally verified Sumant's crop, was the record confirmed.

The rhythm of Nalanda village life was shattered. Here bullocks still pull ploughs as they have always done, their dung is still dried on the walls of houses and used to cook food. Electricity has still not reached most people. Sumant became a local hero, mentioned in the Indian parliament and asked to attend conferences. The state's chief minister came to Darveshpura to congratulate him, and the village was rewarded with electric power, a bank and a new concrete bridge.

That might have been the end of the story had Sumant's friend Nitish not smashed the world record for growing potatoes six months later. Shortly after Ravindra Kumar, a small farmer from a nearby Bihari village, broke the Indian record for growing wheat.

Darveshpura became known as India's "miracle village", Nalanda became famous and teams of scientists, development groups, farmers, civil servants and politicians all descended to discover its secret.

When I meet the young farmers, all in their early 30s, they still seem slightly dazed by their fame. They've become unlikely heroes in a state where nearly half the families live below the Indian poverty line and 93% of the 100 million population depend on growing rice and potatoes.

Nitish Kumar speaks quietly of his success and says he is determined to improve on the record. "In previous years, farming has not been very profitable," he says. "Now I realise that it can be. My whole life has changed. I can send my children to school and spend more on health. My income has increased a lot."

What happened in Darveshpura has divided scientists and is exciting governments and development experts. Tests on the soil show it is particularly rich in silicon but the reason for the "super yields" is entirely down to a method of growing crops called System of Rice (or root) Intensification (SRI).

It has dramatically increased yields with wheat, potatoes, sugar cane, yams, tomatoes, garlic, aubergine and many other crops and is being hailed as one of the most significant developments of the past 50 years for the world's 500 million small-scale farmers and the two billion people who depend on them.

Instead of planting three-week-old rice seedlings in clumps of three or four in waterlogged fields, as rice farmers around the world traditionally do, the Darveshpura farmers carefully nurture only half as many seeds, and then transplant the young plants into fields, one by one, when much younger.

Additionally, they space them at 25cm intervals in a grid pattern, keep the soil much drier and carefully weed around the plants to allow air to their roots. The premise that "less is more" was taught by Rajiv Kumar, a young Bihar state government extension worker who had been trained in turn by Anil Verma of a small Indian NGO called Pran (Preservation and Proliferation of Rural Resources and Nature), which has introduced the SRI method to hundreds of villages in the past three years.

While the "green revolution" that averted Indian famine in the 1970s relied on improved crop varieties, expensive pesticides and chemical fertilisers, SRI appears to offer a long-term, sustainable future for no extra cost.

With more than one in seven of the global population going hungry and demand for rice expected to outstrip supply within 20 years, it appears to offer real hope. Even a 30% increase in the yields of the world's small farmers would go a long way to alleviating poverty.

"Farmers use less seeds, less water and less chemicals but they get more without having to invest more. This is revolutionary," said Dr Surendra Chaurassa from Bihar's agriculture ministry. "I did not believe it to start with, but now I think it can potentially change the way everyone farms. I would want every state to promote it. If we get 30-40% increase in yields, that is more than enough to recommend it."

The results in Bihar have exceeded Chaurassa's hopes. Sudama Mahto, an agriculture officer in Nalanda, says a small investment in training a few hundred people to teach SRI methods has resulted in a 45% increase in the region's yields. Veerapandi Arumugam, the former agriculture minister of Tamil Nadu state, hailed the system as "revolutionising" farming.

SRI's Origins

SRI's origins go back to the 1980s in Madagascar where Henri de Laulanie, a French Jesuit priest and agronomist, observed how villagers grew rice in the uplands. He developed the method but it was an American, professor Norman Uphoff, director of the International Institute for Food, Agriculture and Development at Cornell University, who was largely responsible for spreading the word about De Laulanie's work.

For the time being, if you actually want to develop such ideal asrama, we must have sufficient land, and all other things will gradually grow. For raising crops from the land, how many men will be required—that we must estimate and for herding the cows and feeding them. We must have sufficient pasturing ground to feed the animals all round. We have to maintain the animals throughout their life. We must not make any program for selling them to the slaughterhouses. That is the way of cow protection. Krishna by His practical example taught us to give all protection to the cows and that should be the main business of New Vrindaban. Vrindaban is also known as Gokula. Go means cows, and kula means congregation. Therefore the special feature of New Vrindaban will be cow protection, and by doing so, we shall not be loser. In India of course, a cow is protected and the cowherdsmen they derive sufficient profit by such protection. Cow dung is used as fuel. Cow dung dried in the sunshine kept in stock for utilizing them as fuel in the villages. They get wheat and other cereals produced from the field. There is milk and vegetables and the fuel is cow dung, and thus, they are self-independent in every village. There are hand weavers for the cloth. And the country oil-mill (consisting of a bull walking in circle round two big grinding stones, attached with yoke) grinds the oil seeds into oil. The whole idea is that people residing in New Vrindaban may not have to search out work outside. Arrangements should be such that the residents should be self-satisfied. That will make an ideal asrama. I do not know these ideals can be given practical shape, but I think like that; that people may be happy in any place with land and cow without endeavoring for so-called amenities of modern life—which simply increase anxieties for maintenance and proper equipment. The less we are anxious for maintaining our body and soul together, the more we become favorable for advancing in Krishna Consciousness.

—Srila Prabhupada (Letter to: Hayagriva, Montreal 14 June, 1968)

Given $15m by an anonymous billionaire to research sustainable development, Uphoff went to Madagascar in 1983 and saw the success of SRI for himself: farmers whose previous yields averaged two tonnes per hectare were harvesting eight tonnes. In 1997 he started to actively promote SRI in Asia, where more than 600 million people are malnourished.

"It is a set of ideas, the absolute opposite to the first green revolution [of the 60s] which said that you had to change the genes and the soil nutrients to improve yields. That came at a tremendous ecological cost," says Uphoff. "Agriculture in the 21st century must be practised differently. Land and water resources are becoming scarcer, of poorer quality, or less reliable. Climatic conditions are in many places more adverse. SRI offers millions of disadvantaged households far better opportunities. *Nobody is benefiting from this except the farmers; there are no patents, royalties or licensing fees.*"

For 40 years now, says Uphoff, science has been obsessed with improving seeds and using artificial fertilisers: "It's been genes,

Primitive means very, very old. So whether in the days gone by, people were actually happy or now they are happy?

Even if you say "primitive," the primitive life is very nice. Primitive life means simple life. Keeping pace with the nature's law. It is very nice. Primitive life ... It gives you anxiety-free life, and therefore, even if you take it as primitive, the saintly persons, sages, they used to live long, long years, and their brain was so sharp, because they were taking natural food, fruits, grains, and milk that helps to develop human brain for understanding subtle subject matter. So even Vyasadeva... You have seen the picture of Vyasadeva. He's writing books just near a cottage only. But he's writing. Nobody can create such literature. But he was leading very simple life, in a cottage. Even, say, 2,000 years ago or little more, there was Canakya Pandita. Canakya Pandita, he was a brahmana, but great politician. His politics are studied even now in M.A. class. And because he was a great politician, diplomat, under his name in our India, in New Delhi, the capital, there is a neighborhood which is called Canakya Puri, and all the foreign embassies are there. Your American embassy is also there.

— Srila Prabhupada

(Lecture, Srimad-Bhagavatam 2.3.24, Los Angeles, June 22, 1972)

genes, genes. There has never been talk of managing crops. Corporations say 'we will breed you a better plant' and breeders work hard to get 5-10% increase in yields. *We have tried to make agriculture an industrial enterprise and have forgotten its biological roots.*"

Dominic Glover, a British researcher working with Wageningen University in the Netherlands, has spent years analysing the introduction of GM crops in developing countries. He is now following how SRI is being adopted in India and believes there has been a "turf war".

"There are experts in their fields defending their knowledge," he says. "But in many areas, growers have tried SRI methods and abandoned them. People are unwilling to investigate this. SRI is good for small farmers who rely on their own families for labour, but not necessarily for larger operations. Rather than any magical theory, it is good husbandry, skill and attention which results in the super yields. Clearly in certain circumstances, it is an efficient resource for farmers. But it is labour intensive and nobody has come up with the technology to transplant single seedlings yet."

But some larger farmers in Bihar say it is not labour intensive and can actually reduce time spent in fields. "When a farmer does SRI the first time, yes it is more labour intensive," says Santosh Kumar, who grows 15 hectares of rice and vegetables in Nalanda. "Then it gets easier and new innovations are taking place now."

In its early days, SRI was dismissed or vilified by donors and scientists but in the past few years it has gained credibility. Uphoff estimates there are now 4-5 million farmers using SRI worldwide, with governments in China, Indonesia, Cambodia, Sri Lanka and Vietnam promoting it.

Sumant, Nitish and as many as 100,000 other SRI farmers in Bihar are now preparing their next rice crop. It's back-breaking work transplanting the young rice shoots from the nursery beds to the paddy fields but buoyed by recognition and results, their confidence and optimism in the future is sky high.

Last month Nobel prize-winning economist Joseph Stiglitz visited Nalanda district and recognised the potential of this kind of organic farming, telling the villagers they were "better than scientists". "It was amazing to see their success in organic farming," said Stiglitz, who called for more research. "Agriculture scientists from across the world should visit and learn and be inspired by them."

Bihar, from being India's poorest state, is now at the centre of what is being called a "new green grassroots revolution" with farming villages, research groups and NGOs all beginning to experiment with different crops using SRI. The state will invest $50m in SRI next year but western governments and foundations are holding back, preferring to invest in hi-tech research. The agronomist Anil Verma does not understand why: "The farmers know SRI works, but help is needed to train them. We know it works differently in different soils but the principles are solid," he says. "The biggest problem we have is that people want to do it but we do not have enough trainers.

"If any scientist or a company came up with a technology that almost guaranteed a 50% increase in yields at no extra cost they would get a Nobel prize. But when young Biharian farmers do that they get nothing. I only want to see the poor farmers have enough to eat."

Despite all the claims made by industry-funded hacks that genetically-modified organisms (GMOs) and other industrial agricultural methods are necessary for the future of humanity, it is the traditional growing methods that continue to shine through as the real sustainers of life.

96.

Exit The Cows

Enter The Monsanto

Karnataka is a southern state in India with a population of 61 million. Recently it saw a government change as the ruling party was voted out. The new government, in the first few hours of assuming office made its sinister intentions clear.

The Chief Minister's First Move: Lifting Ban On Cow Slaughter In Karnataka

By Niticentral Staff on May 14, 2013

Karnataka Chief Minister K Siddaramaiah has lifted the ban on cow slaughter in the State.

The erstwhile BJP regime in the State had implemented a ban on cow slaughter by introducing Karnataka Prevention of Cow Slaughter and Preservation Bill, 2012.

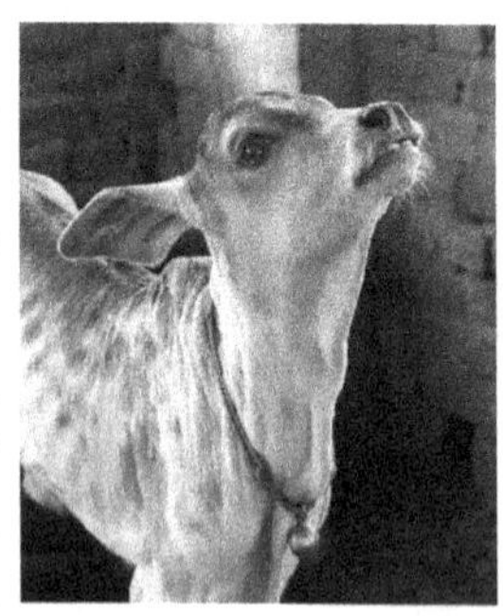

The Bill prohibits slaughter of cattle, sale, usage and possession of beef, puts restriction on transport of cattle and also prohibits sale, purchase or disposal of cattle for slaughter.

The offence was punishable with imprisonment of not less than one year which may extend up to seven years or a fine of Rs 25,000 to Rs 50,000, or both. A second and subsequent offence attracted a fine of not less than Rs 50,000 and up to Rs 1 lakh along with imprisonment.

The Bill provided for stringent punishment upon violation of the Act, and also allowed for powers of search and seizure of any premises including vessels or vehicles.

This was his first file to be signed within hours of taking oath as chief minister. Some members of minority hailed this historic move and praised him for being minority friendly.

Karnataka Government Has Open Mind On GM Crops

PTI, May 21, 2013

Karnataka government has an open mind on the issue of genetically modified crops, and favours giving options for farmers to make informed choices, Agriculture Minister Krishna Byre Gowda has said.

We know when India was more primitive, there were thousands of cows owned by the agriculturists and they used to enjoy life by the agricultural products and sufficient quantity of clarified butter, milk and curd. Even some hundreds of years before during the reign of Nawab Swaesta Khan, rice was selling in India at the rate of nine mounds (40kg) a rupee and today ever since the beginning of scientific knowledge in India, rice is selling now at the rate of nine chatak (9x60gms) a rupee. In the former days, the Indian kings and rich men used to perform yajnas by burning tons and tons of pure clarified butter made out of cow's milk and at the present moment there is not a drop of pure clarified butter made out of cow's milk even for daily use. That is the law of material nature. Leaving aside the stories of Nawab Sawesta Khan's history we can say from our personal experience that my father, say 40 years before at most, used to stock at our house (in Calcutta) always a cart load of rice, 15 mounds (15x40kg), ten seers (10x1kg) of pure ghee, a bag of potato and a cart load of soft coke always ready for use. Our family was not a rich family and my father's income was within Rs. 250/- per month. And it was within his easy reach to stock household provisions in the above manner. But at the present moment at no house in the cities and towns generally there is stock of more than 15 seers (1kg) of rice. Formerly they used to enquire rates of commodities in the terms of mounds (40kg) and now they ask for it in terms of seers (1kg) or chattacks (60gms) although we are able to keep more glittering cars than cows at the present moment.

— Srila Prabhupada (Back To Godhead magazine, Nov. 1956)

He said Bt cotton, first introduced in the State some one-and-half decades ago, has definitely benefitted farmers to improve yields in an eco-friendly manner. "That's why farmers have adopted it". As much as 90 per cent of farmers in Karnataka are using Bt cotton seeds. (He made no mention of thousands of farmers committing suicide in the state every year after Bt cotton's introduction.)

Agricultural universities based in Dharwad and Raichur are currently working on improving the Bt cotton seeds.

"We must keep our minds open", Byre Gowda said when asked to spell out the new Congress government's stand on GM crops.

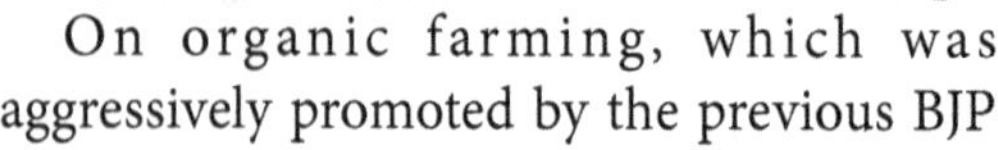

On organic farming, which was aggressively promoted by the previous BJP government, the Minister, in reply to a query, said funds for such initiatives were perhaps misused but added that subject comes under the Horticulture Department, which needs to inquire into it.

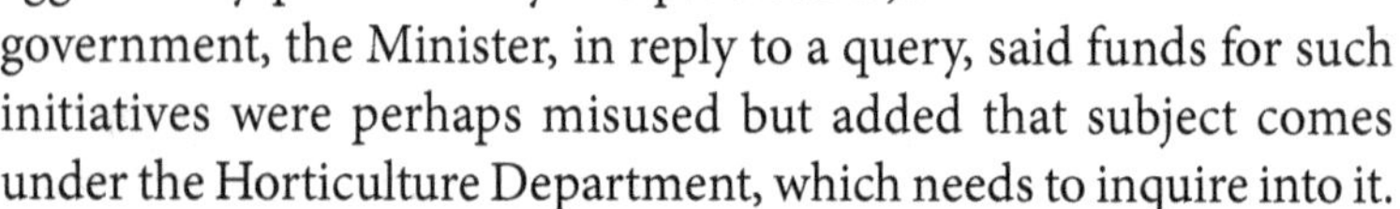

The Minister said the government has geared up to supply seeds and fertilisers to farmers. Agriculture department has estimated that for the 2013 Kharif season, 10.68 lakh quintals of seeds would be needed, which had been stocked.

As against the requirement of 24 lakh tonnes of fertilisers, the government has a stock of nine lakh tonnes, which would continuously get replenished, he said.

The Minister advised farmers not to over-use urea just because it was cheap, saying such an approach would bring down soil fertility.

A special squad has been formed to crack down on elements who seek to create "artificial shortage" by hoarding, he said.

The economic development requires cow protections, but these rascals do not know. Their economic development' is cow killing. Just see, rascal civilization. Don't be sorry. It is sastra.

Therefore kurute vikarma. Simply for little satisfaction of the tongue, the same benefit you can derive from the milk, but because they are rascals, madmen, they think that eating or drinking the blood of the cow is better than drinking milk.

— Srila Prabhupada (Lecture, Srimad Bhagavatam, September 9, 1973)

97.

In Praise Of Cowdung

By Vandana Shiva, ZNet Sustainer Program, November 20, 2002

In India we worship cow dung as Lakshmi, the goddess of wealth. Gobur-dhan puja is literally the worship of gobur (cowdung) dhan (wealth).

Cow dung is worshipped because it is the source of renewal of soil fertility and hence the sustainability of human society. The cow has been made sacred in India because it is a keystone species for agro-ecosystems -- it is key to the sustainability of agriculture.

When Monsanto and biotech industry spokesmen parading as "farmers" presented me with cow dung at the WSSD (World Summit on Sustainable Development) in Johannesburg, I accepted their "award" as a tribute to organic farming and sustainable agriculture.

The small farmers convergence at the WSSD with farmers from across Africa rejected GMO's, and chemicals and committed themselves to organic farming and defense of farmers rights. They are freely choosing seeds they can save and technologies that are sustainable.

Farmers organizations in India and in Africa are saying "no" to GMO's on the basis of their freedom to choose to be organic which means being free of genetic contamination that results from GM crops. Genetic contamination robs farmers of their freedom to be GM free.

Patents and intellectual property rights on seed rob farmers of their freedom to save, exchange, develop seed. Farmers are treated as "thieves" and "criminals" for exercising their rights.

The worst example is that of Parcy Schmeiser whose canola fields were contaminated by Monsanto's GM canola and he was sued for "theft" of genes.

That is why those of us who farm organically and want to maintain our freedom to farm and uphold farmers rights are resisting the irresponsible corporations which are trying to own life on earth, including seed, contaminate our crops and food and have total control over farming and farmers.

GM seeds and chemicals are a threat to farmers survival, a threat to consumer health and a threat to the environment. Farmers in India are committing suicides because the costly seeds and chemicals from corporations like Monsanto/Mahyco have pushed them into deep debts.

The claims of Monsanto and its apologists like Swaminathan Iyer (who called me a "Green Killer" in the Times of India on 22nd Sept 2002, because I practise and promote organic farming) that GM can feed the world is totally false.

Monsanto's Bt cotton has failed across India in its first year of commercial planting. In Khargone in Madhya Pradesh Bt is a 100% failure and farmers are demanding compensation. In Maharastra, the Bt crop has failed on 30,000 hectares and farmers are asking for Rs. 500 crore compensation. In Gujarat, in Bhavnagar, Surendranagar and Rajkot Bt cotton has been destroyed by a heavy infestation of bollworm, the pest for whose control the toxin producing Bt. gene has been engineered into cotton. The genetically engineered Bt cotton is not a miracle, it is a fraud on farmers.

In Rajasthan, the hybrid corn which Monsanto claims will give 20 – 50 quintals per acre is giving 1.5 to 1.7 quintals per acre while demanding intensive water and chemical use, aggravating the draught and famine.

The pseudo scientific claims of irresponsible biotech corporations like Monsanto are killing our farmers, our agriculture, our biodiversity.

Organic agriculture is increasing farm productivity by 2 to 3 times, increasing farmers incomes, and protecting public health and the environment. That is why the Time Magazine identified Navdanya as a pioneer for the new century and stated that "In India atleast, Navdanya sets an eco-friendly standard that agribusiness must show it can out perform. The challenge for genetic engineers is to create seeds adapted to particular locales that enable farmers to reduce, not increase, the use of chemicals" (Time, Aug 26, 2002, "Seeds of self Reliance, p 36)

Monsanto and its lobbyists profit by selling and promoting poisonous, toxic seeds and corporate control. Movements like

Dr. Patel: They have in Bengal this Standard Pharmaceuticals of Bengal, been able to isolate penicillin from cow dung, and they have a big plant in Calcutta producing penicillin from cow dung. It's stated, you know, how cow dung was considered sacred. Perhaps we did not know that, but by experience.

Prabhupada: Before this, one Monmohan Gosh, Dr. Monmohan Gosh, he was pathologist in medical college. He proved the antiseptic properties of cow dung. He was Dr. Gosh's friend. So he was working in his laboratory also. I know. Long ago.

Dr. Patel: And in cow urine, sir, there are so many hormones coming, and a big sample of hormones which can be resynthesized as human hormones. That is why gomutra is being drunk.

Prabhupada: Gomutra is good medicine for liver disease. If you drink urine of...

Dr. Patel: Yes, it is proved scientifically so many hormones and by-products and hormones which can be resynthesized into human hormones, modern science.

That's right, cow urine is considered sacred by we people that we put a drop in the newly born child's mouth.

Prabhupada: Pancha-gavya, gomutra is one of the parts. Cow dung, urine, milk, yogurt, and ghee. This is pancha gavya, pertaining to the cow.

— Srila Prabhupada (Morning Walk — August 14, 1976, Bombay)

Navdanya celebrate biodiversity, farmers freedom and cow dung. The corporations and corporate spokespeople are getting desperate because people are seeing through their lies and deceptions.

With organic farming growing worldwide, and the failures and non-sustainability of genetic engineering and chemical engineering becoming evident, the chemical corporate lobby is getting desperate. I view their personal assaults on me as a symptom of the desperation caused by the failure of non-sustainable industrial, corporate agriculture in removing hunger or improving farmers livelihoods.

Sustainable systems are growing because they offer real solutions to the hunger and poverty crisis. And cow dung, biomass and biodiversity are at the heart of sustainability and the non-violent organic alternative to genetic engineering and chemicals.

Ecologically the cow has been central to Indian civilization. Both materially and conceptually the world of Indian agriculture has built its sustainability on maintaining the integrity of the cow, considering her inviolable and sacred, seeing her as the mother of the prosperity of food systems.

The integration of livestock with farming has been the secret of sustainable agriculture. Livestock perform a critical function in the food chain by converting organic matter into a form that can be easily used by plants.

According to K.M. Munshi, India's first agriculture minister after independence, "The mother cow and the Nandi are not worshipped in vain. They are the primeval agents who enrich the soil - nature's great land transformers - who supply organic matter which, after treatment, becomes nutrient matter of the greatest importance. In India, tradition, religious sentiment and economic needs have tried to maintain a cattle population large enough to maintain the cycle, only if we know it "

A century ago, Sir Alfred Howard, the father of modern sustainable farming wrote in his classic, An Agricultural Testament, that, 'In the agriculture of Asia we find ourselves confronted with a system of peasant farming which, in the essentials, soon became stabilized. What is happening today in the small fields of India and China took place many centuries ago. The agricultural practices of the Orient have passed the supreme test - they are almost as permanent as those of the primeval forest, of the prairie, or of the ocean.'

Howard identified the principles of sustainable agriculture as those of renewability as seen in the primeval forest. The agricultural Testament is a record of practices that had maintained the soil fertility of India over centuries. Historical records indicate that the alluvial soils of the Gangetic plains have produced fair crops year after year, without falling in fertility. According to Howard, this has been possible because a perfect balance had been reached between the manurial requirements of crops harvested and natural processes which recuperate fertility. The conservation of soil fertility has been achieved through a combination of mixed and rotational cropping with leguminous crops, a balance between livestock and crops, shallow and light ploughing, and organic manuring.

That is why we organize the Howard Memorial Lectures on 2nd October as a remembrance of India as the source of non-violent, sustainable agriculture. This year's lecture was given by Fukuoka, the Japanese agriculture thinker and chaired by Dr. Tewolde Egziabher, the Ethiopian Environment Minister who has led the Biosafety negotiations in the United Nations.

Howard saw in India's peasants a knowledge of farming far more advanced than that of the west. He recognized the secret of India's sustainable land use as lying in the return of organic matter and humus to the soil. A balance between livestock and crops was always kept in order to maintain the food cycle and return organic matter to the soil. The method of mixed cropping is part of the adaptation of nature's ways in which cereal crops like millet, wheat, barley and maize are mixed with pulses, providing nutrition to give better results than monocultures; Howard notes that, "Here we have another instance where the peasants of the East have anticipated and acted upon the solution of one of the problems which western science is only now beginning to recognize."

Biodiversity conservation and organic agriculture is increasing food output by 200-300%. Biodiversity intensification rather than chemical intensification is the way forward for Indian agriculture. Organic farming is necessary to increase food production and strengthen food security, conserve natural resources - soil, water, biodiversity, improve farmers incomes and well being, protect rural livelihoods, prevent indebtedness, and stop debt linked farm suicides. It creates freedom from debt, domination and disease.

Corporations are creating poverty by diverting the hard earned income of peasants and farmers to the seed/pesticide industry. The new seeds besides being costly are also ecologically vulnerable to pests and diseases leading to more crop failures and higher use of chemicals. These are killer technologies which are undesirable and unnecessary.

The corporate hijack of agriculture is based on pseudo science and false claims. The violent technologies of genetic engineering and toxic pesticides, and the dishonest, deceitful promotion of these poverty creating capital intensive and non-sustainable technologies is leading to the death of our farmers and the destruction of our ecological security and food security. These are primitive, crude and obsolete technologies that are efficient in destruction, not production.

The agriculture technologies of the future have to work for people, not corporations, they have to work with nature, not against nature. If farmers and farming have to have a future, it has to be organic. Neither the planet nor the poor can afford the waste, inefficiency, deceit, pollution and violence of chemicals and genetic engineering.

98.

Isavasya (God-centered) Farming

By Rupanuga dasa

A God-centered farming conception is relevant because it forms the basis for a workable agricultural life-style which includes a strict consideration of the ecological balance between humans, animals, the land, and God. Although sophisticated modern farmers might concede that the success of their endeavors, including their use of innovative machinery, depends in the end on "acts of Providence or God," or at least upon chance, the Isavasya (God-centered) farmer considers that long-range production and ecological balance require actual God consciousness. Therefore, even today in many parts of India, farmers make a point of gratefully offering God a portion of the crop in the form of prasada, or vegetarian food preparations. These offerings are often part of community celebrations in which the members of the community or village meet, especially in the morning and evening, to chant God's holy names and dance.

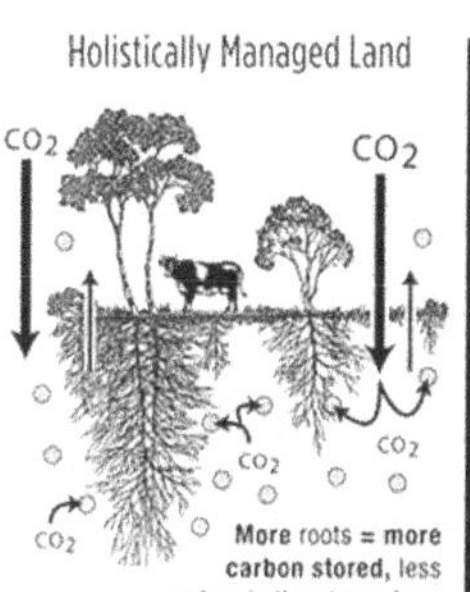
Holistically Managed Land
CO_2
CO_2
More roots = more carbon stored, less carbon in the atmosphere

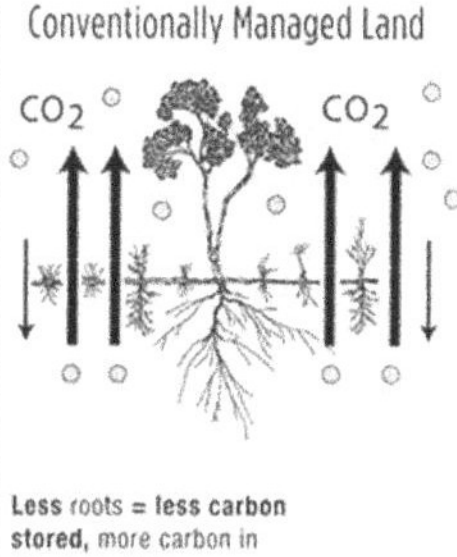
Conventionally Managed Land
CO_2
CO_2
Less roots = less carbon stored, more carbon in the atmosphere

This God-centered attitude does not reflect a "primitive" agrarian culture or mentality of a distant Indian sect, but about a life-style that's in real harmony with the ideals of sustainable living. In fact, some of the most successful of the modern farm communities are based expressly upon isavasya principles.

Those who have got my books, you will see that how much profusely the earth was producing during the time of Maharaja Yudhisthira, because the executive head of the state was a pious, so how nature was helping. Nature was helping. Now India there is scarcity, scarcity of foodstuff. But the same India was producing so much grains, even during British time, that many thousands and thousand tons of rice were being exported from India to other countries. You see? That I have seen. I have seen. My maternal uncle was very rich man by simply exporting rice to the foreign countries. Yes. Spices... And old history you will find that India, they had got their own ships for exporting spices to Greece and other countries of Europe. The history is there. And they were supplying muslin cloth, even just before the British period, Muslim period. So India's export, export, I mean to say, status was far greater than other countries. And these spices and other export attracted persons from Europe, that Vasco de Gama, and the Columbus also wanted to go, but he fortunately came to America. You see? All these Europeans and the Britishers went and established their supremacy. So India was so rich. But now how that India has become so poor? The same land is there. Why? Because they have lost that old culture, God consciousness. You see? And at least my calculation is that, that a state, a secular state... Secular state means he has no... Here in America you have got state religion. You have got state religion. But in India there is no state religion. Every country has state religion. Even Pakistan, it has divided. It is now a part of India. But they have also their state religion. But unfortunately India has no state religion. That means deliberately they are trying to disconnect with God relation, godly relation. But in the same India... You just read the history, five thousand years before, how much profusely the nature was supplying. So nature can give you anything. After all, it is the nature that supplies your necessities, not the industry. Industry simply transformed in a different way, and a certain class make profit out of it. Industry does not mean really economic improvement. Real economic improvement means what you produce from the land. That requires God help. Without raw materials, even your industry cannot go on.

-Srila Prabhupada (Lecture, Bhagavad-gita, New York, April 1, 1966)

A holistic farm community doesn't use technological prowess to try to outwit natural laws. Rather, community members try to do their work in a God-conscious way. "Success cannot come by working at your own risk," says a community member, "You may get good results for a while, but lasting success depends on how conscious you are of your relationship with the actual proprietor of nature."

Gradually, we have to become aware that God is always present—in every place and at every moment. As we learn this art of being conscious of God's presence, we will naturally develop a devotional, serving attitude toward everyone, including humans, plants, and animals. Then we will see all living beings as spiritually equal, because all living beings are equally related with God. Thus, in one sense, returning to the land, to vegetarianism, to nonviolence, to herbal medicine, and to ecological concern—returning to nature—necessitates returning to God consciousness, our natural consciousness. The age-old Vedic literatures describe that consciousness, in clear-cut, scientific terms.

> "Farming is not just about growing food... The way we grow food determines our structure, makes our mega-cities, makes us who we are. Agriculture is culture, at bottom about the integrity of individual lives."
>
> —Richard Manning
>
> Food's Frontier: The Next Green Revolution (North Point Press, 2000)

In fact, in most instances the work of scientists like Howard, Kervran, Baranger, and Hauschka echoes these Vedic conclusions. Howard, for example, simply rediscovered ancient, biologically sound, and ecologically balanced agrarian practices based upon Vedic principles. And Hauschka's assertion that life is not a combination of elements, that instead it "precedes" matter and "originates in a preexistent spiritual cosmos," tells us what the Vedic literatures said thousands of years ago. The Bhagavad-gita, the essence of the Vedas, verifies that individual life is never created or destroyed, but that it is moving (transmigrating) among temporary bodies sustained by God, the original life.

THE AUTHOR

Dr. Sahadeva dasa (Sanjay Shah) is a monk in vaisnava tradition. Coming from a prominent family of Rajasthan, he graduated in commerce from St.Xaviers College, Kolkata and then went on to complete his CA (Chartered Accountancy) and ICWA (Cost and works Accountancy) with national ranks. Later he received his doctorate.
For close to last two decades, he is leading a monk's life and he has made serving God and humanity as his life's mission. His areas of work include research in Vedic and contemporary thought, Corporate and educational training, social work and counselling, travelling in India and aborad, writing books and of course, practicing spiritual life and spreading awareness about the same.
He is also an accomplished musician, composer, singer, instruments player and sound engineer. He has more than a dozen albums to his credit so far. (SoulMelodies.com) His varied interests include alternative holistic living, Vedic studies, social criticism, environment, linguistics, history, art & crafts, nature studies, web technologies etc.
Many of his books have been acclaimed internationally and translated in other languages.

By The Same Author

Oil-Final Countdown To A Global Crisis And Its Solutions

End of Modern Civilization And Alternative Future

To Kill Cow Means To End Human Civilization

Cow And Humanity - Made For Each Other

Cows Are Cool - Love 'Em!

Capitalism Communism And Cowism - A New Economics For The 21st Century

Noble Cow - Munching Grass, Looking Curious And Just Hanging Around

Let's Be Friends - A Curious, Calm Cow

Wondrous Glories of Vraja

We Feel Just Like You Do

Tsunami of Diseases Headed Our Way - Know Your Food Before Time Runs Out

(More information on availability : DrDasa.com)